CHAPTER 12 (pp. 226–227)
Counternull effect size r and percentage (%) coverage of null-counternull interval:

$$r_{\text{counternull}} = \sqrt{\frac{4r^2}{1 + 3r^2}} \qquad \%\,\text{Coverage} = 100\left(1.00 - p_{\text{two-tailed}}\right)$$

CHAPTER 12 (pp. 230–233)
Odds ratio (OR), relative risk (RR), relative risk reduction (RRR), risk difference (RD), and number needed to treat (NNT) in 2 × 2 contingency table:

$$\text{OR} = \frac{A/B}{C/D} \qquad \text{RR} = \frac{A/(A + B)}{C/(C + D)} \qquad \text{RRR} = \left[\frac{\text{Risk difference}}{C/(C + D)}\right]100$$

$$\text{RD} = \left(\frac{A}{A + B}\right) - \left(\frac{C}{C + D}\right) \qquad \text{NNT} = \frac{1}{\text{Risk difference}}$$

with rows and columns labeled :

	Adverse outcome		
Condition	Yes	No	Totals
Treatment	A	B	(A + B)
Control	C	D	(C + D)
Totals	(A + C)	(B + D)	N = A + B + C + D

CHAPTER 12 (p. 234)

Killeen's p_{rep} statistic: $p_{\text{rep}} = \dfrac{1}{1 + \left(\dfrac{p}{1 - p}\right)^{2/3}}$

CHAPTER 13 (pp. 240–242, 248)
Independent-sample t, pooled S^2, and effect size r computed from independent-sample t:

$$t = \frac{M_1 - M_2}{\sqrt{\left(\dfrac{1}{n_1} + \dfrac{1}{n_2}\right)S^2}}, \text{ and } S^2 = \frac{\Sigma(X_1 - M_1)^2 + \Sigma(X_2 - M_2)^2}{n_1 + n_2 - 2} \qquad r_{\text{effect size}} = \sqrt{\frac{t^2}{t^2 + df}}$$

CHAPTER 13 (pp. 244–245)
Cohen's d from independent sample means and pooled population standard deviation:

$$d = \frac{M_1 - M_2}{\sigma_{\text{pooled}}}, \text{ and } \sigma_{\text{pooled}} = S_{\text{pooled}}\left(\sqrt{\frac{df}{N}}\right)$$

CHAPTER 13 (pp. 245–246)
Cohen's d from t and harmonic mean sample size (n_{h}) when $n_1 \neq n_2$:

$$d = \frac{2t}{\sqrt{df}}\left(\sqrt{\frac{\overline{n}}{n_{\text{h}}}}\right), \text{ and } n_{\text{h}} = \frac{2(n_1 n_2)}{n_1 + n_2}$$

which, when $n_1 = n_2$, simplifies to: $d = \dfrac{2t}{\sqrt{df}}$

SEVENTH
EDITION

Beginning Behavioral Research

A Conceptual Primer

RALPH L. ROSNOW
Emeritus, Temple University

ROBERT ROSENTHAL
University of California, Riverside

PEARSON

Boston   Columbus   Indianapolis   New York   San Francisco   Upper Saddle River
Amsterdam   Cape Town   Dubai   London   Madrid   Milan   Munich   Paris   Montreal   Toronto
Delhi   Mexico City   São Paulo   Sydney   Hong Kong   Seoul   Singapore   Taipei   Tokyo

Editorial Director: Craig Campanella
Editor in Chief: Jessica Mosher
Executive Editor: Stephen Frail
Editorial Assistant: Madelyn Schricker
Marketing Manager: Brigeth Rivera
Marketing Assistant: Jessica Warren
Production Manager: Holly Shufeldt
Full-Service Project Management/Composition: Integra Software Services, Ltd.
Cover, Creative Director: Jayne Conte
Cover Designer: Suzanne Behnke
Cover Art: Fotolia
Cover Printer: Lehigh-Phoenix Color/Hagerstown
Printer/Bindery: Edwards Brothers

Library of Congress Cataloging-in-Publication Data
Rosnow, Ralph L.
  Beginning behavioral research: a conceptual primer / Ralph L. Rosnow.—7th ed.
    p. cm.
  ISBN-13: 978-0-205-81031-4 (alk. paper)
  ISBN-10: 0-205-81031-4 (alk. paper)
  1. Psychology—Research—Methodology—Textbooks.   2. Social sciences—Research—Methodology—Textbooks.
  I. Title.
  BF76.5.R64 2013
  300.72—dc23   2011046807

10 9 8 7 6 5 4 3 2 1

ISBN 10:   0-205-81031-4
ISBN 13: 978-0-205-81031-4

Contents

PART II OBSERVATION AND MEASUREMENT

PART III DESIGN AND

IMPLEMENTATION

7 Randomized Experiments and Causal Inference   128

8 Nonrandomized Research and Causal Reasoning   149

9 Survey Research and Subject Recruitment   164

PART IV DESCRIBING DATA AND DRAWING INFERENCES

10 Summarizing the Data 184

11 Correlating Variables 204

12 Understanding p Values and Effect Size Indicators 219

PART V STATISTICAL TESTS

Preface

Welcome to the seventh edition of *Beginning Behavioral Research: A Conceptual Primer*. This book was conceived as a text for students who, as part of a course in research methods, are expected to plan an empirical study, to analyze and interpret the data, and to present their findings and conclusions in a written report. The word *Primer* in the subtitle is intended to communicate the idea that BBR 7th edition is focused on the rudiments, or first principles, of the application of the scientific method in behavioral research. For philosophers of science as well as many philosophically oriented psychologists, the *scientific method* has long been a fascinating and enigmatic part of the puzzle of how scientists arrive at a rational, logically consistent picture of the psychological world in which we live. As one psychologist put it, any metaphor used to characterize the scientific method would have to be a mixed one:

> It is *not* an explanatory web, a predictive network, a descriptive grammar, an experiential map, a technological abacus, a practical almanac, or a moral calculus. It is *not* an arsenal of methods—logical, mathematical, or instrumentative. (Koch, 1959, p. 2)

As we show in this book, the scientific method is all of these things—and much more. Applying it to the wide range of questions of interest to behavioral researchers can be challenging, but also great fun.

Although *Beginning Behavioral Research* was conceived as an undergraduate text for students planning to do research, it has also been used in ways that go beyond that original purpose. For example, it has been used in methods courses in which the production of a research project was not a major goal. It has been used by undergraduate honors students and master's degree students in different disciplines or programs as a primary text and by doctoral students to ease themselves into our advanced text, *Essentials of Behavioral Research* (Rosenthal & Rosnow, 1991, 2008). We have tried to anticipate and confront questions and uncertainties from the student's perspective not necessarily as a potential professional producer of empirical research, but as an intelligent consumer of scientific findings. Our hope is that BBR 7th edition will continue to teach students to understand not only the first principles of behavioral research, but also the difference between good science and pseudoscience and the exacting standards of sound research.

Our Approach

Although much is new in this seventh edition, we have not tinkered with the overall organization of the book, so that instructors who have used a previous edition will have no difficulty integrating this edition into their course outlines and lectures. The chapters follow a linear sequence in which five major parts (Getting Started, Observation and Measurement, Design and Implementation, Describing Data and Drawing Inferences, and Statistical Tests) are subdivided into three chapters each. Once again, there is a sample research proposal (in Chapter 2); instructions on writing a final research report, along with a sample report, in Appendix A; an introduction to meta-analysis in Appendix C; and a glossary of terms. The appendices and glossary are again tabbed so that they are easy to find, and there is a summary list of statistical equations inside the front and back covers. As before, preview questions open each chapter and serve as section headings in the material that follows. Each chapter ends with a summary of ideas, a list of key terms, and multiple-choice and discussion questions and answers for review.

Those familiar with our other work will know that we are not wedded to any single scientific method, theory, or unit of analysis (Rosenthal & Rosnow, 2008; Rosnow, 1981). As the range of interests of psychological researchers is vast, and human behavior is typically fluid, complex, and multifaceted, we are reminded all the time that empirical findings are situated in a sociotemporal context and that observations and interpretations are circumscribed by the observer's perspective and experiential frame of reference (Rosnow & Georgoudi, 1986). Thus, one of the core themes of this book is not to foreclose prematurely on tools, techniques, and ideas that are methodologically and ethically unassailable for usefully addressing a particular question of interest from more than one vantage point. To accentuate the broad base of scientific thinking, we have tried to connect this approach with the empirical reasoning in a number of areas by using both contemporary and classic examples. We have tried to give a sense of the continuity of science and the idea that each generation of researchers builds on the important findings of previous researchers in a chain of discovery and understanding.

Continuity is also implicit in our discussion of data analysis, for example, the important idea that statistical significance tests can be parsed into one or more definitions of effect size multiplied by one or more definitions of study size. Once students have a good grasp of this conceptual relationship, they should begin to perceive that statistical procedures are interconnected at a fundamental level. Though we assume that most students who are assigned this book as a primary text will have had some exposure to basic statistics, we also proceed on the assumption that few will have total recall of the fundamentals or will look forward to having to wrestle again with statistics. Thus, we review basic concepts and procedures, while avoiding the use of any mathematics beyond the high school level. Using tutorial examples, we illustrate statistical procedures not only in the context of the student's research, but also in applications outside a research course so that the student will see and understand what is behind the research that is reported in newspaper, TV, blogs, and online stories of scientific results and claims.

Though the main focus of our discussions of statistical data analysis is on the most popular procedures, we also discuss many recent developments that may not be as well known. Guided by the instructor's lectures, even students with little or no training in statistics should be able to master the basic data-analytic skills by reading these chapters and repeating the steps and exercises that are presented. The speediest method of performing complex calculations is with the aid of a good computer program. As statistician John W. Tukey (1977) counseled, we can also learn much by shifting our point of view and exploring the data in different ways. Our own philosophy of data analysis is to engage with statistics by showing, through intuitive reasoning and examples, what the results tell us. Instructors who teach students to perform their calculations on a computer will find that our emphasis on the concrete and arithmetical aspects of data analysis will complement any statistics program chosen. We also describe useful data-analytic procedures that might not yet be available in popular computer programs but that can be performed on a calculator.

 ## New to This Edition

A primary impetus behind this new edition of *Beginning Behavioral Research* was the release by the American Psychological Association (APA) of a sixth edition of its publication manual. We began by updating the sample report in Appendix A to make it consistent with the APA Manual. However, there are several departures in the student's final report from the strict style of the sixth edition of the APA Manual. Examples include the content of the title page of the student's report in Appendix A and the inclusion of an appendix in that report, as described in the text. Serving as our model was the ninth edition of Rosnow and Rosnow's (2012) *Writing Papers in Psychology*, which emphasizes the APA style while ensuring (a) that instructors will find reported the information they need to assess the originality and quality of their students' research reports and (b) that students who may have no further interest in the APA style after the baccalaureate are not needlessly distracted or bogged down by rules specifically written for authors of papers submitted to journals.

We have added some new box discussions and removed some previous ones, and we have also added several examples. For instance, we have added a section in Chapter 12 that explores what certain effect size indicators tell us of practical importance. The focus of that particular discussion is on randomized clinical trials, 2×2 tables of independent counts, and health-related statistics such as relative risk, the odds ratio, absolute risk, the number needed to treat, and the correlation coefficient (phi). As pointed out recently by Gerd Gigerenzer and his coauthors, confusion about risk statistics is not limited to the general public (Gigerenzer, Gaissmaier, Kurz-Milcke, Schwartz, & Woloshin, 2008), but it is the susceptible public that must ultimately pay the price of that confusion. Stirring misconceptions about the concept of statistical significance into this mix can sometimes produce a bewildering balancing act between statistical significance and relative risk.

Among other changes in this edition of *Beginning Behavioral Research*, the student's sample proposal in Chapter 2 has been updated. In Chapter 4, there is additional emphasis on the issue of plausible rival hypotheses and the third-variable problem as they relate to causal inference. There is a new section in that chapter with illustrations drawn from work on social network analysis. In Chapter 5, there is a new section on the measurement of implicit attitudes. In Chapter 7, we have tightened the narrative and also removed the detailed discussion of the Solomon design. In Chapter 8, the explanation of the use of propensity scores has been made into a new section. In Chapter 10, we propose a way of reporting modes that should increase their informational value (Box 10.2). In Chapter 11, we reordered the sequence in which different correlations are discussed in order to improve the flow of the discussion. In Chapter 12, we added a new section on the counternull statistic. In Chapter 13, we emphasize Cohen's d as an effect size indicator with independent-sample and paired t tests. In Chapter 14, there is more on the use of contrasts and effect sizes in comparisons of more than two conditions. Chapter 15 concludes with the binomial effect-size display (BESD), which had previously been in an earlier chapter.

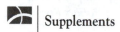 ## Supplements

Instructors have access to **PowerPoint lecture notes**, and an **Instructor's Manual with Tests**, also available through the **Pearson MyTest** computerized test generator.

MySearchLab with eText can be packaged with this text. MySearchLab inlcudes an eText, flashcards, chapter quizzes that report directly to your gradebook, and a wide range of writing, grammar and research tools and access to a variety of academic journals, census data, Associated Press newsfeeds, and discipline-specific readings to hone students' writing and research skills.

Operation ARIES (Acquiring Research Investigative and Evaluative Skills) – Available through MySearchLab or standalone, Operations ARIES is an interactive role-play game that teaches research methods and critical thinking skills. This simulation features a "save the world" plot that requires students to learn and apply critical thinking skills and scientific principles to uncover and foil an extraterrestrial plot to colonize Earth. This supplement was authored by Keith Millis, Northern Illinois University, Art Graesser, University of Memphis, and Diane Halpern, Claremont McKenna College.

 ## Acknowledgments

Margaret Ritchie did the copyediting and also prepared the subject and author indices. Margaret has edited so many of our books for several different publishers that we have lost count, but we always consider ourselves fortunate when she is available to work with us on a new book or a new edition.

The sample research report in Appendix A is based on real data from an unpublished research study by Dr. Bruce Rind. We are grateful to him for allowing us to reanalyze the data to illustrate several points discussed in the later chapters and to represent the study as one by a fictitious student named "Mary Jones."

We thank the following reviewers whose insights and suggestions were helpful to us in preparing this edition of *Beginning Behavioral Research*: Canan Karatekin (University of Minnesota), Thomas Malloy (Rhode Island College), Brenda Russell (Castleton State College), Carey S. Ryan

(University of Nebraska at Omaha), Mark R. Seely (Saint Joseph's College), Pamela Stuntz (Texas Christian University), and Joseph R. Troisi II (Saint Anselm College).

The first edition of this book was published by Macmillan in 1993, where Christine Cardone was our editor. When Macmillan was acquired by Prentice Hall, editors from the second to the fourth edition were Peter Janzow, Jennifer Gilliland, and Jayme Heffler. After Pearson acquired Prentice Hall, we worked with Jayme Heffler on the fifth edition, then with Jeff Marshall on the sixth edition, and on this seventh edition, with Stephen Frail, and his assistant, Maddy Schricker. Each of these people, as well as their associates from production to marketing, contributed to the development and longevity of this book. We are grateful to them all. We also want to acknowledge the skill and professionalism of Abinaya Rajendran and her team of coworkers at Integra-PDY, who worked so diligently on this seventh edition.

Certain tables and figures (noted in the text) have by permission been reproduced in part or in their entirety, for which we thank the authors, representatives, and publishers cited as sources in footnotes.

This is our 18th book together in a collaboration and deep friendship that began back in Massachusetts many years ago while one of us was teaching at Boston University and the other at Harvard University. Throughout this long comradeship, Mimi Rosnow and MaryLu Rosenthal contributed to each one of our books through their feedback, counseling, and skillful assistance. They improved not only our books, but us as well in ways too numerous to count.

MaryLu Rosenthal died in October 2010. Her absence from our lives is a constant reminder of the joy she brought to us and how much we miss her.

Ralph L. Rosnow
Robert Rosenthal

About the Authors

Robert Rosenthal   Ralph L. Rosnow

Photo by Mimi Rosnow

Ralph L. Rosnow is Thaddeus Bolton Professor Emeritus at Temple University in Philadelphia, PA, where he taught research methods for many years in the psychology department and directed the Ph.D. program in social and organizational psychology. He has also taught research methods at Boston University and Harvard University and has been a consultant in basic and applied research and data analysis. He has long been interested in how people make sense of their experiential world and justify their inferences and generalizations. He has explored this topic in research, theory, articles, and books from the perspective of attitude and impression formation, the psychology of rumor and gossip, interpersonal acumen, epistemology, ethics, and data analysis. Since retiring from Temple University, his writing interests have been directed toward focused data analysis, ethical issues and methodological conflicts, and, with his wife, Mimi Rosnow, updating their writing guide for psychology students, now in its ninth edition. He has served on and chaired professional committees in psychology, served on editorial boards of journals and encyclopedias, and was a general editor (with the late Robert E. Lana) of the Reconstruction of Society series of books published by Oxford University Press. He is a Fellow of the American Association for the Advancement of Science, the American Psychological Association and other professional societies, and a Charter Fellow of the Association for Psychological Science. He is a recipient of the Society of General Psychology's George A. Miller Award and in 2006 was honored with a published Festschrift, entitled *Advances in Social and Organizational Psychology*, edited by Donald A. Hantula.

Robert Rosenthal is a Distinguished Professor at the University of California at Riverside and Edgar Pierce Professor of Psychology, Emeritus, Harvard University. His research has centered for many years on the role of the self-fulfilling prophecy in everyday life and in laboratory situations. His special interests include the effects of teachers' expectations on students' performance, the effects of experimenters' expectations on the results of their research, and the effects of clinicians' expectations on their patients' mental and physical health. He also has strong interests in sources of artifact in behavioral research and in various quantitative procedures. In the realm of data analysis, his special interests are in experimental design and analysis, contrast analysis, and meta-analysis. His most recent books and articles are about these areas of data analysis and about the nature of nonverbal communication in teacher-student, doctor-patient, manager-employee, judge-jury, and psychotherapist-client interaction. He served as co-chair of the Task Force on Statistical Inference of the American Psychological Association (APA) and chair of the Research Committee of the Bayer Institute for Health Care Communication. He is a co-recipient of two behavioral science awards of the American Association for the Advancement of Science (1960, 1993) and is an elected Fellow of the American Academy of Arts and Sciences. He is also a recipient of the James McKeen

Cattell Award of the Association for Psychological Science; the Distinguished Scientist Award of the Society of Experimental Social Psychology; the Samuel J. Messick Distinguished Scientific Contributions Award of APA's Division 5—Evaluation, Measurement, and Statistics; the APA's Distinguished Scientific Award for Applications of Psychology; and the American Psychological Foundation's Gold Medal Award for Life Achievement. In 1993, he was honored with a published Festschrift, entitled *Interpersonal Expectations: Theory, Research, and Applications*, edited by Peter David Blanck.

Rosenthal and Rosnow have collaborated on research, articles, and books for many years. Their earliest partnership was on problems of subject effects when the research samples are drawn from a population of volunteers. Their advanced text, *Essentials of Behavioral Research: Methods and Data Analysis* (first published in 1984 and in a third edition in 2008), has been cited over 2,800 times. Among their other books are *Artifact in Behavioral Research* (1969); *The Volunteer Subject* (1975); *Primer of Methods for the Behavioral Sciences* (1975); *Understanding Behavioral Science: Research Methods for Research Consumers* (1984); *Contrast Analysis: Focused Comparisons in the Analysis of Variance* (1985); *People Studying People: Artifacts and Ethics in Behavioral Research* (1997); and (with Donald B. Rubin) *Contrasts and Effect Sizes in Behavioral Research: A Correlational Approach* (2000). Their work has been reprinted in anthologies, and several of their early books have been reissued by Cambridge University Press and Oxford University Press, including a collection entitled *Artifacts in Behavioral Research: Robert Rosenthal and Ralph L. Rosnow's Classic Books* (Oxford University Press, 2009).

CHAPTER 1

Behavioral Research and the Scientific Method

Preview Questions

- Why study research methods and data analysis?
- What alternatives are there to the scientific method?
- How do scientists use empirical reasoning?
- How is empirical reasoning used in behavioral research?
- How do extraempirical factors come into play?
- What does behavioral research cover?
- How does research go from descriptive to relational to experimental?
- What are the characteristics of good researchers?

Why Study Research Methods and Data Analysis?

Traditionally, reading, 'riting, and 'rithmetic—the three Rs—have been viewed as the fundamentals of education that we have been taught since grade school. A fourth R, "researching," is now regarded as another crucial skill for any educated person (Hult, 1996). In high school, you were introduced to the steps involved in "researching" a term paper by systematically "looking things up" (that is, searching for and retrieving information). In college science courses, *researching* implies a different kind of systematic approach to exploring a question, an approach that is traditionally called the **scientific method**. Embracing all branches of science, the applications of this approach vary from one research discipline to another. Researchers in disciplines as varied as anthropology, biology, business, chemistry, communication, economics, geology, physics, political science, psychology, sociology, and many others use some variation of this approach. However, if becoming a researcher is not your goal, you may be wondering why you need to know about the scientific method or to study techniques of research. There are at least five good reasons.

One reason is that our modern way of life is largely the creation of science and technology, and we enhance our understanding of the full range of this influence by learning about the logic and evidence used by researchers to open up the world to scrutiny and explanation. By analogy, viewing paintings, drawings, and sculpture in a museum becomes more meaningful when we know something about the processes and creative ideas that were involved in producing the works of art. Similarly, when we understand how conclusions were reached, we can attach more meaning to hearing that a scientific poll of likely voters found Candidate X ahead of Candidate Y by 4 percentage points with a 5% margin of error, or that a study conducted by developmental psychologists found that higher quality child care is related to advanced cognitive and language skills, or that social psychologists discovered there is a diffusion of responsibility when many people are witnesses to a crisis, or that an epidemiological study reported a statistically significant relation between health problems and exposure to some environmental substance, or that a new drug was found in a randomized clinical trial to reduce the risk of some disease by an impressive percentage.

Besides the richer appreciation of the information that science brings to our lives, a second reason for studying research methods is that *not* clearly understanding how researchers cast and address questions sometimes costs us dearly. Doctors, teachers, lawyers, the clergy, and politicians have an influence on our daily lives, and most of us are familiar with how people in these fields go about their work. But few people seem to have even a vague idea of how researchers in different fields create and test hypotheses and theories that enlarge our understanding of the world. As a consequence, people frequently give credence to misleading generalizations based on faulty data, or accept and repeat conclusions based on bogus data, or succumb to claims for cure-all remedies or panaceas for warding off diseases when there is not a shred of reliable evidence of their effectiveness apart from the power of the placebo effect. Studying the conceptual bases of various research methods, and having the opportunity to conduct an empirical study and then to analyze and interpret the results under the watchful eye of an experienced guide, will begin to sensitize you to the difference between well-grounded scientific conclusions and dubious claims masquerading as generalizable facts.

A third reason is to acquire information and skills you can use later. For example, your attention may be riveted by a pharmaceutical advertisement claiming a new drug's proven effectiveness in reducing the relative risk of a disease by 50% or more. However, it has been noted that most people have exaggerated ideas about the practical and personal implications of statistics like relative risk reduction (Gigerenzer, Gaissmaier, Kurz-Milcke, Schwartz, & Woloshin, 2008). Once you have mastered the material in Chapters 11 and 15, you should be better able to analyze and make sense of the basic information usually reported in the press or on reliable Web sites. You will also be less likely to fall into the trap of mistaking statistical significance for practical significance, a distinction of great consequence that is not limited to health statistics. As the authors of a recent book, *The Numbers Game*, stated, "Numbers now saturate the news, political life. ... For good or for evil, they are today's preeminent public language—and those who speak it rule" (Blastland & Dilnot, 2009, p. x). In business, government, and policymaking, as in any decision-making area, you will be served well by developing a good conceptual understanding of basic methods of data analysis and what summary statistics can and cannot tell you, of how it is possible to generalize from the known to the unknown, and of the risk of "seeing" something that is not there balanced against the risk of *not* seeing something that *is* there.

A fourth reason for studying (and doing) research is to learn about the limits of particular studies and methods, but not only those used in behavioral research. For example, correlational findings in epidemiological studies may be partly (or sometimes entirely) due to variables other than those measured, and results in experimental trials of new drugs administered to young, healthy, mobile volunteer subjects may not apply to aged, infirm, hospitalized patients with advanced diseases (Brody, 2002). In Chapter 3, we explore the limits imposed by institutional review boards that are charged with overseeing the ethical responsibilities of scientific researchers. In research with human participants, another limitation occurs when those whose behavior is being studied know they are being observed for some scientific purpose; they may behave quite differently from those who don't know. In Chapter 7, we describe techniques used by researchers to overcome this problem. These techniques (as indeed all studies and methods) are also limited in some ways. However, despite these limitations, behavioral researchers have formulated empirically grounded answers to questions about how and why people feel, think, and behave as they do (see also Box 1.1).

A fifth reason for studying and doing behavioral research is that some students will find this activity so much fun and so absorbing that they may want to make a career of it!

BOX 1.1 The Provisional Nature of Scientific Knowledge

Because even the most carefully designed research study is limited in some way, the growth and expansion of scientific knowledge is in a constant state of improvement. For many years, philosophers and historians of science have speculated on the characteristics of this unending cycle of development. For example, Thomas S. Kuhn (1962, 1977), a physicist turned scientific historian, believed that major advances in science appear as "paradigm shifts" resulting from revolutionary insights into the physical world in which we live. Another view was proposed by Karl Popper (1963, 1972), an Austrian-born British philosopher of science, who compared progress in science with Charles

Darwin's theory of "survival of the fittest." Popper's idea was that the way scientific knowledge develops is through a continuous process of empirically testing logical conjectures and eliminating those inferences that fail to survive these rigorous trials. No matter whether the growth and expansion of scientific knowledge is viewed as revolutionary or evolutionary, on one point all scientists seem to agree: Scientific knowledge is relative and provisional. As one noted scientist put it, "Scientists know that questions are not settled; rather, they are given provisional answers for which it is contingent upon the imagination of followers to find more illuminating solutions" (Baltimore, 1997, p. 8).

What Alternatives Are There to the Scientific Method?

The scientific method is not the only approach commonly used to make sense of things and give us information. Philosophers, novelists, and theologians seek to give us a coherent picture of our world, but they do not use the scientific method to organize ideas and explain things. What is distinctive about the different approaches used by scientists and nonscientists to formulate a sense of understanding and belief? One scholar who was fascinated by this question was the American philosopher Charles Sanders Peirce (1839–1914). Peirce conceived of the scientific method as being one among four distinctive approaches to explaining things and providing a foundation for strongly held beliefs; he called this process "the fixation of beliefs." Peirce (pronounced "purse") called the other three approaches the *method of tenacity,* the *method of authority,* and the *a priori method.* Each, he implied, is characterized by a formulaic way of thinking and behaving (Peirce, 1966).

Peirce thought the **method of tenacity** was the most primitive approach of all, because it is bound by tradition and involves clinging stubbornly (tenaciously) to claims or beliefs merely because they have been around for a while. It is not easy to shake fixed beliefs or to open up closed minds (Mitchell, 1985). Those who exhibit this kind of behavior resemble an ostrich that buries its head in the sand, Peirce said, because they go through life excluding anything that might challenge or alter their thinking. Some false ideas can endure for centuries. For example, beginning with the Ptolemaic treatise in the 2nd century A.D., people were convinced that the earth was fixed, immobile, and at the center of the universe. It was one of the ancient astronomer Ptolemy's few misconceptions, but it was a whopper that endured for over a thousand years. It was not until Copernicus's insight that the sun, not the earth, is the center of the universe that the geocentric (i.e., earth-centered) design was challenged, though the Copernican system also left much room for improvement (it neglected to show that the sun is a center of force). Indeed, it was not until the advent of modern astronomy, or what one historian called the "witness of the naked eye" (Boorstein, 1985, p. 305), that the geocentric design was finally swept away by the scientific method.

In our own time, the method of tenacity still has a pernicious hold on many people's convictions and superstitions (see, e.g., Box 1.2). Peirce thought that superstitions and other dogmatic beliefs are

BOX 1.2 Flying Saucers, Big Foot, and Other Odd Beliefs

Myth, folklore, and superstition illustrate the method of tenacity's powerful hold on beliefs that can endure for centuries. Carl G. Jung, the noted Swiss psychiatrist and psychologist, theorized about the persistence of stories of "flying saucers," unidentified flying objects (UFOs) piloted by extraterrestrials. This myth, Jung (1910, 1959) theorized, is a projection of people's fears and uncertainties about the world situation and their wish for a redeeming supernatural force. The UFO story usually takes one of two forms: It is said either that benevolent superior beings from another planet have come to save humanity (which was depicted in the 2008 movie The Day the Earth Stood Still), or that menacing creatures threaten humanity and this threat will unify people of diverse ideologies to

make a stand against a common foe (as dramatized in the 1996 movie Independence Day). There are also people who still insist that the earth is flat, that sunrise and sunset are optical illusions, and that the 1969 moon landing was an elaborate hoax staged in a hangar in Arizona (Martin, 2001). In a fascinating case, it was revealed some years ago that a prankster, named Ray L. Wallace, had created the modern myth of Bigfoot (or Sasquatch), the name for the giant, hairy, upright biped rumored to be living in the woods of the Pacific Northwest. After Wallace's death in 2002, his family displayed the carved wooden feet that he had used to stamp a track of oversized footprints. Despite all evidence to the contrary, Bigfoot defenders still insist that the creature exists.

like the cadence that concludes a musical phrase in a symphony and provides closure. Sometimes this closure seems to be based on what social psychologists call a "false consensus" or "pluralistic ignorance"; it means that people have a tendency to misperceive, and frequently to overestimate, the extent to which others believe the same thing (Kelley & Thibaut, 1969; Ross, Greene, & House, 1977). Telling themselves that only *their* beliefs or opinions are correct, they dismiss counterarguments as deviant and seek out information that is consistent with their own biases about how the world should be understood (Marks & Miller, 1987; Ross et al., 1977; Sherman, Presson, & Chassin, 1984). Classic research by psychologist Milton Rokeach (1960) resulted in measures of the degree of dogmatism, or closed-mindedness, showing that people who score high on dogmatism are not only highly defensive about their beliefs but less likely to act on the plausible merits of reliable information independent of their impression of the source (Powell, 1962).

The **method of authority** was Peirce's term for the presumption that something is true because someone in a position of authority says it is. Peirce saw that blind obedience to authority is similar in some ways to the method of tenacity (both imply conformity), but he thought the method of authority superior in some ways, although flawed. To illustrate the negative side, he described the violence that resulted when ordinary people obeyed the word of authority to cruelly punish those accused of witchcraft. Unimaginable atrocities committed in the Holocaust during World War II and "ethnic-cleansing" carnage occurring even today are instances of the heights of cruelty that can be reached in the name of a malevolent authority. Other present-day examples on the negative side include unscrupulous people who pose as authorities, preying on human weakness by using fakery. Think of medical quacks, food faddists, faith healers, TV psychics, cult leaders, and eccentric sexual theorists (M. Gardner, 1957; Shermer, 1997). The authority of these fakers and hucksters is in the eyes of their victims, however, so that it behooves the buyer to beware.

Peirce thought the method of authority was at least a small improvement on the method of tenacity because civilized society would cease to exist without people's willingness to obey just laws and to carry out reasonable orders. Researchers are subject to the benevolent authority of an ever-evolving social contract between science and society concerning the rights of research participants and the privileges granted to researchers (Rosnow, 1997). Other examples on the positive side are the astute physician who prescribes a drug or regimen to cure an illness, the skilled electrician who advises the replacement of wiring that is about to burn out, and the expert mechanic who warns that the brakes on a car are worn and need replacing. We depend on their honesty and the authority of their expertise. On the other hand, not everyone perceives the same source as credible, so some people are quite willing to accept claims that others reject as preposterous. One writer discussed consumers who reject the medical establishment but often unquestionably accept the authority of someone without the slightest medical expertise or qualification who, in their minds, makes a "credible" case for the medicinal value of a health supplement that was never critically tested (R. Walker, 2006).

Even if we know very little about medicine, wiring, or brakes, we can use a third strategy of Peirce's to ask questions to help us better understand the authoritative recommendations. The defining characteristic of this third strategy—the **a priori method**—is that people rely primarily on their individual powers of reason and logic to make sense of the world and to explain it to others. However, as one clever writer put it, "hubris sometimes traps us" into thinking we know more than we do, whereas in reality the understanding we seek is "just out of reach" (Wainer, 2009, p. xv). Nonetheless, the a priori method, Peirce (1966) argued, is "far more intellectual and respectable" than the previous two methods (p. 106); it has proved itself quite robust in the hands of mathematicians and philosophers. In fact, we use the a priori method all the time. When you ruminate on what career path to take, or you successfully figure out what is wrong with your computer, you bring reason and logic into play. Thinking rationally and logically can also sometimes serve as a first line of defense against hoaxes and hucksters who depend on human gullibility. We can approach dubious claims with a questioning mind that, as one psychologist put it, "resists being overly impressed" (Gilovich, 1991, p. 187). However, even highly educated and sophisticated individuals are not immune to wishful and fearful thinking and are therefore susceptible to those who use gimmicks and numbers to trick people into making impulsive decisions. The mathematician who coined the term "innumeracy" (it means a lack of knowledge or understanding of the meaning of numbers) told of how his vulnerability to whim "entrained a series of ill-fated investment decisions" that he still found "excruciating to recall" (Paulos, 2003, p. 1).

Peirce also cautioned that the a priori method is constrained by the limits of pure reason. For example, suppose you make a terrific argument on the basis of reason and logic that A causes B, but I disagree on the basis of my own impeccable reason and logic. Do we just have to let it go at that? What we need, Peirce said, is to figure out a way of drawing on nature to help us resolve our disagreement. This is the role of the scientific method, to provide a framework for drawing on independent realities to evaluate claims rather than to rely only on tradition, authority, or armchair reasoning. As a noted social psychologist stated, we use the scientific method in psychology to help us sort out what we know about human nature from what we only think we know (Milgram, 1977). The scientific method depends heavily on the use of empirical research (**empirical** means "based on observation"). However, as you read further in this book, you will see that the term *scientific method* is actually a misnomer (or "misapplied name"). The reason that we call it a misnomer is that the "scientific method" is not synonymous with a single, fixed empirical method; instead, it embraces a great many procedures and empirical techniques. In particular, it can be distinguished by what we define next as *empirical reasoning*.

How Do Scientists Use Empirical Reasoning?

By **empirical reasoning**, we mean a combination of careful logic, organized observation, and measurement that is open to scrutiny by others. One scientist used the following analogy to describe how this idealized process works: Suppose someone is trying to unlock a door with a set of previously untried keys. The person thinks, "If this key fits the lock, then the lock will spring when I turn the key" (Conant, 1957, p. xii). Similarly, the scientist has a choice of "keys" in the form of empirical techniques, logically decides on one form of organized observation and measurement, and thinks, "I'll try it and see." The same "key" is available to others with the knowledge, resources, and skill to use it to open up the world for empirical scrutiny. In theory, it is this dependence on empirical reasoning (logic, organized observation, and measurement) that unifies research scientists, no matter their specialized fields, empirical strategies and techniques, or the focus of their research. Later in this chapter, we discuss three far-reaching research strategies that use empirical reasoning (characterized here as *descriptive, relational,* and *experimental*), and we give examples of specialized techniques within these broad categories throughout this book.

For example, we will have more to say in later chapters about the different forms that experiments can take, such as different forms of randomized controlled experiments and single-case experimental procedures. Interestingly, the usual dictionary definition of *experiment* does not refer to "randomized" or "controlled" or "single-case." It is more along the lines of a test or "trial" (i.e., as in a clinical trial to test the usefulness of a pharmaceutical or psychosocial intervention) or procedure that is used to discover something, or to try out a principle, or to put a supposition to an empirical test (as in physics). For example, a few years ago, the editors of *Physics Today* invited readers to nominate the "most beautiful experiments of all time" (Johnson, 2002). Ranked first was Thomas Young's famous double-slit experiment, in the early 1800s, in which light passed first from a small source through a slit in a screen to a pair of slits in another screen to fall on an observation screen. The purpose of Young's experiment was to put two rival theories to an empirical test (viz., that light is made of bullet-like particles as opposed to wavelike motion). Young reasoned that if light exists as particles, the final image should make a pattern of two exact lines resembling the paired slits, but if light is wavelike, the final image should spread out (to rediscover the answer yourself, visit http://www.cavendishscience. org/phys/tyoung/tyoung.htm). Ranked second by *Physics Today* was an imaginary (or "thought") experiment of Galileo's in the late 1500s, in which he reasoned that dropping two objects of different weights from the Leaning Tower of Pisa would prove Aristotle was wrong when he concluded that in the same medium, heavier objects always fall faster than lighter ones. (When American astronauts landed on the moon in 1969, they demonstrated for all the world to see that Galileo's empirical reasoning worked on the moon). Another favorite "experiment" of the *Physics Today* readers was Foucault's pendulum, Jean-Bernard-Léon Foucault's 19th-century demonstration of the idea that the earth revolves on its axis. Science museums generally display Foucault's pendulum, which consists of a perpetually swinging iron ball suspended from a wire, with a stylus on the bottom tracing a slightly different clockwise pattern in the sand beneath it with each revolution. (Incidentally, in the Southern Hemisphere the rotation of Foucault's pendulum is counterclockwise, and on the equator, it does not move at all.) (See also Box 1.3.)

 BOX 1.3 Empirical Reasoning in Ancient Times

A far earlier case of empirical reasoning (perverse though it was) was described by Athenaeus of Naucratis (in Egypt), a 2nd-century Greek philosopher (Yonge, 1854). Athenaeus had been convinced by the governor of Egypt that citron ingested before any kind of food was an antidote for "the evil effects from poison" (p. 141). As Athenaeus explained, the governor had condemned some robbers to being given to wild beasts and bitten by asps. On their way to the theater where the execution was to be carried out, they passed a woman who was selling fruit and, taking pity on them, gave them citron to eat. When they were later bitten by the beasts and asps, they suffered no injury. When told about the episode in the marketplace, the governor reasoned that it must have been the citron that had saved their lives. He ordered that the sentence be carried out again the next day and that citron be given to some of the prisoners before they were bitten. Those who ate the citron survived after they were bitten, but the others died immediately. Athenaeus noted that this grotesque experiment was repeated several times to test different preparations of citron.

Empirical reasoning is now deeply inculcated in the way that physicists and other scientists approach many problems. For example, you have probably seen video clips of the space shuttle *Challenger*'s dramatically televised accident on January 28, 1986, in which all seven astronauts lost their lives. Shortly thereafter, a panel of experts and other authorities was convened to look into the disaster and to try to figure out what caused it. One panel member was Richard P. Feynman, a theoretical physicist at the California Institute of Technology and a Nobel Prize recipient. Using empirical reasoning, Feynman came up with a simple way to demonstrate what had gone wrong in the frigid weather on the day of the launch. The rocket that boosted the shuttle contained two rubber seals in the form of rings, called O-rings, which were expected to be resilient but had never been used by NASA (National Aeronautics and Space Administration) in freezing temperature. Feynman reasoned that a lack of resilience of the O-rings when the temperature was below freezing would explain why the rocket had exploded the moment it was ignited. That is, highly flammable fuel would have leaked through the seals, caught fire, and exploded. Feynman wrestled with the question of how best to demonstrate a lack of resilience of those O-rings in a simple way that could be independently corroborated by scientists *and* nonscientists.

At the end of an exhausting day of listening to testimony and arguments, Feynman (1988) had a sudden inspiration when he returned to his hotel room:

> I'm feeling lousy and I'm eating dinner; I look at the table, and there's a glass of ice water. I say to myself, "Damn it. *I* can find out about the rubber *without* having NASA send notes back and forth: I just have to *try* it! All I have to do is get a sample of the rubber." (p. 146)

Early the next day, Feynman went to a hardware store, where he bought screwdrivers, pliers, and the smallest C-clamp he could find. He then went to NASA and used the screwdrivers to peel away a sample of the rubber, which he clamped and placed in a glass of ice water. When he removed the rubber and undid the clamp, the rubber did not spring back. In other words, for more than a few seconds, there was no resilience in the rubber when it was at a temperature of 32°F. It was not only a way of demonstrating the vulnerability of O-rings when it was freezing, but also a simple enough procedure for others to try for themselves.

 How Is Empirical Reasoning Used in Behavioral Research?

Empirical reasoning and experimentation entered into the scientific study of behavior at the end of the 19th century when the creative advances inspired by the applications of the scientific method in physics and biology led to the development of psychology as a distinct science. Wilhelm Wundt (1832–1920), with a background in medicine and experimental physiology, built the first formal experimental laboratory for studying psychological behavior in Leipzig, Germany, around 1879 (Boring, 1957). Around the same time, William James (1843–1910), with a background in philosophy and physiology, announced a graduate course in psychology at Harvard University in which the students participated in demonstration experiments that he arranged. In the 1880s, experimental laboratories were established by two of Wundt's students, G. Stanley Hall at Johns Hopkins University in Baltimore, Maryland, and J. McKeen Cattell at the University of Pennsylvania in Philadelphia. By 1892, James's demonstrational laboratory had also developed into a genuine laboratory under the direction of Hugo Münsterberg, a former student of Wundt's. Incidentally, Wundt was sensitive to the idea that not all aspects of human psychology could be addressed experimentally in the lab. He invested considerable energy in writing a monumental work on the dynamic interrelationship between human nature and societal changes, a work he titled *Völkerpsychologie* (or "folk psychology").

Empirical reasoning was not practiced only in the laboratory or only experimentally. In England, Sir Francis Galton (1822–1911) cleverly demonstrated the application of empirical reasoning to questions that had been previously thought to lie outside science (Forrest, 1974). In one of his many fascinating studies, Galton used longevity data to test the efficacy of certain prayers. In England, the health and longevity of the royal family were prayed for weekly or monthly nationwide. Galton asked: Do members of royal families live longer than individuals of humbler birth? In 1872, in an article entitled "Statistical Inquiries Into the Efficacy of Prayer," Galton reported that, of 97 members of royal families, the mean age attained by males had been 64.04 years. Compared to 945 members of the clergy, who had lived to a mean age of 69.49; 294 lawyers who had lived to 68.14; 244 doctors who had lived to 67.31; 366 officers in the Royal Navy who had lived to 68.40; 569 officers of the Army who had lived to 67.07; and 1,632 "gentry" who had lived to 70.22, members of royal families had fared worse than expectations that were based on the many prayers on their behalf (Medawar, 1969, p. 4). Galton could not, of course, control for individual differences in the sincerity of people's prayers; nor did he reject the idea that faith can have powerful effects. For some people, praying may bring serenity in distress and thereby strengthen their resolution to face hardships, whereas for others, it may itself become a source of further stress and confusion (cf. Exline, 2002; Medawar, 1969; Myers, 2000; Pargament, 2002).

Since the time of Wundt, James, and Galton, there has been phenomenal growth in the scientific study of behavior. Open any introductory psychology text and you will find hundreds of contemporary examples of the application of empirical reasoning to the scientific study of cognition, perception, and behavior, and there are also hundreds of research journals in the behavioral and social sciences that regularly publish reams of empirical studies. Most of these studies closely fit within the contours of the designs described in Chapters 7–9, including many fascinating demonstration experiments. For instance, Jose M. R. Delgado (1963) conducted an unusual demonstration experiment with a charging bull to prove that the electrical stimulation of a part of the brain results in decreased aggressive behavior in animals. Previously, Delgado had done studies with monkeys. In one study, the boss monkey in a colony of monkeys that lived together had an electrode inserted in his caudate nucleus. The switch that turned on the current to the monkey's electrode (through a tiny radio transmitter) was available to the other monkeys. They learned to approach and press the switch whenever the boss monkey began to get nasty, causing him to become less aggressive immediately. In a more dramatic demonstration, Delgado got into a ring with a fierce bull whose brain had been implanted with electrodes. As the bull came charging toward him, Delgado turned on the radio-controlled brain stimulation, causing the bull to stop in midcharge and become passive. Few experimenters have opportunities to demonstrate such confidence in their empirical reasoning.

We mentioned that there are many different forms of experiments, and to anticipate our later discussion a little, let us look at two more examples in two major areas of psychology. One experiment was conducted by Stephen J. Ceci and his coworkers in developmental psychology at Cornell University, and the other (a classic study in the area of social psychology) was conducted by Solomon Asch many years earlier. The experimental designs were very different, as were the participants and the procedures used, but each study was seminal in expanding our understanding of human suggestibility as well as in setting a course for follow-up studies by other behavioral researchers. Considered together, they illustrate a characteristic of behavioral research that has been described as **methodological pluralism**, perhaps an arcane way of saying that, by necessity, researchers use different tools and designs (different methods) because each is limited in some way (Rosnow, 1981, 1986; Rosnow & Georgoudi, 1986). Each method represents and reflects a particular perspective on the phenomenon of interest and the multifaceted complexity of human nature (see also Box 1.4). Another common element in these two experiments is that each used a form of *active deception* that subjected the research participants to false information, a topic explored in depth in Chapter 3.

Ceci and his colleagues focused on the accuracy of children's eyewitness testimony. They designed an experiment in which a character named "Sam Stone" was described to 3- to 6-year-olds as someone who was very clumsy and broke things (Ceci & Bruck, 1993, 1995; White, Leichtman, & Ceci, 1997). A person identified as Sam Stone visited the children's nursery school, where he chatted briefly with them during a storytelling session, but he did not behave clumsily or break anything. The next day, the children were shown a ripped book and a soiled teddy bear and were asked if they knew how the objects had been damaged. Over the course of the next 10 weeks, the children

BOX 1.4 Methodological Pluralism and the "Watcher" Behind the "Look"

An analogy proposed by the existentialist philosopher Jean-Paul Sartre (1905–1980) is relevant to the concept of methodological pluralism. Sartre (1956) described how, when we look at someone who is looking back at us, it is hard to see the "watcher" behind the "look" at the same time that we focus on the person's appearance. We see the face (the eyes, nose, mouth, etc.) of the person watching us, but there is more to the person than just his or her physical appearance. It is as if the personality behind the look is neutralized, put out of play. To catch a glimpse of the whole person, we shift our concentration back and forth, attending first to one thing (such as the person's appearance or manner of expressing himself or herself) and then to another (such as what the person is actually saying, or doing, or has done, or intends to do). Methodological pluralism is a way of shifting our attention to different dimensions of a problem or a phenomenon (such as human suggestibility). The ultimate objective is to try to pull together all these different empirical insights within the conceptual framework of a unified theory.

were reinterviewed. Each time, the interviewer planted clues about the existence of Sam Stone, such as "I wonder whether Sam Stone was wearing long pants or short pants when he ripped the book?" or "I wonder if Sam Stone got the teddy bear dirty on purpose or by accident?" The result of this manipulation was that the planted stereotype of Sam Stone carried over into the indoctrinated children's eyewitness reports. When asked, 72% of the 3- to 4-year-olds said that Sam Stone had ruined either the book or the teddy bear, and 45% of these children claimed that they had actually seen him do it (and they embellished their accounts with other details). The researchers used a comparison group (a *control group*) against which to assess the effect of their experimental manipulation. Children in this comparison condition underwent the suggestive interviews, but they received no planted information about Sam Stone. Ceci's finding was that the children in the comparison group made fewer false claims than the children in whom the stereotype had been planted.

Asch (1952) was interested in the degree to which people with normal intelligence will resist mindlessly conforming to a consensus view when faced with an objective reality that shows the consensus view to be false. In this famous experiment, a participant arrived at the psychology lab along with several other participants, who (unbeknownst to the true subject) were accomplices of the experimenter. Seated together at the same table, all of the participants were told by the experimenter that they would be asked to make judgments about the length of several lines. Each person was to judge which of three lines was closest in length to a standard line. The accomplices always stated their opinions first, after which the true subject expressed an opinion. The accomplices, instructed by the experimenter to act in collusion, sometimes gave obviously incorrect opinions, but they were unanimous. A third of the true subjects, Asch found, gave the same opinion as the accomplices. When they were interviewed later, the true subjects gave different reasons for yielding to the pressure exerted by the incorrect majority: (a) unawareness of being incorrect; (b) uneasiness about their own perceptions; and (c) wanting to appear the same as the majority. The most prevalent reaction of the true subjects, however, was to respond with what was objectively true rather than to go along with the false majority. The theoretical and moral implications of this study continue to be amplified in psychology (Hodges & Geyer, 2006).

How Do Extraempirical Factors Come into Play?

In Asch's experiment, the idea was to see whether people would depend on their own independent observations and resist a majority consensus that was clearly false. The reliance of the scientific method on empirical data and logical reasoning emphasizes the *primary* role of independent observation to ascertain what is true, but extraempirical factors play a role in science just as they do in everyday life (*extra,* as used in this context, means "beyond" independent observation). One reason is that universal laws require a leap of faith because of the limitations of human observation. As an illustration, one of the most powerful laws of science is Newton's first law of motion, which asserts that a body not acted on by any force will continue in a state of rest or, if the body is moving, remain in uniform motion in a straight line forever. Acceptance of this law is based partly on a leap of faith, however, as obviously no scientist can claim to have *observed* "a body not acted on by any force" (e.g., friction or gravity), much less *observed* a body moving "in a straight line forever." Thus, although independent observation is considered primary, there are aspects of physical reality that are beyond the bounds of our ability to observe directly.

We alluded to one of several extraempirical factors previously when we discussed the *Physics Today* informal poll of readers' nominations for "the most beautiful experiments in physics." Philosophers of science and others have discussed this idea of a sense of "beauty" or "elegance" in science, described as the **aesthetic aspect of science** (Chandrasekhar, 1987; Garfield, 1989a, 1989b; Gombrich, 1963; Hineline, 2005; Nisbet, 1976; Wechler, 1978). It is not uncommon to hear a scientist say that some study or finding or theory is "beautiful." A famous case was Albert Einstein's theory of general relativity, which an eminent mathematician (Paul Dirac) said was so beautiful that it *had* to be true (Kragh, 2002). In the *Physics Today* poll, when readers were asked how they defined the concept of *beauty* in science, they mentioned the "economy" of the experimental procedure and what they called an experiment's "deep play," meaning that the experiment was intensely absorbing and engaging. The respondents evaluated the top 10 experiments as epitomizing *beauty* in the "classical" sense of the term. That is to say, the logic and simplicity of the test or demonstration or apparatus or analysis were described "as inevitable and pure as the lines of a Greek monument" (G. Johnson, 2002, p. F3). These impressions are abstract, but perhaps if you have a sense of the aesthetic aspect of science, you may have the makings of a good scientist yourself.

Another extraempirical factor is the persuasive language (*rhetoric*) of science (Gross, 1990), by which we mean not only the tightly logical prose of the verbal modality in written reports but also the way in which numbers fortified by statistical data analysis are used to shore up facts and inductive inferences (Rosnow & Rosenthal, 1989b). We think of this as the **rhetoric of justification**, the concepts and specialized terms that young scientists learn to rely on to build arguments leading to particular conclusions. Of course, every specialized field has its own privileged rhetoric of justification (Gross, 1990; Pera & Shea, 1991): Lawyers sound like lawyers, philosophers like philosophers, doctors like doctors, and so on. To understand what scientists in different fields are saying, we must understand the terms and concepts they are using. In psychological science, McGuire (2006) noted, "When the verbalization is formally scientific (rather than colloquial), it typically takes the form of a hypothesis (proposition, statement) expressing the relation among the two or more variables, usually either a main-effect, interactional, or mediating relation" (p. 356). What are a *hypothesis,* a *main-effect* relation, an *interactional* relation, and a *mediating* relation? We define these and, of course, a great many other specialized terms throughout this book (see the Glossary on pages 344–356).

Professional researchers are expected to publish their empirical results in peer-reviewed journals. (*Peer* means a person who is similar in understanding, and the term *peer-reviewed journals* implies that before the articles are actually accepted for publication, they undergo reviews by other experts in the field.) In Appendix A, you will find a student's report that is structured in the tightly logical way typical of many research reports in psychology and other areas that have adopted the "APA style" (the style recommended in the *Publication Manual of the American Psychological Association*). This structure, which evolved over many years, currently consists of an abstract (or summary), an introduction, a method section, a results section, a discussion section, and a list of references cited in the report. The purpose of having a standardized organization is that it enables busy researchers to read articles in research journals more easily (because they conform to a similar structure) and it encourages authors to organize their thoughts systematically as they report their research to others.

Still another extraempirical factor that has been proposed is frequently called *visualization,* but we prefer the more general term **perceptibility***,* by which we mean that scientists often use images in the form of analogies to explain the operation of complicated phenomena. Metaphors and similes, in which we try to imagine one thing in terms of another, offer us a way of recasting subtle or complex ideas without, as one psychologist has put it, "slipping into trivia and meaninglessness" (Perloff, 2006, p. 315). Much has been written about the use of analogies not only in the rhetoric of science but also in everyday life (e.g., Barker, 1996; Billow, 1977; Gentner, Holyoak, & Kokinov, 2001; Gentner & Markman, 1997; Gigerenzer, 1991; Gross, 1990; Holyoak & Thagard, 1997; Kolodner, 1997; Lakoff & Johnson, 1980; Leary, 1990; A. I. Miller, 1986, 1996; Oppenheimer, 1956; Randhawa & Coffman, 1978; Weiner, 1991). "Her life was an uphill climb" and "He is between a rock and a hard place" are common examples of this usage. Vivid analogies can stimulate thought and can even provoke action, perhaps the reason that they have long been an intrinsic component of effective political oratory. In physics, a powerful image was invoked by Albert Einstein to express his visceral dislike of the uncertainty principle. It was during the period when quantum theorists first tried to convince colleagues that, given a great many atoms, each capable of a certain definite change, the proportion of atoms undergoing each change could be estimated, but it was not possible to state precisely the specific change that any given atom would undergo. A famous remark attributed to Einstein was that God "does not play dice with the world" (Clark, 1971; Jammer, 1966). What makes this imagery so affecting is that we have a sense in our "mind's eye" of what Einstein meant (cf. Bauer & Johnson-Laird, 1993; Johnson-Laird, 1983; Johnson-Laird & Byrne, 1991; Robin, 1993).

What Does Behavioral Research Cover?

The examples that we have mentioned cover a range of disciplines, including psychology, physics, and astronomy. However, this book is not just a trip into the realm of science in general. It is, as the title indicates, a journey into the domain of behavioral research in particular. Therefore, it is important to understand how *behavioral research* is used as an umbrella term throughout this book. That is, **behavioral research** covers the use of empirical reasoning (viz., careful logic, organized observation, and measurement) from different methodological vantage points in an effort to understand how and why people act, perceive, feel, and think as they do. Defined in this broad way, the wide range of interests of behavioral researchers can be said to include the study of early primitive humans; humans as producers, distributors, and consumers of goods and services; humans as political animals, financial animals, social animals, and verbal animals; and humans as logicians. These various aspects of behavior are of scientific, theoretical, and practical interest to psychologists (e.g., clinical, cognitive, counseling, developmental, educational, experimental, organizational, personality, and social psychologists), behavioral economists, political scientists who engage in empirical research, mass communication researchers, sociologists, cultural anthropologists, psycholinguists, behavioral biologists, neuroscientists, and even some mathematicians (who create quantitative models of behavior), physicists (e.g., those who have studied rumor networks!), and statisticians.

For many purposes, it may not matter much whether we can distinguish among all the various behavioral researchers, but there are interesting differences and parallels nonetheless. They are a constant reminder that behavioral researchers use a variety of methods to triangulate on aspects of behavior and related phenomena of interest. They are also a reminder that there is often more than one "right way" to view the causes of behavior, as human nature is complex and behavior is frequently energized by more than one causal agent and channeled toward more than one desired objective. As scientists in different fields continue to strive to develop a more complete picture of human nature, interdisciplinary behavioral research has become increasingly popular. Sometimes a whole new field is created. Familiar examples include cognitive neuroscience, behavioral medicine, and, most recently, experimental political science. Although these behavioral researchers teach in different departments in colleges and universities, the boundary lines of what they teach and study are by no means rigid. Indeed, researchers in different disciplines and different areas of the same discipline are likely to borrow from one another's storehouses of methods and findings; they also contribute new methods and new findings to those storehouses.

A prime example recently has been the application of psychological principles to the understanding of economic behavior. Psychologists Daniel Kahneman (awarded a Nobel Prize in economics in 2002) and his coworker for many years, the late Amos Tversky, did seminal research on people's common use of information-processing rules of thumb (called *cognitive heuristics*) to make quick judgments that not only defy logic but are often wrong (Kahneman & Tversky, 1973; Tversky & Kahneman, 1974). When people frame an event in their minds, they frequently make predictions and then behave in ways that seem to be consistent with those expectations, such as overestimating the likelihood of a particular economic outcome merely because instances of it happen to be salient at that moment. Previously, we mentioned the false-consensus phenomenon (Ross et al., 1977), which is another example of a cognitive heuristic (in this case, overestimating the extent to which others share your beliefs). When people behave in accordance with their predictions, their expectations ultimately become what the sociologist Robert Merton (1948, 1968) called a *self-fulfilling prophecy* (we refer to this term again). It is easy to see how hybrid branches of behavioral research can grow creatively from new interdisciplinary ventures.

So far in this chapter we have sampled fragments of behavioral research in order to give you a sense of the wide range of techniques used. Throughout this book, you will learn about a great many techniques as we explore examples of behavioral research drawn from traditional and interdisciplinary areas of science. In our discussion of the rise of psychological science, we also mentioned the idea of laboratory experiments. In fact, the first journal that was published in psychology had the effect of legitimizing psychology as an experimental science in its own right (Mueller, 1979). So far, however, we have not given an example of what we mean by a "lab experiment," although it remains a fundamental area of psychology reported in many general and specialized journals. Some research questions seem especially suitable to experimental investigation in the lab and also have real-life applications. For example, experimenters working in the lab discovered many years ago that the amount by which stimulus intensity must be increased to produce a just-noticeable change in the perception of the stimulus is a constant proportion of the intensity of the original stimulus. Following this line of empirical reasoning, they showed that it is possible to write a mathematical statement of the theoretical relationship between the intensity of a stimulus and the intensity of a sensation, a statement that can be applied to real-life situations. If, say, your room is lighted by a 100-watt bulb, and if 15 watts of light must be added before you can just detect a difference in the amount of the light, then in a room with a 50-watt bulb, 7.5 watts must be added to make a difference detectable.

 ## How Does Research Go From Descriptive to Relational to Experimental?

We shift our focus now to the idea of three broad strategies of empirical reasoning and research in a progression from descriptive to relational to experimental. First, the traditional goal of **descriptive research** is the careful mapping out of a situation or set of events. Causal explanations are not of direct concern except perhaps speculatively. Suppose we are interested in the study of children's failure in school. A descriptive research strategy might be to spend time carefully measuring and evaluating the classroom behavior of the children who are doing poorly. Our observations of failing students might lead to some revision of traditional concepts of classroom failure, to suggestions about factors that contribute to the development of failure, and possibly to speculative ideas for the remediation of failure.

The descriptive strategy is frequently considered a necessary first step in the development of a program of research because it establishes a logical and empirical foundation of any future undertaking. Observations like these are rarely regarded as enough, however, because we probably also want to know *why* something happens or *how* what happens is related to other events. If our interest is in children's classroom failure, we are not likely to be satisfied for very long with even the most detailed description of that failure. We will want to know the antecedents of the failure and the outcomes of procedures designed to reduce it. Even if we were not motivated directly by the practical implications of knowing the causes of failure and how to alleviate it, we would believe our understanding to be considerably improved if we knew the conditions that increase and decrease failure's likelihood. To learn about the increase or decrease of failure, or any other behavior, we must focus on at least two variables at the same time. That is, we must make two sets of observations and assess the degree of relationship between the two sets.

At this point, the second broad type of strategy, **relational research**, begins. Research is relational (also described as **correlational**) when two or more variables or conditions are measured and their degree of relationship is assessed. Continuing with the classroom example, suppose we had noted that the teachers of many of the failing students rarely looked at or addressed their students and also seldom exposed them to new academic information. We may have an impression about the relation between learning failure and teaching behavior, as such impressions are a frequent, and often valuable, by-product of descriptive research. But if they are to be taken seriously, they cannot be left at the impressionistic level for very long.

To find out whether our impressions are accurate, we might arrange a series of coordinated observations on a sample of students who represent a *target population* (a population of students to whom we would like to generalize our findings). We would note whether or not each student in our sample had been learning anything, or to what degree the student had been learning; we would also note to what degree the teacher had been exposing each student to the material to be learned. We could then make a quantitative statement expressing the relationship (*degree of correlation*) between the amount of exposure to the material that was to be learned (call it *X*) and the amount of that material the students actually learned (call it *Y*). We would want to know not just (a) whether "*X* and *Y* are significantly related" (i.e., whether any observed "nonzero" relationship is unlikely to have occurred by chance), but also (b) the pattern of the relationship (e.g., linear or nonlinear) and (c) the strength of the relationship (i.e., the size of the correlation between *X* and *Y*).

To carry this example into the third general strategy, suppose the students exposed to less information were also those who tended to learn less. We might be tempted to conclude that children learn less because they are taught less. Such an **ad hoc hypothesis** (a conjecture or supposition developed on the spot "for this" special result), although plausible, is not warranted by the relationship observed. It may be that the teachers taught less to those they knew to be less able to learn. In other words, differences in teaching behavior might be a *result* of the students' learning as much as a *determinant* of that learning. To test this proposition, we will need to make further observations that will enable us to examine whether differences in the information presented to students, apart from individual differences among them, affect their learning. We can best answer such a question by experimentally manipulating the conditions that we think are responsible for the effect. In other words, we introduce some change into the situation, or we interrupt or terminate the situation in order to identify causes.

This process is what is meant by an **experimental research** strategy, the objective of which is the identification of causes (i.e., what leads to what). Relational research only rarely provides such information, and then only under very special conditions. The difference between the degree of focus on a causal explanation in relational and experimental research can be expressed in the difference between the statements "*X* is *related* to *Y*" (relational research) and "*X* is *responsible* for *Y*" (experimental research). In our example, teaching is *X* and learning is *Y*. Our experiment will be designed to reveal the effects of teaching on student learning. We will select a sample of youngsters and, by tossing a coin, or by some other unbiased method of selection, randomly assign them to two groups (see Box 1.5). The teachers will give more information to one of these groups (the *experimental group*) and will give the other group (the *control group*) less information. We can then assess whether the experimental group surpassed the control group in learning achievement. If we find this to be true, we might be more inclined to believe that giving the experimental group more information was *responsible* for the outcome.

BOX 1.5 Random Sampling and Random Assignment

Two important concepts that students new to research methods may find confusing are **random sampling** and **random assignment**. In the relational example, we described arranging for a series of observations on a sample of students who represented the target population. To increase the likelihood that the sample will be representative of the population, we use a random sampling procedure (the procedure used by professional survey researchers) to select the sample. In the experimental example just discussed, we described dividing a sample of students into two groups by tossing a coin to decide which condition each student would be assigned to. An unbiased randomizing procedure (a coin toss, for example) to allocate subjects to different conditions is called random assignment and is characteristic of randomized experiments (or randomized trials, the term that is commonly used to describe randomized experiments with new drugs in biomedical research). We will have more to say about these concepts and terms later in this book.

However, there might still be a question of what it was about the better procedure that led to the improvement. Indeed, it is characteristic of research that, when a new procedure is shown to be effective, many questions arise about what elements of the procedure are producing the benefits. In the case of increased teaching, we may wonder whether the improvement was due to (a) the nature of the additional material; (b) the teacher's increased attention to the student while presenting the additional material; (c) any accompanying increases in eye contact, smiles, or warmth; or (d) other possible correlates of increased teaching behavior. These alternatives have in fact been empirically investigated, and it has been reported that the amount of new material teachers present to their students is sometimes predictable not so much by the students' learning ability as by the teachers' beliefs or expectations about their students' learning ability. In other words, teachers' expectations about their students' performance sometimes becomes a self-fulfilling prophecy, in which teachers' expectations become responsible for their students' performance (Babad, 1993; Raudenbush, 1984; R. Rosenthal, 1966, 1976, 1985, 1991; R. Rosenthal & Jacobson, 1968; R. Rosenthal & Rubin, 1978).

As a final illustration in this chapter of the distinction between descriptive, relational, and experimental research, Table 1.1 shows empirically grounded conclusions in psycholinguistics, the psychology of rumor, and research on a methodological issue. As you study these conclusions, you will see that descriptive research tells us *how things are;* relational research tells us *how things are in relation to other things;* and experimental research tells us *how things are and how they got to be that way*.

 ## What Are the Characteristics of Good Researchers?

Some people are better at what they do than others, whether students, teachers, spouses, parents, workers, and so on. This is no less true of researchers, many of whom excel in what they do. Judith A. Hall (1984), a prominent social psychologist and Northeastern University professor, observed that many textbooks on research methods are filled with guidelines for good research but rarely mention what makes a good researcher. We end this chapter by borrowing her list and adding a little to it; these characteristics should also serve you well in everyday life:

1. *Enthusiasm*. Being enthusiastic about what you do is contagious as well as self-motivating, whereas being apathetic can also sap the passion and zeal of everyone around you. This is also true in science. As a wise researcher, Edward C. Tolman (1959), once commented, "In the end,

Table 1.1	Descriptive, Relational, and Experimental Conclusions in Three Research Areas

Psycholinguistics

Descriptive: When a 2-year-old child listens to a message spoken by his or her mother and is asked to repeat it, the child typically repeats only part of the message (R. Brown, 1965).

Relational: On the average, frequently used words tend to be shorter than infrequently used words; this statement is called Zipf's law (G. A. Miller & Newman, 1958; Zipf, 1935, 1949).

Experimental: When interfering background noise is present, a speaker tends to use more words and fewer abbreviations than when there is no interfering background noise (Heise & Miller, 1951).

Psychology of Rumor

Descriptive: In rumor chat groups on the Internet, the participants tend to adopt changing roles, described as the skeptical disbeliever, the positivist, the apprehensive believer, the curious, the anxious, the prudent initiator, and the investigator (Bordia & Rosnow, 1998). In network studies of rumors in organizations, it has been found that there are usually a few well-connected opinion leaders or liaisons who spread rumors (Hellweg, 1987).

Relational: Interview and questionnaire research, anecdotal evidence, and case studies suggest that anxiety, personal relevance, credulity, and uncertainty are related to the spread of rumors in the marketplace (DiFonzo, 2008; DiFonzo & Bordia, 2007; Kimmel, 2004; Kimmel & Audrain-Pontevia, 2010).

Experimental: Children 3–5 years old who overheard a rumor were as likely to report, erroneously, that they had experienced the rumored event as were children who had actually experienced it (Principe, Kanaya, Ceci, & Singh, 2006).

Methodological Research

Descriptive: It has been estimated that perhaps 80% of psychological research on normal adults has used college and university students as research participants (Higbee & Wells, 1972; Jung, 1969; McNemar, 1946; Schultz, 1969; Sears, 1986; Sieber & Saks, 1989; Smart, 1966).

Relational: People who volunteer to participate in behavioral and social research are usually higher than nonvolunteers in education, social class, intelligence, and the need for social approval (Rosenthal & Rosnow, 1975b; Rosnow & Rosenthal, 1997).

Experimental: Research participants made to experience a conflict between "looking good" and cooperating with the experimenter are likely to try to look good, whereas participants not made to experience such a conflict are likely to help the experimenter (Rosnow, Goodstadt, Suls, & Gitter, 1973; Sigall, Aronson, & Van Hoose, 1970).

the only sure criterion is to have fun" (p. 152). He did not mean that good researchers view science as just fun and games without any ethical or societal implications or consequences. What he meant was that for researchers who excel in what they do, choosing a topic, doing research, and analyzing and reporting the results are as absorbing and as much fun as a game that requires skill and concentration and fills a person with enthusiasm.

2. *Open-mindedness.* It is also more gratifying to be with someone who is open-minded, listens to what you have to say, and is reasonable than to be with someone who is dogmatic or a know-it-all. The skillful researcher is open-minded because it is by experiencing the world with a keen, attentive, inquisitive, and open mind that talented individuals come to perceive the world in novel ways. Hall (1984) observed:

> Open-mindedness also means not being too committed to one's preformed ideas and expectations. Such overcommitment can easily lead to biased research results, as well as blind the investigator to interesting results that don't happen to support or bear directly on the main hypothesis. (pp. iv–v)

3. *Common sense.* Common sense is another prized characteristic in every aspect of life. There is an old anecdote about a drunkard who stumbled and dropped his house key in a dimly lit area while trying to open his front door. Instead of looking for it where he had stumbled,

he instead began searching for the key under a streetlight some distance away. Asked why he didn't look where he was more likely to find his key, he answered, "It is a lot easier to look here." Hall (1984) stated, "All the book learning in the world cannot replace good sense in the planning and conduct of research" (p. v). Much effort is lost when students fail to use common sense and instead look only in a convenient place rather than in a place where they are far more likely to find the answers to their questions. In the case of a research study, you need to ask yourself not only whether you are looking in the most likely place for the answer to your question but also whether you are likely to find the answer within the time available.

4. *Role-taking ability.* The ability to see things from others' viewpoints is crucial to success in a wide variety of situations. In research with human participants, it means being able to see your study from the viewpoint of the participants. It also means seeing it from the viewpoint of the person who will evaluate it (in this case, the instructor who will grade it). For students who plan to present their results in a poster, role-taking ability means seeing it from the vantage point of those who will view the poster.

5. *Creativity and inventiveness.* Quoting Hall (1984) again: "One must be creative to be a good researcher." This means not only "asking an interesting question in the first place" but also "finding solutions to problems of financial resources, lab space, equipment, recruitment, and scheduling; responding to emergencies during the conduct of the research; finding new ways to analyze data, if appropriate; and coming up with convincing interpretations of results" (p. v).

6. *Confidence in one's own judgment.* As Hall (1984) remarked:

    > There's hardly ever just one "right way" to do things. … Good researchers will certainly make themselves aware of the accepted practices in their field and of the points on which their work may be subject to criticism, and will seek advice often and without embarrassment. But good researchers, in the end, trust themselves. (pp. v–vi)

    As another writer put it, "You have to believe that by the simple application of your own mind to the facts of experience, you can discover the truth—a little part of it anyway" (Regis, 1987, p. 209). Remember Thomas Kuhn's observation (Box 1.1) that paradigm shifts result from revolutionary insights.

7. *Ability to communicate.* Given the provisional nature of scientific truths (Box 1.1), the end of one study may very well be the starting point for another study. Therefore, it is essential to be able to communicate clearly so that one's findings will be plain to others (Barrass, 1978). To quote Hall (1984) in a similar vein: "Research is not just the doing, it's the telling. If no one knows about your study, or if they can't figure out or remember your results, then you might as well never have done it" (p. vi).

8. *Care about details.* Being careful about details is another characteristic that will serve you well, because others know they can have confidence in your thoroughness and the accuracy of your work. The good researcher is always careful about details, whether preparing a poster for a meeting, a paper for a course, or an article for a scientific journal. It means keeping complete records, carefully organizing the data, copying and adding numbers correctly, stating facts accurately, and proofreading patiently.

9. *Integrity and honest scholarship.* Every good researcher knows that integrity and honesty are paramount. Because "rigged" experiments or presentations of faked results or the suppression of data undermines the credibility of the scientific enterprise, and can also present an imminent danger to the general public, it is the duty of all scientists to guard against dishonesty, and this responsibility is taken very seriously (Committee on Science, Engineering, and Public Policy, 2009). As you think about ethical issues in research, a topic discussed in Chapter 3, you are also forced to confront your own moral presuppositions.

Summary of Ideas

1. Five reasons for studying research methods are (a) to provide a richer appreciation of the information that science and technology bring to modern life; (b) to avoid falling prey to hucksters and imposters whose showy claims are counterfeit; (c) to learn information and skills that are transferable beyond the research setting; (d) to learn that scientific knowledge is relative and provisional (Box 1.1); and (e) to consider research as a career.

2. Peirce's four methods for the "fixation of belief" (the formation of strong beliefs) are (a) the *method of tenacity* (stubbornly and mindlessly clinging to myth, folklore, and superstition, like believing in UFOs or the geocentric design; Box 1.2); (b) the *method of authority* (complying with the word of authority, like Peirce's witchcraft example on the negative side or, on the positive side, obeying reasonable laws that are the basis of civilized society); (c) the *a priori method* (the use of reason and logic to make sense of things and debunk hoaxes); and (d) the *scientific method*.

3. The *scientific method* is a misnomer, in that it is not a single, fixed method but is an approach that depends heavily on *empirical reasoning* (a combination of careful logic, organized observation, and measurement that is open to independent scrutiny by others, e.g., Feynman's demonstration of the vulnerability of O-rings, Galton's study of prayer, Delgado's charging bull, Ceci's experimental study of children's eyewitness testimony, and Asch's use of accomplices in his experimental study of whether a person will conform with a false consensus).

4. One illustration of how empirical methods are limited is that universal laws are based partly on a leap of faith because we simply cannot observe everything (e.g., that objects in motion will stay in motion forever).

5. Three extraempirical factors are (a) the beauty or elegance (the *aesthetic aspect*) of science (e.g., Einstein's general theory of relativity); (b) visualizations in the form of analogies and metaphors to make complex ideas more comprehensible; and (c) the informative and persuasive language (the *rhetoric of justification*) of science, which takes the form of written reports that conform to an accepted basic structure (illustrated in Appendix A).

6. *Behavioral research* covers the use of empirical reasoning from more than a single vantage point, using different methods (called *methodological pluralism*), each of which is limited in some way, to zero in on how and why people act, perceive, feel, and think as they do.

7. *Descriptive research* tells us "how things are" (e.g., describes children's failure in school; other examples are given in Table 1.1).

8. *Relational research* tells us "how things are in relation to other things" (e.g., describes the relation between student failure and teaching behavior; see other examples in Table 1.1).

9. *Experimental research* tells us "how things are and how they got to be that way" (e.g., in studying the effects of teaching on student learning by manipulating the hypothesized causes of student failure; see other examples in Table 1.1).

10. *Random sampling* refers to choosing an unbiased sample that is representative of a targeted population, whereas *random assignment* refers to how participants are allocated by an unbiased procedure to different groups or conditions in a randomized experiment (Box 1.5).

11. Judith Hall listed nine traits of good researchers: enthusiasm, open-mindedness, common sense, role-taking ability, a combination of creativity and inventiveness, confidence in one's own judgment, the ability to communicate, care about details, and integrity and honest scholarship.

Key Terms

ad hoc hypothesis   p. 13
aesthetic aspect of science   p. 10
a priori method   p. 5
behavioral research   p. 11
correlational research   p. 13
descriptive research   p. 12

empirical   p. 5
empirical reasoning   p. 5
experimental research   p. 13
method of authority   p. 4
method of tenacity   p. 3
methodological pluralism   p. 8

perceptibility   p. 11
random assignment   p. 14
random sampling   p. 14
relational research   p. 13
rhetoric of justification   p. 10
scientific method   p. 1

Multiple-Choice Questions for Review
(answers appear at the end of this chapter)

1. John believes that women are more emotionally expressive than men. When asked why he believes this, John says it is because he has "always" believed it, and because "everybody knows it is true." John is using the (a) method of tenacity; (b) scientific method; (c) a priori method; (d) method of authority.

2. Miles, a student at California State University at Sacramento, tells another student, Sasha, that "numbers are infinite," to which she responds, "Prove it!" Miles says, "Would you agree that any number doubled will result in a new number twice the size?" When Sasha answers yes, Miles responds, "Aha, you have just proved that numbers are infinite, because there must be a limitless number of numbers if you are correct." Miles is using the (a) method of tenacity; (b) scientific method; (c) a priori method; (d) method of authority.

3. Julie believes that everyone dreams every night, because her psychology professor told her this is true. Julie is using the (a) method of tenacity; (b) scientific method; (c) a priori method; (d) method of authority.

4. Dr. Smith believes that psychotherapy is generally very effective in treating mental disorders. She claims that her belief is based on empirical research in which therapy was given to some patients but not others, and in which the degree of mental disorder was carefully measured. Dr. Smith's belief is based on the (a) method of tenacity; (b) scientific method; (c) a priori method; (d) method of authority.

5. Which of the following is the *most* distinctive characteristic of science? (a) empirical inquiry and empirical reasoning; (b) images and metaphors; (c) the rhetoric of science; (d) statistical explanation.

6. Behavioral research (a) encompasses many scientific fields; (b) emphasizes multiple methods of observation and explanation; (c) has seen a growth in the number of interdisciplinary fields; (d) all of the above.

7. Which empirical approach is often considered a necessary first step in conducting research but is rarely considered sufficient by itself? (a) relational research; (b) experimental research; (c) descriptive research; (d) none of the above.

8. A researcher at the College of the Southwest conducts a research project on the study habits of students. She reports that, on average, college students study 20 hours per week. This is an example of (a) relational research; (b) experimental research; (c) descriptive research; (d) none of the above.

9. Experimental research (a) can support cause-effect conclusions; (b) involves the manipulation of variables; (c) often involves randomly assigning subjects to conditions; (d) all of the above.

10. A researcher at Grand Valley State University flips a coin to decide whether each person in a sample of research participants will be assigned to the experimental group or the control group. This is an illustration of (a) random sampling; (b) random assignment; (c) both random assignment and randomization because they are synonyms; (d) none of the above.

Discussion Questions for Review (answers appear at the end of this chapter)

1. Philosopher Charles Sanders Peirce described four distinctive approaches (he called them *methods*) on which strongly held beliefs are based. What are these "methods"? Give an example of a belief based on each method.

2. In addition to the use of empirical observation, three other (extraempirical) factors were said to play a role in science. What are those factors? Which of the four is traditionally considered "more fundamental" than the others in science?

3. A Wayne State researcher is interested in the effects of children's viewing TV violence on the children's level of aggression on the playground. The amount and type of viewing will be assessed through a standard procedure: TV diaries sent to parents. Aggression will be rated by two judges. The researcher hypothesizes that children who spend more time watching violent TV at home are more aggressive on the playground than their peers who watch relatively little violent TV at home. Of the three general research types (descriptive, relational, and experimental), which type is this, and why?

4. A Wichita State researcher plans to assign fifth-grade children to one of two conditions. Half the children

(Group A) will be shown a relatively violent movie at 10:30, and half (Group B) will be shown a nonviolent movie at the same time. Each film will be equally engaging. Two observers will code the children's behavior when both groups are brought back together on the playground for their 11:00 recess. This procedure will continue daily for six weeks. The researcher predicts that Group A will be more aggressive on the playground than Group B. Which type of research is this, and why?

5. A researcher at the University of New Hampshire wants to measure the prevalence of shyness in the undergraduate community. She administers the well-standardized Shyness Scale to volunteers in a main dining hall, collecting data on a respectable 35% of all undergraduates. Which type of research is this, and why?

6. A North Dakota State student wants to study other students' creativity, and he wants to use all three types of research approaches (descriptive, relational, and experimental) in this project. Think of a concrete example of each type that he could use.

7. A student at Foothill College claims that it is not possible to study such nonscientific concepts as

prayer because prayer falls in the domain of theology rather than of science. Is the student correct?

8. Alan Turing, who conceived of the computer and was also primarily responsible for breaking the German code (called Enigma) during World War II, proposed a way of demonstrating that a computer simulation of human intelligence actually works. Called the *Turing test*, it consists of people having a dialogue with the computer and seeing whether the computer can fool them into thinking that they are interacting with a human being. How is this an example of empirical reasoning?

9. The chapter ended by describing psychologist Judith Hall's nine "traits of good researchers." List as many as you can recall.

Answers to Review Questions

Multiple-Choice Questions

1. a	**3.** d	**5.** a	**7.** c	**9.** d
2. c	**4.** b	**6.** d	**8.** c	**10.** b

Discussion Questions

1. First, the method of tenacity: believing something because it is an idea that has been around for a long time (e.g., Elvis is alive). Second, the method of authority: believing something said by an expert in the field (e.g., cutting back on fatty foods because the doctor told you to do so and you believe doctors know about this). Third, the a priori method: using pure reason as a basis of belief (e.g., reasoning that $12 \times 100 = 120 \times 10 = 1 \times 1200$). Fourth, the scientific method: using empirical reasoning as a basis of belief (e.g., believing the earth is round because you have circled the globe by foot, boat, and vehicle and not fallen off).

2. The three extraempirical factors are aesthetics (the beauty of science), perceptibility (the use of images and metaphors), and rhetoric (the technical concepts and persuasive language used in science). Empirical reasoning and empirical methods are considered the "most fundamental" in science.

3. This is relational research because it examines the relationship between two sets of observations (TV diary entries and playground aggression). It is not experimental because neither of the variables is manipulated by the investigator.

4. This is experimental research because the investigator has manipulated the type of movie shown.

5. This is descriptive research because the data are collected on student shyness, but these scores are not examined for their relationship to any other variable.

6. For his descriptive research, he might collect data on the creativity scores of other students. For his relational research, he might examine the relationship between creativity scores and SAT (Scholastic Assessment Test) scores. For his experimental research, he might experimentally manipulate the type of music being played in the background while the students' creativity is being measured to see whether Mozart makes students more creative than does hard rock.

7. No, it certainly *is* possible to study the concept of prayer, and Galton conducted a relational study of prayer and longevity. An experimental study might use prayer for a randomly chosen half of 50 people who are ill and no prayer for the remaining people to see whether prayer brings about faster recovery.

8. It is an example of empirical reasoning because it involves logic, observation, and even a kind of measurement. The logic is Turing's reasoning that it may be possible for a computer to trick a person into mistaking it for a human being. The observation is the test itself, and the kind of measurement might consist of judgments made by people at different points in their interaction with the computer, and then a final judgment about whether they were interacting with a person or a computer.

9. The nine traits are (a) being enthusiastic about the topic and process of research; (b) being open-minded so as not to miss a promising lead, and so as to learn from your mistakes and others' criticisms; (c) using good sense rather than doing something only because it is convenient; (d) taking the role of, for example, the research participant, the person who grades your paper, and, if you are presenting a poster, the poster's viewers; (e) being inventive and creative during the planning and implementation of your research and in asking interesting questions; (f) having confidence in your own judgment after applying your mind to the facts; (g) learning to communicate clearly; (h) being careful about details in all phases of your research; and (i) being honest in every aspect of the research.

CHAPTER 2

From Hunches to Testable Hypotheses

Preview Questions

- What is meant by a cycle of discovery and justification?
- What are hypothesis-generating heuristics?
- What is the potential role of serendipity?
- How can I do a literature search?
- How should I go about defining variables?
- What identifies "good" theories and working hypotheses?
- What is the distinction between an independent variable and a dependent variable?
- What belongs in my research proposal?

 What Is Meant by a Cycle of Discovery and Justification?

To give you a sense of the organization of this chapter and what follows in this book, we begin by borrowing a traditional distinction proposed by the German philosopher Hans Reichenbach (1938). Reichenbach described two stages of science, *discovery* and *justification,* and put them into what we call contexts. The **context of discovery** embraces the initial hunches, questions, or insights and the resulting conjectural statements or suppositions that give direction to researchers' observations (as described more fully in this chapter). In particular, we focus on five facets of the context of discovery: (a) coming up with leads, hunches, and interesting questions; (b) doing a literature search to discover what others have found and interpreted; (c) defining the basic variables and concepts; (d) recasting the hunches or questions into technically acceptable hypotheses for empirical evaluation; and (e) pulling the work together in a research proposal. In the next chapter, we discuss ethical accountability, an essential aspect of all research and an important consideration in the research proposal. In the remainder of this book, we explore other topics that are relevant to the context of discovery, but our primary focus in those chapters is methodological and quantitative methods, which largely belong within the context of justification. The **context of justification** (as the expression is used here) includes the empirical evaluation of conjectural statements or suppositions and the evidence-based defense of conclusions and generalizations. Because scientists are trained to ask themselves what others might propose to counter their evidence-based conclusions and generalizations, the discussion sections of research reports are a good place for students to look for promising research leads.

Journals and books that publish detailed reviews of research on particular topics are another good source of promising leads, especially reviews that echo the cycle of discovery and justification in a particular research area. For instance, *Current Directions in Psychological Science* (a journal published by the Association for Psychological Science, or APS) publishes short review articles about research developments and insights in areas such as language, memory and cognition, development, the neural basis of behavior and emotions, aspects of psychopathology, and theory of the mind. Two other highly respected journals that publish longer reviews are the *Psychological Bulletin* and *Behavioral and Brain Sciences* (a special feature of this journal is a section after each article, called Open Peer Commentary, in which others comment on the article). The *Annual Review of Psychology* is another source of longer reviews and is available online as well as in print in many college libraries; it is part of the *Annual Review* series of books, which provide authoritative reviews on just about every topic in science. (Not only may you get some good ideas by browsing literature reviews, but the cited work should also give you a head start when you begin searching and retrieving background material for your proposal.) Public lectures and colloquium presentations (most are also open to the general public) are another possible source of ideas, and there is frequently an opportunity to chat with the speaker after a colloquium presentation. It is important that you take careful notes so that, when writing up your proposal (and your final research report), you are able to give credit to the source of any ideas you used.

Given the provisional nature of scientific knowledge (as mentioned in the previous chapter in Box 1.1), the idea of a cycle of discovery and justification is also a reminder that the end of one study is usually the prelude to another. In the previous chapter, we discussed a progression of interesting questions addressed in a chain of research from descriptive to relational to experimental. Here's another hypothetical case to whet your creative imagination. In a laboratory course in political leadership (where the "laboratory" is frequently the real world), the students were required to visit social studies classes in local high schools and attempt to influence the high school students to vote in the upcoming elections of class officers. For each of the college student visitors, let's assume that records were kept of the percentage of each high school class that later actually did vote. Descriptively, these results showed that about 60% of the high school students actually voted. When the college instructor of this lab course examined the percentage of voters separately for each of her students, she noticed substantial differences (from 35% voting to 85%) voting. Discussing these large differences with her students, the only thing she found related to the variation in voting rates was her students' degree of self-confidence in their ability to influence the high school students they met with to turn out to vote.

It might seem natural to conclude that greater self-confidence in the ability to get out the vote was the cause of particular influencers' effectiveness. It would certainly seem to be the case that self-confidence *predicted* greater success, but that is not the same as *causing* it. If we know what caused a particular outcome, we also know that the cause predicts the outcome. But the converse is not true; being able to specify a "predictor" does not mean we can specify a cause. The influencers who were more effective may also have been smarter, taller, better looking, more interpersonally sensitive, more extraverted, more conscientious, more agreeable, and/or better adjusted than the less effective influencers. Any one of these correlates of self-confidence might have been the "true" cause. Later in this book, we will have a lot more to say about the logic (and the limitations) of causal inference. But when experimenting researchers want to maximize their own confidence that one variable is the cause of an outcome, they often turn to a special case of studying relationships: randomized experiments (see also Box 2.1).

In Chapter 1 (Box 1.5), we mentioned that randomized experiments are often used in medical research. The simplest randomized design consists of two conditions, and each unit sampled (e.g., patients) is assigned to one of the conditions by a randomizing procedure. One condition would be the test medication (e.g., a new drug), and the other condition then serves as a control. When there is an effective treatment already available, it will be given to the sampling units in the control group, so that the comparison is between the test medication and the best currently available treatment. When there is no effective alternative treatment available for comparison with the test medication, the control has traditionally been a placebo (e.g., an inactive "pill" that looks, feels, and tastes the

BOX 2.1 The Importance of Replications

Even in a randomized experiment, there is always the possibility that some uncontrolled variable is responsible for a claimed causal relationship between two other variables. This is one reason why experimenting researchers insist on replications in order to rule out a random "fluke." **Replication** in this context refers to the duplication of an experimental observation, but clearly it is impossible to repeat the identical randomized experiment. At the very least, the participants as well as the experimenters will be different over a series of replications. When specific differences have been pre-programmed into the repeated experiments, they are often described as *varied* replications (meaning that some new variable was intentionally introduced). As the number of varied replications increases, meta-analysis (discussed in Appendix C) is often used to sum up the overall findings and to explore for conditions (called **moderator variables**) that may strengthen or weaken the relationships between *independent and dependent variables* (defined later in this chapter, and we will also have more to say about replications in a later chapter.)

same as the test medication). Suppose that, in our example of getting out the vote, the instructor designs a follow-up randomized experiment with two conditions. In one condition, a randomly selected half of the influencers are told that they can "be confident they will be highly successful in persuading high school students to vote in class officer elections." Two reasons given for this confidence are that (a) the high school students they will try to influence have been specially selected as those that are very susceptible to social influence and (b) the specially selected students are known to have been likely to vote in the past. The other random half of the influencers are given "neutral information" (e.g., they may be told only that the students they will be trying to influence are a fairly typical high school class); this neutral control condition is meant to resemble a "placebo" condition. Here, then, we have another illustration of how the end of one study is the prelude to another in a cycle of discovery and justification.

What Are Hypothesis-Generating Heuristics?

So far, we have discussed in only very generally *how* and *where* hunches, questions, and insights emerge, but there is also a more systematic way of thinking about this puzzle. This more systematic way was suggested by social psychologist William J. McGuire, who coined the expression **hypothesis-generating heuristics** to refer to strategies and circumstances that can lead to testable hypotheses (*heuristic* means stimulating interest as a means of furthering investigation). McGuire began by describing more than four dozen hypothesis-generating heuristics and later went on to propose 20 questions for philosophically oriented psychologists to ponder (McGuire, 1973, 1997, 2006). We will sample four hypothesis-generating heuristics: (a) explaining paradoxical incidents in testable ways; (b) recognizing potential hypotheses in analogies, metaphors, figures of speech, and other assorted imagery; (c) identifying conflicting conclusions for empirical adjudication; and (d) improving on older ideas.

In the first hypothesis-generating heuristic, researchers try to explain a paradoxical incident (a "seemingly contradictory event") in a testable way. A modern classic was the bystander helping research done by social psychologists Bibb Latané and John Darley. The incident that inspired this research was the report of a brutal murder that occurred in the early morning of March 13, 1964, in Queens, New York, when a 28-year-old nurse named Kitty Genovese was returning home from work. The details of what actually happened have been discussed and debated for years, including a fascinating recent account by Charles E. Skoller (2008), who was an assistant district attorney at the time and who served as the prosecutor in the famous trial that took place. The crime was reported in the Police Blotter section of *The New York Times* the day after the murder, but it was a widely read book by a Pulitzer Prize–winning journalist at the *Times* (Abraham M. Rosenthal, 1964) that gave the story legs as it traveled around the world. Entitled *Thirty-Eight Witnesses,* Rosenthal's book details how 38 of Kitty Genovese's neighbors came to their windows to see what was happening but not one went to her aid although it took the murderer over half an hour to kill her. As it turns out, the "38" was merely a made-up number, and most of the bystanders were ear-witnesses rather than eyewitnesses (Takooshian 2009), but the horrific murder was real. Soon, there were other reports of similar bystander "apathy" or "indifference" or "alienation" in the face of other horrendous incidents.

Latané and Darley wondered whether people failed to intervene in these sorts of incidents because each believed someone else was likely to. Calling this phenomenon "diffusion of responsibility," Latané and Darley hypothesized that the larger the number of bystander witnesses to an emergency, the less likely it is that any one of them will offer help. The researchers then went on to test this hypothesis in a series of experiments. For example, in a study at Columbia University, they demonstrated that the larger the number of the students present, the less likely any of them was to volunteer to help in an emergency. The students in this experiment had agreed to take part in a discussion of problems related to life at an urban university. As the discussion progressed, a stream of smoke began to puff into the room through a wall vent. The researchers observed that when one student was in the room, she or he was about twice as likely to report the emergency as when the student was in the room with as few as three others. Instead of reporting the emergency, students in a group tended to be passive and to dismiss their fears through rationalization (Latané & Darley, 1968). In a similar study with introductory psychology students at New York University, who had also agreed to take part in a discussion group, if alone, each was much more likely to report a (simulated) epileptic seizure that he or she happened to hear than if he or she believed that others were also aware of the emergency (Darley & Latané, 1968).

In a second hypothesis-generating heuristic, researchers develop potential hypotheses on the basis of analogies, metaphors, or figures of speech (see also Box 2.2). For example, McGuire (1964) used an inoculation analogy to come up with ideas for inducing resistance to propaganda messages. He assumed that some beliefs (he described them as "cultural truisms") are so widely accepted in a society that they are perceived as indisputably true. Examples of cultural truisms in American society are "Mental illness is not contagious," "It's a good idea to brush your teeth after every meal," and "Cigarette smoking is bad for your health." Using the inoculation analogy as a point of departure, McGuire reasoned that beliefs like these should be especially vulnerable to counterpropaganda for two reasons. First, recipients of propaganda attacking cultural truisms, seldom having

---

 ## BOX 2.2 The Spiral in Nature and Analogy

A favorite analogy is the spiral, because it seems to have such a prominent place in nature. For example, economists speak of "inflationary spirals," and in football, we have "spiral passes." A noted developmental psychologist, Heinz Werner, proposed a "psychogenetic principle of spirality," which he derived from an earlier philosophical analogy about the unfolding of historical events (Werner & Kaplan, 1963). In nature, of course, there are many examples of spirality, such as the DNA double helix that you learned about in a high school science class. Storms that arise in the Northern Hemisphere typically display a counterclockwise spiral rotation, whereas those that arise in the Southern Hemisphere typically display a clockwise rotation. Human hair forms a spiral pattern on the scalp that is generally clockwise in men and counterclockwise in women. Auditory researchers theorized that the spiral shape of the cochlea (the bony sound-perceiving organ in the inner ear) serves to increase sensitivity to low-frequency sounds (Cho, 2006). Spiral forms are also found in pinecones and other varieties of plants. One author told of a researcher who blindfolded a right-handed friend and told him to walk a straight line across a country field; the man walked in a clockwise spiral—that is, until he stumbled on a tree stump (Robin, 1993).

been called on to defend their beliefs, are unpracticed in mustering a defense. Second, they may not be motivated to develop a defense because they view such beliefs as established and unassailable.

Taking the inoculation analogy a step further, McGuire reasoned that, like the unvaccinated person, who is highly vulnerable to an attack of the smallpox virus, a person who has not given very much thought to *why* he or she believes that something is true may also be highly vulnerable to a massive attack of counterpropaganda. Just as vaccinating a person with a weakened dose of small-pox virus stimulates the person's defenses so that he or she can later overcome an attack, perhaps a similar kind of technique would work to "immunize" people's attitudes. Extrapolating from this idea, McGuire theorized that, to immunize people against "viral-like" counterpropaganda, we can simply expose them to some small form of the counterpropaganda in advance, thus stimulating them to build up their own "logical defenses" by rehearsing arguments against the counterpropaganda. Exposing them to too much preliminary counterpropaganda may, however, produce the opposite effect, causing them to reverse their attitude (i.e., it would be like accidentally giving them the disease). The problem, which McGuire worked out in a program of research studies, was to establish the amount of "live virus" in an "inoculation" that, without giving people the "disease," would help build a defense against a future massive attack of the same "virus."

In a third hypothesis-generating heuristic, a researcher who identifies conflicting conclusions (or results) then tries to account for them. For example, social psychologist Robert Zajonc (pronounced "zy-ence," rhymes with *science*) proposed a hypothesis that he termed "social facilitation" to account for some conflicting published data (Zajonc, 1965). Several earlier reports indicated that performance in humans and animals improved when passive observers were present, whereas other reports showed performance becoming poorer in the presence of others. For instance, the participants in one experiment were required to learn a list of nonsense syllables, either alone or in the presence of others. The number of trials needed to learn the list was the criterion variable. Those participants who learned the list alone averaged more than 9 trials, and those who learned the syllables before an audience averaged more than 11 trials (Pessin, 1933). In other experiments, participants who performed a familiar task in groups did better than when they performed the task alone (Bergum & Lehr, 1963). Thus, it seemed that the presence of others enhanced the performance of some tasks but not of others.

How could these seemingly inconsistent results be explained? One important finding in experimental psychology is that a high drive level causes people to give the dominant response to a stimulus. (A drive level refers to the state of readiness of an organism.) When the task is familiar and well learned, the dominant response is usually the right one. However, when the task is novel and the correct responses are unknown or not well learned, the dominant response will probably be wrong. Zajonc started with the idea that the presence of others serves to increase the individual's drive level and thus leads to dominant responses. Therefore, Zajonc hypothesized, the presence of others must inhibit the learning of new responses but facilitate the performance of well-learned responses. In other words, students should study alone, preferably in an isolated cubicle, and then (having learned all the correct responses) take exams with many other students on a stage before a large audience.

Finally, a fourth hypothesis-generating heuristic involves improving on older ideas. A classic case in experimental psychology was B. F. Skinner's improvement on two older theories of conditioning. In the 1930s, two popular conceptualizations were those of Russian physiologist Ivan Pavlov and American psychologist E. L. Thorndike. Skinner's distinction between these two conceptualizations opened the way to a long series of studies by Skinner and others (Ferster & Skinner, 1957; Skinner, 1938). Pavlov had done pioneering research on "classical conditioning." In the experimental proce-dure that produces this type of conditioning, a neutral stimulus is paired with one that consistently brings about some desired behavior or response. Suppose that we, like Pavlov, wish to condition a hungry dog to salivate at the sound of a bell. Once the dog becomes accustomed to the apparatus, we sound the bell to make sure that the dog does not automatically salivate to it. The dog pricks up its ears or barks, but it does not salivate. We now know that the bell will not cause the animal to respond as it does to food. The next step is to ring the bell at the same time we present meat to the dog. If we do this a number of times, we find that the dog begins to salivate at the sound of the bell, before we present the meat. In contrast, Thorndike, who experimented at about the same time as Pavlov, in the early 1900s, worked with "trial-and-error learning." For example, Thorndike studied how cats learned to escape from a puzzle box to gain food. He was convinced that the cats did not reason out a solution, but that their getting out and eating the food he provided somehow strengthened the connection between successful escape movements and the actual escape.

Skinner recognized that, in Pavlovian conditioning, the major factor is the stimulus that precedes the response. In other words, the response is elicited reflexively. In Thorndike's trial-and-error conditioning, the major factor is the stimulus consequence (i.e., the reinforcement of escaping the puzzle box), which follows the response. Skinner focused his own research on the latter type of conditioning, which he called *operant* or *instrumental*. In this type of conditioning, first, the organism responds to a stimulus, and then something is done that will either increase or decrease the probability of the organism's making the same response again. Say that we wish to train a dog to sit on command, and we prepare the animal by withholding food for a time. An operant-conditioning procedure requires that we reward the dog *after* it sits (or approximates sitting) following the command. The laboratory research on operant conditioning paved the way for applications in the military, in educational institutions, and in the treatment of behavior disorders. In his novel, *Walden II* (1948b), Skinner described a whole society organized according to known principles of conditioning.

What Is the Potential Role of Serendipity?

Another important lesson to be learned from what we have discussed so far is that good leads for questions and hypotheses are all around us, and all that is required is to keep our eyes, ears, and minds open. For example, a famous case in the annals of clinical psychology was Leo Kanner's (1943) discovery while he was working with disturbed children. He noticed a striking similarity in their behavior. Not only did they tend to be socially isolated, but they had failed to develop appropriate language skills. Calling this *syndrome* (i.e., a set of symptoms) "infantile autism," Kanner and others began to do research on it, and it was listed in the diagnostic manual used by clinical psychologists and psychiatrists. Kanner's discovery is also an example of **serendipity**, which means a felicitous or lucky discovery (see also Box 2.3). Everyone has an opportunity to benefit from serendipity at one time or another, and like many other researchers, we have benefited from it in our own research.

One of Rosnow's brushes with serendipity happened in 1969, when the Beatles were at the height of their popularity and a rumor about them began to circulate. The rumor alleged that, leaving the recording studio tired and dejected, Paul McCartney had been decapitated in a car accident; to maintain the group, the accident had been covered up, and he had been replaced by a double. The Paul-is-dead rumor, although a preposterous fiction, swept across U.S. colleges with numerous variants and deviations (discussed later in Rosnow & Fine, 1974, 1976). What made the rumor intriguing was that it was not at all like the rumors that had been previously studied by psychologists and sociologists. A classic view of the psychology of rumor had concluded that, in light of the porosity of human memory, rumors will *always* become shorter (Allport & Postman, 1947). To the contrary, however, the Paul-is-dead rumor was not shrinking; instead, it was growing by leaps and bounds as people improvised details and the "clues" multiplied. Rosnow wondered whether the classic view of rumor needed some revision in other respects as well.

Pursuing that lead opened the way to hypotheses, further research, and a modified theory in which rumormongering is viewed as an attempt to deal with emotional stresses and cognitive uncertainties by generating and passing stories and suppositions that interpret nebulous events, address people's anxieties, and attempt to provide a rationale for behavior (Rosnow, 1980a, 1980b, 1991). Another new addendum is that people have a tendency to pass rumors that they perceive as credible, even the most ridiculous stories, but when anxieties are intense, rumormongers are less likely to monitor the logic or plausibility of what they pass on to others (Rosnow, 1991, 2001). Using an analogy to pull together ideas, empirical findings, and their possible implications, Rosnow (1991)

BOX 2.3   Serendipity and the DNA Double Helix

The term *serendipity* (coined by Horace Walpole, an 18th-century English novelist) was inspired by a 16th-century tale told of three princes of Serendip (now called Sri Lanka) who, through sagacity and luck, had felicitous insights. James Watson (1993), the codiscoverer of the DNA double helix, observed, "To have success in science, you need some luck" (p. 1812). Watson went on to note that, had it not been for serendipity, he might never have got interested in genetics in the first place:

> I was 17, almost 3 years into college, and after a summer in the North Woods, I came back to the University of Chicago and spotted the tiny book What Is Life by the

theoretical physicist Erwin Schrödinger. In that little gem, Schrödinger said the essence of life was the gene. Up until then, I was interested in birds. But then I thought, well, if the gene is the essence of life, I want to know more about it. And that was fateful because, otherwise, I would have spent my life studying birds and no one would have heard of me. (p. 1812)

In fact, as Watson (1969) recounted in his lively autobiographical description of the adventure of discovering the structure of the DNA molecule, his encounters with serendipity were not limited to that single incident.

conceptualized some rumormongering as a process akin to loading and firing a gun, where the gun is the rumor public, and the bullet is the rumor, which is loaded in an atmosphere of anxiety and uncertainty. The trigger is pulled when it is believed the bullet will hit the mark, much as an involving rumor is likely to be passed on if it is perceived as credible. But when anxiety is intense or involvement is low, passing on certain rumors is like firing a shot in the dark. Other researchers have uncovered additional patterns in both the content and the level of individual participation in rumor networks, providing insights into malicious rumors and their possible control (DiFonzo & Bordia, 2006, 2007; Fine & Turner, 2001; Kimmel, 2004; Kimmel & Audrain-Pontevia, 2010).

One of Rosenthal's brushes with serendipity occurred while he was a graduate student working on his Ph.D. in clinical psychology, though the serendipitous event hardly seemed felicitous at the time. For his dissertation research, he had been studying the defense mechanism of *projection* (defined as ascribing to another person one's own feelings or thoughts) in college men and women as well as in a group of hospitalized patients with paranoid symptomatology. Each of these groups was divided into three subgroups that received a success, failure, or neutral experience on a task structured to seem like a test of intelligence. Before the participants' treatment conditions were imposed, they were asked to rate the degree to which they perceived success or failure in the faces of individuals pictured in photographs. Immediately after the experiment, the participants rated another set of faces on their degree of success or failure. Rosenthal had hypothesized that being in the success condition would lead the participants to perceive other people as prone to success, and that being in the failure condition would lead those participants to perceive other people as prone to failure (measured by the difference between the preratings and postratings).

Digging into the results, Rosenthal did a number of statistical analyses, and in one of these, to his great surprise and dismay, he found that the *preratings* (the ratings made *before* the treatment was implemented) were biased in favor of his hypothesis. It looked as if the dissertation research was ruined. After discussing the problem with his research adviser, Rosenthal began a frantic search of journals and books for references to this problem, which he called "unconscious experimenter bias." He learned that, as far back as Ebbinghaus (1885), psychologists had alluded to something like this problem, but no one had explicitly designed and conducted experiments to test the hypothesis of unconscious experimenter bias. In a long series of studies of how experimenters' hypotheses may unwittingly influence their results, the concept of unconscious experimenter bias evolved into the concept of *experimenter expectancy bias* (R. Rosenthal, 1966, 1976, 1993). We return to this phenomenon again in a later chapter.

How Can I Do a Literature Search?

The literature search is an indispensable aspect of the context of discovery as it enables researchers to put their ideas into a context of other work that has been done. Previously, we mentioned the journal *Current Directions in Psychological Science,* which publishes short review articles, some of which might be a starting point in your search for and retrieval of relevant work. Because you will be using resources physically located in your college library (e.g., browsing handbooks, encyclopedias, and possibly journals) and, of course, electronic databases that are accessible online, now is the time to familiarize yourself with what is available and how to access it. College libraries provide fact sheets that are usually available on the library's Web page and at an information desk in the library. The fact sheet will tell you where books, journals, and other work are stored in the *stacks* (the shelves in the library). You may also need information on the material that has "restricted access" (meaning that the material is not usually available to the general public) and the books and periodicals that are available for *browsing* (they can be read in the library, but not checked out), which you can also ask about at the information desk or by going to the library's Web page.

If the material that you need is available electronically, you can usually (not always) save it in a file on your computer or your flash memory drive, or you can print it out. You will find it is a lot easier to print out or save abstracts and full-text journal articles than to copy lengthy passages by hand, so it is important to find out whether you can do this at the library or through your own computer. If you are using material in the library that is not available online, it is also easier (and far more accurate) to photocopy pages or paragraphs from books than to copy lengthy passages; you need to know where copying machines are located in the library and whether you need to bring coins or purchase a debit card to use them. All of the library's material is referenced in its automated card catalog, which not only gives you basic information but also tells you where things can be found. It is easy to use the automated catalog, but if you have a question, click on the "Help" key. For bibliographic information (title, author, publisher, ISBN identification, etc.) about books that may not be available in your library's stacks (but may be available through your library's interlibrary loan system), there is the Library of Congress's online catalog (http://catalog.loc.gov). No special training is needed to use this online catalog, which also has fill-in boxes where you can search by title, author, subject, keywords, and so on.

For psychology students, a common way of searching the literature is to use PsycINFO, an extensive reference database maintained by the American Psychological Association, to which most college libraries subscribe. The PsycINFO database has records from the 1800s to the present. The term *database* means it is a filing system (or "base") for storing information. You can typically access PsycINFO using one of your college library's desktop computers, and most colleges allow their students to access this and other electronic databases outside the library using their own computers. Each database has its own language and commands, and experts in information technology suggest that you use several different terms that you intuitively think are relevant to your interest (a process called *free-text searching*). Once you are into PsycINFO, you use these "search terms" (sets of words or phrases, generally called *descriptors*) to pull up relevant abstracts. The trick in using PsycINFO is not to get too much or too little information; you will have to use patience in combining keywords and key phrases until you feel you have the records you need (M. C. Rosenthal, 2006).

Once you feel comfortable using PsycINFO, other computerized databases will be a snap. By going to your college library's Web page, you should be able to find out what reference and *full-text databases* (i.e., databases that contain the entire work, not just an abstract) are available to you online. There are reference databases for just about anything you can think of, including census data (Census Lookup), full-text data from many scholarly publications (Academic Search Premier), bibliographic records of educational resources (ERIC), news reports by topic areas (LEXIS-NEXIS),

BOX 2.4 Tips for Using Electronic Databases

- Begin by writing down the question you have, and then make a list of words or phrases you want to try as search terms. Use several words or phrases, even though this broad search may turn up more than is relevant. It is easier to limit the search after you have inspected what you turned up than to try to anticipate the perfect word or phrase.

- Search not only PsycINFO but also other reference databases. There may be a lot of overlap, but you never know whether something new will turn up, and it will take only a little extra time to do this search online.

- Keep a running list so that you don't waste effort in accidentally retracing your steps. Note down the databases searched, the dates you used them, and the search terms or strategies you used. If you can, copy what you find in a file that you can open later and refer to again if you need to (you can use your antivirus program to make sure the file is not infected).

full-text dissertations and master's theses (ProQuest Dissertations and Theses), and dictionaries and encyclopedias. If you are confused about which database has the information you need, you can ask one of the information specialists in your college library for guidance. Many college library Web sites have a link that you can click, after which you type the name of the journal and/or the title of the article, and you are told whether it is in an electronic database subscribed to by the college. (Box 2.4 provides several tips for using such databases; for a more detailed discussion, particularly if you ever plan to do a meta-analysis, read M. C. Rosenthal, 2006). Incidentally, if you go to www.googlescholar.com and enter a researcher's name, you will see the number of citations of each of the person's works that are listed, which is generally seen in the academic world as a measure of how important and useful the work has been to others interested in the topic. Occasionally, there is a link to a full-text PDF reprint of the work, which you can read, save, or print out by clicking the link.

Once you have turned up relevant abstracts, it is important not to stop with the abstract but to go to the work itself and read it. PsycARTICLES is another APA database, which is linked with PsycINFO in the libraries that subscribe to both. PsycARTICLES offers full-text articles from all the APA journals, the journals of the Canadian Psychological Association (CPA), and a group of other journals. For some articles, PsycINFO gives you the option of requesting the abstract or the full-text article. Full-text articles and books are also available at other sites (such as those noted in the preceding paragraph and elsewhere), sometimes after an "embargo period" (usually a year after the print version of the journal was published). Many of these sites are part of what is called the "deep Web," which means they surface only when you make database queries from within the sites. Search engines like Google or Bing or Yahoo generally seek what are called "statistic Web pages," or thin, digitized layers of information that do not have search functions of their own. It is important, therefore, not to rely only on search engines like these for your literature search and retrieval, but instead to use the deep Web sites.

Our advice about going to the original work applies even to a summary of a classic work that you find consistently cited and described by many authors. Read what you are citing, if only to make sure that you are not passing on a misreported account in a secondary source. Another reason to go to the original work, particularly in the case of a research article, is to see if you agree with the researchers' conclusions. Media accounts of research can be a useful lead, but scientific findings reported in the media usually tend to be oversimplified, so don't depend on them as the final word. Similarly, in a public lecture, the speaker does not have the opportunity to provide the minute details that are required by scientific journals. By the time a research study has been published in a quality journal, the final report has gone through a review by independent consultants. Nevertheless, published research reports are not guaranteed to be error-free, even though the aim of the review process is to detect errors and to raise questions that the author is required to address.

How Should I Go About Defining Variables?

At this juncture, you also need to think about naming and defining the variables in which you are interested, because how you describe something tells others how you conceptualize it and whether you see it the same way they do. We will have more to say about the term *variable* in a moment, but researchers frequently distinguish between two types of definitions of variables, called *operational* and *theoretical*. First, **operational definitions** identify variables on the basis of empirical conditions (the *operations*) used to measure or to manipulate the variables. For example, an experimental psychologist interested in the variable of *hunger* might define it operationally by the degree of stomach contractions. A social psychologist interested in *prejudice* might define it operationally by respondents' scores on an attitude scale designed to measure stereotyping and other elements of attitudinal biases. A child psychologist interested in studying *frustration* might define it operationally by an intervention that thwarts children in some way, such as interrupting play with a set of attractive new toys. A clinical psychologist interested in studying *depression* might define it operationally in terms of scores on a test, such as the Beck Depression Inventory (BDI).

Theoretical definitions define variables in more abstract or more general terms, such as defining *hunger* by a connection between the reported feeling of being hungry and the sensory experience of certain internal and external cues. After looking in the unabridged *Oxford English Dictionary* (which tracks the etymology of all words in the English language), the social psychologist interested in prejudice might discuss how the word *prejudice* derived from the Latin *praejudicium,* meaning a precedent, or judgment, based on prior decisions, and how through centuries of English it has come to mean a "premature judgment, or readiness to prejudge." The child psychologist interested in *frustration* might conceptualize it as "the condition that exists when people feel their goals are blocked by internal or external barriers." After consulting the latest edition of the *Diagnostic and Statistical Manual of Mental Disorders* (published by the American Psychiatric Association), the clinical psychologist interested in *depression* might emphasize symptoms that are associated with it clinically, such as a feeling of sadness or despair, sleep problems, loss of interest in things that were once pleasurable, weight changes, the inability to concentrate, and feelings of hopelessness and death.

How do you begin your quest for good operational and theoretical definitions of the variables you want to study? Before you find yourself reinventing the wheel, you might look in standard references to see how others have conceptualized those variables (see Box 2.5). As an illustration, suppose a student were interested in developing a three-item test that could serve as a quick measure of feelings of depression, not in a clinical or psychiatric sample but in ordinary college students. The instructor suggests that the student think about correlating summed scores on the

---

  BOX 2.5 There's No Need to Reinvent the Wheel!

Whatever concept you are interested in, some psychologist or other behavioral or social scientist has probably written about it somewhere. Concise definitions of the language of psychology can also be found in the *APA Dictionary of Psychology* (VandenBos, 2007) and in specialized encyclopedias such as the APA's Encyclopedia of Psychology (Kazdin, 2000), the *International Encyclopedia of the Social and Behavioral Sciences* (Smelser & Baltes, 2002), the *Encyclopedia of Research Methods* *for the Social Sciences* (Lewis-Beck, Bryman, & Liao, 2003), and the *Encyclopedia of Mental Health* (H. Friedman, 1998). Your library may also have earlier encyclopedic works, which might give you a sense of how experts in the not-too-distant past conceptualized a particular problem, as in the *Encyclopedia of Education* (Deighton, 1971) and the *International Encyclopedia of Psychiatry, Psychology, Psychoanalysis, and Neurology* (Wolman, 1977).

three-item test with the BDI as an indicator of the three-item test's *construct validity*. We will have more to say about construct validity in Chapter 6, but **construct** is another name for a "concept" formulated ("constructed") to serve as a causal or descriptive explanation. By *construct validation,* the instructor means establishing the relation of a concept to variables with which it should, theoretically, be associated positively, negatively, or practically not at all (Cronbach & Meehl, 1955). In this case, the idea would be to show that the three-item test actually correlates positively with the BDI. For a theoretical definition of depression, the instructor recommends that the student read what the author of the BDI, Aaron T. Beck (e.g., Beck, Rush, Shaw, & Emery, 1979; Beck, Steer, & Garbin, 1988), wrote about it. There will be no problem using this material in the student's paper, as long as the source of any material used is properly cited and, when someone is quoted, the page numbers of the quoted passage are given.

Once the preliminary reading and note taking have been completed, the student is ready to draft the three sample items for the instructor to evaluate *before* the student administers them to anyone. One item might focus on sleep problems in depression: "I just don't want to get out of bed in the morning." A second item might focus on procrastination: "I can't get my work done, knowing that it will be really inferior." A third item might ask whether the person has thought about seeking help: "I have been so blue that maybe I should talk to someone about it." These are preliminary items. Expect to be asked to revise and polish your preliminary work based on the instructor's feedback and guidance. You may also have to return to some of your original sources. Try to be as thorough and systematic in your note taking as you can so that you do not have to waste time and energy returning to the same book or article. It is better to record too much than to rely on your memory to fill in the blanks. Try also to make sure your notes will make sense to you when you refer to them later.

 ## What Identifies "Good" Theories and Working Hypotheses?

We have used the terms *theory* and *hypothesis,* but we haven't distinguished between these two concepts. To help you understand this difference, let us look at another example, a formulation created by Leon Festinger (1954) called *social comparison theory*. Basically, this theory assumes that all people need to evaluate their opinions and abilities. People want to know whether they are like or unlike others, or better or worse than others. There are objective standards for many opinions and abilities to help people decide where they stand in relation to others. But for many others, such as opinions about ethnic or racial groups, religion, sex, or environmental pollution, it is not easy to find objective criteria. It follows, Festinger reasoned, that when no immediate objective standard exists, people attempt to evaluate their opinions and abilities by comparing themselves to others. He also theorized that the tendency to compare oneself with another person will decrease as the expected difference between oneself and another increases. Thus, if you wanted to evaluate your opinions about the existence of God, you would be more likely to compare yourself with another student than with a member of the clergy. The theory also states that you will be less attracted to groups whose members' thinking is very different from yours than to groups whose members think more as you do. One reason, according to Festinger, is that people are motivated to elicit reinforcement of the legitimacy of their own opinions.

We see what a "theory" can look like (at least in social psychology), and now let us see what **working hypotheses** look like (frequently called **experimental hypotheses** in experimental psychology). Karl Popper (the philosopher mentioned in the previous chapter in Box 1.1) pointed out that the purpose of scientific hypotheses is to "select" what the researcher will be looking for. To illustrate this function in his lectures, Popper told students, "Take pencil and paper; carefully observe, and write down what you have observed." They immediately asked *what* it was that he wanted them to observe, because a directed observation needs a chosen object, a definite task, an interest, a point of view, and a problem. Popper (1934, 1963) explained to them that their question illustrated why scientists need hypotheses, because they cannot do without a direction for their observations in their empirical research. Here are two of Festinger's (1954) hypotheses: (a) "The tendency to compare oneself with some other specific person decreases as the difference between his opinion or ability and one's own increases" (p. 120), and (b) "The existence of a discrepancy in a group with respect to opinions or abilities will lead to action on the part of the members of that group to reduce the discrepancy" (p. 124).

What does this illustration teach us so far about scientific theories and hypotheses? First, it shows that a **hypothesis** is a conjectural statement or supposition, and a **theory** is an organized set of explanatory propositions connected by logical arguments and by explicit and implicit prior assumptions (or *presuppositions*). Second, we see that hypotheses can be derived from a good theory and that they give direction to researchers' observations. Third, we see that a theory postulates a kind of conceptual pattern, which can then serve as a logical framework for the interpretation of the larger meaning of our observations (Hoover & Donovan, 1995). Finally, it is true of *seminal theories* (those that shape or stimulate other work) that they are constantly evolving as new findings, hypotheses, and interpretations emerge. Good scientific theories are also described as *generative,* which means they encourage others to generate additional hypotheses; social comparison theory measures up well to this standard (e.g., Buunk & Gibbons, 1997; Suls, Martin, & Wheeler, 2000; Suls & Miller, 1977; Wheeler, Martin, & Suls, 1997; Wood, 1989).

Good working hypotheses also have certain identifiable characteristics. First, they are *plausible,* or credible; that is, they are consistent with respected theories and reliable data. Traditionally, the working hypotheses that correspond most closely to accepted scientific truths are assumed to have good "payoff potential" when subjected to empirical jeopardy. That is to say, such hypotheses are expected to be more easily corroborated than conjectures that come out of the blue. It is impossible to be absolutely certain that a working hypothesis will pay off when tested, but the idea is to maximize the odds by ensuring that the hypothesis is credible (hence, the need to do a literature search). Second, good working hypotheses are *testable* in some empirical way. Third, they are *refutable,* or what Popper (1934, 1961) called *falsifiable.* Realizing that it is possible for those with a fertile imagination to find or concoct support for even the most preposterous claims, Popper argued that **falsifiability** is the most essential scientific standard of all. Conjectures that cannot, in principle, be refuted by *any* means are not within the realm of science, he argued. For example, "Behavior is a product of the good and evil lying within us" is not refutable empirically and, therefore, is not within the realm of science.

Finally, a fourth characteristic of good working hypotheses is that they are *succinct.* Traditionally, this requirement implies a combination of **coherence**, which means that the statement of the hypothesis "sticks together" in a logical way, and **parsimony**, which means the statement is not overly wordy or unduly complex. Most scientists believe that, to be acceptable, hypotheses must be only as complex and wordy as is absolutely necessary. Therefore, they "cut away" what is superfluous by means of a ruminative and winnowing process known as **Occam's razor**, after a 14th-century Franciscan philosopher named William of Occam (also spelled Ockham, known to his fellow friars as "doctor invincibilis"), who insisted that we cut away what is unwieldy. What can be stated or explained in fewer words or on the basis of fewer principles is stated or explained needlessly by more, he argued. A word of caution, however: Occam's razor is not a description of nature (because nature is often very complicated); it is a prescription for the *wording* of hypotheses. It is important not to cut off too much—"beards" but not "chins." How can you find out whether your working hypothesis cuts off too much or does not cut off enough? The best way is to ask the instructor for feedback and suggestions.

 What Is the Distinction between an Independent Variable and a Dependent Variable?

We have referred to *variables,* and a **variable** is simply an event or condition that the researcher observes or measures or plans to investigate that is likely to vary (or change). The rhetoric of behavioral and social science also recognizes a further distinction between dependent variables and independent variables (R. A. Fisher, 1973a, p. 129). The **dependent variable** (usually symbolized as Y) is the consequence (or the outcome) in which the researcher is interested; in other words, it *depends* on the changes in one or more other variables, called **independent variables**. In the simplest case of one independent variable (symbolized as *X*) and one dependent variable (*Y*), the idea is that changes in *X* are responsible for changes in *Y*. For example, in the statement "Jogging makes you feel better," the independent variable (*X*) is *jogging or not jogging*, and the dependent variable (*Y*) is *feeling better or not feeling better*. We do not mean that particular variables are always either dependent or independent variables but is simply another conceptual convenience in the rhetoric of behavioral science. In fact, *any* event or condition may be an independent variable *or* a dependent variable.

It is easy to imagine how some independent variable might be transformed into a dependent variable, and vice versa, because a variable derives its label from its context. Earlier in this chapter, we mentioned the idea that rumors are triggered by a combination of anxiety and uncertainty; in that context, anxiety and uncertainty were independent variables, and rumor was the dependent variable. Going back to the 1960s, a commission was established by President Lyndon B. Johnson to study the roots of racial rioting in the United States. It was called the Kerner Commission (after its chairman, Governor Otto Kerner of Illinois), and one of its chief conclusions was that rumors had significantly aggravated tensions and disorder in a substantial proportion of civil disorders (Kerner et al., 1968, p. 136). In the Kerner Commission's conclusion, rumors were the independent variable (i.e., the aggravating condition) and anxiety and uncertainty were dependent variables (i.e., the aggravated tension). In the blink of an eye, the independent and dependent variables have switched places; some rumors can be viewed as independent variables one moment and dependent variables the next (Rosnow, 2001).

You may be wondering whether there is an agreed-upon way of classifying independent and dependent variables, in the way, for instance, that chemists can turn to the periodic table to find out how an element is classified. The answer is no. There are, in fact, scores of independent and dependent variables in the literature of behavioral and social research. As simply an illustration, two general categories of independent variables that encompass a great many specific forms are biological and social variables. We will use eating behavior to illustrate these two categories.

In one classic example, a biological independent variable is seen when blood from a well-fed animal, as compared to the blood of a hungry animal, is injected into another animal that is hungry. The hungry animal stops feeding (Davis, Gallagher, & Ladove, 1967). This finding suggested that a biological independent variable for satiation is somehow carried by the blood: Information about a cell need must be transmitted to a part of the central nervous system that is well supplied with blood and that can control and organize the food-getting activities of the whole animal. Another classic example of a biological independent variable affecting eating behavior was first identified by physicians who observed that tumors in the region of the brain near the hypothalamus and the pituitary gland caused the symptoms of atrophy of the genital organs and tremendous obesity (described as *Froehlich's syndrome*). It was unclear, before experiments on animals were conducted, whether the syndrome was due to damage of the pituitary gland or to damage of the hypothalamus by the tumor. When the pituitary gland of normal animals was surgically removed, no obesity resulted, but later damage to the hypothalamus was followed by obesity (Bailey & Bremer, 1921). The status of the hypothalamus, not the pituitary gland, was the independent biological variable involved in the physiological regulation of food intake.

There are also many examples of social variables affecting eating behavior. The reason, of course, is that feeding by both humans and other species is affected not only by internal factors but also by many external conditions, including attitudes toward food in different cultures. For example, when people in Flemish Belgium, France, the United States, and Japan were surveyed for their beliefs about the diet-health link, whether they worried about food, and other issues related to the consumption of foods perceived as "healthier," the results revealed clear country differences in all domains except the importance of diet to health. Interestingly, among these cultural groups, Americans associated food most with health and least with pleasure (Rozin, Fischler, Imada, Sarubin, & Wrzesniewski, 1999). Having learned to eat at particular times of the day is another social variable that affects one's experiences of hunger (e.g., Schachter, 1968), as anyone who has ever crossed several time zones during an airplane trip can testify. Taste, appearance, and consistency are other obvious independent variables that strongly influence what foods humans prefer and how much food they will eat.

Independent variables can also occur in combinations, or *interactions* (more about this term in Chapter 14). For example, approximately half of the 40%–50% of North American women who crave chocolate or sweets do so primarily during the part of the menstrual cycle surrounding the onset of menstruation, but it is not clear whether this craving is due to biological or social factors, or maybe to a combination of both (Michener, Rozin, Freeman, & Gale, 1999). Another example implying an interaction is that if ice cream is adulterated with quinine in increasing quantities, obese people tend to refuse it before normal-weight people refuse it. Experiments have also found that obese people will tend to eat more of an expensive, good-tasting ice cream than will normal-weight people, but obese people will not work as hard as normal-weight or underweight people to obtain the food (Schachter, 1968).

Dependent variables also have no single classification system. Suppose a behavioral researcher wants to study pain avoidance as a source of drive level somewhat different from the appetitive drives of hunger, thirst, and sex. (As noted earlier, a drive level refers to the state of readiness of an organism, or more specifically in this case, a readiness to engage in physiologically connected behavior.) What should the researcher choose as the dependent measure? Imagining yourself quickly withdrawing your hand from a shock-producing stimulus suggests that measuring the time it takes to withdraw from the stimulus (i.e., the *latency*, or delay, of withdrawal) is a good dependent measure. However, suppose the researcher is interested instead in the pain connected with extreme sexual deprivation in male rats. This topic seems more complex than food or water deprivation, though similarities certainly exist. If the rats are very hungry because they were deprived of food, the researcher might record their actions as they are faced with choosing between food and a female rat in heat.

When you peruse the journal literature in your field, you will see that these examples barely scratch the surface of the many kinds of dependent variables examined by behavioral scientists. Here is a more exotic example from the field of developmental psychology: Infants have always fascinated their parents by balancing precariously on the edge of a chair or table in apparent imitation of a tightrope walker. The parents' fascination is usually liberally mixed with fear for the safety of the infant. Obviously, an infant is not yet a fully competent and accurate judge of size and distance in its exploration of the space around it. The child's ability to perceive depth was a subject of intense interest to Eleanor J. Gibson and Richard D. Walk. These investigators worked with what they called a "visual cliff"—a board laid across a large sheet of glass that was raised a foot or more above the floor. A checkerboard pattern covered half the glass. On the other half, the same checkerboard pattern appeared on the floor directly under the glass. The visual cliff was created by the perceptual experience of the difference between the two sides. In one study, Gibson and Walk (1960) tested infants ranging in age from 6 to 14 months on the visual cliff. Each child was placed on the central board and was called by its mother from the "cliff" side and the "shallow" side successively. Most of the infants moved off the central board onto the glass, and all of these crawled out to the "shallow" side at least once. Only a few moved to the glass suspended above the pattern on the floor; most infants would not cross the apparent chasm to their mothers. The dependent variable was *crossing versus not crossing the apparent chasm*. As a consequence of having developed this not-so-ordinary dependent variable, Gibson and Walk discovered that most human infants discriminate depth as soon as they are able to crawl.

What Belongs in My Research Proposal?

Once you have retrieved relevant work, developed your hypotheses, and have a design and a plan to implement it, you must tell your instructor what you would like to study and how you propose to go about it, including how you propose to deal with ethical issues (discussed in the next chapter). Exhibit 2.1 will give you an idea of what a proposal to be submitted to the instructor might look like. Think of it not as a one-way communication, but as a mutual understanding between you and your

(text continues on p. 37)

Exhibit 2.1 Sample Research Proposal

Mary Jones 1

Proposal for a Research Project

Mary Jones (e-mail address or other contact information)

(Date the proposal is submitted)

Objective of the Research

I propose to conduct a randomized experiment in which college students will simulate the role of a bail judge. There will be two randomized conditions, in both of which the students will be given a "crime scenario" to read. In the experimental condition, the students will read that the suspect tested positive for drugs while in custody. In the control condition, that information will be omitted. Immediately afterward, the students will be asked to set the bail amount between $0 and $50,000. I am interested in exploring whether the experimental group will set a harsher bail amount than the control group.

Background and Hypotheses

Dr. Rind's instructions were to choose a question that can be empirically addressed in an ethical and technically acceptable way in a descriptive, relational, or experimental investigation. Since I hope to go to law school, I was particularly interested in choosing a question that might be relevant to the legal process. This semester, I am taking a political science course. In one of the lectures, the professor spoke about the application of psychological principles and research methods to situations involving the law, or what the *APA Dictionary of Psychology* refers to as *forensic psychology* (VandenBos, 2007, p. 385). We learned about certain classic studies of the distorting effects of misleading questions on the memories of eyewitnesses (e.g., Loftus, Miller, & Burns, 1978), which got me interested in biasing effects in the legal process in general. The

---

Mary Jones 2

professor also played video clips from debates about legal issues, and one of them in particular seemed like it could be the basis of an experimental investigation of biased judgments.

This particular clip was from the ABC television program *Nightline*, back in the summer of 1988, but the professor said that it was still a topical issue today. The debate was between a representative of the American Civil Liberties Union (ACLU) and a spokesperson for a national group of prosecutors. They debated whether mandatory drug testing should be carried out on all persons arrested. The ACLU representative argued, among a number of issues, that providing positive results of mandatory drug testing to bail judges would unfairly bias decisions on how much bail to impose. The prosecutor argued that having the drug information would have no effect on a bail judge's decision. Thinking about that debate, I then consulted my notes from a social psychology course that I took last semester. We learned about Jones and Davis's (1965) classic work on what they called correspondent inference theory, a basic assumption of which was that people tend to selectively focus on certain aspects of behavior to infer character traits.

Though I think of my proposed research as an exploratory study, I do have a hypothesis based on Jones and Davis's work and other classic work in the area of attribution theory which was mentioned by the social psychology instructor. She said that among the kinds of questions that observers ask themselves is whether the particular aspect of behavior that they are focused on is low in social desirability. The idea she stressed was that people have a natural tendency to focus on socially undesirable behavior in judging an actor's traits and, once having inferred such traits, then use this information to predict the actor's future behavior. That idea seems relevant to the question of biasing effects of drug-testing results on bail judgments. On the assumption that drug usage is generally considered low in social desirability in our society, my hypothesis is that

(Continued)

knowledge of positive results from the defendant's drug test will result in harsher bail judgments than when that information is not available to the bail judge.

Proposed Method

Research Participants

It would be unrealistic for me to think I could use real judges in this research, but I have received permission from another instructor to conduct a simulation study in an undergraduate course that he teaches. The students will be responding anonymously. He thought that I might have 30 or more students willing to participate in this study, because it will give them firsthand experience of being a subject in a psychological experiment and they will at some point also be taking a research methods course. Assuming that the estimated sample size is correct, I will be working with statistical power much lower than .80 (the recommended level in the course text). However, since I think of this research as exploratory, all I am really looking for is a directional effect and the magnitude of the effect.

Procedure

I have developed two versions of a "crime scenario" that will be printed out, and the two versions will be randomly ordered and each student will receive a one-page questionnaire having one of the two versions on it. Both versions will state that a man had been arrested as a suspected burglar because he fit the description of a man who had been seen running from the burglarized house. In the experimental condition, the next sentence will state that, while in custody, the man had submitted to a blood test and it determined that he had recently used drugs (the experimental condition). In the control condition, a substitute sentence will simply state that the man had spent enough time in custody to receive two meals and make three phone calls.

On the bottom of the page, there will be a single item that asks the student to assume the role of a bail judge. The student will be asked "what bail would you set?" if limited by a dollar amount from $0 to $50,000. My reason for specifying a range is to give the research participants a common metric. I chose this particular range because it seemed realistic and sufficiently wide to produce differences between the experimental and control groups. Although the participants will be asked to give their age, sex, year in college, and estimated GPA, no name will be asked for, because I believe they will be more forthcoming if they know that they will be responding anonymously.

Data Analysis

I plan to analyze the results using an independent t test and to report the associated p, the effect size, and the 95% confidence interval of the reported effect size. Before I begin writing up the research report, I will go over the results with Dr. Rind once I have the raw data scored and have calculated some basic descriptive statistics. My purpose in consulting Dr. Rind will be to ensure that there are no unanticipated problems that I will need to address with some followup analysis of the data.

Ethical Considerations

Although I have obtained permission to run this study in another instructor's class, I will emphasize at the outset that any student who does not wish to participate can simply return the one-page questionnaire without filling it out. At the point at which I ask the students to return the questionnaires, I will instruct them to fold the page in half with the blank side showing, so that it is impossible for any other student to see how anyone responded (or did not respond). The study does not involve deception, and at the end of the study the instructor has asked me to answer any questions about the study that the students raise.

(Continued)

Exhibit 2.1 Continued

References

Jones, E. E., & Davis, K. E. (1965). From acts to dispositions: The attribution process in person perception. In L. Berkowitz (Ed.), *Advances in experimental social psychology* (Vol. 2, pp. 219-266). New York, NY: Academic Press. doi:10.1016/S0065-2601(08)60107-0

Loftus, E. F., Miller, D. G., & Burns, H. J. (1978). Semantic integration of verbal information into a visual memory. *Journal of Experimental Psychology: Human Learning and Memory, 4*, 19-31.

VandenBos, G. R. (Ed.). (2007). *APA dictionary of psychology*. Washington, DC: American Psychological Association.

instructor (who may require additional information besides that shown in the exhibit or may specify some other variation on it). Once your proposal has been approved, it is expected that you will consult with the instructor should you wish to make significant changes in how you conduct your research, because the proposal constitutes a formal agreement you have made with the instructor.

Turning to Exhibit 2.1, you will notice that the student's name and the page number are repeated in the upper right corner of every page. This repetition serves as a safety device should any page get accidentally detached. Centered at the top of the first page are the words "Proposal for a Research Project"; then the student's name again and her contact information; and the date she will be handing in the proposal. What follows is the *main body of the proposal*, which is divided into sections, each with a center heading in boldface. The proposal concludes with a list of references that Mary has consulted so far. As you study the sample proposal, you will see that Mary Jones uses the first-person style of writing ("I propose to conduct a randomized experiment…" and "I am interested in exploring whether…"). When writing papers for publication, researchers do not typically use the first-person style, although you will find that some do use it (we have used it in a number of articles in professional journals). The reason we encourage this style in your proposal and final report is that it is an opportunity to indicate that this work is your own, as originality is a concern of most instructors. Still, we suggest you check with your instructor to make sure he or she has no objections to the style illustrated here.

Notice next that the main body of the proposal is divided into four sections: (a) the objective of the research; (b) the background and hypotheses; (c) the proposed method; and (d) ethical considerations. (You may want to modify this organization or choose different section headings, which will depend on the nature of the research that you are proposing.) In the first section, Mary begins by briefly stating exactly what she is proposing and in this way gives the instructor a preview of the rest of the proposal. In the next section, Mary leads the instructor through her train of thought as she came up with an initial idea and developed it into a testable hypothesis. Next, she gives a detailed description of the method she proposes to use, beginning with the participants, then the procedure and the materials, and finally the data analysis as she currently envisions it. Finally, Mary discusses ethical considerations.

The references (which begin on a new page) are a preliminary list, which Mary will probably want to expand and modify in the final report. The rule is to reference everything you cited and to cite everything in the references. Mary's citations and references are in the APA writing style, as specified in the most recent edition (the 6th edition) of the *Publication Manual of the American Psychological Association* (APA, 2010), referred to as the "APA Manual." The author-date method is the APA Manual's style of citing articles and books. In the references, notice that the APA Manual's style is to invert all authors' names (last name, first initial, middle initial) and to list the names in the exact order in which they appear on the title page of the cited work, using commas to separate authors and an ampersand (&) before the last author. If you turn to the sample report in Appendix A, you will find more examples of the APA style of citing and referencing books and articles. New in the latest edition of the APA Manual is the requirement that the Digital Object Identifier (doi) of an article (assuming there is a doi and you know it) should be listed at the end of the particular reference as "doi:xxxxxx" without a period.

In this chapter, we have considered the initial phase of a research project as a process of creative insight and critical rumination leading to one or more good hypotheses. However, we do not want to leave you with the idea that behavioral research *must* proceed in a strictly formulaic way. One philosopher asserted that "successful research…relies now on one trick, now on another; the moves that advance it and the standards that define what counts as an advance are not always known to the movers" (Feyerabend, 1988, p. 1). Though a lot of what behavioral researchers do is perhaps also based on myriad phenomena and a kind of surface intuition, there are many tried-and-true research methods. Before we resume our discussion of these methods, it is important to have an understanding of ethical considerations and guidelines, which are now considered an essential component of the scientific method in the behavioral and social sciences, and it is to this subject that we turn in the next chapter.

Summary of Ideas

1. The *context of discovery* was defined as the circumstances leading from initial hunches, questions, or insights to conjectural statements or suppositions that give direction to researchers' observations.

2. The *context of justification* was defined as the empirical evaluation of conjectural statements or suppositions and the evidence-based defense of conclusions and generalizations.

3. Besides getting good ideas for hypotheses and research from the relevant literature, colloquia, and poster presentations (since the end of one study is usually the prelude to another in a cycle of discovery and justification), four hypothesis-generating heuristics that were discussed are (a) explaining paradoxical incidents in testable ways (Latané and Darley's work on bystander intervention); (b) using analogies, metaphors, or figures of speech (McGuire's inoculation model of resistance to "viral-like" counterpropaganda); (c) identifying and trying to resolve conflicting conclusions (Zajonc's social facilitation hypothesis); (d) improving on older ideas (Skinner's distinction between Pavlovian conditioning and Thorndikian learning).

4. Good leads for questions and hypotheses are all around us, and serendipity can play a role if we keep our eyes, ears, and minds open (Rosnow's work on rumor, and Rosenthal's on the self-fulfilling nature of interpersonal expectations).

5. The literature search can be facilitated by computerized databases, including full-text databases, which can be accessed online (such as PsycINFO and PsycARTICLES).

6. *Operational definitions* identify variables on the basis of the empirical conditions (*operations*) that are used to measure or manipulate the variables, whereas *theoretical definitions* assign the meaning of terms abstractly or generally. Before you find yourself reinventing the wheel, look in standard references (e.g., Box 2.5) to see how concepts and variables are defined in the area in which you propose to do research.

7. *Theories* are sets of statements, generally including some hypotheses, connected by a logical argument (Festinger's social comparison theory). Good *working hypotheses* are plausible, empirically testable, refutable (Popper's falsifiability criterion), and succinct (coherent and parsimonious, using "Occam's razor" to cut away what is superfluous).

8. *Constructs* are explanatory concepts that provide a theoretical connection between variables.

9. *Variables* are what the researcher observes or measures, and as the term implies, they are likely to vary.

10. The *independent variable* (X) is the status of the antecedent event or condition, and countless types of events and conditions can qualify as independent variables in different situations. The *dependent variable* (Y) is the status of the consequence, and there is also an infinite variety of dependent variables. Furthermore, the same event or condition may qualify as an independent variable in one situation and as a dependent variable in another, all depending on our particular interest (e.g., anxiety, uncertainty, and rumor). The events or conditions may also occur in combinations.

11. The research proposal is an agreement made between the student and the instructor regarding the student's plans to do a research study; it describes (a) the objective of the research; (b) the background and hypotheses of the proposed investigation, (c) the proposed sample of participants, method, and data analysis, and (d) the ethics of the proposed plan of investigation.

Key Terms

coherence p. 31	hypothesis p. 31	parsimony p. 31
construct p. 30	hypothesis-generating	replication p. 22
context of discovery p. 20	heuristics p. 22	serendipity p. 25
context of justification p. 20	independent variable p. 32	theoretical definitions p.29
dependent variable p. 31	moderator variables p. 22	theory p. 31
experimental hypotheses p. 30	Occam's razor p. 31	variable p. 31
falsifiability p. 31	operational definitions p. 29	working hypotheses p. 30

Multiple-Choice Questions for Review
(answers appear at the end of this chapter)

1. Paul has suffered brain damage in a car accident. Dr. Thaler, a specialist in internal medicine, studies Paul intensively, giving him many clinical interviews and tests to measure his cognitive functioning. Based on his work with Paul, Dr. Thaler comes up with a brilliant new hypothesis, which he and others can test further in empirical research. From what we know so far, we would say that the doctor's hypothesis came

about primarily through (a) serendipity; (b) analogical thinking; (c) an intensive case study; (d) the examination of a paradoxical incident.

2. A researcher at the University of Colorado is interested in studying dynamics in small groups (typically consisting of two to five people). She begins by thinking that people in small groups relate to each other much as the governments of large countries relate to each other. She develops hypotheses about small-group dynamics by thinking about how people in small groups are similar to diplomats at the United Nations. Her hypothesis came about through (a) attempting to resolve conflicting results; (b) improving on older ideas; (c) using analogical thinking; (d) serendipity.

3. A researcher at Monmouth University conducts a study of high school students and finds there is no relationship between the amounts of time spent watching TV and grade point average. A researcher at Emporia University conducts a study of elementary school students and finds that those who watch a lot of TV tend to have very low grades. A third researcher, from Providence College, now develops a new theory stating that the relationship between watching TV and grade point average depends on other variables, including the age of the student. This third researcher's theory has come about through (a) serendipity; (b) using analogical thinking; (c) attempting to resolve conflicting results; (d) examining intensive case studies.

4. Dr. Pearson, a research specialist in urology, sets out to find a new treatment for cancerous tumors. By a lucky coincidence, he discovers that the new treatment he is studying might serve as a treatment for Parkinson's disease, a disease that is totally unrelated to cancer. His discovery would appear (from this limited information alone) to have come about through (a) improving on older ideas; (b) using analogical thinking; (c) examining intensive case studies; (d) serendipity.

5. Edwin H. Land was with his 3-year-old daughter when she asked him why a camera could not produce pictures instantly. Thinking about her question while out for a walk, he hit on the idea for the Polaroid Land Camera. This is an illustration of how (a) circumstances can evoke ideas; (b) ideas are all around us if we keep our eyes, ears, and minds open to discovery; (c) creativity is not limited to art or music; (d) all of the above.

6. A researcher at the Baltimore campus of the University of Maryland is studying *intelligence* and defines it as "a person's general ability to adapt to his or her environment." This statement is (a) an operational definition; (b) a theoretical definition; (c) a dimensional definition; (d) none of the above.

7. The same researcher will be measuring the intelligence of high school students at the Baltimore City College. For this aspect of his study, the researcher defines *intelligence* as "a score on the WAIS (Wechsler Adult Intelligence Scale)," an example of (a) an operational definition; (b) a theoretical definition; (c) a dimensional definition; (d) none of the above.

8. ————is to operational definition as———— is to theoretical definition. (a) Construct, variable; (b) Coherence, parsimony; (c) Parsimony, coherence; (d) Variable, construct

9. A researcher at Saint Anselm College conducts an experiment with volunteers. Half of them are given 1 ounce of colored water and told it is bourbon; the other half are given 4 ounces of the same liquid and told that it is bourbon. The researcher then gives all the participants a test of motor coordination. In this experiment, the test of motor coordination is the————variable. (a) control; (b) dependent; (c) independent; (d) none of the above

10. A researcher at the University of South Carolina, who is collaborating with the researcher at Saint Anselm College, conducts the same experiment with high schoolers in Columbia, South Carolina. In this experiment, the colored water the participants receive is the————variable. (a) control; (b) dependent; (c) independent; (d) none of the above

Discussion Questions for Review
(answers appear at the end of this chapter)

1. A Rowan University student wants to see whether self-esteem affects academic performance. He asks 30 randomly selected students from his dormitory to fill out a self-esteem measure, and he divides the students into groups having high and low self-esteem on the basis of their test scores. He then compares the self-reported grade point average (GPA) of the two groups and concludes that high self-esteem does lead to a higher GPA. How has he operationalized his independent and dependent variables? If he finds these variables to be highly related, how well justified will he be in claiming that self-esteem affects academic performance?

2. A Virginia Tech student is interested in the personality trait of extraversion. Give an example of both an operational and a theoretical definition of this construct that she can use.

3. A friend tells a George Washington University student that astrology is accurate and reminds her that

President Ronald Reagan consulted an astrologer. How should the student respond to her friend? Can you think of a way for her to do an empirical study to test her friend's assertion?

4. A San Diego State student is interested in studying revenge. Can you devise a causal hypothesis for her to test? How can you assess whether your hypothesis is "good" before passing it to her?

5. A "wolf boy" was discovered in Alaska and brought to a learned doctor for study. The doctor conducted many exploratory tests to determine the boy's reactions. The doctor slammed the door, and though everyone else flinched, the boy remained calm and unmoving. The doctor called out to his secretary, who was taking notes, "Write: Does not respond to noise." A nurse who was looking after the boy protested, "But, sir, I have seen the boy startle at the sound of a cracking nut in the woods 30 feet away!" The doctor paused and then instructed his secretary, "Write: Does not respond to *significant* noise." How was the doctor's explanatory observation flawed? How would you instead propose to study the wolf boy?

Answers to Review Questions

Multiple-Choice Questions

1. c
2. c
3. c
4. d
5. d
6. b
7. a
8. d
9. b
10. c

Discussion Questions

1. His independent variable was operationalized by scores on the self-esteem scale; his dependent variable was operationalized by self-reported GPA. Because this is a relational study rather than an experimental study, he would not be justified in drawing the causal inference that either variable led to or affected the other.

2. An operational definition could be the score earned on a standard psychological test purported to measure extraversion. A theoretical definition might be "the degree of social ease and smoothness shown in a group setting."

3. One study of the accuracy of astrological forecasts might ask a panel of "expert" astrologers to prepare a brief description of the personality of persons born under each of the 12 signs of the zodiac. A large number of students would then be asked to rate each of these 12 descriptions on the extent to which each of the descriptions applied to them. As long as the students know nothing about astrology, evidence for the accuracy of astrology would be obtained if the students rated the personality descriptions of their sign as more characteristic of them than the average of the other 11 descriptions. These students' roommates or friends could also rate the students, assuming the roommates or friends also knew nothing about astrology.

4. A causal hypothesis might be that revenge is more likely to occur when people feel they have been harmed intentionally by another. To evaluate this hypothesis, we can assess its plausibility (Is it consistent with accepted truths?); testability (Can it be subjected to empirical scrutiny?); credibility (Is it believable?); refutability (Is it falsifiable if wrong?); and succinctness (Is the statement of the hypothesis coherent and parsimonious?).

5. The doctor did not take the boy's cultural background or context into account. We might study the boy by administering standard medical, neurological, and psychological evaluations; by giving him a wide choice of cultural artifacts (toys, tools, foods, pictures, videos, etc.) to observe, use, and explore; and by accompanying him to settings (e.g., parks, lakes, and forests) more like those in which he grew up in order to observe his behavior in a habitat to which he was more accustomed.

CHAPTER 3

Ethical Considerations and Guidelines

Preview Questions

- How do ethical guidelines in research function?
- What is informed consent, and when is it used?
- How are ethics reviews done and acted on?
- What are obstacles to the rendering of "full justice"?
- How can a "relationship of trust" be established?
- How do scientific quality and ethical quality intertwine?
- Is deception in research ever justified?
- What is the purpose of debriefing, and how is it done?
- How is animal research governed by ethical rules?
- What ethical responsibilities are there when writing up research?

How Do Ethical Guidelines in Research Function?

In Chapter 1 we introduced you to the idea of three general research strategies (descriptive, relational, and experimental), and we noted that within these three approaches there are many different options (some of which are further illustrated in the next two chapters). In Chapter 2, we examined the ways in which good ideas emerge and credible, tightly reasoned, falsifiable hypotheses are created. The primary focus of this chapter is ethical issues as they pertain to research with human participants. We also briefly discuss research with animal subjects later in this chapter and conclude by discussing ethical responsibilities when reporting research findings. The word *ethics* was originally derived from the Greek *ethos*, meaning "character" or "disposition." In current usage, **ethics** is understood as referring to conduct that is considered "morally right" or "morally wrong" as specified by codified and culturally ingrained principles, constraints, rules, and guidelines. Thinking about ethical issues and potential conflicts in conducting and reporting research findings also compels you to confront your own moral presuppositions.

For instance, one major concern of the American Psychological Association (APA) when it first adopted a research code for psychologists was the prevalence of various types of deception in some areas of research (cf. Kelman, 1968; Sieber, 1982a, 1983; M. B. Smith, 1969; Vinacke, 1954). The types of deception included giving misinformation to research participants, misrepresenting the purpose of the study or procedure to participants, and giving incomplete information to the participants but implying it was complete (Geller, 1982). Of course, it is hardly news that the use of

active deceptions (e.g., manipulating the truth) and **passive deceptions** (e.g., spying on people or omitting pertinent information) are far from rare in our society, although their prevalence is not a moral justification for their use in behavioral research. Still, trial lawyers have been known to manipulate the truth in court on behalf of their clients; prosecutors have surreptitiously recorded private conversations; the police have used sting operations to assemble incriminating evidence; and investigative reporters have used undercover practices, hidden cameras, and hidden microphones to get the information they seek (Bok, 1978).

For example, a case involving the use of deception by CBS-TV's news program *60 Minutes* was described by social psychologist Leonard Saxe (1991). On the pretense that they represented a photography magazine owned by CBS, the *60 Minutes* people recruited four polygraph examiners randomly chosen from the telephone directory and asked each of them to help incriminate the magazine employee who had stolen more than $500 worth of camera equipment. No one, in fact, had stolen anything, and a different person was "fingered" by the *60 Minutes* staff for each polygrapher. The deceptively fingered "culprits" were confederates who were promised $50 by the program staff if they could convince the polygraphers of their innocence. A hidden camera filmed the testing situation without the polygraphers' knowing they were the subjects of a televised exposé. Dramatically, the *60 Minutes* report showed that the polygraphers did not necessarily "read" the psychophysiological polygraph information to make their diagnoses; it showed each polygrapher *trying* to get the "guilty" person to confess.

Had this study been proposed to a review panel as a scientific study under the auspices of an academic institution, concerns would undoubtedly have been raised about the ethical propriety of using an elaborate deception to uncover another deception. Saxe (1991) commented, "The demonstration was very clever, but dishonest: CBS lied to the polygraphers. The four polygraphers unwittingly starred in a television drama viewed by millions...yet it is hard to think of a way to do this study without deception" (p. 409). Forewarning the polygraphers they were going to be the subjects of a *60 Minutes* exposé would have made the study—and no doubt the results—quite different. Do you think the elaborate deception used by *60 Minutes* was justified by the investigation's purpose, or would you instead argue that the ends did not justify the means? Do you think that deception is ever morally justified in research? In a 2009 article in the *Journal of Consumer Psychology*, the authors reported that the prevalence of deceptive practices has increased in this area of behavioral research (N. C. Smith, Kimmel, & Klein, 2009). We mention this article again later in this chapter, as the authors also proposed a set of principles to govern when "deception in research is morally permissible" (N. C. Smith et al., 2009, p. 489).

Violations of ethical principles codified by professional organizations, such as the APA, are typically supported by sanctions such as loss of membership in the organization. In the case of the APA ethics code, many psychologists who are engaged in productive, rewarding research careers do not belong to APA. However, federal and state statutes also hold researchers to ethical principles by means of legally enforceable rules. In the 1970s, a federal act created a commission for the protection of human subjects of biomedical and behavioral research. After holding hearings for 3 years, the commission issued *The Belmont Report* of April 18, 1979. The Belmont Report set out three principles as an ethical foundation of human subjects research: (a) respect for persons, (b) *beneficence* (the "doing of good," and the concomitant moral obligation "to do no harm," now called *nonmaleficence*), and (c) justice (see also Box 3.1). The Belmont Report also established the use of informed-consent procedures and a gatekeeping mechanism in the form of *institutional review boards* (IRBs) to weigh the risks and benefits of proposed research and to monitor ongoing research in order to protect human participants from harm.

After the Belmont Report, everything changed permanently for researchers who worked with human participants, as "accountability" became the watchword of the decade (National Commission on Research, 1980). The dilemma for researchers was, as one scholar put it, to justify the use of human subjects as the means to an end that was beneficial in some significant way (e.g., the advance of science, public health, or public policy) while protecting fundamental "ideals of human dignity, respect

BOX 3.1   The Belmont Report and the Tuskegee Study

The **Belmont Report** took its name from discussions that were held in Washington, DC, at the Smithsonian Institution's Belmont Conference Center (National Commission for the Protection of Human Subjects of Biomedical and Behavioral Research, 1979). Before this report, there had been some safeguards to protect subjects in medical research, but serious violations had occurred nonetheless (Beecher, 1970; Katz, 1972). In a notorious study that was conducted by the U.S. Public Health Service (USPHS) from 1932 to 1973, the course of syphilis in more than 400 low-income African-American men in Tuskegee, Alabama, had been monitored without the researchers' informing the men they had syphilis (they were told only that they had "bad blood"). They were not given penicillin when, in 1947, it was found to

effectively treat syphilis. They also were warned not to seek treatment elsewhere or they would be dropped from the study and would lose their free "health care" and free annual medical exam. The researchers even got local doctors to promise not to provide antibiotics to subjects in the study (Stryker, 1997). The Tuskegee study was eventually terminated after details were made public by a lawyer who had once been an epidemiologist for the USPHS. By this time, however, the untreated disease had progressed predictably: The men had experienced skeletal, cardiovascular, and central nervous system damage and, in some cases, death (J. H. Jones, 1993). As a consequence of this infamous study, many minority communities still maintain a "legacy of mistrust" of government and medicine (Stryker, 1997, p. E4).

for persons, freedom and self-determination, and a sense of worth" (Atwell, 1981, p. 89). Over the years, as the basic and applied contexts in which behavioral researchers work have expanded, virtually every facet of research has been scrutinized from the perspective of ethics (e.g., Kimmel, 2007; Panter & Sterba, 2011; Sales & Folkman, 2000; Sieber, 1982b). Not surprisingly perhaps, researchers often find it difficult to "exorcize the devil from the details" when challenged by ethical guidelines that sometimes seem to conflict with the technical imperatives of science (Mark, Eyssell, & Campbell, 1999, p. 48).

Later on in this chapter we define some technical standards of science, and throughout the chapter we emphasize five broad **ethical principles** that serve as a framework for this discussion. These five principles are an amalgamation of rules, institutionalized regulations, and professional ideals (e.g., American Psychological Association, 2002; Committee on Science, Engineering, and Public Policy, 2009; Kimmel, 1996, 2007; Rosnow & Rosenthal, 2011; Sales & Folkman, 2000; M. B. Smith, 2000). Collectively, they can also be understood as reflecting a continually evolving compact (or implicit *social contract*) between researchers and society (Rosnow, 1997). Principle I is respect for persons and their *autonomy* (independence or freedom). Principle II is an obligation not to do psychological or physical harm (*nonmaleficence*) and to strive to do research that is meaningful or potentially beneficial in advancing knowledge or well-being (*beneficence*). Principle III is the pursuit and promotion of justice; *injustice* occurs when an individual is unreasonably denied a benefit or gain to which he or she is entitled, or when some unequal burden is imposed excessively or undeservedly on individuals. Principle IV is the establishment of a relationship of trust between researchers and research participants. Principle V is a fidelity to professional responsibilities, scientific integrity, and accountability.

What Is Informed Consent, and When Is It Used?

Principle I (respect for persons and their autonomy) is the basis of the researcher's ethical and legal responsibility to ensure that each potential participant knows what the study involves and is free to decide whether or not to participate. In practice, the researcher tells prospective participants about the study and obtains their written agreement to participate (called **informed consent**). It is essential not to overcomplicate the disclosure procedure by making the information so detailed and cumbersome that it defeats the purpose for which informed consent was intended (Imber, Glanz, Elkin, Sotsky,

Boyer, & Leber, 1986). However, it is also vital to go beyond the mere ritualized presentation of a consent form (Melton, Levine, Koocher, Rosenthal, & Thompson, 1988). This striking of a balance between too much and too little may be difficult in some situations, but it is crucial nonetheless. For students in search of challenging research leads, the horns of this dilemma offer an opportunity to study a problem with potential ethical, substantive, and methodological implications (for illustrative studies, see Dorn, Susman, & Fletcher, 1995; Susman, Dorn, & Fletcher, 1992).

There are, to be sure, situations in which informed consent is unnecessary or impossible, such as archival studies that use public records (illustrated in the next chapter). Other exempt cases are risk-free experiments in which instituting informed consent would be counterproductive. For example, a team of social psychologists who were interested in studying tipping behavior had servers in a restaurant draw or not draw a happy face on the back of customer checks before presenting them (Rind & Bordia, 1996). The practical reason to be interested in tipping behavior is that more than 2 million people in the United States work as waiters and waitresses and, for most of them, a major source of income is the tips they receive from the dining parties (Bureau of Labor Statistics, 2010–2011). Before initiating this study, the researchers explained everything to the servers and the owner of the restaurant and obtained their permission to proceed. No attempt was made to inform the customers (the subjects in this study) or to ask them to sign a consent form, because telling them about the research in advance would have destroyed the credibility of the experimental manipulation and rendered the study meaningless. (Incidentally, the results were that drawing the happy face was associated with increased tips for the female server but did not increase tips for the male server.)

In the recruitment of subjects for psychological experiments, the prospective participants are typically given a form that describes (a) the nature of the study, (b) any potential risk or inconvenience to them, (c) the procedure for ensuring the confidentiality of the data, and (d) the voluntary nature of their cooperation and their freedom to withdraw at any time without prejudice or consequence. The person is usually asked to sign a second form to indicate that he or she understands the nature and purpose of the research and is willing to participate. However, if the participants are confused about the nature of their involvement, it cannot be said that the informed-consent procedure complies with the spirit of Principle I. Figure 3.1 shows in Section A an illustration of the consent portion of an informed-consent

---

Instructions to participant: Before you participate in this study, please print and then sign your name in the space provided in section A. Once the study is over and you have been debriefed, you will be asked to initial the three statements in Section B to indicate your agreement.

Section A

I, _____, voluntarily give my consent to participate in this project. I have been informed about, and feel that I understand, the basic nature of the project. I understand that I may leave at any time and that my anonymity will be protected.

_____   _____
Signature of Research Participant   Date

Section B

Please initial each of the following statements once the study has been completed and you have been debriefed:

_____I have been debriefed.

_____I was not forced to stay to complete the study.

_____All my questions have been answered satisfactorily.

Figure 3.1   Example of the written-consent portion of the informed-consent agreement.

BOX 3.2 Generalizing Beyond the Student Subject Pool

Concerns have been periodically raised about the limitations of generalizing beyond the student subject pool and the typical lab experiment and questionnaire study to the general population in the "real world" (cf. J. G. Adair, 1973; Levitt & List, 2007; McNemar, 1946; Sears, 1986; Silverman, 1977; Strohmetz, 2006). The concerns are based not only on obvious differences between college students and the general population along many dimensions, but also on the suspicion that those who volunteer for research participation may differ from nonvolunteers in the degree to which they are affected by hints and cues that govern their perception of their role as "research subject" and the experimenter's expectation. We return to this problem in a later chapter, but one consequence of the research on this problem was to call attention to limitations of particular methods of investigation, an idea that we mentioned at the very beginning of Chapter 1 (Rosnow & Rosenthal, 1997). As we also mentioned in that chapter, because every method is limited in some way researchers often try to triangulate on questions of interest from more than one methodological perspective (described previously as *methodological pluralism*).

agreement and, in Section B, an example of what a participant who has been *debriefed* (a process discussed later in this chapter) might be asked to initial after the study has been completed.

Suppose the prospective participants have a limited or diminished capacity to understand the consent form. For example, young children frequently have difficulty understanding the consent agreement (Dorn et al., 1995; Susman et al., 1992). Whenever research calls for children or adolescents to participate, the researcher is required to obtain parental consent before proceeding and is not permitted to make appeals to children to participate before this consent is obtained (Scott-Jones & Rosnow, 1998). If the children do not live with their parents (e.g., they may be wards of some agency), the researcher can speak with an advocate who is appointed to act in the best interests of the child. Once the informed consent of the parent or advocate has been obtained, the researcher asks the child on the day of the study whether he or she wishes to participate, that is, assuming the child is mature enough to be asked about participation. Incidentally, signing an informed-consent form does not mean the person has relinquished certain legal rights, such as the right to sue for negligence (T. Mann, 1994). In fact, the right to sue has long been protected by federal regulations on the use of human subjects (U.S. Department of Health and Human Services, 1983).

Because college and university students are so readily available, they are used frequently in behavioral research studies and have taught us a great deal about cognition, attitude formation, perception, and social behavior. A common assumption in many departments is that there is an educational benefit to the students who participate as subjects, such as a deeper understanding of the research process and, presumably, the material they are learning in a course. In the spirit of Principle I, it is important to prevent coercion or the appearance of coercion. In 2010, the Office for Human Research Protections (OHRP), a unit of the Department of Health and Human Services (DHHS), posted a letter to a company that provided a Web-based system for managing student subject pools. In the letter OHRP stated that it would violate DHHS regulations to penalize students who failed to show up for scheduled research appointments and added that the statement applied not just to commercial Web-based systems but also to any system used for managing student subject pools (see also Box 3.2).

How Are Ethics Reviews Done and Acted On?

Principle II (beneficence and nonmaleficence) is the idea that researchers will attempt to maximize the societal and scientific benefits of their research (**beneficence**) and to avoid doing harm (**nonmaleficence**). Since the Belmont Report, it is now expected that all proposed research studies will be carefully appraised by a panel of evaluators, an **institutional review board (IRB)**, which will conduct a **risk-benefit analysis** of the proposed study (*risk* was defined in the Belmont Report as a "possibility that harm may occur") and also conduct regular reviews of the research. IRBs are now also authorized "to monitor informed consent procedures, gather information on adverse events, and examine conflicts of interest" (Committee on Science, Engineering, and Public Policy, 2009, p. 24). Although conceding that terms such as "small risk" and "high risk" are typically used metaphorically rather than precisely, the risk-benefit ideal advocated in the Belmont Report was to consider enough information to be able to approve a proposed study and any proposed changes in the ongoing research (National Commission for the Protection of Human Subjects of Biomedical and Behavioral Research, 1979). Research appraised by an IRB as of **minimal risk** (the likelihood and extent of harm to participants is no greater than that typically experienced in everyday life) is eligible for an **expedited review** (that is, it can be evaluated without undue delay). Research involving more than minimal risk automatically receives a far more detailed risk-benefit assessment. Student projects in research courses typically fall in the no-risk category and are frequently eligible for evaluation by either the instructor or a surrogate committee responsible to the IRB.

The model in Figure 3.2 is a way of conceptualizing how the risk-benefit decision process is traditionally presumed to work (Rosenthal & Rosnow, 1984). After reviewing a detailed description of the proposed study, and after the researchers have responded to specific questions, the IRB members consider aspects of the research that have risk-benefit implications. The questions that researchers must answer vary from one institution to another (see Table 3.1 for sample questions). Ideally, the risks and benefits of doing a particular study would be evaluated on scales of perceived method-ological and societal values or interests. In typical behavioral research studies, the risks of doing the research might include annoyances or inconveniences to participants and their loss of privacy, whereas the benefits of doing the research might include the advance of scientific knowledge and educational or psychological advantages to participants or to other people at other times and places. Studies that are well thought out and are of minimal risk, and that address important questions or issues, will be judged more scientifically beneficial than studies that are not well thought out, that involve physical or psychological risks, or that address trivial questions or issues. In Figure 3.2, studies falling in the extreme upper left area (labeled A) would not be approved because the risks are high and the benefits low; studies falling in the extreme lower right area (labeled D) are likely to be approved because the benefits are high and the risks low. Studies falling along the B–C diagonal are too difficult to decide without further elaboration and possible modifications that can move the proposal off the "diagonal of indecision."

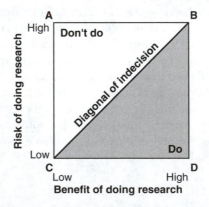

Figure 3.2   Representation of an idealized risk-benefit ethical evaluation. Studies falling at A are unlikely to be approved by an IRB; studies falling at D are likely to be approved; and studies falling along the B–C diagonal are likely to be returned to the investigators for further elaboration and possible modifications.

Table 3.1	Sample Questions for Ethics Review

Investigator

1. Who is the primary investigator, and who is supervising the study?

2. Will anyone be assisting you in this investigation?

3. Have you or the others whose names are listed above had any experience with this kind of research?

Nature of the Study

4. What is the purpose of this research? What is it about?

5. What will the research participants be asked to do, or what will be done to them?

6. Will deception be used? If the answer is yes, why is it necessary?

7. What is the nature of the deception, and when will the debriefing take place?

8. Will the participants risk any harm (physical, psychological, legal, or social) by taking part in this research?

9. If there are any risks, how do you justify them? How will you minimize the risks?

Research Participants

10. How will you recruit the research participants?

11. How do you plan to explain the research to your potential participants and obtain their informed consent?

12. What should be the general characteristics of your research participants (e.g., age range, sex, institutional affiliation, and the projected number of participants)?

13. What, if any, are the special characteristics you need in your research participants (e.g., children, pregnant women, racial or ethnic minorities, mentally retarded persons, prisoners, or alcoholics)?

14. Are other institutions or individuals cooperating in or cosponsoring the study?

15. Do the participants have to be in a particular mental or physical state to participate usefully?

Material

16. If electrical or mechanical equipment will be used, how has it been checked for safety?

17. What standardized tests, if any, will be used? What information will be provided to the participants about their scores on these tests?

Confidentiality

18. What procedure will you use to ensure the confidentiality of the data?

Debriefing

19. How do you plan to debrief the participants?

A limitation of this decision-plane model is that it focuses only on the risks and benefits of *doing research* and ignores the societal and scientific risks of *not doing research*. Suppose an IRB rejected a research proposal for a study of an important health topic because there was no guarantee that the privacy of the participants could be protected. On the other side, the researchers insisted there was no acceptable alternative design that would not compromise the scientific integrity of the project. Rejecting the research proposal and depriving the community of evidence-based information with which to address the important health problem did not make the ethical issue disappear. It merely traded one ethical issue for another, and the risk in human terms of the research not conducted could also be high. Not surprisingly, it has been suggested that, given the subjectivity of an ethical review, there might be considerable variability in the decision making of different IRB panels. In the end, getting a socially sensitive proposal approved could be a matter of the luck of drawing a receptive IRB panel (Ceci, Peters, & Plotkin, 1985; Kimmel, 1991; Rosnow, Rotheram-Borus, Ceci, Blanck, & Koocher, 1993; cf. Rosnow, 1990).

 ## What Are Obstacles to the Rendering of "Full Justice"?

The spirit of Principle III (**justice**) is that the burdens and benefits of the study are intended to be distributed fairly. In the case of the Tuskegee study (Box 3.1), none of the men who participated could have benefited in any significant way; they alone bore the awful burdens. Suppose instead it had been a medical experiment to evaluate the effectiveness of a new drug to *cure* syphilis, and suppose the strategy was to give half the men at random the test drug and the other half a placebo. Do you think it is acceptable to deprive some people (i.e., those who receive the placebo) of the benefits of a potentially lifesaving drug? In 2000, the World Medical Association adopted the principle that a placebo should be used only when no effective alternative treatment is available for comparison with the therapeutic intervention being tested. But even when the control group receives the best available option, there is often a debate as to whether depriving the control patients of a potentially more effective treatment is morally right. In 2010, there was a highly publicized debate over whether testing a new drug for melanoma should require withholding it from some patients (Harmon, 2010). The test drug had been reported to be at least temporarily effective in shrinking tumors in those patients whose tumors carried a particular mutation. Next in the research would be to test the drug in successive phases of clinical trials where patients in the control group would be given not the test drug but the best alternative drug (see also Box 3.3). Critics argued that depriving half the potential beneficiaries of the test drug would cause "needless suffering," as it was well known that no alternative drug could shrink tumors in the right patients even for a limited time (Harmon, 2010, p. 20). For intractable illnesses, do you think that traditional rules on how clinical trials should be conducted need to be more flexible on Food and Drug Administration humane grounds? Or do you think that bending those rules raises another moral issue because it compromises the scientific integrity of the research?

Justice also implies fair-mindedness, or impartiality, but questions about "what is equal?" or "what is unequal?" are often complex and highly nuanced. In the 1970s, a field experiment known as the *Rushton study* was designed to improve the quality of work life in a mining operation owned by the Rushton Mining Company in Pennsylvania (Blumberg & Pringle, 1983). After months of careful preparation by the researchers and the managers of the mine, an appeal was made for volunteers for a work group that would have direct responsibility for the production in one section of the mine. The experiment called for the workers in this group to abandon their traditional roles and to coordinate their own activities after extensive training in safety laws, good mining practices,

---

 ## BOX 3.3 Four Phases of Clinical Trials

In the United States, the Food and Drug Administration (FDA) must approve an experimental drug before it can be marketed. This evidence-based regulatory process typically involves four phases of clinical trials (Everitt, 2006). In Phase I, the drug is tested for safety in a small group of volunteers. Once the drug has been established as safe, Phase II is to conduct a clinical trial in a larger group to establish an optimum dose and to determine the short-term side effects and risks. In Phase III, large multicenter clinical trials are conducted to compare the benefits and risks of the drug to those of standard treatments (these studies are needed to support product license applications by the FDA). In Phase IV, studies are conducted after the drug is licensed and marketed in order to provide additional details about its safety and efficacy.

and job safety analysis. They were also given top-rate wages, those paid for the highest skilled job classification in that section. Not surprisingly, they were enthusiastic proponents of "our way of working." However, trouble soon reared its head. Workers in the rest of the mine (who were the control group) were resentful of the "injustice" of the situation: "Why should the volunteers receive special treatment and higher pay than other miners, some with many more years on the job?" Rumors circulated that the volunteers were "riding the gravy train" and being "spoon-fed," and that the project was a "communist plot" because all the volunteers received the same rate and the company was "making out" at their expense. As a consequence, the study had to be terminated prematurely.

Still, is it reasonable to expect *full justice* to be achieved in any research situation? As life constantly reminds us, it is not always easy to distribute benefits and burdens equally. For example, a drug company announces a new medicine that slows the course of multiple sclerosis, but the company is unable to produce enough of the new medicine to treat everyone who wants it (Lewin, 1994). The ethical issue is how to select patients for treatment in a way that is just. The company's answer is to have people register for a lottery and then to draw names at random as the new medicine becomes available. Each person in the lottery has the same likelihood of being chosen, in the same way, for example, that a lottery was used in the United States in World War II, the Korean War, and the Vietnam War when men were drafted for the military. Was using a lottery to draft men for the military in those wars a "just" procedure because everyone who was eligible was given an equal chance of being selected for life or death? Suppose patients were selected to receive a scarce new medicine not randomly, but on the grounds of who was most likely to benefit from it. Or suppose there was a military draft but soldiers were selected on the basis of who was the biggest and strongest (Broome, 1984). Which approach is more ethical, a random lottery or selection on the basis of who is more likely to benefit or survive?

 ## How Can a "Relationship of Trust" Be Established?

Principle IV (the establishment of a relationship of **trust** with the research participants) proceeds on the assumption that there is informed consent and that nothing will happen to jeopardize this agreement. And yet we asked you earlier if you think it is right to withhold information from participants if you suspect that a full disclosure will bias the research results. Assuming the research is worth doing, researchers deal with situations like these by explaining the reasons for withholding information after the research is over. A traditional way to establish a relationship of trust in the first place is to use confidentiality. For example, one of the oldest obligations in medicine is keeping the patient's disclosures confidential; lawyers are obliged to do the same for their clients, as are priests in hearing confessions (Bok, 1978, p. 147). In the context of research, **confidentiality** implies that participants' disclosures will be *protected against unwarranted access*. This may have the effect of eliciting more open and honest disclosures in some situations, but it is also another important problem that calls for further research and analysis (for discussion, see Blanck, Bellack, Rosnow, Rotheram-Borus, & Schooler, 1992).

To maintain confidentiality in your research, you need to seek advice from your instructor to set procedures in place that can protect participants' disclosures against unwarranted access. For example, with the guidance of the instructor you can devise a coding system in which the names of the research participants are represented by a sequence of numbers that no one else can identify. When participants are not asked to give any personal information that would identify them, privacy is automatically protected. In government-funded biomedical and behavioral research, it may be possible for the researcher to obtain a "certificate of confidentiality," a formal agreement that requires the researcher to keep the individual disclosures confidential (and exempts the data from subpoena). The extent to which such a certificate can actually provide legal protection has not been established in the courts, however, and is complicated by the existence of laws that require the reporting of certain sensitive information (see Box 3.4).

BOX 3.4 The Reporting of Child Abuse and Neglect

The Child Abuse Prevention and Treatment Act of 1974 and its revisions and amendments have mandated that each state pass laws to require the reporting of child abuse and neglect. The nature and wording of the statutes have been left to the discretion of the states, but the lists of people who are obligated to report suspected cases of abuse and neglect in each state have expanded over the years (Liss, 1994). Suppose you were a member of a team of developmental researchers studying child abuse, and you promised to protect the privacy and confidentiality of the respondents' disclosures. Your legal responsibility is to report suspected cases of child abuse, but reporting a suspected victim means violating the trust you established with the respondents when you promised to hold their disclosures confidential. Furthermore, it is possible that charges of abuse will not be proven, although this possibility does not excuse you from your legal responsibility (Liss, 1994).

How Do Scientific Quality and Ethical Quality Intertwine?

The underlying assumption of scientific integrity and accountability of Principle V (fidelity) is that there is a close relationship between faithful adherence to high standards of scientific quality and ethical quality (R. Rosenthal, 1994b). If the scientific quality of the design, implementation, statistical analysis, or reporting of research results is deficient, the research is wasteful of public resources (at a minimum, it wasted the participants' time). Poorly designed or sloppily implemented research, incorrectly analyzed data, and exaggerated conclusions can also be dangerously misleading to decision makers (public policy makers and physicians, for example) who rely on the fidelity and integrity of reported results (Blanck, Schartz, Ritchie, & Rosenthal, 2006; Committee on Science, Engineering, and Public Policy, 2009). Yet, violations of this fundamental ethical principle have been reported. For example, Spielmans and Parry (2010) documented shocking instances in which certain pharmaceutical firms were caught "cherry-picking" research findings and suppressing negative results of clinical trials. Spielmans and Parry called it "marketing-based medicine" and displayed a number of incriminating screen shots of company e-mails to illustrate the violations of fidelity to professional responsibility, scientific integrity, and accountability. In an editorial in *PLoS Medicine* (2009), the editors urged "politicians to consider the harm done by an environment that incites companies into insane races for profit rather than for medical need" and reminded pharmaceutical executives, "After all, even drug company employees get sick."

Table 3.2 is a way of conceptualizing the relationship between ethical quality and scientific quality (Rosnow & Rosenthal, 2011, 2012). The five rows refer, of course, to the five broad ethical principles that provide a framework for this chapter. As to the five columns, first, by *transparent* we mean that the reporting of results is open, frank, and candid; that any technical language used is clear and appropriate; and that visual displays are also clear and understandable. Second, *informative* means enough information is reported to enable sophisticated readers to reach their own independent conclusions and statistically sophisticated readers to perform their own calculations. Third, *precise* means that results are reported to the degree of exactitude required by the given situation. Fourth, *accurate* means not exaggerating results by, for example, making claims that future applications are unlikely to achieve. It also means that data are recorded accurately, as "the best methods will count for little if data are recorded incorrectly or haphazardly" (Committee on Science, Engineering, and Public Policy, 2009, p. 9). Fifth, *grounded* means that the methods and statistical procedures are logically and scientifically justified, the questions and hypotheses addressed are appropriate to the design, and the primary data analysis focuses on the questions or hypotheses as opposed to going off on a tangent or giving answers that are diffuse or unfocused (we have more to say about this problem later in this book).

When there is a conflict between ethical principles and scientific standards, the researcher is expected to resolve the conflict, because scientists are held accountable for both the ethical and

Table 3.2	Ethical Principles Crossed by Scientific Standards				
	Scientific Standards				
Ethical principles	**1. Transparent**	**2. Informative**	**3. Precise**	**4. Accurate**	**5. Grounded**
I. Respect for people's autonomy					
II. Beneficence & nonmaleficence					
III. Justice					
IV. Trust					
V. Fidelity					

the scientific merit of their work. Earlier, we also mentioned the need for further research on topics such as informed consent and confidentiality, as the study of such conflicts can indeed contribute to responsible conduct in research at the same time that the contributions expand knowledge and build a stronger science (Blanck, Bellack, et al., 1992).

Sometimes a conflict between ethical quality and scientific quality can be easily resolved by more accurately and precisely describing the objective of the research so that it does not seem to promise more than the design can reasonably deliver. Suppose an IRB received a proposal for a study that, according to the researchers' statement, "will test whether private schools, more than public schools, improve children's intellectual functioning." As described in the proposal, children from randomly selected private and public schools will be tested extensively, and the hypothesis will be addressed by a comparison of the scores earned by students from private and public schools. The proposal, as written, raises an ethical concern because the relational design does not permit reasonable causal inference ("intellectual functioning" might instead be due to intrinsic differences in the different populations). Resources will be wasted (e.g., funding will be wasted, and people's time will be taken from potentially more beneficial educational experiences), and conclusions that are unwarranted (they are neither grounded nor accurate) will result. If the proposal had instead stated that the objective of the research was to learn about "performance differences" between students in private and public schools, the research design would be suitable, resolving the conflict (Rosenthal, 1994b).

 ## Is Deception in Research Ever Justified?

Earlier in this chapter, we alluded to Stanley Milgram's classic research on obedience to authority, in which he used a "false illusion" to trick the participants into believing they were subjecting another person to increasing levels of electric shock. The research was inspired in part by Solomon Asch's earlier work on conformity (discussed in Chapter 1; see also Box 3.5). Milgram was interested in the psychological mechanism that links blind obedience to destructive behavior, an interest that grew out of his profound dismay about the horrifying obedience to Nazi commands in World War II. In particular, he wanted to see just how far ordinary adults would go in carrying out the orders of a legitimate authority to act against a third person. In the 1960s, Milgram's studies lit a fuse as several prominent psychologists made impassioned pleas for the ethical codification of constraints against deceptive methods and other controversial research practices (Kelman, 1968; M. B. Smith, 1969; cf Blass, 2004, 2009). Milgram's emphasis on "the power of the situation" also influenced the direction of theoretical thinking and research in personality and social psychology (Benjamin & Simpson, 2009).

BOX 3.5 Milgram's Inspiration for His Obedience Experiments

Milgram (1977) later wrote that he had wanted to make the classic work done by Solomon Asch "more humanly significant" (p. 12). Asch had designed his investigation to determine under what conditions people will remain independent of their groups and when they will conform, by using accomplices to influence an individual subject's expressed judgment concerning which of three lines was closest in length to a standard line. Milgram (1977) recalled the moment when he suddenly hit on the idea for his own experiments:

> I was dissatisfied that the test of conformity was judgments about *lines*. I wondered whether groups could pressure a person into performing an act whose human import was more readily apparent, perhaps behaving aggressively toward another person, say by administering increasingly severe shocks to him. But to study the group effect you would also need an experimental control; you'd have to know how the subject performed without any group pressure. At that instant, my thought shifted, zeroing in on this experimental control. Just how far *would* a person go under the experimenter's orders? It was an incandescent moment, the fusion of a general idea on obedience with a specific technical procedure. Within a few minutes, dozens of ideas on relevant variables emerged, and the only problem was to get them all down on paper. (p. 12)[*]

[*]From 'The Individual in a Social World: Essays and Experiments', by Stanley Milgram. Addison-Wesley Publishing Company, 1977, pp. 12, 13. Reprinted with permission.

In Milgram's studies, volunteer participants placed in the role of a "teacher" were made to believe they would be giving increasing levels of painful electric shock to a third person (called the "learner") each time the learner made a mistake in a certain task. Milgram also varied the distance between the teacher and the learner in order to explore whether the "teacher" would be less ruthless in administering electric shocks as he or she got closer and the learner pressed the teacher to quit. The results were, to Milgram as well as to others, almost beyond belief. A great many of the participants (the "teachers") unhesitatingly obeyed the experimenter's "Please continue" or "You have no choice, you must go on" and continued to increase what they believed the level of the electric shocks to be no matter how much the learner pleaded with them to stop. Particularly surprising was that none of the actual participants (the "teachers") ever walked out of the room in disgust or protest. This remarkable obedience was observed time and time again in a number of different settings where the experiment was repeated. "It is the extreme willingness of adults to go to almost any lengths on the command of an authority that constitutes the chief finding of the study and the fact most urgently demanding explanation," Milgram wrote (1974, p. 5).

Though the "learner" in his studies was really a confederate of Milgram's and no electrical shocks were actually administered by the "teacher," concerns about ethics and values dogged these studies from the moment they were first reported. Psychologist Diane Baumrind (1964) quoted Milgram's descriptions of the reactions of some of his subjects—such as "a twitching, stuttering wreck, who was rapidly approaching a point of nervous collapse" (Milgram, 1963, p. 377). Baumrind argued that once Milgram had seen how stressful his deception was, he should have immediately terminated the research on moral grounds. She insisted that there was "no rational basis" for ever using this kind of manipulation, unless the participants were first made fully aware of the psychological dangers to themselves and effective steps were taken to ensure the restoration of their well-being afterward. Milgram responded that the chief horror was not that a stressful deception was carried out, but instead that the participants obeyed. The signs of extreme tension in some participants were quite unexpected, but his intention had not been to create anxiety, he explained.

Before carrying out this research, Milgram had asked professional colleagues about their expectations, and none of the experts had anticipated the blind obedience that resulted. Like the experts, he had thought the participants would refuse to follow orders. Moreover, he was skeptical about Baumrind's contention that there had been psychologically injurious effects on the participants, in spite of the dramatic appearance of anxiety in some of them. To ensure that the participants would not feel worse after the experiment than before, he also took elaborate precautions to debrief them. They were given an opportunity for a friendly reconciliation with the "learner" after the experiment was concluded and were shown that the "learner" had not received dangerous electric shocks but had only pretended to receive them. To find out whether there were any delayed negative effects, Milgram sent questionnaires to the participants to elicit their reactions after they had read a full report of his investigation. Less than 1% of those who received this questionnaire said they regretted having participated; 15% were neutral or ambivalent, and over 80% said they were glad to have participated. Milgram interpreted the tolerant reactions as providing another moral argument (after the fact) for his research:

> The central moral justification for allowing my experiment is that it was judged acceptable by those who took part in it. Criticism of the experiment that does not take account of the tolerant reaction of the participants has always seemed to me hollow. This applies particularly to criticism centering on the use of false illusion (or "deception," as the critics prefer to say) that fails to relate this detail to the central fact that subjects find the device acceptable. The participants, rather than the external critics, must be the ultimate source of judgment in these matters. (Milgram, 1977, p. 93)

In arguing that research participants, not the experimenter, are the ultimate arbiters of whether a particular deception is morally acceptable, Milgram was speaking before the advent of IRBs. In fact, *when* Milgram did his work, it was within the norms of deception then in use. But suppose the study had never been done, and it was you who wanted to do it. The IRB rejects your proposal and responds that the use of deception in any form is unacceptable. "Be open and honest with your participants, and have them sign an informed-consent agreement that indicates they fully understand what the research is about," the IRB tells you. Is getting rid of the deception, and being open and honest, a reasonable requirement? Or could it present a further ethical dilemma? Imagine an experiment like Milgram's in which the experimenter instead greeted the participants by saying something like the following:

> Hello. Today we are going to do a study on blind obedience to a malevolent authority, particularly emphasizing the effects of physical distance from the victim on willingness to inflict pain on her or him. You will be in the "close" condition, which means that you are expected to be somewhat less ruthless in your behavior. In addition, you will be asked to fill out a test of your fascist tendencies because we believe there is a positive relation between scores on our fascism test and blind obedience to an authority who requests that we hurt others. Any questions?

A completely open and honest statement to a research participant of the intention of the experiment might involve a briefing of this kind, but would it result in fewer problems? Clearly, such a briefing would be absurd if you were serious in your wish to learn about blind obedience to authority. If the participants had full information about your experimental purpose, plans, procedures, and hypotheses, it seems unlikely they would behave as Milgram's participants did. They might instead base their behavior on what they *thought* the world was like or what they believed *you* thought the world was like. This is not to say that any scientists would advocate the use of deception merely for its own sake. At the same time, however, there may be few who feel that they can do entirely without certain minimal-risk deceptions (e.g., disguising the name of the "California Fascism Scale" by calling it the "Personal Reaction Inventory"). For example, surely no social psychologist would advocate giving up the study of prejudice or discrimination. But would it be worth the effort and expenditure if all measures of prejudice and discrimination had to be openly labeled? Adopting an uncompromising moral orientation that decries deception as wrong would mean banishing all forms of deception and producing misleading results in some cases.

BOX 3.6 Proposed Principles on Deception in Research

Earlier, we mentioned N. Craig Smith, Allan J. Kimmel, and Jill Gabrielle Klein's (2009) article on deception in consumer research. In that article they also argued that "deception in research is morally permissible to the extent that it is consistent with certain principles" (p. 489). The principles they proposed were predicated on adherence to the following four "minimum conditions" drawn from the 2002 APA ethics code: (a) "respect for human dignity and a commitment to voluntary participation and informed consent"; (b) the assurance to participants that "they can and should withdraw from a study at any time if they have concerns about procedures used"; (c) deception is used only when "forewarning" (see Principle 4 below) and debriefing are employed; and (d) "harmful deceptions are never employed" (N. C. Smith et al., p. 491).

Given that the APA conditions are met, N. C. Smith et al. (2009) proposed six principles as further moral

imperatives: (1) "Deception is a last resort…used only where researchers have established that alternative and valid research procedures are unavailable" (p. 492). (2) "Researchers never expose participants to procedures or risks that they themselves would be unwilling to accept if similarly situated" (p. 492). (3) "Researchers never expose participants to the risks of potential lasting harm" (p. 492). (4) "Researchers explicitly forewarn participants that deception is often used in consumer research" (p. 493). (5) "Researchers plan for participant vulnerability. They anticipate and make allowances for possible vulnerabilities of participants in developing studies that use deception and in seeking informed consent" (p. 493). And finally, based on the assumption that volunteers for research participation can be presumed to have moral responsibilities as well, N. C. Smith et al. added (6) "Research participants cooperate fully and in good faith in a research study they have agreed to participate in" (p. 493).

Some argue that deception in *any* form is wrong, while others argue that there are special circumstances in which deception in research may be morally permissible (see Box 3.6). For example, refraining from telling diners that you are doing a study of tipping behavior, or not telling a participant that an "experiment in the learning of verbal materials is designed to show whether earlier, later, or intermediate material is better remembered," does not seem to be an especially heinous form of deception. The reason most of us would probably not view these deceptions with alarm seems, on first glance, to be that they involve a passive deception rather than an active deception. A truth is left unspoken; a lie is not told. But what if the verbal learning experiment were actively misrepresented as a "study of the effects of the meaningfulness of verbal material on retention or recall"? That is a direct lie, an active deception designed to misdirect the participant's attention from a crucial aspect of the experimental treatment to another factor that really does not interest the scientist. Even this change, however, does not seem to make the deception appalling, although the scientist has not withheld information from, but actively lied to, the participant.

It would appear that it is not the active or passive form of a deception that is its measure, but its effect on the research participant. Few people would care whether the participants focused on a noncrucial aspect of verbal material rather than on a crucial aspect, because the deception does not seem to have perilous consequences. Similarly, not telling diners they are participating in an experiment on tipping behavior does not seem particularly shocking in any way. In other words, it is not deception so much as it is potentially *harmful* deception that we would like to minimize. But how shall we decide what is potentially harmful? Does it come down to someone's opinion? If so, whose opinions should prevail? Individual investigators, their colleagues, the IRB, and, to some extent, ultimately, the general society that enables the research must decide whether a particular deception is worth the possible increase in knowledge. Incidentally, psychologist Jerry M. Burger, at Santa Clara University, conducted a partial replication of the Milgram paradigm with modifications to make the partial replication acceptable to an IRB. An article by Burger (2009) describing these findings, accompanied by commentaries by other psychologists, can be found in the January 2009 issue of the *American Psychologist* devoted to "Obedience—Then and Now."

 What Is the Purpose of Debriefing, and How Is It done?

In a **debriefing** session at the conclusion of their participation, Milgram's "teachers" were given the opportunity to have a friendly reconciliation with the "learner" and to engage in an extended discussion with the experimenter about the purpose of the study and why it was necessary to use the deception. The purpose of such a debriefing is to remove any misconceptions and anxieties the participants may have, so that their sense of dignity remains intact and they do not feel that their time has been wasted (Blanck et al., 1992; Harris, 1988). Debriefing sessions are considered ethically essential in many research situations, but sometimes a debriefing may be either impossible or inadvisable. For example, a full debriefing is inadvisable if it would produce stress or be ineffective, such as when the research participants are children, are mentally ill, or are retarded (Blanck et al., 1992). Debriefing sessions can also be an opportunity to explore what the participants thought about the study, providing the experimenter with an experiential context in which to interpret the results and with good ideas for further analysis and research (Blanck et al., 1992; E. E. Jones & Gerard, 1967).

Milgram's postexperimental debriefing and further efforts were unusually extensive, far more so, in fact, than is characteristic of most experiments. Because he duped the participants into believing that they were administering painful electric shocks to another person, he felt it necessary to go to elaborate lengths to remove lingering stresses or anxieties. He explained to participants that their behavior was normal and that any conflict or tension they may have experienced had also been felt by other participants. At the conclusion of the research, all received a comprehensive written report detailing the experimental procedure and findings and, of course, treating the participants' own part in the research with dignity. They were also administered a questionnaire that asked them again to express their thoughts and feelings about their behavior in the research. A year later, a psychiatrist experienced in outpatient treatment interviewed 40 of the participants and found no evidence of any traumatic reactions.

The following guidelines (Aronson & Carlsmith, 1968; Sieber, 1982a, 1983) may be incorporated into more typical debriefings, particularly when the study involved some form of deception:

1. Give whatever explanation is needed to reveal the truth about the research and the researcher's carefully considered decision to employ a deception. For example, the researcher might explain that often it is necessary to design or implement a study in a particular way, even to use a ruse or pretext sometimes, to control for factors that might jeopardize the scientific integrity (e.g., validity and generalizability) of the results.

2. Despite the researcher's sincere wish to treat the participants responsibly, some of them may leave the study feeling gullible, as if they have been "had" by a fraudulent procedure. Whatever form of deception was used, the researcher should explain that being taken in does not reflect in any way on their intelligence or character; instead, it shows the validity or effectiveness of the study's design. The researcher presumably went to some pains to achieve an effective design in order not to waste the participants' time.

3. Proceed gradually and patiently, with the chief aim of gently unfolding details of any deception that was used. A patient discussion will go far to reduce the participants' negative feelings. Instead of thinking of themselves as "victims," they may more accurately perceive that they have been "coinvestigators" with the researcher in the scientific search for truth.

4. Never use a **double deception**, that is, a second deception in what the participant thinks is the official debriefing. Double deception can be terribly damaging: Instead of restoring the participants to the frame of mind in which they entered the study, a double deception leaves them with a lie and, therefore, is unethical.

How Is Animal Research Governed by Ethical Rules?

Although the primary focus of this book is on research with human participants, we did mention in Chapter 2 the Pavlovian conditioning of a dog and Thorndike's studies of cats in puzzle boxes. The use of animals in experiments has been vigorously debated (Slife & Rubinstein, 1992) because the very assumption of biological continuities between animals and human beings raises ethical dilemmas. That is, it should follow that animals, like humans, must also experience some measure of pain and suffering. Federal laws and licensing requirements spell out the responsibilities of researchers and animal facilities to protect the well-being of experimental animals, consistent with advancements made possible by research.

For example, the federal Animal Welfare Act sets out specific standards for the humane care and treatment of animals used in research, including their handling, housing, feeding, and use in the study of drugs. The Animal Welfare Act also requires the establishment of Institutional Animal Care and Use Committees, which must include both members of the public and experts in the care of animals (Committee on Science, Engineering, and Public Policy, 2009). Research institutions are also subject to unannounced inspections by the U.S. Department of Agriculture at any time. If violations are uncovered, the institution's license to operate animal facilities may be revoked.

Beyond these federal regulations, animal researchers are subject to institutional and professional requirements. Institutions with animal care facilities make a point of underscoring the experimenter's responsibilities, and any proposed animal research also routinely undergoes ethical review. In addition, the APA and other professional and scientific organizations around the world have elaborated on the ethical obligations of investigators of animal behavior. For example, the APA insists that researchers make every effort to minimize discomfort, illness, and pain in their experimental animals. Any procedure that subjects animals to pain, stress, or privation may be used only when no alternative procedure is available and the goal of the research is justified by its prospective scientific, educational, or applied value.

Nevertheless, the confrontation between those who argue for and those who argue against experiments using animals is often quite heated. One point of disagreement concerns whether the interests of human beings supersede the interests of animals. At one extreme, many animal rights activists argue that animals and humans have equal rights and that benefits to humans are not a justification for animal experimentation. On the other side, it has been argued that animals have often benefited from the research, such as from discoveries in veterinary medicine (e.g., vaccines for deadly diseases), and experimental insights that have helped to preserve some species from extinction (e.g., the wild condor). Scientists point out that the use of animals in a variety of behavioral and biomedical studies has directly benefited humans in a great many ways. In medical research, the development of vaccines for rabies and yellow fever was made possible by the use of animal proxies (Paul, Miller, & Paul, 2000).

In behavioral science, research with animals has led to advances in the rehabilitation of persons suffering from spinal cord injuries, in the treatment of disease and eating disorders, and in improvements in communication with the severely retarded. In experiments with cats and monkeys, Roger Sperry, who won a Nobel Prize for his work, demonstrated that severing the fibers connecting the right and left hemispheres of the brain (resulting in a so-called split brain) did not impair a variety of functions, including learning and memory. This important discovery led to a split-brain treatment for severe epilepsy and made it possible for people who would have been confined to hospitals to lead a more normal life (Gazzaniga & LeDoux, 1978; Sperry, 1968).

Animal rights activists argue that enterprising researchers would be forced to think of alternative methods if they were banned from using animals (see Box 3.7). In fact, such advances have been made without any ban on animal experimentation. It has been possible, for example, to use anthropomorphic "dummies" (e.g., in car crash tests), to simulate tissue and bodily fluids in research situations, to use computer models of human beings, to use lower order species (e.g., fruit flies in

BOX 3.7 Another Three Rs in Animal Research

Some years ago, the British zoologist William M. S. Russell and microbiologist Rex L. Burch made the argument that, given scientists' own interest in the humane treatment of the animals used in research, it would be morally prudent to search for ways to (a) *reduce* the number of animals used in research, (b) *refine* the experiments so that there was less suffering, and (c) *replace* animals with other procedures whenever possible. Called the **three Rs principle** by Russell and Burch (1959), this argument defines modern research on animal subjects.

experiments on genetics), and to study animals in their natural habitats (such as Dian Fossey's studies of gorillas; Fossey, 1981, 1983) or else in zoos, rather than to breed animals for laboratory research.

In sum, just as the scientific community recognizes both an ethical and a scientific responsibility for the general welfare of human subjects, it must also assume responsibility for the humane care and treatment of animals used in research. There are laws and ethical guidelines to protect animals in research, and it is also evident that humans and animals have benefited by discoveries made in experiments with animals. Thus, even though there is a continuing debate about the use of animals in research, it is clear that society has benefited in terms of biomedical and behavioral advances and that the ethical consciousness of science and society has been raised with regard to the humane conduct of this research.

What Ethical Responsibilities Are There When Writing Up Research?

In this chapter we have primarily concentrated on the data collection phase of research, but ethical guidelines have implications for other aspects of the research process as well. As mentioned in Chapter 1, the most fundamental ethical principle of good researchers is integrity and honesty, an essential aspect of the research process, from the implementation of the study to the final report of the procedures used, the results, and their implications. As we have also tried to show, many of the guidelines discussed in this chapter, although directed specifically at professional researchers, have implications for students who are conducting research to satisfy an academic requirement. These ethical rules also apply to the final phase of the process, in which you will be writing up your results.

For example, professional researchers are responsible for making accurate, accessible records of what they have done and also making available the data on which their conclusions are based. In consultation with your instructor, you will be shown how to make such a record, indicating not only the raw data but also where and when the data were collected. Students are also expected to be able to produce all of their raw data as required by the instructor. Professional researchers also know that it is unethical to misrepresent original research by publishing it in more than one journal and implying that each report represents a different study. The implication for students is that it is unethical to submit the same work for additional credit in different courses. Authors of published articles are also expected to give credit where it is due; the implication for a student is that if someone gave you an idea, you should credit that person in a footnote. Should your research or some other work of yours be used in a multiple-authored article, the decision about whether you will be listed as a coauthor or in a footnote acknowledgment will depend on the nature of your contribution. For example, analyzing data that the instructor provided or assisting in the literature search and retrieval phase may be a minor contribution deserving a footnote acknowledgment. If the article is substantially based on your research or is based to a large extent on your individual efforts, you will usually be listed as a coauthor.

The most nagging ethical concern of most instructors, however, is conveying to students the meaning and consequences of **plagiarism** and how to avoid it. The term *plagiarism* comes from a Latin word meaning "kidnapper," and to plagiarize means to kidnap another person's idea or work

BOX 3.8 Joel Levin's "Plagiarism-Prevention Practice"

A trick to help you avoid falling into plagiarism accidentally is not to paraphrase a passage while reading it. Arizona University psychologist Joel R. Levin (2011) recommended a four-step practice. First, of course, is to read the passage very carefully. Second is to think about what you read. Third, once you have a sense of what you read, close the source book or article you were reading. Fourth is to write down, in your own words, what you want to say. We would also suggest a fifth step, which is that you compare what you wrote with the original passage to make sure you have not stumbled into plagiarism by accident (and, of course, keep careful notes, so that you can later accurately cite and reference what you paraphrased).

and to pass it off as one's own. "Accidental plagiarism" occurs when one copies someone else's work but "forgets" to credit it or to put it in quotes. It is crucial that you know what constitutes plagiarism, because it is not an acceptable defense to claim that you do not understand what plagiarism is, nor is it ethically defensible to lift a passage from someone's work (without putting it in quotes with a citation) because it was not easy to think of a way to express a thought in your own words. Even if the plagiarism was "accidental," it is important to understand that misappropriating someone else's work as one's own is wrong and that, even if it is unintentional, the penalty can be severe (see also Box 3.8).

Of course, you can quote other's people's ideas or work in your research and writing, but you must always give the author of that material full credit for originality and not misrepresent (intentionally or accidentally) that material as your own original work. For example, suppose a student did a study on cognitive dissonance and then turned in a report that, without a citation, contained the following passage:

> Dissonance—that is, the existence of nonfitting relations among cognitions—is a motivating factor in its own right. By *cognition* is generally meant any knowledge, opinion, or belief about the environment, about oneself, or about one's behavior. Cognitive dissonance can be seen as an antecedent condition that leads to activity oriented toward dissonance reduction, just as hunger leads to activity oriented toward hunger reduction.

The student has cheated by committing plagiarism and will pay the consequences: an F in the course. The reason is that, except for a changed word here and there, the student has lifted this passage directly from Leon Festinger's classic book, *A Theory of Cognitive Dissonance* (1962). On page 5 of that book, Festinger wrote:

> In short, I am proposing that dissonance, that is, the existence of nonfitting relations among cognitions, is a motivating factor in its own right. By the term *cognition,* here and in the remainder of the book, I mean any knowledge, opinion, or belief about the environment, about oneself, or about one's behavior. Cognitive dissonance can be seen as an antecedent condition which leads to activity oriented toward dissonance reduction just as hunger leads to activity oriented toward hunger reduction.

How might the student have used Festinger's work without falling into plagiarism? The student would indicate what is his or hers and what is Festinger's. For example, this student could have written:

> In his book *A Theory of Cognitive Dissonance,* Festinger (1962) described cognition as "any knowledge, opinion, or belief about the environment, about oneself, or about one's behavior" and defined cognitive dissonance as "the existence of nonfitting relations among cognitions" (p. 5). He added, "Cognitive dissonance can be seen as an antecedent condition which leads to activity oriented toward dissonance reduction" (p. 5).

If you find something on the Internet you want to use, the same considerations of honesty apply. Electronic plagiarizing is no more acceptable than plagiarizing from printed matter. Given the availability and effectiveness of dedicated search engines, it has become far easier for instructors to catch perpetrators. You will notice on the cover page of Mary Jones's final research report (in Appendix A) that she expresses responsibility for the originality of her work ("I have written this report of my original research to satisfy the requirements in Psychology 274."), and she also acknowledges specific assistance she received from others.

One final word of advice: Some students, on hearing that cited material is not construed by definition as plagiarism, submit papers that are saturated with quoted material. Such papers are viewed by instructors as **lazy writing**. Although the penalty for lazy writing is not as severe as that for plagiarism, often it means a reduced grade. You may need to quote or paraphrase some material (with a citation, of course), but your written work is expected to result from your own individual effort. Quoting a simple sentence that can easily be paraphrased signals lazy writing.

Summary of Ideas

1. Legal, institutional, and professional *ethical guidelines* help us evaluate the moral "rights" and "wrongs" of particular strategies of doing and reporting research. Thinking about ethical issues in research also forces us to confront our own moral presuppositions, for example, as regards the use of active and passive deceptions.

2. The Belmont Report set out basic principles as a foundation for research ethics and established the requirement of informed consent and the use of institutional review boards (IRBs) to assess the risks and benefits of proposed studies and protect human subjects from harm.

3. The conceptual framework for this chapter consists of five broad ethical principles, partly based on the Belmont Report, the APA ethics code, and an amalgamation of other rules, institutionalized regulations, and professional ideals.

4. Principle I is respect for persons and their independence or freedom (called *autonomy*). In practice, the idea is to ensure that each prospective participant knows what he or she will be getting into (the *informed-consent* agreement, as illustrated in Figure 3.1). It also means respecting participants' right to decide whether they want to participate and remain in the study. In some situations, informed consent may be unnecessary or impossible (e.g., studies that use public records, or risk-free studies in which requiring informed consent would be counterproductive to the purpose of the research). If the participants have diminished capacity to understand the consent form, a legally responsible person may speak on their behalf.

5. Principle II (beneficence and nonmaleficence) instructs us to maximize benefits and minimize risks of research, assessed by an IRB (Figure 3.2). Table 3.1 sampled the kinds of questions that researchers are typically required to answer. *Minimal risk* studies are eligible for *expedited review*. The drawback of the idealized assessment presented in Figure 3.2 is that it focuses only on the risks and benefits of the *doing* of research and, unfortunately, ignores the societal and scientific costs of *not doing* the research.

6. Principle III (justice) underscores the idea that the benefits and burdens of research should be distributed as fairly as possible and that injustices should be avoided. As is true of life itself, full justice is based on an idealized standard that is unlikely to be fully achieved in a world that is never fully just. One reason is that justice (or fair-mindedness, or impartiality) is usually a matter of each person's perspective or subjective judgment (e.g., the Rushton study).

7. Principle IV (relationship of trust) cautions researchers not to do anything that may jeopardize the trusting relationship participants have entered into and to protect the disclosures of the participants against unwarranted access (*confidentiality*). However, there are laws that require the reporting of sensitive information, such as the reporting of child abuse and neglect (Box 3.4), which can present a moral conflict for researchers.

8. Principle V (fidelity to professional responsibility, scientific integrity, and accountability) assumes that researchers are held accountable for both the scientific quality and the ethical quality of their work (Table 3.2). Badly designed or carelessly conducted studies, poorly analyzed data, exaggerated conclusions, ambiguously reported studies, and the "cherry picking" or suppression of results violate both scientific and professional ethical standards. The scientific standards highlighted were (a) transparency; (b) informativeness; (c) precision; (d) accuracy; and (e) groundedness.

9. Milgram's use of a "false illusion" was well within the norms of deception in use at the time. We asked you whether you thought that being open and honest with the participants would have jeopardized the validity of the results. We suggested that it is not the *active* or *passive* nature of deception that seems most problematic but whether a deception could be potentially harmful in some way. Box 3.6 listed a set of proposed principles to govern the use of deception in experimental consumer research.

10. *Debriefing* participants after the data have been collected is the final step in the data collection process and is considered essential when there has been a deception or when there is likely to be any residual anxiety. Deceiving the participant during the debriefing (a *double deception*) is never permissible.

11. Just as the scientific community has an ethical and scientific responsibility for the general welfare of human participants, it also assumes responsibility for the humane care and treatment of animals used in research. The *three Rs principle* (Box 3.7) emphasizes the *reduction* of the number of animals used in research, the *refinement* of experiments so there is less suffering, and the *replacement* of the use of animals with other procedures whenever possible.

12. Ethical guidelines during the reporting stage also require that researchers (a) make available the data on which their conclusions are based (while protecting the confidentiality of their participants); (b) not imply that a study published in more than one journal represents different studies; and (c) give credit where it is due.

13. *Plagiarism* means stealing another person's idea or work and misrepresenting it as one's own idea or work. To avoid "accidental plagiarism," it is important to make careful notes and to cite the sources of any ideas, work, or quotations used in your report. Avoid the *lazy writing* of repeatedly quoting sentences that you can paraphrase (and reference, of course). Do not be tempted to buy "scientific" reports or "term papers" on the Internet, as it is unethical and when discovered is severely punished.

Key Terms

active deception p. 42
Belmont Report p. 43
beneficence p. 45
confidentiality p. 49
debriefing p. 55
double deception p. 55
ethical
  principles p. 43

ethics p. 41
expedited review p. 46
informed consent p. 43
institutional review
  board (IRB) p. 45
justice p. 48
lazy writing p. 59
minimal risk p. 46

nonmaleficence p. 45
passive
  deception p. 42
plagiarism p. 57
risk-benefit
  analysis p. 46
three Rs principle p. 57
trust p. 49

Multiple-Choice Questions for Review

1. Which of the following methodological procedures can cause moral conflicts? (a) invasion of privacy; (b) deception; (c) withholding information from research participants; (d) all of the above

2. Deliberately withholding information from research participants is called _____; deliberately misinforming participants is called _____. (a) active deception, passive deception; (b) active deception, double deception; (c) double deception, passive deception; (d) passive deception, active deception

3. In the Milgram experiments, which of the following actually received electrical shocks? (a) the "teacher"; (b) the "learner"; (c) both a and b; (d) neither a nor b

4. Ethical questions were raised about the Milgram experiments because (a) participants were deceived and apparently stressed; (b) some participants received severe shocks; (c) some participants were physically injured; (d) all of the above.

5. The Rushton study, conducted in a mining company, raised the ethical issue of (a) deception; (b) fair-mindedness; (c) invasion of privacy; (d) all of the above.

6. The participants who objected to the Rushton study were (a) in the control group; (b) in the experimental group; (c) in both the experimental and control groups; (d) subjected to severe shocks.

7. According to the decision-plane diagram in Figure 3.2, if the risks of doing a research project are equal to the benefits of doing the research, then the study is said to fall on (a) the diagonal of ambivalence; (b) the diagonal of equality; (c) the diagonal of indecision; (d) none of the above.

8. Research at virtually all colleges and universities has to be approved by (a) the president of the institution; (b) the U.S. government; (c) professors in the psychology department; (d) an IRB.

9. The procedure of disclosing the full purpose of a study after individuals have participated is called

(a) debriefing; (b) peer review; (c) the Milgram procedure; (d) double deception.

10. Which of the following help ensure that animals used as subjects in research are treated ethically? (a) federal laws; (b) professional codes of conduct; (c) institutional (e.g., university) policies; (d) all of the above

Discussion Questions for Review

1. A study proposal is submitted to the Tufts University IRB for review. The researchers propose to administer a two-hour-long questionnaire to people hanging out on the street in the red light district in Boston. The questionnaire contains items asking about these people's lifestyles and attitudes toward criminal behavior. What are some potential risks to the participants in the study?

2. A University of Richmond student is interested in studying helping behavior. She designs an experiment to take place in a corner drugstore. Enlisting the aid of the owner, the student has confederates, varying in age and manner of dress, commit a robbery at the store. Another confederate, posing as a customer, observes the real customers, noting which of them help, what they do, how long it takes, and so on. What are some ethical problems in this research? What risks and benefits would you consider in deciding whether this project should be done?

3. A student at California State–Fullerton wants to run a study in which he will deceive participants into believing that they have done poorly on a test of their sensitivity to others. At the end of the experimental session, he plans to pay the participants, thank them for participating, and tell them they can call him later

if they have questions about the study. How does the student fail in his ethical responsibilities to the participants? What should he do?

4. An instructor at the University of Nebraska tells a student in her research methods class that, in her view, the student's proposed study falls on the "diagonal of indecision." What does the instructor mean, and what are the implications for the student?

5. An Arlington University researcher proposes to use Texas students to replicate Asch's classic experiment. The IRB requires an informed-consent agreement from the prospective participants. What does this mean, and what are the implications for the researcher?

6. A Whittier College student is interested in conducting a study of the effects of various financial incentive programs in a large organization. Because his research involves no deception or invasion of privacy, he tells his adviser that no ethical issues are raised by his research. The adviser's reply is "Remember the Rushton study!" What does she mean?

7. An instructor at the University of Utah tells her students that they have ethical responsibilities when writing up their research. What are those responsibilities?

Answers to Review Questions

Multiple-Choice Questions

1. d	3. d	5. b	7. c	9. a
2. d	4. a	6. a	8. d	10. d

Discussion Questions

1. Two possible risks include (a) embarrassment at "being studied" in an unsavory location or occupation and (b) the danger of discovery of participants' criminal behavior because someone in law enforcement obtains the questionnaire and can link it to the respondents.

2. Observing the thefts might be quite upsetting to the real customers, who may be put at risk of, say, anxiety reactions or heart attacks. The confederate "robbers" may also be put at risk of being shot by a neighboring armed shopkeeper or attacked by a customer trying to foil the robbery. We need to ask

whether what we might be able to learn from this research is really worth the risk to the real customers, the shopkeeper, and the confederate "robbers."

3. The student has failed to debrief the participants, and therefore they may leave feeling that they are really insensitive to others. He should, of course, debrief them.

4. The instructor means that the risks and benefits are in such balance that it is very difficult for her to reach a decision on whether to let the student go ahead with the research. For removal of the study from the diagonal of indecision, the student needs to decrease the risks of the study, increase the benefits, or both. If there are significant risks, however, the student should start by eliminating them.

5. The IRB requires that the participant must understand what the research will require from her or him, that she or he may leave at any time, and that she or he will remain anonymous. Fully informing the participants about the nature of the Asch experiment would, however, make it impossible to replicate because they would see through the manipulation.

6. The Rushton study also raised no questions of deception or invasion of privacy. However, the issue of fair-mindedness was raised. Were some of the company's workers going to be "treated specially," or would they get to ride "the gravy train" in the eyes of other workers?

7. Their responsibilities include (a) producing all of their raw data if the instructor asks for it, (b) not submitting the paper for credit in another course, (c) giving credit to anyone who helped, and (d) not committing plagiarism, even accidentally.

CHAPTER 4

Methods of Systematic Observation

Preview Questions

- What is meant by systematic observation?
- How do researchers simultaneously participate and observe?
- What can be learned from quantifying observations?
- How are judgment studies done?
- How does content analysis work?
- How are situations simulated in controlled settings?
- What are plausible rival hypotheses and the third-variable problem?
- What is the distinction between reactive and nonreactive observation?

 ## What Is Meant By Systematic Observation?

We use the term **systematic observation** to differentiate the research strategies described in this chapter from the self-report methods described in the next chapter. *Observation* means that the researcher is viewing or noting a fact or an occurrence for a scientific purpose, and *systematic* implies that the observation follows a particular plan or system and can therefore be evaluated by means of technical standards (unlike our daily observations, which are apt to be casual and haphazard). Within this broad definition, systematic observation typically calls for resourcefulness and, more often than not, uses more than just one observational or self-report method. Because all empirical methods are limited in some ways, the use of a single empirical method would confine observations to a narrow range of facts or occurrences. As discussed earlier, the recommended use of multiple methods (*methodological pluralism*) is an underlying thread that runs throughout this book and ties the chapters together. The challenge is to skillfully choose (or create) and implement both technically and ethically acceptable observational methods and measurement procedures in order to zero in on phenomena from more than one vantage point, a plan described as **methodological triangulation** (Campbell & Fiske, 1959).

There are many more observational techniques than we could possibly cover in this chapter, the purpose of which is to sample some of the ways that systematic observation is done. Within the descriptive, relational, and experimental frameworks outlined in Chapter 1, a further distinction is between quantitative and qualitative research. In **quantitative research**, the empirical approach emphasizes numerical data, as distinct from the usual emphasis of **qualitative research** on spoken words, prose descriptions of behavior, and pictorial records (described as *qualitative data*).

BOX 4.1 Observational Studies

Observational study is another commonly used term. In psychology, observational studies are defined as research that is based on direct observation of participants "without any attempt at intervention or manipulation of the behavior being observed" (VandenBos, 2007, p. 638). Longitudinal investigations of risk factors and outcome measures are observational studies, for instance. A well-known example is the Framingham Heart Study, which was begun by the U.S. Public Health Service (USPHS) in 1948. Responding to concerns about soaring coronary disease rates in the United States, the USPHS has systematically collected basic demographic and health data on several thousand residents of Framingham, Massachusetts. In 1960, cigarette smoking was revealed to be a risk factor that statistically predicted cardiovascular disease, and in 1961, high blood pressure was identified statistically as another risk factor. These relational observations led to controlled experiments that confirmed the preventive approach to combating heart disease by exercise (which at one time was considered dangerous for people at risk), not smoking, lowering harmful cholesterol, and reducing stress, blood pressure, and obesity.

This distinction is not unambiguous, however, because it is usually possible to think of ways of quantifying qualitative data. Furthermore, it is often instructive to use quantitative and qualitative methods in the same study (e.g., using open-ended interviews of some of the participants in a rigorously quantified lab experiment to find out how *they* perceived the study). It can also be informative to systematically observe, and describe in prose, the demeanor of the participants. Were they attentive and focused on the instructions and the experimental task, or did they seem uninterested and distracted? Did they appear calm and composed, or were they anxious and unsettled and possibly concerned about how they would be evaluated?

If we think of qualitative and quantitative research as the two ends of a continuum, on the extreme qualitative side would be naturalistic studies in which the researchers are part of the scene and are also observers. We begin by describing two classic examples of these kinds of participant observation studies. Continuing along the qualitative-quantitative continuum, we discuss the use of graphics to map out networks of interpersonal relationships. We then turn to judgment studies, which use raters or coders to evaluate and categorize ongoing behavior. Raters or coders can also classify archival material using a traditional approach called *content analysis,* which is also illustrated later in this chapter. On the extreme quantitative side of the continuum are experimental research studies, including situations simulated in artificial settings. Discussion of such studies leads us into the issue of plausible rival hypotheses. A related issue in the context of relational research is hidden variables that are correlated with each of the variables that comprise an observed relationship and may be a cause of both. Finally, we turn to the distinction between reactive and nonreactive observation, and we illustrate the use of nonreactive observation in field experiments. (See also Box 4.1.)

How Do Researchers Simultaneously Participate and Observe?

One traditional procedure in qualitative research is **participant observation**, where the term *participant* refers to the investigator as opposed to the research participants. For example, in a classic participant observation study in psychology, a team of social psychologists observed a cult from within (as members) for approximately two months before and one month after the date that the cult leader had predicted that the world would end (Festinger, Schachter, & Riecken, 1956). The leader told her followers, who fervently believed every word, that she had received written messages from extraterrestrials about gods and spiritual vibrations on other planets, and that, on a specified day, just before dawn, a flood would engulf most of the continent. In the days before this predicted cataclysm, many members quit their jobs, discarded their possessions, and were careless about their money, believing they would have no need for these things. What gave them emotional consolation was the leader's word that they would be evacuated by a flying saucer that would land in her backyard at 4:00 p.m. on a particular day to transport the "chosen ones" to another planet. Although they waited in anticipation with coats in hand, no flying saucer arrived and the world did not end. Nonetheless, they did not lose faith. Instead, they interpreted their experience as a drill and a rehearsal for the real pickup. Leon Festinger (1957), the noted social psychologist who developed the theory of cognitive dissonance, cited the observations as evidence of how people sometimes cling to ridiculous beliefs even in the face of dissonant events by seeking out new reasons to justify their beliefs.

In another classic example of participant observation, clinical psychologist David Rosenhan (1973) was interested in how people who are labeled as "mentally ill" get to be stigmatized and what determines how they are treated. Rosenhan and a number of volunteer coworkers gained secret admission to psychiatric hospitals in five states on the East and West Coasts by feigning psychiatric symptoms (e.g., complaining of hearing voices). Once admitted, they all behaved quite normally, responded honestly to questions about significant life events, and attempted to interact normally with the staff members (psychiatrists, psychologists, and resident physicians). The staff members were not told that it was *their* behavior that was being studied by Rosenhan and his team of pseudopatients. The reason the staff was not told was that Rosenhan believed that, sensitive to their loss of privacy, the staff members would become selective in cooperating with the researchers.

None of the pseudopatients was detected, and all but one were diagnosed as schizophrenic. Notes about ward life were kept by the pseudopatient researchers, one of whom (Lando, 1976) reported positive aspects of his experience. In contrast, Rosenhan strongly emphasized a feeling of depersonalization and powerlessness. Rosenhan (1973) also conducted a follow-up study in which the hospital staff was alerted to the possibility of pseudopatients. In that study, roughly 10%–20% of new admissions were judged to be faking, even though none of the patients was an experimental pseudopatient. The results were immediately a lightning rod for a heated discussion on the accuracy of the diagnostic labeling of psychiatric patients. One beneficial consequence was that the American Psychiatric Association's diagnostic manual was revised in an effort to reduce the likelihood of future misdiagnoses.

As these cases illustrate, participant observation lets the researcher study complex social interactions as they occur and progress rather than relying on public records of past events. Thus, it is a way of witnessing natural events in their "wholeness," particularly those that would be impossible to simulate in a lab, or that might be too sensitive or risky to try to manipulate experimentally (Weick, 1968). Some have claimed that participant observers approach the field of observation without any preconceived ideas. However, it is hard to believe that researchers would realistically know where, when, how, or what to study without having at least a hunch or theoretical preconception, even if the purpose of the research were exploratory and descriptive. If for no other reason, having some ideas in advance encourages serendipity, or as social scientists Fine and Deegan (1996) noted, "The prepared participant observer hoping to maximize the chances of obtaining data selects just the right time and just the right place" (p. 439). Suppose a researcher wants to observe barroom brawls. The researcher is more likely to witness such behavior by visiting bars on weekend nights than by visiting during afternoons in the middle of the week. "Courting serendipity involves planned insight married to unplanned events," as Fine and Deegan put it (p. 435).

In the early development of this research approach, there was not yet a tradition of how to obtain the most credible qualitative data. Nowadays, participant observers often work in teams and use strategic checks and balances to try to control for individually biased observations, known as **observer bias**. It occurs when observers overestimate or underestimate the occurrence of events or "see" things that are not really there because they think those things exist or operate in a particular way. As one writer commented, scientists, like all human beings, sometimes associate what they *believe* they see, and what they may *want* to see, with what is actually happening (Lane, 1960). One

BOX 4.2 Translation and Back Translation

When people are to be interviewed or given questionnaires to answer, it is important that items be phrased accurately in their own language or dialect. When the language of those observed is not the native language of the researchers, **translation and back translation** are used: One bilingual person first translates the questions from the source to the target language, and then another bilingual person translates the questions back into the source language. The original is compared with the twice-translated version (i.e., the *back translation*) to see whether anything has been lost in the translation and needs correction.

way to identify observer bias is to compare the field notes of two or more independent observers for discrepancies. In making these field notes, observers use several conventions. One rule of thumb for every written note referring to a conversation is to distinguish verbatim quotes from the observer's paraphrases (see also Box 4.2). Whenever possible, it is also advisable to make audio or video recordings (with the permission of those being recorded).

What Can Be Learned From Quantifying Observations?

Quantifying what we "see" (or sense) empirically encompasses not only the expression of observations in numerical form, but also the use of graphics to explore data and help us to visualize their abstract properties. An example is the use of **network analysis**—also called **social network analysis** (SNA) when used to graph pathways of interpersonal behavior in social networks (Kossinets, Kleinberg, & Watts, 2008). The original inspiration for this work goes back to the 1930s and the contributions of Jacob Moreno (1934), a psychiatrist, who pioneered the use of a visual and quantitative technique (he called it *sociometry*) to map out individuals' subjective feelings toward one another. In a recent review article, Borgatti, Mehra, Brass, and Labianca (2009) noted the "explosion of interest in network research across the physical and social sciences" (p. 892). Similarly, Duncan Watts (2003), in his book *Six Degrees*, described the impressive applications of network analysis in a growing number of fields. As an illustration, Kossinets and Watts (2006) mapped out the e-mail traffic of over 43,000 students, faculty, and staff at a large university.

As a simplified example, Part A of Figure 4.1 shows an SNA "map" that helps us visualize a hypothetical cult network (Foster & Rosnow, 2006). Typically in cults, the leader achieves control

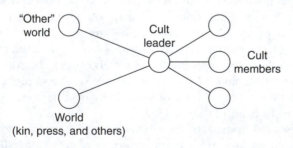

Figure 4.1   Illustrations of social network analysis (SNA) maps (Foster & Rosnow, 2006, pp. 172, 173).

over the cult members by essentially walling them off from the world of kin, the press, and others while playing the role of a spiritual intermediary between the cult members and the "other" (the spiritual) world. A traditional term for reporters who control the flow of news is a *gatekeeper* (White, 1950). The cult leader is also a kind of gatekeeper. However, the cult leader is not only a self-appointed guardian of how cult members are permitted to think and behave but is also the sole keeper at the gate.

In a parallel (if less pathological) situation, Part B of Figure 4.1 represents a hypothetical corporate network where the top executive is both the CEO and the chair of the company or corporate board (Foster & Rosnow, 2006). This executive has a powerful role in being able to control the information flow to each of the three constituent groups (the board, the employees, and the shareholders). Unless the information is leaked, this executive can, in theory, keep each constituent group in the dark about what is happening in the other groups. If there is dissension among board members, and if formal communications have to pass through the top executive, the shareholders may be unaware of this dissension. Several large corporations have recently undergone major makeovers in which the CEO and board chair positions were separated because the vested constituencies perceived that the power of the top executive had become too centralized.

As another example, in Figure 4.2, which was inspired by a graphic in Watts's (2003) book, we show a mobile phone social network where the person in the center is connected to 5 people by one degree of separation, and each of them is connected to 4 people by one degree of separation, and each of them is also connected to 4 people by one degree of separation. Therefore, within three degrees, the person in the center of the network is connected to 105 people. Suppose that, instead of the network in Figure 4.2, each person in another social network is connected to 100 people by one degree of separation. At two degrees of separation, the connection is $100 \times 100 = 10,000$ people. At three degrees of separation, the connection is $100 \times 100 \times 100 = 1,000,000$ (1 million) people. Therefore, within three degrees of separation, we have $100 + 10,000 + 1,000,000$, or $1,010,100$ people. In 2011, it was estimated that the world population was 7 billion people. Within how many degrees of separation would everyone be connected to everyone else in the world in our hypothetical network? However, as Watts (2003) noted, the real world is more complex because there is a lot of redundancy in social networks. That is, people's friends usually know other people's friends, and therefore it is not 100 independent acquaintances for each person in the worldwide network.

The title of Watts's book, *Six Degrees*, comes from the title of a play by John Guare, *Six Degrees of Separation* (later made into a movie). The inspiration for Guare's play was one of Stanley Milgram's clever studies on what he called "the small world problem," an expression that he borrowed from a widely circulated unpublished manuscript by political scientist Ithiel de Sola Pool and mathematician Manfred Kochen (they eventually published this manuscript two decades later as the leadoff article in the first issue of the journal *Social Networks*, 1978–1979). Milgram (1967) was interested in exploring the number of intermediate acquaintances it would take to connect two people in the world who did not know one another. Inspired by a children's game (called "messages"), Milgram thought of an interesting way to study the small world problem empirically.

In the original children's game (described by Jacobs, 1961), the idea was to pick two very dissimilar individuals—say, a head hunter in the Solomon Islands and a cobbler in Rock Island, Illinois—and to try to imagine the shortest plausible chain of individuals through which a message could be communicated from the cobbler to the head hunter. In Milgram's adaptation of this game, he began by writing recruitment letters to a sample of women and men representing different walks of life who resided in Wichita, Kansas. In a replication, Travers and Milgram (1969) recruited women and men residing in Omaha, Nebraska. The letters invited these people to "participate in a study of social contact in American society." The volunteers from Kansas then served as starting points

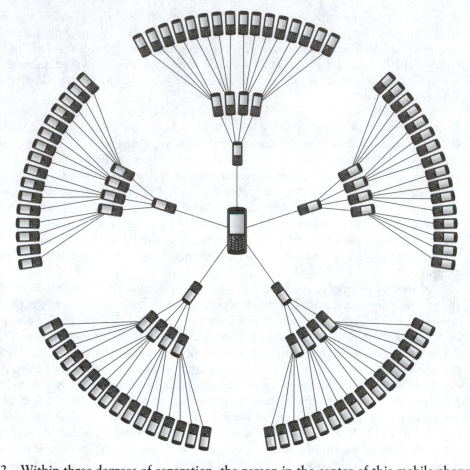

Figure 4.2 Within three degrees of separation, the person in the center of this mobile phone social network is connected to 5 + 20 + 80 = 105 people.

to transmit a message to a specific person identified as residing in Cambridge, Massachusetts. The volunteers from Nebraska were to communicate the message to a person who was identified as working in Boston and residing in Sharon, Massachusetts.

The instructions and a set of postcards addressed to Harvard University (where Milgram was teaching) were enclosed in a mailable folder. Each person in the chain was instructed to write his or her name at the bottom of the communication, so that the next person who received the folder knew where it came from. The name and address of the target person and some other information about the person were also noted in the instructions, which stated that the idea was to transmit the communication to the target person using only a chain of friends or acquaintances. Each person in the chain who received the folder was instructed to mail it within 24 hours to someone that he or she knew on a personal basis and to mail a postcard back to Harvard. There was a roster where each person was to sign his or her name. For example, in one of the shortest chains the document started with a wheat farmer in Kansas, who passed it on to an Episcopal minister in his hometown, who passed it on to an Episcopal minister who taught in Cambridge, Massachusetts, who gave it to the target person, the wife of a Divinity School student. In the Nebraska-to-Massachusetts chain, the median number of intermediaries was 5.5—which, rounded to 6, is the number in the title of John Guare's play, *Six Degrees of Separation*. (See also Box 4.3.)

BOX 4.3   The Kevin Bacon Game

As Watts (2003) noted, small world networks are everywhere—from electronic circuitry, to anatomical and cortical connections, to airport hubs, to gossip networks. Often, the degrees of separation are fewer than six. For example, if you wanted to travel from your home in a small town to a hotel in a big city on another continent, you might drive from your home to your small town airport, then take a plane to a hub airport, and from there take a taxi to your hotel (three degrees of separation). As another illustration, in 1994, a group of fraternity brothers at Albright College invented the game of figuring out actors' degrees of separation from the actor Kevin Bacon.

An actor who had appeared in a movie with him would have a Bacon number of one; an actor who had worked with somebody who had acted with Kevin Bacon would have a Bacon number of two, and so forth. For instance, the actor George Ives has a Bacon number of one because he was in the movie *Stir of Echoes* with Kevin Bacon, and Marilyn Monroe has a Bacon number of two because she was in *Niagara* with Ives. Tabulating the distribution of over a half million actors with Bacon numbers ranging from zero (Bacon himself) to 10, Watts found that the average path from the vast majority of actors to Kevin Bacon was four steps or less.

 How Are Judgment Studies Done?

Another strategy for quantifying qualitative observational data is to use coders or raters in what is generally described as a **judgment study** (Rosenthal, 1987). Among the various methods that are used to choose coders or raters in judgment studies are the following:

1. An informal way is to decide intuitively on the type of judges needed. Suppose a researcher wanted a sample of raters educated at a particular level, in which case the researcher might recruit graduate or undergraduate students. A researcher who wanted ratings of nonverbal expressions of psychopathology might recruit experienced professionals, such as clinical psychologists, psychiatrists, or psychiatric social workers.

2. A formal way of choosing a sample of judges is to consult the research literature for empirically based clues. Suppose a researcher needed a sample of judges to evaluate aspects of people's nonverbal behavior. Consulting the research literature, the researcher learns that college-educated women, people who are cognitively complex, and people who are psychiatrically unimpaired tend to be particularly sensitive to nonverbal cues (Rosenthal, Hall, DiMatteo, Rogers, & Archer, 1979). Another relevant clue is that people who are high in *field independence* (as measured by a psychological test) tend to be more accurate raters than field-dependent persons (Härtel, 1993).

3. Another formal way of choosing judges is to do a "pilot test" that compares the people who volunteered to participate as judges for their accuracy of judgment on some relevant criterion. Suppose the researcher is interested in selecting judges for a study in which they will have to categorize the emotions expressed by adolescents in tutoring sessions. The researcher might begin by showing the potential judges pictures of adolescents exhibiting different emotions (anger, disgust, fear, happiness, sadness, surprise, and so on). The researcher would (a) ask these potential judges to identify the emotion expressed in each picture, (b) score their answers, and (c) then select the most accurate judges for the study.

One advantage of the use of coders or raters in judgment studies is that researchers can measure the judge-to-judge reliability (discussed in Chapter 6); also it is usually possible to use simple statistics (such as the basic statistics described in Chapter 10) to summarize the results. Continuing with our interest in interpersonal behavior, a classic series of judgment studies in which talk was subjected to formal observation and analysis was performed by Robert F. Bales (1950a, 1950b; Bales & Cohen, 1979). He first began to develop a systematic procedure for analyzing social interaction when he "became interested in trying to account for the success of Alcoholics Anonymous in help-ing apparently hopeless drinkers to stop drinking" (Bales, 1955, p. 31). At the meetings, he spoke with members but was reluctant to ask all the questions that occurred to him, and thus he "began to develop crude methods for recording who did what, who spoke to whom, and how" (Bales, 1955, p. 31). Eventually he abandoned the effort when he sensed that it had begun to appear intrusive and sinister. He shifted his attention instead to developing a way of studying people engaged in group discussions within the more scientifically favorable conditions of a laboratory.

A number of laboratories for studying social interaction in small groups had been developed by other investigators. For his research, Bales established at Harvard University a laboratory consisting of a large room for the group under study and an adjoining room for observers to watch and listen from behind windows with one-way vision. For the groups under study, Bales brought several people together, had them read a factual information sheet containing material related to a human relations problem, and asked them to discuss the problem. The discussions usually lasted about 40 minutes, and the group met four times. The observers were trained to code every act that occurred—an *act* being defined as a single statement, question, or gesture.

Figure 4.3 contains the 12 categories developed by Bales for the observing judges to classify the acts. Notice that the acts are divided into *socioemotional relations* and *task relations* classifications,

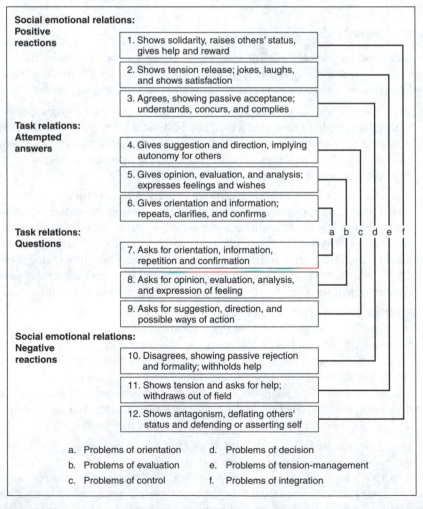

Figure 4.3 Categories of socioemotional (directed at friendship and emotional needs) and task-related (directed at achieving concrete problem-solving interactions) in small groups (Bales, 1950a, p. 258).

the former term referring to positive and negative reactions, and the latter term referring to questions and attempted answers. Typically, there were between 15 and 20 acts per minute, about half of which were coded as problem-solving attempts. The remaining acts consisted of positive and negative reactions and questions. In the first third of a session, giving information tended to be the most frequent act. Opinions tended to be given most during the middle portion of a meeting, and offering suggestions was most frequent in the last third. Of particular interest to Bales was a consistent finding that the acts alternated between socioemotional and task or problem-solving attempts. It seemed that when too much emphasis was given to the human relations problem, socioemotional relations between members became strained; emphasis was then placed on this area until member relations were again harmonious. Then there was a return to the problem, and thereafter acts were directed back and forth between these two areas.

In the next chapter, we turn to self-report methods. A self-report method (a questionnaire) was also used by Bales in his studies. After each meeting, the discussants were given a questionnaire asking them to rank the other participants in the discussion in terms of the quality of their ideas, those members liked best, and so forth. Bales (1955) reported that the individual ranked as having the best ideas was often the one who did the most talking and who offered more than the average number of suggestions and opinions. Bales also reported that, whereas one person would become a specialist in advancing ideas, another would develop a specialization on the socioemotional side. Those most commonly rated "best liked" also had higher-than-average rates of showing tension release and showing agreement. It was not impossible for a person who was ranked at the top in ideas also to be the best liked, but it was rare.

How Does Content Analysis Work?

Observational methods sometimes involve the use of materials stored in archives (**archival material**). Much of this material is qualitative (e.g., print collections, newspapers, public documents such as speeches of legislators in the *Congressional Record*), but quantitative information is also stored in archives (e.g., crime data, census data, and voting records of legislators). A traditional strategy used for sorting through and categorizing the contents of qualitative archival material is called **content analysis**. As an illustration, Air Force Captain Stephanie R. Kelley, for her master's thesis at the Naval Postgraduate School, did a content analysis of nearly a thousand rumors reported in 2003–2004 in *The Baghdad Mosquito*, a daily newsletter produced under the auspices of the Multi-National Forces in Iraq. Once a week, the chief of the *Baghdad Mosquito* sat down with his Iraqi staff, who were representative of the population in Baghdad (including Arab Sunnis and Shi'as, Kurds, and Turkmen), and they discussed the latest circulating rumors. Proceeding from the idea that rumors can be a window into a community's uncertainties and anxieties, Kelley (2004) categorized them using a classic typology developed by psychologist Robert Knapp (1944) for his content analysis of rumors circulating in the United States during World War II. Kelley also content-analyzed the rumors circulating in Iraq using a classification system that she developed for identifying the targets of the rumors. To assess the reliability of her coding, she had a second person content-analyze a random sample of 50 rumors, and the results were satisfactory. In this way, Kelley generated hypotheses about community morale and public opinion in Baghdad during the period of her study (see also Box 4.4).

As a more detailed illustration of the content analysis of qualitative subject matter, social psychologist Peter Crabb and his coworkers (Crabb & Bielawski, 1994; Crabb & Marciano, 2011) were interested in tracking how visual presentations of behavior in children's books portrayed female and male roles. They chose for their study all picture books that had received a prestigious award known as the Caldecott Medal or Honor. The Caldecott awards are given annually to the artists of the chosen children's picture books published in the United States. Crabb and his coworkers reasoned that illustrations in these books might be especially influential in transmitting information about gender roles, as books that win the Caldecott Medal or Honor usually have a high profile in libraries

BOX 4.4 Secondary Observation

Other potentially useful sources of archival material frequently require more effort to track down and obtain permission to use for research purposes (M. C. Rosenthal, 1994; Simonton, 2000). For instance, a researcher might track down sales of airline tickets, or trip insurance policies, or liquor sales at airport bars as indicators of increased anxieties. Other potential "fugitive" (elusive or hard-to-find) materials for the purpose of a content analysis might be certain institutional and industrial records (sicknesses and absences, employee complaints, unsolicited commendations, and accident reports) and personal documents (such as diaries and letters of captured soldiers in wartime). A researcher's observations that are twice removed from the source are described as **secondary observation**. The individual who recorded the information for an archive is presumed to be once removed from the source, and the researcher is removed from the source by a second degree of separation.

and bookstores. Furthermore, other researchers have recently reported that children do attend more to pictures than to textual material (Evans & Saint-Aubin, 2005; Shapiro, Anderson, & Anderson, 1997) and that children generally ask more questions about pictures than about textual material (Yaden, Smolkin, & MacGillivray, 1993).

In the initial study, Crabb and Bielawski (1994) collected 1,613 illustrations, including 416 of female characters and 1,197 of male characters in books that had received the Caldecott Medal or Honor between 1938 and 1989. Instead of content-analyzing *all* this material by hand, the researchers drew a sample of 300 illustrations by gender and decade. The judges were rehearsed in the use of the coding system, and they then coded the sex of the characters shown in the pictures, the nature of any household tools (such as those used in food preparation, cleaning, repair, and family care), nonhousehold tools (such as those used in construction, agriculture, and transportation), tools not falling into the above two groups, and features of the characters using the tools and the situation (such as the age of the character, coded as child, teenager, or adult). The ratings were, when assessed statistically, generally consistent from judge to judge. One finding was that household tools were associated more with female characters, whereas nonhousehold tools were associated more with male characters. Similar observations were later reported by another team of researchers (Poarch & Monk-Turner, 2001), who analyzed a sample of non-award-winning children's books published in the United States between 1963 and 1995. Interestingly, Crabb and Bielawski (1994) also observed that the proportion of male characters shown using household tools in the award-winning books had increased over time, though the proportion of female characters using nonhousehold tools had not changed much over time.

In a more recent follow-up study by Crabb and Marciano (2011), the question of interest was whether changes had occurred in the portrayal of female and male characters in the Caldecott award-winning books since 1989. Crabb and Marciano noted that since 1989, the final publication year of the original content analysis by Crabb and Bielawski, some labor patterns of women and men had changed. According to the Bureau of Labor Statistics, there was still a higher level of participation of men in the workforce, although the participation of women had risen from 57.3% in 1989 to 59.4% in 2008, and the participation of men had declined from 76.3% in 1989 to 72.7% in 2008. Other data also cited by Crabb and Marciano suggested that women generally continued to do the bulk of housework, and the pattern was consistent across different cultures. For this follow-up study, Crabb and Marciano used 490 illustrations in 68 books that had won the Caldecott Medal or Honor between 1990 and 2009. The content analysis procedure was similar to that used in the original study, and the judge-to-judge consistency was again impressive. The main finding was that little had changed from the earlier period in the way that gender roles were visually portrayed in the award-winning books. Female characters were still more likely than male characters to be shown using household tools (e.g., bowls, forks, knives, spoons, and sewing machines) and male characters were more likely than female characters to be shown using production tools (e.g., cars, trucks, and fishing nets).

There are also computer programs for use in content analysis research (P. Stone, 1997, 2000). These programs can sort through written material according to particular research specifications. Sourcebooks on content analysis are quite detailed (C. W. Roberts, 1997; C. P. Smith, 1992), but there are three general guidelines to keep in mind:

1. If you are planning to use judges (or raters or coders), it is important that the analysis of content be reasonably consistent among the judges. That is, the different coders should produce similar results (i.e., there should be good *judge-to-judge reliability*, discussed in Chapter 6). Assuming that each category and unit has been precisely defined, and that the judges were properly trained, the consistency among the judges should be satisfactorily high.

2. It is essential that the specific categories and units be relevant to the questions or hypotheses of the study. In choosing categories for written records, for example, it is a good idea to ask, "What is the communication about?" and "How is it said?" Questions like these help to focus the analysis on the substance (the *what*) and the form (the *how*) of the subject matter. It is also prudent to consider several different units of analysis before settling on any one unit. For example, if you were analyzing textual material, you might consider coding words and word compounds (or phrases) or perhaps themes (or assertions).

3. If you are not planning to analyze the entire universe of data, it is important to decide on a good sampling procedure. We will have more to say about different sampling plans later in this book, including approaches that call for (a) *random sampling* from listings of all relevant units; (b) *stratified sampling*, which breaks up units into subgroups and then selects samples from the subgroups; and (c) *systematic sampling*, in which every *n*th unit of a list is selected.

As we said before, all strategies and procedures are limited in some ways, and the method of content analysis is no exception. Most basically, it is limited by the quality, dependability, and relevance of the material to be analyzed. However, it also has four definite advantages when used properly (Woodrum, 1984). First, developing a coding system and then implementing it requires little more than commonsense logic. Second, content analysis is a "shoestring" methodology in that, although labor-intensive when done by hand, it does not require much capital investment. Third, it is a "safe" methodology, because you can add necessary information if it is missed or incorrectly coded or if there are changes in what is being measured over time. These additions and corrections are far more difficult to implement in the typical experimental or survey study. Fourth, it forces researchers to think carefully about the material to be evaluated and classified.

How Are Situations Simulated in Controlled Settings?

In Chapter 2, we mentioned examples of laboratory experimental observation, including the use of animals in learning and conditioning studies. It is frequently possible to *simulate* (or mimic) a causal relationship in a controlled experimental setting in which we can manipulate the theorized causal condition (we have more to say about the logic and the limitations of causal inference in Chapter 7). Suppose we are interested in why people's ears buzz and tickle as they listen to a hard rock band up close. Our hypothesis is that the intensity of sound waves (measured in decibels) is probably the cause. To test our hypothesis, we can simulate this experience by positioning a loudspeaker next to one or more volunteers in a tightly controlled laboratory setting, manipulate the carefully calibrated sounds, and ask the participants to report the sensations they feel. If they report that their ears buzz and tickle, the sound pressure is probably well above 120 decibels (which can produce feelings of discomfort, prickling, and pain). After each exposure to such high-decibel sounds, the sensitivity of the ear may be temporarily reduced. (If we wanted to find out whether people who have a steady diet of hard rock have more hearing difficulties than those who do not listen to hard rock, we can't ethically expose subjects to such an experience in a controlled setting. However, we can design a relational study in which we sample a population of people and record the minimal audible noise detected by those who report they routinely listened either to a lot of hard rock or to no hard rock at all.)

Experimental simulations in the artificial situation of a "lab" (broadly defined) have also involved scripted role playing. As an illustration, Irving Janis and Leon Mann (1965; Mann, 1967; Mann & Janis, 1968) used a procedure that could be described as "emotional role playing" to get heavy smokers to modify their smoking behavior. Drawing on the "saying is believing" principle in social psychology, Janis and Mann experimented with a scripted simulation that was designed to increase the volunteer participants' emotional involvement. The volunteer subjects were young women, all between the ages of 18 and 23, none of whom had been told that the objective of the research involved modifying their smoking habits and attitudes toward smoking. Before the study began, the women had averaged approximately a pack of cigarettes a day. Randomly assigned to an experimental or a control group, they were all told at the beginning of the study that the purpose of the research was to examine two important problems about the human side of medical practice: (a) how patients react to bad news and (b) how patients feel when a physician tells them to quit smoking.

Each participant in the experimental condition was told to imagine that the experimenter was a physician who had been treating her for a persistent cough, and that on this "third visit" he was going to give her the results of X-rays and other diagnostic tests. The experimenter then outlined five different scenes, and he instructed the participant to "act out" each scene as realistically as possible. The first scene took place in the doctor's office while the patient awaited the diagnosis. She was asked to imagine how she would feel and then to express aloud her thoughts, her concerns, and her feelings about whether to give up cigarettes. The second scene was the imagined interaction with the physician. The participant was told that the diagnostic tests had revealed a small malignant mass in her right lung. She was also told that there was only a moderate chance of surgical success in treating this condition. She was then encouraged to ask questions. In the next scene, she was instructed to express her feelings. The physician could be overheard in the background phoning for a hospital bed. In the fourth scene the physician described the details of imminent hospitalization. He told the participant that chest surgery typically requires a long convalescent period, at least 6 weeks. He raised questions about the woman's smoking history and asked whether she was aware of the relationship between smoking and cancer. He stressed the urgent need for her to stop smoking and encouraged her to talk freely about the problems she thought she might encounter in trying to break the smoking habit.

The women who were randomly assigned to the control group were exposed to similar information about lung cancer in a tape recording of one of the experimental sessions. However, they were not given an opportunity to engage in emotional role playing. As Janis and Mann hypothesized, the impact of the experimental manipulation in the emotional role-play condition exceeded that in the control condition. There was greater fear of personal harm from smoking, a stronger belief that smoking causes lung cancer, and a greater willingness and intent to quit smoking in the emotional role-play condition than in the control condition. To find out about long-term effects, Janis and Mann conducted follow-up interviews at different points over 18 months. The results were essentially as before. On the average, the women in the scripted role-play sessions reported that they had reduced their daily cigarette consumption by more than twice the amount of those randomly assigned to the control group; this difference persisted even after a year and a half.

In many cases, doing research in an artificial setting can be a convenient and effective way of studying a phenomenon of interest in behavioral research (Mook, 1983). However, it is important to proceed with some caution when generalizing from laboratory simulations to real-world situations (cf. Adair, 1973; Levitt & List, 2007; Rosnow & Rosenthal, 1997; Silverman, 1977). For example, suppose we were interested in the effect of frustration on aggression in a controlled laboratory setting. Because frustration can evoke hostile behavior, we might design a simulation experiment in which two volunteer participants engage in a competitive task and are given an opportunity to administer a

BOX 4.5　Virtual Reality in the Lab

Microworld simulations using computer-generated environments are intended to improve realism and increase the generalizability of the findings (Brehmer & Dörner, 1993; DiFonzo, Hantula, & Bordia, 1998; Funke, 1991; Omodei & Wearing, 1995). Virtual-reality technology can simulate various kinds of perceptual phenomena (Biocca & Levy, 1995; Carr & England, 1995; Loomis, Blascovich, & Beall, 1999; Steuer, 1992). The ability to simulate a 3-D environment makes possible tactile, motion, and audio stimulation designed to immerse a person in a "world" that feels the same as the real world. A similar approach has been used by the military and aerospace programs to train pilots and astronauts. Potential advantages of microworld simulations are that (a) volunteer participants may be made to "feel" the way they do in a real-world setting; (b) naturally occurring variables can be manipulated in a controlled setting; (c) the situation is dynamic (rather than static), in the way that real-world settings are; and (d) it may now be possible to study questions that have been too sensitive to study except in passive observational studies or in experiments using written vignettes (cf. Pierce & Aguinis, 1997).

mild electric shock to one another. We frustrate one participant by withdrawing some desired object and then see whether the person administers shock to the other participant. Meta-analytic findings suggest that simulating aggression in the lab yields a faithful representation of certain effects in the real world, but these simulations may overestimate the effects of situational variables (e.g., media violence) and underestimate the effects of individual differences (C. A. Anderson & Bushman, 1997). Efforts to improve the realism and generalizability of so-called microworld simulations have led to innovative applications using virtual-reality technology in the lab (see Box 4.5).

 ### What Are Plausible Rival Hypotheses and the Third-Variable Problem?

Later in this book, we will discuss how to anticipate and control for certain experimental design problems. However, it is not too soon to begin to sharpen your intuitive skills or to get an idea of what your instructor may expect as you begin to put together a background review of the literature on your research topic or to write the discussion section of your research report. The instructor will expect you to think carefully about alternative explanations (also called **rival interpretations** or **plausible rival hypotheses**) for the reported results. The expression *plausible rival hypothesis* was initially proposed by Donald T. Campbell and Julian C. Stanley (1963) in the context of what they called the "degree of confirmation" that can be conferred on a theoretical explanation (p. 36). Their notion was that as the research process progresses, some interpretations can be eliminated in a kind of survival-of-the-fittest hypothesis. Campbell and Stanley reasoned that the fewer the plausible rival hypotheses remaining, the greater is the likelihood of the confirmation of the surviving interpretation(s).

To get you thinking about rival interpretations, let us begin by looking at another set of studies in experimental psychology. These studies focused on how life experiences influence what people select from their perceptual environment as significant objects and events. In one study, the researchers began by giving a questionnaire to a group of participants to measure each person's values and, more specifically, whether a person's value orientation was predominantly aesthetic, theoretical, economic, social, political, or religious (Postman, Bruner, & McGinnies, 1948). Individuals who responded in ways that indicated they valued the search for truth above most other things received a high "theoretical" score, and those whose values were dominated by the usefulness of things were given a high "economic" score. The "political" respondents were concerned about power, "social" respondents about the needs of others, "aesthetic" respondents about criteria of beauty, and "religious" respondents about the meaning of life as related to their conception of God. All respondents were then presented with a series of words through a stachistoscope projector, a device (used before the computer had been invented) that briefly presented various stimuli by flashing them on a screen for a fraction of a second. The words chosen reflected the six value orientations of the respondents.

On the whole, the participants in this influential study identified the words associated with their own value orientation more rapidly than the words not so associated (Postman et al., 1948). This outcome was initially taken as evidence of *subliminal perception* (the impact of stimuli below the person's level of conscious awareness) but was then challenged by another team of experimenters (Solomon & Howes, 1951), who proposed a rival explanation. These challengers argued that people with a specific value orientation may have been exposed to such words in print more often than other people (presumably, individuals read more literature relevant to their own values). In other words, people oriented to "political" words would recognize them more rapidly than other words because of their familiarity and not because they were perceived more quickly subliminally. This plausible rival hypothesis paved the way for follow-up studies that were specifically designed to reconcile these differences in interpretation. Those early investigations, in turn, ultimately led to further research on what is now called *subliminal priming*, defined as "unconscious stimulation that increases the probability of the later occurrence of related cognitive tasks" (VandenBos, 2007, p. 904).

Here is another example on which to practice identifying rival interpretations. Though a great deal is now known about how marijuana acts (e.g., L. L. Iversen, 2000), in the 1960s, when this experiment was done, there were volumes of statistics on the relationship between alcohol use and accident rates, but comparable data for marijuana use were unavailable. A study of the effects of drugs on simulated driving performance was deemed ethically acceptable and could be tightly controlled. What was lost, however, was the actual stress of driving in traffic. In this study (Crancer, Dille, Delay, Wallace, & Haybin, 1969), the effects of marijuana, alcohol, and no drug were compared in three simulated driving tests. In all three driving tests, the participant sat in a specially constructed console mock-up of a car and observed a large screen on which a driver's-eye motion picture was projected. Normal and emergency situations on urban and suburban streets appeared on the screen, and the participant was instructed to respond to them by operating the accelerator, brake, turn signals, and steering, and by checking the speedometer.

In the first driving test, experienced marijuana smokers were tested for 30 minutes on the console mock-up after smoking two marijuana cigarettes, and the same people were tested when their blood alcohol concentration reached 0.10% (the legally defined intoxication level in 1969), the equivalent of about 6 ounces of 86-proof liquor in a 120-pound person. In the no-drug control condition, neither marijuana nor alcohol was given. The second driving test was taken 2½ hours after the first test, and the third driving test was taken 1½ hours after the second test. All the tests were the same, and on each test it was possible to make up to 405 errors. Under the effects of alcohol, the participants did worse than in either the marijuana or the no-drug condition. In the alcohol condition over all three tests, they made a mean of 97 errors, compared with a mean of 85 errors in the control condition. In the marijuana condition, compared to the control condition, the only bad effect was an increase in speedometer errors. Under the effects of alcohol, there was an increase in all types of errors except steering errors. What problems do you see in this study? Compare your answer with the footnote at the bottom of this page.*

The concept of a rival interpretation applies as well to explanations of relationships that take the form of statistical correlations (such as the relationship between two variables, A and B), where it is described as the **third-variable problem** to reflect the idea that some variable that is correlated with

---

* The participants were experienced marijuana users, may have been motivated to do well in the marijuana condition, and may have been motivated to do poorly in the alcohol condition. The drug doses may not have been comparable. Two marijuana cigarettes may not have made the participants as "high" as 6 ounces of 86-proof alcohol. If the participants had been made equally "high" by the alcohol and marijuana treatments, perhaps their error rates would have been more nearly equal and might have been greater than those accumulated in the no-drug condition.

A and B may be a cause of both and may therefore be responsible for the observed relationship. The mathematician John Paulos (1990, 1991) discussed a number of fascinating examples. As an illustration, there is a positive correlation between milk consumption and the incidence of cancer in various societies. Paulos explained this correlation by the fact that people in relatively affluent societies live longer, and increased longevity (the third variable) is associated with an increase in the likelihood of getting cancer. Thus, any health practice (such as milk drinking) that increases longevity will probably correlate positively with cancer incidence. Another example is the small negative correlation observed between death rates and divorce rates (more divorce, less death) in various regions of the United States. The plausible third variable proposed by Paulos to explain this relation is the age distribution of the various regions, because older married couples are less likely to divorce and more likely to die than younger couples. Another Paulos example was the high positive correlation between the sizes of children's feet and their spelling ability. Should we, he asked facetiously, use foot stretchers to increase children's spelling scores? The plausible third variable is age, because children with bigger feet are usually older, and older children spell better.

 What Is the Distinction Between Reactive and Nonreactive Observation?

Another important distinction proposed by Campbell and Stanley (1963) is between *reactive* and *nonreactive* observations and measurements. These two terms are used to differentiate observations and measurements that do (**reactive**) from those that do not (**nonreactive**) affect the behavior or phenomenon that is being observed or measured. For example, in a clinical experiment on therapy for weight control, the initial weigh-in measurement might be a reactive stimulus to weight reduction, even without the therapeutic intervention (Campbell & Stanley, 1963). As another example, a team of researchers demonstrated experimentally that simply asking students (executive M.B.A. students and college undergraduates) about their intent to engage in certain behavior increased the likelihood of their engaging in that behavior (Levav & Fitzsimons, 2006). Any use of a **concealed measurement** or concealed observation illustrates nonreactive observation, such as using a hidden recording device to eavesdrop on conversations. A variant of concealed measurement is called **partial concealment**; the researcher does not conceal the fact that he or she is making observations but does conceal who or what is being observed. For example, in studies of mother-child interactions, the researcher implies that it is the child who is being observed when in actuality *both* the mother and the child are being studied (Weick, 1968). In the previous chapter, we discussed ethical concerns associated with the use of active and passive deceptions; concealment and partial concealment raise an ethical red flag regarding the invasion of people's privacy.

In a classic example of a field experiment that used nonreactive observation, the psychologist George W. Hartmann (1936) examined the role of emotional and rational persuasive communications in an actual voting campaign and election. Hartmann was struck by the fact that much of the persuasive communication to which we are subjected in advertisements and political speeches is designed to appeal more to our emotions than to our reason. The purpose of such communication is to arouse certain needs and to offer simple solutions that, if we adopt them, will seem to satisfy those needs. Every day we are bombarded by a host of advertisements on TV, radio, billboards, the Web, and so forth, each commercial in its own way claiming some product will make us feel better because we will become more sexually appealing or more companionable or more sweet-smelling. Around election time, political commercials become a complex fusion of excitement, resentment, vague enthusiasm, aroused fears, and hopes. While he was at Columbia University in the 1930s as a postdoctoral fellow, Hartmann decided to test whether emotional or rational advertisements are more persuasive in politics.

In the 1935 statewide election campaign in Pennsylvania, Hartmann had his name placed on the ballot as a Socialist Party candidate in Allentown. To study the effects of emotional and rational messages, he created two political leaflets, one designed to appeal to voters' reason and the other to appeal to their emotions. The leaflets were distributed in different wards in Allentown, matched on

BOX 4.6 Unobtrusive Observation

A major work on the use of unobtrusive observation was written by a team of psychologists and sociologists headed by Eugene J. Webb (Webb, Campbell, Schwartz, & Sechrest, 1966; updated by Webb, Campbell, Schwartz, Sechrest, & Grove, 1981). It is a fascinating book that describes hundreds of unobtrusive measures collected by Webb and his group, and classified into four broad categories: (a) archival records (discussed previously), (b) physical traces, (c) simple observations, and (d) contrived observations. **Physical traces** are the kind of material evidence that a detective might consider clues to solving a crime. For example, in one detective case, a car's radio buttons were clues to the driver's geographic location. By studying the commercial station frequencies to which the buttons were tuned, the detective could identify the general area where the car had been garaged. **Simple observation** is unobtrusive observation that does not attempt to influence or manipulate the situation or to affect what is being observed. For example, Webb's group mentioned finding a correlation between the methodological and theoretical disposition of psychologists and the length of their hair; the "tough-minded" psychologists had shorter hair than "tender-minded" psychologists. In **contrived observation**, the researcher introduces a variable of interest and unobtrusively observes its effects. For instance, Webb et al. mentioned the assessment of the degree of fear induced by a ghost story by unobtrusively observing the shrinking diameter of a circle of seated children.

the basis of their size, population density, assessed property valuation, previous voting habits, and socioeconomic status. The nonreactive measurement in this study was the objective record of the polls. The results were that wards that received the emotional leaflet increased their Socialist votes more than in the wards receiving the rational leaflet. Hartmann also found that even the "rational" wards showed a greater increase in Socialist votes than a number of control wards that had received neither leaflet.

Voting behavior is also an example of what is termed an *unobtrusive measurement*, or what is more generally described as **unobtrusive observation** (see also Box 4.6). As another illustration, Arceneaux (2010) noted that there has been a noticeable increase in the use of randomized field experiments to study campaign effects, apparently inspired by the work of Yale University political science researchers Alan S. Gerber and Donald P. Green. In one study, Gerber and Green (2000) conducted a randomized field experiment designed to assess the relative effectiveness of some basic political tools in getting people to vote. Nonpartisan get-out-the-vote messages were conveyed to approximately 30,000 registered voters in New Haven, Connecticut, through direct mail, personal canvassing (face-to-face contact), or telephone calls using a randomized experimental design. The face-to-face contacts proved to be the most effective in mobilizing these registered voters to get out and vote.

You have seen from the wide variety of examples in this chapter (and in previous ones) that systematic observational methods provide much of the empirical content of behavioral and social science, yet our discussion has barely scratched the surface of what is possible. Before we turn to strategies in which the observations are directed "inward" rather than "outward," we want to reiterate an earlier point: Scientists, like all humans, are susceptible to the errors and biases imposed by limitations of perception and cognition. It is for this reason that scientists encourage independent replications as a way of checking on the accuracy of any single observation or set of observations. We will have more to say about this issue in Chapter 6, when we discuss the role of replication in research. We began by urging you not to harbor illusions about the power of any single research method or tool but instead to be mindful that all are limited in some ways. It is a constant challenge to attempt to figure out ways of opening up our world for scientific scrutiny, to evaluate the validity and reliability of these strategies, and, ultimately, to make sensible generalizations that do not mislead by exaggerating what we think we know.

Summary of Ideas

1. Systematic observation is characterized by a plan of action and by preexisting questions or hypotheses in qualitative and quantitative research. As every method is limited in some way, *methodological triangulation* is used to converge on phenomena of interest from more than one perspective. *Observational study* (Box 4.1) is the name given to research (usually longitudinal) based on direct observation, with no attempt to intervene or manipulate the behavior being observed.

2. Participant observers study a social situation from within by watching and recording how people behave and what they talk about (e.g., Festinger et al.'s study of a cult that predicted the end of the world on a specified date and Rosenhan's study of the staff in mental hospitals). One possible limitation of this research (and not only of this research) is called *observer bias* because the observer overestimates or underestimates an event or "sees" something that is not there. Using more than one independent observer is a traditional way of identifying discrepancies in observations.

3. *Social network analysis* (SNA) can be used to map out pathways in social communication networks. Milgram's studies of the small world problem inspired the idea of six degrees of separation.

4. Bales's study of socioemotional relations and task relations in discussion groups illustrates what can be learned by quantifying qualitative behavior using coders or raters in judgment studies. Three ways of choosing coders or raters are (a) intuitively, based on one's notions of the type of judges needed; (b) by looking for empirically based clues in the research literature; and (c) by doing a "pilot test" in which a pool of volunteers is evaluated for their accuracy of judgments.

5. *Content analysis* can be used to enumerate variables in *archival material* (e.g., Kelley's use of published rumors as a window into uncertainties and anxieties, and Crabb et al.'s analysis of pictorial representations of gender roles in children's books). Three important guidelines for content analysis are (a) checking for intercoder reliability, (b) using relevant categories, and (c) using a good sampling procedure.

6. Simulating a phenomenon in the lab can in many cases be a convenient and effective way of studying it in a more controlled situation (e.g., studying why people's ears buzz and tickle as they listen to a hard rock band up close). Scripted role playing is another kind of simulation approach (e.g., Janis and Mann's effort to get heavy smokers to modify their behavior).

7. All studies, including tightly controlled laboratory experiments and relational studies, are subject to critical examination for *plausible rival hypotheses* or *rival interpretations* (such as the tachistoscopic study of word recognition, the mock-driving study of the effects of marijuana smoking, and the examples of the *third-variable problem*).

8. *Nonreactive observation* includes *concealed measurement* (hidden recording devices), *partial concealment* (not revealing who or what is being observed), and *unobtrusive observation* (Hartmann's study of the effect on voting behavior of emotional and rational messages in a statewide election campaign). Besides archival records, three additional types of unobtrusive observation used are *physical traces, simple observation,* and *contrived observation* (Box 4.6).

Key Terms

archival material p. 71	observational study p. 64	rival interpretations p. 75
concealed measurement p. 77	observer bias p. 65	secondary observation p. 72
content analysis p. 71	partial concealment p. 77	simple observation p. 78
contrived observation p. 78	participant observation p. 64	social network analysis p. 66
judgment study p. 69	physical traces p. 78	systematic observation p. 63
methodological	plausible rival hypotheses p. 75	third-variable problem p. 76
triangulation p. 63	qualitative research p. 63	translation
network analysis p. 66	quantitative research p. 63	and back-translation p. 66
nonreactive observation p. 77	reactive observation p. 77	unobtrusive observation p. 78

Multiple-Choice Questions for Review

1. In a classic study, several social psychologists "joined" a religious cult that believed that the world would soon end. After they were accepted as members of the group, they made careful observations of the behavior of the group. This type of research is known as (a) a field experiment; (b) participant observation; (c) ethnocentric research; (d) all the above.

2. A student at the University of Hawaii wants to study gossip and rumor among Asian cultures. In this

research, interview questions must be translated from English into other languages. To ensure that the translations are accurate, the researcher must use (a) ethnographic research; (b) linguistic relativism; (c) back translation; (d) dual translation.

3. In 1935, psychologist George Hartmann ran for political office in Pennsylvania. In some areas, he distributed leaflets with an emotional appeal to voters. In other areas, he distributed leaflets with a rational appeal. He then observed the voting records for these different areas. In Chapter 2, we discussed the difference between an independent variable and a dependent variable. In this study, the type of leaflet was the _____ variable, and the voting records were the _____ variable. (a) independent, experimental; (b) experimental, independent; (c) dependent, independent; (d) independent, dependent

4. Suppose you are conducting an observational study, and you want judges (or raters) who are very sensitive to nonverbal cues. You should choose judges who are (a) psychiatrically unimpaired; (b) college-aged; (c) female; (d) all of the above.

5. A researcher at Montclair State University carefully observes whether or not people lock their car doors when parked in the university's parking lot. The people do not realize that they are being observed for a research study. This is an example of (a) reactive observation; (b) partial concealment; (c) unobtrusive observation; (d) none of the above.

6. A researcher at Florida International University conducts an observational study of job satisfaction in a large corporation. She tells the research participants that she is studying their behavior but does not tell them what aspect of their behavior she will be observing. This is an example of (a) quasi disclosure; (b) partial concealment; (c) unobtrusive observation; (d) residual disclosure.

7. To determine which classrooms are used most heavily at Akron University, a researcher measures the amount of wear on floor tiles. This is an example of the use of (a) physical traces; (b) simple observations; (c) contrived observations; (d) archival records.

8. A researcher at Colby College observes how far apart people stand from each other at a party. This is an example of the use of (a) physical traces; (b) simple observations; (c) contrived observations; (d) archival records.

9. A researcher at the University of Colorado at Denver reports that marriage rates are associated with the size of the city. She obtained both the marriage rates and the population estimates from government statistics available in the library. This is an example of the use of (a) physical traces; (b) simple observations; (c) contrived observations; (d) archival research.

10. Which of the following is not an unobtrusive measure? (a) physical traces; (b) simple observations; (c) contrived observations; (d) interviewing people

Discussion Questions for Review

1. An Iowa State student is given the task of describing two possible uses of archival measures not mentioned in this chapter. Can you suggest some possibilities?

2. An Arizona State student wants to test the hypothesis that people's level of aggression predicts their preference of sports; that is, more aggressive people like more aggressive sports. How might the student test this hypothesis using nonreactive measures?

3. A Towson State student wants to use content analysis to study the comic pages in the *Baltimore Sun*. Can you think of a particular hypothesis to guide the data collection? What steps would you advise the student to take in carrying out her study?

4. A Fitchburg State College student wants to do a participant-observer study of tourists and local residents

in Provincetown. What advice would you give him about systematizing his observations?

5. A student at the University of Massachusetts at Boston wants to illustrate the application of methodological triangulation to the question of whether inhaling cigarette smoke is unhealthy. Can you help by giving an example of a descriptive, a relational, and an experimental study, all addressing the same question?

6. An Ohio State University student has found that teachers' ratings of their students' intellectual abilities are highly correlated with the students' IQ test scores and concludes that this correlation reflects the effects of teachers' expectations on students' intellectual performance. What might be a plausible rival hypothesis to that interpretation?

Answers to Review Questions

Multiple-Choice Questions

1. b	3. d	5. c	7. a	9. d
2. c	4. d	6. b	8. b	10. d

Discussion Questions

1. Archival materials could be used as follows: to learn the "effects" of legislation on some outcome behavior (e.g., drunk driving) by comparing the change in behavior in states (or counties) that have enacted new laws with the change in behavior in states that have not enacted new laws; to predict legislators' votes from an analysis of their past votes or the style of communication revealed in their earlier speeches; to predict future intelligence, personality, and psychopathology from archived early-childhood drawings.

2. The student could correlate the frequency of reported fights, stampedes, and riots with the aggressiveness of various sports as defined by the average number of injuries per player sustained in each sport.

3. The student could examine the hypothesis that comic strips featuring children are designed for a younger readership. The mean word length in comic strips featuring children could be compared to the mean word length in comic strips not featuring children. The student should check the reliability of two judges' (a) classifying the strips as featuring or not featuring children and (b) counting the word lengths and computing their average. The student might also want to sample the comic strips over a period of several weeks or months.

4. The most important advice is that he should be clear about what he wants to learn from this research. He should pay heed to the problems of interpreter bias and observer bias.

5. A descriptive study may reveal a high rate of wheezing, coughing, illness, and death among those exposed to cigarette smoke. A relational study may show that those who are exposed to greater amounts of cigarette smoke suffer from higher rates of illness and death. An experimental study may show that animals experimentally exposed to higher dosages of cigarette smoke have higher rates of illness and death than do animals exposed to lower dosages.

6. A rival hypothesis might be that the teachers' ratings of their students' intellectual ability were nothing more than the teachers' accurate diagnosing of IQ. It would take an experimental manipulation of teachers' expectations to demonstrate that they played a causal role.

CHAPTER 5

Methods for Looking Within Ourselves

Preview Questions

- What are the uses and limitations of self-report measures?
- What are open-ended and fixed-choice items?
- How are personality and projective tests used?
- What is meant by measuring implicit attitudes?
- What are numerical, forced-choice, and graphic ratings?
- What are rating errors, and how are they controlled?
- What is the semantic differential method?
- What are Likert scales and Thurstone scales?
- How are items prepared for a questionnaire or an interview?
- How are face-to-face and telephone interviews done?
- How are behavioral diaries used in research?

 ### What Are the Uses and Limitations of Self-Report Measures?

Researchers who study human behavior not only watch and record, frequently calling on judges (raters or coders) to make systematic observations, but they also often ask people to look within themselves and disclose their own attitudes, feelings, perceptions, and beliefs in order to elicit a kind of information that is unique (Baldwin, 2000). These inner-directed observations are described as **self-report measures**, and their use in behavioral and social research goes back more than a century. In the formative years of psychology, experimental researchers had subjects reflect and verbally report on their sensations and perceptions (a process known as *introspection*). Later on, with the development of behavioral methodology, verbal reports fell out of favor in experimental psychology and were largely replaced by behavioral responses and observational methods.

Nonetheless, self-report is used quite regularly in many areas. When you go to the eye doctor to be fitted for glasses, after you are shown the letter chart you are shown a series of paired images and asked which of the two you find easier to see. When you go to your family doctor, you are asked how you feel. When an athlete experiences a sports-related head trauma, the symptoms that are checked at the time of the injury, then 2–3 hours, 24 hours, 48 hours, and 72 hours later (or until these, and all other, symptoms have cleared) include dizziness, drowsiness, feeling "in a fog," headache, nausea, and a ringing in the ears (Brody, 2009). Psychological researchers who use **standardized measures** (meaning that they were developed and are administered and scored according to certain rules, or standards) to study "subjective well-being" also ask the respondents how they feel (e.g., Diener, 2000). Many behavioral and social researchers use a variety of self-report

BOX 5.1 Personality Testing of Professional Athletes

Psychologists have shown that it is possible to estimate future performance in some occupations from well-constructed measures of normal personality, given to potential employees before employment (Hogan, Hogan, & Roberts, 1996). For example, an article in *The New York Times* reported that the Giants football organization gives its own personality test to prospective players, including asking them to answer true or false to statements like "When a person 'pads' an income tax report so as to get out of some taxes, it is just as bad as stealing money from the Government," and "I am often said to be hotheaded" (T. W. Smith, 1997, p. 11). According to the *Times* article, the prospective player's responses to these and other items are used to create a personality profile that is believed to be as informative as the required physicals.

measures in their work (A. A. Stone et al., 2000), including personality inventories (Box 5.1), opinion polls and attitude questionnaires, and procedures in which people are asked to reflect on their inner feelings or to "think aloud" (Ericsson & Simon, 1993). In pain research, self-report measures are used to gather specific information about the duration, intensity, and kind of pain (Turk & Melzack, 1992). Neuroscientists who are interested in identifying neural networks of physical and social experiences of pain and pleasure usually rely to some degree on the experiential feedback from the volunteer participants to identify and triangulate on sensations correlated with the observed brain activity (Lieberman & Eisenberger, 2009).

The purpose of this chapter is to acquaint you with a range of self-report methods and to discuss the uses and limitations of each. Most of the instruments described are readily available to student researchers, but some require supervised training and certification. If you are looking for a specialized psychological measure in the public domain to use in your research, a good place to begin is the *Directory of Unpublished Experimental Mental Measures,* edited by B. A Goldman, D. Mitchell, and their colleagues (1995, 1996, 1996, 1997, 2003). This series of volumes contains brief descriptions of several thousand noncommercial psychological instruments for use in research situations, including various measures of aptitude, attitude, concept meaning, creativity, personality, problem solving, status, and so on. Another huge database of information on questionnaires, interview schedules, checklists, coding schemes, and rating scales was developed by Evelyn Perloff. Called *Health and Psychosocial Instruments* (HaPI), it is available on the Ovid and EBSCO databases (host systems that also offer PsycINFO, discussed in Chapter 2). In this chapter, we also discuss different forms of rating scales, questionnaires designed to reveal implicit attitudes, the use of interviews and behavioral diaries, and rating errors and how they are controlled. In addition, we illustrate three traditional scaling procedures that use rating methods (the semantic differential, the Likert item-analysis procedure, and the Thurstone equal-appearing interval procedure).

When using self-report measures, there are four important issues to consider, one of which is the dependability of the resulting data. A basic assumption when self-report measures are used is that what people say about themselves is true and not merely a strategy to "look good." However, when people are apprehensive about being evaluated, their responses to questions are frequently evasive or not completely forthcoming. This anxious state is called **evaluation apprehension** (Rosenberg, 1969), and allowing people to respond privately (Schaeffer, 2000), anonymously (Thomas et al., 1979), or confidentially (Esposito, Agard, & Rosnow, 1984; Singer, Von Thurn, & Miller 1995) may reduce it. In Chapter 3, we mentioned that researchers can sometimes obtain a formal "certificate of confidentiality" to protect their participants' disclosures against unwarranted access, but the extent to which such a certificate can provide legal protection has not been established in the courts. In survey research, it has been reported that elaborate assurances of confidentiality increase respondents' expectation that questions concerning their opinions will touch on highly sensitive issues that they may be reluctant to talk about (Frey, 1986; Singer,

Hippler, & Schwarz 1992). In experiments in which the manipulation contains an element of surprise or has an aura of mystery, it has been reported that the level of evaluation apprehension may also be intensified (Rosenberg, 1969).

A second issue is the right to privacy. Research participants have the right to withhold information and the right not to have the information they disclose made public or used against them (Bersoff & Bersoff, 2000). Suppose we are studying young children or adolescents, and we learn that the child has a suicidal tendency or that the parents are abusing the child (LaGreca, 1990). Obviously the moral, clinical, and legal implications are profound. Because such situations are possible, a concern of ethicists is whether it is appropriate for a clinically untrained and inexperienced researcher (such as a college student) to ask people about such things as depression, anxiety, sexuality, and traumatic life experiences (Bersoff & Bersoff, 2000). As discussed in Chapter 3, proposed research is usually evaluated for its risks and benefits. Your instructor will be sensitive to ethical imperatives in behavioral and social research, particularly to potential conflicts that beginning researchers might not anticipate.

A third issue is whether self-report research participants, even the most well intentioned, can provide information that is as valid and reliable as other behavioral data. Some psychologists have argued that people simply cannot look within themselves nor have a clear sense of themselves apart from the immediate situation (Nisbett & Wilson, 1977). For example, it has been theorized that people have a general tendency to overvalue themselves. Cornell University psychologist David Dunning, coauthor of a detailed review of self-assessment measures (Dunning, Heath, & Suls, 2004), mentioned in an interview in the Association of Psychological Science's August 2005 *Observer* (p. 9) the finding that 94% of college professors who were questioned rated themselves as doing "above average" work! In other words, almost all those questioned saw themselves as above average, a result that defies statistical probability. As another example of the questionable validity of self-report data, parents who were interviewed as they were leaving an HMO immediately after their children had received one or more vaccinations mistakenly reported what had occurred a few minutes earlier (Willis, Brittingham, Lee, Tourangeau, & Ching, 1999). As an illustration of long-tem unreliability, in a longitudinal study men were asked about experiences they had reported 30 years earlier when they were adolescents (Offer, Kaiz, Howard, & Bennett, 2000). Whereas 61% of them as adolescents had reported that sports and other physical activities were their favorite pastimes, 23% of them, as adults, gave the same answer when asked to "recollect" their favorite pastimes. When they were young, 28% of them had reported that they disliked schoolwork, but 58% as adults "remembered" they hated it. As adolescents, 70% had said they found religion personally helpful, but as adults, only 26% of them remembered it the same way (see also Box 5.2).

A fourth issue has to do with the interpretation of individual scores. Suppose you propose to use a standardized test for which there are **norm-referenced** values for the respondents in some specified population (such as the Scholastic Assessment Test that many high school seniors take, and that is used by many colleges and universities in their selection process). By comparing your respondents' scores with those of the normative group, you can estimate the percentile in which each of your respondents' scores falls (more about percentiles in a later chapter). But what if you have constructed your own rating instrument? It might be misleading to compare the rating scores of one individual with those of another individual (Bartoshuk, 2002). Suppose Persons A and B independently rate the extent to which they are "feeling stressed" as 3 on a scale from 0 (no stress) to 7 (extreme stress). Although both have given the same response, how do you know that A's score means the same thing as B's? Suppose they have different thresholds of stress. On the other hand, if all you want to know is whether each person's feeling of stress changed over time, you have the original scores as base rates in a repeated-measures design (we have more to say about repeated-measures designs later in this book). Similarly, there is no problem if all you want to do is compare the average rating scores for stress in two randomly assigned groups, because we presume that randomly occurring differences (called *random errors* in the next chapter) will have a tendency to cancel out in the long run (Norwick, Choi, & Ben-Shachar, 2002).

BOX 5.2 The Seven Sins of Memory

Daniel L. Schacter (1999), a Harvard cognitive psychologist, described what he called the "seven sins of memory." Three of them refer to types of forgetting: (a) absent-mindedness, (b) the blocking out of certain information, and (c) the gradual deterioration of details over time. Another three refer to different kinds of distortions or inaccuracies: (d) attributing something to the wrong source, (e) unconscious biases due to stereotypes and prejudices, and (f) human suggestibility to implanted ideas. As a demonstration of (f), in Chapter 1 we mentioned the research of Stephen J. Ceci and his colleagues on children's eyewitness testimony, in which the researchers planted stereotypical information about someone named "Sam Stone." In another well-known study, Elizabeth F. Loftus (1975) experimented with the phrasing of questions that were asked subjects who had just been shown films of complex, fast-moving events such as automobile accidents or classroom disruptions. She found that simply planting false details about an object in those questions increased the likelihood that the subjects would later report having seen the objects. Finally, the seventh memory "sin" listed by Schacter refers not to forgetting or memory gaps, but to (g) the nagging persistence of images that are instantaneously, and seemingly forever, imprinted in some people's memories (such as the shocking images of September 11, 2001, which were imprinted in the memory of all those who watched the tragedy unfold on television). Schacter theorized that these seven sins of memory are like "spandrels," an architectural term referring to the leftover spaces in structural components of buildings, except that these memory spandrels are leftover effects gone astray in an evolutionary process that is imperfect.

What Are Open-Ended and Fixed-Choice Items?

All of the methods that are described in this chapter, whatever their limitations, have been used in basic and applied behavioral research. In fact, few people escape the opportunity to participate in one of these two types of research, although not everyone agrees to volunteer or to participate. Suppose you receive the following telephone call:

> Hello, is this _____? My name is _____, and I'm calling from the Survey Institute at Central University. We are conducting a short random survey to determine how people feel about gun control issues so that we can get a true picture of people's attitudes. It will only take about 5 minutes, and we would greatly appreciate your help. May I ask you some questions?

If you answer yes, you will be a participant in a study using self-report data to measure people's behavior or state of mind.

You will be read a series of questions and asked to say how you personally behave, feel, or think (Lavrakas, 1987). Some of the questions that you are asked may be **open-ended items**, so called because they offer you an opportunity to express your feelings and impressions spontaneously. The doctor's asking "How do you feel?" is an example of an open-ended question. Your answer not only gives the doctor a clue to *what* to observe or diagnose but also gives her or him a sense of how *you* (as an individual) experience things. In the telephone survey example, the researcher is looking for individual responses, although the goal is to generalize (cautiously) about similar individuals in some specified population. An example of an open-ended question that the researcher might ask is "How do you feel about the National Rifle Association?" When analyzing the data, the researcher will code the responses to this question and then correlate the coded data with the responses to other questions (another example of relational research).

Like any observational or self-report method, an open-ended format has advantages and disadvantages (Scott, 1968). The advantages of open-ended items is that (a) this method does not lead the respondent by suggesting specific answers; (b) the method is exploratory, allowing the researcher to find out whether the person has anything at all to say; and (c) the respondent can answer in his or her own language, which helps to increase rapport. The disadvantages of open-ended items are that (a) they are time-consuming for the researcher (who must record responses); (b) they may elicit rambling and off-the-mark responses that never actually touch on the topic the researcher is interested in; and (c) they may be hard to assess for reliability (discussed in the next chapter).

Thus, another approach is to use **fixed-choice items** (also known as *structured, precoded,* or *closed items*), which take their name from the fact that they use a more controlled format, giving the respondent specified options such as yes-no or multiple-choice alternatives. An example of a fixed-choice item is "How do you feel about a 10-day waiting period for permission to buy a gun? Would you say you are strongly in favor, moderately in favor, moderately against, or strongly against this idea?" A response that would not be read to the respondent is "Don't know," but if that is the spontaneous answer, the interviewer would note it down. In general, the advantages and disadvantages (or limitations) of fixed-choice items tend to be the reverse of open-ended items. For most researchers, the major advantage of the fixed-choice method is that it forces the respondents' answers into the dimensions of interest to the researcher rather than producing irrelevant answers (Scott, 1968). Later on, we will describe how open-ended and fixed-choice methods are used in personality inventories, attitude questionnaires, face-to-face and computer-assisted telephone interviews. The rule of thumb is that the measures chosen should match the dimensions of interest and the kind of information that is desired.

 ## How Are Personality and Projective Tests Used?

As ideas of personality have developed, from the time of Sigmund Freud to the present, methods of assessing various personality characteristics, particularly as part of the therapeutic process, have also evolved. Much of the early testing of personality consisted of diagnosing the mental state of the individual by examining that part of the personality relevant to therapy, a process that led to the development of a variety of personality measures. The particular configuration of an individual's personality is believed to have profound consequences for her or his behavior. Although there is disagreement about the factors that are most influential in a given situation, there is theoretical speculation that a small number of factors may transcend cultural differences (McCrae & Costa, 1997). That is, there is presumed to be a human universal in the structure of personality, similar to the universality of the human skeletal structure—even though individuals differ from one another in, for example, their girth and height (see also Box 5.3).

 ## BOX 5.3 OCEAN: The Big Five

Current thinking in personality assessment generally supports the idea of five broad domains of individual personality, often referred to as the **Big Five factors** (Goldberg, 1993; McCrae & Costa, 1997; Wiggins, 1996). The acronym *OCEAN* is an easy way to remember these five factors, although each factor may be made up of hundreds of specific traits:

1. *Openness to experience* (O), or the degree of imagination, curiosity, and creativity.

2. *Conscientiousness* (C), or the degree of organization, thoroughness, and reliability.

3. *Extraversion* (E), or the degree of talkativeness, assertiveness, and activity.

4. *Agreeableness* (A), or the degree of kindness, trust, and warmth.

5. *Neuroticism* (N), or the degree of nervousness, moodiness, and temperamentality.

Measures of the structure of personality take many different forms, including the use of open-ended and fixed-choice formats. One of the oldest psychological measures of personality is the **projective test**. This class of instruments, of which the **Rorschach test** is perhaps the most familiar example, uses an open-ended format. The Rorschach comprises 10 inkblots, shown one by one to the respondent in a standard order, each for as long as the respondent likes. The Rorschach test is open-ended because the presenter instructs the respondent to describe whatever he or she sees in the blot. The presenter keeps a verbatim record of everything the person says, also noting any peculiarity of facial expression or bodily movement. Once the person has responded to all the test plates, the task of scoring begins. The 10 test plates were originally created by psychiatrist Hermann Rorschach, who also provided a scoring method. Interpreting the Rorschach has been modified and expanded by other researchers over the years (e.g., S. J. Beck, Beck, Levitt, & Molish, 1961; Exner, 1993; Huprich, 2006; Kleinmuntz, 1982; I. B. Weiner, 2003). Scoring and interpreting the Rorschach calls for professionally supervised experience, so the Rorschach is out of the reach of undergraduate students doing research. Illustrative of its use in research was a study that used a scoring system that the researchers developed to assess the verbal responses of Japanese, Algerian Arabs, and Apache Native Americans in order to identify certain universal concepts and symbols (De Vos & Boyer, 1989). (We discuss the validity and reliability of the Rorschach test in the next chapter.)

Another classic open-ended projective test, but not as well known to the general public, is the **Thematic Apperception Test (TAT)**. Created by Henry Murray, the TAT consists of a number of picture cards of people in various life contexts, and the respondent is asked to make up a story explaining each picture. Because the situations depicted are adaptable to a large number of interpretations, different stories are appropriate. The cards include different subsets for men, women, boys, and girls. The stories the respondent tells are presumed to disclose the respondent's perception of interpersonal relationships. In a landmark study in personality research, David McClelland and his coworkers (McClelland, Atkinson, Clark, & Lowell, 1953) used the TAT to profile people who were high and low in the "need to achieve." The researchers asked college students to construct a story from TAT pictures. As each picture was presented, the student was asked: (a) What is happening? Who are the persons? (b) What has led up to this situation? That is, what has happened in the past? (c) What is being thought? What is wanted? By whom? and (d) What will happen? What will be done? Once the students had made up their stories, they were scored on the need for achievement. The researchers also used other tools of personality measurement to elicit the respondents' high and low levels of need for achievement. McClelland and his colleagues described the structure and intensity of the need for achievement in each respondent and also developed a model of situational factors that, they theorized, might increase or decrease a need for achievement.

A widely used psychological measure of personality, which you may also come across in your reading, is the **Minnesota Multiphasic Personality Inventory (MMPI)**. Using a fixed-choice format, the MMPI contains several hundred statements such as "I often cross the street to avoid meeting people," "I am afraid of losing my mind," "I believe I am no more nervous than most others," and "I have a great deal of stomach trouble." The test taker responds "true" or "false" to each statement. The statements were originally selected by researchers after studies had revealed which items best differentiated normal individuals from various types of psychiatric patients. Some statements were also selected to reflect general health, sexual attitudes, emotional states, and so on. From these statements, clinical scales were created, which are related to diagnostic categories such as depression, paranoia, and schizophrenia. Those taking the MMPI are usually scored on all scales, and the scores are then compared with those of normal control respondents (e.g., A. F. Friedman, Lewak, Nichols, & Webb, 2001). The tools described in the remainder of this chapter can be used routinely by most students (with the ethical stipulation noted previously), but the availability of the MMPI (like the Rorschach and the TAT) is restricted to testers who have had supervised training. (See Box 5.4 for an approach that is more generally available to all researchers.) (We discuss the validity and reliability of the MMPI in the next chapter.)

BOX 5.4 The Three Faces of Eve

Although access to the Rorschach test and the TAT is limited to those with supervised training and experience, there are (as cited at the beginning of this chapter) many instruments that are in the public domain. It is also possible to construct our own measures using the scaling procedures discussed in this chapter. One such procedure, discussed later in this chapter, is the *semantic differential*, which has been employed in a wide variety of experimental and applied contexts, including clarifying the meaning of the Rorschach and the TAT and as a diagnostic test. If you are an old movie buff who has seen the 1957 film *The Three Faces of Eve*, you will be particularly interested in a classic article by Osgood and Luria (1954)

in which they described how they used the semantic differential in a blind analysis of Eve's multiple personality. The article also contains a set of graphics resembling a Tinkertoy, where the circles are descriptive words, and the sticklike lines that connect the circles are the quantified psychological distances that Osgood and Luria calculated. The graphics are representations of each of Eve's purported three personalities ("Eve White," "Eve Black," and "Jane") based on her responses on a semantic differential created by the researchers for this specific research. If you enjoyed the old film, we think you will be fascinated by Osgood and Luria's interpretations of Eve's semantic-differential responses.

Students interested in learning more about professional testing principles will find a detailed discussion in a manual titled *Standards for Educational and Psychological Testing,* developed jointly by the American Educational Research Association (http://www.aera.net), the American Psychological Association (http://www.apa.org), and the National Council on Measurement in Education (http://www.ncme.org). Look for the latest edition of the manual, which is updated periodically and should be available in your library or through its interlibrary loan system. For further information about the manual, you can use your computer to search on the title or visit one of the Web sites listed above.

What Is Meant By Measuring Implicit Attitudes?

Among the various core constructs in the field of social psychology is the concept *attitude*. The terms *attitude* and *opinion* are often used interchangeably in ordinary conversation, but the traditional distinction between them in social psychology is that *opinions* are verbal entities that can be measured directly, whereas *attitudes* are inferred entities (see also Box 5.5). Experiments that are described as "attitude change" or "attitude formation" studies usually imply that the research attempted to influence participants' verbal or nonverbal behavior in some measurable way that is related to a presumed underlying attitude. One customary way for researchers to get a sense of attitudes is to ask people for their opinions on a controversial issue using an "attitude questionnaire." As illustrated later in this chapter, these questionnaires contain items designed to bring out explicit verbal responses (opinions) that reflect, and thereby presumably reveal, the person's underlying attitude.

A conventional attitude questionnaire is by no means a foolproof way of inferring a person's underlying attitude. What people are willing to disclose about themselves in a questionnaire may not be a true reflection of their attitudes because of the problem of evaluation apprehension (discussed earlier in this chapter). Also, as mentioned earlier, people cannot always easily look within themselves, nor do they have a clear sense of themselves apart from the immediate situation (Nisbett & Wilson, 1977). An alternative approach, developed by social psychologists Anthony G. Greenwald and Mahzarin R. Banaji (1995), is intended to measure what they called *implicit attitudes*—"manifest as actions or judgments that are under the control of automatically activated evaluation, without the performer's awareness of that causation" (p. 1464). To expose these implicit attitudes, Greenwald and Banaji's **Implicit Attitude Test (IAT)** focuses on people's automatic associations with certain target concepts and the time it takes to make these associations.

BOX 5.5 What Is an Attitude?

Since the 1930s and 1940s, social psychologists have generally conceptualized an *attitude* as a relatively enduring set of tendencies (or "mental readinesses") built around an idea that can lead to specific verbal and behavioral action (cf. Allport, 1935; Chein, 1948). Most social psychologists also still seem to proceed on the assumption that attitudes are comprised of three separate dimensions (or components)—called the *cognitive* (referring to people's beliefs and the way they see things), the *affective* (referring to the way a person evaluates things, or how the person feels about them), and the *conative* (referring to whether or not the person will be moved to act).

These three components are not always interrelated simply or consistently. A person might know very little about a controversial issue and yet have strong feelings, even to the point of demonstrating in favor or against one side. Another person might know a great deal about the issue and also have strong feelings about it, yet not act on that knowledge or those feelings. For instance, there is the old observation that many smokers, despite knowing the hazards of cigarette smoking, and the tendency to believe that cigarette smoking is harmful to health, nevertheless do comparatively little to change their behavior (Bernstein, 1969).

To give a sense of how the IAT works, Greenwald, McGhee, and Schwartz (1998) described a pair of thought experiments, each consisting of three tasks. First, imagine being shown a series of faces and asked to respond by saying "hello" if the face is male and "goodbye" if it is female. Next, imagine being shown a series of names, to which you are to respond "hello" if the name is male and "goodbye" if it is female. These are easy tasks so far. The third task is also easy to do. It simply alternates the other tasks, sometimes showing you a male or female face and sometimes a male or female name. All you need do is respond "hello" if the face or name is male and "goodbye" if the face or name is female.

Now imagine participating in a second experiment. The first task is the same. Again, you are shown a series of faces and asked to respond by saying "hello" if the face is male and "goodbye" if it is female. No problem so far. However, the second task is reversed. You are now shown the series of names, but you are to respond "goodbye" if the name is male and "hello" if it is female. Each task, by itself, is easy. But when mixed together so that faces and names alternate, the new final task is not easy. If you don't want to make mistakes, you will respond more slowly than in the first thought experiment. The nature of your responses, including the time it takes you to respond, is presumed to be an indicator of your *implicit attitude*. However, the best way for you to get a sense of the IAT approach is to go to https://implicit.harvard.edu/implicit/demo and try one of the tests yourself.

What Are Numerical, Forced-Choice, and Graphic Ratings?

Researchers who want to have people rate themselves (or to have judges rate others, as discussed in the previous chapter) often create their own **rating scales**. The most commonly used scales in behavioral and social research are the numerical and graphic kinds, but we will also describe a third kind, the forced-choice rating scale. Whether you are testing people and scoring the results yourself or are using a computer-assisted procedure, you will find these three types easy to use, easy to score, and widely applicable. Standardized questionnaires also typically use one of these three formats. Where there are response options that are labeled with **cue words** (guiding labels), it is prudent to give the respondent an example (illustrated later in this chapter).

Numerical scales, which are the most popular of these three types, take their name from the idea that respondents work with a sequence of defined numbers. The numbers may be stated for the person to see and use, or they may be implicit (e.g., 1 vs. 0 for "yes" vs. "no"). To illustrate, here is a 5-point item from a questionnaire that was designed to measure attitudes toward mathematics (Aiken, 1963):

My mind goes blank, and I am unable to think clearly when working with math.

_____strongly disagree

_____disagree

_____undecided

_____agree

_____strongly agree

In this example, the numbers are implicit rather than explicit. For instance, we can score *strongly disagree* as −2, *disagree* as −1, *undecided* as 0, *agree* as +1, and *strongly agree* as +2. Or we can score *strongly disagree* as 1, *disagree* as 2, *undecided* as 3, *agree* as 4, and *strongly agree* as 5. Either way, we will get equivalent results when we analyze the data. Notice in the item above that the respondent is given the option to answer "undecided" (neutral). However, some researchers prefer pushing respondents to one or the other side rather than giving them the neutral option, for example:

My mind goes blank, and I am unable to think clearly when working with math.

_____strongly disagree

_____disagree

_____agree

_____strongly agree

Most survey researchers regard neutral responses as a form of "missing data" that reduces their ability to detect statistical differences (Schuman & Presser, 1996). In the illustrative item above, the positive and negative scoring will remain the same, but there is no zero. Alternatively, we can score *strongly disagree* as 1, *disagree* as 2, *agree* as 3, and *strongly agree* as 4.

To illustrate the second form of rating scales, called **forced-choice scales**, suppose you were asked to respond to the following question:

Which characteristic *best* describes your best friend—honest or intelligent?

This question forces you to choose between two positive attributes (thereby implying that the one you did not choose is less characteristic of your friend). Because many people dislike having to make a forced choice, you might ask why use forced-choice scales at all? The answer is that they were created to overcome a type of response bias called the **halo effect** (Thorndike, 1920), which occurs when the person doing the rating of someone (the target person) forms a very favorable impression of the target person based on one central trait and extends that impression to the target person's other characteristics. For example, suppose a target person who is athletic and good-looking is judged to be far more popular than she or he really is. A numerical scale would allow the rater to pile up favorable scores, but on a forced-choice scale the rater is *required* to make a difficult choice.

The forced-choice format that seems to arouse the least antagonism (and produces the most valid results) presents four positively valenced options and asks respondents to select the two *most descriptive ones* in this group (Guilford, 1954). Suppose we are interested in evaluating a new incentive program designed to improve the reward system and morale in a company. As a way of experimentally assessing the effectiveness of the program, we expose a sample of workers (the experimental group) to a 1-month treatment condition and compare their reactions with those of other workers (the control group) who did not receive the experimental treatment. In the spirit of methodological pluralism, our dependent measures consist of self-ratings, ratings by managers, and nonreactive measures of performance, which we will use to triangulate on the effectiveness of the new program. Among the self-ratings are some forced-choice items, such as:

Circle the *two* characteristics that *best describe* how you feel in your work:

rewarded   relaxed   appreciated   trusting

Our hypothesis is that, if the incentive program has the effect of improving the reward system and morale, the experimental group is more likely than the control group to circle characteristics such as "rewarded" and "appreciated."

Finally, **graphic scales** are a third basic type of rating scale. A graphic scale is a straight line resembling a thermometer, presented either horizontally or vertically. It can be used as either an observational or a self-report tool (just as numerical and forced-choice scales can be used in both situations). For example, teachers might be asked to use the following items to rate each student in their homeroom (an observational method), or students might be asked to rate themselves (a self-report method):

Unpopular _____ Popular

Shy _____ Outgoing

Solitary _____ Gregarious

The respondent makes a check mark, and the scorer then transforms that mark into a number by placing a ruler under the line and reading the number from the ruler. Of course, it would be a lot easier to present the items on a computer screen so that the responding and scoring are both done more efficiently. Notice in this case that the items above are what would be described as *bipolar,* which in this context means that the cue words at the ends of these scales are extreme opposites. (Using bipolar items can be a problem, however, when respondents have mixed emotions about what they are rating. In that situation, we generally recommend that researchers use unipolar rather than bipolar items, where *unipolar* means that the scores run from a low amount to a high amount on a particular dimension.)

For scoring purposes, it is also usually preferable to divide the straight line into segments. In the case above, dividing the straight line into six segments would transform the "thermometer scale" into a numerical rating scale (also described as a *segmented graphic scale*):

Unpopular _____:_____:_____:_____:_____:_____ Popular

Shy _____:_____:_____:_____:_____:_____ Outgoing

Solitary _____:_____:_____:_____:_____:_____ Gregarious

Here, the researcher asks the teacher or student to make a decision that reflects only positively or negatively on the person being rated, because a scale with an even number of segments does not allow for an undecided response. This example is reminiscent of a forced-choice measure, except that it gives the person a range of positive and negative options.

 ## What Are Rating Errors, and How Are They Controlled?

The use of rating scales assumes that respondents are capable of an acceptable degree of rating precision and objectivity. In constructing questionnaires that use such measures, it is important to think about how to overcome certain **rating errors** (also called *response biases* or *rater biases*), such as the halo effect mentioned above. Some researchers have questioned the seriousness of the halo effect and whether it is as prevalent as earlier researchers claimed (Murphy, Jako, & Anhalt, 1993). Should it occur, it seems more likely to do so when the rater relies on global impressions rather than on recently observed behavior. Halo errors also seem more likely to occur when the rater is only casually acquainted with the person being rated, or when earlier judgments involve dimensions that are logically related to the rater's global evaluation of the person. Early research suggested other situations in which halo errors seem more likely to occur, such as when the trait or characteristic to be rated cannot be easily observed, or is not clearly defined, or involves relations with other people, or is of some moral importance (Symonds, 1925). When there is concern about halo effects, the forced-choice procedure is the traditional control. The Implicit Attitude Test is also thought to be a way of overcoming halo effects (Greenwald & Banaji, 1995).

For other suspected rating errors, statistical adjustments are often possible (Hoyt, 2000), but there are also simpler ways of attempting to overcome the biases by choosing or modifying a particular numerical or graphic rating scale. For example, another type of rating error is called **leniency bias** because it occurs when judges rate someone who is very familiar, or someone with whom they are ego-involved, in an unrealistically positive manner. If you were using a graphic scale, a way to overcome this bias would be to give only one unfavorable cue word (e.g., *poor*); the rest of the range is then made up of favorable responses in different degrees (e.g., *fairly good, good, very good, excellent*), as in the following extended scale:

Poor	Fairly good	Good	Very good	Excellent

However, you would treat or analyze the cue words numerically so that *Good* is only a 3 on a 5-point scale from *Poor* (scored 1) to *Excellent* (scored 5).

Another type of rating error, **central tendency bias**, occurs when respondents hesitate to give extreme ratings and instead cluster their responses around the center choice. This potential bias can be addressed in the same way that the positive range was expanded in the case above. Suppose you wanted to have a range of at least 5 points in a segmented-graphic scale, in which case you might use a 7-point scale, on the assumption that some respondents are reluctant to use the end points under any circumstances. Similarly, if you wanted to have a range of at least 7 points, you might use a 9-point scale.

Another circumstance is a rating scale used as a before-and-after measure. Suppose you want to use 5-point numerical or segmented-graphic scales as before-and-after measures (or "tests") in an experiment using a manipulation designed to move the participants' responses in a given direction. If the participants make extremely high or extremely low scores on the *pretest* (i.e., the measure taken before the manipulation), there will be a problem if you then want to produce further change in that direction. That is, you will have a **ceiling effect** or a **floor effect**, which restricts the amount of change that can be produced. You could try extending the ends of the scale after pilot-testing it, so that a 5-point scale becomes a 9-point or an 11-point scale. If you find no changes from pretest to posttest, you must make sure the data were not artificially restricted by a ceiling or floor effect, that is, that there really was no room for respondents to move their scores on the after measure.

In another type of response bias, the **logical error in rating**, the respondents give similar ratings for variables or traits that they themselves feel to be logically related but that may not occur together in the person being rated. This bias is similar, in a way, to the halo effect in that both erroneously intercorrelate variables or traits that are being rated. The difference between the two is that, in the halo effect, the respondent extends one favorable trait to the person as a whole, whereas in the logical error, the respondent interrelates certain variables or traits irrespective of the individual being rated. The standard way to overcome a logical error in rating is to construct very precise definitions and to make the instructions as explicit as possible.

In still another type of response bias, the **acquiescent response set**, some respondents (sometimes called *yea-sayers*) are overly agreeable. Rather than weighing each statement on its merits, they go along with almost any statement. If they are asked whether they agree or disagree with even the most unlikely item, they will almost invariably agree with it. This bias is addressed by the use of both anti and pro items so that the yea-sayers can easily be identified by their agreement with both types of items and dropped from the study or at least considered separately. In reporting the results, we would indicate the number of such respondents identified and how we decided to deal with them. Our expectation is that there will be few if any yea-sayers, although if there are many of them, we need to figure out why our questionnaire is so vulnerable to the acquiescent response set.

The examples above give a flavor of response biases and their control, but there are other possibilities as well. In the next chapter, we will describe classic research on "socially desirable responding," in which the person answering has a tendency to give responses that will make him or her look good. The MMPI, mentioned earlier in this chapter, has a set of items (called the *L Scale,* or *Lie Scale*) that was designed to identify respondents who are *trying* to appear socially desirable. Socially desirable responding was originally seen by researchers as simply a nuisance variable to be controlled or eliminated in some way (R. J. Fisher, 1993), but it is also viewed as a personality variable of interest in a wide variety of settings (Crowne, 1979; Nouri, Blau, & Shahid, 1995; Ones, Viswesvaran, & Reiss, 1996). We now turn to three traditional approaches that have often been used to develop specialized attitude questionnaires: the semantic differential method, the Likert method of item analysis, and the Thurstone equal-appearing intervals method.

 ## What Is the Semantic Differential Method?

In Box 5.4, we mentioned the **semantic differential method**, which was created for the study of the subjective (or representational) meaning of things (including any explicit or implicit entities) in an individual's experiential world (Osgood, Suci, & Tannenbaum, 1957). The semantic differential method uses a fixed-choice format with segmented-graphic scales. The developers of this method observed that most things in life (puppies, kittens, chairs, continents, ethnic groups, flowers, under-graduate majors, and so forth) tend to be universally perceived in terms of three primary dimensions of subjective meaning. Calling them *evaluation, potency,* and *activity,* the developers (Osgood et al., 1957) defined each of them in terms of bipolar cue words. Though they also isolated other dimensions, those other dimensions usually accounted for only a tiny portion of people's subjective associations. In some instances, however, one or more of those lesser dimensions (described as *stability, tautness, novelty,* and *receptivity*) might be highly relevant as well.

Suppose we wanted to compare potential voters' associations about two rival political candidates in terms of their respective evaluation, potency, and activity meanings to samples of different age groups and people's political affiliations. To tap into the evaluation dimension, we could choose from among the following statistically related bipolar anchors: *bad-good, unpleasant-pleasant, negative-positive, ugly-beautiful, cruel-kind, unfair-fair,* and *worthless-valuable.* To measure the potency dimension, we could choose from among *weak-strong, light-heavy, small-large, soft-hard,* and *thin-heavy.* For the activity dimension, any of the following could be used: *slow-fast, passive-active,* and *dull-sharp.* Incidentally, it has been informally observed that potency and activity tend to be conflated in people's minds in many instances, so that we may end up with an evaluation dimension and a conflated (potency-plus-activity) dimension. If we thought that one or more of the lesser dimensions might be relevant, we could choose from (a) *changeable-stable, intuitive-rational,* and *rash-cautious* for the stability dimension; (b) *rounded-angular, curved-straight,* and *blunt-sharp* for the tautness dimension; (c) *old-new, usual-unusual,* and *mature-youthful* for the novelty dimension; and (d) *tasteless-savory, boring-interesting,* and *insensitive-sensitive* for the receptivity dimension.

Suppose we chose one bipolar scale each for evaluation, potency, and activity and one bipolar scale each for stability and novelty, in which case our segmented-graphic scales might consist of the following:

Ugly _____:_____:_____:_____:_____:_____:_____ Beautiful

Soft _____:_____:_____:_____:_____:_____:_____ Hard

Dull _____:_____:_____:_____:_____:_____:_____ Sharp

Rash _____:_____:_____:_____:_____:_____:_____ Cautious

Old _____:_____:_____:_____:_____:_____:_____ New

We instruct the participants to rate each candidate by checking the appropriate space. To score people's responses, we assign numbers to their ratings as follows:

Dull _____:_____:_____:_____:_____:_____:_____ Sharp

$$-3 \quad -2 \quad -1 \quad 0 \quad +1 \quad +2 \quad +3$$

If we wanted to graph those results, we could compute the median (the midmost score) or the mean (both statistics are reviewed in Chapter 10) for each bipolar scale and then simply connect the medians or means by a line drawn from one median or mean to another. We would do this for each sampled group so it would be easy to compare them. We could do more in-depth statistical comparisons using the contrast procedures described later in this book (Chapter 14). In the next chapter, we will turn to reliability and validity in measurement. You will learn that increasing the number of items generally increases the *internal-consistency reliability* (defined in Chapter 6) of the instrument as a whole. With that concept in mind, we would probably want to choose more than just one bipolar scale for each dimension of interest to us.

Previously, we noted the importance of ensuring that the participants understand what each response category signifies, particularly when the segments in graphic scales are unlabeled. In the example, the numbers above stand for something like "extremely sharp candidate" (+3), "quite sharp candidate" (+2), "slightly sharp candidate" (+1), "neutral" (0), "slightly dull candidate" (−1), "quite dull candidate" (−2), and "extremely dull candidate" (−3). If these labels make sense to you in terms of the purpose of your study, then the rating scale will do. Figure 5.1 shows a typical set of instructions, based on those provided by the inventors of the semantic differential, which would appear on the front page of our questionnaire booklet. For the instructions in Figure 5.1, we have shifted the focus of our semantic differential study from political candidates to popular music groups. Suppose our interest is in comparing people's associations about some particular music groups in

The purpose of this questionnaire is to measure the *meanings* of some music groups to various people by having them judge these groups against a set of descriptive scales. We would like you to judge each group on the basis of what the group listed means *to you.* On each page of this booklet, you will find a different group to be judged and beneath it a set of scales. You are to rate the group on each of these scales in order.

If you feel that the group at the top of the page is *very accurately described* by the word at one end of the scale, place your check mark as follows:

Dull _____ : _____ : _____ : _____ : _____ : _____ : _✔_ Sharp
                                    or
Dull _✔_ : _____ : _____ : _____ : _____ : _____ : _____ Sharp

If you feel that the group is quite (but not extremely) *accurately described* at one end of the scale, place your check mark as follows:

Dull _____ : _____ : _____ : _____ : _✔_ : _____ Sharp
                                    or
Dull _____ : _✔_ : _____ : _____ : _____ : _____ : _____ Sharp

If the group seems *only slightly described* by one end as opposed to the other end (but is not really neutral), place your check mark as follows:

Dull _____ : _____ : _____ : _____ : _✔_ : _____ : _____ Sharp
                                    or
Dull _____ : _____ : _✔_ : _____ : _____ : _____ : _____ Sharp

The placement of your check, of course, depends on which of the two ends of the scale seems more descriptive of the music group you are judging. If you see the group as *neutral* on the scale (that is, if both ends of the scale are *equally descriptive* of the group), or if the scale is *completely irrelevant* (that is, unrelated to the group), place your check mark in the middle space:

Dull _____ : _____ : _____ : _✔_ : _____ : _____ : _____ Sharp

Figure 5.1   Semantic differential instructions.

terms of their respective evaluation, potency, and activity meanings. Notice that these instructions incorporate a number of examples so that the respondents will know what each check mark is intended to represent. In reporting the results, we can create profiles of the groups being rated by showing the median ratings on each dimension (evaluation, potency, and activity) or on each pair of adjectives. For example, marketing researchers have used the semantic differential procedure to develop profiles of products and advertising campaigns. Incidentally, if you are able to find an old book by Snider and Osgood (1969), it contains articles that describe interesting ways in which semantic differential results have been presented and interpreted in the past.

What Are Likert Scales and Thurstone Scales?

The semantic differential method gives us a *multidimensional* picture of what is being scaled, as there are usually the three principal dimensions of evaluation, potency, and activity and sometimes one or more of the lesser dimensions (stability, tautness, novelty, or receptivity). Another traditional scaling procedure, the **summated ratings method**, gives a *one-dimensional* picture of attitudes on controversial issues. The summated ratings method was created by Rensis Likert in the 1930s; attitude questionnaires that are developed by this method are known as **Likert scales**. Some researchers use the expression "Likert items" to describe any 5-point numerical items ranging from *strongly agree* to *strongly disagree,* but this usage is misleading if the summated ratings method is not also used. Though most students will not have occasion to create their own Likert scales, it is useful to know how they are constructed in case you refer to a Likert questionnaire in your work.

The first step is to compose a large number of pro-and-con statements on the controversial issue. The second step is to give these statements to a sample of people from the target population, along with instructions to indicate their evaluations of each statement. Usually, these evaluations are made on a 5-point scale: *strongly agree, agree, undecided, disagree, strongly disagree.* The final step is for the researcher to sort through these data in order to select the best 20 or so statements for the Likert questionnaire. This selection involves computing the extent to which the responses to individual statements are correlated with the *total score* (the sum of all the items). Statements that correlate well with the total score are prospects for the final Likert questionnaire. The theory behind this item selection process is that statements that have low correlations with the total score will not be as good at discriminating between those people with positive attitudes and those with negative attitudes.

The result of using this method is illustrated in Figure 5.2. It shows a questionnaire that was pared down to 20 items (Mahler, 1953). Items 2, 4, 6, 9, 10, 11, 14, and 15 are in favor of a compulsory health program. Items 1, 3, 5, 7, 8, 12, 13, 16, 17, 18, 19, and 20 are opposed to a compulsory health program. When using this Likert scale, the researcher scores the responses to the pro-compulsory-health-program statements from 5 *(strongly agree)* to 1 *(strongly disagree).* For the anti-compulsory-health-program statements, the researcher reverses this scoring and instead scores the responses from 1 *(strongly agree)* to 5 *(strongly disagree).* A person's score is the sum of these weighted responses. Thus, a high score total indicates an accepting attitude toward a compulsory health program and a low score indicates an attitude opposed to a compulsory health program. In this example, the highest and lowest possible scores, respectively, are 100 (most strongly in favor of a compulsory health program) and 20 (most strongly against a compulsory health program).

Another traditional scaling procedure for constructing an attitude questionnaire was called the **method of equal-appearing intervals** by its developer, L. L. Thurstone (1929, 1929–1934). It takes its name from the idea that judges, who are asked to sort statements into different piles, are able to keep the piles psychologically equidistant. Attitude questionnaires developed by this method are often known as **Thurstone scales**. Thurstone also invented other scaling methods and conceptualized theoretical rationales for all these methods, and his ideas have been absorbed into modern scaling methodology and theory (a field known as *psychometrics*). However, when you see

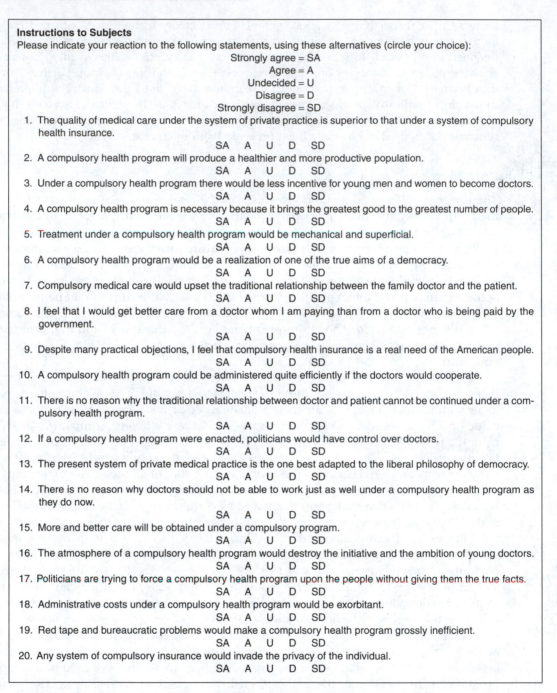

Instructions to Subjects

Please indicate your reaction to the following statements, using these alternatives (circle your choice):

Strongly agree = SA

Agree = A

Undecided = U

Disagree = D

Strongly disagree = SD

1. The quality of medical care under the system of private practice is superior to that under a system of compulsory health insurance.

   SA   A   U   D   SD

2. A compulsory health program will produce a healthier and more productive population.

   SA   A   U   D   SD

3. Under a compulsory health program there would be less incentive for young men and women to become doctors.

   SA   A   U   D   SD

4. A compulsory health program is necessary because it brings the greatest good to the greatest number of people.

   SA   A   U   D   SD

5. Treatment under a compulsory health program would be mechanical and superficial.

   SA   A   U   D   SD

6. A compulsory health program would be a realization of one of the true aims of a democracy.

   SA   A   U   D   SD

7. Compulsory medical care would upset the traditional relationship between the family doctor and the patient.

   SA   A   U   D   SD

8. I feel that I would get better care from a doctor whom I am paying than from a doctor who is being paid by the government.

   SA   A   U   D   SD

9. Despite many practical objections, I feel that compulsory health insurance is a real need of the American people.

   SA   A   U   D   SD

10. A compulsory health program could be administered quite efficiently if the doctors would cooperate.

    SA   A   U   D   SD

11. There is no reason why the traditional relationship between doctor and patient cannot be continued under a compulsory health program.

    SA   A   U   D   SD

12. If a compulsory health program were enacted, politicians would have control over doctors.

    SA   A   U   D   SD

13. The present system of private medical practice is the one best adapted to the liberal philosophy of democracy.

    SA   A   U   D   SD

14. There is no reason why doctors should not be able to work just as well under a compulsory health program as they do now.

    SA   A   U   D   SD

15. More and better care will be obtained under a compulsory program.

    SA   A   U   D   SD

16. The atmosphere of a compulsory health program would destroy the initiative and the ambition of young doctors.

    SA   A   U   D   SD

17. Politicians are trying to force a compulsory health program upon the people without giving them the true facts.

    SA   A   U   D   SD

18. Administrative costs under a compulsory health program would be exorbitant.

    SA   A   U   D   SD

19. Red tape and bureaucratic problems would make a compulsory health program grossly inefficient.

    SA   A   U   D   SD

20. Any system of compulsory insurance would invade the privacy of the individual.

    SA   A   U   D   SD

Figure 5.2   A Likert Scale to Measure Attitudes Toward a Compulsory Health Care System.

Source: I. Mahler, *Journal of Social Psychology* (1953), 38. Taylor & Francis Group. http://www.informa.com. Used with permission.

some reference to a "Thurstone attitude scale," you can usually assume that the writer means the questionnaire was constructed by the method of equal-appearing intervals.

This method also begins with a large number of statements. Before the invention of personal computers, the statements were usually printed on index cards and then judges (not the people to be given the questionnaire) would be asked to sort the statements into 11 piles, numbered from 1

Instructions to Subjects

This is a study of attitudes toward war. Below you will find a number of statements expressing various degrees of attitudes toward war or tendencies to act in case of war.

In expressing your agreement or disagreement with the statements, please put yourself in three possible situations. First, imagine that the United States had declared a *Defensive War* (war for the purpose of defending the United States in case of an attack). Please indicate in the first set of parentheses, designated by Roman numeral I, your agreement, disagreement, or doubt. Put a check mark (✓) if you agree with the statement, put a minus sign (−) if you disagree with the statement, and a question mark (?) if you are in doubt about the statement.

Second, imagine that the United States has declared a *Cooperative War* (war in cooperation with the democratic countries of Europe for the defense of democracy). Go over the statements again and indicate in the second set of parentheses, designated by Roman II, your agreement, disagreement, or doubt in a similar way.

Third, imagine that the United States has declared an *Aggressive War* (war for the purpose of gaining more territory). Read the statements again and indicate in the third set of parentheses, designated by Roman III, your agreement, disagreement, or doubt by a similar method.

I	II	III	
( )	( )	( )	1. I would support my country even against my convictions.
( )	( )	( )	2. I would immediately attempt to find some technicality on which to evade going to war.
( )	( )	( )	3. I would immediately go to war and would do everything in my power to influence others to do the same.
( )	( )	( )	4. I would rather be called a coward than go to war.
( )	( )	( )	5. I would offer my services in whatever capacity I can.
( )	( )	( )	6. I would not only refuse to participate in any way in war but also attempt to influence public opinion against war.
( )	( )	( )	7. I would take part in war only to avoid social ostracism.
( )	( )	( )	8. I would not go to war unless I were drafted.
( )	( )	( )	9. If possible, I would wait a month or two before I would enlist.
( )	( )	( )	10. I would go to war only if my friends went to war.
( )	( )	( )	11. I would refuse to participate in any way in war.
( )	( )	( )	12. I would disregard any possible exemptions and enlist immediately.
( )	( )	( )	13. I would not enlist but would give whatever financial aid I could.

Figure 5.3   A Thurstone Scale to Measure Attitudes Toward Three Types of War.

Source: From "Attitudes Toward Defensive, Cooperative, and Aggressive War", D. Day, O.F. Quackenbush, *Journal of Social Psychology* (1942) Heldref Publications. Copyright © 1942 Taylor & Francis Group. Used with permission. http://www.informaword.com

(labeled "most unfavorable statements") to 11 ("most favorable statements"). The judges would be allowed to place as many statements as they wish in any pile. A *scale value* would be calculated for each statement, usually defined as the median of the responses of all the judges to that statement. In selecting statements for the final questionnaire, the idea is to try to choose statements (a) that are most consistently rated by the judges and (b) that are spread relatively evenly along the entire attitude range.

Shown in Figure 5.3 is an attitude questionnaire that, although developed many years ago, is still topical (Day & Quackenbush, 1942). If you were administered this questionnaire as a respondent, you would be asked to reply to each statement three times, that is, once for each type of war described in the instructions. Another team of researchers (Shaw & Wright, 1967) obtained scale values for these 13 items by having 15 women and 35 men respond to each statement; these values are shown in Table 5.1. The lowest scale value (0.8 for Statement 3) corresponds to what was described as the most pro-militaristic item, and the highest scale value (8.4 for Statement 6) to the most anti-militaristic item in this set. The researcher would calculate the median scale value of statements checked by the respondent for each type of war (defined in the scale as defensive, cooperative, and aggressive). The higher the median, presumably the more unfavorable the respondent's attitude toward that particular type of war. For example, if a respondent checks Statements 2, 4, 6, and 11 under Roman numeral I, it is presumed that the person is very strongly opposed to defensive war (median = 8.05, or midway between the scale values of 7.9 for Statement 4 and 8.2 for Statement 11).

Table 5.1	Scale Values for the Questionnaire in Figure 5.3		
Statement	Scale value	Statement	Scale value
1	2.5	8	5.9
2	7.5	9	4.6
3	0.8	10	5.1
4	7.9	11	8.2
5	2.5	12	1.4
6	8.4	13	3.5
7	6.3			

Note: The scale values are median scores (or midmost values), based on the responses of 15 men and 35 women to each particular item (Shaw & Wright, 1967).

 ## How Are Items Prepared for a Questionnaire or an Interview?

In developing a questionnaire—as much as in developing an interview (discussed next)—pilot testing is absolutely essential. This testing enables the researcher to determine whether the items are worded properly, for example, whether terms like *approve* and *like* (or *disapprove* and *dislike*) are being used as synonyms or whether there are differences in implication. Suppose that a company president wants to examine a team of workers' opinions of the quality of a manager's job performance, and the president directs that a fixed-choice item be phrased as follows: "How do you feel about the manager? ____I like the manager. ____I dislike the manager." The item is useless because it does not distinguish between liking and approving. It is possible to like someone without approving of his or her job performance, and vice versa (Bradburn, 1982).

If you were assigned the job of writing items, you would also have to be sure that the wording and presentation of your items do not lead the respondent into giving an unrealistically narrow answer. A poor question will produce a very narrow range of responses or will be misunderstood by respondents. Take the following item: "Do you approve of the way the manager is handling her duties? ____Yes. ____No." Respondents might approve of the way the manager handled one crisis but not another, or they might disapprove of the way the manager handled the dress code but not the rumor about possible layoffs. Thus, a number of different items are needed to cover the various issues on which you want an opinion about the manager's effectiveness, and the issues must be spelled out if you are to avoid misunderstanding on the part of the respondents. Suppose the dress code crisis was resolved amicably, but the layoff crisis involved union confrontations. You will need a separate question, or set of questions, regarding each situation and whether the respondent approved or disapproved of the way each was handled.

You must also avoid asking *leading questions* (items that "lead" the respondent to answer in a particular way), because they can constrain responses and produce biased answers. An example of a leading question is "Do you agree that the manager has an annoying, confrontational style? ____Yes. ____No." The phrasing of the question practically directs the respondent to be overly negative or critical. How should the question be properly phrased? It depends on what you are trying to find out. However, in coming up with an alternative, you need to be sure that the new item is not worded so as to produce another meaningless answer: "Do you agree with the manager's work philosophy? ____Yes. ____No." What would a "yes" or "no" really tell you? You need to be more precise and specific, and also to do some probing to get meaningful information.

Problems such as these can be identified during the pilot testing and can often be resolved with rewording or with a set of probing items instead of a single item. The issue of whether to use open-ended or more structured items (or a combination of both) can also be answered by pilot testing. Like personality measures, the questionnaires used by many survey researchers come in a variety of open and fixed-choice formats. The latter may, for example, comprise multiple-choice, yes-no, either-or, or acceptable-unacceptable items. A fill-in-the-blank form may be useful when more specific, unprompted responses are sought. Of course, these structured forms are effective only if the material to be covered allows this amount of simplification.

In your pilot testing, you might think about asking exploratory questions such as "What did the item mean to you?" "What was it you had in mind when you said '_____'?" "Consider the same question this way, and tell me what you think of it: _____." "You said '_____,' but would you feel differently if the question read '_____'?" (Converse & Presser, 1986, p. 52). It is also important that the answers elicited reflect what the respondent really feels or believes. As a rule, people have not thought very much about most issues that do not affect them directly or immediately; their answers may reflect a superficial understanding, or they may try to "put on a good face." Thus, survey researchers may also ask the respondent how he or she feels about a topic (e.g., "How *deeply* do you feel about it?"). In this way, they attempt to determine whether the respondent believes what he or she has reported (Labaw, 1980). Still another technique is to ask respondents to rate their confidence in their answer so that they might reveal how much they are guessing.

If you plan to use open-ended questions, a method that was designed to prevent vague, rambling, irrelevant responses is the **critical incident technique** (Flanagan, 1954). It involves having the respondent describe an observable action the purpose of which was fairly clear to the respondent and the consequences sufficiently definite to leave little doubt about its effects. A typical use of this technique would begin with the interviewer saying something like "We are making a study of [specific activity], and we believe you are especially well qualified to tell us about this activity." The interviewer next asks, "What would you say is the primary purpose of [specific activity]?" and "How would you summarize the general aim of this activity?" Then the respondent is asked to think of the last time that he or she was personally involved in this activity and to describe exactly what transpired. For example, a team of researchers used this technique in a study of company managers in the United States and India who were interviewed as part of an investigation of how managers usually tend to cope with destructive rumors (DiFonzo, Bordia, & Rosnow, 1994). Managers were asked to describe as concretely and fully as possible an actual situation that had been important to their company and they had been required to confront a harmful or a potentially harmful rumor. The data revealed some circumstances in which rumor control strategies are likely to succeed and that were also found to be consistent with empirically-based theorizing. If you would like to use the critical incident technique, we suggest you read a classic article by John Flanagan (1954), the inventor of this technique, which gives a more detailed example and a rationale for its use.

How Are Face-to-Face and Telephone Interviews Done?

Before we turn to the **face-to-face interview**, it is also important for those who are thinking of using interviews and questionnaires to have a sense of their relative advantages. Advantages of using questionnaires are that (a) they can be efficiently administered to large numbers of people (e.g., in mail surveys, assuming that they will be mailed back to you); (b) they are relatively economical (a mail survey eliminates travel time and cost); and (c) they provide a type of "anonymity" (instead of meeting the researcher face to face, the respondent may be instructed to return the completed survey, for example, to an impersonal research center). Advantages of using a face-to-face interview are that (a) it provides an opportunity to establish rapport and to stimulate the trust and cooperation needed to explore sensitive issues; (b) it provides an opportunity to clarify questions (if the participant is confused); and (c) it allows flexibility in determining the wording and sequence of questions by giving the researcher greater control (e.g., by letting the interviewer determine on the spot the amount of probing required).

Just as researchers who use questionnaires need to do pilot testing, researchers who use an **interview schedule** (the script containing questions to be asked in the interview) should always try it out before actually implementing the study full scale. This pilot testing and all the planning that precedes it typically involve four steps: (a) thinking about the study's objectives and any specific questions or hypotheses to be addressed; (b) deciding how the interviewees will be recruited; (c) outlining and structuring the interview schedule; and (d) testing the interview schedule and making appropriate revisions. The first step is self-explanatory. The second step is a matter of defining the population to which we want to generalize, and then devising a plan for recruiting a representative sample from that population (discussed in more detail in Chapter 9). In the final step (pilot testing), the researchers interview a few people from the target population and listen *analytically* to their responses to each item (Downs, Smeyak, & Martin, 1980). Good interviewers will have good listening skills. That is, good interviewers are patient, hear the facts, and do not jump in or interrupt before the person being interviewed has developed an idea (Weaver, 1972).

The third step (structuring the interview schedule) needs a little more explanation because it involves writing the items and checking each one for relevancy, determining ranges of responses for some fixed-choice items, and establishing the best sequence and wording of questions. Each item or question should be carefully considered for its bearing on the specific hypotheses or the exploratory aims of the study. Because fatigue or boredom is apt to set in during a tediously long interview, the interview schedule will require the pruning of undesirable or unnecessary items. If we need to know income levels, we will need to decide on ranges of responses rather than bluntly ask the interviewee for an exact amount. If we are planning to ask questions that rely on people's memories (e.g., critical incident questions), we want to make sure that we are not making unrealistic demands. A prominent researcher who has studied and written extensively about memory errors in survey research observed that effective jogs to a person's memory about a particular event are those that help the person to differentiate the event from others that might be brought to mind (Tourangeau, 2000). However, this researcher also cautioned that even the best cues to help people recall experiences cannot trigger the retrieval of a memory that was not fully or accurately stored in the person's memory in the first place.

The sequence in which the sets of questions should be presented also needs to be established. Specific questions appear to be less affected by what preceded them than are general or broadly stated questions (Bradburn, 1982; Schuman & Presser, 1996). When sensitive issues are touched on, it is usually better to ask these questions at the end of the interview. People may view questions about their age, education, and income as an invasion of their privacy. When asked at the beginning of an interview, questions like these may interfere with the establishment of trust. Even when they are asked at the end of the interview, it is helpful to preface such questions with a reassuring statement. In one study, the interviewer was unusually candid: "Some of the questions may seem like an invasion of your privacy, so if you would rather not answer any question, just tell me it's none of my business" (C. Smith, 1980). The researcher also needs to work out the best wording of the items to ensure that all the interviewees understand the wording in equivalent ways. The final step (pilot testing) should reveal what jargon and expressions are "inhibitors" and "facilitators" of understandable communication. Especially important will be the phrasing of the opening question, which should show the person immediately that the interviewer is pursuing the stated purpose. As noted in Chapter 3, we also want to be as open and honest as possible with the respondents, just as we want them to be open, honest, and forthcoming in their responses.

Beginning back in the 1960s, several factors led many researchers in the United States to turn to the **telephone interview** and the mail survey as substitutes for the face-to-face interviews used in household surveys. Among the factors contributing to this shift were (a) the increased costs of conducting face-to-face interviews; (b) the invention of random digit-dialing methods for random (area probability) sampling of land-line telephone households; and (c) the development of computer-assisted methods of recording responses (called *computer-assisted telephone interviewing*, CATI), in which questions are flashed on a computer screen and the interviewer directly keys in responses for computer scoring (Rossi, Wright, & Anderson, 1983; Saris, 1991).

Like all research methods, telephone interviewing has advantages and limitations (Downs et al., 1980; Lavrakas, 1987; P. V. Miller & Cannell, 1982). Among the various advantages are that it allows a quick turnaround (information is obtained immediately rather than waiting to discover whether a mailed questionnaire will be returned). It has been reported that refusal rates are usually lower in telephone interviewing than when households are canvassed by field interviewers. A problem with telephone interviewing is that many people use only mobile phones, but using area probability sampling is restricted to households that have a land-line telephone linked to a specific geographical location. Another problem is that telephone interviewing is, of course, restricted to those that answer the phone, instead of having an answering machine or a caller ID constantly on duty to screen calls. It is also harder to establish rapport in a telephone interview. As a result, fewer questions, and less probing questions, can be asked of people who tend to be impatient to conclude the telephone interview. In large-sample surveys, however, the advantages of using telephone interviewing, particularly CATI, could far outweigh other options (cf. Groves & Mathiowetz, 1984; Watson, Firman, Heywood, Hauquitz, & Ring, 1995).

Whether telephone or face-to-face interviewing is used, similar procedures are used in developing an interview schedule and training interviewers. As noted above, a telephone interviewer has less time to establish rapport; the person who is called can always hang up without listening to the full introduction. If the person does not immediately hang up, then a strategy used to foster "commitment" on the part of the person is to point out the important goals of the research and to use positive feedback to reinforce what the researcher perceives as good responding: "Thanks…this is the sort of information we are looking for in this research…it's important to us to get this information…these details are helpful" (P. V. Miller & Cannell, 1982, p. 256).

 ## How Are Behavioral Diaries Used in Research?

As we said before, a nagging problem in self-report measures is that autobiographical questions may yield inaccurate answers when the participants are asked to rely on memory (e.g., how often they have done something or how much of something they have bought or consumed). Some examples are "How many weeks have you been looking for work?" and "How much have you paid for car repairs over the previous year?" As previously discussed in Box 5.2, problems surface because the storing of events in memory is fallible, memory is porous, recall is limited, and people fill in the gaps of what they cannot retrieve (H. B. Bernard & Killworth, 1970, 1980; Reed, 1988; D. L. Schacter, 1999; A. A. Stone et al., 2000; Tourangeau, 2000; Webber, 1970; Zechmeister & Nyberg, 1982). Suppose we want to study lying in everyday life. If we ask people to estimate, for example, the number of "little white lies" they tell each day, the results can hardly be considered valid because of all the factors mentioned above and also the respondents' possible wish to give a socially desirable response.

An innovative tool that is thought by its users to overcome the various memory problems is the **behavioral diary** (Conrath, 1973; Wickesberg, 1968). The basic procedure is to ask people to keep diaries of certain events at the time they occur. As an illustration, social psychologists Bella M. DePaulo and Deborah A. Kashy, and their coworkers used this method in studies of the lies that college students tell (DePaulo & Kashy, 1998; DePaulo, Kashy, Kirkendol, Wyer, & Epstein, 1996; Kashy & DePaulo, 1996). The participants in this research were asked to keep meticulous records of their lying. Assuming that the records they turned in were truthful, the findings were quite revealing. For example, people who indicated they had told more lies were also found to be more manipulative and more concerned about self-presentation and, not surprisingly, to have told more self-serving lies.

As another illustration, Csikszentmihalyi and Larson (1984) used this tool to study teenagers' day-to-day lives. The participants in this study were 75 teenagers who were given beepers and were then signaled at random by the researchers. When the beeper went off, the teenager was supposed to record his or her thoughts and feelings at that moment. Collating this information with what the teenager was doing at that moment (e.g., viewing TV, eating, being in class) was used to reveal mood swings from happiest to unhappiest as the teenager tried to cope with everyday events.

Researchers who use this method assume that such a diary gives more reliable data than questionnaires or interviews that elicit answers to autobiographical questions. To evaluate this assumption, a team of researchers (Conrath, Higgins, & McClean, 1983) collected data from managers and staff personnel in three diverse organizations (a manufacturer of plastic products, an insurance brokerage company, and a large public utility). Each participant in this study was instructed to keep a diary of 100 consecutive interactions, beginning on a specific date and at a specific time. The instructions were to list the other party to the interaction, the initiator of the activity, the mode of interaction, the elapsed time, and the process involved. The diary was constructed in such a way that the participant could quickly record all this information with no more than four to eight check marks next to particular items. At a later time, each participant was asked to answer a questionnaire covering the same interactions.

The data from all the behavioral diaries and questionnaires were compared afterward. If one person reported talking to others, the researchers checked the diaries and questionnaires of those others to see whether they had also reported that activity. In this way, a separate measure of reliability was obtained for the behavioral diary and for the questionnaire data (i.e., concerning the reporting of specific events at the time of the events as opposed to a later time). The results were that the questionnaire data (the recalls from autobiographical memory) were less reliable than the behavioral diary data. In spite of these encouraging results, other researchers have challenged the accuracy of diary information and have argued that the participants may be overly attentive to events that "stick out" in their minds and may underreport other behavior (Maurer, Palmer, & Ashe, 1993). Nonetheless, it is another interesting method that, in conjunction with observational methods, might be used to triangulate on the behavior in question.

Summary of Ideas

1. Four fundamental issues in the use of *self-report measures* concern (a) the truthfulness of what people report, especially when the information is personal and sensitive; (b) the ethical and potentially risky implications of such information, particularly when the researchers have not been professionally trained; (c) the validity of information that depends on remembering some past event (Schacter's "seven sins of memory" in Box 5.2); and (d) the comparison of people's scores when individual sensitivities or thresholds of response are so different that cue words on rating scales mean different things to different people.

2. Two forms of self-report measures are those that allow respondents to express their feelings and impressions quite spontaneously (*open-ended)* and those that use a structured format with precoded response options (*fixed-choice);* the general advantages and limitations of open-ended measures are essentially the reverse of the advantages and limitations of fixed-choice measures.

3. The *Big Five factors* of personality (OCEAN) are openness to experience, conscientiousness, extraversion, agreeableness, and neuroticism (Box 5.3).

4. The *Rorschach inkblot test* and the *TAT* (which are both open-ended measures) operate on the principle that, in the spontaneous responses that come to mind, respondents will project some unconscious aspect of their life experience and emotions onto ambiguous stimuli. The *MMPI* (which has a fixed-choice format) contains hundreds of statements to which the respondent answers true or false.

5. An attitude (see Box 5.5) is an example of a construct (defined in Chapter 2), as is the concept of prejudice. Greenwald and Banaji's *Implicit Attitude Test (IAT)* methodology focuses on the automatic associations that people make with target concepts and the time it takes them to make such associations. This method was designed to ferret out implicit attitudes that people may be reluctant to disclose in a traditional attitude questionnaire (such as their prejudices).

6. Three kinds of popular *rating scales* are the *numerical* (in which the numbers may be implicit or explicit), the *forced-choice* (which was developed to overcome the *halo effect*), and the *graphic* (resembling a thermometer that may or may not be segmented).

7. Other *rating errors* (besides the halo effect) include the *error of leniency,* the *error of central tendency,* the *logical error in rating,* and the *acquiescent response set*—each of which can be controlled in a particular way by the choosing or modifying of a numerical or graphic rating scale. When a rating scale is used as a before-and-after measure, it is quite important for the researcher to be sensitive to possible *ceiling effects* and *floor effects* that can restrict the amount of change that might otherwise naturally occur.

8. The *semantic differential* method was invented to measure the multidimensional subjective meaning of things in a person's experiential world. It uses a fixed-choice format and bipolar anchors that take the form of *segmented graphic scales* (see Figure 5.1). The three primary dimensions, those most commonly measured, are *evaluation, potency,* and *activity* (potency and activity are often conflated into a single dimension), but there are also lesser dimensions (*stability, tautness, novelty,* and *receptivity*) that may be relevant in some situations.

9. *Likert's method of summated ratings* is used to construct a one-dimensional numerical attitude scale (such as the Likert attitude scale in Figure 5.2, used to measure attitudes for and against a compulsory health program). *Thurstone's method of equal-appearing intervals* is another traditional scaling procedure that is used to construct one-dimensional attitude scales (such as the Thurstone attitude scale in Figure 5.3, used to measure attitudes toward defensive, cooperative, and aggressive war).

10. The purpose of pilot-testing a *questionnaire* or *interview schedule* is to enable the researcher to fine-tune the data collection instrument and procedures. Four steps in the development of an interview schedule are (a) working out the objective; (b) formulating a general strategy of data collection; (c) writing the questions and establishing the best sequence; and (d) pilot-testing the material.

11. The *critical incident technique* is a way of focusing open-ended responses by concentrating on an actual incident and asking the respondent a series of highly specific questions.

12. *Telephone interviews* first became popular because they were more cost-efficient than *face-to-face interviews* and could be implemented easily with *random digit-dialing* and computer-assisted interviewing and data-recording methods. Nowadays, the problem is that many people use mobile phones rather than land-line telephones, making it increasingly difficult for researchers to do telephone interviewing with representative (area probability) samples.

13. The *behavioral diary* records events as they happen, and there is no need to rely on longer term recall (e.g., the study about lying and the real-time study of teenagers' day-to-day lives).

Key Terms

acquiescent response set   p. 92
behavioral diary   p. 101
Big Five factors   p. 86
ceiling effect   p. 92
central tendency bias   p. 92
critical incident technique   p. 99
cue words   p. 89
evaluation apprehension   p. 83
face-to-face interview   p. 99
fixed-choice (structured)
   items   p. 86
floor effect   p. 92
forced-choice scales   p. 90
graphic scales   p. 91

halo effect   p. 90
Implicit Attitude
   Test (IAT)   p. 88
interview schedule   p. 100
leniency bias   p. 92
Likert scales   p. 95
logical error in rating   p. 92
method of equal-appearing
   intervals   p. 95
Minnesota Multiphasic Personality
   Inventory (MMPI)   p. 87
norm-referenced   p. 84
numerical scales   p. 89
open-ended items   p. 85

projective test   p. 87
rating errors   p. 91
rating scales   p. 89
Rorschach test   p. 87
self-report measures   p. 82
semantic differential
   method   p. 93
standardized measures   p. 82
summated ratings
   method   p. 95
telephone interview   p. 100
Thematic Apperception
   Test (TAT)   p. 87
Thurstone scales   p. 95

Multiple-Choice Questions for Review

1. A researcher at Southwestern University decides to use self-report methods in his study of caffeine use. His survey contains the following item: "In the past week, did you drink any coffee? Yes or no." This item is an example of (a) a fixed-choice question; (b) an open-ended question; (c) a neutrally worded question; (d) a negatively worded question.

2. A researcher at Baylor is conducting a study of the self-concept of college students. His survey contains the following item: "In your own words, please describe your self-concept. In other words, what kind of person are you?" This item is an example of (a) a negatively worded question; (b) an open-ended question; (c) a neutrally worded question; (d) a fixed-choice question.

3. A researcher at Case Western Reserve gives a participant an ambiguous picture of people in a social situation and asks the participant what the people in the picture are doing, what they are thinking, and what they will be doing in the future. This is an example of

a (a) fixed-choice format question; (b) reverse-scored question; (c) projective test; (d) none of the above.

4. Some research participants are likely to agree with almost any question that is asked of them. This tendency is generally referred to as (a) an acquiescent response set; (b) an affirmation bias; (c) a nonnegation bias; (d) an affirmation tendency.

5. To avoid problems with the "halo effect," a researcher might want to use (a) forced-choice scales; (b) graphic rating scales; (c) equal-appearing interval scales; (d) segmented graphic scales.

6. Observers often assume that, if a person is physically attractive, he or she also has many other positive qualities, including being intelligent and outgoing. This is an example of (a) the error of central tendency; (b) the halo effect; (c) the error of misperception; (d) none of the above.

7. According to research on the semantic differential method, which of the following is a useful dimension

of subjective meaning? (a) potency; (b) activity; (c) evaluation; (d) all of the above

8. Which of the following is also known as the method of summated ratings? (a) the semantic differential method; (b) the Thurstone method; (c) the Likert method; (d) the equal-appearing intervals method

9. Which of the following is also known as the method of equal-appearing intervals? (a) the semantic differential method; (b) the Thurstone method; (c) the Likert method; (d) the graphic rating method

10. A researcher at Rhode Island College wants to ask people the following question during an interview: "Describe as fully and concretely as possible a real situation that was important to you in which you acted in some way that was a cover for your true feelings." This is an example of (a) a self-recorded diary; (b) the critical incident technique; (c) the semantic differential method; (d) an interview schedule.

Discussion Questions for Review

1. An Austin Peay student wants to develop numerical and graphic items to measure attitudes about abortion. What advice would you give the student on how to get started?

2. A Central Michigan student is asked by the instructor to tell which rating error each of the following descriptions represents: (a) rating too positively someone you know; (b) tending to respond in an affirmative direction; (c) not using the extremes of a scale; (d) rating a central trait and other traits in the same way. Do you know the answers? Do you also know how to control for each of these errors?

3. A Northwestern University student who has a job selling used cars is thinking about developing a questionnaire to explore the motivations of people who buy and don't buy used cars. What methodological pointers would you give the student?

4. A student at Wheaton College in Norton, Massachusetts, wants to develop a Thurstone scale to measure attitudes about eliminating final exams for graduating seniors. Describe the steps she will need to take in developing this scale.

5. The student in Question 4 has a boyfriend who is a psychology major at Brown University. He tells her that he is planning to develop a Likert scale to measure the same attitudes. Do you know the difference between these two approaches?

6. A student at the City University of New York wants to use the semantic differential to study people's reactions to certain *New York Times* advertisements.

If you were this student, how would you design this instrument?

7. A student with a dual major in psychology and political science at Ohio Wesleyan, who is running for student body president, reads *The Selling of the President,* in which the author, Joe McGinniss, wrote about the use of the semantic differential by advertising researchers who worked for Richard M. Nixon when he began assembling a team for his 1968 presidential campaign. The researchers traveled all through the United States asking people to evaluate the presidential candidates (Nixon, Hubert Humphrey, and George Wallace). They then plotted an "ideal presidential curve" (i.e., a line connecting the points that represented what the researchers thought would be the ideal candidate) and compared the candidates' profiles with this ideal. The Ohio Wesleyan student is also running against two rivals and wonders whether it might be possible to do a similar study. What methodological pointers would you give her?

8. A student at the University of South Africa, a correspondence university, works in a company that wants to study the morale of its employees. The student thinks it might be instructive to ask a sample of the employees one or two critical incident questions. How should they be worded?

9. A Haverford College student is asked by his instructor to state, in one succinct sentence, the major advantage of the behavioral diary method over using a questionnaire. How should he answer?

Answers to Review Questions

Multiple-Choice Questions

1. a	**3.** c	**5.** a	**7.** d	**9.** b
2. b	**4.** a	**6.** b	**8.** c	**10.** b

Discussion Questions

1. Define the aspects of attitudes about abortion you want to cover with your measure, and be sure the items are easily understood. Decide how many response categories you want to use in your numerical and segmented graphic scales.

2. Leniency bias, acquiescent response set, central tendency bias, and halo effect (or logical error in rating), respectively. The section on rating errors gives suggestions on how to control for each of these rating concerns.

3. Most of the chapter contributes to an answer to this question, but you might begin with the answer to discussion Question 1 above.

4. Have a large number of judges sort a large number of items into 11 piles numbered 1 to 11 in order of item favorableness. Compute the median rating of favorableness of each item, and select the items for the final scale on the basis of (a) the judges' agreement on each item's degree of favorableness and (b) the items' being spread fairly evenly throughout the range of attitudes from 1 to 11. The format of the final attitude scale might resemble the sample scale in Figure 5.3 (the sample scale values are shown in Table 5.1).

5. The major difference is that the Likert 5-point (or 7-point or 9-point) items are used only if they correlate highly enough with the total score. A sample scale based on the Likert method is shown in Figure 5.2.

6. Select a sample of bipolar cue words from the lists in this chapter that seem to best represent the evaluative, potency, and activity dimensions. Sample instructions are shown in Figure 5.1.

7. Instead of supposing what the ideal candidate might be like, it might be better to ask respondents which characteristics of candidates would elicit their votes.

8. One wording might be: "Describe in detail a situation in which you felt pleased and proud to be an employee of the company. What led up to the situation, and what was its outcome?" The same question might well be asked again, this time with "unhappy and ashamed" substituted for "pleased and proud."

9. It has been shown to lead to more accurate data.

CHAPTER 6

Reliability and Validity in Measurement and Research

Preview Questions

- What is the difference between validity and reliability?
- What are random and systematic errors?
- What is the purpose of retest and alternate-form reliability?
- What is internal-consistency reliability, and how is it increased?
- What are acceptable test-retest and internal-consistency reliabilities?
- How is the reliability of judges measured?
- How is reliability related to replication and external validity?
- How are content and criterion validity defined?
- How is construct validity assessed in test development?
- How is construct validity relevant to experimental design?
- What is the importance of statistical-conclusion validity and internal validity?

What Is the Difference Between Validity and Reliability?

The purpose of this chapter is to explain different applications of two important criteria of how well measurements and certain research designs fulfill their functions. **Validity** is one of these criteria. In the most general terms, it shows how well the measure or design does what it purports to do. The measure in question might be a psychological test of some kind, or a group of judges who rate things, or a functional MRI scanner for monitoring brain activity, or it could be any other instrument or measuring tool. Consider an aptitude test that is designed to predict whether applicants to law school will succeed if admitted. We would be interested in the test's *criterion validity* because it would tell us how well scores on the test are correlated with the particular criterion of success used to assess it. We would also be interested in the test's *construct validity,* as it provides insurance that we are measuring the concept (or *construct*) in question. There are other uses of validity that are of interest to us as well, such as the test's *content validity,* which tells us how adequately the test has sampled the universe of content it purports to measure.

The concept of validity also has several different uses in research design, and in the following chapters we will examine specific experimental and nonexperimental designs and how well each fulfills its function. Suppose a new report found a statistically significant correlation between the living habits and the health outcomes in a particular society and implied that the relationship was causal. In Chapter 4, we discussed the importance of thinking about the possibility of *rival interpretations* or *plausible rival hypotheses* for statistical relationships. If we can think of a plausible rival hypothesis for the inferred causal relationship, the implication is that we are skeptical about its *internal validity*. Quite apart from the inferred causal relationship, we would also be interested in the generalizability (or *external validity*) of the observed association between living habits and health outcomes. That is, we would still want to know how dependable the data are, for example, whether the correlational findings can be replicated and generalized across different societies. In this chapter, we have much more to say about these and the other kinds of validity previewed in Table 6.1.

Reliability is the second important criterion. In the most general terms, it implies consistency or stability, but it may also imply dependability. The concept of external validity (defined below) can be said to be a bridge between reliability and validity, because external validity implies not only generalizability but also whether, for example, an observed relationship can be replicated with different participants and in different settings. By stability, we mean, for example, that if we measure a person's IQ as 110 in January, we would expect to obtain a similar score when we test the person again in December. That is, we expect the person's IQ score to be steady over this period of time, although we anticipate observing some random fluctuations in the IQ scores (discussed next).

Table 6.1   Types of Reliability and Validity

Reliability

Alternate-form reliability: The degree of relatedness of different forms of the same test.

Internal-consistency reliability: The overall degree of relatedness of all items in a test or all raters in a judgment study (also called *reliability of components*).

Item-to-item reliability: The reliability of any single item on average (analogous to *judge-to-judge reliability*, which is the reliability of any single judge on average).

Test-retest reliability: The degree of temporal stability (relatedness) of a measuring instrument or test, or the characteristic it is designed to evaluate, from one administration to another; also called *retest reliability*.

Validity

Construct validity: The degree to which the conceptualization of what is being measured or experimentally manipulated is what is claimed, such as the constructs that are measured by psychological tests or that serve as a link between independent and dependent variables.

Content validity: The adequate sampling of the relevant material or content that a test purports to measure.

Convergent and discriminant validity: The grounds established for a construct based on the convergence of related tests or behavior (convergent validity) and the distinctiveness of unrelated tests or behavior (discriminant validity).

Criterion validity: The degree to which a test or questionnaire is correlated with outcome criteria in the present (its *concurrent validity*) or the future (its *predictive validity*).

External validity: The degree of generalizability of a relationship over different people, settings, manipulations (or treatments), and research outcomes.

Face validity: The degree to which a test or other instrument "looks as if" it is measuring something relevant.

Internal validity: The soundness of statements about whether one variable is the cause of a particular outcome, especially the ability to rule out *plausible rival hypotheses*.

Statistical-conclusion validity: The accuracy of drawing certain statistical conclusions, such as an estimation of the magnitude of the relationship between an independent and a dependent variable (a statistical relationship that is called the *effect size*) or an estimation of the degree of statistical significance of a particular statistical test.

We would also be interested in the reliability of the test as a whole (its *internal-consistency reliability*), which tells us how well all of the items in the test "hang together." If we are using judges to make ratings, we want to know how coherent all their ratings are as a group (*their* internal-consistency reliability) as well as the average reliability of any *single* judge (the *judge-to-judge reliability*). These and other applications of the concept of reliability, which are discussed in this chapter, are also previewed in Table 6.1.

Reading about all these types of validity and reliability may seem confusing at this point, but what each connotes and how they are all interrelated will become clearer as you delve deeper into this chapter. After you finish this chapter, you will find it instructive to go back and read this introduction again as a reminder of how the various types of validity and reliability are practically interrelated. For example, generally speaking, if the measure you want to use is unreliable, it is often less likely to be valid. However, it is quite possible for a measure to be reliable and *not* be valid with regard to a specific criterion. For example, it is possible to imagine that individuals blink their eyes roughly the same number of times a minute under a variety of circumstances (the measure has high reliability), but we cannot predict someone's IQ or success in law school from the person's eye-blink rate (i.e., it is neither a valid measure of IQ nor a forecaster of grades in law school).

In sum, when assessing the measuring tools that are used in research (whether they are based on physical measures, test items, judges' ratings, etc.), researchers usually prefer validity and reliability to be as high as possible. The bottom-line criterion is always validity, however, as it rarely serves a researcher's objectives to have a highly reliable measure that correlates with nothing of any consequence.

What Are Random and Systematic Errors?

Before we turn to the specialized uses of reliability and validity listed in Table 6.1, there are two other important concepts that are not only related to reliability and validity but also relevant to the statistical procedures discussed in later chapters. These are the concepts of random error and systematic error. **Random error** (often described as "noise") is the name for chance fluctuations, or haphazard errors. **Systematic error**, on the other hand, is the name for fluctuations that are not random but are slanted in a particular direction (another name for systematic error is *bias*). In classical test theory, the idea is that the scores obtained (also called the *raw scores* or *observed scores*) comprise the theoretically "true scores" (the actual or "real" values) plus random errors (called *errors of measurement*). Errors of measurement are understood as randomly pushing the raw scores up and down around the true scores. The greater these random fluctuations (i.e., the more noise there is), the less consistent or dependable (i.e., the less reliable) the raw scores are (see also Box 6.1).

Random errors are not confined to psychological measures; they are characteristic of all measurements, no matter how well controlled and precisely calibrated the instruments. As an illustration, the National Bureau of Standards in Washington, DC, checks all the weights and measures used in the United States by comparing them with prototypes that are owned by the bureau. One prototype, the standard weight of 10 grams (the weight of two nickels), is designated as NB10. This prototype, which was acquired around 1940, has been weighed approximately once a week ever since. At each weighing, an attempt has been made to control all the factors known to affect the results (like air pressure and temperature), but still there have been fluctuations. In one series of five weighings of NB10, for example, the results were

9.999591 grams
9.999600 grams
9.999594 grams
9.999601 grams
9.999598 grams

BOX 6.1 The Logic of Classical Test Theory

In the technical language of classical test theory, if we use the symbol Y_o to represent an observed (or raw) score on some dependent measure, Y_t for the true score, and e for random error, the relationship among these variables can be expressed as $Y_o = Y_t + e$. This expression presumes that the variability of true scores and their random errors of measurement are statistically independent of each other. In other words, they are uncorrelated.

If you have taken a course in statistics, you know that one popular measure of variability is the variance (σ^2) of a set of scores (which we discuss later, in Chapter 10). The classical test model is based on the idea that the variance of all the observed scores (σ_o^2) is equal to the variance of the true scores (σ_t^2) plus their random error of measurement variance (σ_e^2), which can be expressed simply as $\sigma_o^2 = \sigma_t^2 + \sigma_e^2$.

Suppose we now divide the variance of the true scores (σ_t^2) by the variance of the observed scores (σ_o^2); this gives us the proportion of variance due to true scores. Similarly, suppose we also divide the random error of measurement variance (σ_e^2) by the variance of observed scores (σ_o^2); this gives us the proportion of variance due to random errors of measurement. Because the two proportions, taken altogether, consume all of the observed variance, it follows that summing these two proportions must equal 1. In other words, $\Sigma\left[(\sigma_t^2/\sigma_o^2) + (\sigma_e^2/\sigma_o^2)\right] = 1.0$.

In the technical language of classical test theory, the smaller the random error variance (i.e., the less the noise), the more reliable the raw scores will be and, therefore, the more *precise* our estimate of any particular true score should be.

As you can see, although the first four digits are identical, the last three digits are shaky. As careful and precise as these measurements were, we see errors of measurement in the form of chance fluctuations (*random error*) (Freedman, Pisani, Purves, & Adhikari, 1991).

As an illustration of systematic error (or bias), suppose the measuring instrument is off by a known percentage. Because all the results will be biased by the same percentage, we can correct for it. However, imagine a situation in which we know the direction but not the amount of the bias. For example, suppose we buy a bunch of grapes from a grocer who has an annoying habit of putting his thumb on the scale every time he weighs something, thereby inflating the cost of our grapes (*systematic error*, but we don't know by exactly how much). A systematic error may also occur quite innocently. Suppose your sample of research participants consists only of men, but you want to generalize your research results to both women and men. Systematic error due to a biased sample may jeopardize the generalizability of your conclusions.

Another way of thinking about the difference between systematic errors and random errors is that random errors are likely to cancel one another, on the average, over a great many repeated measurements (i.e., they are likely to have an average of about zero). Systematic errors, on the other hand, do not cancel one another and do affect all measurements in roughly the same way (i.e., they do *not* have an average of about zero). Thus, if we want a single, unbiased estimate of the true weight of NB10, all we need do is calculate the arithmetic mean of all the different values, on the assumption that (a) the random errors will cancel out, and (b) the measurement apparatus is unbiased (i.e., there is no systematic error).

In the case of the dishonest grocer with the heavy thumb, perhaps we could figure out approximately how much his thumb on the scale inflates what he weighs. Simply by using another scale to weigh several bunches of grapes that he weighed, we can use the average difference in values to estimate the bias imposed by his heavy thumb. But imagine we have two scales, and we know that one is consistently too high and the other is inconsistent all the time. Which scale is better? We would prefer the first scale, because a little bias is better than a lot of random error when we know the amount of bias and can adjust for it (J. C. Stanley, 1971).

What Is the Purpose of Retest and Alternate-Form Reliability?

As noted in Table 6.1, one type of reliability is **test-retest reliability** (also referred to simply as **retest reliability**). Suppose you want to use a psychological test or other assessment procedure to empirically examine some prediction of interest. Test-retest reliability is an estimate of the degree of fluctuation of the instrument, or of the characteristic it is designed to measure, from one administration to another. If it is a standardized test (such as an IQ test, or a personality test like the MMPI), you should be able to find out about its test-retest reliability in your literature search. You can also estimate the test-retest reliability of a test that you developed by administering the instrument to a sample of people and then administering it again to the same people later on. The test-retest reliability can be represented by a correlation coefficient between the scores on the test administered at those two different times.

We will have more to say about correlation in Chapter 11, but if you have had a course in statistics, you know that the basic measure of association is the Pearson r correlation coefficient. If you are unfamiliar with the Pearson r, or need your memory of correlation jogged a little, all you need to know at this point is that the Pearson r measures the strength of association (the degree of relatedness) of two measured variables, such as height and weight. One characteristic of the Pearson r is that it ranges from -1.0 through 0 to $+1.0$. A value of exactly zero (0) means that the two variables being correlated have no linear relation. Suppose, for instance, that taller people are not heavier (or lighter) on average than shorter people; this would be indicated by finding a Pearson r of 0. A value of $+1.0$ means that the two variables have a perfect positive relation: As the scores on one variable increase, there are perfectly predictable increases in the scores on the other variable. A value of -1.0 means the opposite: As the scores on one variable increase, there are perfectly predictable decreases in the scores on the other variable. Knowing these characteristics of the Pearson r, what would you *generally* want the correlation (r) to be between the scores at the initial testing and at the retesting, if you were thinking about using a particular test or other instrument in your research?

The answer is that you would probably want the r to be a positive value as high as possible, as the higher the test-retest correlation, the more dependable or temporally stable the instrument. By *temporal stability* or *dependability* in this example, we mean that those who scored high initially scored high on retest, and that those who scored low initially scored low on retest. Thus, the retest reliability depends on maintaining one's *relative* position from initial test to retest; it is not affected by changes in *everyone's* scores from pretest to retest. If everyone earns, for example, 10 points more on retest because of practice effects (or 10 points less on retest because of fatigue effects), the test-retest reliability correlation is not affected even though the scores have changed quite a bit from pretest to retest. If you are measuring something that you believe is very stable over time, the closer the r is to $+1.0$, the more theoretically impressive is the temporal stability of the measuring instrument. On the other hand, if you are measuring a volatile or changeable variable (such as mood), you will expect much lower test-retest reliability if there have been changes in circumstances affecting that variable. That is, you want a measuring instrument that is *sensitive* to the volatility or change. Thus, published reports of the test-retest reliability of an instrument ordinarily indicate not only the interval over which the retesting was done, but also the nature of the sample on which the test-retest reliability is based.

On the other hand, a common concern when people take the same test twice is that the test-retest r may be artificially inflated because of their familiarity with the test. One way to prevent this kind of inflation is to create two statistically and theoretically comparable forms of the test with different items that measure the same content. Not all tests have more than one form, but many of the most popular ones do. If the forms are reliable, higher scores on one form should be associated with higher scores on the other forms as well. The correlation coefficient is again used to assess the reliability of the sets of scores, that is, their **alternate-form reliability**. Suppose we want to test vocabulary skills. We can randomly draw several samples of words from the dictionary and let each random sample constitute one form of our test. The correlation between each form with another form at a particular time is one indication of alternate-form reliability (Guilford, 1954). Other indications are that the forms have similar variances as well as similar intercorrelations with theoretically relevant criteria (Gulliksen, 1950; Nunnally & Bernstein, 1994).

Before we turn to another important application of reliability, we want to reiterate the conceptual difference between the simple correlations we have just discussed. In the case of test-retest reliability, the correlation is between scores on the same form administered to the same people at different times. Thus, it can be understood as a measure (or coefficient) of *stability*. In the case of alternate-form reliability, the correlation is between scores on different forms that were administered to the same people at approximately the same time. Thus, it is conceptualized as a measure (or coefficient) of *equivalence*. The situation becomes more complicated, however, if the correlation is between one form of the test at Time 1 and another form at Time 2, which is called a *cross-lag correlation*. We will have more to say about it later in this book (Chapter 8), but the complication is that cross-lag correlations can be affected by instability, nonequivalence, or both.

 ## What Is Internal-Consistency Reliability, and How Is It Increased?

Internal-consistency reliability is a general expression that refers to the degree of relatedness of the individual items on a test. Put another way, it tells us how well the separate items (or *components* of the test) "hang together." It is also called the **reliability of components**. There are several ways of estimating this reliability. One traditional approach (illustrated below) is to use the Spearman-Brown formula, which in turn is based on the average intercorrelation of all the items symbolized as r_{ii} to denote the mean item-to-item Pearson (r) correlation. Two other traditional approaches, which you may come across in your reading, are K-R 20 and Cronbach's alpha coefficient, which are described briefly in Box 6.2. It has been demonstrated that when all the item variances are equal, the estimates of internal-consistency reliability obtained from the two methods in Box 6.2 and the Spearman-Brown formula should be identical (Li & Wainer, 1998). In this discussion, we use the capital letter R to denote an estimate of internal-consistency reliability (to emphasize that it refers to the composite, or overall, measure of reliability), and we use the superscript *SB* to indicate that the estimation procedure is based on the Spearman-Brown formula (R^{SB}).

 ## BOX 6.2   K-R 20 and Cronbach's Alpha

K-R 20 gets it name from its originators, G. F. Kuder and M. W. Richardson (1937); the *20* comes from its being their 20th-numbered equation. K-R 20 is useful when test items are scored dichotomously, for example, scored 1 if marked correctly and 0 if not marked correctly. **Cronbach's alpha**, named after Lee J. Cronbach (1951), is not restricted to dichotomously scored items. If you have had a course in statistics, you may recall that another name for the *p* value is *alpha*. That alpha, which refers to the probability of a Type I error (discussed in Chapter 12), is not the same thing as Cronbach's alpha, which refers only to the degree of internal-consistency reliability. It is beyond the scope of this text to give examples of how K-R 20 or Cronbach's alpha are calculated, but if you are interested, you will find a detailed discussion in our advanced methods text (Rosenthal & Rosnow, 2008, pp. 94–98). Generally speaking, the same rule applies whether we use K-R 20, Cronbach's alpha, or the Spearman-Brown formula: The more comparable items there are in a test and the longer the test, the greater is its internal-consistency reliability. Another way of expressing this general rule is that *the internal-consistency reliability will increase with increased test length as long as the items being added are relevant and are not less reliable than the items already in the test* (Li, Rosenthal, & Rubin, 1996).

To illustrate, suppose you have made up a three-item questionnaire in which respondents are to indicate their agreement or disagreement with three attitudinal statements on a 5-point numerical scale from *strongly agree* to *strongly disagree*. You want to have a single summary score for each respondent based on your assumption that the items tap into conceptually related aspects of the attitudinal issue. You administer the questionnaire to a sample of people, score the results, and then correlate responses to Item 1 with responses to Item 2, Item 1 with Item 3, and Item 2 with Item 3. We can represent these Pearson correlations by the letter r with numerical subscripts indicating the specific items that were correlated with one another. Let us say you find $r_{12} = .45$ between Items 1 and 2; $r_{13} = .50$ between Items 1 and 3; and $r_{23} = .55$ between Items 2 and 3. Summing the values gives us $.45 + .50 + .55 = 1.50$. Dividing this total by the number of pairs (three pairs) tells us the *mean* item-to-item correlation ($r_{ii} = 1.50/3 = .50$), that is, the **item-to-item reliability**. Think of this value as the estimate of the *reliability of any single item on average*.

You can now use the **Spearman-Brown formula** to estimate the internal-consistency reliability of your three-item test from the information above. Created by Charles Spearman and William Brown, who came up with it independently (and simultaneously published their work in the same issue of the *British Journal of Psychology* in 1910), the formula can be written as

$$R^{SB} = \frac{nr_{ii}}{1 + [(n - 1)r_{ii}]},$$

where n = the number of items in the test, and r_{ii} = the average intercorrelation of the items. To use the summary results noted above, you would set n equal to 3 (because you have a three-item test) and r_{ii} equal to .50. Substituting in the formula above, you find

$$R^{SB} = \frac{3(.50)}{1 + [(3 - 1).50]} = \frac{1.5}{1 + 1.0} = .75.$$

The beauty of this formula is that you can experiment with different values of n and forecast what the effect will be on the internal-consistency reliability by increasing the length of your test. Thus, the formula is also known as the Spearman-Brown *prophecy formula*. For example, suppose you used six relevant items instead of three. Assuming that the average intercorrelation remains at $r_{ii} = .50$, you would prophesy as follows:

$$R^{SB} = \frac{6(.50)}{1 + [(6 - 1).50]} = .86.$$

What if you are thinking about increasing the length of your test to nine items? With $n = 9$ and the same average intercorrelation, your prophecy is:

$$R^{SB} = \frac{9(.50)}{1 + [(9 - 1).50]} = .90.$$

There is not much difference between .90 and .86. However, what is striking is that you can keep on improving the internal-consistency reliability by steadily adding new items, as long as the average item-to-item correlation (r_{ii}) remains unchanged. If the new items are not as relevant or as reliable as the items already in your test, then the r_{ii} will be reduced, and if this reduction is great enough, the internal-consistency reliability will be reduced (Li et al., 1996). Also, items with very low test-retest reliability will increase the error of measurement and reduce the internal-consistency reliability (Wainer & Thissen, 1993). Of course, you cannot simply add items forever, because there is a psychological limit to how long a test should be. If you make the test too long, the respondents will become fatigued and lose their concentration.

What Are Acceptable Test-Retest and Internal-Consistency Reliabilities?

In case you are wondering how many items are optimal to achieve the reliability you want, without making the test or questionnaire so cumbersome as to burden respondents or give them headaches, there is no simple answer. The acceptable range will depend on the context in which your instrument is to be used and the objective of the research. For example, if you need an instrument with a high degree of test-retest reliability, you might not be comfortable settling for a test-retest correlation less than .80. And yet, there are many acceptable instruments with test-retest correlations below .80, including many medical tools for detecting or diagnosing illness (such as the instrument for measuring the pressure of blood in an artery, called the *sphygmomanometer*). Scores on many medical tests vary as a function of patients' feelings of anxiety, changes in the patient's diet, and so on. Besides asking your instructor for guidance on acceptable test-retest and internal-consistency reliabilities, you can begin to develop a sense of the optimal test length in any particular case by looking up test reviews in primary sourcebooks (such as the *Mental Measurements Yearbook*) or by browsing the *Directory of Unpublished Experimental Mental Measures* (e.g., Goldman & Mitchell, 2003) for relevant measures.

To give you a reference point, the test-retest *r* on the Scholastic Assessment Test (SAT) for essay scores in the humanities is usually between .3 and .6, while for the SAT in chemistry, it is usually between .6 and .8 (Braun & Wainer, 1989). You will recall that in the previous chapter we described both the Minnesota Multiphasic Personality Inventory (MMPI) and the Rorschach inkblot test. Using the information they found in articles between 1970 and 1981, a team of psychologists (Parker, Hanson, & Hunsley, 1988) compared the internal consistency and test-retest reliability of these instruments and another well-known psychological test, the Wechsler Adult Intelligence Scale (WAIS). Developed by David Wechsler (a clinical psychologist who was connected with New York's Bellevue Hospital for many years), the WAIS is the most widely used individually administered intelligence test for adults. It is divided into verbal and performance subtests, the verbal part depending more on academic-related abilities than the performance part. Parker et al. estimated the average internal-consistency reliability was .87 for the overall WAIS, .84 for the MMPI, and .86 for the Rorschach test. They also estimated the average test-retest correlation at .82 for the overall WAIS, .74 for the MMPI, and .85 for the Rorschach.

Internal-consistency reliability is usually expected to be higher than test-retest reliability, unless the test-retest intervals are very short. Parker et al.'s findings, then, are consistent with that expectation, though in the case of the Rorschach the difference is hardly noticeable. Only limited claims can be made about multidimensional instruments, such as the Rorschach and the MMPI, but the typical level of criterion-related validity of the Rorschach has been estimated at $r = .29$, and of the MMPI at $r = .30$, based on a comparative meta-analysis (Hiller, Rosenthal, Bornstein, Berry, & Brunell-Neuleib, 1999). These values contradict earlier claims of higher mean validity coefficients for the same instruments (Atkinson, 1986; Parker et al., 1988).

More is known about the reliability (and the validity) of the WAIS, the MMPI, and the Rorschach than about most other psychological tests in current use, but we do not want to leave you with the idea that these three tests are without controversy. For example, the limitations of projective tests as tools in diagnosing psychopathology have been debated, including the use of the TAT (e.g., Sharkey & Ritzler, 1985) and the Rorschach (Garb, Wood, Lilienfeld, & Nezworski, 2005). In an extensive review article, Garb et al. (2002) specifically cautioned clinicians not to take the Rorschach at face value in diagnosing psychopathology, as the use of certain standard norms for interpreting Rorschach protocols sometimes leads to diagnoses in which relatively normal individuals are identified as having severe psychopathology. Regarding the values noted by Hiller et al. (1999) for the criterion-related validity of the Rorschach ($r = .29$) and the MMPI ($r = .30$), they may actually be about as high as can be expected for personality tests (see Cohen, 1988, p. 81). There is also an extensive literature on intelligence testing arguing that other aptitudes besides those measured by the WAIS are characteristic of other forms of intelligence (e.g., Ceci, 1990, 1996; H. Gardner, 1983, 1986, 1993; H. Gardner, Kornhaber, & Wake, 1996; Sternberg, 1985, 1990, 1997; Sternberg & Detterman, 1986).

Far less is known about the reliability and validity of the two attitude questionnaires reprinted in Chapter 5. Regarding the Thurstone questionnaire designed to measure attitudes toward defensive, cooperative, and aggressive war (Figure 5.3 in Chapter 5), the developers of this scale (Day & Quackenbush, 1942) reported only its internal-consistency reliability, which was in the .80 to .87 range for all three referents measured. For the Likert questionnaire measuring attitudes for and against compulsory health care (Figure 5.2 in Chapter 5), all we know is that its internal-consistency reliability was reported by its developer (Mahler, 1953) to be .96. However, this 20-item scale is interesting for another reason having to do with alternate-form reliability because the questionnaire in Figure 5.2 actually comprises two comparable 10-item forms, with alternate-form reliability in the .81 to .84 range.

How Is the Reliability of Judges Measured?

Similarly, reliability procedures are applicable when researchers select judges to classify or rate things in observational studies. To cite an instance, in a procedure used by developmental psychologists to study attachment behavior in infants and the maternal responses, the judges code positive and negative actions in a number of situations. They usually do this coding, for example, when the mother and the infant are together, when the mother leaves the infant in the presence of a stranger, when the mother returns, and when the infant is left alone (Ainsworth, Blehar, Waters, & Wall, 1978; de Wolff & Van Ijzendoorn, 1997; Main & Solomon, 1990). Suppose that a developmental researcher has three judges (A, B, and C) code the maternal behavior of five mothers (the family names are Smith, Jones, Brown, Kelly, and Blake) in one situation on a 7-point scale from *very secure* (1) to *very anxious* (7). The results of this hypothetical study are shown in Part A of Table 6.2. After calculating the Pearson correlations between all pairs of judges (A with B; A with C; and B with C), the researcher obtains the mean of all the correlations. These results are given in Part B of Table 6.2, in which the mean of all the interjudge correlations is $r_{jj} = .676$ (the subscript j stands for "judge"). This mean correlation can be described as the **judge-to-judge reliability**, or the *reliability of any single judge on average*.

Table 6.2	Ratings and Intercorrelations for Three Judges

A. Judges' ratings

| Mothers | Judges | | |
	A	B	C
Smith	5	6	7
Jones	3	6	4
Brown	3	4	6
Kelly	2	2	3
Blake	1	4	4

B. Judge-to-judge correlations

$r_{AB} = .645$
$r_{AC} = .800$
$r_{BC} = .582$
$r_{jj} = .676$

Note: We typically report correlations to two decimal places, but when we are going to use correlations in further calculations, it is often helpful to use three decimal places.

We would also like to know the reliability of the group of three judges as a whole, that is, the internal-consistency reliability. We find it by using the Spearman-Brown formula, now expressed as

$$R^{SB} = \frac{nr_{jj}}{1 + [(n-1)]r_{jj}},$$

where n = the number of judges (3 in this case, for Judge A, Judge B, and Judge C), and r_{jj} = the average judge-to-judge reliability (indicated as .676 in Table 6.2). Substituting in the above formula gives us

$$R^{SB} = \frac{3(.676)}{1 + [(3-1).676]} = \frac{2.028}{1 + 1.352} = .862.$$

It can now be reported that the reliability of the three judges' ratings as a whole (the group of judges' internal-consistency reliability) is R^{SB} = .862, and the reliability of any single judge is r_{jj} = .676 (the average judge-to-judge reliability). We would, of course, label each to avoid reader misunderstandings. Suppose we want to predict the amount by which internal-consistency reliability will increase if we add one more judge whose ratings are intercorrelated approximately .68 with those of the other judges. We find our prediction by substituting in the Spearman-Brown formula, with the number (n) of judges now indicated as 4 instead of 3, and we round r_{jj} to .68, which gives us

$$R^{SB} = \frac{4(.68)}{1 + [(4-1).68]} = .895.$$

This result tells us that using four similar judges instead of three similar judges is likely to boost the internal-consistency reliability of the group as a whole from .86 to roughly .90. This result assumes, of course, that the four judges are in fact similar, which assumes that the judge-to-judge reliability (r_{jj}) will not be altered dramatically by the addition of this fourth judge.

Table 6.3 pulls together what we discussed in this section and in the previous section. That is, the table can be used whether we are interested in the reliability of judges or items for a test. The column headings, which range from .05 to .95, denote the average judge-to-judge reliability (r_{jj}), or the average item-to-item reliability (r_{ii}). The first column on the left, labeled n, represents the

Table 6.3 Estimation of Spearman-Brown Internal-Consistency Reliability (R^{SB}) Based on Number (n) of Judges or Test Items and Mean Judge-to-Judge (r_{jj}) or Item-to-Item (r_{ii}) Reliability

	Mean judge-to-judge (r_{jj}) or item-to-item (r_{ii}) reliability																		
n	.05	.10	.15	.20	.25	.30	.35	.40	.45	.50	.55	.60	.65	.70	.75	.80	.85	.90	.95
1	.05	.10	.15	.20	.25	.30	.35	.40	.45	.50	.55	.60	.65	.70	.75	.80	.85	.90	.95
2	.10	.18	.26	.33	.40	.46	.52	.57	.62	.67	.71	.75	.79	.82	.86	.89	.92	.95	.97
3	.14	.25	.35	.43	.50	.56	.62	.67	.71	.75	.79	.82	.85	.88	.90	.92	.94	.96	.98
4	.17	.31	.41	.50	.57	.63	.68	.73	.77	.80	.83	.86	.88	.90	.92	.94	.96	.97	.99
5	.21	.36	.47	.56	.62	.68	.73	.77	.80	.83	.86	.88	.90	.92	.94	.95	.97	.98	.99
6	.24	.40	.51	.60	.67	.72	.76	.80	.83	.86	.88	.90	.92	.93	.95	.96	.97	.98	.99
7	.27	.44	.55	.64	.70	.75	.79	.82	.85	.88	.90	.91	.93	.94	.95	.97	.98	.98	.99
8	.30	.47	.59	.67	.73	.77	.81	.84	.87	.89	.91	.92	.94	.95	.96	.97	.98	.99	.99
9	.32	.50	.61	.69	.75	.79	.83	.86	.88	.90	.92	.93	.94	.95	.96	.97	.98	.99	.99
10	.34	.53	.64	.71	.77	.81	.84	.87	.89	.91	.92	.94	.95	.96	.97	.98	.98	.99	.99
12	.39	.57	.68	.75	.80	.84	.87	.89	.91	.92	.94	.95	.96	.97	.97	.98	.99	.99	1.0
14	.42	.61	.71	.78	.82	.86	.88	.90	.92	.93	.94	.95	.96	.97	.98	.98	.99	.99	1.0
16	.46	.64	.74	.80	.84	.87	.90	.91	.93	.94	.95	.96	.97	.97	.98	.98	.99	.99	1.0
18	.49	.67	.76	.82	.86	.89	.91	.92	.94	.95	.96	.96	.97	.98	.98	.99	.99	.99	1.0
20	.51	.69	.78	.83	.87	.90	.92	.93	.94	.95	.96	.97	.97	.98	.98	.99	.99	.99	1.0

number of judges or the number of items. The values in the body of the table refer to the Spearman-Brown internal-consistency reliability (R^{SB}) at the intersection of n and the value of r_{jj} or r_{ii}.

To illustrate, consider the following two questions pertaining to the reliability of judges and the detailed answers to each question:

1. *Question:* Given an obtained or estimated average judge-to-judge reliability, r_{jj}, and a sample of n judges, what is the approximate Spearman-Brown internal-consistency estimate, R^{SB}, of the judges' ratings as a whole?
   Answer: The value of R^{SB} is read from the table at the intersection of the appropriate row (n) and column (r_{jj}). Suppose we want to work with a variable believed to show a mean reliability of $r_{jj} = .50$ and can afford only four judges. We believe we should go ahead with our study only if the internal-consistency reliability (R^{SB}) will reach or exceed .75. Shall we go ahead? The answer is yes, because the table shows $R^{SB} = .80$ at the intersection of $n = 4$ and $r_{jj} = .50$.

2. *Question:* Given the value of the obtained or desired internal-consistency reliability, R^{SB}, and the number of judges actually available, n, what will be the predicted value of the mean reliability, r_{jj}?
   Answer: The table is entered in the row corresponding to the n of judges available and is read across until the value of R^{SB} closest to the one desired is reached; the value of r_{jj} is then read as the corresponding column heading. Suppose we will settle for internal-consistency reliability no less than $R^{SB} = .90$ and we have a sample of $n = 20$ judges available. For each variable to be rated by these judges, what should be the judges' minimally acceptable average judge-to-judge reliability? From this table we see the answer is $r_{jj} = .30$.

Now suppose we shift our focus from the reliability of judges onto test items. We still use the table in the same way, but we think of n as the number of test items and the column headings are now the average item-to-item reliabilities (r_{ii}). To illustrate, consider the following question pertaining to the reliability of test items:

3. *Question:* Assuming an obtained or estimated average item-to-item reliability, r_{ii}, and also an obtained or desired internal-consistency reliability, R^{SB}, what is the corresponding number of items (n) required?
   Answer: The table is entered in the column corresponding to the average item-to-item reliability, r_{ii}, and is read down the column until the value of R^{SB} closest to the desired internal-consistency reliability is reached. The value of n is then read as the corresponding row title. Suppose our choice of test items has an average item-to-item reliability of $r_{ii} = .40$, and we want an internal-consistency reliability of .85 or higher. Reading down the $r_{ii} = .40$ column, we come to $R^{SB} = .86$ (the closest to our desired internal-consistency level), and on the far left we see that we will need 9 items to achieve our desired level of R^{SB} (assuming the items still average $r_{ii} = .40$).

 ## How Is Reliability Related to Replication and External Validity?

We turn now to the concept of validity, beginning with an application that is sometimes a source of confusion because it encompasses aspects of both reliability and validity. Called **external validity**, the term was originally coined by Donald T. Campbell (1957), who also coined a counterpart term he called *internal validity*. We will mention internal validity again later in this chapter, and we also discuss two other concepts added to Campbell's original lexicon in work in which he collaborated with Thomas D. Cook (Cook & Campbell, 1976, 1979)—the traditional concept of *construct validity* and a newer one that they called *statistical-conclusion validity*. For now, however, we concentrate only on the concept of external validity and its relevance to the importance of **replication** (i.e., the repeatability of observations). The *APA Dictionary of Psychology* broadly defines *external validity* as "the extent to which the results of research or testing can be generalized beyond the sample that generated the results to other individuals or situations" (VandenBos, 2007, p. 358). In another collaborative update of Campbell's original expanded work (cf. Campbell & Stanley, 1963; Cook & Campbell, 1976, 1979), William R. Shadish, Cook, and Campbell (2002) defined *external validity* as specifically referring to "inferences about the extent to which a *causal relationship* [our emphasis] holds across variations in persons, settings, treatments, and outcomes" (p. 82). In other words, just as we are interested in the dependability of measurements, we are also interested in the dependability of causal generalizations in replicable experimental research.

We will have more to say about the logic of causal inference in experimental research in the next chapter. However, using the broad APA definition of external validity, suppose we obtained a particular result at one point in time in a psychology or educational or child development experiment. We want to know not only whether it will stand up over time, but also whether it is generalizable across different kinds of participants and different investigators (see also Box 6.3). Or, using the Shadish et al. (2002) definition of external validity, suppose we have successfully conducted not one, but a series of experiments on learning or cognition, and although the causal results are reliable, the volunteer subjects in these experiments were psychology students. Can we assume that the same results will apply to a general population of nonvolunteers that is not as literate or as well educated? Suppose the subjects in a biomedical experiment are male volunteers. Can we generalize to all women, or even to all men, including those who, if asked, would decline to participate in the research? Or suppose we used one standard treatment in all experiments designed to study a particular phenomenon. Can we safely assume that the causal result will hold up across other treatment variations in other settings? These are the kinds of questions that external validity addresses.

In reality, the *same* experiment can never be "exactly" repeated, because at the very least the participants will be older. Therefore, researchers tend to think of all replications, even the ones most closely modeled on the original study, as *relative replications* (Cook & Campbell, 1979; R. Rosenthal, 1990c; Shadish et al., 2002; Sidman, 1960). With the use again of the Shadish et al. definition of external validity, the issue is whether the size of the effect (or *effect size*, discussed in detail in later chapters) of an independent variable (X) on a dependent variable (Y) is similar in the original and the replication study. One convenient way to operationalize the concept of effect size is by computing the correlation between membership in the experimental or control group (coded, for example, as 1 vs. 0) and scores on Y. Effect size correlations that scatter slightly around zero tell us that not much is going on between X and Y in either study. However, suppose we want to replicate an experiment in which the effect size was $r_{XY} = .50$ (these subscripts indicate that the correlation is between variable X and variable Y, also often symbolized in lower case as r_{xy}), and suppose the effect size in our replication attempt is $r_{XY} = .40$. The two correlations (.50 and .40) are positive, far from zero, and are not terribly far apart, possibly leading us to conclude that the replication attempt was successful.

BOX 6.3 The Problem of Correlated Replicators

In the evaluation of a set of replication studies, it is often assumed that the replications are independent of one another. But what does "independence" mean in practical terms? The usual minimum requirement is that the study participants be different persons. But what about the independence of the people who conducted the research? Are 10 replications conducted by one investigator as independent of one another as 10 replications each of which was conducted by a different investigator? One way to approach this puzzle is to separate the replications into subsets (a procedure called *blocking*) and to compare the different subsets. For example, we might block on the particular interests of the investigators (Did they hold similar theoretical views and expectations, or were they at odds with one another?) or their background and training (Were they all affiliated in some way?). Once relevant characteristics have been identified, it is possible to assign a set of weights to the results that reflect some theoretically defined degree of independence, and to use these weights in a meta-analysis of the different studies (meta-analysis is discussed in Appendix C of this book).

We can also compare the two effect sizes statistically (using a procedure described in Appendix C) to learn how likely it is that the differences found are due to simple chance variation.

Although replications are possible only in a relative sense, we can still think of a distribution of possible replications in which their overall variability is a function of the degree of similarity to the original study that characterizes each possible replication. If researchers choose the study designs of their replications to be as similar as possible to the study being replicated, they may be more true to the original ideal of replication, but they may also pay a price because of the *limited generalizability* across other variations in settings and treatments. Broadly speaking, the threats to the external validity of causal inferences that experimenters typically worry about fall into two categories (Shadish et al., 2002): (a) variables that *were not* in the experiment (variations in persons, settings, and treatments) and (b) variables that *were* in the experiment (operationalizing the variable of interest too narrowly, or using a highly specialized group of research participants, or conducting the research in a setting that is clearly unlike the circumstances to which we want to generalize). Because it would be impossible to rule out every potential threat to external validity, researchers must be sensitive to the limitations of their study designs and must not make false or imprudent causal generalizations.

 ## How Are Content and Criterion Validity Defined?

Before turning to the three other applications of the concept of validity in experimental research (construct validity, statistical-conclusion validity, and internal validity), we will first examine its application in instrument (e.g., test) construction. To review, the concept of *validity*, in the context of instrument construction, refers to the degree to which a test or measuring instrument actually does what it purports to do. This assessment is considered the most important criterion in instrument construction and typically involves accumulating evidence in three categories, called *content validity, criterion validity,* and *construct validity*. Test developers are expected to provide this information so that (a) test users know the capabilities and limitations of each instrument before using it, and so that (b) test takers are not misled or their time and effort wasted when they are administered these instruments. In this section, we will discuss content and criterion validity, and in the following section we will focus on construct validity in instrument construction (later in this chapter, we discuss construct validity in experimental design). Before we begin, however, another type of validity that you may come across in your reading is **face validity**; the term simply means whether the instrument seems on the surface (or "face") to be measuring something relevant. It should not be confused with content validity, as face validity refers not to what the test (or some other instrument) measures but only to what it appears to measure. The idea of face validity is that if a test or questionnaire, for example, does not *appear* to be relevant, some respondents may not take it seriously (Anastasi & Urbina, 1997). Of course, there are many tests (projective tests such as the Rorschach and the TAT) that purposely do not contain a clue to what they are specifically measuring, but they seem at least on the surface to be delving into something deeply psychological.

Content validity means that the test or questionnaire items represent the kinds of material (or content areas) they are supposed to represent, generally a basic consideration in the construction phase of any test or questionnaire. Thus, reporting that a test or questionnaire has "good content validity" means that it adequately covers all major aspects of the content areas that are presumed to be relevant. For example, when the MMPI was developed, the researchers sought to select a range of statements that would be endorsed in a certain direction by each of several different clinical groups. For this purpose, they began by developing a set of specifications, with the idea that the items could then be judged against these specifications. In this way, they hoped to differentiate among a number of different clinical conditions by including a range of items that tapped different content areas. To assess whether the test items were consistent with the original specifications, they called on expert judges to make subjective evaluations of the relevance or appropriateness of each item to assessing different content areas.

Less formal methods can be used in other situations. Suppose an instructor is making up a final exam and wants it to have content validity. The instructor may start by thinking, "What material should students be able to master after studying the readings and listening to my lectures?"

The instructor drafts a list of the material the exam should cover and then writes questions to represent this material. As students we have all experienced exams with poor content validity. They are the ones about which we say, "The instructor never mentioned this material, and it appeared in a two-line footnote in the appendix!" Thus, content validity has little to do with statistical aspects of the test or questionnaire (Cronbach & Quirk, 1971). The instructor is not interested in items that are highly intercorrelated, because such high intercorrelations would impose restrictions on the range of material the instructor wants the test to sample. Also, a test that is content-valid one semester is not necessarily going to be content-valid when the course is taught again, because there may be a new textbook or the instructor may have updated the lectures. The instructor must also make sure that all items can be easily understood, so that if a student gives the wrong answers, it is not because of some "irrelevant difficulty" but because the student did not know the right answers (Cronbach & Quirk, 1971, p. 168).

Criterion validity has more to do with statistical aspects of the test, as it refers to the degree to which the test or questionnaire is correlated with one or more outcome criteria (a variable with which the instrument should be reasonably correlated). For example, suppose researchers want to develop a test of college aptitude. They might use as their criterion the successful completion of the first year of college or maybe the grade point average (GPA) after each year of college. If they are instead developing a test to measure anxiety, they might use as the criterion the pooled judgments of a group of highly trained clinicians who are asked to rate the degree of anxiety of each person to whom the researchers administer the test. In assessing criterion validity, researchers select the most sensitive and meaningful criterion in the present (called **concurrent validity**) or future (called **predictive validity**) and then statistically correlate the participants' performance on the test or questionnaire with that criterion.

For example, clinical diagnostic tests are ordinarily assessed for concurrent validity, as the criterion of the patient's "real" diagnostic status is in the present with respect to the test being validated. The concurrent validity of shorter forms of longer tests is also typically evaluated, the longer test being used as the criterion. The practical advantage to researchers of using a criterion in the present is that it is less expensive and less time-consuming than using a criterion that is in the future. It also controls for any possible complicating effect of temporal instability (Anastasi & Urbina, 1997). Frequently, researchers must also consider the validity of the criterion itself. Suppose a researcher wants to develop a short test of anxiety that will predict the scores on a longer test of anxiety. The longer test serves as the researcher's criterion, and the new short test may be relatively valid with respect to the longer test. But the longer test may be of dubious validity with respect to some other criterion (e.g., clinicians' judgments). In other words, criteria must often be evaluated with respect to other criteria, although there are no firm rules (beyond the use of logic and the consensus of other researchers in that area) about what constitutes an "ultimate" criterion.

All the same, predictive validity also plays an important role in measurement. Tests of college aptitude are normally assessed for predictive validity because the criteria of graduation and GPA are of the future. The students' aptitude test scores are saved until the future-criterion data become available, and the test scores are then correlated with the future-criterion data. The resulting correlation coefficient serves as an *index of criterion validity*. GPA tends to be a fairly reliable criterion, but clinicians' judgments (e.g., about complex behavior) may be a less reliable criterion. We can usually increase the internal-consistency reliability (R^{SB}) of pooled judgments by adding new similar judges to the group whose pooled judgments are to serve as the criterion (as was shown in Table 6.3).

 ## How Is Construct Validity Assessed in Test Development?

More sophisticated views of the validation of tests require that researchers be sensitive not only to the correlation between their measures and some appropriate criterion, but also to the correlation between the measures and some "inappropriate" criterion. Suppose that a researcher in clinical psychology develops a new test of psychological adjustment, and she wants to use the test in a field experiment. She next does some pilot studies to assess the validity of the new test. In one aspect of this pilot work, she has expert clinicians rate the psychological adjustment of patients who were given the test. When she finds that the test scores correlate positively and substantially with the pooled judgment of the expert clinicians, she can correctly interpret this correlation as an attractive outcome of a *concurrent validation* effort.

Suppose she also gives the same patients a standard test of verbal aptitude and finds that their scores on the verbal aptitude test and on her new test of psychological adjustment correlate positively and substantially with one another. Should she conclude that the new test of psychological adjustment is a reasonably valid measure of psychological adjustment, of verbal aptitude, of both, or of neither? This question is not an easy one to answer, though one thing that is clear is that she cannot claim on the basis of these results to understand her new test of psychological adjustment very well. It is not intended, after all, to be a measure of verbal aptitude. In short, her new test has good concurrent validity but fails to discriminate: It should, but does not, correlate differentially with very different criteria. A test's *ability to discriminate* is a basic characteristic of **construct validity**, which itself is considered the most "fundamental and all-inclusive validity concept, insofar as it specifies what the test measures" (Anastasi & Urbina, 1997, p. 114). To put it another way, *construct validity has to do with what a test really does assess*. Content and criterion validity provide us with valuable information in their own right but are also generally regarded as improving our understanding of the construct assessed by the test.

How one should establish the construct validity of a test has been explored and debated for years in psychology. One traditional approach is to use logical analysis, and another procedure involves manipulating the respondents' experience before the test or during the test to see whether the manipulation will produce differences in responding as the construct would imply (Cronbach & Quirk, 1971). Campbell and Fiske (1959) proposed a way of formalizing the construct validation procedure both logically and statistically. They recommended that researchers test for two kinds of validation evidence: (a) the testing for *convergence* across different measures or manipulations of the same behavior (**convergent validity**) and (b) the testing for *distinctiveness* between measures or manipulations of related but conceptually different traits or behaviors (**discriminant validity**). For example, finding that a new test of psychological adjustment correlates positively and substantially with expert clinicians' ratings would be regarded as evidence of convergent validation. Finding that the new test correlates positively and substantially with a test of verbal aptitude (which is distinct from the construct of psychological adjustment) would be regarded as contrary to the necessary discriminant validation evidence. Recently, focused statistical procedures, besides the use of simple correlations, have been applied to the quantification of construct validity (Westen & Rosenthal, 2003).

To give you a further sense of the practical process of testing for construct validation, we turn to a landmark program of research by personality psychologists Douglas Crowne and David Marlowe, in which a number of different strategies were used, including logical analysis, correlation, and laboratory studies. The original purpose of Crowne and Marlowe's research was to develop a psychological scale that would measure *socially desirable responding*. As noted in the previous chapter, in this type of behavior people respond in ways that make them look good (rather than give their most candid and honest responses). As their work progressed, Crowne and Marlowe realized that the scale they were building might be assessing a more general personality variable, which they termed the *need for social approval* to reflect the idea that people differ in their need to be thought well of by others. In developing this scale—called the Marlowe-Crowne Social Desirability (MCSD) scale—the researchers wanted not only to measure the degree to which people vary on the need-for-approval dimension independent of their level of psychopathology, but also to validate the need-for-approval construct.

Crowne and Marlowe began by considering hundreds of personality test items (including a few from the MMPI) that could be answered "true" or "false." To be included, an item had to reflect socially approved behavior but also had to almost certainly be untrue (behavior too good to be true!). In addition, responses could not have any implications of psychological abnormality or psychopathology, or the MCSD scale could not be said to be measuring the need-for-approval dimension apart from the respondent's level of psychopathology. By having a group of psychology graduate students and faculty judge the social desirability of each item, Crowne and Marlowe developed items that seemed to reflect behavior that was too virtuous to be probable, but behavior that would not be primarily influenced by personal maladjustment. The final form of the MCSD scale, consisting of 33 items chosen by item analysis and ratings by experienced judges (Crowne, 1979; Crowne & Marlowe, 1964), showed a high degree of relationship statistically to variables with which the scale scores were expected to converge (i.e., evidence of convergent validity). For example, high scorers on the final MCSD scale preferred low-risk behaviors and avoided being evaluated by others. The final form also showed only a low degree of relationship statistically to variables with which the MCSD scale was expected not to converge. For example, correlations with measures of psychopathology were smaller than was the case for an earlier developed scale of social desirability, a result implying that the MCSD scale was a better measure of social desirability because it was not confounded by psychopathology. Also encouraging was an impressive correlation ($r = .88$) between the responses of people who were tested and then retested a month later (evidence of test-retest reliability).

These were promising beginnings for the MCSD scale, but it remained to be shown that the concept of need for social approval (and Marlowe and Crowne's scale developed to measure it) was meaningful beyond predicting responses on other paper-and-pencil measures. As part of their program of further validating their new scale and the construct that was its basis, the researchers undertook an ingenious series of studies relating scores on the MCSD scale to research participants' behavior in other, non-paper-and-pencil test situations. Crowne and Marlowe reasoned that "dependence on the approval of others should make it difficult to assert one's independence, and so the approval-motivated person should be susceptible to social influence, compliant, and conforming" (Crowne, 1991, p. 10). A series of relational-type studies produced results that were generally consistent with this logical expectation. For example, in the first of these studies, the participants began by completing various tests, including the MCSD scale, and then were asked to get down to the serious business of the experiment. This "serious business" required them to (a) pack a dozen spools of thread into a small box, (b) unpack the box, (c) repack the box, (d) unpack the box, and so on for 25 minutes while the experimenter appeared to be timing the performance and making notes about them. After these dull 25 minutes had elapsed, the participants were asked to rate how "interesting" the task had been, how "instructive," and how "important to science" and how much they wanted to participate in similar studies in the future. Those persons who scored above the mean on social desirability said they found the task more interesting, more instructive, and more important to science and were more eager to participate again in similar studies than those persons who had scored below the mean. In other words, just as Crowne and Marlowe had predicted, the participants who were higher in the need for social approval were more compliant and said nicer things to the experimenter about the task that he had set for them.

In still other research, Crowne and Marlowe used a variant of Asch's (1952) conformity procedure (described in Chapter 1). That is, a group of people are asked to make judgments on specific issues, and all the confederates make the same uniform judgment, one that is quite clearly in error. Conformity was defined as the real subject's "going along with" the majority in his or her own judgment rather than giving the objectively correct response. In one study, Crowne and Marlowe had the real subject listen to a tape recording of knocks on a table and then report his or her judgment of the number of knocks. Each subject was led to believe that he or she was the fourth participant. To create this illusion, the experimenter played for the subject the tape-recorded responses of three prior participants to each series of knocks that was to be judged. The earlier three participants were confederates of the experimenter, and they all gave an incorrect response in 12 of 18 trials. It was therefore possible to count the number of times out of 12 that the real subject yielded to the wrong but unanimous majority. The results were consistent with Crowne and Marlowe's hypothesis that the approval-motivated person is conforming: The real subjects who had scored higher in the need for social approval went along with the majority judgment of the confederates more than did the subjects who scored lower in the need for social approval.

Many additional studies have been performed by these and other investigators (e.g., Allaman, Joyce, & Crandall, 1972; Crowne, 1979; Crowne & Marlowe, 1964; Paulhus, 1991; Weinberger, 1990). Some of the follow-up studies produced different results. In current usage, the word *need* in Crowne and Marlowe's *approval need* construct is no longer fashionable (Paulhus, 1991), and other researchers have also suggested relabeling the construct *evaluative dependence* (Millham & Jacobson, 1978) or simply calling it *approval motivation* (Strickland, 1977). These developments are consistent with the course of any successful research program, in which researchers build on, and attempt to improve our understanding of, the earlier work. However, the main point of this example is to pull together some of the ideas that we have discussed in this chapter and to illustrate a systematic approach to construct validity. If you are interested in seeing the final form of the MCSD scale, it is reproduced in Robinson, Shaver, and Wrightsman's (1991) *Measures of Personality and Social Psychological Attitudes* (another useful resource for available tests in the public domain), along with commentary by D. L. Paulhus on related measures.

 ## How Is Construct Validity Relevant to Experimental Design?

As noted earlier, *external validity* and *construct validity* are two of four types of validity that are of major interest to experimenters, the other two being *statistical-conclusion* and *internal validity*. We discuss statistical-conclusion validity and internal validity in the following section, but first we want to say a little more about construct validity in the context of experimental design. To review briefly the distinction between construct validity and external validity, you will recall that *external validity* is (broadly speaking) synonymous with "generalizability." In the case of experimental design, Shadish et al. (2002) equated external validity with "causal generalization" or, more specifically, with "whether a causal relationship holds over variations in persons, settings, treatments, and outcomes" (p. 21). To borrow an example noted by Shadish et al., suppose we are reading the results of an experiment on the effects of a kindergarten Head Start program to improve the reading ability of poor African American children in the grammar schools in a particular city. The generalizability issue might be whether similar causal effects would result with poor Hispanic or other poor children in another city.

By contrast, we know that *construct validity* is concerned with the conceptualization of variables. In research in which causal generalizations are the primary objective, construct validity refers to the validity of the hypothetical idea linking the independent (X) and dependent (Y) variables, but it also refers to the conceptualization of X and Y. An illustration was Latané and Darley's (1968, 1970) experiments (in Chapter 2) using the construct of "diffusion of responsibility" to explain why the more witnesses there are to an emergency (X), the less likely it is that any one of them will offer help (Y). The connection between independent and dependent variables has been conceptualized as a kind of theoretical scaffolding (Cronbach & Meehl, 1955). In this case, the idea is that diffusion of responsibility is the theoretical scaffolding between X and Y. One of the more common threats to construct validity is *vagueness in defining or operationalizing the concepts or variables of interest*. For example, what precisely is meant by "diffusion of responsibility," "witnesses," and an "emergency"?

Although in the past some leading psychologists had claimed that it is quite possible to do research without using constructs, Shadish et al. (2002) argued that it is a logical impossibility for three reasons. First, researchers need constructs to connect the operations they use in their studies to pertinent theory and to the way that causal generalization will be used in practice. Not using constructs to connect operations is like speaking in gobbledygook, that is, without any substance or deeper meaning. Second, constructs shape our perceptions and, because they also invariably have rich connotations, invite discourse and debate that stimulate further ideas for operationalizing and measuring these constructs. Third, the "creation and defense of basic constructs" is the essence of what science is about (Shadish et al., 2002, p. 65). In chemistry, the periodic table is a basic construct. In physics, the atom is another basic construct. In behavioral and social research, there are countless constructs that are considered essential (the *self,* the *body, groups, society, culture, environment, evolution, attitude,* and on and on). Indeed, the very idea of a *construct* is itself a construct in our thinking, and that we can talk about it in a meaningful way is further tacit evidence of the validity of Shadish et al.'s argument.

 ## What Is the Importance of Statistical-Conclusion Validity and Internal Validity?

This brings us to the concepts of statistical-conclusion validity and internal validity. First, going back to Chapter 3 and looking again at Table 3.2 will remind you that one of the five technical standards of scientific quality is the logical and scientific grounding of the methods and statistical procedures that researchers use. We added that this standard also encompasses the assumption that the questions and hypotheses addressed are appropriate to the research design and that the primary data analysis focuses on those questions or hypotheses as opposed to going off on a tangent or giving answers that are diffuse or unfocused. The term **statistical-conclusion validity** echoes a similar sentiment, as it refers to whether statistical conclusions are well grounded, such as conclusions about the size of the effect (frequently operationalized as the correlation between treatment and outcome, or between the independent variable and the dependent variable) or conclusions about the effect size's statistical significance (Shadish et al., 2002). For instance, when statements are made about correlations, the question pertaining to statistical-conclusion validity is whether there is in fact a likely relationship between two variables or whether some observed statistical association was due merely to chance fluctuations. When experimenters are interested in drawing a causal inference (that *X* causes *Y*), they first need to show that the presumed cause and the presumed effect actually occur together (i.e., that they *covary*). A "real" causal relationship may be occurring, but the statistical circumstances may not be conducive to observing (or "detecting") it at the given level of significance (more on this topic in later chapters).

The final type of validity in experimental research, **internal validity**, is concerned with what was described in Chapter 4 as **plausible rival hypotheses**. As defined by Shadish et al. (2002), the term *internal validity* refers specifically to whether an observed covariation between *X* and *Y* truly reflects a causal relationship from *X* to *Y*. In Chapter 4, we gave some examples of plausible threats to internal validity without invoking the term *internal validity*. It is, however, considered another fundamental concept in the lexicon of behavioral and social research. In the following chapter, we will discuss this concept in more detail.

To anticipate, suppose a pair of students (a male student and a female student) decided to conduct an experiment on verbal learning. Their particular interest is in the causal effect of stress, in the form of loud noise, on the learning of certain prose material. In order to divide the work fairly, the students flip a coin to determine which of them will run the participants in the stress condition and which of them will run the participants in the no-stress condition. The problem is that, even if these researchers were to find the hypothesized relationship, they could not ascribe it to the experimental stress, because there would be plausible rival hypotheses to consider. One rival hypothesis might be that the results were due to experimenter differences (e.g., personality and gender differences). This rival hypothesis could have been ruled out if each of the students had run half the participants in the stress condition and half the participants in the no-stress condition. Such a design would prevent the methodological *confounding* (or intermixing) of the effects of stress and the effects of plausible experimenter differences and, in turn, would strengthen the internal validity of the argument.

If you are confused about the difference between internal validity and construct validity, one way to separate them is simply to remember that *ruling out plausible rival hypotheses is the essential characteristic of internal validity.* That is, *internal validity* refers to whether we can logically rule out competing explanations for the observed covariation between a presumed independent variable (*X*) and the presumed effect of *X* on the dependent variable (*Y*). Construct validity, on the other hand, concerns the validity of the concepts we use in our measurements and causal explanations. Whenever you ask what is *really* being measured (e.g., "What does this test really measure?")

BOX 6.4 Being Wrong Versus Being in a Weak Position

Professor Judith A. Hall (1984), whose ideas about what makes a good researcher were discussed in Chapter 1, has also proposed a good intuitive distinction among the four kinds of validity in experimental research. When either construct or internal validity is poor, researchers may be actively misled because they are at risk of making causal inferences that are plain "wrong." When either statistical-conclusion or external validity is poor, researchers are at risk of being in a "weak position" to make *any* causal inferences or sweeping conclusions because limits are imposed on what can be learned or what can be generalized to other situations.

or what is *really* being investigated (e.g., "What is this experiment really investigating?"), you are asking about construct validity rather than about internal validity. Stated another way, construct validity addresses whether the concepts being measured or manipulated are properly identified (i.e., whether we have a clear conception of what we are measuring or manipulating), and internal validity addresses whether a variable other than *X* (the causal variable we *think* we are studying) may have caused *Y* to occur (see also Box 6.4).

Summary of Ideas

1. Generally speaking, *validity* refers to the degree to which something does (or is) what it claims to do (or to be), whereas *reliability* refers to consistency, stability, or dependability.

2. All measurements are subject to *random errors* (frequently described as *noise*), which are chance fluctuations that are presumed to cancel out, on the average, over many repeated measurements. By contrast, *systematic error* (also called *bias*) pushes measurements in one direction.

3. According to the logic of classical test theory, observed (raw) scores comprise the true scores and their random errors of measurement (Box 6.1).

4. *Test-retest reliability,* or simply *retest reliability* (a measure of *stability*), is the correlation between scores on a test given to the same people on two different occasions. *Alternate-form reliability* (a measure of *equivalence*) is the correlation between scores on different forms of the same test given to the same people at approximately the same time.

5. *Internal-consistency reliability* is the overall degree of relatedness of the components of a test (also called *reliability of components*) or a group of judges. One way to measure it is to use the *Spearman-Brown formula,* which is based on the average item-to-item or judge-to-judge correlation and the number of items or judges (Table 6.3). Other useful measures of internal-consistency reliability are *K-R 20* and *Cronbach's alpha coefficient* (Box 6.2), which (along with the Spearman-Brown

procedure) give similar results when the item variances are equal.

6. The degree of reliability of widely used tests (e.g., the MMPI, the Rorschach, and the WAIS) gives some indication of what convention specifies as acceptable reliability.

7. *External validity,* one of four major types of validity based on empirical research, is the dependability of generalizations across persons, settings, treatment, and outcome variations.

8. To say that a replication attempt was successful generally implies that the research procedure was modeled on the original study, the overall pattern of results was similar, and the effect sizes (e.g., the correlation between the independent variable, *X*, and the dependent variable, *Y*) of the studies were fairly similar.

9. Validity in test development usually means accumulating evidence in three categories: (a) *content-related validity;* (b) *criterion-related validity* (e.g., *predictive, concurrent*); and (c) *construct validity* (based, for example, on *convergent* and *discriminant validity*). This process was illustrated by Crowne and Marlowe's validation of the construct of "approval need" and the MCSD scale they created to measure it.

10. Besides *external validity* and *construct validity,* two other major types of validity of interest to experimenters are *statistical-conclusion validity* (whether certain statistical conclusions are well grounded, such as the effect size and the *p* value) and *internal validity* (whether plausible rival hypotheses can be ruled out).

Key Terms

alternate-form reliability   p. 110
concurrent validity   p. 119
construct validity   p. 120
content validity   p. 118
convergent validity   p. 120
criterion validity   p. 119
Cronbach's alpha   p. 111
discriminant validity   p. 120
external validity   p. 116
face validity   p. 118

internal-consistency
  reliability   p. 111
internal validity   p. 123
item-to-item reliability (r_{ii})   p. 112
judge-to-judge reliability (r_{jj})   p. 114
K-R 20   p. 111
plausible rival hypotheses   p. 123
predictive validity   p. 119
random error   p. 108
reliability   p. 107

reliability of components   p. 111
replication   p. 116
retest reliability   p. 110
Spearman-Brown prophecy
  formula   p. 112
statistical-conclusion
  validity   p. 123
systematic error   p. 108
test-retest reliability   p. 110
validity   p. 106

Multiple-Choice Questions for Review

1. Random error is error that (a) isn't worth worrying about; (b) is always in the same direction; (c) has an average of about zero; (d) is also known as *bias*.

2. Broadly speaking, _____ refers to the consistency or stability of measurement. (a) validity; (b) modulation; (c) reliability; (d) invalidity

3. A researcher at Wheelock College administers a test of chronic anxiety. One month later, she administers the same questionnaire and finds that scores on the two administrations of the test correlate highly (r = .85). This outcome demonstrates the _____ of the test. (a) internal validity; (b) internal-consistency reliability; (c) external validity; (d) test-retest reliability

4. A researcher at Roosevelt University constructs a five-item measure of attitudes toward national health insurance. The average intercorrelation among the items is r_{ii} = .40. Using the Spearman-Brown equation, he calculates that R^{SB} = .77. This researcher has calculated the _____ of the attitude scale. (a) internal validity; (b) internal-consistency reliability; (c) test-retest reliability; (d) convergent validity

5. In Question 4, in which the researcher determined that R^{SB} = .77, what is the reliability of the scale as a whole? (a) .77; (b) .50; (c) .40; (d) cannot be determined from the information given

6. One intelligence test has two separate forms. Both measure intelligence, but they contain different questions. A researcher at Eastern University in Radnor, Pennsylvania, finds that the scores of students on Form A correlate highly with their scores on Form B (r_{AB} = .92). This correlation demonstrates the _____ reliability of the test. (a) internal consistency; (b) external consistency; (c) test-retest; (d) alternate-form

7. In determining whether one study replicates the results of another, scientists often examine _____, which are statistics that reflect the magnitude of the relationship between X and Y. (a) significance levels; (b) alpha coefficients; (c) effect sizes; (d) data on the manipulation checks

8. "A test should correlate with theoretically related external variables; for example, the SAT should correlate with grade point average." This statement defines _____ validity. (a) statistical-conclusion; (b) content; (c) consistency; (d) criterion

9. "A test should not correlate with variables from which it is theoretically distinct." This statement defines _____ validity. (a) convergent; (b) content; (c) discriminant; (d) criterion

10. The degree of generalizability of the results of a study is referred to as the _____ of the study. (a) internal validity; (b) external validity; (c) construct validity; (d) discriminant validity

Discussion Questions for Review

1. An Emory University student is trying to make her mark in the field of psychology by developing a new scale measuring fear of public speaking. How might she assess her scale's predictive and construct validity?

2. On a quiz, a University of Toronto student is asked how we know that the Marlowe-Crowne scale (MCSD) measures need for social approval. What is the answer?

3. A University of Houston student has piloted his observational study using two judges and has found a moderate judge-to-judge reliability (r_{jj} = .50). Because he wants to achieve a higher overall

reliability, he is distressed by the prospect of having to modify his coding criteria and training procedures. Another student suggests, "Don't bother with all that. Simply add two more judges to improve the internal-consistency reliability." Would you consider the second student's advice sound?

4. A Kansas State University researcher wants to study the effects of the texture of toys on the frequency with which toddlers touch them. She uses the following toys: a brown teddy bear, a smooth blue plastic ball, a green wooden cube, and an orange corduroy-covered rattle. She finds that male toddlers are more likely to touch the ball and the cube than the teddy bear and the rattle, whereas female toddlers are more likely to touch the teddy bear and the rattle than the other two toys. When she reports the results, a member of the audience raises the possibility that male toddlers must therefore prefer hard, less variegated textures to soft, more variegated textures, whereas female toddlers show the reverse preference. What is one rival hypothesis that would also be consistent with the researcher's results? How might the rival hypothesis be ruled out?

5. A Northeastern University researcher wants to build a 20-item test to measure need for power. She assigns several students to use the Spearman-Brown formula to measure the internal-consistency reliability of her new test based on data recently collected from a large sample. They tell her that $R^{SB} = .50$ and that the mean interitem reliability (r_{ii}) equals .40. She asks them to check their work. Why?

6. A student at the State University of New York at Binghamton is interested in assessing a new 20-item scale of optimism-pessimism. How should she assess the reliability of this scale? The student is also advised by her instructor to measure several different traits using several different methods to demonstrate empirically the convergent and discriminant validity of the new scale. Why did the instructor give this advice?

7. A student at Bridgewater State College weighs a 10-pound object 5 times and obtains readings on the scale of 14, 8, 7, 10, and 11 pounds. Describe the systematic error and the random errors characterizing the scale's performance.

Answers to Review Questions

Multiple-Choice Questions

1. c		3. d		5. a		7. c		9. c
2. c		4. b		6. d		8. d		10. b

Discussion Questions

1. She can assess her scale's predictive and convergent validity by showing that her scale correlates substantially with future symptoms of fear when people are asked to speak in public. In addition, the new scale should not correlate substantially with such less relevant variables as height, spatial relations abilities, and political party preference (discriminant validity). Convergent and discriminant validity are aspects of construct validity.

2. We know the MCSD scale measures need for social approval because it correlates highly with behaviors defined as reflecting high need for social approval, but not as highly with behaviors not reflecting high need for approval.

3. Yes, the second student's advice is sound because a total of four judges will yield an internal-consistency reliability of .80 when the typical judge-to-judge reliability is .50 (see Table 6.3).

4. A plausible rival hypothesis is that female toddlers prefer more complex shapes than do male toddlers.

A new study might add four new stimuli: a smooth, hard teddy bear and rattle, and a soft, fuzzy ball and cube. If the plausible rival hypothesis is correct, female toddlers will prefer the new smooth, hard teddy bear and rattle to the new fuzzy ball and cube. Considering all eight stimuli, then, female toddlers will prefer the four complexly shaped stimuli, whereas male toddlers will prefer the four simply shaped stimuli if the rival hypothesis is accurate. Still another rival hypothesis is that the color differences of the toys determine the frequencies with which toddlers touch them. To address this alternative, similar toys would have to be created in different colors, such as wooden cubes that are brown, blue, green, and orange but are identical in all other respects.

5. The reason the students were asked to check their work is because Table 6.3 shows that, for 20 items, a mean item-to-item reliability of .40 is associated with an internal-consistency reliability of .93, not .50.

6. The student can assess the test-retest reliability of the new 20-item scale by administering the test twice to the same people (e.g., 4 weeks apart) and computing the correlation between the two administrations. The internal-consistency reliability can be computed from correlating all the items with each other and then applying the Spearman-Brown formula to the average intercorrelation of the items (or using Table 6.3) to get the overall internal-consistency reliability. The reason for administering several different measures is that the student can show convergent validity with the measures with which her new scale should correlate substantially and discriminant validity with the measures with which her new scale should not correlate substantially.

7. There is no systematic error because the average reading is accurate (10 pounds). The random errors are $+4$, -2, -3, 0, and $+1$ on the five readings, or errors of $+40\%$, -20%, -30%, 0%, and $+10\%$, respectively, a not very precise performance.

CHAPTER 7

Randomized Experiments and Causal Inference

Preview Questions

- What is the purpose of randomized experiments?
- How is random assignment accomplished?
- What are between-subjects designs?
- What is the formative logic of experimental control?
- What are within-subjects designs?
- What are factorial designs?
- What is meant by counterbalancing the conditions?
- Why is causality said to be "shrouded in mystery"?
- How do scientists logically puzzle out efficient causality?
- What conditions pose a threat to internal validity?
- What are artifacts in research?

 ### What Is the Purpose of Randomized Experiments?

Inferring causality is both an evolutionary necessity and something we all do constantly. Yet, as one scholar, Judea Pearl (2000), remarked, it is "a notion shrouded in mystery, controversy, and caution" (p. 331). In this chapter we explore that observation within the context of randomized designs and the logic of causal inference. We will also mention some statistical procedures that are typically used to analyze the designs described in this chapter as well as suggest, in some cases, alternative procedures that are discussed in more detail later. In this chapter and in the later chapters, we use the term *focused* to describe statistical procedures that ask precise questions of data. *Focused statistical tests* include (a) all *t* tests, (b) only *F* tests with 1 degree of freedom in the numerator, and (c) only chi-square tests with 1 degree of freedom. If you can hardly remember the difference between *t* tests, *F* tests, and chi-square tests, think of these abbreviated descriptions as an introduction to data-analytic procedures that are described in detail in the final six chapters. We will also resume our discussion of threats to *internal validity* (discussed briefly in the previous chapter). Finally, recalling the distinction between random error (*noise*) and systematic error (*bias*), as described in the previous chapter, we conclude with a discussion of two sources of systematic error that have been studied empirically, one referred to as *demand characteristics* and the other, as *expectancy effects*.

As we first noted in Chapter 1 (Box 1.5), the identifying characteristic of **randomized experiments** is that the allocation of sampling units (e.g., volunteer subjects) to groups or conditions is done by a process of **random assignment** (also described as **randomization**). In biomedical research, randomized experiments (often called *randomized controlled trials*) have long been regarded as the "gold standard" of causal inference for empirically assessing whether a therapeutic intervention can ultimately make a beneficial difference to individuals treated in clinical or medical practice. For example, the intervention might be psychotherapy and/or a medication to treat a behavioral or psychological disorder, a drug to be prescribed for a patient in a physician's office, an over-the-counter remedy to reduce pain, or a vaccine for use in a public health immunization program to eradicate a preventable disease. Of course, just as the value of gold can fluctuate, it is also true that health care decisions can fluctuate in value as a consequence of obscured or uncontrolled factors that jeopardize the external or internal validity of the study. Furthermore, the statistical tests that researchers and pharmaceutical companies frequently emphasize can be confusing. Put another way, in an imperfect world there exists always the possibility of unaccounted for extraneous factors and alternative explanations that could help to explain the presumed contributory relationship between the assumed treatment and observed outcome (see also Box 7.1).

We will have more to say about randomized controlled trials in biomedical research and, of course, in behavioral and social research, but perhaps the most famous example of a randomized biomedical trial was the classic Salk vaccine study (Francis et al., 1955; Meier, 1988). The purpose of this study was to quantify the effects of inoculating over 200,000 young children with the Salk poliomyelitis vaccine compared with a placebo (consisting of a simple salt solution) given to over 200,000 other children (Francis et al., 1955). Writing in a prominent statistical journal, K. A. Brownlee (1955) pointed out a number of serious flaws in the original design and implementation of the study. Nevertheless, he concluded that there was "convincing evidence for the effectiveness of the vaccine" (p. 1010). What would you guess was the magnitude of the convincing correlation between (a) receiving or not receiving the Salk vaccine and (b) contracting or not contracting polio? We pose this question now only to get you thinking about *effect size correlations;* the answer will be given later in this chapter. Incidentally, another illustration of a quite different randomized experiment was the one proposed by Mary Jones in Exhibit 2.1 (see Chapter 2). Her sampling units were male and female students in a simulation experiment designed to investigate whether telling "judges" about a defendant's prior drug usage would cause them to make harsher bail judgments.

 ### BOX 7.1 Imperfect Randomized Trials

In his book on causality, Judea Pearl (2000) noted several potential problems. First, perfect control is often hard to achieve because patients who suspect that they are in a placebo control group may attempt to obtain the experimental drug on their own from other sources. Second, patients who experience adverse reactions to an experimental drug may, without telling the researchers, decide to reduce their assigned dosage. Third, assigning patients with a terminal illness to a placebo group could have legal ramifications, as they are being denied access to a potentially lifesaving drug or an experimental treatment. (As we mentioned in Chapter 3, one option in many cases is to give the control group the best available treatment, so the comparison is between the experimental drug or treatment and the best available alternative rather than a placebo.) Fourth, simply knowing that randomization is being used may make some patients wary of volunteering. The generalizability of the results could be jeopardized if the volunteers' responses to the treatment were different from the (unobserved) responses of those who chose not to volunteer and participate.

Traditionally, there are three principal reasons why random assignment is used. One reason is that it is intended to provide a safeguard against the possibility of the researchers' subconsciously letting their opinions or preferences influence which sampling units will receive a given treatment (Gigerenzer et al., 1989). As you may already have guessed, the expression *sampling units* is a general way of referring to the participants, subjects, groups, or objects being studied (the units sampled from the population), although these units might also be animals, schools, countries, or agricultural crops. The term *treatment* is commonly used both as a general name for the manipulation or intervention and as a way of referring to the conditions to which the sampling units are allocated. For example, in the Salk vaccine trial, the vaccine was the treatment that children in the experimental group received and children in the control group did not receive (but instead received a placebo). In Mary Jones's study, the experimental treatment was the version of the crime scenario that stated that a man, while in custody, had submitted to a drug test and tested positive. The control condition version of the scenario did not mention the drug testing.

A second reason for using random assignment (and one that most experimenters would probably mention) is that it distributes the characteristics of the sampling units over the experimental and control conditions in a way that should not bias the outcome of the experiment (Kirk, 2000). There is no absolute guarantee, however, because it is always possible that some unintended or uncontrolled variable related to the dependent variable might systematically affect the outcome in one condition more than another. For example, it has been reported that volunteers for research participation are often highly responsive to typically uncontrolled treatment-related cues (Orne, 1962, 1969; Rosenthal & Rosnow, 1975b, 2009). An unintended consequence of using volunteer subjects might be to amplify the observed difference between experimental and control groups on the dependent variable. Or suppose, in a randomized psychological experiment with five participants each in the experimental group and the control group, that two extremely tense individuals happened, by sheer coincidence, to end up in the experimental group. If prior tenseness affected the outcome in the experimental group, the exceptionally high prior tenseness of the two extremely tense individuals would be a threat to the validity of inferences about whether the observed association (the correlation) between the presumed treatment (X) and the presumed outcome (Y) reflects a causal relationship from X to Y (Shadish, 2010). In sum, random assignment does not guarantee equality in the characteristics of the sampling units that are assigned to different conditions. All it does is to give each unit at each draw an equal chance of being assigned to a particular condition.

The third reason for using random assignment (and one that most psychological statisticians and textbooks in statistics underscore) is that random assignment permits the computation of statistics that require particular characteristics of the data (Kirk, 1995, 2000; Maxwell & Delaney, 2000). Specifically, it provides a mechanism to derive probabilistic properties (p values) of estimates based on the normal distribution of data (the distinctive bell-shaped curve, as discussed in Chapter 10). This assumes that certain requisite statistical requirements of the significance tests were not seriously violated (discussed later in this book). However, suppose we want to study the effects of high dietary cholesterol on human longevity. It would be an ethical absurdity to think that we could randomly assign people to a high-cholesterol diet in order to see how many more would die than those assigned to a low-cholesterol diet. In observational studies with very large samples, one option (discussed in the next chapter) is to use a statistically sophisticated matching procedure called *propensity matching*. This procedure reduces relevant characteristics of the "naturally treated" and "untreated" individuals to a single composite variable and then estimates the "treatment effect" by comparing the results in subclassifications of those composite (*propensity*) scores (Rosenbaum & Rubin, 1983; Rubin, 1973; Rubin & Thomas, 1996). (We will give an example in the next chapter.)

How Is Random Assignment Accomplished?

Statisticians speak of random assignment *rules* (or plans). For example, suppose a researcher has designed an experiment with two conditions (treatment and control), and each condition and set of measurements is to be presented in the form of a booklet (or perhaps in a questionnaire, as in Mary Jones's research).

On the surface, the materials look the same, but the booklet given to the experimental group incorporates a treatment or manipulation not present in the booklet the control group receives. One possible randomization rule in this case would be to presort the booklets into pairs so that each pair contains an experimental and a control booklet. The first participant is to receive Booklet A or B (which can be decided by a flip of a coin), and the next participant gets the other booklet. For the next two participants the same procedure is repeated, so the experimenter ends up with an equal number of sampling units in each of two conditions. An alternative assignment rule might be to arrange the booklets so that, of every 4 or 6 or 8 booklets, half are Booklet A and half are Booklet B (again determined by coin flips). If the study can be run on a computer, the computer can do the random assignment.

As another illustration of the use of random assignment, suppose you wanted to assign 40 volunteer subjects at random to either an experimental or a control condition. You might use a table of random digits such as the one in Chapter 9 (Table 9.1), from which the following 120 single-digit integers were taken:

10097	32533	76520	13586	34673
37542	04805	64894	74296	24805
08422	68953	19645	09303	23209
99019	02529	09376	70715	38311
12807	99970	80157	36147	

First, you would make a list of all 40 individuals. Next, you have to decide in advance how you will use the table of random digits. Suppose you decide to read across and down the five-digit sets of numbers in the columns, one column at a time, beginning with the first column (10097, 37542, 08422, 99019, 12807, 32533, 04805, etc.). Suppose you also plan to have numbers 1, 3, 5, 7, and 9 designate the participants (coded as numbered subjects) to be randomly assigned to the experimental group, and to have numbers 0, 2, 4, 6, and 8 designate those in the control group. You would assign the first person on your list (Subject 1) to the experimental group because the first digit in 10097 is the number 1. Subjects 2 and 3 are assigned to the control group (0, 0, the second and third digits in 10097), Subjects 4–8 are assigned to the experimental group (9, 7, 3, 7, 5), Subjects 9–15 to the control group (4, 2, 0, 8, 4, 2, 2), Subjects 16 and 17 to the experimental group (9, 9), Subject 18 to the control group (0), Subjects 19 and 20 to the experimental group (1, 9), and so forth.

What Are Between-Subjects Designs?

When participants are exposed to one condition each, this arrangement is known as a **between-subjects design**. For example, Mary Jones's experiment uses a "two-group between-subjects design." The template for a two-group between-subjects design with a total of 10 units is shown in Table 7.1, where we see that 5 participants receive Condition A and 5 other participants receive Condition B. The logic behind this design is that if there is a causal effect of the treatment, it would be present in

Table 7.1	Between-Subjects (Nested) Design With Two Conditions

Condition A	Condition B
Subject 1	Subject 2
Subject 3	Subject 4
Subject 5	Subject 6
Subject 7	Subject 8
Subject 9	Subject 10

Table 7.2	Salk Vaccine (Between-Subjects) Trial	
Condition	Paralytic polio present	Paralytic polio absent
Salk vaccination	33	200,712
Placebo	115	201,114

Condition A and absent in Condition B. Another name for the between-subjects design is a **nested design**, as the units are regarded as "nested" within their own groups or conditions. A traditional way of statistically analyzing two-condition between-subjects designs is by the *t* test for independent samples, which compares the mean outcome in Condition A with the mean outcome in Condition B (discussed in Chapter 13).

In biomedical trials, the outcome (the dependent variable) is often a dichotomous measure (e.g., die vs. live, or sick vs. well, or disease present vs. disease absent), and the data (frequencies) are usually arranged not in two columns, but in a 2 × 2 chi-square table of frequencies of occurrence (also called *counts*). There are ordinarily far more than just a few subjects in each condition. Previously, we mentioned the Salk poliomyelitis vaccine study, described by Meier (1988) as "the biggest public health experiment ever." As shown in Table 7.2, there were over 400,000 children in that study (Francis et al., 1955). The rows in this table are the two levels of the independent variable (Salk vaccine vs. placebo), the columns are the two levels of the outcome variable (polio present vs. polio absent), and the cell values are the independent counts (or frequencies). A typical statistical test would be the chi-square (χ^2) procedure on the independent counts (discussed in Chapter 15). If the frequencies in the table are not independent of one another, computing an accurate *p* value from chi-square is not possible, but computing an effect size correlation on a 2 × 2 table of counts can easily be done (illustrated in Chapter 15).

Between-subjects designs are not limited to two groups or two conditions. Suppose we want to study the effects of nutrition on the academic performance of children who are to be randomly assigned to one of four different conditions. In one condition (Group 1), the children will receive a hot lunch daily. In another condition (Group 2), the children will be given free milk. In a third condition (Group 3), the children will get a vitamin supplement. The fourth condition (Group 4) will be a "zero control group" that will get nothing extra. Suppose our prediction is that the observed group means will be highest in Group 1, followed by Group 2, then followed by Group 3, and the lowest of all in the zero control group (Group 4). Later in this book, we will come back to this hypothetical case, where our hypothesis can be expressed as $M_1 > M_2 > M_3 > M_4$ (where *M* denotes the group mean, the subscript indicates the particular group, and the symbol > stands for "greater than"). The mean of Group 1 (M_1) is predicted to be greater than (>) the mean of Group 2 (M_2), and so forth. This design is quite commonly analyzed by an *F* test with numerator *df* = 3, but the numerator *df* > 1 tells us that it is not a focused statistical procedure that will actually address the precise prediction above. A preferable alternative would be a specialized application of *t* or *F* that focuses on the $M_1 > M_2 > M_3 > M_4$ prediction (called a *contrast*, illustrated in Chapter 14).

What Is the Formative Logic of Experimental Control?

Before we describe some other basic randomized designs, we want to give you a sense of the logic of *experimental control*. Later on in this chapter we will also have some more to say about the formative logic of causal inference, but remember that causal inference is always subject to some degree of uncertainty—which is why good scientists are careful not to make exaggerated claims. Though some degree of uncertainty is a constant in science (just as it is in everyday life), randomized controlled experiments (such as the common control-group design in Table 7.1) have traditionally been assumed to be a way to tease out patterns of likely (or *probable*) causal relationships between variables.

The philosophical rationale for this assumption derives from what, in the discipline of philosophy of science, is known as **Mill's methods**, a name given to certain logical propositions that were popularized by the 19th-century English philosopher John Stuart Mill. Two of Mill's methods—called *agreement* and *difference*—together provide the formative logical basis of the design in Table 7.1.

The idea, in principle, is that when two independent groups are comparable in all respects except for some intervention or manipulated variable (the *experimental treatment*) that is operating in one group but not in the other, that experimental treatment is implicated as the probable agent responsible for the observed differences between the two groups on the dependent measures. To see where this idea came from, you need to understand what Mill meant by the method of agreement and the method of difference:

First, the **method of agreement** states, "If X, then Y," X symbolizing the presumed cause and Y the presumed effect. The statement means that if we find two or more instances in which Y occurs, and if only X is present on each occasion, then X might be at least a **sufficient condition** of Y. Describing X as a "sufficient condition" implies that it is *adequate* (i.e., capable or competent enough) to bring about the effect. Stated another way, an effect will be present when the sufficient cause is present. In baseball, we would say there are several sufficient conditions for getting the batter to first base, such as the batter's getting a hit (X_1), being walked by the pitcher (X_2), or being struck by a pitch (X_3), or the catcher's not holding onto the ball after a third strike and then failing to tag the batter or toss him out at first base (X_4).

Second, the **method of difference** states, "If not-X, then not-Y." The statement implies that if the presumed effect (Y) does not occur when the presumed cause (X) is absent, then X is probably suspected to be a **necessary condition** of Y. Calling X a "necessary condition" implies that it is *indispensable;* that is, X is believed to be essential to bring about the effect. Stated another way, the effect will be absent when the necessary cause is absent. For example, to win in baseball (Y), it is *necessary* for your team to score more runs than the other team (X); not scoring any runs at all (not-X) will inevitably result in not winning (not-Y).

To take these ideas one step further, suppose that X represents a new and highly touted tranquilizer, and Y represents a change in measured tension. We give people who complain of tension a certain dosage of X, and we find a noticeable reduction in their measured tension. Can we conclude from our before-and-after observations that the tranquilizer was responsible for the reduction in tension? Not yet, because even if we repeatedly find that giving X is followed by tension reduction, we can infer only that X might be a *sufficient condition* of Y. Using the logic of Mill's methods, what we need is a **control group** with which to compare the reaction in the first group. For our control group, we need a comparable group to whom we do not give drug X. If the people in the comparable group show no tension reduction, the further implication is that X may also be a necessary condition of Y.

We can diagram this design along the lines of the randomized between-subjects design in Table 7.1, and we observe that the two groups correspond to Mill's methods of agreement and difference:

Experimental group	Control group
If X, then Y	If not-X, then not-Y

Assuming the groups are comparable in other respects, can we now conclude that taking the drug led to tension reduction? Yes, although with the stipulation that "taking the drug" implies something more than just getting a chemical into the bloodstream. "Taking the drug" means, among other things, (a) having someone give the person a pill; (b) having someone give the person the attention that goes with pill giving; (c) having the person believe that relevant medication has been administered; and (d) having the active ingredients of the drug find their way into the person's bloodstream.

Usually, when testing a drug in a randomized clinical trial, the researchers are interested only in the patients' reactions to the active ingredients of the medication. The researchers do not care whether the patients will feel better if they merely *believe* they are being helped, because this fact (the power

BOX 7.2 Placebo: "I Shall Please"

The term placebo means in Latin "I shall please." It is generally recognized that **placebo effects** (i.e., the "healing" effects of inert substances or nonspecific treatments) are ever-present in clinical practice and research, including the healing effects of a placebo on angina, blood pressure, the common cold, cough, fever, panic disorder, headache, psoriasis, insomnia, pain, rheumatoid arthritis, and warts; even placebo vaccines have an effect (Turkkan & Brady, 2000). Recently, a team of researchers reported that it was possible to augment a placebo effect by progressively combining certain therapeutic rituals in the patient-practitioner relationship (Kaptchuk et al., 2008). Other researchers have reported that if patients receive a real treatment but are told they are receiving a placebo, there is usually less placebo effect (L. White, Tursky, & Schwartz, 1985). Though expectations and the context of the situation apparently play an important role in the placebo effect, the biobehavioral and/or neural mechanism mediating the healing remains unexplained. Some have theorized that it involves the classical conditioning interaction of the central nervous system and particular organ systems (Turkkan & Brady, 2000).

of suggestion) has already been established in other research. But if researchers know about the power of suggestion, how are they to separate the effects of the drug's ingredients from the effects of pill giving, of the patients' expectations of being helped, and possibly of other factors that may be sufficient conditions of *Y*? The traditional answer is by the choice of a different (or additional) control group. So this time, we use not a group given nothing, but a *placebo control group* given something that differs only in lacking the active ingredients whose effects we would like to know. The general finding, incidentally, is that placebos are often effective and sometimes even as effective as the far more expensive pill for which they serve as the control (see also Box 7.2).

 ## What Are Within-Subjects Designs?

In some randomized experiments, the researchers might plan to have participants make repeated judgments or repeated responses based on two or more different conditions that each participant receives. Called a **within-subjects design**, the simplest case is shown in Table 7.3, where we see that all 10 subjects received both Condition A and Condition B. Assuming that their judgments or actions were measured after each condition, this arrangement can also be described as a **repeated-measures design**. Another name for the basic within-subjects design is **crossed design**, because

Table 7.3	Within-Subjects (Crossed) Design With Two Conditions
Condition A	Condition B
Subject 1	Subject 1
Subject 2	Subject 2
Subject 3	Subject 3
Subject 4	Subject 4
Subject 5	Subject 5
Subject 6	Subject 6
Subject 7	Subject 7
Subject 8	Subject 8
Subject 9	Subject 9
Subject 10	Subject 10

the participants are thought of as "crossed" by conditions (i.e., observed under two or more conditions) rather than nested within them. The *t* test is usually used to analyze such data, but the researcher would use a *t* test for nonindependent samples (discussed in Chapter 13).

Within-subjects designs are not limited to two groups. Say we want to study the degree to which students' performance on a certain cognitive task improves over time. We will measure the students' performance at specified intervals, referred to as *repeated occasions of measurement*. Suppose we had hypothesized that the students will improve by an equal amount each time they perform the task over four occasions 1 month apart (i.e., equal intervals of 1 month). Using *M* to denote mean performance, we predict that $M_1 < M_2 < M_3 < M_4$ (where the symbol $<$ stands for "less than"). That is, we hypothesize that the mean performance will be lower on the first occasion of measurement (M_1) than on the second occasion (M_2), that mean performance on the second occasion will be lower than on the third occasion (M_3), and that mean performance will be lower on the third occasion than on the fourth occasion (M_4). (We return to this case in Chapter 14 to illustrate the focused statistical procedure used to assess this predicted *linear increase in means*.)

What Are Factorial Designs?

When we think of the conditions as arranged (also described as *arrayed*) along a continuum or single dimension, the design is described as a *one-factor* or *one-way design*, where the term *factor* is a general name for the independent variable of interest. Now suppose that women and men are randomly assigned to a drug or a placebo group, and we are interested in gender as well as treatment. This experimental design would be described as a two-factor study or, more specifically, as consisting of two *levels* of the variable of gender (women and men) and two levels of the variable of treatment (drug vs. placebo). This arrangement is more generally called a **factorial design**. Because we have two levels of each of the two factors, the arrangement can be specifically described as a 2 × 2 factorial study (where "2 × 2" is read as "two by two") or a 2^2 (or 2-squared) factorial design. The hypothetical experimental design is illustrated in Table 7.4.

Suppose that, using the symbols in Table 7.4, we predict Group A will, on average, be most responsive on the dependent measure, and that there will be no differences among Groups B, C, and D. In other words, our prediction, stated in terms of the group means, is $M_A > M_B = M_C = M_D$. Though this is a 2 × 2 study, for our focused statistical analysis we would conceptualize it for data-analytic purposes as a 1 × 4 study, that is, one dimension consisting of four conditions (A, B, C, D).

If a researcher who used the design in Table 7.4 really had no prediction or even a hunch, the traditional way of analyzing the data would be by a 2 × 2 analysis of variance (ANOVA). However, it seems a remote possibility that a researcher who has gone to the trouble of designing an experiment, submitting it as a proposal to a review board, recruiting participants, and carefully implementing the study would not have an expectation of some kind. Still, in that unlikely case, the researcher could explore (a) the between-group variation of the women and men (the two levels of the *row factor* in Table 7.4); (b) the between-group variation of the drug versus the placebo (the two levels of the *column factor*); and (c) the interaction of these two factors (the interaction of the two levels of the row factor with the two levels of the column factor).

Table 7.4 Two-by-Two Factorial Study		
	Manipulated conditions	
Gender	Drug	Placebo
Women	A	B
Men	C	D

We can also have a factorial design with more than two factors and more than two levels of each factor, although it may stretch the number of sampling units too thinly. For example, if all we have to work with is $N = 24$ units, there will be $n = 12$ in each group of a two-group between-subjects design. Working with a 3×4 factorial design and the same number of sampling units ($N = 24$), there will be 12 conditions and 2 units in each condition. Suppose we were using a randomized factorial design with three between-subjects factors (A, B, C) and two levels of each factor. A $2 \times 2 \times 2$ ANOVA could look into the following seven sources of variation: (a) between levels of Factor A; (b) between levels of Factor B; (c) between levels of Factor C; (d) interaction of levels of Factor A with levels of Factor B; (e) interaction of levels of Factor A with levels of Factor C; (f) interaction of levels of Factor B with levels of Factor C; and (g) interaction of all three factors.

What Is Meant By Counterbalancing the Conditions?

Suppose that instead of a factorial study with two between-subjects factors, we have a within-subjects design with repeated treatments and measurements on men and women. Now we have a more complex design, in which one factor is between subjects (men and women) and the other is within subjects (repeated treatments and measurements). We are using a *mixed factorial design*, a design that consists of both between- and within-subjects factors. In within-subjects studies with repeated treatments and measurements, a potential problem is that the *order* in which the treatments are administered to the same participants may be confounded with the treatment effect. Suppose the treatment conditions are administered to young children who are immediately measured after each treatment (a repeated-measures study). The children may be nervous when first measured, and they may perform poorly. Later, they may be less nervous and they may perform better. To deal with the problem of systematic differences between successive treatments (or measurements), we would use **counterbalancing**, which means rotating the sequences. In this example, some children will randomly receive Condition A before Condition B, and the others will randomly receive B before A.

A specific statistical design that has counterbalancing built in is called the **Latin square design**. It is characterized by a square array of letters or numbers (representing treatment conditions), where each letter appears once and only once in each row and in each column. The 4×4 Latin square in Table 7.5 uses letters (A, B, C, D) to represent a case in which four treatments (or conditions) are administered to all participants in a counterbalanced pattern. Those who are randomly assigned to Sequence 1 receive treatments in the sequence A, then B, then C, and finally D. In the remaining sequences (Sequences 2 through 4), the treatments (or conditions) are administered in sequences BCDA, CDAB, and DABC, respectively. In the 1920s, the noted British statistician R. A. Fisher applied the idea of Latin squares to studies of crop rotation. In Chapter 14, we illustrate the analysis of a Latin square design by means of Fisher's F statistic in behavioral research.

Table 7.5	A 4 × 4 Latin Square Design			
		Order of administration		
	1	2	3	4
Sequence 1	A	B	C	D
Sequence 2	B	C	D	A
Sequence 3	C	D	A	B
Sequence 4	D	A	B	C

Why Is Causality Said to Be "Shrouded in Mystery"?

Earlier in this chapter we quoted Pearl's (2000) statement that causality is "a notion shrouded in mystery, controversy, and caution" (p. 331). Yet, we all think in causal terms as we go about our daily activities, although giving hardly a moment's consideration to the *notion* of causality. For example, when we turn the key or push a button in a car's ignition, we implicitly expect our action to *cause* the motor to get going. We also implicitly expect that gorging on fatty foods will *cause* a person to put on weight, that pulling a sleeping dog's tail will usually *cause* the dog to growl or snap at us, and that smoking cigarettes over a long period can cause emphysema, heart disease, and lung cancer. All these are causal relations, which is to say they entail a relation between a presumed *cause* (in the form of a responsible human or physical agent or force) and a presumed *effect* (in the form of an event, a state, or an object). So what's mysterious about the notion of causality?

Part of the answer has to do with what you mean by *causality*. The great Greek philosopher Aristotle (384–322 B.C.) distinguished among four kinds of causality, traditionally referred to as *material, formal, final,* and *efficient.* Briefly, **material causality** has to do with the substance or substances that are thought to be necessary for the movement of something or for the coming into being of an event. **Formal causality** has to do with the plan or the development that gives meaning to the event. **Final causality** (also described as *teleological causality*, which means the action is "goal-directed") refers to the objective or purpose of the event. **Efficient causality** refers to the activating (or energizing) force responsible for the event.

To illustrate, imagine the flight of a curve ball that is thrown by a pitcher in a major league baseball game. It takes a fraction of a second for the ball to travel from the pitcher's hand to home plate. The batter swings and misses, and suppose you ask, "What *caused* the ball to break that way?"

- If you mean the *material cause*, the answer is that roughness on the surface of the ball and the nature of fluid flow comprise the material cause of the baseball's unusual movement. A ball with a smooth surface tends to have a smooth flight, especially if it passes through air at a speed of less than 50 miles per hour. But a ball with rough seams, traveling over 50 miles per hour, will encounter turbulence, especially when the ball is thrown in a special way to take advantage of the nature of airflow (R. K. Adair, 1990).
- If you mean the *formal cause*, the answer is the "idea" of "throwing a curve ball" as formally initiated in the mind of the catcher, who communicated it by finger signals to the pitcher, who thought "curve ball" up to the moment that the ball was released.
- If you mean the *final (or teleological) cause*, the answer is the "objective" of having a ball break as it nears the plate so that the batter will be unable to hit the pitch squarely.
- If you mean the *efficient cause*, it was the "act" of throwing the ball. That was the energizing force that caused the ball to travel at an optimal velocity and caused its trajectory to deviate from the original horizontal direction of motion.

Let's now apply these ideas to the "causes" of human development. First, we might think of cellular structure as constituting the *material cause* (the "stuff" of development). Second, DNA or genetics is the *formal cause* (the biological blueprint). Third, we might think of physiological maturation as the *final cause* (the goal or "end purpose"). Fourth, we can think of parenting as an environmental variable as the *efficient cause* (the activating or instigating cause that makes things happen). To some degree, researchers who are interested in human development pay attention to all four kinds of causality. But it is efficient causality that researchers usually have in mind when conducting randomized controlled experiments.

This brings us back to the question of what's puzzling about the idea of causality—by which we specifically mean *efficient causality*. The answer was provided by the great 18th-century Scottish philosopher David Hume. In a classic work (published in 1739–1740), *A Treatise of Human Nature*,

Hume reflected on the example of a billiard ball that is lying on a table with another ball rapidly moving toward it. They strike, the ball previously at rest is set in motion, and we quickly conclude that one ball *caused* the other to move. Yet, as Hume noted, all that we really observed was that "the two balls touched one another before the motion was communicated, and that there was no interval betwixt the shock and the motion" (Hume, 1739–1740/1978, pp. 649–650). Continuing in his words, "Beyond these three circumstances of contiguity, priority, and constant conjunction, I can discover nothing in this cause...In whatever shape I turn this matter, and however I examine it, I can find nothing farther" (pp. 649–650).

In other words, it appeared to Hume that the idea of an efficient cause was an illusion created by the sensation of *contiguity, priority,* and *a constant conjunction*. In essence, we are hard-wired to think "the cause and effect must be contiguous in space and time"; and that "the cause must be prior to the effect"; and that "there must be a constant union betwixt the cause and effect," that is, "the same cause always produces the same effect, and the same effect never arises but from the same cause" (p. 173). Although contiguity, priority, and a constant conjunction might be stipulated as necessary requisites of efficient causality, merely because a physically or temporally contiguous event invariably precedes another event—and therefore predicts the second event perfectly well—does not automatically implicate the prior event as the *cause* of the latter. Monday and Tuesday are temporally contiguous, and there is a constant union between them, and Monday is always prior to Tuesday, but we wouldn't think that Monday is the *cause* of Tuesday. Hume's example was that a rooster's "cock-a-doodle-do" stands in prior constant conjunction to sunrise but doesn't *cause* the sun to rise (Pearl, 2000). On what logical grounds, then, are scientists' inferences of efficient causality traditionally predicated?

 ## How Do Scientists Logically Puzzle Out Efficient Causality?

In practice, scientists emphasize as a further stipulation that it is possible to use empirical reasoning to rule out rival explanations for the presumed causal relationship between X and Y. Ideally, they do this before implementing the study by anticipating plausible threats to internal validity and designing the study in a way that reduces those threats (e.g., the use of a randomized controlled experimental design, although no design is absolutely perfect). When experiments are done in social settings (field experiments), the sheer number of possible threats to internal validity (37, by Shadish et al.'s 2002 count) can be mind-boggling. Trying to control them all simultaneously in one randomized controlled experiment would rival the circus act of one person trying to spin 37 plates on the ends of sticks. Nonetheless, modern scientists use empirical reasoning to puzzle out efficient causality by emphasizing what we refer to in this section as *covariation, temporal precedence,* and *internal validity,* defined as follows:

- By **covariation**, we mean a fusion of what Hume called "contiguity" and "constant conjunction," but with the qualification that the conjunction between cause and effect is not necessarily constant but is a *likely* or *probable* conjunction between X and Y.
- By **temporal precedence**, we mean what Hume called "priority," the assumption that the cause (X) does, in fact, precede the effect (Y). On the other hand, some relationships can become a vicious circle of bidirectional causes and effects, where X is first the cause of Y and then Y is the cause of X, and so forth (as discussed below).
- By **internal validity** (also discussed in the previous chapter), we mean that the scientist attempts, on logical and empirical grounds, to rule out plausible rival explanations for the observed relationship between the presumed cause and the presumed outcome.

To flesh out these three criteria, first, the scientist looks for evidence that the independent variable (X) and the dependent variable (Y) are mutually related (covary). That is, the scientist asks whether the presence (and the absence) of X (the presumed cause) is associated with the presence (and the absence) of Y (the presumed effect). On the assumption that X and Y show a satisfactory correlation, we have evidence of *covariation*. What constitutes a "satisfactory" correlation? This is not a question with a one-size-fits-all answer. If I fall whenever you push me, obviously there is a perfect degree of association between the two events, pushing (X) and falling (Y). However, when a pill is taken to lower cholesterol or to prevent cancer or a heart attack, the statistical association in the large samples studied is likely to be a lot smaller, because the rate at which the adverse events (cancer and heart attack) occur are usually relatively low in the population sampled over the course of the study. Remember our asking you to guess the correlation between (a) receiving or not receiving the Salk polio vaccine and (b) not contracting or contracting polio in the landmark 1954 clinical trial? Based on the results that were shown in Table 7.2, you would find the effect size correlation between (a) and (b) is .011. This small r (or phi, which we show how to calculate in Chapter 15) is close to zero. The correlation is small because polio was not a common event in the general population of children studied over the course of the clinical trial, not because the vaccine was ineffective (it was decidedly more effective than a placebo). The incidence of paralytic polio in the untreated group was a little greater than half-a-percentage point (115 out of 201,229 = 0.057%), and in the vaccinated group the incidence of the disease was far smaller (33 out of 200,745 = 0.0164%). That 0.057 is nearly three-and-a-half times larger than 0.0164 would seem consistent with Brownlee's conclusion (quoted earlier) of "convincing evidence for the effectiveness of the vaccine" (Brownlee, 1955, p. 1010).

Second, though causation implies covariation, covariation does not automatically imply causation. Therefore, a second stipulation was evidence that Y did not occur until after X occurred—or what Hume called "priority" and we term *temporal precedence*. Because a later event cannot be the cause of an earlier one, scientists seek evidence that X preceded Y. In relational research it is often difficult to obtain incontrovertible evidence of such temporal precedence, because we are looking at X and Y *in retrospect* (i.e., looking back at them). As noted previously, a further complication is that some causal relationships are *bidirectional* (X is a cause of Y, and Y is a cause of X). For instance, given an optimal combination of uncertainty and anxiety, rumors are likely to take root, and some rumors can also contribute to people's anxieties and uncertainties (Rosnow, 2001). Of course, temporal precedence and covariation still are insufficient grounds to conclude that the prior variable was clearly the efficient cause of the later variable. The barometer falls before it rains, but a falling barometer does not *cause* the rain (Pearl, 2000, p. 336).

Third, then, what scientists also need is a suitable model (a conceptual mock-up) of the presumed causal relationship between X and Y and, by implication, a way of ruling out reasons why factors other than the treatment (X) may be a plausible rival explanation for a causal relationship between X and Y. Traditionally, scientists use "cause-probing research" (Shadish et al., 2002, p. 98) and critical reasoning to rule out plausible threats to *internal validity*. Because humans are not omniscient, the success of these logical efforts to rule out rival explanations has limits. To encourage critical thinking about causal claims, Campbell (1957) and his coworkers (e.g., Campbell & Stanley, 1963; Cook & Campbell, 1979; Shadish et al., 2002) have, over many years, identified over three dozen possible threats to internal validity, and we sample a few general categories next.

What Conditions Pose a Threat to Internal Validity?

Among the plausible threats to internal validity that have been cataloged by the Campbell group of methodologists (e.g., Campbell & Boruch, 1975; Campbell & Kenny, 1999; Campbell & Stanley, 1963; Cook & Campbell, 1976, 1979; Shadish et al., 2002) are many that pose a problem primarily in research in which the designs resemble randomized experiments but do not use random assignment. Research that uses these particular nonrandomized designs is traditionally referred to as **quasi-experimental**, where *quasi* means "resembling" a randomized design, or "seemingly, but not actually" a randomized experiment. For example, in the next chapter we refer to *nonequivalent-groups designs*, in which the sampling units are allocated to the experimental and control groups by means other than randomization, and, typically, observations are made both before and after the experiment. In this section, however, we focus on six general categories of threats to internal validity that occur in quasi-experimental research, and that are also taken into account in other situations whenever the relationship between two variables is purported to be causal: (a) biased selection, (b) bias due to history, (c) bias due to maturation, (d) bias due to attrition, (e) bias due to testing, and (f) instrumentation bias.

First, **biased selection** (more commonly *selection*) refers to how the sampling units assigned to different conditions were selected for those conditions. The term *biased* implies that the selection procedure resulted in groups that, even before the experimental intervention or manipulation, were systematically dissimilar in respondent characteristics relevant to the observed outcome. In survey research (discussed in Chapter 9), *biased selection* has a very different meaning, as it refers to the nonrepresentativeness of a nonrandom survey with regard to the population of interest (*external validity* as opposed to internal validity). (As we stated earlier, in survey research, *random sampling* is the traditional method of controlling for biased selection, whereas *random assignment* is the device used to control for biased selection for assignment to groups or conditions in experimental research.) There are also commonly used designs that Campbell and Stanley (1963) described as **preexperimental designs**, because they were viewed as so primitive as to be especially vulnerable to biased selection and causal misinterpretations. For example, suppose that children who were administered a new educational intervention designed to improve their concentration skills were given an achievement test after the intervention, and there was no independent control group. This preexperimental design was called a **one-shot case study**, symbolized as X-O, where X = exposure to the intervention (experimental treatment), and O = observation or measurement. In the X-O design, we are unable to assess each child's prior level of performance on the achievement test before the intervention.

Second, **bias due to history** (more commonly described simply as *history*) refers to the presence of an event other than (but typically concurrent with) the treatment, the idea in this case being that the event (not the treatment) may be responsible (or partly responsible) for the observed effect. For example, imagine another preexperimental design with a slight improvement over the one-shot case study. This type of preexperimental design again consists of just a single condition, but the condition incorporates a pretreatment measurement (i.e., an observation prior to the intervention or manipulation). Described as a **one-group pre-post design**, it would be symbolized as O-X-O. In our continuing example, the O-X-O design would address one deficiency of the X-O design by enabling us to measure each child's level of performance on the achievement test prior to the educational intervention. Like the X-O design, however, the O-X-O design lacks a non-X comparison (control) group. Suppose an unexpected weather event resulted in the cancellation of classes, interrupting the schedule of X treatments. Because the design lacks a randomly assigned non-X condition, we cannot rule out *bias due to history* (the concurrent weather event) as a threat to internal validity (see also Box 7.3).

 BOX 7.3 The O-X-O Design in the Doctor's Office

A variant of the O-X-O design where it is, in fact, possible to have a control condition is the one used by dermatologists. Suppose you have a skin rash that, the dermatologist tells you, is contact dermatitis produced by an allergic reaction to some substance to which you are overly sensitive. To figure out what substance produces that reaction, the dermatologist gives you an allergen patch test. A patch with tiny substances on it, each numbered, is attached to your skin, and you are told to wear the patch for a couple of days to see whether your skin reacts to any of the substances. The patch also has a *negative-control spot*, a place with nothing on it. Its purpose is to enable the dermatologist to control for the patch itself, that is, to detect whether the patch material irritates your skin.

Third, **bias due to maturation** (commonly described as *maturation*) refers to certain "naturally occurring changes over time" in the research participants (Shadish et al., 2002, p. 55). For example, the children's levels of concentration may have changed *without* the intervention. In other kinds of research in which causal inferences are drawn, bias due to maturation could pose a threat to internal validity if the participants' having grown older, wiser, stronger, more experienced, and so forth, could be the reason for the observed effect, quite apart from the intervention or treatment. The researchers would probably use a design such as that in Table 7.1, and to control for bias due to maturation they would ensure that the children who were randomly assigned to the treatment and control groups were generally the same age (an attempt to hold the maturation levels similar in both groups). Shadish et al. (2002) also recommended that the children in such a study be sampled "from the same location so that local secular trends are not differentially affecting them" (p. 57). (A *secular trend* means a fairly long-term pattern.)

Fourth, **bias due to attrition** (commonly described simply as *attrition*) refers to the differential loss of units in some conditions, the problem in this case being that the remaining units are dissimilar in the treatment and control groups. Imagine a within-subjects design with repeated measurements and a sample of volunteer subjects in both the treatment and control groups. Suppose that many more volunteers who were randomly assigned to the experimental group failed to keep their appointments (described as *no-shows*). If some characteristics of these no-shows were highly correlated with the dependent variable, the differential attrition might help to explain the obtained differences between the treatment and control groups. In biomedical research, *mortality* is the usual way of describing attrition resulting from deaths. A high mortality rate can also be a threat to *statistical-conclusion validity*, by reducing the statistical power of the significance tests used in the study (more about this in Chapter 12).

Fifth, **bias due to testing** implies that being measured, tested, or observed initially (or repeatedly) can affect subsequent performance on the dependent variable. (Bias due to testing is frequently described as *testing*, but this term is also used in many other connections and can be confusing when it is not put in context.) In Chapter 4, where we described the distinction between reactive and nonreactive observations and measurements, an example we mentioned was a study of therapy for weight control, where the initial weigh-in measurement was a reactive stimulus to subsequent weight reduction without the therapeutic intervention (Campbell & Stanley, 1963). As another example, Entwisle (1961) used a complex control-group design (called *the Solomon design*, after its inventor, Richard L. Solomon, 1949) to study children's ability to learn the state locations of large U.S. cities. Entwisle found that pretesting aided recall for the high-IQ children and was "mildly hindering" for the average-IQ children. In an attitude-change study, also using the Solomon design, Rosnow and Suls (1970) found that pretesting the research participants resulted in different effects for those identified as nonvolunteers compared with volunteers. In other studies, bias due to pretesting has sometimes been reported and in some cases ruled out as a possible threat to internal validity (Lana, 1959, 1969; Rosnow, Holper, & Gitter, 1973; Solomon & Howes, 1951; Solomon & Lessac, 1968).

Sixth, **instrumentation bias** (or simply described as *instrumentation*) refers to the possibility that the posttreatment effect that was measured or observed was due to changes in the measuring instrument. Suppose the "instruments" were students recruited as judges, who were instructed to rate the subjects' behavior in a tediously long experiment. If fatigue were to set in over time, any diminution in effects (as rated on the dependent measure) might be explained away as instrumentation bias due to tired judges. Or suppose over time that the students became more proficient in their ratings, so that the problem was not *instrument deterioration* but *instrument improvement*, which might be confused with the effects of the presumed treatment on the dependent variable.

 ## What Are Artifacts In Research?

In this final section, we turn to a problem described as "artifacts in research," where an **artifact** is regarded as "a type of error that occurs systematically rather than randomly and, if ignored or left uncontrolled or uncorrected, can jeopardize the validity of conclusions concerning the research hypotheses" (Rosnow, Strohmetz, & Aditya, 2000, p. 242). Artifacts can affect not only internal validity, but also construct and external validity. Artifacts can also occur in the measuring of human attributes (Fiske, 2000), a problem that we alluded to when we discussed reactive measures in Chapter 4. In this section, we review some empirically based insights about artifacts in research and the procedures for dealing with them (an area of research called "the social psychology of the experiment"). Viewed in the context of experimental research, the artifact problem (like the problem of threats to internal validity) is the concern that findings may be the result of conditions other than those intended by an experimenter. We will touch on some of the work in this area, beginning with artifacts that appear to be associated with the role and motivations of the research participants (often described as *subject-related artifacts*) and then turning our attention to *experimenter-related artifacts*.

Although insightful theoretical speculations about artifacts in research go back to the 1930s (Rosenzweig, 1933), it was not until the late 1950s and early 1960s that the problem began to be empirically investigated from the perspective of both the subjects (as research participants were commonly described) and the experimenter. Pioneering work on certain subject-related artifacts was done by Martin T. Orne, a psychologist and psychiatrist at the University of Pennsylvania, whose interest in artifacts grew out of his research on hypnosis. Observations in that research led him to theorize that the trance manifestations that participants exhibit on entering hypnosis are partly determined by their motivation to "act out" the role of a hypnotized subject. Orne believed that his volunteer participants' preconceptions of how a hypnotized person ought to act, along with the hypnotist's cues indicating how research subjects should behave (called **demand characteristics** by Orne, 1962, 1969, 1970), were likely to determine how his participants thought they should enact this role. He also theorized that typical volunteers for psychology experiments may have a tendency to enact the role of what he called "the good subject," that is, a participant who is sensitive to demand characteristics and tries to give experimenters what they seemingly want to find.

The extent to which some research participants will comply with demand characteristics sometimes surprises even an experimenter. At one point in his research on hypnosis, Orne (1962) tried to devise a set of dull, meaningless tasks that nonhypnotized persons would refuse to do or would try for a short time and quit. One task that he concocted was to ask volunteers for research participation to add thousands of rows of two-digit numbers. Five and a half hours after the participants began, the experimenter gave up! Remarkably, even when they were told to tear each worksheet into a minimum of 32 pieces before going on to the next, they *still* persisted. In another instance, Orne (1962) simply asked a number of casual acquaintances to do an experimenter a favor and, when they agreed, then asked them to do five push-ups. They seemed amazed and incredulous, and each of them responded "Why?" But when he asked a similar group of individuals whether they would take part in a brief experiment and, on their acquiescence, asked them to do five push-ups, their typical response was "Where?" Orne theorized that "good subjects," the volunteers who complied with the request to do five push-ups, may have reasoned they were helping the cause of science (see also Box 7.4).

In Chapter 5, we spoke of Milton Rosenberg's (1969) view of the human participants in psychological research as usually being apprehensive about being evaluated, a condition he referred to as *evaluation apprehension*. Although Rosenberg argued that typical subjects are motivated to "look good" rather than to help the cause of science (Orne's assumption), Rosenberg and Orne agreed that typical subjects frequently find meaning in even the most meaningless cues. Orne theorized that most research subjects (especially those who volunteer for participation) believe that, no matter how trivial and inane the task outwardly seems (such as adding thousands of rows of two-digit numbers or doing push-ups), the experimenter must surely have an important scientific purpose that justifies their experimental cooperation. Feeling that they have a stake in the outcome of the study, these "good subjects" believe they are making a useful contribution by complying with the demand characteristics of the experiment. The puzzle, Orne recognized, was to figure out a way to tease out artifact-producing demand characteristics in a given experiment.

BOX 7.4 Demand Characteristics in Hypnosis?

In one of his early experiments, Orne (1959) used students in an introductory psychology course as participants. In two sections, a demonstration of hypnosis was carried out on several of these student participants. Demonstration participants in one section were given the concocted suggestion that, on entering a hypnotic trance, they would manifest "catalepsy of the dominant hand." All of the students in this section were told that catalepsy of the dominant hand was a standard reaction of the hypnotized person, and the class's attention was called to the right-handed person's catalepsy of the right hand and the left-handed person's catalepsy of the left hand. In the other section, the demonstration of hypnosis was carried out, but without the display of Orne's concocted symptom of "catalepsy" (characterized by muscular rigidity and a suspension of sensation).

In the next phase of the study, Orne asked for volunteers for hypnosis from each section and had them tested in such a way that the experimenter could not figure out which lecture they had attended until after the completion of the experiment. Of the nine volunteers from the first section, five showed catalepsy of the dominant hand, two showed catalepsy of both hands, and two showed no catalepsy. None of the volunteers in the control section showed catalepsy of the dominant hand, but three showed catalepsy of both hands. Because catalepsy of the dominant hand was known not to occur spontaneously, Orne interpreted its occurrence in the first group but not in the second as confirmative evidence for his hypothesis that "trance behavior" is affected by the person's preconceptions of the hypnotic state. That three of nine volunteers in the control group spontaneously displayed catalepsy of both hands was explained in terms of the experimenters' repeated testing for catalepsy, which Orne suspected might be an implicit source of demand characteristics (a reactive measure).

To help researchers in this quest, Orne (1962, 1969) proposed the use of **quasi-control subjects**. These are individuals who are asked to step out of the traditional role of the "research subjects" and to think of themselves as "coinvestigators" in a scientific search for knowledge. They are drawn from the same population as the experimental and control participants, but the quasi-control subjects are asked to reflect and free-associate on the context in which the experiment is being conducted. For example, the participation of a few individuals in the experimental group might be terminated at different points during the course of the study. These participants then become quasi-control subjects, who are carefully interviewed about what they perceived to be the demand characteristics of the experiment. The key to the success of the quasi-control method is how forthcoming these individuals will be with the interviewer. Thus, it is important not to cue them with new demand characteristics. Orne found it was helpful to have someone other than the original experimenter do the interviewing, so that the quasi-control subjects clearly perceive that, for them, the experiment is over and they really are "coinvestigators."

On the other side of the subject-experimenter artifact coin are experimenter-related artifacts, that is, sources of bias (or systematic error) resulting from uncontrolled intentions or actions of the experimenters. A number of such sources have been identified (R. Rosenthal, 1966), though the one we describe here is particularly intriguing because it occurs when people's expectations unwittingly serve as self-fulfilling prophecies. When the "prophet" is the experimenter and the subjects' behavior is at issue, the self-fulfilling prophecy is called an **experimenter expectancy effect**. (In Chapter 2, we described how serendipity had played a role in an early sighting of this particular artifact.) In one early study of experimenter expectancy, each of a dozen student experimenters was given five rats to teach to run a maze with the aid of visual cues (R. Rosenthal & Fode, 1963). Half the students were told their rats had been specially bred for maze-brightness, and the remaining students were told their rats had been specially bred for maze-dullness. Actually, there were no prior differences in the rats; they had been randomly labeled as "maze-bright" or "maze-dull." At the end of the experiment, however, there were observable differences. The rats run by student-experimenters who expected maze-bright behavior performed better than the rats run by student-experimenters who had expected maze-dull behavior. When the study was repeated, this time in a series of learning experiments each conducted in a Skinner box, similar results were observed (R. Rosenthal & Lawson, 1964). Allegedly brighter rats performed better than allegedly duller rats did. The essential point here is that the experimenters' expectations had apparently acted on the performance of the animals, not merely on the perception of the animals' performance. Neither of these studies showed any evidence that the student-experimenters were trying to generate false data (i.e., there was no evidence of cheating).

A common procedure for dealing with the experimenter expectancy effect is to use **blind experimenters**, that is, experimenters who are unaware of ("blind to") which subjects are to receive the experimental treatment and which the control treatment. The idea is that, if the experimenters do not know what treatment the subject receives, they are unlikely to communicate expectancies about the nature of the treatment. The necessity of keeping the experimenters *blind* (unaware) is well recognized in randomized drug trials. Ideally, these trials use **double-blind procedures**, in which neither the human participants nor the experimenters know which individuals are in the experimental and control groups. (See also Box 7.5.)

Using the logic of experimental control, as discussed earlier in this chapter, another approach to the experimenter expectancy problem is to use a factorial design that not only assesses whether an expectancy effect is present but also allows a direct comparison of that effect with the phenomenon of theoretical interest. Such a design, also called an **expectancy control design**, is shown in the 2 × 2 factorial arrangement in Part A of Table 7.7. Group A is a condition in which the experimental treatment is administered to subjects by data collectors who expect the occurrence of the experimental effect in this sample. Group D is a condition in which the absence of the experimental treatment is associated with data collectors who expect the nonoccurrence of the experimental effect in this sample. Ordinarily, researchers are interested in the experimental effect unconfounded with experimenter expectancy; the addition of the appropriate expectancy control groups permits the researchers to evaluate the experimental effect separately from the expectancy effect. Subjects in Group B receive the experimental treatment but are contacted by data collectors who do not expect an experimental effect in this sample. The subjects in Group C do not receive the experimental treatment but are contacted by data collectors who expect an experimental effect.

You can see that it is an expensive design, because it calls for many data collectors who are randomly assigned to the four cells. Illustrative of its use in animal research was a study reported by J. R. Burnham (1966), with the results shown in Part B of Table 7.7. Each of about two dozen student-experimenters ran one rat in a discrimination task in a T-maze (a runway with the starting box at the base and the goal at one end of the crossbar). Portions of the brains of approximately

---

 BOX 7.5 Blindfolding to Ensure "Blindness"

The principle of ensuring "blindness" may also be applicable to the role of other participants in the research. For example, developmental psychologists Kathy Hirsh-Pasek and Roberta Michnick Golinkoff (1993, 1996) used a novel method to study language comprehension in infants and toddlers, a model the researchers called the "preferential looking paradigm." Suppose we want to study noun comprehension to find out how early in their lives infants and toddlers are able to distinguish a shoe from a hat. An infant is seated on a blindfolded parent's lap approximately $2\frac{1}{2}$ feet away from a pair of television monitors. By means of a concealed speaker, the word shoe is sounded at the same time that one of the monitors shows a shoe and the other monitor shows a hat. A camera records the child's preferential looking behavior over a series of trials using many different pairs of stimuli. Blindfolding the parent eliminates the possibility of the parent's unintentionally signaling the correct responses.

Table 7.7   The Expectancy Control Design

A. Basic 2 × 2 factorial design

Treatment conditions	Expectancy conditions	
	Experimental treatment	Control treatment
Experimental	Group A	Group B
Control	Group C	Group D

B. Burnham's (1966) study of discrimination learning in rats

Treatment conditions	Expectancy conditions		Row means
	Lesioning of brain	No lesioning	
Lesioning of brain	46.5	49.0	47.75
No lesioning of brain	48.2	58.3	53.25
Column means	47.35	53.65	

half the rats had been surgically removed (*lesioned*). The remaining rats had received only sham surgery, which involved a cut through the skull but no damage to brain tissue (so that it was impossible for the student-experimenters to tell which rats had actually undergone brain lesioning). The purpose of the study was explained to the student-experimenters as an attempt to learn the effects of lesions on discrimination learning. Expectancies were manipulated by the labeling of each rat as "lesioned" or "unlesioned." Some of the really lesioned rats were labeled accurately as lesioned, but some were falsely labeled as unlesioned. Similarly, some of the really unlesioned rats were labeled accurately as unlesioned, but others were falsely labeled as lesioned.

By comparing the means in the row and column margins, we get an idea of the relative effectiveness of the surgical and the expectancy treatments. The higher these scores, the better was the rats' performance in that row or column. Note that rats that had been surgically lesioned did not perform as well as those that had not been lesioned. Note also that rats that were *believed* to have been lesioned did not perform as well as those that were believed to be unlesioned. The logic of this design is that it enables the researcher to compare the magnitude of the effect of experimenter expectancy with the magnitude of the effect of actual removal of brain tissue. In this case, the two effects were similar in magnitude. Of course, we are not limited to comparing the differences in row means and column means, and previously in this chapter we mentioned how it is possible to compare all four cell means by computing a contrast that compares the group means with predicted values.

Summary of Ideas

1. In *randomized experiments*, each sampling unit has an equal chance of being assigned to any group or condition, a procedure that guards against potential sources of allocation bias.

2. Random assignment cannot guarantee equality of the groups or conditions (Box 7.1), but it increases the likelihood of such equality; it also increases the probability of drawing accurate causal inference.

3. *Random assignment rules* (or plans) include flipping coins and using random digits to eliminate bias in the allocation of the sampling units or treatment conditions.

4. In *between-subjects designs* (described as *nested designs*), the subjects or units are exposed to one condition each; these designs are not limited to two groups or two conditions.

5. The formative logic of experimental control derives from *Mill's methods of agreement (If X, then Y)* and *difference (If not-X, then not-Y),* which correspond to the experimental and control groups (e.g., a placebo control, as in Box 7.2), respectively.

6. *Within-subjects designs* (described as *crossed designs*) are distinguished by *repeated occasions of measurement.*

7. Designs may have more than one dimension (*factorial designs*), and there are also combinations (mixed factorial designs) as well as *counterbalanced* repeated-measures designs (e.g., *Latin square designs*).

8. Aristotle described four kinds of causality: *material, formal, final,* and *efficient*. Hume's idea of efficient causality was that it was an illusion created by the sensation of *contiguity, priority,* and *constant conjunction*.

9. In practice, modern scientists use critical empirical reasoning to justify causal inferences on the basis of what this chapter described as (a) *covariation* (a fusion of Hume's "contiguity" and "constant conjunction"); (b) *temporal precedence*; and (c) *internal validity*.

10. Among the possible threats to internal validity identified by Campbell and his coworkers are (a) *biased selection*, (b) *bias due to history*, (c) *bias due to maturation*, (d) *bias due to attrition*, (e) *bias due to testing*, and (f) *instrumentation bias*.

11. *Preexperimental designs,* as illustrated by the *one-shot case study* (X-O) and the *one-group pre-post design* (O-X-O), make no effort to control for threats to internal validity.

12. *Artifacts* are findings that result from conditions other than those intended (and controlled for) by the experimenter, such as (a) *subject-related artifacts* due to *demand characteristics* (which can be ferreted out by the use of *quasi-control subjects*) and (b) *experimenter expectancy effects* (controlled by the use of *blind experimenters* and, typically in randomized clinical trials, *double-blind procedures*). Based on the logic of experimental control discussed earlier in this chapter, an *expectancy control design* is used to isolate and compare the expectancy effect with the effect of the main independent variable (e.g., Burnham's study of discrimination learning in rats).

Key Terms

artifact   p. 141
between-subjects design   p. 131
bias due to attrition   p. 141
bias due to history   p. 140
bias due to maturation   p. 141
bias due to testing   p. 141
biased selection   p. 140
blind experimenters   p. 144
control group   p. 133
counterbalancing   p. 136
covariation   p. 138
crossed design   p. 134
demand characteristics   p. 142
double-blind procedures   p. 144
efficient causality   p. 137

expectancy control design   p. 144
experimenter expectancy
   effect   p. 143
factorial design   p. 135
final causality   p. 137
formal causality   p. 137
instrumentation bias   p. 141
internal validity   p. 138
Latin square design   p. 136
material causality   p. 137
method of agreement   p. 133
method of difference   p. 133
Mill's methods   p. 133
necessary condition   p. 133
nested design   p. 132

one-group pre-post design
   (O-X-O)   p. 140
one-shot case study (X-O)   p. 140
placebo effects   p. 134
preexperimental designs   p. 140
quasi-control subjects   p. 143
quasi-experimental
   designs   p. 139
random assignment   p. 129
randomization   p. 129
randomized experiments   p. 129
repeated-measures design   p. 134
sufficient condition   p. 133
temporal precedence   p. 138
within-subjects design   p. 134

Multiple-Choice Questions for Review

1. Which of the following is considered a defining characteristic of randomized clinical trials in medical research? (a) random sampling; (b) random assignment of the sampling units to the experimental and control conditions; (c) use of a placebo control group; (d) use of a quasi-control group

2. Randomization is (a) selecting a sample at random from a larger population; (b) manipulating a random sample of variables within an experiment; (c) ensuring that each subject has an equal chance of being assigned to any condition; (d) randomly determining which experimenter will conduct which experimental condition.

3. Which of the following is a type of cause that was identified by Aristotle? (a) final; (b) efficient; (c) formal; (d) all of the above

4. To conclude that X causes Y, scientists must be able to rule out plausible rival hypotheses. This is called the criterion of (a) covariation; (b) temporal precedence; (c) internal validity; (d) material causation.

5. Philosopher J. S. Mill stated, "If *X*, then *Y*." This is known as Mill's method of (a) agreement; (b) disagreement; (c) difference; (d) covariation.

6. Which of the following was described as a possible threat to internal validity? (a) bias due to maturation; (b) bias due to covariation; (c) bias due to time-series data; (d) none of the above

7. The name for a preexperimental design in which there is only one group, and that group is measured only after the treatment, is the (a) Solomon design; (b) one-shot case study; (c) Latin square design; (d) factorial design.

8. A study is conducted in which there is only one group, and the group is measured before and after the treatment. This design is vulnerable to which of the following threats to internal validity? (a) history; (b) maturation; (c) selection; (d) all of the above

9. We defined covariation as (a) a fusion of what Hume called "contiguity" and "constant conjunction"; (b) synonymous with Hume's idea of "contiguity"; (c) synonymous with Hume's idea of a "constant conjunction; (d) unrelated to Hume's ideas.

10. Cues given off by an experimental procedure and context that communicate to participants how they should behave are called (a) artifacts; (b) demand characteristics; (c) experimenter expectancy effects; (d) none of the above.

Discussion Questions for Review

1. A Colby College student wants to evaluate the effectiveness of a popular method of boosting self-esteem called "I'm-better-than-OK therapy." In this therapy, people read pop psychology books, compliment themselves while looking in a mirror, and have group touch-a-lot sessions. What kind of control group(s) would you recommend?

2. A Villanova University student believes that positive reinforcement increases self-esteem. To test this hypothesis, she administers a self-esteem scale to 40 other students and correlates the scores with their grade point averages. Can you think of any limitations in this research design?

3. An Auburn University student tells his participants that he is interested in identifying the characteristics associated with good leadership skills. He then administers two measures titled Social Intelligence Survey and Interpersonal Problem-Solving Ability. Do you see any potential problem in this method?

4. A student at the University of New Mexico wants to prove that eating a lot of chocolate chip cookies will cure depression. What basic requirements of inference would he have to meet, according to J. S. Mill?

5. An American University student wants to use an expectancy control design to assess a program offering individual tutoring to enhance students' performance on achievement tests. How might she set up this design?

6. A manufacturer of pain relievers wants to market what seems to be a revolutionary new product: a near-cure for the common cold. Researchers in the R & D division select 1,000 persons to participate in a test study. Each participant is observed for 6 months. For the first 3 months, baseline data are collected. For the last 3 months, the participants take a weekly dose of the common-cold cure. Sure enough, 15% of the participants contract a cold during the first 3 months, whereas only 5% do so in the second 3 months. The investigators rush their findings to the company president, who must decide whether the data are convincing enough for the product to be put on the market. Can you think of any weakness in the research design?

7. On a quiz, University of Arkansas students are asked to define four threats to internal validity described on the quiz in shorthand terms as "history," "maturation," "selection," and "instrumentation." Do you know the answers?

8. A Howard University medical student designs an experiment to test the effects of a new drug. In consultation with her faculty mentor, she decides to include both a placebo control and a zero control group. Do you know the difference?

Answers to Review Questions

Multiple-Choice Questions

1. b	3. d	5. a	7. b	9. a
2. c	4. c	6. a	8. d	10. b

Discussion Questions

1. A placebo control group might be used to which clients are randomly assigned. This placebo control group would receive a pseudomethod of boosting self-esteem, for example, reading material believed to be irrelevant to self-esteem and watching irrelevant movies. The clients assigned to this placebo control group should believe that their "treatment" will have beneficial effects to the same degree as do the clients assigned to the "real" treatment.

2. Because the positive reinforcement (grades) was not experimentally manipulated, there is no basis for her concluding that it "caused" the self-esteem scores even if there is a positive correlation between self-esteem and GPA. Self-esteem may as well "cause" grades, or some other variable may "cause" both grades and self-esteem.

3. Telling participants the hypothesis and the names of the measuring instruments is likely to result in strong demand characteristics.

4. According to Mill's methods, the student would have to show that eating chocolate chip cookies is followed by a reduction in depression (method of agreement) and that not eating chocolate chip cookies is not followed by a reduction in depression (method of difference).

5. The basic plan could be implemented by use of the following four conditions, analogous to those shown in Table 7.7:

	Expectancy	
Actual treatment	Experimental	Control
Tutoring	A	B
Control	C	D

6. As in all one-group pre-post studies, history, maturation, and instrumentation all threaten the internal validity of the research.

7. History refers to the presence of an event other than, but usually concurrent with, the treatment that could be responsible for the observed effect. Maturation refers to certain naturally occurring changes over time (e.g., the participants' growing older, wiser, stronger, or more experienced), which might be responsible for the observed effect. Selection refers to how the sampling units assigned to different conditions were selected for those conditions. Instrumentation refers to changes in the instruments (including judges as "instruments) that might be confused with the observed effect (e.g., instrument deterioration, such as fatigued judges).

8. A placebo control group offers a treatmentlike condition that serves to control for research participants' beliefs or expectations about the efficacy of any treatments that might be administered. A zero-control group is characterized by the absence of any intervention, "real" or "pseudo" (placebo).

CHAPTER 8

Nonrandomized Research and Causal Reasoning

Preview Questions

- How is causal reasoning attempted in the absence of randomization?
- How is the third-variable problem relevant?
- What is meant by subclassification on propensity scores?
- What are time-series designs and "found experiments"?
- What within-subjects designs are used in single-case experiments?
- How are correlations interpreted in cross-lagged panel designs?
- What is the difference between longitudinal and cross-sectional research?

 How Is Causal Reasoning Attempted in the Absence of Randomization?

In the previous chapter, we described how researchers do randomized controlled experiments in an attempt to create the equivalence they need to make causal inferences. Randomized controlled experiments are not always possible, however. Suppose your arm was bitten by a dog. You go to a doctor, who prescribes a tetanus shot and an oral antibiotic. You ask the doctor to give the tetanus shot in the arm that has been bitten so that you have the use of your other arm. But the doctor points out that if she did so and you had a reaction to the tetanus, she would not be able to separate it from the possible continued reaction to the dog bite, which could, in the worst-case scenario, cause the arm to swell. For this reason, she gives the shot in your good arm so any swelling due to an allergy to the tetanus will not be confounded with a reaction to the dog bite. Her causal reasoning was in some ways suggestive of the simplest *single-case experiment* (discussed later in this chapter). The doctor's "single-case experiment" will use **prospective data**; that is, she will collect data by following your reaction forward in time (*prospective* means "of or in the future"). Prospective data are also often used in *longitudinal research* (also discussed in this chapter), the defining characteristic of which is that individuals are observed and measured repeatedly through time. In Chapter 4, we mentioned the Framingham Heart Study (Box 4.1), a longitudinal observational investigation that was started by the U.S. Public Health Service in the 1940s.

The purpose of this chapter is to sample several families of nonrandomized designs that are frequently used for generalized causal inference, including *nonequivalent-groups designs*, *interrupted time-series designs*, *cross-lagged panel designs*, *single-case experimental designs*, and *cohort designs*. Sometimes the data are collected back in time, and they are called **retrospective data** (*retrospective* means "looking or directed backward"). Table 8.1 shows a hypothetical example of retrospective data (derived from an illustration by Kahane, 1989). Suppose 12 people ate at a

Persons	Ate rare hamburger	Ate tuna sandwich	Ate fries	Ate salad	Drank shake	Got food poisoning
Mimi	Yes	No	Yes	No	No	Yes
Gail	No	No	No	Yes	Yes	No
Connie	No	No	Yes	No	No	No
Jerry	No	Yes	No	Yes	No	No
Greg	No	Yes	No	No	Yes	No
Dwight	No	No	No	Yes	No	No
Chris	Yes	No	Yes	Yes	No	Yes
Richard	No	Yes	Yes	Yes	No	No
Kerry	No	No	No	Yes	No	No
Michele	Yes	No	Yes	Yes	Yes	Yes
John	Yes	No	Yes	Yes	No	Yes
Barbara	Yes	No	No	No	No	Yes

Table 8.1   Causal Reasoning With Retrospective Data

fast-food restaurant, and 5 of them (Mimi, Chris, Michele, John, and Barbara) got food poisoning (*Y*). Epidemiologists generally deal with far more complex data, but suppose you were given the data in Table 8.1 and asked to figure out the reason (*X*) that the five people became sick. All you have to work with is the circumstantial evidence of covariation (i.e., the foods they ate and whether they got food poisoning) and temporal precedence (i.e., retrospective information on what each person said they had eaten). The challenge now is to try to emulate the causal reasoning of Mill's methods (discussed in Chapter 7) in order to arrive at causal hypotheses that are as sound as possible within the limitations of the retrospective database.

Table 8.1 indicates that Michele had a milk shake, but we cannot think of a way that the milk shake might have caused food poisoning (though spoiled milk could cause stomach upsets). But Gail and Greg also had milk shakes, and they did not get an upset stomach. Of those people who got sick with food poisoning, some of them reported they ate a salad (Chris, Michele, and John), and it is possible that a salad might have contained spoiled dressing. Some people ate a salad and did not get sick (Gail, Jerry, Dwight, Richard, and Kerry), but maybe their salads did not have the same dressing. The table also shows that some of the people who got sick ate greasy french fries, but Connie and Richard also ate french fries and were not affected. The most striking finding in the table is that all those who got sick ate a rare hamburger, and no one who did not get sick ate a rare hamburger. It is easy to imagine how a rare hamburger might contain bacteria that were not destroyed in the cooking process.

On the surface, the one common factor was the rare hamburger. But suppose the owner tells us that one of the food handlers was feeling ill the day these people were served. That food handler worked for a while, but after he complained of feeling dizzy and nauseated, the owner told him to leave work early. Suppose the food handler touched some, but not all, of the foods eaten while he was there that day. Maybe he passed on his germs by serving the five people who got food poisoning, Maybe his handling of Mimi's and Barbara's hamburger, Chris's salad dressing, and Michele's and John's fries would be another factor common to all the cases.

Once we think about this situation some more, we think we can safely rule out the food handler because he must have served others and touched more items than those suggested above. If he were the cause (*X*), then others who ate at the restaurant should have become ill (*Y*). Maybe they did and just did not report it, but all we have is Table 8.1. It shows that 7 people did not get food poisoning (not-*Y*) even though they ate some of the same things the others ate (*X*), except for the rare hamburger (the true *X*?). Only the rare hamburger was absent in every reported case in which there was no food poisoning. On the basis of the available retrospective data, we suspect that the rare hamburger was the necessary and sufficient condition (*X*) that brought about food poisoning (*Y*). Perhaps there were also variables that moderated the relation between *X* and *Y*, but there is not enough information to explore that possibility. Furthermore, it appears from the retrospective reports that everyone who ate the rare hamburger got food poisoning. (We will return to these results in Chapter 11, where we will show how the association between eating the rare hamburger and becoming sick can be quantified by a correlation statistic.)

How Is the Third-Variable Problem Relevant?

You know that causality implies correlation, as causality entails the covariation of the presumed cause (*X*) and the presumed effect (*Y*). However, finding that *X* and *Y* covary does not reveal *why* they are related. In the previous chapter, we explained that, besides covariation and *temporal precedence* (that *X* preceded *Y*), another requirement of causal inference is the exclusion of plausible rival explanations of the covarying relationship between *X* and *Y*. Back in Chapter 4, we first mentioned the concept of a rival explanation described as the **third-variable problem**. That is, in nonrandomized research, a "third variable" that is correlated with both *X* and *Y* could cause *X* and *Y* to covary. We cited Paulos's (1991) clever example of the high positive correlation between (*X*) the size of children's feet and (*Y*) their spelling ability. The implication is not that stretching a child's feet will result in better spelling, but that as children mature, and their feet grow, they also usually spell better. In other words, a third variable (age) that is correlated with *both X* and *Y* can also account for the correlation *between X* and *Y*.

As a practical illustration of this problem, imagine that we have discovered an outbreak of strange medical symptoms and want to explain them in causal terms. Time is of the essence, but we don't want to mislead people, and possibly cause further harm, by making a spurious causal inference. We might begin by drawing a representative sample of those afflicted and then interview them, with the aim of finding some event they have in common. As it turns out, *before* they experienced the strange new medical symptoms, they had all been ill and, as result, had been prescribed a new drug whose side effects have not been fully established. We suspect that a side effect of the new drug may be the cause of the strange new symptoms. The most direct way to dispel our suspicion would be to design a randomized experiment in which we take a sample of *asymptomatic* people (people without these strange new symptoms) and randomly give half of them the suspected drug and give a placebo to the other half. Although this "gold standard trial" would allow us to compare these two groups of people to see whether those given the new drug are more likely to develop the strange new symptoms, the ethical cost of such a study would obviously be unacceptable. We cannot deliberately expose people to a drug we have good reason to suspect is harmful.

Another alternative might be to track down patients who were diagnosed with the original illness and separate from that group the patients who were prescribed the new drug. We then compare them with those patients whose physicians did not prescribe the new drug. If only those given the new drug have developed the strange new medical symptoms, the new drug would seem to be more seriously implicated as the causal agent. However, its causal role is still not fully established, because patients given the new drug may differ on some unknown variable (a "third variable") from those not given the drug. That is, using the same logic we used when thinking about rival hypotheses in randomized experiments (threats to internal validity), we think it is plausible that not the new drug but an unknown correlate of being given the new drug might be the causal variable.

Suppose in our exploratory research we discover that not all patients who took the new drug were given the same dosage levels. Another strategy might be to correlate the dosage levels with the outcome variable. If it turns out that patients on larger dosages suffer more severely with the strange new medical symptoms, would this evidence clearly implicate the drug more strongly as the cause of those symptoms? Unfortunately, the answer is the same as the one above, which is that we still cannot be sure about the causal role of the new drug, because those given larger dosages may have initially been more severely ill. In other words, we wonder whether the *severity* of the illness for which the different dosages of the drug were prescribed, rather than the drug itself, might be the unknown third variable that is responsible for the strange new symptoms.

How have we done so far? "Not very well," you might answer. To confidently establish temporal precedence, we need to show that taking the new drug preceded the strange new medical symptoms. Unless our medical records go back far enough, we may not be able to prove that the symptoms did not occur until after the drug was taken. The covariation assumption requires us to show that the new drug is related to the strange new medical symptoms. However, even if we can show that taking the new drug is correlated with the mysterious symptoms, it might be argued that, in order to be susceptible to the drug, a patient already had to be in a given state of distress. According to this argument, it was not the new drug—or maybe *not only* the new drug—that was related to the strange symptoms. If the patients who were in a state of distress were the only ones given the new drug, it is possible that the state of the patients' distress determined the particular group in which they found themselves.

Despite the ambiguity of causal inference in this case, we might still be convinced by strong circumstantial, though inconclusive, correlational evidence. If patients who had been taking the new drug were more likely to display the strange new medical symptoms, if those taking more of the new drug displayed more of the strange symptoms, and if those taking it over a longer period of time also displayed more of the strange symptoms, we would be reluctant to conclude that the new drug was *not* the cause of the strange symptoms. Even if we were unwilling to state that the new drug was definitely at the root of the strange symptoms, at least on the basis of the type of correlational evidence outlined above, it might be prudent to act "as though" it were. On this basis, we might think about designing a randomized experiment using an animal model (primates, for example) to simulate the strange medical symptoms, because we also now have a causal model with which to work. Still, failure to produce the symptoms in primates would not rule out a causal relationship in human patients.

What Is Meant By Subclassification on Propensity Scores?

In the previous chapter we alluded to a family of nonrandomized designs described as **nonequivalent-groups designs**. Nonequivalent-groups designs traditionally take the form of between-subjects designs in which the sampling units (the subjects, groups, etc.) are allocated to the experimental and control groups by means other than randomization and are also observed or tested before and after the experimental intervention. Imagine we want to investigate the effect of a new therapy for treating hyperactive children. If it were a randomized experiment, we would use an unbiased procedure to assign the hyperactive children to the experimental treatment or the control group. However, suppose that circumstances beyond our control dictate that we must use two intact groups of children: one group at School A and the other at School B. We could flip a coin to decide which school will be the experimental group, but we are unable to allocate children *within* each school to the two groups.

Assuming these children will be observed and measured at both the beginning and the end of the study, the nonrandomized design can be diagrammed as follows:

School A   NR   O   X   O
School B   NR   O   O

where X = treatment or intervention, O = observation or measurement, and NR = nonrandomized allocation of sampling units to conditions (see also Box 8.1). One potentially significant problem is that the children in School A may be different from those in School B in a basic way that systematically biases the results when we compare one intact group (from School A) with another intact

| **BOX 8.1 Wait-List Controls**

If the researcher cannot use a random assignment procedure in a particular case because of concerns about depriving the control group of the experimental treatment, the researcher might propose a randomized design with a **wait-list control group**. Such a design can also have other benefits. Here is an example of a randomized design with a wait-list control group:

Group 1	R	O	X	O	O
Group 2	R	O		O	X	O

where R = random allocation of the participants to groups or treatment conditions, O = observation or measurement, and X = treatment or intervention. Those participants assigned to Group 1 receive the experimental treatment (X) at the beginning of the study, and (assuming the treatment is found to be beneficial) those assigned to Group 2 (the control condition) are later given an opportunity to receive the treatment once the beneficial result is observed. If we measure Group 1 after the treatment and again after Group 2 receives it, and we compare the results with those in Group 2, a further benefit of the design is that we have information about the immediate and delayed effect of the treatment as well as a replication of the immediate effect.

group (School B). The general nature of this problem was recognized years ago by an Iowa State University statistician, E. F. Lindquist (1953), who called it "Type G Error" (for "group error"); it means that relevant extraneous factors exist that are characteristic of the group from School A but uncharacteristic of the group from School B. The group from School A might have been assigned to better teachers, or the home lives of most of the group from one school might be more supportive than those from the other school, and so on. Much has been written about these nonequivalent-groups designs by the Campbell group of methodologists (most recently by Shadish et al., 2002), and we will describe an innovative statistical way of improving this situation when sample sizes are large enough and there are relevant subgroups that are also well stocked with sampling units.

This procedure, described as **subclassification on propensity scores**, reduces all of the variables on which the "treated" and "untreated" sampling units differ to a single composite variable (Rosenbaum & Rubin, 1983; Rubin, 2006). This composite variable, called a **propensity score**, is a summary statistic of all the differences on all variables on which the "treated" and "untreated" units differ. The procedure requires a computer program (Rubin, 2006), and the technical details are beyond the scope of this book, but Table 8.2 provides a summary illustration (Rubin, 2006, p. 43). In Part A of the table are the data from a study (Cochran, 1968) of the death rates for nonsmokers (N), cigarette smokers (C), and cigar and pipe smokers (CP) in each of three geographic databases

Table 8.2 Comparing Death Rates for Nonsmokers (N), Cigarette Smokers (C), and Cigar and Pipe Smokers (CP) in Three National Databases

	Canada			United Kingdom			United States		
	N	C	CP	N	C	CP	N	C	CP
A. Death rates per 1,000 person years									
	20.2	20.5	35.5	11.3	14.1	20.7	13.5	13.5	17.4
B. Average age in years									
	54.9	50.5	65.9	49.1	49.8	55.7	57.0	53.2	59.7
C. Adjusted death rates based on at least nine subclasses of age in each subpopulation									
	20.2	29.5	19.8	11.3	14.8	11.0	13.5	21.2	13.7

(Canada, the United Kingdom, and the United States). Notice that the death rates are highest for the cigar and pipe smokers (CP) and lower for the nonsmokers (N) and cigarette smokers (C) in all three geographic databases. What surprises us is that the death rates of the nonsmokers (N) and the cigarette smokers (C) in the United States sample are identical, a finding that would suggest that cigarette smoking is not harmful to health!

Part B of the table, however, shows substantial discrepancies in the average age of each subpopulation. Because age and mortality are correlated, age in this example is a confounding variable. We would need to adjust for the average differences in age before reaching any conclusions about death rates of nonsmokers (N), cigarette smokers (C), and cigar and pipe smokers (CP). An adjustment for age would subdivide each subpopulation into age categories of roughly equal size. The next step would compare the death rates within the age categories. The final step would be adjusting the death rates by averaging over the age-group-specific comparisons in order to get overall estimates of the death rates. Part C of Table 8.2 shows the final results of this subclassification-on-propensity-scores analysis. In this case, the adjusted death rates were based on dividing the subpopulations into nine or more subcategories of roughly equal size. Now we see very clearly that the death rate was actually consistently highest among the cigarette smokers and lowest in the nonsmoking U.S. database and lowest in the cigar- and pipe-smoking Canadian and United Kingdom databases. Although the procedure required a technically complex analysis, its beauty was that it corrected for the statistical artifacts in the original nonequivalent groups.

What Are Time-Series Designs and "Found Experiments"?

In **time-series designs**, the defining characteristic is the study of variation across some dimension over time. When the effects of some intervention or "treatment" are inferred from a comparison of the outcome measures obtained at different time intervals before and after the intervention, the data structure is called an **interrupted time-series design**. The term *time series* means there is a data point for each point in time, and an *interrupted* time series means there is a dividing line at the beginning of the intervention (a line analogous to the start of the "treatment"). For example, Gottman (1979) described how certain cycles of social behavior might be studied in the context of a time-series design. He mentioned earlier work by Kendon (1967) showing that when two people converse, there are cycles of gazing and averting gazing at one another as a function of who is speaking. The person who begins speaking has a tendency to look away from the listener and then to increase eye-to-eye contact toward the end of the speech, which is an implicit signal for the listener to begin looking away and speaking. This cycle, Gottman thought, is suggestive of cycles of sine and cosine waves. Another example of cycles is regular repetitions of brain waves when people are awake, drowsy, or in different stages of sleep.

The statistical analysis of time-series designs has its own terminology and can be quite complex (e.g., Cryer, 1986; Judd & Kenny, 1981; Gottman, 1981), but we will give a simplified application that was inspired by the work of sociologist David P. Phillips. He referred to his studies as "found experiments" because they are essentially *found* (or discovered) in naturally occurring situations (cf. Phillips & Glynn, 2000). In one such set of studies, Phillips explored the clustering of imitative suicides after a series of televised news stories and televised movies about suicide (see Phillips, Lesyna, & Paight, 1992, for a review). The variations in the results were difficult to explain, however. For example, a New York City study found that teenage suicides had increased after three televised fictional films about suicide (Gould & Shaffer, 1986), but a follow-up study (Phillips & Paight, 1987) done in California and Pennsylvania did not find an increase in teenage suicides after the same three films were televised. In another study, conducted in Austria, Phillips and Carstensen (1986) reported evidence of what appeared to be copycat imitations of suicides in news stories.

In Vienna, Austria, there was a sharp increase in the number of subway suicides in 1984. Persuaded by the evidence generated by Phillips and others, the Austrian Association for Suicide Prevention, Crisis Intervention, and Conflict Resolution argued that there might be a connection

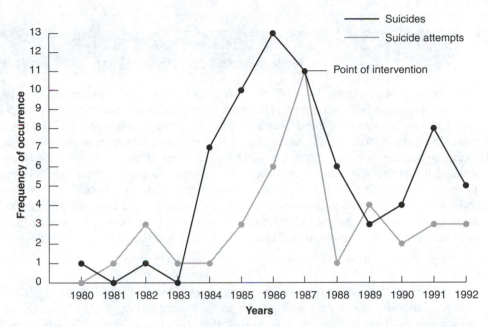

Figure 8.1   Subway suicides and suicide attempts from 1980 to 1992 in Vienna, Austria.

Source: Reprinted from G. Sonneck, E. Etzersdorfer, S. Nagel-Kuess, Imitative suicide on the Viennese subway, Social Science & Medicine, Volume 38, Issue 3, February 1994, Pages 453–457, ISSN 0277-9536, Copyright © 1994 Elsevier Science. Reprinted with permission from Elsevier.

between this increase and the then heavy emphasis in newspaper stories on subway suicides. The organization drew up media guidelines and convinced two large-circulation Viennese newspapers to curtail the publicity given to subway suicides. The change in policy occurred in June 1987, and Figure 8.1 shows time-series data based on an article by Sonneck, Etzersdorfer, and Nagel-Kuess (1994, p. 454). The data reveal a dramatic reduction in subway suicides and suicide attempts after this policy was enacted (Sonneck, Etzersdorfer, & Nagel-Kuess, 1994). Using the symbols that we used earlier (X = treatment or intervention; O = observation or measurement), we can diagram this interrupted time-series design as:

$$O\ O\ O\ O\ O\ O\ O\ X\ O\ O\ O\ O\ O\ O$$

where O is the number (or frequency of occurrence) of subway suicides and suicide attempts in a particular calendar year, and X is the intervention of the media curtailment agreed to by the leading newspapers.

 ## What Within-Subjects Designs Are Used in Single-Case Experiments?

A family of nonrandomized designs that is a mainstay of behavior modification research is called **single-case experimental research** (also called *small-N experimental research* and *N-of-1 experimental research*). Characteristic of all single-case experimental designs is that they incorporate "treatments" (interventions) that are manipulated and controlled for within a repeated-measures design. What distinguishes them from other experimental and nonexperimental designs is that, in single-case experiments, (a) only one sampling unit is studied, or only a few units are studied; (b) repeated measurements are taken of the unit (a within-subjects design); and (c) random assignment is rarely used. It would, of course, be impossible to assign a single subject at random to the various treatment procedures. Instead, the occasions (at intervals of days, weeks, or months) may be assigned at random to the various treatment procedures, and the results can then be compared (Hineline & Lattal, 2000).

BOX 8.2 Superstition in the Pigeon and the Financial Market

In a fascinating single-case study by B. F. Skinner (1948a), the unit was eight hungry pigeons. The birds were housed in cages in which there was a food hopper (containing grain) that swung into and away from the cage at regular intervals. A timing mechanism automatically moved the hopper into the cage so that all the pigeon had to do was reach into the hopper and eat. But six of the birds developed "superstitious" movements, in that whatever they had been doing in the moment when they were first rewarded with food became imprinted. One pigeon made counterclockwise motions about the cage before taking the grain; another performed a tossing motion of the head; and others persisted in making pendulum-type motions of the head and body or brushing movements toward the floor. Some behavioral economists theorize that this behavior is similar to what goes on in financial markets, where people infer causal connections between two occurrences when, in fact, there is no causal link (Fuerbringer, 1997).

Although the sampling unit in a single-case design is frequently the single unit (human or animal), the unit might be a group, such as an assembly line, a class of students, a shift of workers in a plant, or a set of hungry pigeons (see Box 8.2). In one study, the unit was the offensive backfield on a football team of 9- to 10-year-olds; the purpose of the single-case experiment was to test a schedule of feedback to improve their execution of plays (Komaki & Barnett, 1977). In another case, the unit was a community, and the objective was to encourage drivers to obtain and use child safety seats by presenting them with coupons they could exchange for a seat and training in its use (Lavelle, Hovell, West, & Wahlgren, 1992). In another study, a single-case design was used to evaluate the effect of a national antismoking campaign on the reduction of smoking in a large urban hospital (Hantula, Stillman, & Waranch, 1992).

Single-case experimental designs are often used in educational, clinical, and counseling settings to evaluate the effects of operant conditioning interventions (e.g., I. H. Iversen & Lattal, 1991; Johnston & Pennypacker, 1993a, 1993b; Kazdin, 1992). In operant conditioning (described in Chapter 2), one way to strengthen behavior is to reward the behavior, and one way to weaken behavior is to use extinction (no longer rewarding the response). Such designs employ as a **behavioral baseline** the observations of a consistent pattern in the subject's behavior before the experimental treatment (or intervention). That is, a relatively stable pattern of behavior before the treatment or intervention serves as a kind of "pretest" with which details about the pattern of behavior after the treatment can be compared. In this way, the unit serves as its own control in a within-subjects design.

As an illustration, a team of psychologists employed a single-case design to track the effects of interventions used in the classroom to shape the behavior of a child named Robbie (R. V. Hall, Lund, & Jackson, 1968). The results of this study are shown in Figure 8.2. During the baseline period (a class spelling period), the psychologists recorded that Robbie's study behavior was consistently low, ranging from a low point of about 15% of the time to a high point of slightly over 40%, with an average of about 25%. The rest of the time, they observed, Robbie's behavior was disruptive: He snapped rubber bands, played with toys in his pocket, slowly drank his milk, played with the milk carton, and laughed with those around him. Almost 55% of his teacher's attention was absorbed by this disruptive behavior.

The psychologists believed that the teacher's attention was actually maintaining Robbie's disruptive behavior. To modify his behavior, they decided to use a twofold intervention: (a) ignoring the nonstudy and disruptive behavior (extinction) and (b) attending to the appropriate study behavior (positive reinforcement). Whenever he engaged in 1 minute of continuous study, the observer would quietly signal the teacher and she would come over and compliment Robbie, saying such things as "Good work, Robbie." The second part of Figure 8.2 shows Robbie's increased study behavior during the nine sessions of this stage of the experiment. Then, to verify the effect of the teacher's

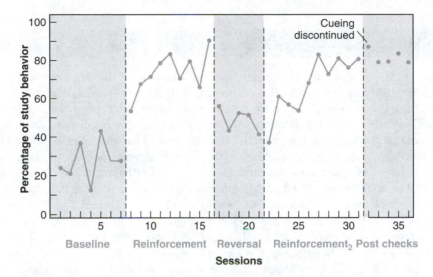

Figure 8.2   Robbie's study behavior record.

Source: "Effects of Teacher Attention on Study Behavior," Journal of Applied Behavior Analysis (1968). Used with permission.

attention, the consequences were reversed. The teacher ignored Robbie, remaining with the group. Robbie's study behavior decreased to about 50% over these sessions. When reinforcement was restored, Robbie's study behavior increased to and leveled off at about 75%. A checkup over the following weeks, when the teacher continued to praise Robbie's study behavior, showed that Robbie continued to study. Robbie's spelling performance also improved, with a jump from fewer than 5 words correct out of 10 to an impressive 9 words correct out of 10.

Instead of Xs and Os, single-case researchers use a different notation system to represent their specific designs. The basic model is called an **A-B-A design**, which evolved out of an even simpler prototype, the **A-B design** (which is the simplest of all single-case designs). In the A phase, no treatment (or intervention) is in effect, and in the B phase a treatment (or intervention) is operating. The first A in the A-B-A and A-B designs is, therefore, the baseline period. Once the researcher observes steady, continuous behavior in the baseline phase, the treatment (B) is introduced. In other words, the researcher is observing and recording the behavior repeatedly within all phases of the design: the A phase and the B phase. In an A-B design, the dependent variable is measured repeatedly throughout the baseline and intervention phases of the study. In the A-B-A design, the treatment is withdrawn at the end of the B phase and the behavior is measured; that is, there are repeated measures before the treatment, during the treatment, and then when the treatment has been withdrawn.

A number of other single-case designs are used in clinical intervention assessment. In the **A-B-BC-B design**, for example, the B and C are two different therapeutic interventions. The symbols tell us that the individual's behavior is measured or observed (a) before the introduction of either intervention, (b) during Intervention B, (c) during the combination of Intervention B and Intervention C, and (d) during B alone. The purpose of this design is to evaluate the effect of B both in combination with C and apart from C. Notice in this case that the sequence ends with a treatment phase, the reason being that if the intervention is beneficial, the researcher does not want to end the study on a negative note.

Still another basic variant is the **A-B-A-B design**. The strategy ends in a treatment phase of B, but this model provides two occasions (B to A and then A to B) for demonstrating the positive effects of the intervention (Hersen & Barlow, 1976). Returning to the illustrative study in Figure 8.2, we can see that it is a simple variant on this design, that is, an **A-B-A-B-A design**. Robbie's behavior was observed (a) before the reinforcement intervention, (b) during the intervention, (c) after removal of the intervention, (d) during its restoration, and (e) after the desired behavior had been shaped by

BOX 8.3 Randomization in Single-Case Research

On occasion, single-case researchers use designs that are hard to distinguish from randomized experimental designs. An example was a study done by psychologists at the University of Notre Dame (Anderson, Crowell, Hantula, & Siroky, 1988), in which the unit consisted of workers in a student-managed bar. The bar was a haunt of many students and faculty members, but the state board of health threatened to close it after citing health problems (e.g., pervasive accumulations of grease, as well as garbage disposal areas strewn with debris). The psychologists agreed to try to modify the behavior of the students who worked at the bar, using a variant on what is called the **A-B-C design**. The B phase consisted of exposing workers to a task clarification treatment, and the C phase was a feedback period. What is particularly striking about this single-case study is that the researchers allocated the workers to three groups *at random* in an effort to control for the delay of

feedback. The A phase was the baseline period, in which the workers' usual behavior was recorded. During the B phase, all the workers were instructed in how to work more neatly, and a set of criteria was posted for all to see (e.g., put refrigerated items in the refrigerator, pick up garbage in the men's bathroom, clean bar utensils, and wipe off all games). A week later, each worker in Group 1 was given feedback, which continued for 2 more weeks. The feedback treatment in Group 2 did not begin until 1 week after it had been initiated in Group 1, and the feedback in Group 3 was initiated another week later. Thus, it was possible to compare the effects of immediate and delayed feedback in this combination of a between-subjects (delay of feedback) and within-subjects (A-B-C) design. The result of the behavior modification effort was that sanitary conditions in the bar improved markedly, so much so that it was not closed (to the gratification of the students and the researchers).

the prior intervention. The advantage of this design is that it allows us to compare Robbie's behavior during different phases, although, as noted, it does not control for threats to internal validity (such as the instrumentation problem). Though the interpretation of single-case results typically depends on visual inspection, there are statistical techniques for testing predictions in the evaluation of these within-subjects results (e.g., Kazdin, 1976; Kratochwill & Levin, 1992; Rosenthal & Rosnow, 1985; Rosenthal, Rosnow, & Rubin, 2000). (See also Box 8.3.)

How Are Correlations Interpreted in Cross-Lagged Panel Designs?

A **cross-lagged panel design** is called *cross-lagged* because some of the data points are treated as temporally "lagged" (delayed) values of the outcome variable. It is called a *panel design* because, in social survey terminology, a *panel study* is another name for a **longitudinal study** (a study that examines the change in a person or a group of people over an extended period of time). Figure 8.3 shows the simplest cross-lagged design, where A and B denote two variables, each of which has been measured individually over two successive time periods. The figure shows paired correlations, where the symbol r denotes correlation, and the subscripts are the correlated variables. You will recall that the Pearson r can range from -1.0 (a perfect negative relationship) through 0 (no relationship) to $+1.0$ (a perfect positive relationship). Let us see what each of the correlations in Figure 8.3 tells us.

We will start with r_{A1A2} and r_{B1B2}, which refer to the correlation, respectively, between A at Time 1 and A at Time 2 and between B at Time 1 and B at Time 2. Both these correlations are like **test-retest correlations** that tell us the reliability of each A and B over two time periods. Next, there are r_{A1B1} and r_{A2B2}, which refer to the correlation, respectively, between A and B at Time 1 and A and B at Time 2. These correlations are called **synchronous correlations** (*synchronous* means that A and B are observed or measured in the same period); when we compare them, these two correlations tell us the reliability of the association between A and B over the two time periods. Finally, there are r_{A1B2} and r_{B1A2}, which refer to the correlation, respectively, between A at Time 1 and B at Time 2

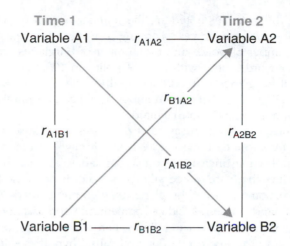

Figure 8.3   Design for cross-lagged and other correlations between Variables A and B.

and between B at Time 1 and A at Time 2. Both of these correlations are **cross-lagged correlations**, which show the relationships between two sets of data points, where one point is treated as a lagged value of the outcome variable.

The causal question concerns whether A is a more likely cause of B than B is of A, or whether A might cause B to a greater extent than B might cause A. The logic used to arrive at the answer is that, given equally reliable test-retest correlations (r_{A1A2} and r_{B1B2}) and synchronous correlations equal in magnitude (r_{A1B1} and r_{A2B2}), comparing the cross-lagged correlations (r_{A1B2} and r_{B1A2}) will enable us to conclude which is the more likely causal direction, or which variable (A or B) implies the preponderance of causal influence. Assuming there is any causal relation, we suspect that A is a more likely (or more important) "cause" of B than B is of A if r_{A1B2} is appreciably higher than r_{B1A2}. On the other hand, we suspect that B is a more likely (or more important) "cause" of A than A is of B if r_{B1A2} is appreciably higher than r_{A1B2}. An example will show how this design is used and will illustrate the hidden problem of *confounded hypotheses* (competing confounded pairs of hypotheses).

Figure 8.4 is taken from an unpublished correlational study by Louise Kidder, Robert Kidder, and Paul Snyderman (1976). The correlations are based on archival data in the *FBI Uniform Crime Reports*

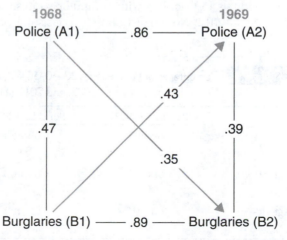

Figure 8.4   Correlation of number of police and number of burglaries per capita measured in 1968 and 1969 in 724 cities.

Source: Based on Kidder, Kidder, and Snyderman, 1976.

for 1968–1969; the variables noted are the number of police (A) and the number of burglaries (B) in 724 U.S. cities during each year. Looking first at the test-retest correlations (.86 and .89), we see that both the number of police and the number of burglaries were quite reliable during this 2-year period. In other words, cities with a lot of police in 1968 had a lot of police in 1969, and also cities with a lot of burglaries in 1968 continued to have a lot of burglaries in 1969. The synchronous correlations of .47 and .39 between number of police and number of burglaries for 1968 and 1969, respectively, were substantial in magnitude.

At first glance, our intuition says that burglaries may cause an increase in the number of police. The problem of confounded hypotheses is that it might just as well be hypothesized that increasing the number of police may increase recorded burglaries, because the more police there are available, the more opportunities there are to keep thorough records of all the burglaries reported. When there are not many police, some reported burglaries may go unrecorded. The cross-lagged correlations do not allow us to definitively rule out either competing hypothesis and, in fact, provide some support for both (.43 and .35). If you think carefully, you are sure to come up with other rival hypotheses. There are statistical ways of trying to rule out rival causal hypotheses in cross-lagged designs, but they are not without problems (Campbell & Wainer, 1963; Kenny, 1979; Pelz & Andrew, 1964; Rogosa, 1980; Rozelle & Campbell, 1969). Though the cross-lagged panel strategy is no longer as popular as it once was, some leading methodologists emphasize its usefulness as an exploratory procedure in the analysis of longitudinal data (Campbell & Kenny, 1999; cf. Kenny & Campbell, 1984, 1989).

What Is the Difference Between Longitudinal and Cross-Sectional Research?

Earlier, we mentioned the Framingham Heart Study as an example of longitudinal research. You will recall that the defining characteristic of this kind of research is that individuals or groups are observed or measured repeatedly through time. This kind of nonrandomized design can be contrasted with a **cross-sectional design**, in which the outcomes are measured for each individual or group during one period. The distinction between longitudinal and cross-sectional designs is illustrated in Table 8.3, called a *cohort table*. The sociological term **cohort** traditionally refers to a collection of individuals who were born in the same period, implying a "generation" that has experienced certain similar life events at the same period (Ryder, 1965). The table shows hypothetical percentages of cohort members with computer sophistication (as measured by a specially designed test) in three age ranges (20–30, 30–40, and 40–50) and three periods (1992, 2002, 2012). For example, the members of Cohort 3 are 20–30 years old in 1992, 30–40 years old in 2002, and 40–50 years old in 2012. The percentage of individuals in Cohort 3 with computer sophistication increases from 70% in 1992, to 75% in 2002, to 80% in 2012. Note that Cohort 1, consisting of people 40–50 years of age in 1992,

Table 8.3	Percentages of People Ages 20–30, 30–40, and 40–50 With Computer Sophistication in 1992, 2002, and 2012 (Hypothetical Data)*

	Period 1 (1992)	Period 2 (2002)	Period 3 (2012)
Age 20–30	Cohort 3 70	Cohort 4 80	Cohort 5 90
Age 30–40	Cohort 2 60	Cohort 3 75	Cohort 4 85
Age 40–50	Cohort 1 50	Cohort 2 70	Cohort 3 80

* Each column of results gives us a cross-sectional perspective on computer sophistication in three age ranges at a particular period (as illustrated by Period 3), whereas tracking the cohorts diagonally gives us a longitudinal perspective (as illustrated by Cohort 3).

is not tracked after the first period because they are 50–60 in 2002, which is beyond the age range of this hypothetical study. Similarly, the table does not track Cohort 5 beyond the 20–30 age range because 2012 is the final period reported.

It is simpler, and certainly less costly, to sample individuals or groups cross-sectionally during one time period than to try to follow individuals or groups over several periods. However, a vital question is whether the cross-sectional results will give as accurate an account of the temporal course of the variable of interest as a longitudinal study in which we follow individuals or groups over time. Typically, the answer is no. For example, suppose we propose to do a cross-sectional survey in 2015 to study the maturational effects of some variable of interest in cohorts born in 1965, 1975, 1985, 1995, and 2005 who are 50, 40, 30, 20, and 10 years old in 2015. A *generation* is frequently defined as 20 years, so a "generation gap" generally implies a 20-year separation between cohorts (e.g., between the cohort born in 1965 and the cohort born in 1985, and between the cohort born in 1985 and the cohort born in 2005). Gaps like these pose a serious problem because cohorts separated by a generation have experienced different life events. The problem is that a possible confounding of cohort and maturation is hidden in a design that fails to look at several cohorts longitudinally. If life experiences are associated with the variable of interest, the researcher may draw spurious conclusions about maturational effects by relying solely on a cross-sectional design.

Behavioral researchers who use longitudinal designs—including some animal researchers (e.g., Fairbanks, 1993)—also attempt, when possible, to study several cohorts cross-sectionally and longitudinally. In this way they learn about cohort changes as well as age group changes as a function of period. Other informative uses of longitudinal designs are possible, but each design is limited in certain predictable ways, and the data analysis is usually complex because it must deal with knotty methodological issues (e.g., Diggle, Liang, & Zeger, 1996). There is a discussion of a number of these designs and related issues in our advanced text (Rosenthal & Rosnow, 2008, pp. 250–256). As emphasized earlier, it is prudent to use several strategies that allow convergence on the question or phenomenon of interest. Each approach and procedure is always limited in some way, but the idea is to choose methods whose individual strengths can improve our overall understanding of the phenomenon.

Summary of Ideas

1. The observed data in nonrandomized research may be *prospective* (collected as behavior or a reaction is followed forward in time, as in the anecdote about the doctor treating a patient for a dog bite) or *retrospective* (collected back in time, e.g., as extracted from historical records in the epidemiological study of cause of food poisoning).

2. The relevance of the *third-variable problem* in nonrandomized research is that an uncontrolled or unmeasured variable that is correlated with X (a presumed causal variable) and Y (the presumed effect of X) may account for the association between X and Y, so that this "third variable" is the actual determinant of both X and Y (e.g., age as a determinant of foot size and spelling ability, and the case of the strange medical symptoms).

3. In nonequivalent-groups designs with large relevant subgroups, comparability of the "treated" and "untreated" subjects may be achieved by subclassification on *propensity scores* (e.g., the study of nonsmokers, cigarette smokers, and pipe and cigar smokers in three large databases).

4. The use of *wait-list controls* may overcome objections to a randomized design if the objections are based on the ethical cost of depriving control subjects of the benefits of the treatment given to the experimental subjects (Box 8.1).

5. *Interrupted time-series designs* compare the "effects" of an intervention in a situation before and after it occurs (e.g., the Vienna subway study).

6. *Single-case experimental designs* come in many different forms (e.g., *A-B-BC-B* and *A-B-A-B*); the unit of study may be an N of 1 (e.g., the study of Robbie) or a few subjects (Skinner's study of superstition in pigeons in Box 8.2) or several groups of individuals with one of the treatments randomized (the *A-B-C* study in Box 8.3).

7. In the *cross-lagged panel approach*, some data points are treated as temporally delayed values, and the *cross-lagged correlations* are analyzed along with the *test-retest* and the *synchronous correlations* for the direction of causation (e.g., the retrospective data study of the number of police and the number of burglaries).

8. *Longitudinal research* means that the variable of interest is observed in such a way as to uncover changes that occur over time, such as studying the "life course" of some variable.

9. In studies in which age is the independent variable, a *cross-sectional analysis* of a life course variable may lead to spurious conclusions because of a possible confounding of cohort and maturation.

Key Terms

A-B design   p. 157
A-B-A design   p. 157
A-B-A-B design   p. 157
A-B-A-B-A design (the Robbie study)   p. 157
A-B-BC-B design   p. 157
A-B-C design   p. 158
behavioral baseline   p. 156
cohort   p. 160
cross-lagged correlations   p. 159
cross-lagged panel design   p. 158

cross-sectional design   p. 160
interrupted time-series design   p. 154
longitudinal study   p. 158
nonequivalent-groups designs   p. 152
propensity score   p. 153
prospective data   p. 149
retrospective data   p. 149
single-case experimental research   p. 155

subclassification on propensity scores   p. 153
synchronous correlations (in cross-lagged panel designs)   p. 158
test-retest correlations (in cross-lagged panel designs)   p. 158
third-variable problem   p. 151
time-series designs   p. 154
wait-list control group   p. 153

Multiple-Choice Questions for Review

1. Which of the following is typically not characteristic of single-case experiments? (a) experimental intervention; (b) randomization; (c) control condition; (d) repeated measurement

2. A researcher at North Carolina State University develops a new treatment program for alcoholism. He allows the participants to choose whether they want to be in the experimental group or the control group. This is an example of a (a) true experimental design; (b) nonequivalent-groups design; (c) time-series design; (d) cohort design.

3. In large-sample nonequivalent-groups designs, the comparability of "treated" and "untreated" subjects (a) may be improved by subclassification on propensity scores; (b) is also going to be suspect whatever we do; (c) is no worse than in a similar randomized experiment; (d) all of the above.

4. One type of research design involves measuring a single variable on many separate occasions and assessing the impact of interventions on this variable. This type of design is called a (a) correlational design; (b) cohort design; (c) cross-sectional design; (d) time-series design.

5. A behavioral therapist at Northeastern University is working with autistic children. He decides first to observe their baseline levels of disruptive behavior and then to observe their behavior several times after administering his intervention. He then removes his intervention to determine whether the disruptive behavior will return to baseline levels. This type of design can be described as an

(a) A-B design; (b) A-B-C design; (c) A-B-A design; (d) A-B-A-C design.

6. A study examining changes in individuals over an extended period of time is called a (a) longitudinal study; (b) quasi-longitudinal study; (c) nonequivalent-groups design; (d) time-series study.

7. A researcher at the University of Montana conducts a study on the relationship between watching TV (Variable A) and violent behavior (Variable B). She measures both variables at two points in time. She calculates the correlation between watching TV at Time 1 and watching TV at Time 2. This is an example of a(n) _____ correlation. (a) internal validity; (b) test-retest; (c) synchronous; (d) cross-lagged

8. The same researcher calculates the correlation between watching TV at Time 2 and violent behavior at Time 2. This is an example of a(n) _____ correlation. (a) internal consistency; (b) test-retest; (c) synchronous; (d) cross-lagged

9. In the study above, this researcher also calculates the correlation between watching TV at Time 1 and violent behavior at Time 2. This is an example of a(n) _____ correlation. (a) internal validity; (b) test-retest; (c) synchronous; (d) cross-lagged

10. The same researcher finds that $r_{A1B2} = .30$ and $r_{B1A2} = .02$. These results suggest that (a) it is more likely that watching TV causes violent behavior; (b) it is more likely that violent behavior causes TV watching; (c) there is no causal relationship between watching TV and violent behavior; (d) watching TV and violent behavior have reciprocal causal effects.

Discussion Questions for Review

1. A University of Toledo student wants to assess the possible causal relationship between therapist approval, which is expressed in tone of voice, and degree of patient progress. Using a sample of 45 therapist-patient dyads, he measures these variables at the beginning and end of treatment. From the results shown below, what do you think he will conclude?

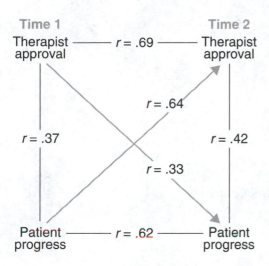

Time 1   Time 2

Therapist approval —— $r = .69$ —— Therapist approval

$r = .64$

$r = .37$ $r = .42$

$r = .33$

Patient progress —— $r = .62$ —— Patient progress

2. Using a cross-sectional design, an Oklahoma University student found a lower degree of androgyny in women aged 40–45 than in women aged 20–25. What confounding variable prevents him from concluding that androgyny decreases with age? Can you think of a better way to do the study?

3. A Catholic University student wants to do a time-series analysis of the effects of assassination attempts against U.S. presidents but cannot decide on the dependent variable. What dependent variable would you advise her to track, and how would you suggest she locate the kind of data she needs for such a study?

Answers to Review Questions

Multiple-Choice Questions

1. b	**3.** a	**5.** c	**7.** b	**9.** d
2. b	**4.** d	**6.** a	**8.** c	**10.** a

Discussion Questions

1. Because (a) the test-retest correlations are similar to each other, (b) the synchronous correlations are similar to each other, and (c) the cross-lagged correlations differ appreciably from each other (.64 versus .33), it might be reasonable for him to conclude a preponderance of causal influence of the patient progress variable over the therapist approval variable.

2. The cohort of women is confounded with their age, so the student cannot tell whether age or cohort differences or both are reflected in the obtained differences. For example, it may be that the women aged 40–45 have been showing an *increasing* degree of androgyny as they developed from age 20–25 to age 40–45. A longitudinal design of the type shown in Table 8.3 would be a better way to do this study.

3. Some dependent variables that may reflect presidential assassination attempts are stock market figures, mental-health-facility-usage data, gun-control legislation activity, the number of people announcing for elective positions, views of the United States reflected in the foreign press, and changes in party affiliation. Reference librarians can help her find the government and other documents that carry the needed information. These documents are also a rich source of ideas for other dependent variables for which data are available.

CHAPTER 9

Survey Research and Subject Recruitment

Preview Questions

- What are opportunity and probability samples?
- What is meant by bias and instability in survey research?
- Why do we not know "for sure" the bias in sampling?
- How is simple random sampling done?
- What are stratified random sampling and area probability sampling?
- What did the *Literary Digest* case teach pollsters?
- What are point estimates and interval estimates?
- What are the benefits of stratification?
- How is nonresponse bias handled in survey research?
- What are the typical characteristics of volunteer subjects?
- How is volunteer bias in opportunity samples managed?

 ## What Are Opportunity and Probability Samples?

In the two preceding chapters, we examined the logic and limitations of randomized and nonrandomized designs for empirical studies. We turn our attention in this chapter to the logic and limitations of the methods used to select research participants. As Donald Rubin (1974) noted, "In a sense all studies lie on a continuum from irrelevant to relevant with respect to answering a question" (p. 699). For instance, randomized laboratory-type experiments that use **opportunity samples** of the first available students in college settings have a restricted sample of participants but usually have a high degree of control over the variables of interest. By contrast, researchers who do survey studies select the potential respondents using special sampling procedures in order to generalize their descriptive findings to a specific larger pool (a **population**) of people. If survey researchers used opportunity samples, spurious results and misleading generalizations about the specific population of interest would seriously compromise the scientific integrity of their work.

There is a wide range of topics of interest to survey researchers. Pollsters use survey designs to map out some specified population's opinions on important societal issues, such as the community's fears of crime or its choice of political candidates. Similar methods are sometimes used in epidemiological research, forensic research, economic research, and many other areas in which scientific surveys are conducted. When health officials wanted to find out about national trends in cases of tuberculosis contracted on the job, they did scientific surveys of hospitals to count employees reported to have TB (Kilborn, 1994).

As the federal courts became inundated with mass torts involving asbestos cases (averaging 1,140 per month in 1990, or one third of the federal criminal caseload), one solution was to sample asbestos cases from the larger pool within a court's jurisdiction. The assessed damages in randomly chosen cases from each of five disease categories were then applied to each larger pool (Saks & Blanck, 1992). More recently, when researchers wanted to study the prevalence of psychological resilience after a traumatic event, they chose a probability sample of New Yorkers to survey in the 6 months following the September 11, 2001, terrorist attack on the World Trade Center. The researchers reported that resilience was present in two thirds of the sample and never fell below one third even among highly exposed individuals with posttraumatic stress disorder (Bonanno, Galea, Bucciarelli, & Vhahov, 2006).

Instead of trying to question every member of the population (which is usually impossible), this type of research focuses on a segment (or **sample**) that is believed to be typical of the population. How can researchers be certain that the segment is **representative** (or typical) of the population? How can they be certain, for example, that the percentage of fear of crime in the sample is typical of the percentage in a whole specified population, or know for sure that the reported TB cases in sampled hospitals are representative of trends in all similar hospitals, or be absolutely confident that a sample of a couple of thousand New York residents adequately represents the broader New York population? They might compare the sample with the most recent census data, but it is well known that census data are problematic because it is impossible to contact every member of the population. In other words, researchers who use a sample can never be 100% sure of their generalizations. They can make a reasonable guess, however, by first developing an accurate sampling frame that defines the target population and then relying on a carefully designed blueprint (the **sampling plan**) to select the sample by means of probability sampling. The term **probability sampling** implies that randomness enters into the selection process at some stage so that the laws of mathematical probability apply; **probability** refers to the mathematical chance of an event's occurring. Examples of probability are the likelihood of getting "heads" when you flip a coin once (1 chance in 2) or getting a 2 when you throw a die once (1 chance in 6).

Though survey studies can take many different forms, all use sampling plans in which some method of probability sampling determines the random selection of the households or people to be contacted. These plans enable the researcher to assume reasonably—but with no 100% guarantee of being correct—that the sample is representative of its population. Practical problems may impose limits on the representativeness of the sample. Even in the most carefully conducted survey, not every household or person in the sample can be reached and, of those who are actually contacted, not everyone will agree to be interviewed. In the study of psychological resilience after the September 11, 2001, terrorist attack on the World Trade Center in New York, a random digit-dialing approach was used to contact members of the sample. When the number of completed and partial interviews was summed and this total was divided by the sum of all numbers that were either eligible as residential phone numbers or of unknown eligibility, the response rate was estimated to be 34% (Bonanno et al., 2006). Later in this chapter, we will discuss how survey researchers deal with the nonresponse problem, and also how experimenters who use volunteer subjects deal with another kind of bias. We will begin, however, by describing some basic concepts in survey sampling and then illustrate the logic of probability sampling plans. (Remember not to confuse *random selection* with *random assignment*. As noted earlier, random *assignment* is the unbiased allocation of units to groups or conditions; its purpose is to control differences in the groups or conditions to be compared.)

 ## What Is Meant By Bias and Instability in Survey Research?

Survey research is done not only by private organizations (the Gallup Organization and Louis Harris & Associates, among others), but by individual researchers working alone or with ties to private organizations (e.g., the Research Triangle Institute in North Carolina), and in the United States at university-based institutes that can implement face-to-face and telephone interviewing in national probability surveys (such as the University of Chicago's National Opinion Research Center and the University of Michigan's Institute for Social Research). Although this research takes many different forms, all valid survey research is characterized by sampling plans in which every element, or sampling unit, in the population has a known nonzero probability of being selected at each draw. Two very important statistical requirements of a probability sampling plan are (a) that the sample values be unbiased and (b) that there be stability in the samples.

To be **unbiased**, the values produced by the sample must, on average, coincide with the true values of the population—but we can never actually be absolutely sure that this requirement has been met in a given study unless we already know those values. **Stability** means that there is not much variability (or spread) in the sample values. Stability is estimated by statistical procedures such as the variance and the standard deviation (which are discussed in the next chapter). Figure 9.1 will help you to conceptualize the role of these two technical requirements. In the figure, the letter X refers to a particular sampling unit, the arrow points to the true population mean, and the horizontal line represents the underlying continuum on which the relevant values are determined. The beauty of sampling theory is that it can be applied not only to individual respondents but also to teams in a population of teams (e.g., Little League baseball teams), or to products on an assembly line, or to any other specified population of animate or inanimate units.

Suppose we want to estimate the number of widgets made by assembly-line workers in a given period. In Figure 9.1, we would think of X as a work team's output; ↑ indicates the value that we are trying to estimate (the true population value, or number of widgets, on average, that are made by all the teams of assembly-line workers). The distance between the true population value (↑) and the midpoint of the values of the five output units (i.e., the *sampling units*) indicates the amount of **bias** (or systematic error). The spread (or variability) among the sampling units indicates their degree of instability. We can see that the amount of instability is constant within each row, going from a high amount of instability (or spread) in row 1 to no instability in row 3. The amount of bias is constant in each column, going from a high bias in column 1 to zero bias in column 3. We can sum up our observations by saying that, in the three cases in column 3, the sample values are balanced around the true population mean, but with much instability in row 1, some instability in row 2, and none in row 3. In the three cases in row 3, there is no instability, but there is much bias in column 1, some in column 2, and none in column 3.

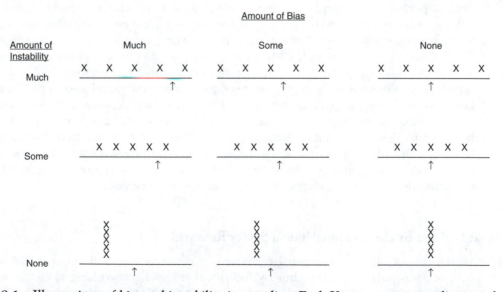

Figure 9.1   Illustrations of bias and instability in sampling. Each X represents a sampling unit located on a dimension represented by the horizontal line, and the arrow points to the true population mean.

BOX 9.1 The Wine Taster

In the manufacture of red wine, grapes are crushed and the residue is put into huge vats in which fermentation occurs. The wine is then drawn off into barrels, where fermentation continues, and the product is periodically sampled by the wine taster. The wine taster needs to draw only a small sample in order to evaluate the quality of the wine in the barrel. It is the same in survey research: The more homogeneous the population, the smaller the sample that needs to be drawn.

The hypothetical case at the intersection of row 3 and column 3 represents the best of all situations, but it is highly unlikely that we would ever find such complete agreement.

Generally speaking, the more *homogeneous* (the more "alike") the members of the population are, the fewer of them will need to be sampled. If all widget makers are exactly alike (the situation in row 3, column 3), *any* sampling unit will provide complete information about the population as a whole. The more *heterogeneous* (dissimilar) the different teams are, the more sampling units we will need to ensure a sample of the full range of dissimilarity (see also Box 9.1).

Why Do We Not Know "For Sure" the Bias in Sampling?

We said that we can never really know "for sure" the bias in sampling results. However, there *is* one way to know for certain, and that is to examine every single member of the population and the sample *at the same time* the sampling is done. If the pattern of replies in the sample exactly matched the pattern of replies in the population, we would know for sure that there was no sampling bias in the surveyed sample. Later in this chapter, we give an illustration where we are, in fact, able to sample from a completely known population of values. Practically speaking, if we already knew for certain how everyone in the population of interest would respond in a survey, it would make no sense to go to the trouble and expense of sampling the population.

It is sometimes thought that election forecasting allows us to detect bias in a sample because we can compare the predicted voting results with the actual votes. However, the problem in this case is that we are comparing data obtained at one point in time with the results at another point in time. Still, a well-designed and carefully implemented selection process involving probability sampling can usually produce data that are remarkably close to the election results. For example, Gallup Survey records in U.S. presidential elections show discrepancies that are quite small. In the 1996 election, the final election poll conducted by the Gallup Organization for *USA Today* and CNN, using 1,448 "likely voters" who were sampled on November 3–4, 1996, predicted that Bill Clinton would win 48%, Robert Dole 40%, and Ross Perot 6% of the vote. The prediction that Clinton would top Dole by 8% was right on the mark, and the specific vote predictions were close to the actual election result of 49% for Clinton, 41% for Dole, and 8% for Perot (Kagay, 1996). Polls that are conducted close to the election are usually better predictors than early polls, but there is no guarantee that voters will not change their minds between the poll and the election, or that they might not show up to vote. In the 1996 election, early polls reported a landslide 15 percentage point lead by Clinton, which may have made some Clinton supporters complacent and less likely to show up to vote.

Some elections are so close that even polls right up to the day of voting disagree. In the 2000 election, the final difference between George W. Bush and Al Gore was razor thin in some states, and final polls were in some disagreement about which candidate would ultimately be the victor. In the 2004 presidential election, most of the polls taken in the final days just before the election had George W. Bush winning the popular vote by a percentage point or two, and those polls that did not were usually within the margin of error of plus-or-minus 3 percentage points. Research firms that designed the exit polling system used by news organizations in the 2004 election mistakenly showed

John Kerry leading. One suspected reason for this glitch was that half the surveyors were 34 or younger, and it appears that they were more successful in securing interviews with Kerry supporters as they left polling places than with Bush supporters (Steinberg, 2005).

How Is Simple Random Sampling Done?

The basic prototype of probability sampling is called **simple random sampling**. The *simple* tells us that the sample is selected from an undivided population; *random* means that the sample is to be chosen by a process that will give every unit in the specified population the same chance of being selected at each draw (see also Box 9.2). In order for this to occur, the selection of one unit must have no influence on the selection of other units. A further assumption of simple random sampling is that we have an understanding of the existence of all the units in the population. For this illustration, let us assume we have a list of names of everyone in a specific population. The procedure is to draw individuals one at a time until we have as large a sample as we need. The process of selecting units might consist of having a computer draw units at random, using a table of random digits, or even spinning a roulette wheel or drawing well-mixed capsules from an urn. In doing telephone interviewing, random digit dialing is used to include households with unlisted numbers. The area code and first three digits can be selected according to the geographic area of interest, and then a computer program is used to randomly select the last four digits.

A famous case illustrating the hazards of inadequate randomization occurred in 1970. The previous year, while the war in Vietnam was in progress, the U.S. Congress had passed a bill allowing the use of a random lottery to select conscripts for the armed forces. To give each individual an equal chance of being selected or not selected, the planners decided to pick birthdays out of an urn. The 365 days of the year were written on slips of paper and placed inside tiny cylindrical capsules. Once all the capsules were inside the urn, it was shaken for several hours, and then the capsules were removed, one by one. However, the results were found to be biased in spite of the precautions taken to ensure an unbiased sample: The birth dates in December tended to be drawn first, those in November next, then those in October, and so on. The reason was that the January capsules were put in the urn first, the February capsules next, and so forth, and layers were formed with the December capsules on top. Even shaking the urn for several hours did not produce a thorough mixing of the capsules (Broome, 1984; Kolata, 1986).

The use of a table of random digits, such as Table 9.1, should help us to avoid such pitfalls. The 2,250 digits in this list came from a million random digits that were generated by an electronic roulette wheel programmed to produce a random frequency pulse every tiny fraction of a second (Rand Corporation, 1955). A computer then counted the frequency of 0s, 1s, 2s, and so on in the final

---

BOX 9.2 Randomness and Aimlessness

Don't confuse randomness with *aimlessness,* or "hit-or-miss" sampling, which, in fact, can seldom be called random. You can prove the difference to yourself by asking a friend to write down "at random" several hundred one-digit numbers from 0 to 9. Afterward, tabulate the 0s, 1s, 2s, and so on. If the numbers were truly random, there would be few obvious sequences, and each digit would occur approximately 10% of the time. You will find, however, that the results are inconsistent with the hypothesis of randomness. You will see obvious sequences and notice that some digits occur with high frequency, whereas others appear hardly at all (Wallis & Roberts, 1956). Using a single-case experimental strategy, psychologist Allen Neuringer (1992) was able to reinforce pigeons into making left-right choices that looked pretty random. He then used feedback to reinforce Reed College students to generate sequences of numbers that resembled random sequences (Neuringer, 1996; Neuringer & Voss, 1993).

Table 9.1   2,250 Random Digits

Rows	1–5	6–10	11–15	16–20	21–25	26–30	31–35	36–40	41–45	46–50
1	10097	32533	76520	13586	34673	54876	80959	09117	39292	74945
2	37542	04805	64894	74296	24805	24037	20636	10402	00822	91665
3	08422	68953	19645	09303	23209	02560	15953	34764	35080	33605
4	99019	02529	09376	70715	38311	31165	88676	74397	04436	27659
5	12807	99970	80157	36147	64032	36653	98951	16877	12171	76833
6	66065	74717	34072	76850	36697	36170	65813	39885	11199	29170
7	31060	10805	45571	82406	35303	42614	86799	07439	23403	09732
8	85269	77602	02051	65692	68665	74818	73053	85247	18623	88579
9	63573	32135	05325	47048	90553	57548	28468	28709	83491	25624
10	73796	45753	03529	64778	35808	34282	60935	20344	35273	88435
11	98520	17767	14905	68607	22109	40558	60970	93433	50500	73998
12	11805	05431	39808	27732	50725	68248	29405	24201	52775	67851
13	83452	99634	06288	98083	13746	70078	18475	40610	68711	77817
14	88685	40200	86507	58401	36766	67951	90364	76493	29609	11062
15	99594	67348	87517	64969	91826	08928	93785	61368	23478	34113
16	65481	17674	17468	50950	58047	76974	73039	57186	40218	16544
17	80124	35635	17727	08015	45318	22374	21115	78253	14385	53763
18	74350	99817	77402	77214	43236	00210	45521	64237	96286	02655
19	69916	26803	66252	29148	36936	87203	76621	13990	94400	56418
20	09893	20505	14225	68514	46427	56788	96297	78822	54382	14598
21	91499	14523	68479	27686	46162	83554	94750	89923	37089	20048
22	80336	94598	26940	36858	70297	34135	53140	33340	42050	82341
23	44104	81949	85157	47954	32979	26575	57600	40881	22222	06413
24	12550	73742	11100	02040	12860	74697	96644	89439	28707	25815
25	63606	49329	16505	34484	40219	52563	43651	77082	07207	31790
26	61196	90446	26457	47774	51924	33729	65394	59593	42582	60527
27	15474	45266	95270	79953	59367	83848	82396	10118	33211	59466
28	94557	28573	67897	54387	54622	44431	91190	42592	92927	45973
29	42481	16213	97344	08721	16868	48767	03071	12059	25701	46670
30	23523	78317	73208	89837	68935	91416	26252	29663	05522	82562
31	04493	52494	75246	33824	45862	51025	61962	79335	65337	12472
32	00549	97654	64051	88159	96119	63896	54692	82391	23287	29529
33	35963	15307	26898	09354	33351	35462	77974	50024	90103	39333
34	59808	08391	45427	26842	83609	49700	13021	24892	78565	20106
35	46058	85236	01390	92286	77281	44077	93910	83647	70617	42941
36	32179	00597	87379	25241	05567	07007	86743	17157	85394	11838
37	69234	61406	20117	45204	15956	60000	18743	92423	97118	96338
38	19565	41430	01758	75379	40419	21585	66674	36806	84962	85207
39	45155	14938	19476	07246	43667	94543	59047	90033	20826	69541
40	94864	31994	36168	10851	34888	81553	01540	35456	05014	51176
41	98086	24826	45240	28404	44999	08896	39094	73407	35441	31880
42	33185	16232	41941	50949	89435	48581	88695	41994	37548	73043
43	80951	00406	96382	70774	20151	23387	25016	25298	94624	61171
44	79752	49140	71961	28296	69861	02591	74852	20539	00387	59579
45	18633	32537	98145	06571	31010	24674	05455	61427	77938	91936

Source: From *A Million Random Digits with 100,000 Normal Deviates,* The Free Press 1955. Reprinted with permission.

results, on the assumption that an impartial probability method would produce an approximately equal number of 0s, 1s, 2s, and so on in the overall table of a million random digits. This equality was confirmed. In Chapter 7, we showed how to use the random numbers in this table to do random assignment of participants to experimental and control conditions.

To see how you might use this table if you wanted to do random selection in a survey, imagine you want to interview 10 men and 10 women individually after choosing them at random from a list of 96 men and a list of 99 women. You would begin by numbering the population of men consecutively from 01 to 96 and the population of women from 01 to 99. You are now ready to use the random digits in Table 9.1. To do so, you can put your finger blindly on a starting position. You can start anywhere in the table and then move your finger in any direction, as long as you do not pick a set of numbers because they "look right" or avoid a set of numbers because they "don't look right." Suppose you put your finger on the first five-digit number in row 5, column 1. Beginning with this number, 12807, you would read across the line two digits at a time, selecting the men numbered 12, 80, 79, 99, and so on, until you had randomly chosen the 10 male interviewees. You would do the same thing, beginning at another blindly chosen point, to select the 10 female interviewees. If you had fewer than 10 persons on each list, you would read only one digit at a time. If you had between 100 and 999 persons on your list, you would read three digits at a time, and so forth.

Suppose you chose the same two-digit number more than once, or suppose you chose a two-digit number not represented by any member of the population. In either case, you would go on to the next two-digit number in the row (that is, unless you were *sampling with replacement*, as discussed next). What if your population was so small that you were forced to skip many numbers in the table because they were larger than the largest number of people in your population? For example, what if there were 450 people in the population and you wanted to select 50 people at random? Because the population is numbered from 001 to 450, you would have to skip approximately one half the three-digit numbers in the section of the table you chose (those from 451 to 999). As a simple solution (also acceptable in terms of randomness), you can subtract 500 from any number in the range from 501 to 999. This additional option will result in fewer unusable selections.

Another option in some situations is sampling with or without replacement. **Sampling with replacement** means that the selected units are placed in the selection pool again and may be reselected on subsequent draws. Every unit in the population continues to have the same probability of being chosen every time a number is read. To do sampling with replacement, you have to select units one at a time. For example, suppose the units are days of the year sealed in tiny capsules in an urn stirred so completely that there are no layers or nonrandom clusters. You select a capsule, read it, and put it back in the urn (making sure the urn is well mixed), so the same capsule may be randomly selected more than once.

In **sampling without replacement**, a previously selected unit cannot be reselected, and the population shrinks each time you remove a unit, but all the units remaining have the same likelihood of being drawn on the next occasion. If you scoop a handful of capsules, record each, and then discard those you picked, this would be sampling without replacement. Either option is technically acceptable, but survey researchers usually prefer sampling without replacement because they do not want to draw the same individuals twice or more. Another example of sampling without replacement is the wine taster (Box 9.1), who draws and then spits out a sample of wine. We wouldn't have it any other way!

 What Are Stratified Random Sampling and Area Probability Sampling?

Simple random sampling is useful when the population is known to be homogeneous or when its precise composition is unknown. When we know something about the exact composition, a more efficient method of sampling is to sample from the different substrates of the population. Professional polling organizations typically use this approach to probability sampling, that is, randomly selecting sampling units (persons or households) from several subpopulations (termed *strata* or *clusters*)

into which the population is divided. For example, if we know the population is 60% female and 40% male (a ratio of 3 to 2), and that gender is a pertinent variable, we can improve our sampling procedure by selecting subsamples proportionate in size to this 3:2 ratio of females to males.

Described as **stratified random sampling**, this procedure can be an efficient method of probability sampling. A separate sample is randomly selected from each homogeneous stratum (or "layer") of the population. The stratum means are then statistically weighted to form a combined estimate for the entire population. In a survey of political opinions, for example, it might be useful to stratify the population according to party affiliation, gender, socioeconomic status, and other meaningful categories related to voting behavior. This method ensures that we have enough women, men, Democrats, Republicans, and so on to draw descriptive or correlational conclusions about each respective subgroup. We will have more to say about this method of sampling shortly.

A popular variant of this sampling approach is called **area probability sampling**, because the population is divided into geographic areas (i.e., population clusters or strata). This method is applicable to any population divisible into meaningful geographic areas related to the variables of interest. For example, depending on the variables of interest, meaningful geographic areas might be people living in urban neighborhoods, Inuits in igloos, or nomads in tents. The assumption is that, within each of the areas, the units will have the same probability of being chosen. The sampling procedure can be more complicated than those described above, but the method is cost-effective because the research design can be used repeatedly with only minor modifications. Suppose a polling organization needs an area probability sample of 300 out of 6,000 estimated housing units in a city, and a good list of all the dwellings in the entire city does not exist (and would be too costly to prepare). Using a city map, the pollsters can instead select a sample of dwellings by focusing on small clusters of blocks.

To do this in the simplest case, they divide the entire map of the city into blocks of equal size and then select 1 of, say, every 20 blocks for the sample. If they define the sample as the housing units located within the boundaries of these equal-sized sample blocks, the probability of selection for *any* unit is the selection of its block—set at 1/20 to correspond to the desired sampling rate of 300/6,000 (Kish, 1965). In other cases, researchers categorize the blocks by taking into account their size or some other factor of interest and then treat this factor as a stratum to sample in a specific way. The procedure can become more complicated as the area gets bigger, but the key requirements are to ensure (a) that all areas will have some chance of selection and (b) that the units within the areas are chosen impartially (Fowler, 1993). For the same plan to be used again, all that must be altered are the randomly selected units within each area.

 ## What Did the *Literary Digest* Case Teach Pollsters?

The late George Gallup, the pioneering survey researcher who founded the Gallup Survey, once noted some of the methodological lessons learned by survey researchers going back to 1936 (Gallup, 1976). That year, Franklin D. Roosevelt (the Democratic presidential candidate) was running against Governor Alfred Landon of Kansas (the Republican candidate). Most people thought that Roosevelt would win easily, but a pseudoscientific poll conducted by a current events magazine, the *Literary Digest,* predicted that Landon would win an overwhelming victory. What gave the prediction credence was that the *Digest* had successfully predicted the winner in every presidential election since 1916. Moreover, this time, it announced it had based its prediction on a sample of 2.4 million respondents!

The magazine got these 2.4 million by generating a nonrandom sample of 10 million people from sources like telephone directories, automobile registration lists, and club membership lists. Straw vote ballots were then mailed to each name. The lists had actually been compiled for solicitation purposes, and advertising was included with the straw vote ballot (Katz & Cantril, 1937). One problem was that few people in 1936 had a telephone (only one in four households), or owned a car or belonged to a club, so that the final list was biased in favor of wealthy Republican households. Another problem was that there were a great many nonrespondents, and subsequent statistical analyses suggest that had they responded and been counted, the results would have been very different.

As it turned out, the election voting was split pretty much along economic lines, the more affluent voting for Landon and the less affluent voting for Roosevelt. The *Digest* predicted that Landon would win by 57% to Roosevelt's 43%, but the election results were Roosevelt 62% and Landon 38% (Freedman et al., 1991). The *Digest* could have used the information that the sample was top-heavy in upper-income Republicans to correct its estimate, but it deliberately ignored this information. Instead, the *Digest* proudly (but naively) proclaimed that the "figures had been neither weighted, adjusted, nor interpreted." After making the largest error ever made by political prognosticators in a presidential election, the *Digest* (which had been in financial trouble before the election) declared bankruptcy.

A lesson learned from this episode was that, if we seek to generalize to an entire population the percentage differences we have found in a sample, the sampling plan and its execution must be properly implemented in a precise, scientific way, and sampling weights must be used to correct for potential biases. Yet, similar pseudoscientific public opinion polls are conducted daily by many "news shows" that pose a yes-or-no or multiple-choice question about some current issue and invite the viewers to register their opinions by phone or online. The external validity of the reported results is so low as to render any generalization useless, as in all likelihood those who respond are not only nonrepresentative of the general population but also nonrepresentative of even the regular viewing audience. In one case, a television station skipped its polling one night and still received 20 calls voting "yes" and 38 voting "no" (Rosnow & Rosenthal, 1970). It may be "entertaining" to see the results of such polls, but what they reveal is the inexperience of those conducting the polls and the gullibility of the audience that believes them.

George Gallup was just getting started during the days of the *Literary Digest* flop. Using his own polling method, he was able to predict that Roosevelt would win (although Gallup was off by 6 percentage points)—as well as to predict what the *Literary Digest* results would be. His method, called **quota sampling**, was an early precursor of current methods; it assigned a quota of people to be questioned and let the questioner build up a sample that was roughly representative of the population. The interviewers were given ranges of variables and told to identify by sight people who seemed to fit this quota. For example, an interviewer might be told to talk to so many people of ages 21–35, 36–55, and 56 or over. We do not know how much of this interviewing took place on busy street corners and at trolley stops rather than in house-to-house canvassing, but bias might be introduced simply as a consequence of the interviewed individuals' being more accessible than others (Rossi et al., 1983). Now, of course, we would use random selection procedures instead of leaving the selection of units to the judgment of the questioner. However, another lesson that Gallup and others in the 1930s learned from the *Literary Digest* episode was that large numbers do not, in and of themselves, increase the representativeness or the predictive accuracy of a sample.

Because of that experience, the methodology of survey sampling has been improved in other ways as further unexpected problems have been encountered and additional lessons learned. In the congressional election of 1942, for example, pollsters had not reckoned with voter turnout, which was at an all-time low because people were changing their places of residence to work in war factories or to enter the military during World War II. Gallup's polls correctly predicted that the Democrats would retain control of the House of Representatives, but the margin of victory turned out to be much closer than either Gallup or any other pollsters had predicted. The important lesson learned this time was to give far more attention to the factor of voter turnout in making predictions. In the 1948 presidential election, Harry S Truman, by luring Democratic defectors back into the fold during the last 2 weeks before Election Day, turned the tide against his Republican opponent, Thomas E. Dewey. However, many public opinion polls predicted that Dewey would win. This time, Gallup and other pollsters learned the lesson that political polling had to be done as close to Election Day as possible (see also Box 9.3).

After 1948, the Gallup Survey (and other respected polls) adopted area probability sampling, in which election districts are randomly selected throughout the nation, and then randomly chosen

BOX 9.3 Push Polls

Don't confuse the legitimate type of polling with what are called **push polls**—an insidious form of negative political campaigning that is designed to push opinions in a particular direction rather than scientifically sample them. Push polls use rumors, gossip, lies, innuendoes, and half-truths to manufacture negative voter attitudes by posing questions like "Would you be more or less likely to vote for [name of candidate] if you knew he/she had been arrested/failed to pay child support/failed to pay income taxes/falsified his/her résumé?" If you are asked questions like these in a telephone "interview," ask about the sponsors of the survey and how the information is being used. The American Association for Public Opinion Research (AAPOR) has campaigned against push polling, including issuing repeated warnings to the public and the media about the iniquity of these pseudoscientific polls. For more information, visit http://www.aapor.org and enter *push polls* in the "Search Our Site" space.

households within these districts are contacted by interviewers. This procedure, and the lessons learned from the mistakes made in the *Literary Digest* episode and its aftermath, brought about further improvements. By 1956, the Gallup Survey, based on a little more than 8,000 respondents, was able to predict with a margin of error of only 1.7% that Dwight D. Eisenhower would be reelected president. The **margin of error** means that, in this case, the prediction (based on the laws of mathematical probability) was that the anticipated percentages would fall within an interval bounded by plus-and-minus 1.7 percentage points. Poll watchers now expect an error of no more than 2 or 3 percentage points in national elections, if the probability sampling plan is properly implemented.

What Are Point Estimates and Interval Estimates?

The margin of error is an example of an *interval estimate*, and survey researchers are also interested in making point estimates of population values. **Point estimates** tell us about some typical characteristic of the target population. For instance, in a probability survey of a college population, we might want a point estimate of the number of seniors who plan to continue their education after graduating. Other examples of point estimates noted earlier in this chapter were the average number of widgets made by assembly-line workers, the number of cases of tuberculosis contracted on the job, and the incidence of psychological resilience among New Yorkers after the September 11, 2001, terrorist attack on the World Trade Center. **Interval estimates**, on the other hand, tell us how much the point estimates are likely to be in error (e.g., because of variability in the composition of the population).

Suppose we do a simple random survey of 100 college students out of a population of 2,500 graduating seniors at a certain university. Each student is asked, "Do you plan to continue your education after you graduate from college, by going on to graduate school, business school, medical school, dental school, or law school?" In answer to our question, 25 of them reply yes. In order to make a frequency estimate of the population value, we multiply the sample proportion replying yes (.25) by the total number of students in the population (2,500). We estimate that 625 out of the 2,500 graduating seniors plan to continue their education.

How "approximate" is this estimate? The **confidence interval** will indicate the probability that the estimated population value is correct within plus-or-minus some specified interval. Suppose we want to state with 95% confidence (i.e., 95 chances in 100) that the estimated population value of 625 is likely to be correct within plus-or-minus some specified interval (the *95% confidence interval*). In our polling a sample (*n*) of 100 graduating seniors, we found that .25 (symbolized as *prop,* for "proportion") of that sample planned to continue their education. To obtain an approximate 95% confidence interval around *prop*, we compute

$$\text{Lower limit} = prop - 2\sqrt{\frac{prop\,(1 - prop)}{n}}$$

and

$$\text{Upper limit} = prop + 2\sqrt{\frac{prop\,(1 - prop)}{n}}.$$

In this example, $n = 100$, $prop = .25$, and $1 - prop = .75$, so

$$2\sqrt{\frac{prop(1 - prop)}{n}} = 2\sqrt{\frac{(.25)(.75)}{100}} = .09,$$

with a resulting lower limit of $.25 - .09 = .16$, and an upper limit of $.25 + .09 = .34$. Applying these proportions to the population (*N*) of 2,500 yields $.16(2,500) = 400$ as the lower limit, and $.34(2,500) = 850$ as the upper limit of our approximate 95% confidence interval for the number of graduating students planning to continue their education. (In Chapters 10 and 12, we will show how to compute confidence intervals for other important values.)

What Are the Benefits of Stratification?

In the illustration above, we randomly selected individual sampling units, using the population of graduating seniors as a single heterogeneous cluster. In most cases of survey research, sampling several strata or clusters is more efficient if the population can be separated into more homogeneous strata. As an illustration of the benefits of stratification, and also a further illustration of an unbiased sampling plan, suppose we wanted to use probability sampling to estimate the average hourly production of widgets by teams of assembly-line workers. To keep this example simple, we will imagine that the entire population consists of four such teams and that the mean number of widgets produced per hour is as follows:

Team A	11.5
Team B	12.5
Team C	13.0
Team D	19.0

14.0 (true population value)

Adding the average hourly production rates $(11.5 + 12.5 + 13.0 + 19.0 = 56.0)$ and dividing by 4 $(56.0/4 = 14.0)$ tells us that the true population value is 14.0. But for this example, we ask, "How accurate an estimate of the true population value will we obtain by simple random sampling or stratified random sampling?" Finding the answer to this question will illustrate what an **unbiased sampling plan** is.

We must initially decide on the size of the sample (the *n*) we wish to use to estimate the population value. To keep it simple, we will define the sample size as any two teams selected at random $(n = 2)$. For example, were we to randomly select Team A and Team B, we would obtain a point estimate of 12.0, computed as $(11.5 + 12.5)/2 = 12.0$. How good is this estimate? The answer, called the **error of estimate**, is the closeness of 12.0 to the true population value of 14.0. We figured this answer out by subtracting the population value from the sample mean, or $12.0 - 14.0 = -2.0$. In other words, this particular sample underestimates the true population by 2.0 (the negative difference tells us it is an underestimate; a positive difference would indicate an overestimate).

Table 9.2	Results for All Possible Simple Random Samples of Size Two		
Sample	Sample values	Estimate of population value	Error of estimate
Team A, Team B	11.5, 12.5	12.00	−2.00
Team A, Team C	11.5, 13.0	12.25	−1.75
Team A, Team D	11.5, 19.0	15.25	+1.25
Team B, Team C	12.5, 13.0	12.75	−1.25
Team B, Team D	12.5, 19.0	15.75	+1.75
Team C, Team D	13.0, 19.0	16.00	+2.00
Total		84.00	0.00
Mean		14.00	0.00

Table 9.2 lists all possible combinations of two-member samples, the estimates derived from them, and the error of estimate for each sample. The average of the errors of estimate (when we take account of their signs) gives the amount of *bias* of the general sampling plan. Not surprisingly, we see (at the bottom of the last column) that the general sampling plan is *unbiased* (even though there is error associated with individual sample values).

In stratified random sampling (to which we now turn), we begin by dividing the population into a number of parts. We then randomly sample independently in each part. To get started, notice that the last column in Table 9.2 shows that every simple random sample containing Team D overestimates the population value, and that every random sample without this team underestimates it. If we had reason to suspect this fact before the sampling, we could make use of such information to form strata so that a heterogeneous population is divided into two parts, each of which is fairly homogeneous (Snedecor & Cochran, 1989). One stratum will consist of Teams A, B, and C, and the second stratum will consist of Team D alone, as Table 9.3 shows. This table helps us to see clearly why this general sampling plan is called *unbiased* and also to see the advantages of stratification in probability sampling.

Starting with the first row in Table 9.3, notice under "Weighted sample values" that Team A's score is 11.5 × 3 = 34.5, whereas Team D's score is not weighted (19.0). The reason we weight Team A's score by multiplying it by 3 is that it is one of three members of Stratum 1. We did not weight Team D's score because it is the sole occupant of Stratum 2. To compute the scores under "Estimate of population value," we add Team A's weighted score to Team D's unweighted score and then divide by the total number of members, which gives us (34.5 + 19.0)/4 = 13.375. We obtain the "Error of estimate" by subtracting the true population mean from this result, or 13.375 − 14.0 = −0.625 (which indicates that the Team A + Team D sample underestimates the true population value by a small amount). This table shows the results of all possible stratified random samples of size two. Again, we find (not unexpectedly) that the general sampling plan is unbiased in that the average of the errors of estimate (bottom of last column) is zero.

Table 9.3	Results for All Possible Stratified Random Samples of Size Two				
Sample	Stratum 1	Stratum 2	Weighted sample values	Estimate of population value	Error of estimate
1	Team A	Team D	34.5, 19.0	13.375	−0.625
2	Team B	Team D	37.5, 19.0	14.125	+0.125
3	Team C	Team D	39.0, 19.0	14.500	+0.500
Total				42.000	0.000
Mean				14.000	0.000

By comparing the results in Tables 9.2 and 9.3, you will see in quantitative terms the advantages of separating selections from strata of the population. The most extreme errors in Table 9.2 range from −2.00 to +2.00, a difference of 4.00. By contrast, the most extreme errors in Table 9.3 range from −0.625 to +0.500, a difference of 1.125. Notice that fewer samples are possible of size two in Table 9.3 than in Table 9.2. In summary, the error of an individual sample is greater in simple random sampling of a heterogeneous population than in stratified random sampling of that same population divided into homogeneous strata, in this case by a magnitude of 4.00/1.125 = 3.56, or more than three times the size. The potential for error is also greater in simple random sampling than in stratified random sampling. Some forethought based on reliable information is needed when you are dividing a population into homogeneous strata; this kind of planning can often pay off handsomely in the utility of stratification.

How Is Nonresponse Bias Handled in Survey Research?

Nonresponse bias is systematic error due to nonparticipation. For example, a problem in the use of phone interviews is that random samples become harder to obtain because busy people might hang up the phone, or they might feel their privacy is being invaded, or adults might not be available because they work away from home, or people might not have land lines (but only mobile phones). A typical answer by one person who turned down a phone request to interview her about where she shops was "It was 7 o'clock, I was putting the kids to bed, and it was zoo time around here, which is when these people call" (Rothenberg, 1990, p. 1). Statisticians and survey researchers have devoted considerable effort to studying the effects of nonresponse bias. Not only might this bias result in a smaller **effective sample size** (the size of the actual final sample) than the researcher had planned on for statistical reasons (discussed in a later chapter), but the accuracy of estimates of population values may be jeopardized as well.

Table 9.4 illustrates in quantitative terms the basic idea of nonresponse bias, and it also illustrates one way that companies and researchers who still use mailed questionnaires may attempt to reduce this bias by sending out questionnaires more than once. The data in this table are based on three waves of questionnaires that were mailed out to peach growers in North Carolina (Finkner, 1950; cited in Cochran, 1963). It is unusual to have data about both the respondents and the nonrespondents. But when we have such relevant information on all members of the population surveyed, we can use it to compare those who respond with those who don't respond. In this case, one variable was the number of peach trees owned, and data were available for the entire population of growers. For this variable, then, we can quantify the amount of bias due to nonresponse remaining after the first, second, and third mailings.

Table 9.4   Example of Bias Due to Nonresponse in Survey Research

Basic data:	First wave	Second wave	Third wave	Total nonrespondents	Total population
a. Number of respondents	300	543	434	1,839	3,116
b. Percentage of population	10	17	14	59	100
c. Mean trees per respondent	456	382	340	290	329

Cumulative data:					
d. Mean trees per respondent (Y_1)	456	408	385		
e. Mean trees per nonrespondent (Y_2)	315	300	290		
f. Difference ($Y_1 - Y_2$)	141	108	95		
g. Percentage of nonrespondents (P)	90	73	59		
h. Bias $= (P)(Y_1 - Y_2)$	127	79	56		

The first three rows of Table 9.4 provide the basic data in the form of (a) the number of respondents to each wave of questionnaires and the number of nonrespondents; (b) the percentage of the total population (3,116) represented by each wave of respondents and nonrespondents; and (c) the mean number of trees owned by the respondents in each wave. To calculate the effective sample size after each mailing, we cumulate (sum) the number of respondents to that point. The effective sample size is 300 after the first mailing; $300 + 543 = 843$ after two mailings; and $843 + 434 = 1,277$ after three mailings. To convert the values in row a into the percentages in row b, we divide the row a values by the total population size and multiply by 100 to change a proportion into a percentage. For example, dividing the number of respondents to the first mailing by the total population value gives us $300/3,116 = .096$, which, when rounded to .10 and multiplied by 100, tells us that 10% of the growers responded to the first mailing.

The remaining five rows of data are based on the cumulative number of respondents after the first, second, and third mailings. For each wave, five items of information are shown: (d) the mean number of peach trees owned by the respondents up to that point in the survey; (e) the mean number of trees owned by those not yet responding; (f) the difference between these two values; (g) the percentage of the population not yet responding; and (h) the magnitude of the bias (defined in terms of peach trees owned) up to that point in the survey. The bottom row (h) shows that, with each successive wave of respondents, there was a decrease in the magnitude of the bias (a fairly typical result). The implication is that increasing the effort to recruit the nonrespondents should lessen the bias of the point estimates.

Knowing the magnitude and direction of the nonresponse bias can help us adjust our estimate of the generalizability of the results. To make this adjustment, we need to have information about the nonrespondents as well as the respondents on some variable that is related to our area of interest. Without this information, we can compute the proportion of population participants (P) and the statistic of interest (the point estimate) for the respondents (Y_1), but we cannot compute the statistic of interest (the corresponding point estimate) for those people who did not respond (Y_2). We may be in a position to suspect bias but may be unable to give an estimate of its magnitude. We will come back to this problem in a moment (in our discussion of volunteer bias), but (as Table 9.4 implies) one way to reduce nonresponse bias may be to try to increase the rate of response of the likely nonrespondents.

In the case of mail surveys, more nonrespondents may be drawn into the sample by one or more follow-up mailings or reminders. Survey researchers who do mail surveys often advise phoning the nonrespondents if the response rate is still not satisfactory. Professional pollsters attempt to increase the initial rate of participation by using incentives and attention-getting techniques, such as using special delivery as opposed to ordinary mail, using hand-stamped rather than postage-permit envelopes, and sometimes including a token gift at the time of the request for participation (Linsky, 1975). In Chapter 5, we discussed the creation of questionnaires; to increase response rates to mailed questionnaires, it is important that the instructions be clear, that the items be easy to read and the layout attractive, and that the task of answering questions not be burdensome (Fowler, 1993; Tryfos, 1996). In the case of phone surveys, polling companies can attempt to increase participation by sending an advance letter that spells out the importance of the study, by pilot-testing probing questions to ensure that the persons contacted will not feel intimidated by them or by the uses to which the data will be put, and by carefully screening out less effective interviewers. One or more follow-up phone calls on evenings and weekends might improve the response rate (Fowler, 1993; Tryfos, 1996), but only if the calls are not perceived as annoying and intrusive.

What Are the Typical Characteristics of Volunteer Subjects?

So far, we have focused on the prototypical survey study. We turn now to a problem similar to nonresponse bias that occurs in other research (e.g., experimental research) in which the participants are individually recruited. As we noted earlier, experimenters do not usually concern themselves with the particulars of a probability sampling plan when recruiting their participants; instead,

BOX 9.4 The Disgruntled Volunteer

When scientists recruit volunteers for randomized trials involving risk (e.g., an experiment testing the effects of different diets on cholesterol), those people already at high risk may be most likely to volunteer. However, volunteer bias is not limited to experimental studies. Suppose a cable TV company randomly selects subscribers to be interviewed in a telephone survey. The dissatisfied subscribers may be more likely to participate because they have grievances they want to voice (Tryfos, 1996). Unless the cable company is interested only in discovering problems that need to be corrected, the difficulty would be trying to generalize from the disgruntled volunteers to all the company's cable customers.

they use opportunity samples. One reason for this lack of concern is that it may be impossible to work within the confines of a probability sampling plan. A second reason is that, even when random selection is feasible, experimenters typically assume that "people are people" in terms of the psychological factors or mechanisms that are being studied. A common assumption is that as long as people are randomly assigned to the treatment conditions, it should make little difference whether those assigned to the experimental and control groups are volunteer subjects or a random sample of some specified population. In some situations, however, using strictly volunteer subjects may unwittingly lead to biased conclusions (discussed in the following section), and using random assignment would not address this problem (see also Box 9.4).

You may be wondering how anyone can possibly know how typical volunteer subjects might differ from typical nonvolunteers, as nonvolunteers are, by definition, unavailable. One strategy is to study the characteristics of people in a population for which information is available on just about everyone in the population (e.g., biographical data and psychological test results). Formal requests for research volunteers are then made some time later, and those individuals who volunteer are compared with those who do not volunteer on the relevant items of information. For instance, most colleges routinely administer psychological tests and questionnaires to all incoming students during an orientation period. The results, assuming they are ethically obtainable by the researchers (having received the IRB's permission, as discussed in Chapter 3), have been used not only to compare the students who volunteered with those who did not volunteer for a certain psychological experiment or other type of study later that year, but also to compare the respondents with nonrespondents to an alumni-organization questionnaire sent out years later. This discussion assumes that permission has been granted by the student to use this personal information and that the student's anonymity and confidentiality are protected.

Table 9.5, based on an analysis of hundreds of studies comparing volunteers and nonvolunteers, lists nine general characteristics that are hypothesized to be typical of volunteers for research participation

Table 9.5 Characteristics of the Typical Research Volunteer
1. Better educated
2. Higher social class
3. Higher IQ scores
4. Higher need for social approval
5. More sociable
6. More arousal-seeking
7. More unconventional
8. More often female
9. Less authoritarian

(R. Rosenthal & Rosnow, 1975b). The characteristics in the table are ranked in the descending order of their approximate reliability, based on the data that were examined in that analysis. The list of characteristics has been simplified to make it easier to refer to when we return to these characteristics in the next section, but all are context-dependent to some degree. The following are examples:

1. Volunteers for research participation tend to be better educated than nonvolunteers, especially for studies in which personal contact between the investigator and the participant is not required.

2. As defined by the volunteers' own status (rather than by parental status), volunteers for research participation tend to be higher in social class status than nonvolunteers.

3. People who volunteer for somewhat less typical types of research (such as hypnosis, sensory isolation, sex research, and small-group and personality research) tend to score higher on IQ tests than nonvolunteers do.

4. Volunteers tend to be higher than nonvolunteers in need for social approval (the variable studied by Marlowe and Crowne, discussed in Chapter 6).

5. As measured by their scores on tests of sociability, volunteers typically score higher than nonvolunteers do.

6. When volunteering is for research involving stress, sensory isolation, or hypnosis, volunteers tend to be identified as more arousal-seeking than nonvolunteers.

7. When the volunteering is for studies of sexual behavior, volunteers tend to be identified as more unconventional than nonvolunteers.

8. Women are more likely to volunteer for research in general, but women are less likely than men to volunteer for physically and emotionally stressful research (e.g., electric shock, high temperature, sensory deprivation, and interviews about sexual behavior).

9. Volunteers for research participation tend to be less authoritarian than nonvolunteers (a characteristic implying that volunteers are usually less rigid thinkers and are likely to put a high value on individual freedom).

 ## How Is Volunteer Bias in Opportunity Samples Managed?

In connection with this topic, the term **volunteer bias** is used to refer to systematic error resulting when the responses of people who volunteer differ from those of individuals in the general population (Rosenthal & Rosnow, 1975b, 2009; Rosnow & Rosenthal, 1997). On the basis of knowing that research volunteers, compared to nonvolunteers, have a tendency to be brighter (Item 3), higher in approval need (Item 4), less authoritarian (Item 9), and so on, we can sometimes predict the direction of the potential volunteer bias.

For example, imagine that a research consulting firm is hired by a company to find out how persuasive an advertisement is before using it in a heavily funded television campaign. The consulting firm proposes to pilot-test the advertisement on volunteer participants assigned at random to an experimental group that views the advertisement or a control group that views something else to fill the same amount of time. The manager of the company (who took a research methods course in college and learned about characteristics of typical volunteer subjects) thinks that the volunteer participants may be relatively high in approval need (Item 4). The manager also recalls (from a course in personality psychology) that people who score high in approval need tend to be more easily influenced than those who score low in approval need. Putting this information together, the knowledgeable manager reasons that the consultants' results could overestimate the persuasive effect of the advertisement. Because volunteers in the experimental condition might overreact to the advertisement, the effect of the advertising campaign in the general population may be exaggerated by the pilot-study results.

Knowing that biased conclusions are possible, researchers can try to avoid this problem. For example, the use of volunteer subjects may lead to biased conclusions in the standardization of a new test. In

Chapter 5, we noted that many standardized tests are norm-referenced. That is, each person's score can be compared with those of a normative reference group by means of a table of values representing the typical performance of a given group. These *norms* provide a standard of comparison so that we can see how much any person's score deviates from the average of a large group of representative individuals.

For example, if you plan to apply to law school, you will want to know how much your score on the Law School Admission Test (LSAT) deviates from the scores of other highly qualified college students with similar career plans. In the next chapter, we will describe how to interpret a "standard score," but what is more relevant here is that a crucial assumption of researchers in developing norms for new tests is that the resulting values are representative of the target population. The developers of the LSAT have such information on everyone in the target group because everyone in the group must take this test. However, suppose a researcher uses volunteer subjects to standardize a brand-new intelligence test but wants to use the test and the resulting norms in a population consisting of typical volunteers *and* nonvolunteers. In light of Characteristic 3, our best guess is that the researcher's estimates of population norms will be inflated values, because volunteers may be expected to score higher on intelligence tests than nonvolunteers in the same population. The researcher needs to think of some noncoercive way of encouraging nonvolunteers to participate in the research.

Previously, we summarized some techniques used to stimulate participation by typical nonrespondents in survey research. Researchers can use a number of other incentives to stimulate participation by typical nonvolunteers (Rosenthal & Rosnow, 1975b; Rosnow & Rosenthal, 1997). Increasing such participation should, in turn, lessen the likelihood of selection bias by drawing a more representative sample of participants. For example, one recruitment technique is to explain to the potential participants why they will find the research interesting and worthwhile. This approach is based on evidence that people who are more interested in the research are more likely to participate (Rosenthal & Rosnow, 1975b). Another technique is to explain the research in a way that is nonthreatening, so that potential participants are not put off by fears of unfavorable evaluation (i.e., by their evaluation apprehensions). The basis of this technique is another set of findings that people who expect to be unfavorably evaluated by the investigator are less likely to volunteer, and those who expect to be favorably evaluated are more likely to volunteer. Some other empirically based techniques for stimulating research participation are emphasizing the scientific importance of the research, offering small courtesy gifts to potential participants for taking the time to consider participating, and avoiding unnecessary procedures that may be perceived as psychologically or biologically stressful.

A hasty reading of these techniques might give the impression that they are designed only to increase rates of participation. However, there is another, more subtle, benefit. When researchers tell prospective participants as much as possible about the significance of the research and avoid doing unnecessary psychologically or biologically stressful research, it follows that the researchers probably put more care and thought into planning to ensure that the research would withstand the scrutiny of critical evaluations. The researchers are treating the potential participants as if they were another "granting agency"—which in a sense they are, granting their valuable time and cooperation. Thus, another benefit of these techniques is that they provide incentives to researchers to be ethically responsible and humane when deciding what kind of research to do and how to go about it (Blanck et al., 1992; R. Rosenthal, 1994b; Rosnow, 1997).

Whatever your research project, whether it involves a survey, a randomized experiment, a single-case experiment, or some other strategy of collecting data directly from people, the final step before implementing the study is to pilot-test the materials. For example, suppose we want to study a sensitive topic and are concerned that people might be reluctant to tell the truth (Lee, 1993). We might pilot-test more than one version of the questionnaire or interview schedule. If we are concerned about nonresponse bias, we might test different recruitment procedures. Interestingly, even when conducting the actual survey, researchers use embedded randomized experiments on subsets of the sample, which can be an opportunity to pilot-test different recruitment methods to help prevent incurably flawed data in future research (e.g., Fienberg & Tanur, 1989; Schuman & Presser, 1996; Tanur, 1994). As the old saying goes, an ounce of prevention is worth a pound of cure.

Summary of Ideas

1. *Opportunity samples* use the first units that are available, whereas *probability sampling plans* use a random procedure for selecting a *sample* that is expected to be representative of the target *population*. However, to be absolutely sure that a sample is representative, we would have to know the true population value in advance, in which case (practically speaking) there would be no reason to study the sample.

2. A *biased* sample overestimates or underestimates the true population value. An *unstable* sample is characterized by sampling units that vary greatly from one another. Generally speaking, the more homogeneous the population, the fewer the sampling units needed.

3. In *simple random sampling,* the sample is selected from an undivided population (or from a relatively homogeneous stratum), and each unit has the same chance of being selected on any draw. Two options are (a) *sampling with replacement* and (b) *sampling without replacement* (e.g., the wine taster).

4. *Area probability sampling* is a variant of *stratified random sampling* in which the strata are geographic clusters.

5. The *Literary Digest* case (and its aftermath) taught political pollsters that (a) valid sampling must be done in a precise, scientific way that uses random selection (not, e.g., *quota sampling*); (b) large samples do not, in and of themselves, ensure representativeness; and (c) polling close to Election Day usually yields better predictions, but attention to voter turnout (or the predicted turnout) is important. "Push polls" (Box 9.3), an insidious form of political campaigning, are bogus "polls" designed to manufacture negative voter attitudes.

6. *Point estimates* predict typical population characteristics, whereas *interval estimates* tell us how much the point estimates are likely to be in error. *Confidence intervals* tell us the probability that the estimated population value is correct within some specific interval.

7. As the widget example illustrated, both the error of estimate of an individual sample and the likelihood of making that error tend to be greater in simple random samples than in stratified random samples.

8. In survey research that uses a probability sampling plan, bias due to nonresponse is likely to diminish with each successive wave of respondents (e.g., the survey of peach growers). Other ways to reduce nonresponse bias in survey research include (a) using reminders and follow-up communications; (b) personalizing the contact; and (c) offering an incentive to respond.

9. On practical, ethical, and theoretical grounds (e.g., the idea that people are similar), behavioral experimenters generally use opportunity samples of volunteer participants.

10. The typical volunteer for research participation (compared to the typical nonvolunteer) is (a) better educated; (b) higher in social class status; (c) higher in IQ; (d) higher in need for social approval; (e) higher in sociability; (f) more arousal-seeking; (g) more unconventional; (h) more often female; and (i) less authoritarian. Knowing the relationship between these characteristics of volunteer participants and the variable of interest, we can sometimes predict the direction of volunteer bias in experimental and nonexperimental studies.

11. Procedures for stimulating participation (e.g., telling people as much as possible about the significance of the research and avoiding stressful manipulations) also provide incentives to researchers to act ethically and humanely.

12. Pilot-testing the research materials can produce valuable information that will help us avoid making certain costly, intractable mistakes.

Key Terms

area probability sampling   p. 171
bias   p. 166
confidence interval   p. 173
effective sample size   p. 176
error of estimate   p. 174
interval estimates   p. 173
margin of error   p. 173
nonresponse bias   p. 176
opportunity samples   p. 164

point estimates   p. 173
population   p. 164
probability   p. 165
probability sampling   p. 165
push polls   p. 173
quota sampling   p. 172
representative   p. 165
sample   p. 165
sampling plan   p. 165

sampling without
  replacement   p. 170
sampling with replacement   p. 170
simple random sampling   p. 168
stability   p. 166
stratified random sampling   p. 171
unbiased   p. 166
unbiased sampling plan   p. 174
volunteer bias   p. 179

Multiple-Choice Questions for Review

1. Which of the following is most commonly used in public opinion polling? (a) random selection; (b) random assignment; (c) random processing; (d) opportunity sampling

2. A _____ is the total group of those in whom one is interested; a _____ is a segment of the total group that will be studied more closely. (a) universe of subjects, population; (b) population, sample; (c) sample, population; (d) sample, microsample

3. The true population mean is 4. A sample is chosen with the following values: 2, 3, 4, 5, 6. This sample is (a) unbiased; (b) biased; (c) random; (d) nonrandom.

4. The true population mean is 4. Sample A has the following values: 3, 4, 4, 5. Sample B has the following values: 0, 4, 4, 8. Compared to Sample B, Sample A is more (a) unbiased; (b) biased; (c) stable; (d) random.

5. A sampling plan is created in which each member of the population has an equal probability of being selected. This is called a(n) _____ plan. (a) quota sampling; (b) simple random sampling; (c) stratified random sampling; (d) area probability sampling

6. A public opinion pollster divides the population into subpopulations of males and females, and of Democrats and Republicans. She then takes a random sample from each of these subpopulations. This approach is called (a) area probability sampling; (b) stratified random sampling; (c) simple random sampling; (d) quota sampling.

7. A researcher concludes that 1,000 students at a particular college plan to go to graduate school. This is an example of a(n) (a) reliable measure; (b) interval estimate; (c) point estimate; (d) judge's rating.

8. The same researcher states that it is 95% likely that between 900 and 1,100 students at the college plan to go to graduate school. This is an example of a(n) (a) observation measure; (b) confidence interval estimate; (c) point estimate; (d) judge's rating.

9. In some circumstances, people who agree to participate in survey research are noticeably different from people who refuse to participate. This problem is sometimes called (a) lack of randomization; (b) sampling without replacement; (c) instability in sampling; (d) nonresponse bias.

10. Compared to nonvolunteers, those who typically volunteer to participate in psychological research tend to be (a) less authoritarian; (b) higher in arousal-seeking; (c) more sociable; (d) all of the above.

Discussion Questions for Review

1. Do you know the answer to the following questions asked of a University of Vermont student? Given a true population mean of 12 and the following participants' scores, (a) which group is measured with greatest stability, and (b) which group is the most biased?

Group 1	Group 2	Group 3
10	10	9
11	12	12
12	14	15
13	16	18

2. Fed up with studying for midterms, four Smith College students—Susan, Valerie, Ellen, and Jane—decide to throw darts at Susan's encyclopedia, which contains one volume for each letter of the alphabet. Because the word *midterm* begins with the letter *M*, the *M* volume is chosen as the target. Each person gets three darts. Susan hits the *M* volume every time; Valerie hits the *N* volume every time; Ellen hits the *L* volume, the *M* volume, and the *N* volume once each; and Jane hits the *M* volume, the *N* volume, and the *O* volume once each. Assuming that each volume of the encyclopedia is the same size, interpret the performance of each person in terms of bias and instability.

3. A Virginia Polytechnic Institute student is interested in the relationship between IQ and sociability. He designs a questionnaire to study this relationship and sends it out to hundreds of people. Twenty percent of the people complete and return the questionnaire. What is a possible source of bias in the results this student will obtain? How would you improve on his design?

4. A University of Kansas student is asked by his instructor to think up experimental cases in which the difference between typical volunteer participants and nonvolunteers might lead the researcher (a) to overestimate the effectiveness of the experimental treatment and (b) to underestimate the effectiveness of the experimental treatment. Can you help the student? Can you also think of how these situations might be remedied?

5. A University of Michigan student wants to sample the opinions of all graduating seniors on various issues. However, because the graduating class is so large, she decides it would be best to sample a representative group rather than try to contact every one of the graduating seniors. Describe the steps she should

take to develop a representative sampling plan, as well as some further steps she might take to deal with the problem of nonresponse bias.

6. A Cabrini College student wants to conduct an interview study using married adults who frequent the King of Prussia shopping mall. Because she is worried about volunteer bias, she would like to make every reasonable effort to obtain as representative a sample as she possibly can. What can she do to encourage people to participate in her study?

Answers to Review Questions

Multiple-Choice Questions

1. a	**3.** a	**5.** b	**7.** c	**9.** d
2. b	**4.** c	**6.** b	**8.** b	**10.** d

Discussion Questions

1. Group 1 is measured with the greatest stability; its members' scores range only from 10 to 13, whereas Groups 2 and 3 range from 10 to 16 and from 9 to 18, respectively. The means of Groups 1, 2, and 3 are 11.5, 13.0, and 13.5, respectively; therefore, the mean of Group 3 is the most biased.

2. Susan showed no bias with respect to the target volume (her average hit was M, the target volume) and no instability (she hit the same volume each time). Valerie showed a one-volume-away bias, hitting N on average, instead of volume M; she showed no instability, hitting the same volume each time. Ellen showed no bias (her average volume hit was M, the target volume, but she showed a three-volume instability, hitting three adjacent volumes). Jane showed a one-volume-away bias, hitting volume N on average instead of volume M; she showed a three-volume instability, hitting three adjacent volumes. We can summarize the results as follows:

	Bias	No bias
Some instability	Jane	Ellen
No instability	Valerie	Susan

3. Because volunteers or respondents tend to be more intelligent and more sociable than the general population, the correlation between IQ and sociability found in this self-selected sample may be quite different from the correlation we would find in the general population. One way to improve on the design might be to use follow-up questionnaires to increase the representativeness of the sample. Another way to improve on the design might be to try to locate data archives that include data from almost all of a given target population, for example, a college sample all of whom were tested at the time of admission or orientation.

4. In a study of the effects of a placebo on self-reported happiness, volunteers might show a larger placebo effect (i.e., the difference between the placebo and the no-treatment conditions) than nonvolunteers because volunteers are more likely to want to please the experimenter. In a study of the effects of a treatment designed to increase sociability, volunteers might show a smaller treatment effect than nonvolunteers because volunteers might already score so much higher on sociability that it might be hard to show further changes. Any procedures reducing volunteer bias would help reduce these potential problems.

5. She might draw a random sample of graduating seniors and contact them several times to reduce nonresponse bias. If she knew what characteristics were likely to be highly correlated with responses to her questionnaire, she might do her random selection within the various strata formed by her subdividing the sample into relatively more homogeneous subgroups.

6. She can try to make her appeal for volunteers as interesting, nonthreatening, and rewarding as possible.

CHAPTER 10

Summarizing the Data

Preview Questions

- How is visual integrity ensured when results are graphed?
- How are frequencies displayed in tables, bar graphs, and line graphs?
- How do stem-and-leaf charts work?
- How are percentiles used to summarize part of a batch?
- How is an exploratory data analysis done?
- How does asymmetry affect measures of central tendency?
- How do I measure how "spread out" a set of scores is?
- What are descriptive and inferential measures?
- How do I estimate a confidence interval around a population mean?
- What is distinctive about the normal distribution?
- Why are *z* scores called *standard scores,* and how are they used?

How Is Visual Integrity Ensured When Results Are Graphed?

In this chapter we review older and newer procedures that will help you summarize and evaluate tendencies of the data using frequency distributions, summary measures of central tendency and variability, descriptive and inferential measures, and standard (*z*) scores. If you are writing a research report for a course assignment, some procedures will be applicable as you analyze and interpret your results. But you should also find them useful beyond the bounds of this course. In the following chapters we will describe how the concepts discussed in this chapter provide the basic ingredients of common data-analytic procedures. Once you understand the logic and limitations of these concepts and procedures, you will also have a better understanding of the results you obtain if you are learning to use a computer to run a statistics program (see Box 10.1). You should also be in a stronger position to recognize phony claims based on statistical gimmicks that are used to trick people.

It is said that a picture is worth a thousand words, a statement that often seems true of research data. We will begin by showing some ways of graphing results to reveal tendencies of the data. With computer programs, it is easy to recast quantitative data in a visual display. It is important not to overcomplicate the results, as confusion and clutter will elicit vacant stares rather than easy comprehension. A properly prepared visual display is informative (one of the standards noted in Table 3.2 in Chapter 3) and easy to understand. Edward R. Tufte (1983), a statistician specializing in these designs, suggested that to ensure visual integrity and easy comprehension, it is important to keep in mind three criteria of all good visual displays: (a) *clarity* (representing data in a way that is closely integrated with the numerical meaning); (b) *precision* (representing results with the needed

BOX 10.1 What If You're Using a Computer Program?

If you are learning to use a computer to run a statistics program (such as SPSS, SAS, SYSTAT, or Minitab), you will find that most (but not all) of the statistical methods described in this book are among the most common statistical tools. To improve your understanding of what the computer program tells you, enter the raw data numbers from the examples as you go through the chapters. Most of the procedures described in this book are also simple enough to allow you to work them out on a pocket calculator. Even a calculator that computes only the standard deviation and variance of a sample (S, S^2) and a population (σ, σ^2) can get you started.

exactness, and not exaggerating numbers); and (c) *efficiency* (presenting the numbers in a reasonably compact space, so that the reader is encouraged to think about important details and is not distracted by unnecessary ones). As another expert in the visual display of quantitative information cautioned, the surest ways to impair the clarity, precision, and efficiency of graphics are to crowd them with too many numbers and statistics, to layer trivial information on important information, and to use a font that is hard to read and labels that are unfamiliar to most people (Wainer, 1997).

Cognitive psychologist Stephen M. Kosslyn (1994), who has written about how the brain perceives and processes visual information, suggested keeping in mind three interrelated principles that he characterized as (1) the mind is not a camera; (2) the mind judges a book by its cover; and (3) the spirit is willing, but the mind is weak:

1. *The mind is not a camera*. This means that we do not see things only as they are, because our experiences, hopes, anxieties, and expectations also come into play. You know the old saying that "seeing is believing." Well, it is also true that "believing is seeing," in that people have a tendency to perceive things in ways that seem to fit into their belief systems. For example, the more cluttered the graphic design is with ambiguous or superfluous information, the more likely it is that people will perceive something that, although irrelevant, *seems* to be relevant to their belief systems.

2. *The mind judges a book by its cover*. This means that people often take physical appearance as a clue to reality. For example, imagine a bar graph that uses side-by-side bars to report the results of two groups, labeled the Blue Team and the Red Team. But suppose the student who prints the graph gives little thought to the colors used to represent these results, and he uses blue ink to represent the Red Team and uses red ink to represent the Blue Team. The graph will create confusion, because the mind gravitates to physical appearance—or in this case, to the color of the ink to infer the meaning of the words written on the graph.

3. *The spirit is willing, but the mind is weak*. Neurological limitations dictate what the human brain can process properly. You may remember perceiving a halo around a blue streetlight at night and thinking it was due to fog; actually, that halo was caused by your eyes' inability to focus the image properly. The same would be true of cobalt blue used in a visual display: Cobalt blue is a mixture of red (which has a relatively long wavelength) and blue (which has a relatively short wavelength) and is hard to keep in focus.

How Are Frequencies Displayed in Tables, Bar Graphs, and Line Graphs?

When researchers want visual emphasis on the data's overall pattern, they often decide to use a **frequency distribution**. Such a display shows the number of times that each score or other unit of observation occurs in a set of data. A frequency distribution usually takes the form of a chart (e.g., a bar graph or a

Table 10.1	Evaluation by Focus Group Members of Two Smartphone Apps	
Score	Current App	New App
−3	2	1
−2	4	2
−1	14	10
0	28	20
+1	20	29
+2	8	12
+3	4	6

line graph), but frequencies can also be displayed in a tabular format. For example, Table 10.1 contains hypothetical data showing the frequency distribution of ratings by 80 focus group members of a Current App and a New App made for smartphones. Instead of a numerical rating scale with cue words such as *terrible, very poor, poor, average, good, very good,* and *excellent,* the members were given the pictorial scale in Figure 10.1. In the scoring of the results, each of the faces was assigned a number (or score) in the sequence −3, −2, −1, 0, +1, +2, +3. Table 10.1 shows the *frequency* (number) of members who chose each option in the face scale. For example, in the top row of Table 10.1, two members rated the current app −3 and one member gave the new app that same rating.

Figure 10.2 recasts the results clearly and efficiently as two **bar graphs**, where the height of the solid bars represents the number (frequency) of focus group members who chose each option. The scale values (which were implicit in Figure 10.1) are explicit on the horizontal axis (called the ***x axis***) in Figure 10.2, and the number of members is read from the vertical axis (the ***y axis***). Another name for the horizontal (*x*) axis is the **abscissa**; another name for the vertical (*y*) axis is the **ordinate**. (To keep these names straight, remember that the "abscissa sits," or rests on the bottom.) Comparing the two bar graphs allows us immediately to see that the new app was rated, in general, as more agreeable than the current product.

Bar graphs are especially useful for representing categories of responses and frequencies (or proportions) within those categories. **Line graphs** are an efficient way of graphing *changes* in the frequency (or proportion) of scores over time. An example was shown in Chapter 8, where Figure 8.1 (page 155) is a line graph of up-and-down change in the frequency of subway suicides and suicide attempts from 1980 to 1992 in Vienna, Austria. To identify the year in which the number of suicides or suicide attempts was greatest, we find the highest point and look at the horizontal axis (the abscissa) to read the year. The value of the visual display in Figure 8.1 is not only that it shows the increases and decreases at a glance, but that it also allows us to compare the change over time in two line graphs (shown together) before and after the intervention.

PLEASE CHECK THE BOX UNDER THE PICTURE THAT EXPRESSES HOW YOU
FEEL TOWARD THE PRODUCT YOU ARE RATING.

Figure 10.1 A 7-point pictorial rating scale.

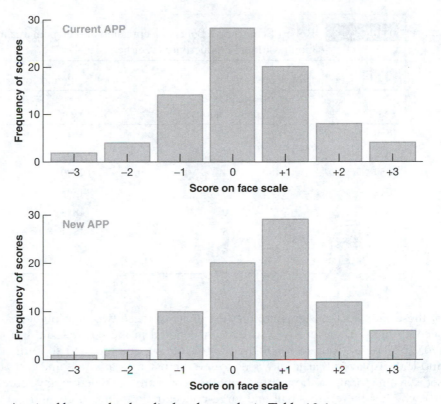

Figure 10.2 **A pair of bar graphs that display the results in Table 10.1.**

How Do Stem-and-Leaf Charts Work?

No hard-and-fast rule requires the representation of all frequency distributions to resemble the types discussed above. Another display alternative, called the **stem-and-leaf chart** (created by statistician John W. Tukey), provides a clear, precise, and efficient technique for displaying and interpreting a "batch" of data. A stem-and-leaf chart is a hybrid between a table and a graph, inasmuch as it presents original numbers and simultaneously gives an economical summary view of them. Constructing a stem-and-leaf chart involves no elaborate statistical theory. It relies on the question of interest to the researcher who decides to use it, possibly to do an exploratory data analysis (as illustrated later in this chapter) or to test a prediction or working hypothesis (Chambers, Cleveland, Kleiner, & Tukey, 1983; Emerson & Hoaglin, 1983; Tukey, 1977).

To illustrate how a stem-and-leaf chart is constructed, suppose we asked 15 students to rate a famous rapper, known for his social statements and wry political observations, on a scale from 0 ("the most shallow") to 100 ("the most profound"), and we obtain the following results: 66, 87, 47, 74, 56, 51, 37, 70, 82, 66, 41, 52, 62, 79, 69. Figure 10.3 shows a stem-and-leaf display

Stems	Leaves			
8	2	7		
7	0	4	9	
6	2	6	6	9
5	1	2	6	
4	1	7		
3	7			

Figure 10.3 **A stem-and-leaf chart of students' ratings of a famous rapper.**

Table 10.2	Robert Schumann's Bouts of Depression and Hypomania and His Compositional Productivity (Weisberg, 1994)		
Periods of depression		**Periods of hypomania**	
Year	Number of compositions	Year	Number of compositions
1830	1	1829	1
1831	1	1832	4
1839	4	1840	25
1842	3	1843	2
1844	0	1849	28
1847	5	1851	16
1848	5		

of these ratings. The stems are the first digits of these two-digit numbers, and the leaves are the second digits. There are two scores concentrated in the 80s (82 and 87), three scores in the 70s (70, 74, and 79), four scores in the 60s (62, 66, 66, and 69), and so forth. The beauty of the stem-and-leaf display is that it allows us to see the batch as a whole and to note (a) whether the data set is symmetrical, (b) how spread out the scores are, (c) whether any scores are outside the batch, (d) whether there are small and large concentrations of scores, and (e) whether there are any gaps (Emerson & Hoaglin, 1983). Thus, stem-and-leaf charts score high on the criteria of clarity, precision, and efficiency.

As a further illustration of the use of the stem-and-leaf display in research, we turn to the frequency distribution results in Table 10.2, based on a correlational study done by cognitive psychologist Robert W. Weisberg (1994). Weisberg was interested in an old theory that madness fosters creativity, and he decided to test this theory on the case of the prolific German composer Robert Schumann (1810–1856). Schumann suffered from what is now called bipolar disorder (previously described as manic depression) and eventually committed suicide. Weisberg first compiled a complete list of Schumann's musical compositions, then noted those compositions that experts considered works of genius, and also documented the specific years in which Schumann suffered from depression or hypomania (a mild form of mania, characterized by elation and quickness of thought). Weisberg found no support for the idea that madness fostered brilliance in Schumann's work. However, Table 10.2 shows that he had a tendency to produce more compositions when in a hypomanic than in a depressive state.

Another way of representing the data in Table 10.2 is shown in Figure 10.4, which plots the rates in adjoining stem-and-leaf charts, called a **back-to-back stem-and-leaf chart**. Figure 10.4 lets us see at a glance that the rates are spread out more for hypomania than for depression, and that the rates during bouts of depression are concentrated in a single stem.

Depression	Stems	Hypomania
	2	5 8
	1	6
5 5 4 3 1 1 0	0	1 2 4

Figure 10.4   A back-to-back stem-and-leaf chart of Schumann's number of compositions during his bouts of depression and hypomania (based on Table 10.2).

How Are Percentiles Used to Summarize Part of a Batch?

So far, the charts we have looked at display *all* the data, but researchers also find it useful to summarize *part* of the batch. For example, there is often a practical value in knowing the point in the distribution below and above which a certain percentage of scores falls. Called the **percentile**, 25% of the scores fall at or below the 25th percentile, 75% of the scores fall at or below the 75th percentile, and so on. When producing stem-and-leaf charts, researchers usually accompany the charts with a quantitative summary of the data, which includes a listing of the scores falling at the 25th, 50th, and 75th percentiles.

In many cases, it is highly useful to know the location of the typical score and the spread of scores around that location (we turn to measures of spread shortly). One very useful measure of typical location is the 50th percentile, called the **median** (symbolized as *Mdn*). It is one of several popular measures of **central tendency**, which tells us that it is one measure of the location of central or typical values. The median is the score above and below which an equal number of scores fall. In other words, the median is the midmost score in a distribution of scores. When the total number of scores (symbolized as *N*) is an odd number, the median is the middle score. In the series 2, 3, 3, 4, 4, 5, 6, 7, 7, 8, 8, the *Mdn* = 5 because it is in the middle, leaving five scores below it (2, 3, 3, 4, 4) and five scores above it (6, 7, 7, 8, 8).

When there is an even number of scores (so that there are two midmost scores), the median is computed as half the distance between the two middle numbers. In the series 2, 3, 3, 4, 4, 7, the *Mdn* = 3.5, halfway between the 3 and the 4 at the center of the set of scores. Tied scores create a small problem, however. Consider the series 1, 2, 3, 3, 3, where we see the number 3 listed three times, including in the middle. Simply imagine this series of five numbers as made up of a 1, a 2, a "small" 3, a "larger" 3, and a "still larger" 3. The assumption is that using a more precise measurement procedure would have allowed us to break the ties, so we conceptualize the "small 3" as the median (because there are two scores below this particular 3 and two above it). In reporting this result, however, we would simply report *Mdn* = 3.

An easy way to locate the median (the 50th percentile) is to multiply *N* + 1 (where *N* is again the total number of scores in the ordered set) by .50. In the back-to-back stem-and-leaf in Figure 10.4, Schumann's annual rate of musical compositions was 0, 1, 1, 3, 4, 5, 5 scores when he was depressed. The location of the median is given by .50(*N* + 1), which is .50(7 + 1) = 4th score in the set of seven ordered scores (counting from left to right), or *Mdn* = 3 compositions. Similarly, Schumann's rate of compositions was 1, 2, 4, 16, 25, 28 scores when he was hypomanic. The median rate is given by .50(6 + 1) = 3.5th score in this set (counting from left to right), or halfway between the number 4 and the number 16, yielding *Mdn* = 10.

We can also use this procedure to locate other percentiles. The location of the 75th percentile is .75(*N* + 1), and the location of the 25th percentile is given by .25(*N* + 1). In the 0, 1, 1, 3, 4, 5, 5 set, the 75th percentile is .75(8) = 6th score, or 5 compositions. The location of the 25th percentile in this set is given by .25(8) = 2nd score, that is, 1 lone composition. In the 1, 2, 4, 16, 25, 28 set, the location of the 75th percentile is .75(7) = 5.25th score (i.e., 25% of the distance between the 5th and 6th scores), which is 25.75 compositions. For these same six scores, the location of the 25th percentile is given by .25(7) = 1.75th score (i.e., 75% of the distance between the 1st and 2nd scores), which is 1.75 compositions. The distance between the 25th and 75th percentiles is called the **interquartile range**. In the 1, 2, 4, 16, 25, 28 set, the interquartile range indicates that, when Schumann was in a hypomanic state, the middle 50% of his annual work was between 1.75 and 25.75 compositions.

 How Is an Exploratory Data Analysis Done?

Previously, we mentioned that the stem-and-leaf chart can be used not only to do hypothesis testing (known as **confirmatory data analysis**), but also to do exploratory data analysis. **Exploratory data analysis** is detective work because we are looking for clues, and to do it properly, we must

Stems	Leaves
.4	0 1 2
.3	0 0 1 2 6 6 7 7 7 8
.2	4
.1	0 2 4 6 9
.0	3

Figure 10.5   A steam-and-leaf chart of the proportion of no-show volunteers in 20 studies (Rosenthal & Rosnow, 1975b).

look in the right place. Therefore, we would not stop with a visual display of the overall batch of data but would also look for patterns in parts of the batch. Let us see how to do this using only the stem-and-leaf chart and the calculation of percentiles.

In the previous chapter, we referred to research on volunteer characteristics. A number of investigators were also interested in what kind of volunteers become "no-shows" (people who fail to show up for their scheduled research appointments). Suppose we want to estimate the number of people we need to recruit in order to make it likely that at least 40 will show up. Some years ago, we explored a variation on this question in a meta-analytic review of 20 studies that reported the proportion of no-shows (R. Rosenthal & Rosnow, 1975b). Those proportions are listed in the stem-and-leaf chart in Figure 10.5. The proportion of no-shows (reading from top to bottom) was .42 in one study, .41 in another study, .40 in another study, .38 in another study, and so forth. To continue our detective work, we will compute the 25th, 50th (*Mdn*), and 75th percentiles on these data.

Reading now from the lowest to the highest score in Figure 10.5, the sequence of values is as follows:

1. .03	**6.** .19	**11.** .32	**16.** .37
2. .10	**7.** .24	**12.** .36	**17.** .38
3. .12	**8.** .30	**13.** .36	**18.** .40
4. .14	**9.** .30	**14.** .37	**19.** .41
5. .16	**10.** .31	**15.** .37	**20.** .42

The location of the median in this ordered series is the $.50(20 + 1) = 10.5$th score. That is, the median is halfway between the 10th score (.31) and the 11th score (.32), or $Mdn = .32$ (i.e., .315 rounded to the nearest even value).

The location of the 25th percentile score is given by $.25(N + 1)$. Therefore, $.25(21) = 5.25$th score (i.e., 25% of the distance between the 5th and 6th scores), which gives us .17. The location of the 75th percentile score is $.75(N + 1)$, which we calculate as $.75(21) = 15.75$th score, 75% of the distance between the 15th and 16th scores. In this case, the 15th and 16th scores are both .37, so 75% of the distance between them is zero, and therefore the 75th percentile $= .37$. To summarize this stem-and-leaf chart in certain key values of the distribution, we would report that (a) the maximum value $= .42$; (b) the 75th percentile $= .37$; (c) the *Mdn* (50th percentile) $= .32$; (d) the 25th percentile $= .17$; and (e) the minimum value $= .03$.

What have we learned? The interquartile range (the distance between the 25th and 75th percentiles) reveals that the 50% of the studies that were midmost have values between .17 and .37. From the fact that the median no-show rate of volunteers is .32, we now have a recommendation: If we were counting on 40 volunteer participants to show up for our research, we might schedule about 60 (i.e., one third of 60 = 20, and 60 − 20 = 40), or half again as many volunteers as we absolutely need. Of course, this recommendation is based on the assumption that the results in Figure 10.5 are, in fact, typical and that the median no-show rate is still about the same. Answering these sorts of questions would require a follow-up meta-analysis. The results of later studies of no-show rates could be compared with the results in Figure 10.5 in a back-to-back stem-and-leaf chart. For example, in a 20-year follow-up meta-analysis done by a graduate student for his master's thesis, he reported that the median no-show rate had remained relatively unchanged at about one third (Aditya, 1996).

How Does Asymmetry Affect Measures of Central Tendency?

Besides the median, another measure of central tendency is the **mode**. It is the score, or category of scores, that occurs most often. In the series 3, 4, 4, 4, 5, 5, 6, 6, 7, mode = 4. The series 3, 4, 4, 4, 5, 5, 6, 7, 7, 7 has two modal scores (at values 4 and 7) and is thus described as *bimodal* (having two modes). For the stem-and-leaf chart in Figure 10.5, we would refer to the modal *category* as the ".30s" (stem of .3 and leaves of 0, 0, 1, 2, 6, 6, 7, 7, 7, 8). Sometimes there is no distinct mode, in which case the central tendency of the data is better described by another measure, such as the median or the ordinary mean. Another problem with reporting the mode is that it tells us nothing about the proportion of the total (N) scores falling on the mode, which can range from $2/N$ to 1.00. The larger the proportion of scores falling on the mode, the more useful is the reporting of the mode (see Box 10.2).

The ordinary sample mean (or *arithmetic mean*), called the **mean** for short, is generally symbolized in psychology research reports as M. An older symbol, still recognized in the *Publication Manual of the American Psychological Association* (APA, 2010) is $\overline{X}$ Whether you see M or $\overline{X}$ the arithmetic mean that is reported is the sum of the scores (ΣX) divided by the total number (N) of scores in a set (or n for a subset of scores, that is, a sample of scores). Where the denominator is N, the formula for the mean is

$$M = \frac{\Sigma X}{N},$$

where Σ (the uppercase Greek letter sigma) tells us to "sum" the X scores. In the series 1, 2, 3, 3, 3, the sum of the scores is 12, the total number of scores is 5, and therefore, M = 12/5 = 2.4. For the stem-and-leaf values in Figure 10.5, the mean is calculated as the sum of the reported proportions (5.65) divided by 20, which gives M = .28 (i.e., .2825 rounded to two decimal places is .28) as the mean proportion of no-shows. You can think of the mean as the "center of gravity" of a distribution of numbers. For example, if you turned a stem-and-leaf on its side and balanced it, the balance point is the mean (Wilkinson & Engelman, 1996). Reporting more than one measure of central tendency will give readers a clearer idea of the distribution of the data set. When the distribution of scores is symmetrical, the median and the mean give the same value. The mode and the proportion of scores falling on the mode offer a good way to show that there were many identical scores, and the median is useful when there are extreme high or low scores, because it is unaffected by only a few extreme scores. When scores are tightly bunched, the mean is close to all the scores, though averaging in a few extremely high or extremely low scores may give a misleading picture of the central tendency of the data set.

BOX 10.2   The Modal Representativeness

An index for reporting the proportion of N scores falling on the mode might be as a subscript (in parentheses) of the mode. So a mode having only 2 scores out of 50 falling on the mode could be reported as mode$_{(.04)}$, whereas a mode having 10 scores out of 50 falling on the mode would be reported as mode$_{(.20)}$. In the series 3, 4, 4, 4, 5, 5, 6, 6, 7, the mode = $4_{(.33)}$. In the series 3, 4, 4, 4, 5, 5, 6, 7, 7, 7 (having two modes), the modes are $4,7_{(.6)}$. The modal category for the stem-and-leaf chart in Figure 10.5 is .30s$_{(.5)}$, because 10 scores out of 20 fell in that category. We describe this information as the **modal representativeness index**.

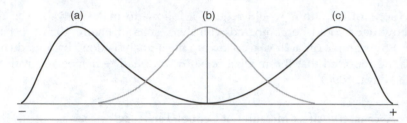

Figure 10.6   Illustrations of symmetry and asymmetry. Only distribution (b) is symmetrical, in that both sides of the middle line are identical. When the long, pointed tail is toward the positive end (i.e., a long right tail) as represented by (a), the distribution is said to be positively skewed. When the long, pointed tail is toward the negative end (i.e., a long left tail) as illustrated by (c), the distribution is said to be negatively skewed.

Figure 10.6 further illustrates these relationships. The (b) curve displays a **symmetrical distribution**, which means there is a correspondence in arrangement on the opposite sides of the middle line. When the right side is not the reverse of the left side of the distribution, we have an **asymmetrical distribution**. When the mean of the distribution is much larger than the median, the stretched-out tail points conspicuously toward the positive end (in a **positively skewed distribution**), as shown by the (a) curve. When the mean is much smaller than the median, the stretched-out tail points toward the negative end (in a **negatively skewed distribution**), as shown by the (c) curve. The (b) curve also shows what we meant when we said that the median and the mean have the same value in a symmetrical (or nonskewed) distribution.

Suppose that a few scores lie far outside the normal range. These far-out scores are called **outliers**. When a distribution of scores is strongly asymmetrical because of outliers, researchers often prefer a **trimmed mean** to an ordinary mean because an ordinary mean is very sensitive to extreme values. Trimming implies giving the data set a "light haircut" by cutting off not just the one or more outliers from one side, but the same percentage of scores from both ends of the series of scores. Consider, for example, a strongly asymmetrical series: −20, 2, 3, 6, 7, 9, 9, 10, 10, 10. The −20 is an outlier that clearly disrupts the homogeneity of the series. To expunge outliers fairly, we trim an equal number of scores at each end. In this case, trimming one score from each end leaves 2, 3, 6, 7, 9, 9, 10, 10. What if we had not trimmed the series? Would leaving the outlier in have distorted the average by very much? It depends on how the "average" is defined. The trimmed mean = 7.0 and the untrimmed mean = 4.6, so the answer is yes in the case of the ordinary mean (M). The median is unaffected by trimming, so for these scores $Mdn = 8$ with or without trimming. The mode, which may be affected by trimming, is 10 for the scores before trimming but is bimodal at 9 and 10 after trimming (see also Box 10.3).

 BOX 10.3 Unusual Scores and Wild Scores

Medians and trimmed means protect us in certain cases from possibly misleading interpretations based on very unusual scores. For example, if we calculated the benefits of a proposed tax plan for 10 families and found 9 of them with a $100 benefit and 1 with a $9,100 benefit, the mean benefit of $1,000 would be highly unrepresentative of the "typical benefit" compared to the trimmed mean, the median, or (in this case) even the mode. Medians and trimmed means also protect us somewhat against the intrusion of certain extreme scores recorded erroneously (called **wild scores**). Imagine the series 4, 5, 5, 6, 6, 6, 7, 7, 8, of which the mean, median, mode, and trimmed mean are all 6. However, suppose we erred and entered the data as 4, 5, 5, 6, 6, 6, 7, 7, 80. Our new (erroneous) mean would now be 14, though our median or trimmed mean would remain unaffected.

However, do not be tempted just to drop any outliers. Until you know whether the outliers are errors (scoring or recording mistakes), dropping them could be discarding important information that warrants further examination. There are also statistical procedures for "reeling in" outliers and making them part of the group (Rosenthal & Rosnow, 2008, pp. 309–311). These procedures also increase the homogeneity of the variability found in the two or more groups or conditions that we might want to compare statistically, as homogeneity of variability is one of the statistical assumptions underlying t tests and F tests. The calculated value of the statistical tests will be more accurate if the variabilities of the populations from which the obtained data were derived are more nearly equal. In the sample paper in Appendix A, Mary Jones approaches this problem in another acceptable way, using a procedure described in her report.

How Do I Measure How "Spread Out" a Set of Scores Is?

The term *variability*, used above, refers to how "spread out" the scores are. For example, besides knowing the central tendency (or "typical value") of a set of scores, we also want to know the *interval estimate* (as it was described in Chapter 9). That is, we also want to know how far the scores deviate from the value of the central tendency measurement. Just as there are different measures of central tendency, there are several different measures of what is alternatively described as *spread, dispersion,* or *variability*. For example, we mentioned the interquartile range (the distance between the 25th and 75th percentiles), which tells us the variability that is characteristic of the middle 50% of the scores. Other measures of spread include the range (the crude range and extended range), the variance, and the standard deviation.

We will start with the ordinary **range** (or **crude range**), which is the difference between the highest and lowest scores. If you were administering a scale, you would want to report the *potential* crude range as well as the *observed* (or obtained) range. If the potential crude range is quite narrow, it might be impossible to produce appreciable differences among the participants; that is, there is a flaw in the design. On the other hand, it does not follow that simply having a very wide potential range will automatically result in a substantial observed range. The way we interpret the range depends on the purpose of the study and the nature of the instruments used. For example, if you used a scale consisting of 20 five-point items, and each item is scored from 1 to 5, the potential crude range is from 20 to 100. You would report the potential crude range (CR) as being the highest score (H) minus the lowest score (L), so potential $CR = H - L = 80$ points. Using the same method, you would also report the crude range for the observed scores.

A further distinction is made between the crude range and the **extended range** (sometimes called the **corrected range**). In the series 2, 3, 4, 4, 6, 7, 9, the crude range is the highest score minus the lowest score, or $CR = 9 - 2 = 7$. The extended range (ER) assumes that, in more precise measurements, a score of 9 will fall somewhere between 8.5 and 9.5 and that a score of 2 will fall somewhere between 1.5 and 2.5. To adjust for this possibility, we think of the extended range in this case as running from a high of 9.5 to a low of 1.5. The extended range is then $9.5 - 1.5 = 8$. The extended range thus adds a half unit at the top of the distribution and a half unit at the bottom of the distribution, or a total of 1 full unit, and can be computed as $ER = (H - L) + 1$. The crude range and the extended range tell us about the extreme scores in a set of scores. The next two measures of spread—the variance and the standard deviation—are based on information from all the scores.

The **variance** of a set of scores tells us the deviation from the mean of the scores, but instead of using deviation values directly, it squares the deviations and averages them. In other words, it is the mean of the squared deviations of the scores (X) from their mean (M). The variance of a set of scores is also commonly referred to as the **mean square** (i.e., the mean of the squared deviations), and you will see this term again in our discussion of the F test (which is used in the statistical procedure known as *analysis of variance*). The symbol used to denote the variance of a population is σ^2 (read as "sigma-squared"), and the formula used to calculate the population variance is

$$\sigma^2 = \frac{\Sigma(X - M)^2}{N},$$

where the numerator instructs us to sum (Σ) the squared deviations of the individual scores from the mean of the set of scores, and the denominator tells us to divide that sum by the total number of scores.

The **standard deviation** is by far the most widely used and reported of all measures of spread around the average. Symbolized as σ, the standard deviation of a population is the square root of the population variance. That is,

$$\sigma = \sqrt{\sigma^2},$$

or calculated from the original data as

$$\sigma^2 = \sqrt{\frac{\Sigma(X - M)^2}{N}}.$$

Incidentally, some statistics programs use the term **root mean square** (RMS) as another name for the standard deviation, since the standard deviation is the square root of the mean of the squared deviations, as the equation above shows.

If you do not have a calculator that allows you to compute the standard deviation and the variance directly from "raw" (i.e., obtained) scores (and are not using a computer with a statistics package), it is still easy to compute these values with any handy calculator. Practicing with the summary data in Table 10.3 is a way of teaching yourself what the variance and standard deviation represent in five easy steps:

Step 1 (in the first column) is to add up the six raw scores ($\Sigma X = 30$), and then to find their mean by dividing the sum by the number of scores ($M = 30/6 = 5$).

Step 2 (in the second column) is to subtract the mean from each raw score. As a check on your arithmetic, you will find that these deviation scores sum to zero, that is, $\Sigma(X - M) = 0$.

Step 3 (in the last column) is to square the deviation scores in column 2, and then to add up the squared deviations, which gives $\Sigma(X - M)^2 = 24$.

Step 4 is to compute the population variance (σ^2) by substituting the value obtained in Step 3 in the numerator, and the number of scores in the denominator, which gives you

$$\sigma^2 = \frac{\Sigma(X - M)^2}{N} = \frac{24}{6} = 4.$$

Table 10.3   Summary Data for Computing the Variance and the Standard Deviation

Raw scores	$X - M$	$(X - M)^2$
2	-3	9
4	-1	1
4	-1	1
5	0	0
7	2	4
8	3	9
$\Sigma X = 30$	$\Sigma(X - M) = 0$	$\Sigma(X - M)^2 = 24$
$M = 5$		

Step 5 is to find the standard deviation, either by obtaining the square root of the value in Step 4, that is,

$$\sigma = \sqrt{4} = 2,$$

or by direct substitution in the formula noted earlier, that is,

$$\sigma = \sqrt{\frac{\Sigma(X - M)^2}{N}} = \sqrt{\frac{24}{6}} = 2.$$

 ## What Are Descriptive and Inferential Measures?

Another distinction is that made between descriptive and inferential measures. Suppose we were interested in the variability of the batting averages of a favorite baseball team. We can collect the scores of *all* the players and compute the standard deviation using the formula described above. In this case, the formula used for measuring variability is classified as a **descriptive measure** because it describes a *complete population* of scores or events, with Greek letters (not italicized) used to symbolize the particular measure (e.g., σ or σ^2).

As discussed in the previous chapter, researchers are also interested in generalizing from a sample of known scores or events to a population of unknown scores or events, which may be finite or infinite (see Box 10.4). Suppose we were interested in the variability of the population of major-league baseball players' batting averages as a whole. We can collect a sample of scores and then make inferences about the variability of scores in the population from which they were drawn. The equation we now use to measure variability is classified as an **inferential measure**, with roman type (italicized) used to symbolize the particular measure (e.g., S or S^2).

Except for the denominator and the symbol (Greek or roman), the descriptive and inferential formulas for computing variances (σ^2 and S^2)—and, therefore, standard deviations (σ and S)—are similar. In the descriptive formulas for variances and standard deviations, the numerator value is divided by N (as previously shown). In the inferential formulas, the numerator value is divided by $N - 1$ (because it can be shown statistically that, with repeated sampling, this procedure gives the most accurate inferences). Thus, if you want to estimate the variance (σ^2) of a population from a sample, you use the statistic S^2 (referred to as the **unbiased estimator of the population value of** σ^2) and the following formula:

$$S^2 = \frac{\Sigma(X - M)^2}{N - 1},$$

where N is the sample size. And if you want to estimate the σ of a population from a sample, you use the statistic S and the following formula:

$$S = \sqrt{S^2} = \sqrt{\frac{\Sigma(X - M)^2}{N - 1}}.$$

 ## BOX 10.4 Finite and Infinite

In the baseball example, we are dealing with both a finite sample and a finite population. **Finite** means that all the units or events can, at least in theory, be completely counted. **Infinite**, on the other hand, means "boundless" or "without limits." Suppose, based on samples of sand that have been randomly collected, we want to make a generalization about the variability of all the sand at Long Beach Island, New Jersey. Here, we are attempting to make an inference from a finite sample to a population of unknown "events" that is regarded as infinite (because of ecological changes and so on).

For example, if you think of the 6 raw scores in the first column of Table 10.3 (scores of 2, 4, 4, 5, 7, 8) as a sample from a larger population, and you want to generalize from this sample of $N = 6$ scores to the larger population, you compute

$$S^2 = \frac{\Sigma(X - M)^2}{N - 1} = \frac{24}{5} = 4.8,$$

and

$$S = \sqrt{4.8} = 2.19.$$

How Do I Estimate a Confidence Interval Around a Population Mean?

In our discussion of survey research (Chapter 9), we introduced the idea of confidence interval estimates, which tell us about the degree to which the point estimates are likely to be in error. The most commonly reported confidence interval estimate (symbolized as CI) is the 95% CI. This interval runs from a value below our obtained point estimate to a value above it, both values having been chosen so that there is a 95% probability that the true (but unknown) population value falls between the lower and upper limits. Because confidence intervals tell us how accurately or precisely we have estimated some quantity (e.g., a specific number of people, a proportion of a population, or a population mean), they are valuable pieces of information to have in a research report. We turn now to a procedure for obtaining confidence limits around an estimate of a population mean. (In a later chapter, we will describe a procedure for obtaining confidence limits around an estimate of a population effect size.)

Three quantities are required to compute a 95% CI around an obtained estimate of a population mean: N, S, and $t_{(.05)}$, where N is the number of scores upon which the observed mean (M) is based, and S is the standard deviation of the N scores obtained, computed again as

$$S = \sqrt{\frac{\Sigma(X - M)^2}{N - 1}}.$$

If you have had a course in statistics, you know that t is the symbol for Student's t test (discussed in Chapter 13), but for this application, all you will need to know is how to find the value of $t_{(.05)}$. Looking at Table B.2 in Appendix B (page 327), you see, at the very top, a row labeled "two-tailed" and a value of ".05" in the fourth column. You know you are looking at the right column if you see 12.706 as the first value (corresponding to what in the far left is labeled "$df = 1$") and 1.960 as the last value (corresponding to "$df = \infty$"; ∞ is the symbol for infinity). We explain these terms in a later chapter, but for this application the df (which stands for *degrees of freedom*) is defined as $N - 1$ (the number of sample scores minus 1). We obtain the quantity $t_{(.05)}$ from Table B.2 by looking down the column headed ".05 two-tailed," until we reach the row label indicating the number of df on which our obtained mean was based (i.e., $N - 1$).

Consider again the data of Table 10.3, in which $N = 6$ raw scores. These scores are 2, 4, 4, 5, 7, 8, with mean (M) = 5 and (as calculated in the previous section) $S = 2.19$. We find that $t_{(.05)} = 2.57$, because $df = N - 1 = 5$, and Table B.2 shows the value 2.571 at the intersection of the column headed ".05 two-tailed" and the row labeled 5 df. To obtain a 95% confidence interval around the estimated population mean, we find

$$\text{Lower limit} = M - \frac{(t_{(.05)})(S)}{\sqrt{N}}$$

Table 10.4	Values of x and $t_{(x)}$ (for $df = 5$) for Five Different Confidence Intervals	
CI (%)	x	$t_{(x)}$ (for $df = 5$)
99.9	.001	6.87
99	.01	4.03
95	.05	2.57
90	.10	2.02
80	.20	1.48

and

$$\text{Upper limit} = M + \frac{\left(t_{(.05)}\right)(S)}{\sqrt{N}}.$$

For our example in Table 10.3, after rounding 2.571 to 2.57, we calculated

$$\text{Lower limit} = 5 - \frac{(2.57)(2.19)}{\sqrt{6}} = 5 - 2.30 = 2.70$$

and

$$\text{Upper limit} = 5 + \frac{(2.57)(2.19)}{\sqrt{6}} = 5 + 2.30 = 7.30$$

Because we computed a 95% CI around the obtained estimate of the population mean, we state that "there is a 95% probability that the estimated population mean falls between 2.70 and 7.30."

Although 95% confidence intervals are the most commonly used, we can choose any size CI we like. The APA Publication Manual recommends that "As a rule, it is best to use a single confidence level, specified on an a priori basis (e.g., a 95% or 99% confidence interval), throughout the manuscript" (American Psychological Association, 2010, p. 34). To choose other than a 95% confidence interval, we need only replace the quantity $t_{(.05)}$ with the quantity $t_{(x)}$, where $x = 1$ minus the desired CI. Table 10.4 shows the values of x and $t_{(x)}$ (for $df = 5$) for five different confidence intervals. Values of $t_{(x)}$ are larger for the more demanding confidence intervals (99% and 99.9%), as we would expect in general, but these values of $t_{(x)}$ are especially large (4.03 and 6.87) because of the small sample size in our example ($N = 6$).

 ## What Is Distinctive About the Normal Distribution?

When scores on a variety of types of measures (intelligence test scores, physical performance measures, scores on an attitude scale, and so forth) are collected by means of a representative sampling procedure, the distribution of these scores often forms a curve that has a distinct bell-like shape (as shown in Figure 10.7). This curve is called a **normal distribution** because of the large number of different kinds of measurements that are assumed to be ordinarily ("normally") distributed in this manner.

The normal distribution is particularly useful in providing a mathematical description of populations because it can be completely described from our knowledge of just the mean and the standard deviation. For example, we can say that roughly two thirds of the area of the normal distribution is within one standard deviation of the mean, and so on. Specifically (as represented in Figure 10.7), 68.3% of normally distributed scores fall between -1σ and $+1\sigma$; 95.4% fall between -2σ and $+2\sigma$;

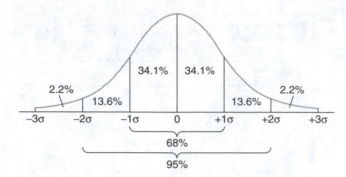

Figure 10.7   The normal distribution divided into standard deviation units.

and 99.7% fall between -3σ and $+3\sigma$. Even though over 99% of the scores fall between -3σ and $+3\sigma$, the left and right tails of the normal curve never do touch down on the abscissa; instead, they stretch into infinity.

One reason the normal distribution is so useful is that, by some simple arithmetic, we can translate raw scores obtained by different measures into standard deviation units. Not only does this process make the different scores comparable, but we can also usually estimate what proportion of normally distributed scores in the population can be found in any region of the curve. Because so many measurements are distributed normally in the population, the statistics derived from this bell-shaped curve are also very important in the testing of hypotheses. We will return to this topic in Chapter 12, but let us see how you might translate a raw score into a standard deviation unit, or a standard score.

 Why Are z Scores Called *Standard Scores,* and How Are They Used?

A normal curve with a mean set equal to 0 and the standard deviation set equal to 1 is described as a **standard normal curve**. Any individual raw score can be put through a statistical translation (referred to as **transformation**) into a **standard score** corresponding to a location on the abscissa of a standard normal curve. A standard score (called a ***z score***) expresses, in standard deviation units, the raw score's distance from the mean of the normative group. We make the transformation by subtracting the mean of the group (*M*) from the individual raw score (*X*), and then dividing this difference by the standard deviation (σ) of the normative group, that is,

$$z \text{ score} = \frac{X - M}{\sigma}.$$

For example, scores on the Scholastic Assessment Test (SAT) have a normative group mean of 500 and a standard deviation of 100. Suppose you want to transform an individual raw score of 625 into a *z* score with a distribution mean of 0 and a standard deviation of 1. You simply calculate as follows:

$$z = \frac{625 - 500}{100} = 1.25$$

and find that the raw score of 625 corresponds to a *z* score of 1.25, which tells you how far above the mean (in terms of the standard deviation of the distribution) this score is. To transform the *z* score back to the original raw score, you multiply the *z* score by σ and add it to *M*:

$$X = (z \text{ score})(\sigma) + M = (1.25)(100) + 500 = 625.$$

Table B.1 in Appendix B (see page 326) provides a listing of *z* scores (standardized normal deviates). The *z* column (with rows ranging from .0 to 4.0) lists *z* values to one decimal place.

The remaining columns (.00 to .09) carry z to two decimal places. The body of the table shows the proportion of the area of the normal distribution that includes and is to the right of (i.e., above) the value of any particular z on the abscissa. You can use this information to estimate the proportion of normally distributed scores in the population that is higher (or lower) than the raw score of 625 (corresponding to a z score of 1.25) on the SAT. Given $z = 1.25$, you simply locate the intersection that corresponds to 1.2 (row 13) and .05 (column 6). That value is .1056, which estimates the proportion of SAT scores including and higher than an obtained score of 625 in the normative group of students taking the SAT. Multiply .1056 by 100 to transform the proportion into a percentage, which tells you that 10.56% of those tested ordinarily score as high as 625 or higher. Subtracting this percentage from 100 tells you how many ordinarily score lower than 625 (i.e., $100 - 10.56 = 89.44\%$ score lower).

The title of Table B.1 refers to "one-tailed" p values. We will have more to say about "one-tailed" (or "one-sided") significance levels in other chapters, but basically the term means that we are concentrating on one part of the normal distribution. In the case of a positive z score, we are focusing on the part from the midpoint (0) to the end of the right tail. If the z were a negative score, we would be concentrating on the part from the midpoint to the end of the left tail. In summary, then, a positive z score is above the mean; a negative z score is below the mean; and a zero z score is at the mean.

Another practical value of reporting z scores is that scores on different tests or instruments need not be normally distributed to be transformed into z scores and then compared in terms of this common metric. For example, by calculating z scores for height and weight, you can tell whether a person is taller than he or she is heavy, relative to others in the normative distribution of height and weight. However, only if they are distributed approximately normally in the population can you estimate from a z score how many scored above or below a given z score. You can do so for SAT scores because they are approximately normally distributed in the population.

As a practical illustration of the utility of z scores, imagine that an instructor has two measures of course grades on five male and five female students, as shown in Table 10.5. One set of scores

Table 10.5	Raw and Standard Scores on Two Exams				
Student ID and gender	Exam 1		Exam 2		Average of z_1 and z_2 scores
	X_1 score	z_1 score	X_2 score	z_2 score	
1 (M)	42	+1.78	90	+1.21	+1.50
2 (M)	9	−1.04	40	−1.65	−1.34
3 (F)	28	+0.58	92	+1.33	+0.96
4 (M)	11	−0.87	50	−1.08	−0.98
5 (M)	8	−1.13	49	−1.13	−1.13
6 (F)	15	−0.53	63	−0.33	−0.43
7 (M)	14	−0.62	68	−0.05	−0.34
8 (F)	25	+0.33	75	+0.35	+0.34
9 (F)	40	+1.61	89	+1.16	+1.38
10 (F)	20	−0.10	72	+0.18	+0.04
Sum (Σ)	212	0	688	0	0
Mean (M)	21.2	0	68.8	0	0
SD (σ)	11.69	1.0	17.47	1.0	0.98

BOX 10.5 "How" and "What" to Report

In the remaining chapters, we continue our discussion of the analysis and reporting of statistical information. But before we resume our discussion, we want to remind you again of the scientific standards discussed in Chapter 3. To ensure scientific quality when reporting quantitative results, it is important to be (a) *transparent* (open, frank, and candid, using language that is clear and appropriate); (b) *informative* (reporting enough basic information to enable sophisticated readers to reach their own conclusions and more statistically sophisticated readers to perform their own calculations); (c) *appropriately precise* (avoiding false precision or needless precision); (d) *accurate* (being careful to identify and correct any mistakes in measurements, calculations, or the reporting of numbers); and (e) *grounded* (choosing methods or procedures that are justified and appropriate to your hypotheses, predictions, or hunches).

(X_1) is based on an essay exam of 50 points with $M = 21.2$ and $\sigma = 11.69$, and another (X_2) is based on a multiple-choice exam of 100 points with $M = 68.8$ and $\sigma = 17.47$. The instructor transforms the raw scores into standard scores, with the results shown in the z_1 and z_2 columns. For example, Student 1 received a raw score of 42 on Exam 1, which the instructor converts to a z score by computing $(42 - 21.2)/11.69 = 1.78$. Student 1's score on Exam 1 is almost 2 standard deviations above the mean, but Student 2's score on the same exam is approximately 1 standard deviation *below* the mean.

The z scores take this information into account, allowing the instructor to make easy comparisons within and across students. Here, the instructor counted the two exams equally to get the average score (in the last column), but it is easy enough to weight them. Suppose she had wanted to count the second exam twice as much as the first exam; she would double the z scores for Exam 2 before averaging the two exams and then divide by 3 instead of 2. Notice also that the standard deviation (*SD*) at the bottom of the last column is not 1.0; the reason is that the averages of two or more z scores are not themselves distributed as z scores with $\sigma = 1.0$. If the instructor wanted the averages of these z scores to be distributed as z, she would first have to z-score these averages (see also Box 10.5).

Summary of Ideas

1. Clarity, precision, and efficiency are important criteria of graphic integrity when we want to represent numerical data in a visual display.

2. In a *frequency distribution,* a set of scores is arranged according to the incidence of occurrence either in a table or in a figure such as a *bar graph* or, if we want to show change over time, a *line graph.*

3. In a *stem-and-leaf chart,* the original data are preserved with any desired precision so that we can visually detect the symmetry, spread, and concentration of the batch as well as any outliers.

4. A *percentile* locates a score in a distribution by defining the point at or below which a given proportion (or percentage) of the cases falls. The *interquartile range* is the distance between the 25th and 75th percentiles.

5. The *median* (*Mdn,* or 50th percentile) is the midmost score of a distribution.

6. The *mode* is the score (or the batch of scores in a stem-and-leaf chart) occurring with the greatest frequency.

7. The *mean* (*M*) is the arithmetic average of a set of scores and can be thought of as the "center of gravity" of a set of scores.

8. In a *symmetrical distribution,* the median and the mean have the same value. *Trimmed means* are useful when distributions are strongly *asymmetrical,* and (like medians) they can often protect us against the intrusion of "wild scores" (Box 10.3).

9. The *range* is the distance between the highest and lowest scores (the *crude range*), sometimes *extended* (also called *corrected*) to increase precision.

10. The *variance* (or *mean square*) is the average squared distance from the mean of all the scores.

11. The *standard deviation* (or *root mean square*) is the square root of the variance.

12. *Descriptive measures* (e.g., σ and σ^2) are used to calculate population values, and *inferential measures* (S and S^2) are used to estimate population values based on a sample of values.

13. A *confidence interval* (CI) around an estimated population mean tells us how accurately we have

estimated the mean within certain lower and upper limits.

14. The *normal distribution* is a bell-shaped curve that is completely described by the mean and the standard deviation.

15. We calculate *standard scores* (*z scores*) by *transforming* raw scores to standard deviation units.

16. Standard scores permit the comparison (and averaging) of scores from different distributions of widely differing means and standard deviations.

Key Terms

abscissa   p. 186
asymmetrical distribution   p. 192
back-to-back stem-and-leaf
  chart   p. 188
bar graphs   p. 186
central tendency   p. 189
confirmatory data analysis   p. 189
corrected range   p. 193
crude range   p. 193
descriptive measure   p. 195
exploratory data analysis   p. 189
extended range   p. 193
finite   p. 195
frequency distribution   p. 185
inferential measure   p. 195
infinite   p. 195

interquartile range   p. 189
line graphs   p. 186
mean (*M*)   p. 191
mean square (S^2)   p. 193
median (*Mdn*)   p. 189
modal representativeness
  index   p. 191
mode   p. 191
negatively skewed distribution
  p. 192
normal distribution   p. 197
ordinate   p. 186
outliers   p. 192
percentile   p. 189
positively skewed distribution
  p. 192

range   p. 193
root mean square   p. 194
standard deviation   p. 194
standard normal curve   p. 198
standard score (*z*)   p. 198
stem-and-leaf chart   p. 187
symmetrical distribution   p. 192
transformation   p. 198
trimmed mean   p. 192
unbiased estimator of the population value of σ^2 p. 195
variance   p. 193
wild scores   p. 192
x axis   p. 186
y axis   p. 186
z score   p. 198

Multiple-Choice Questions for Review

1. A graph in which the horizontal axis contains the score values, and in which the vertical axis reflects the frequency of a given score, is called a (a) stem-and-leaf chart; (b) cascade plot; (c) data summary graph; (d) frequency distribution.

2. Participants in a study at Iona College are asked to take a test of anxiety. Forty percent of the subjects receive scores lower than 12 on this test. For this sample, the value 12 is considered the (a) mean; (b) 40th percentile; (c) 60th percentile; (d) median.

3. Which of the following is considered a measure of central tendency? (a) mean; (b) 50th percentile; (c) mode; (d) all of the above

4. In a data set consisting of 0, 0, 0, 2, 2, 8, what is the mode? (a) 0; (b) 1; (c) 2; (d) 8

5. In the data set shown above, what is the *M*? (a) 0; (b) 1; (c) 2; (d) 8

6. In the same data set, what is the *Mdn*? (a) 0; (b) 1; (c) 2; (d) 8

7. Consider the following set of data points: 0, 1, 2, 3, 4. What is the crude range of these scores? (a) 2.5; (b) 0; (c) 4; (d) 5

8. Formulas that are used to calculate information about a population are called _____. (a) popular; (b) descriptive; (c) inferential; (d) none of the above

9. A standard normal distribution has a mean of _____ and a standard deviation of _____. (a) 0, 1; (b) 1, 0; (c) 1, 1; (d) cannot be determined from this information

10. A DePaul researcher administers an attitude scale to a group of industrial/organizational psychology students. The average score is 2, and the standard deviation is 2. Suppose that you receive a score of zero. What is your *z* score? (a) 2; (b) −2; (c) 0; (d) −1

Discussion Questions for Review

1. A University of Oregon student conducted a study on anxiety in 11 business executives. Their scores on a standardized test of anxiety were 32, 16, 29, 41, 33, 37, 27, 30, 22, 38, and 33. Can you reconstruct the student's stem-and-leaf chart for these scores? What is the median of these scores, and what are the extended range and the interquartile range?

2. A Fordham University student is interested in studying ways of cutting down noise pollution in Manhattan. Her first step is to buy a machine that will measure the loudness of various sounds. In order to decide which machine to buy, she tests four brands against a standard tone of 85 decibels for five trials each, with the results shown below. Assuming that all the machines are the same price, which should be her first choice?

	Machine A	Machine B	Machine C	Machine D
	76	84	83	85
	82	87	89	81
	78	83	91	93
	84	85	77	89
	80	86	105	77
M	80	85	89	85
S	3.16	1.58	10.49	6.32

Oops ... she finds that the manufacturer has discontinued her first-choice brand. Which machine would you recommend as a second choice, and why?

3. A Haverford College student recorded the following scores: 22, 14, 16, 24, 13, 26, 17, 98, 11, 9, and 21. What measure of central tendency would you advise him to calculate? Why?

4. A Florida State University student was looking at her grades for the midterm and the final exam. On the midterm she got a score of 58 and the class mean was 52 with a standard deviation of 12. On the final she got a score of 110; the class mean was 100 with a standard deviation of 30. On which test did she do better?

5. A Brandeis University student calls home to tell his family that he just received a score of 2 on a new IQ test. As they wonder why they are spending so much money on his tuition, he reassures them that 2 is his z score. What percentage of the population did he score above?

6. A University of Missouri professor has three sections with three graduate assistants—Tom, Dick, and Harry—each of whom has six students. The time has come to grade papers. In order to ensure uniform grading standards across the sections, the professor instructs the assistants to give an average score of 8.0 (equivalent to B−) on a scale of 1 to 12 (where 1 represents a grade of F, and 12 represents a grade of A). The assistants submit the following sets of grades:

Tom	Dick	Harry
12	8	7
6	8	7
5	10	8
5	7	5
8	8	6
12	7	9

The professor calls in Harry and says, "You have not followed my instructions. Your scores are biased toward having your section do better than it is supposed to." Calculate the means of each section, and then argue the truth or falsity of the professor's accusation. The professor next calls in Tom and Dick and says, "Although both of your sections have a mean grade of 8.0, Tom's scores look more spread out." Calculate, and then compare, the standard deviation of the scores in the sections to decide whether the professor is right. Which is a better grade (relative to one's own section), a 5 in Tom's section or a 7 in Dick's section?

7. Compute the σ, σ^2, S, and S^2 on the no-show data in the stem-and-leaf chart shown in Figure 10.5.

Answers to Review Questions

Multiple-Choice Questions

1. d	3. d	5. c	7. c	9. a
2. b	4. a	6. b	8. b	10. d

Discussion Questions

1. The stem-and leaf plot is

Stem	Leaf
4	1
3	0 2 3 3 7 8
2	2 7 9
1	6

The median score can be found from $.5(N + 1) = .5(12) = 6$. Because the sixth score is 32, that is our median. The extended range is the crude range $(41 - 16)$ plus 1 unit, or $25 + 1 = 26$. The interquartile range is from the $.25(N + 1)$th to the $.75(N + 1)$th score, or from 27 to 37.

2. Her first choice is Machine B because it shows no bias and the least instability or variability. Her second choice might be Machine D because it shows no bias or Machine A because, although it shows a 5-decibel bias, it measures volume more consistently. As long as she remembers to correct for the 5-decibel bias, she might be well advised to get Machine A.

3. Because of the outlier score of 98, he should prefer the median or a trimmed mean to the ordinary mean. In this example, the mean of the 11 untrimmed scores is 24.6, whereas the median is only 17 and the trimmed mean (trimmed by 1 on each end) is 18.2.

4. She did better on the midterm, where the z score $= (58 - 52)/12 = .50$, than on the final, where the z score $= (110 - 100)/30 = .33$.

5. He scored above 97.7% of the normative population.

6. The professor is correct in thinking Harry's grading is biased. However, the professor is wrong about the direction of the bias. Harry's average grade is a C+ (7) instead of a B− (8). The professor is correct in thinking Tom's grades are more spread out than Dick's grades. The three standard deviations are 3.00, 1.00, and 1.29 for Tom, Dick, and Harry, respectively. Students earning scores of 5 in Tom's section performed the same as those earning scores of 7 in Dick's section; in both cases, $z = -1.00$.

7. The answers are $\sigma = .115$, $\sigma^2 = .013$, $S = .118$, and $S^2 = .014$.

CHAPTER 11

Correlating Variables

Preview Questions

- What are different forms of correlations?
- How are correlations visualized in scatter plots?
- How is a product-moment correlation calculated?
- How is dummy coding used in correlation?
- When is the phi coefficient used?
- How is a correlation calculated on ranks?

 What Are Different Forms of Correlations?

You have seen that researchers view variables not in isolation, but as systematically and meaningfully associated with, or related to, other variables. In this chapter we will elaborate on how, using a single number (called the **correlation coefficient**), you can indicate the strength of association between two variables (X and Y). In particular, we describe correlations that reflect the degree to which mutual relations between X and Y resemble a straight line (called **linearity**). The **Pearson r**, short for Karl Pearson's product-moment correlation coefficient, is the correlation coefficient of choice in such situations. Values of r of 1.0 (positive or negative) indicate a perfect linear relation (a fixed change in one variable is always associated with a fixed change in the other variable), whereas 0 indicates that neither X nor Y can be predicted from the other by use of a linear equation (see also Box 11.1). A positive r tells us that an increase in X is associated with an increase in Y, whereas a negative r indicates that an increase in X is associated with a decrease in Y.

We begin by examining what different values of r might look like. Then we go through the steps in computing the correlation coefficient when raw data have different characteristics, as previewed in Table 11.1. The common names "Pearson r," "point-biserial r," and "phi" listed in the table communicate whether the values of X and Y are continuous or dichotomous, although the name *Pearson r* also is often used in a general way to refer to any correlation computed as a product-moment r. The term **continuous variable** means that it is possible to imagine another value falling between any two adjacent scores, and a **dichotomous variable** means that the variable is divided into two distinct or separate parts. For example, someone who studies the discrimination of pitch (the highness or lowness of a tone) might be interested in correlating the changes in the frequency of sound waves (X) with the differing ability of individuals to discriminate those changes (Y). Both variables are continuous, in that we can imagine a score of 1.5 between 1 and 2, or 1.55 between 1.5 and 1.6. Suppose a researcher was interested in

BOX 11.1 Galton, Pearson, and *r*

In Chapter 1, where we first discussed the idea of how empirical reasoning is used in behavioral research, we mentioned Francis Galton's fascinating relational study using longevity data to test the efficacy of certain prayers. Galton was also very intuitive about statistics, and he instinctively came up with a way of measuring the "co-relation" between two variables. At the time, another of his many interesting projects concerned the relationship between the traits of fathers and their adult sons. One day, while he was strolling around the grounds of a castle, it started to rain and Galton sought refuge in the recess of a rock by the side of the pathway. It was there, he later recalled, that, while thinking about his research, the notion of statistical correlation initially flashed across his mind. Though the word *correlation* was already in widespread use in physics, it is believed that Galton's initial spelling of "co-relation" might have been a way of distancing his creation from the commonly used concept (Stigler, 1986, p. 297). Though the statistical concept for which he is best known is correlation, Galton did not develop the idea beyond its use in some of his relational studies. The reason that *r* is called the *Pearson r* is that it was Karl Pearson (1857–1936) who perfected Galton's "index of co-relation" in a more mathematically sophisticated way (Stigler, 1986).

correlating participants' gender with the ability to discriminate pitch. Pitch discrimination is a continuous variable, whereas gender is dichotomously coded as male and female.

Correlation (*r*-type) indices have other useful applications besides those that are mentioned in this chapter. In the case of dichotomous variables, we might create dichotomies in what is called a *median split,* by dividing variables at the median point. A researcher might report "*r*-type effect sizes" on more than two conditions, which we discuss in Chapter 14, where we turn to comparisons (*contrasts*) on more than two conditions. Some other important applications are beyond the scope of this book but are illustrated in our advanced text (Rosenthal & Rosnow, 2008). For example, in a *partial correlation,* a researcher can measure the correlation between two variables when the influence of other variables on their relation has been eliminated statistically. As correlations usually shrink in magnitude when the variability of either of the two samples being correlated shrinks, there is a statistical solution (proposed by Karl Pearson) to correct for this "restriction of variability" (also discussed in our advanced text). The main purpose of this chapter, however, is to give you a working knowledge of the basics of computing and interpreting correlations in the situations that you are most likely to encounter.

Table 11.1 Four Forms of Correlations and Their Common Names

Common name	Characteristics of the data
Pearson *r*	Two continuous variables, such as the correlation of scores on the Scholastic Assessment Test (SAT) with grade point average (GPA) after 4 years of college
Point-biserial *r* (r_{pb})	One continuous and one dichotomous variable, such as the correlation of subjects' gender with their performance on the SAT-Verbal
Phi coefficient (φ)	Two dichotomous variables, such as the correlation of subjects' gender with their "yes" or "no" responses to a specific question
Spearman rho (r_s)	Two ranked variables, such as the correlation of the ranking of the top 25 college basketball teams by sports writers (Associated Press ranking) with the ranking of the same teams by college coaches (*USA Today* ranking)

Table 11.2   Raw and Standardized Data for Product-Moment Correlation

Student ID and gender	Exam 1		Exam 2		Product of z_1 and z_2 scores
	X_1 score	z_1 score	X_2 score	z_2 score	
1 (M)	42	+1.78	90	+1.21	+2.15
2 (M)	9	−1.04	40	−1.65	+1.72
3 (F)	28	+0.58	92	+1.33	+0.77
4 (M)	11	−0.87	50	−1.08	+0.94
5 (M)	8	−1.13	49	−1.13	+1.28
6 (F)	15	−0.53	63	−0.33	+0.17
7 (M)	14	−0.62	68	−0.05	+0.03
8 (F)	25	+0.33	75	+0.35	+0.12
9 (F)	40	+1.61	89	+1.16	+1.87
10 (F)	20	−0.10	72	+0.18	−0.02
Sum (Σ)	212	0	688	0	+9.03
Mean (M)	21.2	0	68.8	0	.90
SD (σ)	11.69	1.0	17.47	1.0	

How Are Correlations Visualized in Scatter Plots?

In addition to the graphics described in the preceding chapter, another informative visual display is called a **scatter plot** (or a *scatter diagram*). It takes its name from looking like a cloud of scattered dots. Each dot represents the intersection of a line extended from a point on the *X* axis (the horizontal axis, or abscissa) and a line extended from a point on the *Y* axis (the vertical axis, or ordinate). To illustrate, Table 11.2 repeats the data that we used at the end of the previous chapter to explain *z* scores, and we will continue to discuss these data in this chapter. For now, we will concentrate on the raw scores (the X_1 and X_2 scores) of these 10 students on the two exams.

Figure 11.1 displays the scores shown in Table 11.2 in a scatter plot. Imagine a straight line through the dots. The higher the correlation is, the more tightly clustered along the line are the dots in a scatter plot (and, therefore, the better is the linear predictability). The cloud of dots slopes up for positive correlations and slopes down for negative correlations, and the linearity becomes clearer as the correlation becomes higher. From this information, what would you guess is the value of the Pearson *r* represented by the data in Figure 11.1?

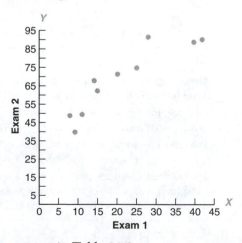

Figure 11.1   Scatter plot of raw scores in Table 11.2

How Is a Product-Moment Correlation Calculated?

There are many useful formulas for calculating different forms of the product-moment correlation coefficient (r). The following formula (which defines the Pearson r conceptually) can be used quite generally in most situations:

$$r_{xy} = \frac{\Sigma z_x z_y}{N}.$$

This formula indicates that the linear correlation between two variables (X and Y) is equal to the sum of the products of the z scores (the *standard scores*, as defined in Chapter 10) of X and Y divided by the number (N) of pairs of X and Y scores. The name **product-moment correlation** came from the idea that the z scores (in the numerator) are distances from the mean (also called *moments*) that are multiplied by each other ($z_x z_y$) to form "products."

To use this formula, we begin by transforming the raw scores (the X and Y scores, or in the case of Table 11.2, the X_1 and X_2 scores) to z scores by following the procedure described in the previous chapter. In other words, we calculate the mean (M) and the standard deviation (σ) of each column of X and Y scores and then substitute the calculated values in the ($X - M$)/σ formula, where X is any student's score. In Table 11.2 we see such z scores corresponding to the students' raw scores on Exam 1 and Exam 2. Notice that, for Student 5, the z score for Exam 1 is identical to the z score for Exam 2 even though the raw scores are very different. The reason is that the z scores for Exam 1 were computed from the mean and standard deviation of Exam 1 (21.2 and 11.69, respectively), whereas the z scores for Exam 2 were computed from the mean and standard deviation of Exam 2 (68.8 and 17.47, respectively). Instead of averaging all the z scores (as we did in the previous chapter for a different purpose), the last column in Table 11.2 gives the products of the z scores and their mean, that is,

$$r_{xy} = \frac{\Sigma z_x z_y}{N} = \frac{9.03}{10} = .903,$$

where r_{xy} is, in this application, the correlation between the X_1 and X_2 scores, and z_x and z_y are the z-transformed X_1 and X_2 scores. Rounding .903 to two decimal places, we would report that $r_{xy} = .90$.

Although we use the conceptual formula above as a teaching tool in this chapter, it is far easier (particularly in large data sets) to obtain the Pearson r by using a computer program (such as SPSS, SAS, SYSTAT, or Minitab) or a handy calculator that allows you to punch a few buttons to compute r. We can also calculate the Pearson r from raw scores rather than z scores, using the following formula:

$$r_{xy} = \frac{N\Sigma XY - (\Sigma X)(\Sigma Y)}{\sqrt{[N\Sigma X^2 - (\Sigma X)^2][N\Sigma Y^2 - (\Sigma Y)^2]}},$$

where N = the number of X and Y pairs of scores, and the Σ directs us to sum a set of values. This formula may look difficult, but it is actually far easier to use than the conceptual formula. All we need are the sums of the scores and of the squared scores. Table 11.3 has the basic data we need to compute r from the raw scores that were listed in Table 11.2. All that is different in Table 11.3 is that the scores on Exam 1 are symbolized as X scores and the scores on Exam 2 are symbolized as Y scores. Substituting the summary data of Table 11.3 into the formula above gives

$$r_{xy} = \frac{10(16{,}430) - (212)(688)}{\sqrt{[10(5{,}860) - (212)^2][10(50{,}388) - (688)^2]}} = \frac{18{,}444}{\sqrt{(13{,}656)(30{,}536)}} = .90.$$

When using this formula, don't forget to take the square root of the denominator (see also Box 11.2).

| | Exam 1 | | Exam 2 | | |
Student	X	X²	Y	Y²	XY
1	42	1,764	90	8,100	3,780
2	9	81	40	1,600	360
3	28	784	92	8,464	2,576
4	11	121	50	2,500	550
5	8	64	49	2,401	392
6	15	225	63	3,969	945
7	14	196	68	4,624	952
8	25	625	75	5,625	1,875
9	40	1,600	89	7,921	3,560
10	20	400	72	5,184	1,440
Sum (Σ)	212	5,860	688	50,388	16,430

Table 11.3 Basic Data for Computing Pearson r from Raw Scores

How Is Dummy Coding Used in Correlation?

Another case of the product-moment r is called the **point-biserial correlation (r_{pb})**. The *point* means that scores for one variable are points on a continuum, and the *biserial* means that scores for the other variable are dichotomous. In many cases, the dichotomous scores may be arbitrarily applied numerical values, such as 0 and 1, or −1 and +1. The quantification of two levels of a dichotomous variable is called **dummy coding** when numerical values such as 0 and 1 are used to indicate the two distinct parts. Dummy coding is a tremendously useful method because it allows us to quantify any variable that can be represented as dichotomous (also called *binary*, meaning there are two parts or two categories). For example, suppose you have performed an experiment in which there were two groups (an experimental and a control group) and you want to correlate group membership with scores on the dependent variable. To indicate each participant's group membership, you code 1 for experimental group and 0 for control group. Another dichotomous independent variable that is typically recast into 1s and 0s is gender. Not only dichotomous independent variables can be dummy-coded in this way, but also dichotomous dependent variables can be recast into 1s and 0s, such as success rate (1 = succeed vs. 0 = fail).

BOX 11.2 Linearity and Nonlinearity

Remember that the Pearson r is a measure of linearity. Though this r is close to 1, even a Pearson r near 0 does not automatically imply zero relationship between X and Y but only indicates there is no *linear relationship*. You need to inspect the scatter plot before ruling out the possibility of a nonlinear relationship. **Nonlinearity** can take many different forms (e.g., U-shaped, J-shaped, or wave-shaped curves). Suppose you are studying the relationship between age and the latency (delay) of some response, and you find that the latency decreases up to a certain age and then gradually increases. If you plot the results by means of a line graph, your curve showing this nonlinear relation will resemble a ∪ with age plotted on the abscissa (the X axis) and latency (delay) of response (from low to high) on the ordinate (the Y axis). Other examples of nonlinear relations include curves for learning, extinction, dark adaptation, and response rate as a function of the amount of reinforcement.

Going back to our earlier example in Table 11.2, suppose we wanted to compare males with females on Exam 1. The scores on that exam were as follows:

Males	Females
42	28
9	15
11	25
8	40
14	20

Though we see two groups of scores, this arrangement does not look like the typical one for a correlation coefficient, where we would expect to see *pairs* of X and Y scores, not two columns labeled Males and Females. In this example, the scores on variable Y (exam scores) are shown, but X is hidden, the reason being that the group identification (male vs. female) implies the variable X scores.

The same data rewritten in a form that looks more correlational are shown in Table 11.4. The first column shows the identification (ID) and gender information. Under "Exam 1," we see again the raw and standardized (z) scores for the first exam. Under "Student's gender," the first column shows the dummy-coded scores for gender, with the female students coded 1 and the male students coded 0. In this particular case, we would think of the dummy-coded variable as "femaleness" because 1 and 0 imply the presence and absence of femaleness, respectively. (If we had coded the male students 1 and the female students 0, we would then think of the dummy-coded variable as "maleness.") The next column under "Student's gender" shows the z scores after the dummy-coded values are standardized. For instance, to get the z score for Student 1's gender, we computed

$$z = \frac{X - M}{\sigma} = \frac{0 - 0.5}{0.5} = -1,$$

Table 11.4 Raw, Dummy-Coded, and Standardized Data for Point-Biserial Correlation

Student ID and gender	Exam 1		Student's gender		Product of z scores
	Raw score	z score	Dummy code	z score	
1 (M)	42	+1.78	0	−1	−1.78
2 (M)	9	−1.04	0	−1	+1.04
3 (F)	28	+0.58	1	+1	+0.58
4 (M)	11	−0.87	0	−1	+0.87
5 (M)	8	−1.13	0	−1	+1.13
6 (F)	15	−0.53	1	+1	−0.53
7 (M)	14	−0.62	0	−1	+0.62
8 (F)	25	+0.33	1	+1	+0.33
9 (F)	40	+1.61	1	+1	+1.61
10 (F)	20	−0.10	1	+1	−0.10
Sum (Σ)	212	0	5	0	+3.77
Mean (M)	21.2	0	0.5	0	.38
SD (σ)	11.69	1.0	0.5	1.0	–

Source: From Perception of Risk, P Slovic, Science 17 April 1987: 236 (4799), 280–285. Reprinted with permission from AAAS.

where X = the dummy score of 0 for Student 1, M = the mean of the column of dummy scores ($M = 5/10 = 0.5$), and σ = the standard deviation (SD) shown at the bottom of that column (0.5). Notice that, as always, the z scores sum to zero. (Seeing a total score other than zero tells us there must be a computational or recording mistake.) Note also that the standard deviation scores within the column of z scores are -1 for a dummy code of 0 and $+1$ for a dummy code of 1. This situation is always found when the number of 0 scores equals the number of 1 scores, but it is not always the case when the number of 0 scores does not equal the number of 1 scores. Finally, the sum of the products of the z scores (shown at the bottom of the last column of data) is $+3.77$. Dividing this value by the number of students ($N = 10$) yields the point-biserial correlation (r_{pb}) between femaleness and scores on Exam 1, that is,

$$r_{pb} = \frac{\Sigma z_x z_y}{N} = \frac{3.77}{10} = .38.$$

Because of the way we coded gender (1 = female vs. 0 = male), this positive correlation tells us that female students scored relatively higher on the exam than did the male students. If the correlation had been negative and of the same magnitude, it would have indicated that female students scored relatively lower on the exam than did male students.

When Is the Phi Coefficient Used?

Not infrequently in biomedical trials, both of the variables to be correlated are dichotomous. One variable (the independent variable) might be whether patients were randomly assigned to a drug group or a placebo group, and the other variable (the dependent variable) might be improvement rate (e.g., improved or not improved). As another illustration, in Chapter 8 we discussed a case in which people who had eaten a rare hamburger became sick. Looking again at Table 8.1 (on page 150), suppose we are interested in quantifying the relation between these two variables. We now have another special case of the product-moment r, called the **phi coefficient** (symbolized by ϕ, the lowercase Greek letter phi). In this case, both of the variables are dichotomous (with applied numerical values such as 0 and 1 or -1 and $+1$).

We can find the value of the phi coefficient (ϕ) in several ways; two of them are shown here. The conceptual procedure, represented in Table 11.5, illustrates why we say that ϕ is another special case of the product-moment r. Under the "Ate burger?" heading, the first column shows the dummy-coded scores of Yes = 1 and No = 0. The next column shows the standardized scores (the z scores) corresponding to the dummy-coded values. For instance, we computed the z score corresponding to Mimi's 1 as

$$z = \frac{X - M}{\sigma} = \frac{1 - .417}{.493} = +1.183.$$

Similarly, under the "Got food poisoning?" heading, the dummy coding is again Yes = 1 and No = 0, followed by the corresponding z scores.

The last column in Table 11.5 shows the mean of the product of the z scores as 1.00, and we report it as the phi (ϕ) coefficient because both variables are dichotomous, but we compute it as

$$r = \frac{\Sigma z_x z_y}{N} = \frac{12.012}{12} = 1.00.$$

In other words, we have treated phi (ϕ) no differently from any product-moment r calculated on the basis of z scores. The positive correlation tells us that answering "yes" to the question "Ate burger?" is directly related to answering "yes" to the question "Got food poisoning?" and the 1.00 tells us that we can predict who got food poisoning perfectly from the knowledge of

Table 11.5	Dummy-Coded and Standardized Data for Phi Coefficient				
Persons	Ate burger?		Got food poisoning?		Product of
	Y = 1; N = 0	z score	Y = 1; N = 0	z score	z scores
Mimi	1	+1.183	1	+1.183	1.400
Gail	0	−0.846	0	−0.846	0.716
Connie	0	−0.846	0	−0.846	0.716
Jerry	0	−0.846	0	−0.846	0.716
Greg	0	−0.846	0	−0.846	0.716
Dwight	0	−0.846	0	−0.846	0.716
Chris	1	+1.183	1	+1.183	1.400
Richard	0	−0.846	0	−0.846	0.716
Kerry	0	−0.846	0	−0.846	0.716
Michele	1	+1.183	1	+1.183	1.400
John	1	+1.183	1	+1.183	1.400
Barbara	1	+1.183	1	+1.183	1.400
Sum (Σ)	5	0.00	5	0.00	12.012
Mean (M)	.417	0.00	.417	0.00	1.00
SD (σ)	.493	1.000	.493	1.000	.337

who ate a burger. If the 1.00 correlation were negative, there would be a perfect inverse relation between eating the burger and getting food poisoning. Thus, when interpreting phi coefficients, we must pay close attention to how the two dichotomous variables were dummy-coded and labeled.

There is an easier way to compute ϕ by using an alternative formula that takes advantage of the fact that the data can be represented in a 2 × 2 table of frequencies (or *counts*), also called a *chi-square contingency table* (more about chi-square in Chapter 15) or simply a *contingency table*. You will see this 2 × 2 format in Table 11.6, which shows that all five people who ate the burgers then got food poisoning and that the seven people who did not eat them remained well. Notice that the cells are labeled A, B, C, D. With this code, we now use the following formula to calculate the phi coefficient:

$$\phi = \frac{BC - AD}{\sqrt{(A + B)(C + D)(A + C)(B + D)}}.$$

Table 11.6	Contingency Table Coded for Computation of Phi Coefficient			
Ate burger?	Got food poisoning?			Totals
	Yes	No		
No	**A** 0	**B** 7		**(A + B)** = 7
Yes	**C** 5	**D** 0		**(C + D)** = 5
Totals	**(A + C)** = 5	**(B + D)** = 7		

Substituting in this formula yields

$$\phi = \frac{(7)(5) - (0)(0)}{\sqrt{(7)(5)(5)(7)}} = \frac{35 - 0}{\sqrt{1,225}} = \frac{35}{35} = 1.00,$$

which (not unexpectedly) is the same result that we obtained using the conceptual formula for the Pearson r.

We will have more to say about the point-biserial correlation (r_{pb}) and the phi coefficient (ϕ) in the following chapters, as r_{pb} and ϕ are also useful indices of the effect size. It is becoming increasingly important in empirical research that scientists report and interpret the effect size, and (as we show in the following chapters) correlation-type (r-type) indices are easily computed and readily interpreted in a wide variety of situations. However, the real-life importance of an effect size depends on the context of the research and the nature of the dependent variable. Nonetheless, knowing the size of the effect is another important piece of information that can help you decide whether it is meaningful in a practical or personal way.

 ## How Is a Correlation Calculated on Ranks?

Most of the useful correlation coefficients are product-moment correlations, and they are typically the special cases of the Pearson r we have been discussing. Now let us suppose the data are in the form of ranks rather than scores on a rating scale or dummy-coded dichotomous independent and dependent variables. Ranked numbers are more predictable than unranked numbers because knowing only the number of pairs of scores (N) immediately tells us both the mean and the standard deviation of the scores obtained. The correlation coefficient for data in the form of ranks is called the **Spearman rho (r_s)** and is computed as

$$r_s = 1 - \frac{6\left(\Sigma D^2\right)}{N^3 - N}$$

where 6 is a constant value, and D is the difference between the ranks assigned to the two scores representing each of the N sampling units.

To illustrate the use of this formula, Table 11.7 shows a portion of the data collected by Paul Slovic (1987) in his investigation of the perception of risk. He was interested in comparing the judgments people make when they are asked to characterize and evaluate hazardous activities and technologies. This table shows the overall rankings by 15 experts on risk assessment and 40 members of the League of Women Voters (LWV). We see, for example, that the experts ranked motor vehicles as most hazardous (Rank 1) and skiing as least hazardous (Rank 30), but the LWV members ranked nuclear power as most hazardous (Rank 1) and vaccinations as least hazardous (Rank 30). Notice that the sums of the ranks are equal for the two variables (465). The column headed D lists the differences between the ranks. For instance, the difference in ranking of nuclear power is computed as $D = 1 - 20 = -19$. The sum of the D scores is always 0. The column headed D^2 shows such differences squared, so that $(-19)^2 = 361$.

To use the computational formula for the Spearman rho, we substitute the sum of the squared differences (indicated in Table 11.7 as 1,828 at the bottom of the column headed D^2) as follows:

$$r_s = 1 - \frac{6\left(\Sigma D^2\right)}{N^3 - N}$$

$$= 1 - \frac{6\left(1,828\right)}{30^3 - 30} = .59.$$

Table 11.7	Ordering of Perceived Risk for 30 Activities and Technologies			
Activity or technology	League of Women Voters	Experts	D	D^2
Nuclear power	1	20	−19	361
Motor vehicles	2	1	1	1
Handguns	3	4	−1	1
Smoking	4	2	2	4
Motorcycles	5	6	−1	1
Alcoholic beverages	6	3	3	9
General (private) aviation	7	12	−5	25
Police work	8	17	−9	81
Pesticides	9	8	1	1
Surgery	10	5	5	25
Firefighting	11	18	−7	49
Large construction	12	13	−1	1
Hunting	13	23	−10	100
Spray cans	14	26	−12	144
Mountain climbing	15	29	−14	196
Bicycles	16	15	1	1
Commercial aviation	17	16	1	1
Electric power (nonnuclear)	18	9	9	81
Swimming	19	10	9	81
Contraceptives	20	11	9	81
Skiing	21	30	−9	81
X-rays	22	7	15	225
High school and college football	23	27	−4	16
Railroads	24	19	5	25
Food preservatives	25	14	11	121
Food coloring	26	21	5	25
Power mowers	27	28	−1	1
Prescription antibiotics	28	24	4	16
Home appliances	29	22	7	49
Vaccinations	30	25	5	25
Sum (Σ)	465	465	0	1,828

Source: From "Perception of Risk," by P. Slovic, 1987, *Science, 236,* p. 281. Copyright © by American Association for the Advancement of Science. Reprinted with permission of Paul Slovic and the American Association for the Advancement of Science.

In interpreting rank correlations, we use the D scores and the ranks to help us illuminate similarities and differences in the results. Here, a positive difference score tells us that the LWV members perceived the activity or technology as less risky than did the experts, whereas a negative difference score indicates the opposite conclusion. We see, for instance, that the two groups of raters disagreed little about the high risks associated with motor vehicles, handguns, and motorcycles (D of +1 or −1). There was little disagreement about the much lower risk associated with power mowers ($D = -1$), but there was strong disagreement about nuclear power ($D = -19$), X-rays ($D = 15$), and mountain climbing ($D = -14$).

Table 11.8   Raw Data from Table 11.2 Ranked for Spearman Rho Correlation

| | Exam 1 | | Exam 2 | | | |
Student	X_1 score	Rank	X_2 score	Rank	D	D^2
1	42	1	90	2	−1	1
2	9	9	40	10	−1	1
3	28	3	92	1	2	4
4	11	8	50	8	0	0
5	8	10	49	9	1	1
6	15	6	63	7	−1	1
7	14	7	68	6	1	1
8	25	4	75	4	0	0
9	40	2	89	3	−1	1
10	20	5	72	5	0	0
Sum (Σ)	212	55[a]	688	55[a]	0[b]	10

[a]Note that the sum of the ranks is equal for the two variables.
[b]Note that the sum of D is always 0.

The Spearman rho is typically used when the scores to be correlated are already in ranked form, as in the case that we have been discussing, or if you have judges rank a set of sampling units. However, suppose we are working with raw scores that are continuous (such as the exam grades of the 10 students in Table 11.2), but we now want to recast them as ranks and then compute a Spearman rho. Table 11.8 shows how we would do this. The students in Table 11.8 are now ranked from 1 (the highest raw score) to 10 (the lowest raw score), and again the D value is the difference between the ranks. The sum of the squared differences (indicated as 10 at the bottom of the column headed D^2) is simply substituted in the numerator of the Spearman rho formula:

$$r_s = 1 - \frac{6\left(\Sigma D^2\right)}{N^3 - N}$$

$$= 1 - \frac{6\left(10\right)}{10^3 - 10} = .94,$$

which is not the same correlation we obtained when working with the standardized raw scores ($r = .90$ in Table 11.2), but a slightly higher value ($r_s = .94$).

The reason for the different values is that transforming the raw scores improved their symmetry, but transforming a set of raw scores to ranks sometimes does lead to a lower correlation. Students often ask, "Which is the 'right' correlation?"—or in this case, the r of .90 based on the raw scores versus the r_s of .94 based on the ranked scores? The answer is that they are *both right*. The only difference is that they are based on different values: continuous raw score values or ranks of scores. If there were an outlier in the distribution of continuous raw scores, correlating the scores might change the magnitude of r a lot. In this case, we can (if it seems justified) use the trimming method (discussed in the previous chapter) and correlate the remaining continuous scores. If the sample is already quite small, however, we might prefer to rank the scores and then correlate those ranked scores (to avoid reducing the sample size any further). Whatever procedure we use, we should describe it exactly.

Summary of Ideas

1. The *Pearson r* is a standard index of *linear* relationship, with the possible values running from -1.0 to $+1.0$ (Box 11.2).

2. *Scatter plots* let us visualize the clustering and slope of dots that represent the relationship between X and Y. The cloud of dots slopes up for positive correlations and slopes down for negative correlations.

3. The Pearson r, defined as $(\Sigma z_x z_y)/N$, is called the *product-moment correlation* because z scores (i.e., standardized distances from the mean) are also known as *moments*.

4. The *point-biserial correlation* (r_{pb}) is the Pearson r where one of the variables is *continuous* (e.g., exam scores) and the other is *dichotomous* (e.g., student's gender). *Dummy-coding* the dichotomous variable (e.g., female vs. male, live vs. die, or succeed vs. fail) allows us to calculate r_{pb} by the Pearson r formula.

5. The *phi coefficient* (ϕ) is the Pearson r where both variables are dichotomous (e.g., "Ate burger?" and "Got food poisoning?"). To calculate the correlation between two dichotomous variables, we can (a) dummy-code both variables (e.g., 1 = Yes and 0 = No) and then use the corresponding z scores to compute the Pearson r or (b) compute ϕ directly from a 2 × 2 contingency table.

6. The *Spearman rho* (r_s) is calculated on scores that happen to be in ranked form (e.g., the data on perceptions of risk) and is sometimes a quick estimate of correlation.

7. Calculating r on the original unranked scores typically results in a value for the correlation different from calculating r_s on the ranks of the original scores. Calculating r on the original unranked scores is preferred in most cases.

Key Terms

continuous variable   p. 204
correlation coefficient   p. 204
dichotomous variable   p. 204
dummy coding   p. 208
linearity   p. 204

nonlinearity   p. 208
Pearson r p. 204
phi coefficient (ϕ)   p. 210
point-biserial
   correlation (r_{pb})   p. 208

product-moment
   correlation   p. 207
scatter plot   p. 206
Spearman rho (r_s)   p. 212

Multiple-Choice Questions for Review

1. A correlation coefficient reflects the degree of _____ relationship between two variables.
(a) linear; (b) curvilinear; (c) any kind of; (d) positive

2. Correlation coefficients range from ____. (a) 0 to 1; (b) -1 to 0; (c) 1 to 10; (d) -1 to $+1$

3. A variable (such as gender) with two possible values is called a _____ variable. (a) continuous; (b) dichotomous; (c) quadratic; (d) linear

4. A graph is created in which the X variable is plotted along one axis and the Y variable is plotted along the other axis. Each data point is then represented as a dot in this graph. This kind of graph is called a (a) partial plot; (b) multivariate plot; (c) scatter plot; (d) median-split plot.

5. Another name for the Pearson r is the (a) Spearman rank correlation; (b) product-moment correlation; (c) phi coefficient; (d) point-biserial correlation.

6. Consider the following set of data:

	X	z_x	Y	z_y	$z_x z_y$
	8	1.34	16	1.34	1.80
	6	0.45	12	0.45	0.20
	4	-0.45	8	-0.45	0.20
	2	-1.34	4	-1.34	1.80
Sum (Σ)	20	0.00	40	0.00	4.00

What is the correlation between X and Y? (a) .1; (b) $-.1$; (c) 1; (d) -1

7. A distance from a mean is called a(n) _____; the result of two numbers that are multiplied together is called a _____. (a) deviation, sum; (b) deviation, divisor; (c) error, multiplicative index; (d) moment, product

8. A correlation between two variables that are ranked is most specifically called a (a) point-biserial correlation; (b) phi coefficient; (c) Pearson *r;* (d) Spearman rho.

9. A student at Eastern Connecticut University hypothesizes that being female or male is related to one's position on abortion (measured as "prochoice" or "prolife"). To test this hypothesis, the correlation that the student is most likely to use is a (a) Spearman rho; (b) phi coefficient; (c) point-biserial correlation; (d) none of the above.

10. A student at the London School of Economics wants to determine whether political party affiliation (Labour or Conservative) is related to intelligence (measured by an IQ test that yields a series of continuous scores). To test this hypothesis, the student is most likely to use a (a) Spearman rho; (b) phi coefficient; (c) point-biserial correlation; (d) none of the above.

Discussion Questions for Review

1. A St. Bonaventure University researcher administers tests of IQ and reading ability to four high school students. In addition, their grade point averages are obtained from their school records, with the following results:

	IQ	Reading	GPA
Student 1	105	13	2.6
Student 2	113	17	3.4
Student 3	87	10	2.0
Student 4	125	19	3.8

The correlation between IQ and reading ability is $r = .98$. Without doing any direct calculation, the researcher says he knows the correlation between reading and GPA. Do you know this correlation? What about the correlation between IQ and GPA—without any direct calculation?

2. Twenty students take part in a University of Minnesota study on the relationship between socioeconomic status (SES, coded as rich = 1, poor = 0) and shyness (coded as shy = 1, not shy = 0). Given the results shown below, what is the correlation between these two variables? What specific type of Pearson correlation is this?

	SES	Shyness		SES	Shyness
Student 1	0	1	Student 11	0	0
Student 2	0	1	Student 12	1	1
Student 3	0	0	Student 13	0	0
Student 4	0	1	Student 14	1	0
Student 5	1	1	Student 15	0	1
Student 6	0	0	Student 16	1	0
Student 7	1	1	Student 17	1	0
Student 8	1	0	Student 18	1	1
Student 9	0	1	Student 19	0	1
Student 10	1	0	Student 20	1	0

3. A student at the University of Waterloo had two judges rate infants' fussiness, with the following results:

	Rater 1	Rater 2
Infant 1	60	30
Infant 2	40	50
Infant 3	30	60
Infant 4	50	40

The interjudge agreement, in terms of *r,* was not what the student had hoped for; it was $r = -1.0$. So he got himself two more raters, whose ratings were as follows:

	Rater 3	Rater 4
Infant 1	60	130
Infant 2	40	150
Infant 3	30	160
Infant 4	50	140

What is the agreement, in terms of *r,* between Raters 3 and 4?

4. A Georgia State University student has a job managing a 200-seat summer-stock theater that is filled to capacity on Saturday nights. To study the effect of staff courtesy on audience enjoyment, she asks the ticket taker to smile at randomly selected patrons. After the show, each member of the audience rates his or her enjoyment of the performance on a 7-point scale. Can you identify the independent and dependent variables and then figure out a way to calculate the correlation between them?

5. A student at California State University at Chico administered two tests to five participants (coded as Subjects 1–5) with the following results:

	Test A	Test B
Subject 1	1	4
Subject 2	2	3

(continued)

	Test A	Test B
Subject 3	3	2
Subject 4	4	1
Subject 5	5	100

Show a scatter plot of the relationship between the scores on Test A and Test B. Is anything troubling

about this plot? Can you adjust this problem by using a different version of a Pearson r? Show a scatter plot of the revised or transformed scores on Tests A and B. What is the correlation between the tests if you use (a) the original scores and (b) the revised or transformed scores?

Answers to Review Questions

Multiple-Choice Questions

1. a
2. d
3. b
4. c
5. b
6. c
7. d
8. d
9. b
10. c

Discussion Questions

1. The correlation between the students' reading ability and GPA is 1.00, because the z scores for reading and for GPA are identical. Careful inspection of the original reading and GPA scores shows that the GPA scores are always one fifth the size of the reading scores. If a variable (X) is multiplied by any constant (c), it yields a new variable (cX) that is correlated 1.00 with the original variable (X). The reason is that the old scores are multiplied by c, the old mean is multiplied by c, and the old σ is multiplied by c. Thus,

$$\text{old}\, z = \frac{X - M}{\sigma},$$

and in turn,

$$\text{new}\, z = \frac{cX - cM}{c\sigma} = \frac{X - M}{\sigma}.$$

Because reading ability and GPA have the same z scores, the students' GPA z scores can be substituted for their reading z scores, and GPA will be correlated .98 with IQ just as reading is correlated .98 with IQ. You can check this out by computing the z scores for all three variables (IQ, reading, and GPA) and computing the correlations among these three variables. What you will find are IQ z scores of –0.1810, 0.3982, –1.4843, and 1.2671 for students 1, 2, 3, and 4, respectively. For both reading and GPA, the z scores are –0.5013, 0.6445, –1.3606, and 1.2174 for students 1, 2, 3, and 4, respectively.

2. The correlation is −.20, computed by ϕ, the two-dichotomous-variables version of the Pearson r. It can be computed by the z-score method or by the 2×2 contingency table method; that is,

$$\phi = \frac{\Sigma\, z_x z_y}{N}$$

or

$$\phi = \frac{BC - AD}{\sqrt{(A + B)(C + D)(A + C)(B + D)}}.$$

3. The correlation between Raters 3 and 4 is also −1.00. We can compute that directly, or we can notice that Rater 3 rates identically to Rater 1 and that Rater 4 rates identically to Rater 2, except for adding a constant of 100 points to each of Rater 2's ratings. Adding a constant (c) to each score also adds the constant to the mean, so adding a constant to the raw scores does not change the z scores because

$$\text{old}\, z = \frac{X - M}{\sigma},$$

and

$$\text{new}\, z = \frac{(X + c) - (M + c)}{\sigma} = \frac{X - M}{\sigma}.$$

4. The independent variable is smiling (scored 1) or not smiling (scored 0). The dependent variable is the rating of enjoyment. For the 200 patrons, we correlate the scores on the treatment variable (1 or 0) with the scores on the 7-point enjoyment scale.

5. The scatter plot of the relationship between the scores on Test A and Test B would look like this:

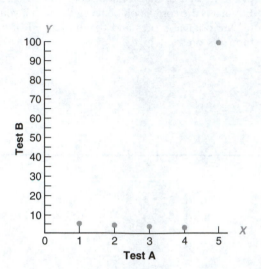

The score of 100 on Test B appears to be an outlier. We can solve the outlier problem by using ranks instead of scores:

Test A		Test B	
Score	Rank	Score	Rank
1	5	4	2
2	4	3	3
3	3	2	4
4	2	1	5
5	1	100	1

Our scatter plot based on ranks would look like this:

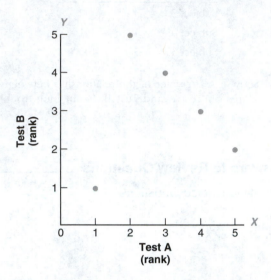

The correlation between Test A and Test B is .69 if we use the original scores; it is .00 if we use the ranks. A discrepancy that large is unusual and needs to be evaluated further before we can confidently say we "know" the correlation between Test A and Test B.

CHAPTER 12

Understanding *p* Values and Effect Size Indicators

Preview Questions

- Why is it important to focus not just on statistical significance?

- What is the reasoning behind null hypothesis significance testing?

- What is the distinction between Type I error and Type II error?

- What are one-tailed and two-tailed *p* values?

- What is the counternull statistic?

- What is the purpose of doing a power analysis?

- How do I estimate a confidence interval for an effect size correlation?

- What can effect sizes tell us of practical importance?

- What does Killeen's p_{rep} tell me?

 ## Why Is It Important to Focus Not Just On Statistical Significance?

Besides describing data (Chapter 10) and measuring relationships (Chapter 11), many behavioral researchers are usually interested in making comparisons using statistical tests such as *t* (Chapter 13), *F* (Chapter 14), and chi-square (Chapter 15). We will explore the reasoning behind the traditional procedure, called **null hypothesis significance testing (NHST)**. Though much has been written about common misconceptions regarding *statistical significance*, it remains a source of confusion for many people. For example, J. D. Miller (2007) noted that many medical specialists mistakenly view "statistical significance" as a proxy for the "degree of improvement a new treatment must make for it to be clinically meaningful" (p. 1832). Statistical significance tells us nothing about the degree of improvement a new treatment must make for it to be clinically meaningful, but effect size indicators, properly interpreted, can often give us insights about the practical significance of an obtained effect. On the other hand, misconceptions and illusions abound about the implications of certain effect size indicators and can result in people drawing unwarranted conclusions. Later in this chapter, we will compare a number of indices from three families of effect sizes in the context of randomized clinical trials (see Box 12.1). The purpose of this comparison is to begin to give you a deeper understanding of the meaning, practical implications, and limitations of these particular effect size measures. This discussion will serve as a prelude to further discussions in the following chapters and an illustration of the advantages of considering more than one effect size indicator.

BOX 12.1   Three Families of Effect Sizes

We call the three families of effect sizes (a) the **correlation** (or **r-type**) **family**, (b) the **difference family**, and (c) the **ratio family** (Rosnow & Rosenthal, 2003). Following up on our discussion of correlation in the previous chapter, the emphasis in this chapter is on *r*-type effect size indicators, such as the point-biserial *r* and the phi (ɸ) coefficient. In the next chapter, we discuss the use of the standardized difference between two means as an effect size measure, and later in this chapter we illustrate

another member of the difference family, called the *risk difference*. We also explain the *odds ratio* and *relative risk* (both belong to the ratio family of effect size indicators). As you will learn later in this book, an advantage of *r*-type effect size indicators is their usefulness when predictions specifically involve more than two groups or more than two conditions. Difference-type and ratio-type effect size indicators are not so naturally applicable in such situations.

A common thread that also runs through the remaining chapters in this book is the general relationship between the *p* value and the effect size, as given by the following conceptual equation:

$$\text{Significance test} = \text{Size of effect} \times \text{Size of study}$$

This general relationship (which we will refer to frequently) simply means that any test of statistical significance (such as *t*, *F*, or chi-square) can be shown to consist of two components: (a) an indicator of the size of the effect and (b) an indicator of the number of sampling units (e.g., the total *N*). The conceptual equation shows that the value of the significance test is the *product* of these two components. Thus, unless the size of the obtained effect is exactly zero (which is quite rare), the larger the size of effect component or the larger the size of study component (e.g., the larger the *N*), the larger is the value of the significance test and, therefore, the smaller (and usually more coveted) is the *p* value. In other words, focusing our attention only on statistical significance (the *p* value) would not tell us whether the effect size, the total *N*, or both were primarily responsible for the level of statistical significance reached. Furthermore, even if the effect size component of the significance test were mainly responsible, a question would still linger concerning which aspect of the effect size indicator was the primary contributing factor. Another common mistake is to equate "nonsignificance" (frequently defined as $p > .05$) as equivalent to estimating an effect size equal to zero. Later in this chapter, we will describe a useful statistic (the *counternull statistic*) that can eliminate this error. We will also explain the concept of *statistical power* and illustrate how a *power analysis* is done.

 ## What Is the Reasoning Behind Null Hypothesis Significance Testing?

To help you understand intuitively what NHST and some related concepts mean, we begin with an analogy (based on Wainer, 1972). Imagine you are strolling along the Atlantic City boardwalk when a shady character approaches and whispers he has a quarter that he is willing to sell you for "*only* five dollars." You ask the man, "What makes this coin worth so much more than its face value?" He answers, "This is a quarter with a special property. When properly used, it could win an enterprising person a lot of money because it does not always come up heads and tails with equal regularity. Instead, one outcome is far more likely than the other, and a person with a touch of larceny in his soul could bet on the outcome and win a tidy sum." Because you haven't walked away yet, he adds, "It might sound like a cock-and-bull story, but flip the coin and see for yourself."

If the coin is not what the boardwalk huckster says it is—that is, if the coin is an ordinary one—then the probability of heads or tails is always one chance in two (see also Box 12.2). Let's assume you accept his challenge and decide to test whether the probability of heads does or does not equal

BOX 12.2   How Are Probabilities Determined?

One characteristic of probabilities is that if all outcomes are *independent* (i.e., one outcome is not influenced by any other), the sum of all the probabilities associated with an event is equal to 1. If, for example, you throw an ordinary six-sided die, there are six possibilities, and (unless the die is loaded) the probability of any particular outcome is 1/6, or .167. Summing all of the independent probabilities gives us .167 × 6 = 1.00. Instead of throwing a die, suppose you have two fair coins and flip both at the same time. There are four possible combinations of heads (H) and tails (T): HH, HT, TH, TT. In determining probabilities, the general rule is to count the total number of possible outcomes and then to count the number of outcomes yielding the event you are interested in. The probability of that event is the ratio of the number you are looking for (the favorable event) to the total number of outcomes. For example, the probability (*p*) of two heads (out of the four possible events) can occur in only one way (HH) and is therefore 1 divided by 4, so *p* = .25. The probability of only one head (out of these four possible events) can occur in two ways (HT or TH) and is therefore 2 divided by 4, so *p* = .5.

the probability of tails. You flip the coin once and heads appears. You flip the coin again, and again it comes up heads. Suppose you flip the coin nine times and each time it comes up heads. Would you believe him now? If your answer is yes, would you believe him if, in nine tosses, the coin had come up heads eight times and tails once? This is the essential question in NHST. You can be as stringent as you like in setting a rejection criterion, but you may eventually pay for this decision by rejecting what you perhaps should not. Let us now restate these ideas more precisely using the concepts involved in NHST.

When you decided to test whether the probability of heads "does or does not" equal the probability of tails, two hypotheses were implied. One was that the quarter is *unbiased* (the probability of heads *does* equal the probability of tails); the second implicit hypothesis was that the coin is biased (the probability of heads *does not* equal the probability of tails). You can think of the "experiment" of tossing a coin as a way of trying to determine which of these hypotheses you cannot logically reject. In statistical terms, the name for the first hypothesis (that the quarter is unbiased) is the **null hypothesis** (symbolized as H_0), and the name for the second hypothesis (that the quarter is biased) is the **alternative hypothesis** (symbolized as H_1). That is,

H_0 *(null hypothesis):* The probability of heads equals the probability of tails in the long run because it is an ordinary quarter, and therefore getting a head or a tail is the result purely of chance (i.e., the coin is not biased).

H_1 *(alternative hypothesis):* The probability of heads is not equal to the probability of tails in the long run because it is not an ordinary quarter (i.e., the coin is biased).

Notice that these two hypotheses are *mutually exclusive*; that is, when one hypothesis is true, the other must be false. Experimenters who do NHST are usually interested in testing the specific H_0 (i.e., no difference) against a general H_1 (i.e., some difference). In a between-subjects design with an experimental and a control group, the null hypothesis generally implies no difference in the success rate between the experimental group and the control group (e.g., no difference in survival rates, performance rates, or however else the "success rate" may be defined). The idea behind NHST is to see whether we can reject H_0 and yet be reasonably sure that we will not be wrong in doing so. This leads to the further idea that there are two kinds of decision risks of general concern in NHST, called *Type I error* and *Type II error*.

What Is the Distinction Between Type I Error and Type II Error?

Type I error implies that the decision maker mistakenly rejected the null hypothesis (H_0) when it is, in fact, true and should not have been rejected. **Type II error** implies that the decision maker mistakenly failed to reject the null hypothesis when it is, in fact, false and should have been rejected. The risk (or probability) of making a Type I error is called by three different names: **alpha (α)**, the **significance level**, and the **p value**. The risk (or probability) of making a Type II error is known by one name: **beta (β)**. To make the most informed decision, researchers who do NHST would, of course, like to know what each type of risk (Type I *and* Type II) is in a given case, so that they can balance these risks in some way. Let us return with this newfound knowledge to the analogy of the boardwalk huckster with the coin for sale.

Suppose you decide that you do not want to be wrong more than 1 time out of 20, which is called the *5% significance level* (see also Box 12.3). You flip the coin 9 times and get 8 heads and 1 tail. To make an informed decision, you need to know about the chances of obtaining this result or a result even more extreme. That is, you need to know the probability of obtaining this result (or a more extreme result) if the null hypothesis (H_0) is true. Therefore, you think, "If this probability is less than 1/20 (i.e., $p < .05$), I will reject the null hypothesis and buy the coin; if not (i.e., $p > .05$), I will not buy the coin." Because the probability of 8 or 9 heads in 9 tosses is less than 1 out of 20 (p approximately .02, or 1 out of 50), let's suppose you decide to reject the null hypothesis and buy the coin. Purely on a statistical basis (ignoring any pangs of conscience about purchasing a crooked coin and using it to win bets), you are doing so for two reasons: (a) because the resultant probability leads you to reject the null hypothesis of a fair coin, with 50% heads, at your chosen significance level (or alpha) of 5%, and (b) because you believe that the alternative hypothesis (i.e., the coin is biased) is tenable and that the data (8 heads and 1 tail, or 89% heads instead of 50%) support this hypothesis.

The analogy we used is actually a simplified one, not exactly a true representation of what goes on in NHST. One reason the coin example falls short is that it is not a "relational event." That is, there is only one variable: the result of the coin toss. The researcher who does NHST, however, usually wants to know the probability of claiming that two variables (X and Y) are related when, in fact, they are unrelated, or that the average "success rate" of one group (e.g., the experimental group) has surpassed that of another group (the control group). In practical terms, then, Type I error can be understood as mistakenly claiming a relationship that does not truly exist; it is the likelihood of this

 BOX 12.3 The 5% Solution

The ultimate day-to-day decision about what is a reasonable risk is a personal one. But as you do your literature search, you will notice that many researchers who do NHST use the .05 significance level as a critical demarcation point for deciding whether to reject the null hypothesis. The logic behind this procedure begins with the proposition that one does not want to accept an alternative hypothesis that stands a fairly good chance of being false (i.e., one ought to avoid Type I errors). The logic goes on to state that one either accepts an alternative hypothesis as probably true (not false) or rejects it, concluding that the null is too likely for one to regard it as rejectable. The .05 alpha is regarded by many scientists as a good "fail-safe" standard because it is stringent enough to protect us from too often concluding that the null hypothesis is false when it is actually true (and, traditionally, it was convenient because statistical tables typically showed 5% values).

Table 12.1	Analogies of Type I and Type II Errors	
	True state	
Your decision	The coin is unbiased	The coin is biased
The coin is biased (i.e., it won't come up heads and tails equally)	"Type I" (gullibility risk)	No error of inference
The coin is unbiased (i.e., it is an ordinary coin)	No error of inference	"Type II" (blindness risk)

risk that initially most interests researchers who rely on NHST. The question they want answered is "What is the probability of a Type I error?"

Although most researchers who do NHST are not indifferent to the probability of making a Type II error (i.e., failing to claim a relation that truly does exist), many of them do tend to attach greater psychological importance to the risk of making a Type I error than to the risk of making a Type II error. Of course, in daily life, people also give greater weight to some decision risks than to others (see Box 12.4). But the reason the researcher attaches greater weight to the risk of making a Type I error is explained in Table 12.1. In the context of the coin example, the risk of making a "Type I error" would imply an *error of gullibility*, or being fleeced by the huckster's claim that an ordinary coin is biased. A "Type II error" implies *blindness*, or the failure to perceive that a not-so-ordinary coin is *really* biased as claimed. Though this analogy is a long stretch, the fact is that scientific researchers have been traditionally taught that it is far worse to risk being "gullible" than it is to risk being "blind" to a real (or true) relationship. Some philosophers have characterized this choice as the "healthy skepticism" of the scientific method (Axinn, 1966; Kaplan, 1964).

To show how Type I and Type II error risks are conceptualized in the tactical reasoning and language of NHST, we turn to Table 12.2. For researchers, the null hypothesis is usually the assumption that no relationship between two variables is present in the population from which the sample was drawn, or that there is no difference in "success rates" in the different groups or conditions. The researcher considers the possibility of making a Type I error whenever a true null hypothesis is tested. As defined by the upper-left cell in this table (which corresponds to the "gullibility risk" cell of Table 12.1), a Type I error results when the researcher mistakenly rejects the null hypothesis by incorrectly claiming a relationship that does not exist (i.e., the relationship was an illusion). As defined by the lower-right cell of Table 12.2 (corresponding to the "blindness risk" cell of Table 12.1), a Type II error results when the researcher mistakenly accepts the null hypothesis by failing to claim a relationship that does exist.

BOX 12.4   Innocent or Guilty?

Imagine that a man is being tried for a brutal murder, and suppose that, if convicted, he is likely to be executed. As a member of the jury, you have to vote on whether he is innocent or guilty of the charges against him. If you vote "guilty" and in fact he is not guilty, you may be sending an innocent man to be executed. If you vote "innocent" and in fact he is not innocent, you could be turning a brutal murderer loose in the community. In the legal system in the United States, it is generally accepted that mistakenly convicting an innocent person is a more serious risk than mistakenly permitting a guilty person to go free. The lesson? Just as most scientists who do NHST do not weight Type I and Type II errors equally, in everyday life we also give greater weight to some decision risks than to others.

Table 12.2	Implications of the Decision to Reject or Not to Reject the Null Hypothesis (H_0)	

	True state	
Scientist's decision	H_0 is true	H_0 is false
To reject H_0	Type I error	No error of inference
Not to reject H_0	No error of inference	Type II error

What Are One-Tailed and Two-Tailed *p* Values?

Now, let us see how you can determine and interpret the statistical significance of an effect size *r* by using a table. For this purpose, we turn to Table 12.3, which contains a portion of the information in a larger table in Appendix B (Table B.5). Both tables show the *p* levels associated with different values of *r*. The first column lists $N - 2$ (where N is the total number of units or observations, e.g., the number of participants), and the other columns indicate the *p* levels (i.e., Type I error risk levels). Notice in Table 12.3 that both "one-tailed" and "two-tailed" *p* levels are given and that two-tailed *p* values are always twice the size of the one-tailed. The **two-tailed *p* value** is applicable when the alternative hypothesis (H_1) did *not* specifically predict in which side (or tail) of

Table 12.3	Significance Levels of *r*				
	Probability level (*p*)				
	.10	.05	.02	.01	two-tailed
$N - 2$	.05	.025	.01	.005	one-tailed
1	.988	.997	.9995	.9999	
2	.900	.950	.980	.990	
3	.805	.878	.934	.959	
4	.729	.811	.882	.917	
5	.669	.754	.833	.874	
10	.497	.576	.658	.708	
20	.360	.423	.492	.537	
30	.296	.349	.409	.449	
40	.257	.304	.358	.393	
50	.231	.273	.322	.354	
100	.164	.195	.230	.254	
200	.116	.138	.164	.181	
300	.095	.113	.134	.148	
500	.074	.088	.104	.115	
1,000	.052	.062	.073	.081	

Note: For a more complete table, see Appendix B, Table B.5. However, notice in Table B.5 that all *p* values are shown as two-tailed.

the probability distribution the significance would be detected. The **one-tailed p value** is applicable when the alternative hypothesis requires the significance to be in one tail rather than in the other tail. However, as you search the journals for background information for your research proposal, you will find that many researchers ignore the one-tail versus two-tail distinction and report only two-tailed p values, a conservative convention that is also acceptable in most cases.

As an illustration of how to read Table 12.3 (and Table B.5), suppose you conduct an exploratory study to examine the relationship between people's level of self-esteem (as measured by a stan-dardized personality inventory) and the extent to which they are reported as engaging in gossip (measured by peer ratings). However, you are unsure of the direction that the relationship will take because (based on your literature review) you think that a positive *or* a negative correlation is possible. The reason you are unsure is that some authors portray the inveterate gossip as a social isolate, the least popular member of a group, characterized by feelings of little self-worth, social anxiety, and a need for esteem from others, who gossips in order to become the center of attention and to obtain status or esteem from others. By contrast, other authors view the typical gossip as sensitive, curious, social, and involved, a person who gossips out of a need to control or manipulate those perceived to be subordinates. Because you are unsure about hypothesizing a positive or a negative relationship, you decide the safe bet is to report a two-tailed p value.

Suppose also that, in your total N of 52 participants, you calculated the correlation between self-esteem and the tendency to gossip to be $r = .33$. In your literature search, you noticed that effect size correlations of this magnitude were sometimes referred to as "moderate" or "medium-sized" in psychology. That usage is based on operational definitions proposed by Jacob Cohen (1988) for use with the power analysis tables he developed, where the operational definitions of "small," "medium," and "large" effect sizes for r were approximately .1, .3, and .5, respectively. Assuming you recall from Chapter 7 that the effect size r in the Salk polio vaccine trial was .011, then you are aware that even an effect size r far smaller than .1 can be meaningful and important. For now, though, all we are interested in is how to use Table 12.3.

That the effect size r was a positive value is consistent with the idea that people who confess that they gossip a lot are higher in self-esteem, whereas a negative r would have implied that the high gossipers are lower in self-esteem. Let's suppose you selected the .05 significance level (the "5% solution" in Box 12.3) to serve as a helpful (though not critical) alpha. Looking at the intersec-tion of $N - 2 = 50$ and the column indicated as ".05 two-tailed" in Table 12.3, you see that r must be at least .273 to be beyond the 5% level of risk that you chose as your basis for rejecting the null hypothesis. As this table indicates, your obtained p is somewhere between .02 and .01 two-tailed, because your effect size r of .33 is larger than the listed value for $p = .02$ two-tailed (indicated as .322) and smaller than the listed value for $p = .01$ two-tailed (indicated as $r = .354$). It is that easy to use a table to find the significance level of the effect size r, and now let's assume you must report what you found.

Not all instructors insist on the same reporting conventions, but suppose you are expected to report the actual descriptive level of statistical significance. Reporting the actual descriptive level of statistical significance obviously carries more information than the phrases "significant difference" or "no significant difference at the .05 level." The problem in stating that there was "no significant difference at the .05 level" is that we have no idea whether the exact p was .06 (which is not very different from .05) or a value much greater than .05, such as .50 (no better than flipping a fair coin). Of course, if you are limited to using a table to look up p values, you may not have the option of estimating the exact p unless you still remember from high school math how to interpolate values. However, you might state that the p is less than (<) one particular level and greater than (>) another particular level as, for example, $.01 < p_{two-tailed} < .02$. Suppose you know the actual descriptive p and are expected to report a small p value to more than two or three decimal places. You might use scientific notation to indicate the exact p instead of reporting a string of zeros. For instance, instead of reporting $p = .00000025$, you can report $p = 2.5^{-7}$. The superscript "-7" tells us to count 7 places to the left of the decimal in 2.5 and make that the decimal place (see also Box 12.5).

BOX 12.5 *r*-Equivalent

Suppose an experimenter decided to use a data-analytic procedure for which no effect size index has yet been generally accepted. For example, some statistical tests described as "nonparametric" or "distribution-free" can give us exact *p* values but may have no generally accepted effect size indicators (cf. Higgins, 2004; Marascuilo & McSweeney, 1977; Siegel, 1956; Siegel & Castellan, 1988). However, if all we have is the exact *p* value associated with a statistical test and the total sample size (*N*), we still may be able to estimate an *r*-type or difference-type (such as Cohen's *d*) effect size (Rosenthal & Rubin, 2003). In the case of the *r*-type index, the effect size is called "*r*-equivalent" because it is equivalent to a sample point-biserial correlation (r_{pb}) between the dummy-coded treatment indicator and a normally distributed outcome in a two-condition experiment with an equal number of units in each group and the obtained *p* value.

Notice in Table 12.3 that the correlation can be significant at $p = .05$ no matter whether it is a very large correlation or a very small correlation. What counts most is whether the "$N - 2$" is sufficiently large to detect the particular magnitude of *r* at $p = .05$. Even an *r* as small as .062 would be significant at $p = .05$ two-tailed with $N = 1,002$, whereas an *r* that is 9 times larger would not be significant at $p = .05$ two-tailed with $N = 12$. Stating only that the effect size *r* is "significant" would not give anyone a clue to whether it was as small as .062 (in this table) or as large as 1.0. Furthermore, it is risky to ignore or dismiss a sizable *r* that was not "statistically significant" ($p > .05$) because the total *N* was too small. Surely it is more prudent to try to replicate the study with a larger *N* before concluding that "nothing happened." (A more immediately available procedure, using the counternull statistic, is described next.)

 ## What Is the Counternull Statistic?

The **counternull statistic**, proposed by Rosenthal and Rubin (1994), is useful for minimizing two common errors in thinking about effect sizes (these errors are different from Type I and Type II errors but are related to them). One error in thinking about effect sizes occurs when a researcher mistakenly infers that failure to reject the null hypothesis also implies an effect size of zero. The second common error occurs when a researcher mistakenly equates the rejection of the null hypothesis with having demonstrated a scientifically important effect. These two errors can be avoided by the routine computation and reporting of the counternull statistic in addition to the *p* value. The counternull statistic tells us the nonnull magnitude of the effect size that is supported by exactly the same amount of evidence as is the null value of the effect size.

Suppose an experimenter calculated an obtained effect size *r* of .10, with the null hypothesis defined as $r = 0$, and found $p = .20$ (two-tailed). The researcher can use the following formula to estimate the counternull value of a point-biserial *r* (Rosenthal et al., 2000):

$$r_{\text{counternull}} = \sqrt{\frac{4r^2}{1 + 3r^2}}$$

where *r* in the formula is the obtained value of the effect size. Squaring $r = .10$ gives us $r^2 = .01$, and therefore

$$r_{\text{counternull}} = \sqrt{\frac{4(.01)}{1 + 3(.01)}} = \sqrt{\frac{.04}{1.03}} = \sqrt{.0388} = .197,$$

which, rounded to .20, is the counternull value that is as likely as the null value of the effect size r of zero. Rather than conclude that "nothing happened" because the obtained p value exceeded .05, the experimenter instead accepts the conclusion that an effect size r of .20 is just as tenable as an effect size of zero. In fact, concluding that the population r is closer to .18 would be more defensible than concluding that the population r is no different from zero.

Shortly, we will also illustrate how to compute a confidence interval for an effect size r, as it is now generally accepted that significance tests and p values are not nearly as informative as effect sizes and interval estimates (Wilkinson & the Task Force on Statistical Inference, 1999). The null-counternull interval can be understood as conceptually related to confidence intervals. The difference is that confidence intervals provide limits for such fixed probabilities as, for example, 95% and 99%, whereas the null-counternull interval ranges from the null value of the effect size (which is typically zero) to the counternull value based on the obtained effect size. To calculate the percentage coverage of the null-counternull interval, we use

$$\% \text{ Coverage } = 100(1.00 - p_{\text{two-tailed}}),$$

which, given an r of .10 and an associated two-tailed p value of .20, yields $100(1.00 - .20) = 80\%$. Had the reported p been one-tailed, we would multiply the p value by 2 before subtracting it from 1.00, that is,

$$\% \text{ Coverage } = 100[1.00 - 2(p_{\text{one-tailed}})].$$

Our interpretation is that, with 80% confidence, the population value of r falls between zero (the null value) and .20 (the rounded counternull value).

What Is the Purpose of Doing a Power Analysis?

Before we discuss the confidence interval for an effect size r, let us first return to another important concept mentioned earlier. Described as **statistical power**, it has to do with the sensitivity of a significance test (such as t, F, or chi-square) to provide an adequate opportunity to reject the null hypothesis when it warrants rejection. When the null hypothesis has not been rejected in a given study, the reason might be that there was not enough statistical power to reject it. The purpose of doing a **power analysis** in this case might be to see (a) whether there was actually a reasonable chance of rejecting the null hypothesis and (b) whether the statistical power should be increased in any future study to increase the sensitivity of the statistical test. One way to increase the power of a significance test is to estimate in advance how many units (e.g., participants) are needed to achieve the desired p level (e.g., the total N). And, as noted earlier, a researcher sometimes performs a power analysis after finding a statistically nonsignificant result, in order to assess the *effective power* of the statistical test after the fact.

For example, suppose that young researcher Smith conducted an experiment (with $N = 80$) on productivity and reported that Managerial Style A was better than B (the old standard), with two-tailed p less than .05 and $r_{\text{effect size}} = .22$. Old researcher Jones, the inventor of Style B, is skeptical and challenges his students to replicate Smith's results. Accepting Jones's challenge, the students begin by recruiting 20 volunteers to participate in their replication attempt. To Professor Jones's perverse delight, the students report their failure to replicate Smith's results. Their obtained two-tailed p value, they tell Professor Jones, was *greater* than .30. Before savoring his victory, Jones reminds the students to calculate the effect size of their result. They report that the effect size was *identical* ($r_{\text{effect size}} = .22$) to Smith's!

In other words, Jones's students actually found exactly what Smith reported, even though the p values of the two studies are not very close. The problem is that Jones's students were working with a level of statistical power that was too low to obtain the p value reported by Smith. Because of the smaller sample size of 20, their statistical power to reject the null hypothesis at alpha = .05 two-tailed was about .15, whereas the statistical power of Smith's significance test was around .50

(based on an N of 80), more than three times as great as the power of the significance test used by Jones's graduate students (but .50 is no better than a coin flip: 50:50).

You will recall that beta (β) is the probability of a Type II error (i.e., the probability of failing to claim a relationship that does exist). **Power** is simply $1 - \beta$, or the probability of not making a Type II error. In the language of NHST, *statistical power* can be understood as the probability of rejecting the null hypothesis when it is false and needs rejecting. For any given statistical test of a null hypothesis (e.g., t, F, or chi-square), you remember that "Significance test = Size of effect $\times$ Size of Study." The statistical power of a significance test is determined by (a) the level of risk of drawing a spuriously positive conclusion (the p level); (b) the size of the effect; and (c) the size of the study (e.g., the total N). Thus, given the values of (a) and (b), we should be able to estimate how large a total N would be needed to achieve the desired level of statistical significance.

Table 12.4 is a compact way of estimating the total number of sampling units (e.g., participants) that are needed to detect different effect size r values at the .05 (two-tailed) level of significance. Suppose a researcher expected to work with power = .8 or better—which is typically the recommended level (Cohen, 1988). Suppose the researcher anticipated a "small" effect (around $r_{effect\ size}$ = .10) based on the researcher's review of the relevant literature. Given this magnitude of effect (r = .10) and power (.8), Table 12.4 shows that the researcher would need 784 participants (i.e., total N) to reject the null hypothesis at .05 two-tailed. This is a lot of volunteer participants to recruit. Had the researcher chosen to work in an area with typically larger effect sizes, recruiting participants would have been made much easier. For example, with an effect size r = .30 and power = .8, the table shows that the researcher would need a total of 86 participants. Or suppose the researcher anticipated an even larger effect size of .50. With $r_{effect\ size}$ = .50, a total N of only 30 participants would be needed, according to Table 12.4.

A complicating factor, however, is that if the researcher is recruiting volunteer participants, we suspect that not everyone who agrees to participate is likely to show up. From our discussion in Chapter 10 (of how an exploratory data analysis might be done), you recall that, on the average, about a third of those who say they will participate may be "no-shows." To be on the safe side, the researcher can multiply the estimated sample size N by 1.5, on the (risky) assumption that a third of the volunteers may not show up. However, the good news is that, in addition to increasing the total N (which can be expensive and time-consuming), there are other techniques as well to increase power. (In the next chapter, you will find a discussion of some other ways to improve the statistical power of a t test.)

Table 12.4 Rounded Sample Sizes (Total N) Required to Detect Effects at p = .05 Two-Tailed

Power	\multicolumn{14}{c}{Effect size correlation (r)}
	.05	.10	.15	.20	.25	.30	.35	.40	.45	.50	.55	.60	.65	.70
.25	664	168	76	44	29	21	16	13	10	9	8	7	6	5
.50	1,538	386	172	97	63	44	33	25	20	16	14	11	10	8
.60	1,960	491	218	123	79	55	41	31	25	20	16	14	12	10
.70	2,469	617	274	154	99	68	50	38	30	24	20	16	14	12
.80	3,138	784	348	195	124	86	63	48	37	30	24	20	17	14
.85	3,589	896	397	222	142	98	71	54	42	34	27	22	19	16
.90	4,200	1,048	464	260	165	114	83	62	49	39	31	26	21	18
.95	5,193	1,295	573	320	203	140	101	76	59	47	38	31	25	21
.99	7,341	1,829	808	451	286	196	142	106	82	65	52	42	34	28

Source: Based on Arno Ouwehand's Power Calculator 2, available via UCLA Department of Statistics (http://calculators.stat.ucla.edu).

How Do I Estimate a Confidence Interval for an Effect Size Correlation?

Just as we were interested in confidence intervals for proportions (Chapter 9) and means (Chapter 10), we are also interested in confidence intervals for effect size correlations. Suppose we are interested in the 95% confidence interval (CI) for an effect size r. We can make such an estimate in four steps using the tables in this book:

- Step 1 is to consult Table B.6 in Appendix B (p. 336), which is used to transform the $r_{effect\ size}$ to a Fisher z_r (which is a log-based transformation of r). The transformation changes the finite scale of r values (the scale ranges from -1.0 to $+1.0$) into a normal distribution without limits. To distinguish the Fisher z_r from the standard score z noted in previous chapters, we use the subscript "r" (not italicized) as a reminder that this z is related to r.

- Step 2 is to substitute the value of N in your study (i.e., the total sample size of your study) in the following expression:

$$\left(\frac{1}{\sqrt{N-3}}\right)1.96,$$

where 1.96 is the standard score z for $p = .05$ two-tailed, and $1/\sqrt{N-3}$ defines the *standard error* of a Fisher z_r. You will find discussions of the standard error in statistics texts, but in general, it refers to the standard deviation of the given statistic. (In the next chapter, where we describe the computational formula for a t test as resembling a "signal-to-noise" ratio, you can think of the standard error as a more technical definition of "noise" in the denominator of the t formula.)

- Step 3 is to find the limits of the 95% CI by subtracting (to create the lower limit) the result in Step 2 from, and adding it (to create the upper limit) to, the Fisher z_r transformed effect size in Step 1.

- Step 4 is to consult Table B.7 in Appendix B (p. 337) to transform these lower and upper z_r values back to $r_{effect\ size}$ values to define the 95% CI around the effect size r.

To illustrate, suppose we find that $r_{effect\ size} = .33$ based on a total sample size of $N = 80$, and we want to estimate the 95% CI. The first step is to look in Table B.6 at the intersection of the row labeled .3 and the column labeled .03, where we find Fisher $z_r = .343$. The second step is to substitute $N = 80$ in the denominator of the standard error, so we have

$$\left(\frac{1}{\sqrt{N-3}}\right)1.96 = \left(\frac{1}{\sqrt{77}}\right)1.96 = 0.2234.$$

The third step is to subtract the result in Step 2 from the result in Step 1 to find the lower limit of z_r (i.e., $.343 - .2234 = .1196$, rounded to .12), and to add the result in Step 2 to the result in Step 1 to find the upper limit of z_r (i.e., $.343 + .2234 = .5664$, rounded to .57). The last step is to transform both results of Step 3 into effect size r values, which we do by consulting Table B.7. For $z_r = .12$, we see at the intersection of the row labeled .1 and the column labeled .02 that the number .119 (rounded to .12) is the lower limit of our $r_{effect\ size}$ of .33. For $z_r = .57$, we see at the intersection of the row labeled .5 and the column labeled .07 that .515 (rounded to .52) is the upper limit of our $r_{effect\ size}$ of .33. Thus, we estimate, with 95% confidence, that the population value of $r_{effect\ size}$ is between .12 and .52.

To see how the confidence interval is affected by a smaller or larger N, suppose that the N is 20 instead of 80. Substituting in the expression in Step 2 gives

$$\left(\frac{1}{\sqrt{N-3}}\right)1.96 = \left(\frac{1}{\sqrt{17}}\right)1.96 = 0.4754,$$

which, when we carry out the remaining calculations, results in a 95% CI ranging from −.13 to .67. A negative effect size r means the pattern of the observed effect is opposite that predicted, so in this case, the confidence interval is so wide that it includes unexpected as well as expected directional patterns. What if we increase the sample to 320? Substituting in the expression in Step 2 gives us

$$\left(\frac{1}{\sqrt{N-3}}\right)1.96 = \left(\frac{1}{\sqrt{317}}\right)1.96 = 0.1101,$$

which, when we follow through with the remaining steps, yields a 95% CI from .23 to .42. Thus, we see that working with a smaller N tends to widen the confidence interval, and working with a larger N shrinks the confidence interval. Because we prefer a narrower rather than a wider confidence interval, ideally we would like to work with the largest reasonable N possible.

Also, we need not restrict ourselves to a 95% CI if we prefer working with some other interval. The table below shows values of alpha (i.e., p levels), confidence intervals, and the corresponding standard score z for p = .10, .05, and .01 two-tailed:

alpha (α)	.10	.05	.01
Confidence interval (CI)	90%	95%	99%
Two-tailed z	1.64	1.96	2.58

Suppose we prefer to work with a 90% CI. We simply substitute 1.64 for 1.96 in the expression in Step 2, or if we prefer a 99% CI. We would substitute 2.58. Increasing the confidence interval from 95% to 99% will, in turn, widen the confidence interval, and vice versa. If you ask yourself how wide an interval you need to be 100% sure about some risky event, you will see intuitively why increasing the confidence level results in a wider confidence interval.

What Can Effect Sizes Tell Us of Practical Importance?

So far, we have focused primarily on technical details when estimating statistical significance (p values) and interval estimates of effect size correlations (such as confidence intervals and null-counternull intervals), and we now turn to what certain effect size indicators tell us of practical importance. For now, we will focus on certain effect size indicators for use with a 2 × 2 contingency table of independent frequencies (and we have more to say about interpreting effect size indices in the following chapters). As a practical venue for this discussion, we will concentrate on random-ized clinical trials in which a treatment is contrasted with a control condition and the dependent variable is whether or not the participants experienced a specified adverse event. An example was the 2 × 2 table for the Salk vaccine trial in Chapter 7 (see Table 7.2 on page 132), where the row variable was the condition to which the children were randomly assigned (Salk vaccine or placebo) and the column (dependent) variable was a binary outcome (i.e., paralytic polio present or absent). Table 12.5 is modeled on this data-analytic arrangement, in which the four cells are coded A, B, C, D (as they were in Table 11.6 on page 211). Five effect size indicators that are often reported are the *odds ratio* (OR), the *relative risk* (RR), the *relative risk reduction* (RRR), the *risk difference* (RD, often described as the *absolute risk reduction*, ARR), and the *number needed to treat* (NNT).

Next we direct your attention to Table 12.6, which shows the hypothetical results of six 2 × 2 randomized controlled trials. Notice there are 2,000 total units in each study, so we have a similar basis of comparison in all six cases. The rate of occurrence of the adverse outcome (often termed the *event rate*) is set at 1% in Studies 1 and 4, 25% in Studies 2 and 5, and 50% in Studies 3 and 6. In Studies 1 and 4, for instance, the adverse outcome was experienced by 20 people, and therefore the event rate is calculated as (20/2,000)100 = 1%. Notice that the total number of adverse outcomes in the first column (i.e., cells A + C) is fixed at 20 in Studies 1 and 4; 500 in Studies 2 and 5; and 1,000

Table 12.5   Template for 2 × 2 Contingency Table of Counts

Condition	Adverse outcome Yes	No	Totals
Treatment	A	B	(A + B)
Control	C	D	(C + D)
Totals	(A + C)	(B + D)	

in Studies 3 and 6. The p values and confidence intervals in these examples are omitted only because the primary focus of the table is intended to be on the specified effect size indicators. For further guidance on confidence intervals for biomedical statistics, we recommend Altman, Machin, Bryant, and Gardner (2000), listed in the references.

The first measure listed beneath each study in Table 12.6 is the **odds ratio** (**OR**). Sometimes also described as the *relative odds* or the *cross-product ratio*, OR is the ratio of treated patients who experienced a specified adverse outcome (cell A) to treated patients who did not experience it (cell B) divided by the ratio of control patients who experienced the adverse outcome (cell C) to control patients who did not experience it (cell D), that is,

$$OR = \frac{A/B}{C/D}$$

or alternatively OR = AD/BC. OR < 1 tells us the experimental treatment was relatively more effective in preventing the adverse outcome when compared to the control, and OR > 1 tells us there were relatively more occurrences of the adverse outcome in the treatment group than in the control. In other words, assuming OR < 1, the smaller the value of OR, the more favorable the odds ratio. In Studies 1, 2, and 3, notice that the value of OR decreases from an impressive 0.05, to a slightly more impressive 0.03, to a still more impressive 0.003. In Studies 4, 5, and 6, the odds ratios are, as expected from inspection of the cell frequencies, noticeably higher values (starting at 0.82 and decreasing to 0.77 and then to 0.67, respectively).

Second is the **relative risk** (**RR**). Also frequently described as the *risk ratio*, RR is the ratio of the proportion of treated patients at risk of a specified adverse outcome to the proportion of control patients at risk of such an outcome, computed as

$$RR = \frac{A/(A + B)}{C/(C + D)}.$$

Finding RR < 1 tells us the treatment reduced the risk of the adverse outcome relative to the control, in which case the **relative risk reduction** (**RRR**) is typically reported, where

$$RRR = \left[\frac{RD}{C/(C + D)} \right] \times 100,$$

and the calculation of RD (*risk difference*) in the numerator will be described shortly. Notice in Table 12.6 that both RR and RRR remain unchanged at 0.05 and 94.7%, respectively, in Studies 1, 2, and 3. Similarly, RR and RRR never deviate from 0.82 and 18.2%, respectively, in Studies 4, 5, and 6. In other words, these measures were insensitive to the differences in the overall event rates, which would seem to be a serious limitation of these risk ratios.

In Chapter 1, we mentioned some of the work of Kahneman and Tversky (1973) on cognitive heuristics. They observed that people often personalize the implications of low-probability events when they identify with a characteristic of the data that distracts them from the probable consequences of the evidence. For example, when people read that a new pharmaceutical reduces

| Table 12.6 | Comparisons of Effect Size Indicators in Six Hypothetical Trials |

Condition	Study 1 (N = 2,000) (Event rate = 1%) Adverse outcome		Study 2 (N = 2,000) (Event rate = 25%) Adverse outcome		Study 3 (N = 2,000) (Event rate = 50%) Adverse outcome	
	Yes	No	Yes	No	Yes	No
Treatment	1	999	25	975	50	950
Control	19	981	475	525	950	50
Odds ratio (OR)	0.05		0.03		0.003	
Relative risk (RR)	0.05		0.05		0.05	
Relative risk reduction (RRR)	94.7%		94.7%		94.7%	
Risk difference (RD)	0.018		0.45		0.90	
NNT = 1/RD	55.6		2.2		1.1	
RD(10,000)	180		4,500		9,000	
r (phi)	.09		.52		.90	

Condition	Study 4 (N = 2,000) (Event rate = 1%) Adverse outcome		Study 5 (N = 2,000) (Event rate = 25%) Adverse outcome		Study 6 (N = 2,000) (Event rate = 50%) Adverse outcome	
	Yes	No	Yes	No	Yes	No
Treatment	9	991	225	775	450	550
Control	11	989	275	725	550	450
Odds ratio (OR)	0.82		0.77		0.67	
Relative risk (RR)	0.82		0.82		0.82	
Relative risk reduction (RRR)	18.2%		18.2%		18.2%	
Risk difference (RD)	0.002		0.05		0.10	
NNT = 1/RD	500		20		10	
RD(10,000)	20		500		1,000	
r (phi)	.01		.06		.10	

the risk of an adverse outcome by over 94%, they might be expected to react instinctively to an inner urgency that their own personal risk is highly likely to be reduced, instead of basing their judgment on the calculus of chance. It may be effective advertising, and certainly reporting relative risk indicators (especially RRR) cues us that something has happened, but these indicators could foster an illusion of representativeness because they are insensitive to base rate probabilities. This limitation of relative risk and relative risk reduction is more vividly illustrated in Figure 12.1, which recasts the six cases of Table 12.6 as histograms (the darkened areas of the bars indicate the number of adverse outcomes experienced in the treatment and control groups). Though hearing about relative risk reduction strikes a personally resonant chord in most people, Figure 12.1 is a way of illustrating when the resonance may be based on an illusion.

Next in Table 12.6 is the **risk difference** (**RD**). Also frequently described as the *absolute risk reduction* (ARR), RD is the difference between the proportion of treated patients at risk of experiencing an adverse outcome and the proportion of control patients at such risk, that is,

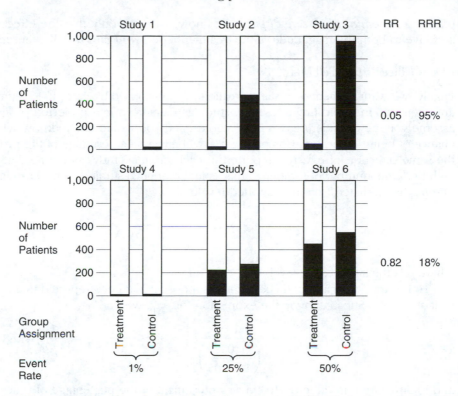

Figure 12.1   Histograms based on the hypothetical studies in Table 12.6, where darkened areas indicate adverse outcomes.

$$RD = \left(\frac{A}{A + B}\right) - \left(\frac{C}{C + D}\right).$$

If you compute RD by hand, the result will be a negative difference when the treatment is found to be more effective than the control, although the convention is to report the absolute value of RD (as in Table 12.6). To convey the clinical usefulness of the consequences of treatments, as indicated by RD (or ARR), the **number needed to treat** (**NNT**) was proposed by Laupacis, Sackett, and Roberts (1988). NNT estimates the number of patients that need to be treated in order to prevent a single adverse outcome (or the number of patients treated for one patient to benefit), that is,

$$NNT = 1/RD.$$

Multiplying RD by 10,000 estimates the number of cases in a group of 10,000 that are predicted to benefit from the treatment, but we can substitute another number for 10,000 (e.g., the number of cases in a group of 1,000). Table 12.6 shows these measures behaving exactly as expected as we go from Study 1 to Study 2 to Study 3, and again from Study 4 to Study 5 to Study 6.

Lastly, phi, as described in the previous chapter, is the product-moment correlation, where both variables are scored dichotomously. As illustrated earlier, this *r*-type effect size indicator can be computed directly on the frequencies in a 2 × 2 table of counts by

$$\phi = \frac{BC - AD}{\sqrt{(A + B)(C + D)(A + C)(B + D)}}.$$

Notice in Studies 1, 2, and 3 that the (*r*) phi increases from .09 to .52 to .90 as the event rate also increases from 1% to 25% to 50%. In Studies 4, 5, and 6, phi again reacts as expected, this time increasing from .01 to .06 to .10. In Chapter 15, we illustrate a simple way of recasting the effect size *r* into a display that can help us convey its practical importance in a standardized population (called a *binomial effect-size display*). For now, we note only that the effect size r appears to be sensitive to both the magnitude of the treatment effect *and* the overall event rate.

 ## What Does Killeen's p_{rep} Tell Me?

Finally, we want to mention a statistic called $\boldsymbol{p_{rep}}$, proposed by Peter R. Killeen (2005). Suppose you are interested in replicating a research study as a first step in a projected program of research. Let's assume you are considering two prior studies, and you would like to know which one has a greater chance of being replicated. Computing p_{rep} will give you an estimate of the probability of replicating the same direction of effect as reported in each original study, assuming that you will be working with the same number of sampling units as in the original studies, as well as with similar procedures. The p_{rep} is estimated from the reported p value by

$$p_{rep} = \frac{1}{1 + \left(\dfrac{p}{1-p}\right)^{2/3}}$$

where p is the significance level.

To illustrate with a hypothetical study, suppose it had been reported that the results were significant at $p = .05$. Substituting in the expression for p_{rep}, we find

$$p_{rep} = \frac{1}{1 + \left(\dfrac{.05}{1-.05}\right)^{2/3}} = \frac{1}{1 + \left(\dfrac{.05}{.95}\right)^{2/3}} = \frac{1}{1.14} = .88$$

and multiplying this value by 100 gives an estimate of the percentage of times (88%) that the effect should "replicate." In the context of p_{rep}, *replication* is defined as "an effect of the same sign as that found in the original experiment" (Killeen, 2005, p. 346). Next, you would perform the same calculations on the second study, and you would factor these p_{rep} values into your decision about which study is more likely to replicate the direction of the earlier results.

Table 12.7 lists p_{rep} values for significance (p) levels from .40 to .001. Notice that the probability of replication (p_{rep}) increases as the p value gets smaller and smaller. Although p_{rep} is intended to be used primarily as a measure of robustness of the direction of effects found in individual studies, Killeen (2005) provided support for the statistic in some meta-analytic findings in which the median p_{rep} was similar to the percentage of replication reported in each meta-analysis. The use of p_{rep} in the technical literature of psychological science has come in for considerable discussion (e.g., Cumming, 2010; Iverson, Wagenmakers, & Lee, 2010; Killeen, 2010; Lecoutre, Lecoutre, & Poitevineau, 2010; Maraun & Gabriel, 2010; Serlin, 2010).

Table 12.7   Probability of Replicating Directional Effect

p Value	Probability of replication (p_{rep})
.40	.57
.30	.64
.20	.72
.15	.76
.10	.81
.05	.88
.01	.96
.001	.99

Summary of Ideas

1. *Significance test = Size of effect × Size of study* is a general relationship that applies to all significance tests (such as *t*, *F*, and chi-square). It explains conceptually why reporting only the *p* value does not tell us the degree to which the effect size and the study size (e.g., the total *N*) contributed to the level of significance reached.

2. Three families of effect size indicators are the *correlation* or *r-type*, the *difference family*, and the *ratio family* (Box 12.1).

3. The probability of a specified favorable outcome is the number of favorable events divided by the total number of possible events (Box 12.2).

4. The *null hypothesis* (H_0) and the *alternative hypothesis* (H_1) are mutually exclusive: When one is true, the other must be false.

5. A *Type I error* is a mistake in rejecting H_0 when it is true, whereas a *Type II error* is a mistake in failing to reject H_0 when it is false. The probability of a Type I error is called *alpha* (α) when set in advance, the *significance level,* and the *p value.* The probability of a Type II error is called *beta* (β).

6. When doing NHST, scientists try to see whether they can reject the null hypothesis and yet be reasonably sure that they will not be wrong in doing so. Traditionally, scientists have believed that it is worse to make a Type I error (an error of "gullibility") than to make a Type II error (an error of "blindness to a relationship").

7. *One-tailed p values* are applicable when the alternative hypothesis requires the significance to be in one tail rather than in the other tail of the probability distribution, but *two-tailed p values* are also acceptable in most cases and are a conservative convention that is generally recommended by many instructors.

8. Failure to reject the null hypothesis does not automatically imply "no effect," and therefore statistical significance should not be confused with the presence or absence of an effect, or with the practical importance of an obtained effect. The *counternull statistic* can provide insurance against mistakenly equating statistical nonsignificance (e.g., $p > .05$) with a zero magnitude effect.

9. *Statistical power,* defined as $1 - \beta$, refers to the probability of not making a Type II error. A *power analysis* enables us to learn (a) whether there is a reasonable chance of rejecting the null hypothesis and (b) whether we should increase the statistical power by increasing the total *N*. Given a particular estimated effect size *r* and a preferred level of power, we can use Table 12.4 to determine how large the total *N* must be to allow detection of the effect at $p = .05$ two-tailed.

10. To create a *confidence interval* (CI) around an effect size *r*, the Fisher z_r transformation is used to locate upper and lower limits of the *r*, and the Fisher z_r limits are translated back into the upper and lower limits of the $r_{\text{effect size}}$. The smaller the *N,* or the higher the desired level of confidence (e.g., 99% instead of 95%), the wider is the confidence interval.

11. The advantage of using more than one effect size indicator is that different families of effect sizes give us different perspectives on the practical importance of the obtained effect (Table 12.6). The *relative risk* and *relative risk reduction* are not sensitive to differences in overall event rates (Figure 12.1), whereas RD (the *risk difference* and its associated indicators, such as the *number needed to treat*) and the effect size *r* are sensitive to the overall event rate.

12. The p_{rep} statistic, which assumes the same number of participants as in the original study and a similar level of sampling error, estimates the probability of a same-direction replication.

Key Terms

alpha (α)   p. 222
alternative hypothesis (H_1)   p. 221
beta (β)   p. 222
correlation family of effect
   sizes   p. 220
counternull statistic   p. 226
difference family of effect
   sizes   p. 220
null hypothesis (H_0)   p. 221
null hypothesis significance testing
   (NHST)   p. 219

number needed to treat
   (NNT)   p. 233
odds ratio (OR)   p. 231
one-tailed *p* value   p. 225
p_{rep} p. 234
power ($1 - \beta$)   p. 228
power analysis   p. 227
p value   p. 222
ratio family of effect
   sizes   p. 220
r-type effect sizes   p. 220

relative risk (RR)   p. 231
relative risk reduction
   (RRR)   p. 231
risk difference (RD)   p. 232
significance
   level   p. 222
statistical power   p. 227
two-tailed *p* value   p. 224
Type I error   p. 222
Type II error   p. 222

Multiple-Choice Questions for Review

1. "There will be no difference between the experimental group and the control group." This statement is an example of a(n) (a) alternative hypothesis; (b) experimental hypothesis; (c) directional hypothesis; (d) null hypothesis.

2. "The experimental group will score higher than the control group." This statement is an example of (a) H_0; (b) H_1; (c) H_2; (d) H_3.

3. Rejecting the null hypothesis when it is true is called a (a) Type 0 error; (b) Type I error; (c) Type II error; (d) Type III error.

4. Failing to reject H_0 when it is false is called a (a) Type 0 error; (b) Type I error; (c) Type II error; (d) Type III error.

5. A Type II error can be thought of as an error of (a) imprecision; (b) deafness; (c) gullibility; (d) blindness.

6. Scientists usually consider a _____ error to be more serious than a _____ error. (a) Type I, Type II; (b) null hypothesis, alternative hypothesis; (c) alternative hypothesis, null hypothesis; (d) Type II, Type I

7. A student at Lincoln University conducts a study with 52 participants and finds the correlation between authoritarianism and prejudice to be $r = .273$. According to Table 12.3, what is the two-tailed significance level associated with this correlation? (a) .10; (b) .05; (c) .01; (d) .001

8. A student at Central Arkansas University wants to conduct a study with power of .60 and, based on previous research, expects to get an effect size r of .20. According to Table 12.4, how many participants should she obtain to reject the null hypothesis at the .05 level two-tailed? (a) 10; (b) 20; (c) 60; (d) 123

9. A student at the University of Alaska expects to find an effect size r of .40 but unfortunately can obtain only 25 participants. According to Table 12.4, what will be the power (to reject the null hypothesis at the .05 level, two-tailed) of his study? (a) .20; (b) .25; (c) .30; (d) .50

10. The *number needed to treat* is the reciprocal of (a) the odds ratio; (b) the relative risk; (c) the risk difference; (d) the phi coefficient.

Discussion Questions for Review

1. A Notre Dame University student was asked by her professor to define the Type II error in the context of the Salk vaccine trial (Chapter 7, page 132) and to tell how it is related to the power of a test. Do you know the answer? Do you know what factors determine the power of a test of significance?

2. A panicking friend asks a University of Texas student for help with a project she is doing at Southern Methodist University on sex differences in scores on a new test of assertiveness. Her study will involve a randomly sampled group of males and a randomly sampled group of females. She tells the University of Texas student that effect sizes in this area of research have tended to be approximately $r_{effect\ size} = .20$. She wants to present her findings at the Southeastern Psychological Association meeting in New Orleans but worries that the study will not be accepted for presentation unless the group difference reaches a significance level (alpha) of $p = .05$ two-tailed. She also tells her University of Texas friend that the power level she is seeking for her study is .7. Given all this information, how many male and how many female subjects should the friend advise her to run?

3. A St. Lawrence University student conducts a study and finds $p = .05$ based on a statistical significance test. Exactly what does this p value tell him? What doesn't it tell him that is also important to know?

4. A Gallaudet University student is asked by her professor to create a 95% confidence interval for an effect size correlation of .034, based on a randomized clinical trial with a total sample size (N) of 22,071 participants. Would you know how to do it?

5. Dr. Squadrito, an experienced medical specialist, is consulted by a biomedical researcher who is interested in pursuing a particular line of research. The biomedical researcher wants to begin by replicating one of two earlier studies as a basis of her grant application, and she asks Dr. Squadrito which study, in his opinion, has the higher replication potential. He advises her to compute the p_{rep} value for each study. What will doing so tell the biomedical researcher?

6. To give first-year residents experience in calculating certain effect size indicators, Dr. Squadrito asks them to calculate the odds ratio (OR); the relative risk (RR); the relative risk reduction (RRR); the risk difference (RD); the NNT (the number needed to treat); RD multiplied by 10,000; and phi on the results of the classic Salk vaccine trial (Table 7.2 on page 132). Can you do these calculations?

Answers to Review Questions

Multiple-Choice Questions

1. d	**3.** b	**5.** d	**7.** b	**9.** d
2. b	**4.** c	**6.** a	**8.** d	**10.** c

Discussion Questions

1. A Type II error would have occurred if it had been concluded that there was a correlation of zero between being vaccinated and getting paralytic polio when that correlation was not really zero. The power of a test is the probability that results will be found significant at a given p value when the null hypothesis is false. Power is defined as $1 - \beta$, where $\beta =$ the probability of making a Type II error. The power of a particular test of significance depends on the alpha (α) we set, the actual size of the effect being investigated, and the size of the sample.

2. In Table 12.4, the intersection of the column headed .20 and the row labeled .70 shows the required total N to be 154. Therefore, she should run 77 females and 77 males.

3. It tells him that only 5% of the time would he obtain a result that significant, or more significant, if the null hypothesis (H_0) were really true. It does not tell him about the size of the effect.

4. Step 1 is to use Table B.6 (on p. 336) to get the Fisher z_r that corresponds to $r_{effect\ size} = .034$, and we find $z_r = .034$ (i.e., not different from r in this particular case). Step 2 is to substitute the N of 22,071 in the expression

$$\left(\frac{1}{\sqrt{N-3}}\right)1.96,$$

which gives us .0132. Step 3 is to subtract this value from .034 to get the lower limit of z_r (.02 rounded), and to add the value to .034 to get the upper limit of z_r (.05). Step 4 is to use Table B.7 (on p. 337) to transform the lower and upper limits of z_r to $r_{effect\ size}$. The student can report to the professor that, with 95% confidence, the effect size r is between .02 and .05 in the population from which the 22,071 participants were sampled.

5. Choosing the study with the higher p_{rep} will increase the replication potential. Multiplying p_{rep} by 100

reveals the percentage of time that the directional result is likely to be replicated, that is, given similar sample sizes and similar procedures to those in the original study.

6. With cells labeled A, B, C, and D as in Table 12.5 (page 231), the Salk vaccine results were:

Condition	Polio present	Polio absent	Totals
Salk vaccination	33	200,712	200,745
Placebo	115	201,114	201,229
Totals	148	401,826	401,974

$$OR = \frac{A/B}{C/D} = \frac{33/200,712}{115/201,114} = \frac{0.0002}{0.0006} = 0.288$$

$$RR = \frac{A/(A+B)}{C/(C+D)} = \frac{33/200,745}{115/201,229} = \frac{0.0002}{0.0006}$$
$$= 0.288$$

$$RRR = \left[\frac{RD}{C/(C+D)}\right] \times 100 = \left[\frac{0.0004}{115/201,229}\right] \times 100$$
$$= 70\% \text{ (rounded)}$$

$$RD = \left(\frac{A}{A+B}\right) - \left(\frac{C}{C+D}\right)$$
$$= \left(\frac{33}{200,745}\right) - \left(\frac{115}{201,229}\right) = -0.0004$$

$$NNT = 1/RD = 1/0.0004 = 2,500$$

$$RD\ (10,000) = 0.0004(10,000) = 4$$

$$\phi = \frac{BC - AD}{\sqrt{(A+B)(C+D)(A+C)(B+D)}} = .011$$

CHAPTER 13

The Comparison of Two Conditions

Preview Questions

- What do signal-to-noise ratios have to do with t tests?
- How do I compute an independent-sample t test?
- What can a table of p values for t teach me?
- What is an effect size index for an independent-sample t?
- How do I interpret Cohen's d for independent groups?
- How do I compute interval estimates for Cohen's d?
- How can I maximize the independent-sample t?
- How does a paired t test differ from an independent-sample t test?
- What is an effect size index for a paired t?

 ### What Do Signal-to-Noise Ratios Have to Do With t Tests?

We have examined the logic of using statistics and probabilities to test hypotheses, and with this chapter we begin our discussion of the three most popular statistical tests: the t test (described in this chapter), the F test (Chapter 14), and the chi-square (χ^2) test (Chapter 15). The question or hypothesis in which you are interested will determine the statistical test you choose. If you are interested in comparing the means of two groups (e.g., experimental and control groups), you will find the **t test** a convenient and powerful tool (see also Box 13.1). It will allow you to test the likelihood that the population means represented by the two groups are equal (i.e., the null hypothesis), by setting up a signal-to-noise ratio. In this ratio, the *signal* is represented by the difference between the two means, and the *noise* is represented by the variability of the scores within the samples. The larger the signal is relative to the noise, the more likely it is that the null hypothesis will be rejected.

As an illustration of how t tests can be thought of as signal-to-noise ratios, suppose that a researcher is conducting an experiment on the effect of vitamins on the academic performance of children from families below the poverty level. In Chapter 7, we described the statistical design of this research as a between-subjects randomized design. The researcher has randomly assigned the children to an experimental group (administered vitamins at regular intervals) or to a control group (given a placebo instead of vitamins). The experimenter's working hypothesis is that vitamins will have a positive effect on the children's academic performance, and the null

BOX 13.1   Student's *t*

The *t* test is also called **Student's *t*** in honor of William Sealy Gosset, its inventor. Introduced in 1908 by Gosset, it "revolutionized the statistics of small samples" (Snedecor & Cochran, 1989, p. 54). Trained as a chemist, Gosset worked for Guinness, the Irish brewery. For security reasons, the staff members were prohibited from publishing their research, but Gosset quietly published under the pseudonym "Student." Before Gosset's development of the *t* test, researchers who did experiments in small samples with varying effects were in a quandary over how to generalize the effects to populations whose variability was unknown. Gosset's genius was to perceive a way of testing the equality of population means whose variability was unknown, given only the means and the variability of samples (Gigerenzer et al., 1989). The noted statistician R. A. Fisher (1973a) later wrote of Gosset's profound contribution that, "important as it was in itself, [it] was of far greater importance in inaugurating the first stage of the process by which statistical methods attained sufficient refinement to be of real assistance in the interpretation of data" (p. 4).

hypothesis is that vitamins will have *no* effect on their academic performance. Table 13.1 and Figure 13.1 show two alternative outcomes of this experiment and help to illustrate the signal-to-noise idea.

We see that the means of the vitamin groups are identical ($M = 15$), as are the means of the control groups ($M = 10$). The only difference between Results A and Results B is that one set of results (B) is more variable. That is, the scores of B are less tightly bunched than the scores of A. When we compare the mean differences *between* the groups ($15 - 10 = 5$), it seems we should also take into consideration the amount of variability *within* the groups. That is, the 5 points of difference between the groups look larger to us when seen against the backdrop of the small within-group variation of Results A than when seen against the backdrop of the larger within-group variation of Results B.

This is the way the **independent-sample *t* test** works. It is a test of statistical significance that examines the difference between two independent means (the *signal*) against the background of the within-group variability (the *noise*). The larger the difference between the means (i.e., the greater the signal), and/or the smaller the within-group variability for a given size of study (i.e., the less the noise), the greater will be the value of *t* (see also Box 13.2). Because large *t* values are associated with differences between means that are more statistically significant, researchers generally prefer larger *t* values. That is, larger *t* values have a lower level of probability (the *p* value) and, in turn, allow researchers to reject the null hypothesis that there is no difference between means. (Later in this chapter, we will discuss design strategies to maximize the independent *t*.)

Table 13.1   Between-Subjects Design With Alternative Results A and B

	Results A		Results B	
	Vitamins	Control	Vitamins	Control
	13	8	9	4
	15	10	15	10
	17	12	21	16
Mean (*M*)	15	10	15	10

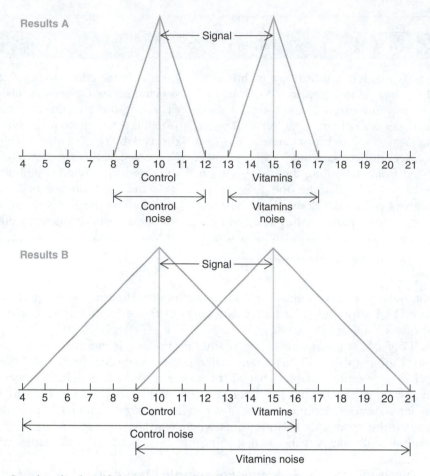

Figure 13.1 Graphic display of the data in Table 13.1. Note that Results A have no overlapping data but that Results B overlap from the scores of 9 to 16.

BOX 13.2 Shouting to Make Yourself Heard!

Suppose you are trying to conduct an intimate conversation in a noisy restaurant. You have to shout to make your words (the signal) understood over the background din (the noise). However, if there is not much noise, you can whisper and your conversation will be easily picked up. By analogy, *t* tests are more sensitive to differences between groups (the signal) when the variability within groups (the din, or noise) does not overwhelm the magnitude of a real difference.

How Do I Compute an Independent-Sample *t* Test?

In the example we have been considering, the two groups are presumed to be *independent* of one another; that is, the results in one group are not influenced by the results in the other group. This is also true of Mary Jones's experiment in Appendix A. Had she used a repeated-measures design, the two scores on each sampling unit would not be independent. We will explain the use of *t* tests with nonindependent data later in this chapter, but when we want to compare two independent samples, a general-purpose formula for the independent-sample t is

$$t = \frac{M_1 - M_2}{\sqrt{\left(\dfrac{1}{n_1} + \dfrac{1}{n_2}\right)S^2}},$$

in which M_1 and M_2 are the means of the two independent groups; n_1 and n_2 are the number of units (the number of participants) in each of the two groups, and S^2 is what (in Chapter 10) was called the *unbiased estimator of the population variance.*

You will see the same formula repeated on the first page of the appendix of Mary Jones's report, along with her calculation of the independent-sample t based on the data she summarized in the body of her report (in her Table 1). Think of S^2 in the t formula noted above as the "pooled estimate" of the population variance (i.e., a single estimate of the variance associated with both populations from which these two samples were drawn), computed as

$$S^2 = \frac{\Sigma(X_1 - M_1)^2 + \Sigma(X_2 - M_2)^2}{n_1 + n_2 - 2},$$

where X_1 and X_2 are individual raw scores, and the other symbols are as defined above. If you are using a computer to calculate statistics but want to try your hand with another set of data to check your understanding of these formulas, you can work with Mary Jones's raw scores.

A good way to get an intuitive feeling for what goes into t and the pooled estimate of S^2 is to go through the steps of computing them by hand on a calculator. Table 13.2 provides all the basic data needed to compute t for the sets of results in Table 13.1. Notice that the measures of spread (S, S^2, and σ) confirm what we perceived when we inspected Table 13.1 earlier, which is that the scores of Results B were more "spread out" than the scores of A. For each group, Table 13.2 shows the sum of squares of the deviations of the scores from their mean, which we now enter into the formula for the pooled estimate of the population variance.

With Results A we find

$$S^2 = \frac{\Sigma(X_1 - M_1)^2 + \Sigma(X_2 - M_2)^2}{n_1 + n_2 - 2} = \frac{8.0 + 8.0}{3 + 3 - 2} = \frac{16.0}{4} = 4.0,$$

so

$$t = \frac{M_1 - M_2}{\sqrt{\left(\dfrac{1}{n_1} + \dfrac{1}{n_2}\right)S^2}} = \frac{15 - 10}{\sqrt{\left(\dfrac{1}{3} + \dfrac{1}{3}\right)4.0}} = \frac{5}{1.63} = 3.06.$$

Performing the same calculations on Results B gives us

$$S^2 = \frac{\Sigma(X_1 - M_1)^2 + \Sigma(X_2 - M_2)^2}{n_1 + n_2 - 2} = \frac{72.0 + 72.0}{3 + 3 - 2} = \frac{144.0}{4} = 36.0,$$

and therefore

$$t = \frac{M_1 - M_2}{\sqrt{\left(\dfrac{1}{n_1} + \dfrac{1}{n_2}\right)S^2}} = \frac{15 - 10}{\sqrt{\left(\dfrac{1}{3} + \dfrac{1}{3}\right)36.0}} = \frac{5}{4.90} = 1.02.$$

Table 13.2   Basic Data for Calculating t for Results A and B in Table 13.1

Results A:

	Vitamin group			Control group		
	X_1	X_1-M_1	$(X_1-M_1)^2$	X_2	X_2-M_2	$(X_2-M_2)^2$
	13	−2.0	4.0	8	−2.0	4.0
	15	0.0	0.0	10	0.0	0.0
	17	+2.0	4.0	12	+2.0	4.0
Sum (Σ)	45	0	8.0	30	0	8.0
Mean (M)	15			10		
S	2.0			2.0		
S^2	4.0			4.0		
σ	1.6			1.6		

Results B:

	Vitamin group			Control group		
	X_1	X_1-M_1	$(X_1-M_1)^2$	X_2	X_2-M_2	$(X_2-M_2)^2$
	9	−6.0	36.0	4	−6.0	36.0
	15	0.0	0.0	10	0.0	0.0
	21	+6.0	36.0	16	+6.0	36.0
Sum (Σ)	45	0	72.0	30	0	72.0
Mean (M)	15			10		
S	6.0			6.0		
S^2	36.0			36.0		
σ	4.9			4.9		

Not surprisingly, in view of the larger denominator in the t test for Results B (4.90) than for Results A (1.63), the value of t is larger for Results A than for Results B. We expected this result because of the difference in variability (the difference in noise levels) between Results A and B. You can look up the approximate p values corresponding to these results in a suitable table, or your calculator may give you this information if you click a few keys. As larger values of t are rarer events, we expect a smaller p to be associated with Results A than with Results B. You can consult a table of p values for t to see whether you are right.

What Can a Table of p Values for t Teach Me?

Though it is convenient to think of t as a single test of statistical significance, it can be thought of as well as a family of curves (called the **t distribution**). There is a different curve (each one resembling the standard normal distribution) for every possible value of what are called the **degrees of freedom** (symbolized as df) of the t test. In the case that we have been considering (the independent-sample t test), the degrees of freedom are defined as $n_1 + n_2 - 2$ (see also Box 13.3). One of the great contributions of the inventor of the t test, W. S. Gosset (Box 13.1), was to figure out the curve for each number of degrees of freedom. Table 13.3 provides a summary of the most pertinent information from those curves for selected p values. This table gives us the areas found in one or both tails of the selected t curves. That is, for one-tailed p values, this table gives the areas found in the right-hand tail, and for two-tailed p values, it gives the areas found in both right-hand and left-hand tails.

Looking carefully at Table 13.3, we see that for any level of p, the value of t required to reach that level is smaller and smaller as the degrees of freedom (df) increase. In addition, for any df, a higher t

BOX 13.3 Degrees of Freedom

The origin of degrees of freedom (*df*) has to do in a way with the standard deviation, which in turn depends on the deviations from the mean (the *X* − *M* values). Suppose you have five raw (*X*) scores: 1, 3, 5, 7, 9, with $\Sigma X = 25$ and *M* = 5. The sum of the deviations from the mean has to be zero. That is, $\Sigma(X - M) = 0$ because $(1 - 5) + (3 - 5) + (5 - 5) + (7 - 5) + (9 - 5)$ equals zero. Knowing this, if you were given all but one value, you could easily determine the missing value because one deviation in the group is not free to vary. In other words, 1 *df* is eliminated. Therefore, with a batch of five scores, you have 4 *df* remaining. In the case of a *t* test on two independent samples, you lose 1 *df* for each group, so that $df = n_1 + n_2 - 2$.

value is required to reach more extreme (smaller) *p* values. One way to think about *t* is that when the null hypothesis of "no difference" or "no effect" is true (i.e., when the means in the population do not differ), the most likely value of *t* is zero. However, even if the population mean difference were zero, we would often find nonzero *t* values by chance alone. Suppose the direction of the effect was predicted to be in one tail and not in the other, in which case we might be primarily interested in the one-tailed *p* values. With *df* = 8, we would obtain a *t* value of 1.40 or greater (favoring the predicted outcome) about 10% of the time (i.e., one-tailed *p* = .10), or of 1.86 or greater about 5% of the time (one-tailed *p* = .05), or of 3.36 or greater about 0.5% of the time (one-tailed *p* = .005). Notice also that the values of *t* in each column become more stable as the degrees of freedom increase. The reason is that the *t* distribution gradually approximates the standard normal distribution as the size

Table 13.3   *t* Values Required for Significance at Various *p* Levels

	\multicolumn{4}{c}{Probability level (*p*)}	
	.20	.10	.05	.01	two-tailed
df	.10	.05	.025	.005	one-tailed
1	3.08	6.31	12.71	63.66	
2	1.89	2.92	4.30	9.92	
3	1.64	2.35	3.18	5.84	
4	1.53	2.13	2.78	4.60	
5	1.48	2.02	2.57	4.03	
6	1.44	1.94	2.45	3.71	
8	1.40	1.86	2.31	3.36	
10	1.37	1.81	2.23	3.17	
15	1.34	1.75	2.13	2.95	
20	1.32	1.72	2.09	2.84	
25	1.32	1.71	2.06	2.79	
30	1.31	1.70	2.04	2.75	
40	1.30	1.68	2.02	2.70	
60	1.30	1.67	2.00	2.66	
80	1.29	1.66	1.99	2.64	
100	1.29	1.66	1.98	2.63	
1,000	1.28	1.65	1.96	2.58	
∞	1.28	1.64	1.96	2.58	

Note: For a more complete table, see Appendix B, Table B.2.

of the samples is increased. At 30 *df*, the *t* distribution is fairly close to that of the standard normal distribution. When *df* = infinity (∞), the *t* distribution gives values identical to those for the standard normal distribution.

Based on what you have learned, let us now look up our two *t* values in the more comprehensive listing found in Table B.2 (pp. 327–328). The rows show the degrees of freedom (*df*), which will be 4 for both sets of results because we eliminate 1 *df* in each group when computing an independent-sample *t*. We put a finger on the row labeled 4 *df* and read across the columns until we find a value that is the same as or larger than the obtained value of *t*. For Results A, the *t* of 3.06 is larger than the value listed for *p* = .025 one-tailed (2.776) but smaller than the value listed for *p* = .01 one-tailed (3.747). Thus, the one-tailed *p* of *t* = 3.06 is less (<) than .025 but greater (>) than .01 (more succinctly expressed as .01 < $p_{\text{one-tailed}}$ < .025). For Results B, the *t* of 1.02 is larger than the value listed for *p* = .25 one-tailed (.741) but smaller than the value listed for *p* = .10 one-tailed (1.533). Thus, the one-tailed *p* for *t* = 1.02 with 4 *df* can also be more succinctly expressed as .10 < $p_{\text{one-tailed}}$ < .25.

You must decide for yourself whether you will regard any given *t* as an event rare enough to make you doubt that the null hypothesis is true. Still, you cannot simply decide, say, that "*p* < .20 is a reasonable risk" and then expect the instructor (or others) to automatically accept your decision. By tradition in psychology and many other fields, most researchers who do NHST prefer the .05 significance level. In Chapter 12, we described this traditional preference as the "5% solution" (Box 12.3 on page 222). By this standard, you would conclude that Results A are "statistically significant" and that Results B are "not statistically significant." Of course (as discussed in Chapter 12), you will also want to examine effect sizes and interval estimates (confidence intervals and, possibly, null-counternull intervals), as you know that the *p* values alone fail to tell the whole story.

Before we turn to the question of an effect size for an independent-sample *t*, we want to revisit a point mentioned in Mary Jones's report in Appendix A (and also alluded to in Chapter 10). Mary refers to an assumption of the *t* test as homogeneity of variance. There are additional assumptions of *t* that, when violated, may lead to incorrect inferences from *t* tests. These same assumptions are also applicable to *F* tests (which are discussed in the next chapter). Without going into too much detail, **homogeneity of variance** means that the population variance of the groups being compared is assumed to be equal. When this assumption is seriously violated, reported *p* values may be off, and the effect size calculated from *t* may also be inaccurate. Mary describes one traditional approach for determining whether there has been a serious violation of the homogeneity-of-variance assumption. She compares the highest and lowest estimated population variance by means of the *F* test and concludes that the homogeneity-of-variance assumption has, in fact, been violated. She then uses another procedure (described as *Satterthwaite's method*) to adjust the degrees of freedom of her *t* test. More commonly used to deal with *heterogeneity* of variance are transformations of the raw data in order to make the variances more nearly equal, and afterward, the *t* test is computed on the transformed data. Among the more commonly used transformations are (a) the square root of each raw score, (b) the log transformation of each raw score, and (c) the reciprocal value of each score. If you are interested in knowing more about assumptions of statistical tests, and about ways of dealing with serious violations, you will find more detailed discussions in our advanced text (Rosenthal & Rosnow, 2008).

 ## What Is an Effect Size Index for an Independent-Sample *t*?

When a *t* test is used, the most commonly reported effect size indicator is a statistic symbolized as *d*, for **Cohen's *d***. Proposed by Jacob Cohen (1969), *d* is a way of expressing the effect size as a "pure number" (free of the original measurement unit) in standard deviation units. Previously, we showed that we can transform a raw score (*X*) into a standard score (a *z* score) by dividing the difference between the raw score and the mean (*M*) of the normative group by the standard deviation (σ); that is, *z* score = (*X* − *M*)/σ. Cohen's *d* for use with an independent-sample *t* test is computed from the raw scores by division of the difference between the two independent means (M_1 and M_2) by the pooled population σ (the combined standard deviation of Group 1 and Group 2), that is,

$$d = \frac{M_1 - M_2}{\sigma_{\text{pooled}}},$$

and the pooled population σ is

$$\sigma_{\text{pooled}} = S_{\text{pooled}}\left(\sqrt{\frac{df}{N}}\right).$$

Cohen's d can also be directly estimated from the independent-sample t, and we will illustrate how in a moment. We will discuss the interpretation of this particular form of Cohen's d in the next section, but for now let us see what the two formulas above give us when we use the data in Table 13.2. A word of caution, though: In studies with very small samples, there is a danger that one or more outliers may inflate the denominator of the formula for d, causing the d to be small even when there is a sizable difference between the means (Wilcox, 2005). As noted in Chapter 10, a far-out score that is not an error is a signal to explore the data further.

For Results A in Table 13.2, we solve for the pooled population σ by

$$\sigma_{\text{pooled}} = S_{\text{pooled}}\left(\sqrt{\frac{df}{N}}\right) = 2.0\left(\sqrt{\frac{4}{6}}\right) = 1.633$$

and then solve for Cohen's d by

$$d = \frac{M_1 - M_2}{\sigma_{\text{pooled}}} = \frac{15 - 10}{1.633} = 3.06.$$

For Results B, we find

$$\sigma_{\text{pooled}} = S_{\text{pooled}}\left(\sqrt{\frac{df}{N}}\right) = 6.0\left(\sqrt{\frac{4}{6}}\right) = 4.90,$$

and therefore

$$d = \frac{M_1 - M_2}{\sigma_{\text{pooled}}} = \frac{15 - 10}{4.90} = 1.02.$$

There is, however, a far easier way to estimate d if we have the independent-sample t value. If the two samples are equal in size (i.e., $n_1 = n_2$), we can estimate d from

$$d = \frac{2t}{\sqrt{df}}.$$

For Results A in Table 13.2, the independent sample t value was 3.06 with $df = 4$, which gives us

$$d = \frac{2t}{\sqrt{df}} = \frac{2(3.06)}{\sqrt{4}} = 3.06.$$

For Results B, the t value was 1.02, again with $df = 4$, yielding

$$d = \frac{2t}{\sqrt{df}} = \frac{2(1.02)}{\sqrt{4}} = 1.02.$$

When the two sample sizes are *not equal*, the formula for obtaining d from t should be modified as follows:

$$d = \frac{2t}{\sqrt{df}}\left(\sqrt{\frac{\bar{n}}{n_h}}\right),$$

where $\bar{n}$ is the mean sample size, that is, $(n_1 + n_2)/2$. The value n_h is called the *harmonic mean sample size* and is computed as

$$n_h = \frac{2(n_1 n_2)}{n_1 + n_2}.$$

In studies with equal-sized independent groups, the mean sample size $(\bar{n})$ is always equal to the harmonic mean sample size (n_h), in which case the unequal-n formula is identical to the equal-n formula for estimating d from an independent-sample t.

How Do I Interpret Cohen's *d* for Independent Groups?

Cohen (1969, 1988) described several ways of thinking about d. One way involved visualizing the distributions of the populations from which the independent groups were sampled, based on the assumption that the population distributions of the groups being compared are normal (bell-shaped). We might envision the effect size d in this case either in terms of the percentage (%) overlap or the percentage nonoverlap of the population distributions. For example, Cohen's $d = 0$ implies that one population distribution is perfectly superimposed on the other, that is, 100% overlap and 0% nonoverlap. In other words, the percentage nonoverlap is simply 100 minus the percentage overlap. Table 13.4 shows these percentages for eight values of d, ranging from 0 to 4.0. Notice that the d values of .2, .5, and .8 are labeled "small," "medium," and "large," respectively.

Calling a d of .2 *small* (i.e., two means separated by one fifth of a standard deviation), Cohen observed that it was comparable to the magnitude of the difference between the mean height of 16-year-old girls and 15-year-old girls. Calling a d of .5 (half a standard deviation) *medium*, he described it as a difference just "visible to the naked eye" and provided as an example the higher mean IQ of professionals and managers versus clerical and semiskilled workers. And calling a d of .8 (four fifths of a standard deviation) *large*, he provided as an example the mean IQ difference of typical Ph.D.s versus typical college freshmen. Because the tails of a normal distribution stretch into infinity, there is always some overlap when d is greater than zero, even if the gap is minimal. Even with $d = 4.0$ (indicating that one of two means is 4 standard deviations above the other), Table 13.4 shows there is still 2% overlap. (See also Box 13.4.)

Table 13.4   Rounded Values of Percentage Overlap and Nonoverlap, r, and r^2 for Different Values of Cohen's d

d	Percentage overlap	Percentage nonoverlap	r	r^2
0.0	100	0	.00	.00
0.2 ("small")	85	15	.10	.01
0.5 ("medium")	67	33	.24	.06
0.8 ("large")	53	47	.37	.14
1.0	45	55	.45	.20
2.0	19	81	.71	.50
3.0	7	93	.83	.69
4.0	2	98	.89	.80

BOX 13.4 Bigger Is *Almost* Always Better

In general, it is probably the case across the many domains in which treatment effects are of interest that larger values of *d* are associated with greater practical importance as well. However, it is also possible to imagine an infinitely large *d* of little or no practical consequence. Suppose a bring-your-temperature-down medication is tested on 100 pairs of identical twins with too-high temperatures. One twin (chosen at random) in each pair is given the medication, and suppose the treated twin loses exactly 1/10th of 1 degree more than the control twin in each and every pair. In this case, the obtained *d* is infinite because of zero variability. But most physicians would not think of the result as reflecting a benefit of any consequence.

In Chapter 11, we showed how to compute a point-biserial *r* by dummy-coding two levels of an independent variable (using 0 and 1) and correlating the dummy-coded values with the scores on the dependent measures. Cohen suggested that another way of thinking about the effect size *d* with two independent groups is in terms of the point-biserial *r*, where group membership can be dummy-coded (e.g., 1 and 0, respectively, for experimental and control), and the dummy-coded scores are correlated with the continuous scores on the dependent measure. The next-to-last column in Table 13.4 shows values of *r* corresponding to values of *d*. Previously, we noted that Cohen labeled effect size *r* values of .1, .3, and .5 as "small," "medium," and "large." But notice in the table that there is not an exact correspondence between Cohen's labeling systems for *d* and *r*. Whereas a *d* of .2 ("small") corresponds exactly with *r* = .10 ("small"), notice that a *d* of .5 ("medium") corresponds with *r* = .24, and a *d* of .8 ("large") corresponds with *r* = .37. One lesson is that it is essential to specify the particular index that you are using, but another lesson is to think twice before using these labels for effect sizes, as they may be misconstrued as implying that "small" means inconsequential. Cohen (1988) cautioned that "the *meaning* of any given ES [effect size] is, in the final analysis, a function of the context in which it is embedded" (p. 535).

Cohen (1988) also noted that a traditional way to think about *r* is "as a proportion of common elements between variables," but he also cautioned that "this interpretation is not compelling for most behavioral science applications" (p. 78). He was referring to the *r*-squared interpretation, also called the **coefficient of determination (r^2)**. The last column in Table 13.4 shows squared values of *r* corresponding to Cohen's *d*. The interpretation of r^2 is as the proportion of variance among the *Y* scores that is statistically attributable to variation in the *X* scores, as well as the proportion of the variance among the *X* scores that is attributable to variation in the *Y* scores. This relationship is traditionally expressed as $r^2 + k^2 = 1.00$, where k^2 is called the *coefficient of nondetermination* (the proportion of variance "not accounted for"). Though it is useful in some other statistical applications, we caution against using r^2 as an effect size indicator because (a) the obtained effects are likely to be misconstrued as far less important than may actually be true, and (b) squaring the *r* loses important information on directionality (Is the treatment helping or hurting, or is the obtained correlation positive or negative?). Table 13.4 shows that "small" (but meaningful; cf. Abelson, 1985; Ozer, 1985) obtained effects can virtually disappear when the effect size *r* is squared. For example, the effect size *r* that we computed for the Salk vaccine trial was phi = .011, which, when squared, virtually disappears (r^2 = .000, or to 5 decimal places, r^2 = .00012).

To convert *d* to *r*, you will again need to take into consideration whether the sample size (*n*) is the same in both independent groups. In an unequal-*n* design, the conversion of *d* to *r* is obtained from

$$r = \frac{d}{\sqrt{d^2 + 4\left(\dfrac{\bar{n}}{n_h}\right)}},$$

where $\bar{n}$ is the arithmetic mean sample size, and n_h is the harmonic mean sample size. In an equal-n design, the conversion formula simplifies to one given by Cohen (1988, p. 23) as

$$r = \frac{d}{\sqrt{d^2 + 4}}.$$

To illustrate the unequal-n formula, suppose group means of $M_1 = 6.0$ and $M_2 = 4.8$, sample sizes of $n_1 = 85$ and $n_2 = 15$, and a Cohen's d of 0.6. The harmonic mean sample size (n_h) is

$$n_h = \frac{2(n_1 n_2)}{n_1 + n_2} = \frac{2(85 \times 15)}{85 + 15} = 25.5.$$

As $\bar{n} = (85 + 15)/2 = 50$, we find r is

$$r = \frac{d}{\sqrt{d^2 + 4\left(\dfrac{\bar{n}}{n_h}\right)}} = \frac{.6}{\sqrt{(.6)^2 + 4\left(\dfrac{50}{25.5}\right)}} = .21.$$

To illustrate the effect size (point-biserial) r computed from an independent-sample t, we return to Results A in Table 13.2 and use

$$r_{\text{effect size}} = \sqrt{\frac{t^2}{t^2 + df}},$$

and, as before, df is defined as $n_1 + n_2 - 2$ for an independent-sample t. With $t = 3.06$ and $df = 3 + 3 - 2 = 4$, we find

$$r_{\text{effect size}} = \sqrt{\frac{t^2}{t^2 + df}} = \sqrt{\frac{(3.06)^2}{(3.06)^2 + 4}} = .84,$$

a "jumbo-sized" magnitude of effect for r. And for Results B in Table 13.2, with $t = 1.02$ and the same df, we find

$$r_{\text{effect size}} = \sqrt{\frac{t^2}{t^2 + df}} = \sqrt{\frac{(1.02)^2}{(1.02)^2 + 4}} = .45,$$

a substantial magnitude of effect in spite of the failure of the t test to achieve significance at the conventional 5% level. If you turn to the appendix of Mary Jones's report, you will see the same formula and other sample calculations. One final point about reporting effect sizes for independent groups is that it is also advisable to report and interpret interval estimates whenever possible (later in this chapter, we note a situation in which the estimation of the confidence interval of an effect size is currently a matter of debate).

How Do I Compute Interval Estimates for Cohen's d?

Before we turn to interval estimates for Cohen's d, we remind you that in Chapter 12 we showed how to compute confidence intervals for an effect size r in four easy steps. To refresh your memory, we will reiterate those steps using the example at the end of the previous section, where the effect size r was .84 and the total N was 6. Assuming we are interested in lower and upper limits with 95% confidence, the first step is to use Table B.6 (page 336) to find the corresponding Fisher z_r, which in this case is 1.221. In Step 2, we substitute $N = 6$ in the expression

$$\left(\frac{1}{\sqrt{N - 3}}\right)1.96 = \left(\frac{1}{\sqrt{6 - 3}}\right)1.96 = 1.1316,$$

BOX 13.5 Crossing Over

At the end of the Results section of Mary Jones's report (Appendix A), she notes that her 95% CI crossed over into the negative side. If you wondered why it happened, it is explained by a special relationship between confidence intervals and the alpha (α) levels (the level of p specified in advance) on which they are based. The width of a confidence interval, expressed in percentage (%) units, is given by $100(1 -$ two-tailed α). If the obtained effect size is found significant at the two-tailed α level (or at $\alpha/2$ one-tailed), the end of the confidence interval closer to .00 will

not cross over the .00 point. That is, the interval will be entirely on the positive side of .00, or entirely on the negative side of .00 when the two-tailed p is statistically significant at .05. Thus, if we find the 95% CI is entirely between $+.00$ and $+1.00$, or entirely between $-.00$ and -1.00, it means that it must be significant at least at $p = .05$ two-tailed or .025 one-tailed. Similarly, if the 90% CI is entirely between $+.00$ and $+1.00$, or entirely between $-.00$ and -1.00, it means that it must be significant at least at $p = .10$ two-tailed or .05 one-tailed.

where 1.96 represents the 95% CI, but we can (as noted in Chapter 12) select another confidence level. In Step 3, we subtract the value of 1.1316 obtained in Step 2 from 1.221 to find the lower limit of z_r (0.0894, rounded to .09) and add 1.1316 to 1.221 to find the upper limit of z_r (2.3526, rounded to 2.35). In the final step, we use Table B.7 (page 337) to transform these lower and upper z_r values back into r values. In this example, with 95% confidence, we expect $r_{\text{effect size}}$ in the population to be between .09 and .98 (see also Box 13.5).

Turning now to Cohen's d on independent means, we obtain the 95% confidence interval (95% CI) for d by

$$95\% \, \text{CI} = d \pm t_{(.05)}(S_{\text{Cohen's}\,d}),$$

where $t_{(.05)}$ is the critical value of t at $p = .05$ two-tailed for $df = n_1 + n_2 - 2$, and $S_{\text{Cohen's d}}$ is the square root of the variance of Cohen's d, given by

$$S^2_{\text{Cohen's}\,d} = \left[\frac{n_1 + n_2}{n_1 n_2} + \frac{d^2}{2(df)} \right] \frac{n_1 + n_2}{df}.$$

Suppose $d = .50$, n_1 and n_2 are each 40, and thus $df = 40 + 40 - 2 = 78$, which gives us

$$S^2_{\text{Cohen's}\,d} = \left[\frac{40 + 40}{(40)(40)} + \frac{(.50)^2}{2(78)} \right] \frac{40 + 40}{78} = .053,$$

and therefore $S_{\text{Cohen's}\,d} = \sqrt{.053} = .230$. With $df = 78$, the critical value of $t_{(.05)}$ is 1.99. Substitution yields 95% CI $= .50 \pm 1.99(.230) = .50 \pm .458$, which indicates that there is a 95% probability that the population value of d falls between .042 and .958.

In Chapter 12, we also discussed another kind of interval estimate, described as the *null-counternull interval*. We said that a common mistake is equating failure to reject the null with the estimation of the effect size as equal to zero. We illustrated how to estimate the counternull value of an effect size r by

$$r_{\text{counternull}} = \sqrt{\frac{4r^2}{1 + 3r^2}}.$$

The counternull value of Cohen's d is easier to estimate because it is simply twice the obtained d in most cases (Rosenthal & Rubin, 1994).

To illustrate, let us assume a simple randomized design with 9 participants in each of two independent groups, and suppose $t(16) = 1.25$, $p = .23$ two-tailed, so

$$d = \frac{2t}{\sqrt{df}} = \frac{2(1.25)}{\sqrt{16}} = 0.625.$$

As in a confidence interval (Box 13.5), the percentage (%) coverage of a null-counternull interval is also given by $100(1.00 - p_{\text{two-tailed}})$. Finding that $100(1.00 - .23) = 77\%$, we can conclude, with 77% confidence, that the population value of d is between 0.00 and 1.25. We can correctly report that the obtained d of 0.625 does not differ significantly (two-tailed $p = .23$) from 0.00 (the null in this example), but the counternull value of d confronts us with the fact that the obtained effect size of d is also not significantly different from 1.25 (the counternull). This example reminds us not to treat a statistically nonsignificant result as necessarily indicating a zero effect size.

 How Can I Maximize the Independent-Sample t?

As mentioned in Chapter 12, a t test, like any significance test, can be shown to consist of two components, one having to do with the size of the effect and the other, with the size of the study. You will recall that the conceptual relationship between these components was expressed as

$$\text{Significance test} = \text{Size of effect} \times \text{Size of study},$$

a fundamental relationship that can help us plan specific ways of maximizing the t test in a given situation (i.e., ways of strengthening the statistical power of the t test).

For example, in the following equation, the independent-sample t test is conceptually broken down into an effect size and a study size component:

$$t = d \times \left[\frac{\sqrt{n_1 n_2}}{n_1 + n_2} \times \sqrt{df} \right],$$

where the effect size is defined in the equation as Cohen's d, and the study size (shown in brackets) is defined by the sample sizes of the two groups (n_1 and n_2). When sample sizes are equal (i.e., $n_1 = n_2$), this equation simplifies to

$$t = d \times \frac{\sqrt{df}}{2}.$$

When we think about these equations, we can see that there are three ways of increasing the value of an independent-sample t.

First, because we know that an all-purpose expression of Cohen's d in the case of two independent means is

$$d = \frac{M_1 - M_2}{\sigma_{\text{pooled}}},$$

it follows that one way to increase the value of t is to use a stronger treatment to drive the means of the two comparison groups further apart. Suppose we are interested in studying the effects of two different amounts of after-school tutoring on students' performance in a particular academic area, and we are thinking about comparing 60 minutes with 30 minutes of tutoring per week in two independent samples. To maximize the value of $M_1 - M_2$ in the numerator of Cohen's d (i.e., the definition of the effect size component in the conceptual relationship), it seems far more advisable to use 5 hours versus 2 hours of tutoring per week (assuming it is practical to do so). Or suppose we are interested in comparing age groups in terms of their performance in some area, but we have limited resources and can compare only two age groups. The more disparate the age groups we choose, the further apart the average performance in the two groups should be (though we might be missing a subtle nonlinear relationship by sampling only two age groups).

Returning to the all-purpose expression of Cohen's d, we see that a second way to maximize t is to decrease the variability within the two groups (the σ_{pooled} term in the denominator of the all-purpose expression of d). If you go back to Table 13.2, you will see that this is what happened in Results A, where the variability of responses within groups ($\sigma = 1.6$) was substantially less than that in Results B ($\sigma = 4.9$). One way to decrease the variability of response might be to standardize the research procedures to make them more uniform. Another option might be to recruit volunteer subjects who are similar in characteristics that we know to be substantially correlated with the dependent variable. In other words, we attempt to recruit a homogeneous sample of volunteers. On the other hand, we need to ask ourselves whether selecting a homogeneous sample might be trading away generalizability (external validity) for statistical power.

A third way of strengthening the power of a significance test was discussed in Chapter 12. It involves doing a power analysis to estimate how many participants might be a requisite number to achieve a particular level of statistical power. By increasing the size of the study, we increase the size of the t value. Incidentally, given a total available study size N (where $N = n_1 + n_2$), it is also prudent to try to keep the sample sizes equivalent in the two groups. The reason is that having an unequal-n can drain the efficiency of a significance test, and the more unequal the sample sizes, the greater the drain. Suppose we have a two-group design with a total N of 100. Compared with a study with $n_1 = n_2 = 50$ participants in each group, a study with $n_1 = 70$ and $n_2 = 30$ participants reduces the efficiency of the study by 16%, which would be like working with a total N of 84 rather than a total N of 100 (Rosenthal & Rosnow, 2008, p. 384).

How Does a Paired t Test Differ From an Independent-Sample t Test?

So far, we have used t to compare the means of two *independent* groups. That is, we regarded the scores in one group as having no inherent relationship to the scores in the other group. However, suppose we measure the same participants more than once (e.g., before and after they are exposed to a learning experience) and we want to compare the means of these two measures. Now the two groups of scores are no longer independent because of the repeated-measures (within-subjects) design. A less obvious example of samples that are not independent occurs when there is a filial relationship between participants. Suppose the two groups consist of pairs of children who are related by birth, and one member of the pair is randomly assigned to Group 1 and the other to Group 2. The shared family membership introduces a degree of prior relatedness between the scores in Group 1 and those in Group 2.

If samples that are not independent are compared by an independent-sample t test, the value of the obtained t will be biased (it will usually be too small, but sometimes it can be too large). To avoid this problem, researchers instead use a **paired t test** for samples that are not independent (also called a **one-sample t test**, or a **correlated-sample t**, or a **matched-pair t**). To illustrate, we refer to the basic data in Table 13.5. The data represent the results of a hypothetical study in which girls were predicted to be more sociable than boys. The scores are the ratings of a judge on a 9-point scale of sociability. What makes this study appropriate for a paired t test is that these are six *pairs* of girls and boys, each pair of children from a specified family. When we examine the judge's ratings over these pairs, we find that a child's sociability score is to some degree predictable from family membership. That is, we see that both the Smith girl and the Smith boy were rated below average, as were the Jones children, and both of the Simpson and Brown children were rated above average.

In t tests for matched (or correlated) data, we perform the calculations on the difference score (D) for each pair of lined-up scores, using the following formula:

$$t = \frac{M_D}{\sqrt{\left(\dfrac{1}{N}\right) s_D^2}}.$$

	Group 1	Group 2				
Family	X_1 (girls)	X_2 (boys)	Mean (M_X)	D	$D - M_D$	$(D - M_D)^2$
Smith	4	3	3.5	1	−1	1
Ross	6	4	5.0	2	0	0
Simpson	8	5	6.5	3	1	1
Jones	4	3	3.5	1	−1	1
Hill	6	4	5.0	2	0	0
Brown	8	5	6.5	3	1	1
Sum (Σ)	36	24	30.0	12	0	4
Mean (M)	6	4	5.0	2.0		

Table 13.5   Basic Data for Paired t Test

Note: The value of M_D is shown as 2.0 at the very bottom of the column of differences (D) between Groups 1 and 2 (i.e., $D = X_1 - X_2$), and the value of $\Sigma(D - M_D)^2$ is shown as 4 at the bottom of the last column.

In this formula, M_D is the mean of the $D = X_1 - X_2$ scores; N is the number of D scores (the number of lined-up pairs); and S_D^2 is the unbiased estimate of the population value of σ_D^2, where

$$S_D^2 = \frac{\Sigma(D - M_D)^2}{N - 1}$$

and N is the number of paired scores. For this paired t, the values of one of the correlated samples was subtracted from the corresponding values of the other correlated sample, creating a new *single* sample of difference scores.

Using the data in Table 13.5, we compute

$$S_D^2 = \frac{\Sigma(D - M_D)^2}{N - 1} = \frac{4}{6 - 1} = 0.800,$$

and

$$t = \frac{M_D}{\sqrt{\left(\frac{1}{N}\right)S_D^2}} = \frac{2.0}{\sqrt{\left(\frac{1}{6}\right)0.800}} = \frac{2.0}{0.365} = 5.477.$$

Because we predicted that girls would score higher than boys, we have the option of looking up p as a one-tailed value. Turning to Table B.2 (pp. 327–328), we read across the row labeled 5 *df* (because the degrees of freedom for a single sample are defined as $N - 1$, or $6 - 1 = 5$). Our t of 5.48 is between 4.773 and 5.893. The one-tailed p is therefore less (<) than .0025 and greater (>) than .001, which might be succinctly reported as $.001 < p_{\text{one-tailed}} < .0025$. The actual descriptive level of statistical significance turns out to be $p = .0014$ one-tailed and, using scientific notation, might be reported as $p = 1.4^{-3}$ one-tailed or as $p = 1.4/10^3$.

What Is an Effect Size Index for a Paired t?

Just as the independent-sample t was shown to consist of a size-of-effect component and a size-of-study component, parsing the paired t reveals a similar conceptual relationship:

$$t = d \times \sqrt{N - 1},$$

where the size-of-effect component is Cohen's *d* for paired observations, and the size-of-study component is the number (*N*) of paired observations minus 1. Cohen's *d* for paired observations is given by

$$d = \frac{M_D}{\sigma_D}$$

where M_D is again the mean of the $D = X_1 - X_2$ scores, and σ_D is the standard deviation of the *D* scores, defined as

$$\sigma_D = \sqrt{\frac{\Sigma(D - M_D)^2}{N}}.$$

If we rearrange the conceptual equation for the paired *t*, it follows that this version of a Cohen's *d* can be obtained from a paired *t* by

$$d = \frac{t}{\sqrt{N - 1}} = \frac{t}{\sqrt{df}}.$$

To illustrate the application of these formulas, we return to Table 13.5 and begin by calculating the standard deviation of the *D* scores as

$$\sigma_D = \sqrt{\frac{\Sigma(D - M_D)^2}{N}} = \sqrt{\frac{4}{6}} = 0.816,$$

and substitution gives us

$$\text{Cohen's } d = \frac{M_D}{\sigma_D} = \frac{2.0}{0.816} = 2.451.$$

Using the conceptual equation for a paired *t*, we compute

$$t = d \times \sqrt{N - 1}$$

$$= 2.451 \times \sqrt{5} = 5.481,$$

and as a check on our calculations, we compute *d* from the paired *t* by

$$\text{Cohen's } d = \frac{t}{\sqrt{N - 1}} = \frac{5.481}{\sqrt{5}} = 2.451.$$

To express the effect size in units of *r*, the same formula illustrated earlier in this chapter for estimating an effect size *r* from an independent sample *t* can be used:

$$r_{\text{effect size}} = \sqrt{\frac{t^2}{t^2 + df}} = \sqrt{\frac{(5.481)^2}{(5.481)^2 + 5}} = .926.$$

Statistically, the interpretation of the effect size *r* based on correlated observations is more complex than the effect size *r* from the independent-sample *t*. Though it is beyond the scope of this book, it is discussed in detail elsewhere (Rosenthal & Rosnow, 2008, pp. 398–400). The estimation of a confidence interval for an effect size based on correlated observations is currently a matter of debate.

Summary of Ideas

1. The *t test* operates like a signal-to-noise ratio used to compare two means relative to the variability of scores within each group. The larger the signal is relative to the noise, the more likely the null hypothesis is to be rejected (Box 13.2).

2. The *independent-sample t* test is used to compare two group means when the scores in one group are not influenced by the scores in the other group. The *degrees of freedom (df)* of the independent-sample *t* are defined as $n_1 + n_2 - 2$ because, in each group, one deviation from the mean is not free to vary (Box 13.3).

3. There is a different *t* curve (or distribution) for every possible value of the degrees of freedom of the *t* test, each curve resembling the standard normal distribution, which the *t distribution* gradually approximates as the size of the samples is increased. At 30 *df*, the *t* distribution is fairly close to the standard normal distribution.

4. To find a one- or two-tailed *p* for an obtained *t*, we need to know the degrees of freedom (*df*) as well as the value of *t*. Reporting a one-tailed *p* implies that we predicted in which side (or *tail*) of the *t* distribution the *p* value would be situated.

5. A popular index of the effect size when the *t* test is used to compare two independent means is *Cohen's d*, which measures the standardized difference between two independent means. It is important to consider the context in which the effect is embedded in order to assess the practical implications of an effect size; it is possible to imagine even an infinitely large *d* of little or no practical consequence (Box 13.4).

6. One way of visualizing the *d* for independent groups is in terms of the percentage (%) overlap or non-overlap of the normal (bell-shaped) population distributions from which the groups were sampled. Another way is in terms of the point-biserial *r*, and we showed how to convert *d* into *r* for equal and unequal sample sizes. We also showed how to obtain *d* from the independent *t* for equal or unequal sample sizes, and how to compute a confidence interval (and a null-counternull interval) for it. Though r^2 (the *coefficient of determination*) is another common interpretation, it is problematic because (a) small (but important) effect size correlations virtually disappear when squared and (b) squaring the *r* loses information on directionality.

7. Like any significance test, the *t* test is made up mathematically of two components: the size of the effect and the size of the study. We can maximize the statistical power of an independent-sample *t* by (a) drawing the means further apart (which increases the value of the effect size); (b) decreasing the variability within groups (again increasing the value of the effect size); and (c) increasing the effective size of the study (i.e., increasing the total *N*). Unequal sample sizes can reduce the efficiency of the *t* test and are like working with a smaller total *N*.

8. One of the assumptions in the use of *t* tests to compare independent groups is that the population variance is similar for the two groups, called *homogeneity of variance*. In Appendix A, Mary Jones illustrates the use of a serviceable procedure for dealing with heterogeneity of variance that involves adjusting the degrees of freedom of the *t* (described as *Satterthwaite's method*).

9. The *paired t test* (also commonly described as a *correlated-sample t*, or a *matched-pair t*, or a *one-sample t*) can be used to compare two groups of scores that are not independent, in which case the $df = N - 1$ (*N* is the total number of paired scores). Mistakenly using an independent-sample *t* in this situation yields a biased value of *t* (usually too small, but also sometimes too large).

10. We showed how to compute a Cohen's *d* and an effect size *r* for paired (correlated) observations, but at this time there is no consensus on a confidence interval for an effect size based on correlated observations.

Key Terms

coefficient of determination
  (r^2) p. 247
Cohen's *d* p. 244
correlated-sample *t* p. 251
degrees of freedom (*df*) p. 242

homogeneity of variance p. 244
independent-sample *t* test p. 239
matched-pair *t* p. 251
one-sample *t* test p. 251
paired *t* test p. 251

Student's *t* p. 239
t distribution p. 242
t test p. 238

Multiple-Choice Questions for Review

1. In a t test, the difference between the two means can be thought of as the (a) significance level; (b) noise; (c) signal; (d) none of the above.

2. In a t test, the variability of scores within samples can be thought of as the (a) significance level; (b) noise; (c) signal; (d) none of the above.

3. A student at Bryn Mawr College conducts a study with 5 participants in the experimental group and 6 participants in the control group. She then calculates a t test. How many degrees of freedom are associated with this test? (a) 4; (b) 5; (c) 6; (d) 9

4. A researcher at the University of Saskatchewan computes a t test for independent samples. There is a total of 8 participants, and $t = 5$. What is the appropriate one-tailed p value? (a) $<.05$; (b) $<.0025$; (c) $<.005$; (d) $<.001$

5. A very small p value (e.g., .001) automatically means that you have a (a) large effect; (b) moderate effect; (c) small effect; (d) cannot be determined from this information.

6. A student at Williams College conducts a study with an experimental group and a control group. There are 4 participants in each group. He calculates that $t = 3$. The effect size r is the square root of (a) 9/15; (b) 3/13; (c) 3/4; (d) 3/7.

7. Fill in the blanks in the following conceptual equation: Significance test = _____ × _____. (a) t, r; (b) t, Size of study; (c) Effect size, Size of study; (d) r, Effect size.

8. Which of the following can be used in maximizing t? (a) decreasing the difference between the means; (b) calculating r instead of t; (c) decreasing the variability within groups; (d) all of the above

9. Scores on two variables might not be independent because they were obtained (a) from the same participants; (b) with a within-subjects design; (c) from brother-sister pairs from the same family; (d) all of the above.

10. A study is conducted in which scores were obtained from 4 participants on two separate occasions. In other words, there are 8 total observations from 4 participants. The data are analyzed by means of a paired t test. How many degrees of freedom will there be? (a) 3; (b) 4; (c) 7; (d) 8

Discussion Questions for Review

1. A Kent State University researcher hypothesizes that marijuana use decreases short-term memory. He brings five volunteers to his laboratory. Each volunteer is given a test of short-term memory. Each is then given marijuana and administered another test of short-term memory. The results are given below (high scores indicate good memory):

	Test 1	Test 2
Subject 1	5	2
Subject 2	7	5
Subject 3	4	5
Subject 4	8	3
Subject 5	8	4

Can you set up the formula and insert the numbers that would be used to test the hypothesis that the scores on Test 2 are significantly lower than the scores on Test 1? What would be the degrees of freedom? If you found a significant difference and a large effect size, should you conclude that marijuana causes a decrease in short-term memory? Why or why not?

2. A Loyola University student conducted a study comparing the creativity scores of four biology and four history majors. The results were

Biology	History
4	7
6	3
3	5
3	6

Can you set up the formula that would be used to compute a t test? What would be the degrees of freedom? How would you compute and interpret the effect size?

3. An experimenter at the University of California at San Diego conducted a study of sex differences in nonverbal sensitivity using an independent-sample design, with 32 women and 32 men. Her results showed that the women were significantly better than the men at decoding nonverbal cues, $t = 2.34, df = 62, p < .05$ two-tailed, and Cohen's $d = 0.594$ and $r_{effect\ size} = .28$. Suppose the experimenter added an additional 30 women and 30 men, randomly selected from the same population as the

original sample. When the analysis is recalculated with the extra participants, should the new t be larger, smaller, or about the same size? Should the p value be larger, smaller, or about the same size? Should Cohen's d and the $r_{effect\ size}$ be larger, smaller, or about the same size relative to the original effect size values? Should the 95% confidence interval be wider, narrower, or about the same size?

4. A student at Virginia Commonwealth University, who is writing a master's thesis based on the research she conducted, found the two-tailed p of her independent-sample t test was .10 two-tailed. She also found Cohen's d for her obtained effect to be 0.6. Her faculty adviser suggests that she compute the counternull d and factor that information into her conclusions. What should the student report back to her adviser?

5. A Santa Fe College student has developed a brief training program that increases sensitivity to nonverbal cues. He plans to compare it to a brief training program that increases sensitivity to people in general. He plans to randomly assign 10 volunteer participants to each treatment, the participants having been found through newspaper ads. He describes his plan to his professor, who suggests he think hard about trying to obtain a larger t than he is likely to get in the planned study. What might the student do to get a larger independent-sample t?

Answers to Review Questions

Multiple-Choice Questions

1. c	**3.** d	**5.** d	**7.** c	**9.** d
2. b	**4.** b	**6.** a	**8.** c	**10.** a

Discussion Questions

1. The difference or change scores (D) for the five participants are $-3, -2, +1, -5, -4$. The paired t can be computed from

$$t = \frac{M_D}{\sqrt{\left(\frac{1}{N}\right)S_D^2}} = \frac{[(-3) + (-2) + (+1) + (-5) + (-4)]/5}{\sqrt{\left(\frac{1}{5}\right)5.30}} = 2.53$$

obtaining S_D^2 from

$$S_D^2 = \frac{\Sigma(D - M_D)^2}{N - 1}$$

$$= \frac{[(-3) - (-2.6)]^2 + [(-2) - (-2.6)]^2 + [(+1) - (-2.6)]^2 + [(-5) - (-2.6)]^2 + [(-4) - (-2.6)]^2}{5 - 1}$$

$$= 5.30.$$

The df are $N - 1 = 5 - 1 = 4$. Had we found a significant and large change in memory test scores, we would not be able to conclude that the change was due to marijuana use. There was no control group to rule out plausible rival hypotheses. Had we been able to compute the significance level and effect size, we would have used Table B.2 (on pp. 327–328) and found our t with 4 df to be significant at $p < .05$ one-tailed (but not quite significant at $p = .025$ one-tailed). The effect size could have been computed from

$$\text{Cohen's } d = \frac{t}{\sqrt{N - 1}} = \frac{2.53}{\sqrt{5 - 1}} = 1.265$$

or from

$$r_{effect\ size} = \sqrt{\frac{t^2}{t^2 + df}} = \sqrt{\frac{(2.53)^2}{(2.53)^2 + 4}} = .78.$$

2. We would compute t from

$$t = \frac{M_1 - M_2}{\sqrt{\left(\frac{1}{n_1} + \frac{1}{n_2}\right)s^2}} = \frac{4.00 - 5.25}{\sqrt{\left(\frac{1}{4} + \frac{1}{4}\right)2.46}} = 1.13.$$

The df would be $n_1 + n_2 - 2 = 6$, and the effect size could be computed from

$$d = \frac{2t}{\sqrt{df}} = \frac{2(1.13)}{\sqrt{6}} = 0.923$$

or from d as

$$r = \frac{d}{\sqrt{d^2 + 4}} = \frac{0.923}{\sqrt{(0.923)^2 + 4}} = .42$$

or directly from t as

$$r_{\text{effect size}} = \sqrt{\frac{t^2}{t^2 + df}} = \sqrt{\frac{(1.13)^2}{(1.13)^2 + 6}} = .42,$$

substantial effect sizes though t is not statistically significant ($p = .30$ two-tailed).

3. From *Significance test = Size of effect × Size of study*, it follows that increasing the size of the study would increase the value of the significance test, and the result would be a smaller (more significant) p value. However, the effect size would not be systematically affected by the addition of more participants of the same type. To illustrate, we assume the following original ingredients of t:

$$t = \frac{2.585 - 2.000}{\sqrt{\left(\frac{1}{32} + \frac{1}{32}\right)1.00}} = 2.34,$$

and $p = .023$ two-tailed, Cohen's $d = 0.59$, and $r_{\text{effect size}} = .28$. We then add 30 participants to each group, yielding

$$t = \frac{2.585 - 2.000}{\sqrt{\left(\frac{1}{62} + \frac{1}{62}\right)1.00}} = 3.26,$$

and $p = .0014$ two-tailed, Cohen's $d = 0.59$, and $r_{\text{effect size}} = .28$. With nothing changing but n_1 and n_2, we see that the independent-sample t increases, the p value decreases, and the effect size measures remain unchanged. The 95% confidence interval will shrink with the additional participants.

4. The counternull value of d is $2d = 2(0.6) = 1.2$. The percentage coverage of the null-counternull interval is $100(1.00 - .10) = 90\%$. With 90% confidence, the student can correctly conclude that her obtained d of 0.6 is between the null of 0.00 and the counternull of 1.2. She can also correctly assert that the obtained effect size d is not significantly different from the null value (0.00), but the counternull value forces her to confront the fact that this assertion is no truer than the assertion that the obtained effect size d is not significantly different from the counternull value of 1.2.

5. The student might try three approaches. First, he might try to drive the means further apart by using a control group that is not as similar to the treatment group. Second, he might use participants who are more homogeneous than the people who answer newspaper ads. Third, he might use larger sample sizes for each condition.

CHAPTER 14

Comparisons of More Than Two Conditions

Preview Questions

- What is analysis of variance (ANOVA), and how are F and t related?
- How is variability apportioned in a one-way ANOVA?
- How are ANOVA summary tables set up and interpreted?
- How can I test for simple effects after an omnibus F?
- How is variability apportioned in a two-way ANOVA?
- How do I interpret main and interaction effects?
- How do I compute a two-way ANOVA and set up a summary table?
- What are contrasts, and how do I compute them on more than two groups?
- What do $r_{effect\ size}$, $r_{alerting}$, and $r_{contrast}$ tell me?
- How are contrasts on multiple repeated measures computed?
- How are Latin square designs analyzed?

 What Is Analysis of Variance (ANOVA), and How Are F and t Related?

Though the t test is often used whenever there are only two means to be compared, later in this chapter we will describe how this statistical test can be used to examine a predicted trend in more than two conditions. Another popular statistic that you are bound to see in your literature search is the F test, which is the primary focus of this chapter. We will explain how F tests divide up variability in a procedure called **analysis of variance (ANOVA)**. (See also Box 14.1.) Even if you are using a computer program to analyze data, you will find that working through the examples in this chapter improves your understanding of the results provided by the computer program. Some concepts and formulas discussed in this chapter are so relatively new that they may not yet be available in your computer program, but they are usually simple enough to compute by hand with a good calculator. The summary ingredients that are provided by your computer program can be used with these formulas.

There is a basic relationship between F and t that is important to understand. Simply stated, it is that *squaring t always produces F, but taking the square root of F does not always produce t*. The reason for this conundrum will become clearer as you read this chapter. For the moment, all you need to remember is that taking the square root of F always produces t when two groups are to be compared. Because squaring t always produces F, and when you recall from Chapter 13 the following formula for computing an **effect size r** from t:

$$r_{effect\ size} = \sqrt{\frac{t^2}{t^2 + df}},$$

BOX 14.1 Fisher, ANOVA, and the "Lady Tasting Tea"

The F test (or F ratio) takes its name from its inventor, R. A. Fisher (1890–1962), a giant in the field of statistics, who also introduced a wide variety of other fundamental concepts. The F ratio is based on the *analysis of variance* (ANOVA), which Fisher originally used to separate the effects of different treatments on crop variations in agricultural experiments. In Chapter 10, we described the variance (S^2 or σ^2) as a measure of the spread of scores around the mean. ANOVA, when used in between-subjects (also referred to as *between-group*) comparisons, compares the spread of scores *between* the conditions ($S^2_{between}$) with the spread of scores *within* the conditions (S^2_{within}). Thus, in the F ratio of $S^2_{between}$ divided by S^2_{within},

you can think of $S^2_{between}$ as the *signal spread* and S^2_{within} as the *noise spread*. For a fascinating popular account of Fisher's work and how statistics revolutionized 20th-century science, read David Salsburg's *The Lady Tasting Tea* (2001). The title refers to a summer tea party of university professors, their wives, and some guests in Cambridge, England, in the late 1920s. One of the guests insists that tea tastes different depending on whether the tea is poured into the milk or the milk is poured into the tea, and Fisher proposes a strategy for testing the hypothesis and works out the probabilities of different outcomes—although the results of the afternoon's tea tasting are never reported (Salsburg, 2001, pp. 3–4).

it follows that, whenever only two samples (or two groups) are to be compared, an effect size r of F can be computed as

$$r_{\text{effect size}} = \sqrt{\frac{F}{F + df_{\text{within}}}},$$

where df_{within} is the degrees of freedom "within conditions," which we obtain by summing all the $n - 1$ degrees of freedom within each group (illustrated later). When specific predictions involve more than two samples (or two groups), the estimation of r-type indices of the effect size from F (and t) is more subtle, also illustrated later in this chapter.

Because we cover a great deal of ground in this chapter, it is useful to have an overall sense of what is in this chapter. We begin by explaining the logic of F tests and the analysis of variance in between-subjects designs, using as our illustration a randomized design with four independent groups. In the illustrative analysis, the F test is what we have called an *omnibus F* (identified as any F test with numerator $df > 1$). A problem with all omnibus tests is that they seldom address questions of real interest to researchers and are typically less powerful than *focused tests* (which include all F tests with numerator $df = 1$ and all t tests). Effect sizes indexed in association with focused statistical tests are commonly referred to as **one-degree-of-freedom effects**, and effect sizes indexed in association with omnibus statistical tests are referred to as **multiple-degree-of-freedom effects**. The first focused procedure that we illustrate in this chapter is the use of t tests after an omnibus F. If we find it useful to think of the analysis in terms of a factorial design, then we can use F tests to carve up the variability associated with main effects and interaction effects. When specific predictions that involve more than two groups are of interest, we can use focused F tests (called *contrasts*), contrast t tests, and r-type indices to assess the one-degree-of-freedom obtained effects. And finally, we will illustrate the use of contrasts in designs with more than two repeated measures (including a Latin square design described in Chapter 7).

In Chapter 13, we began with a hypothetical example to illustrate the signal-to-noise ratio of the t test. If we look at another example, we will see that the logic is essentially the same for

| Table 14.1 | Between-Subjects Design with Alternative Results A and B |

Results A:

	Group 1 Zero	Group 2 Milk	Group 3 Vitamins	Group 4 Hot lunch
	8	10	13	17
	10	12	15	19
	12	14	17	21
Mean (M)	10	12	15	19

Results B:

	Group 1 Zero	Group 2 Milk	Group 3 Vitamins	Group 4 Hot lunch
	4	6	9	13
	10	12	15	19
	16	18	21	25
Mean (M)	10	12	15	19

the analysis of variance. In this example, we imagine that an experimenter who is interested in the effects of nutrition on the academic performance of children decides to use a four-group instead of a two-group randomized design. One group of randomly assigned children is given a hot lunch daily, another group is given free milk, the third group is given a vitamin supplement, and the fourth group gets nothing extra. Once again, imagine two sets of results, as represented by A and B in Table 14.1. We would describe A and B as 1×4 ("one by four") between-subjects designs because the configuration consists of four independent groups in a one-way arrangement.

In examining these results, what conclusions would you be willing to draw on the basis of A compared to B? Notice that the outcome in the group receiving no nutritional bonus (Group 1) has an average of 10 units of academic performance, whereas the average performance of the group receiving milk (Group 2) is 12, that receiving vitamins (Group 3) is 15, and that receiving hot lunches (Group 4) is 19. By applying the logic about the within-group variance described in Chapter 13, we find ourselves feeling more impressed by Results A than by Results B. In Results A, the participants never varied in their performance by more than 2 points from the average score of their group. The few points of difference between the mean scores of these four groups look larger when seen against the backdrop of the small within-group variation of Results A and look smaller when examined against the backdrop of the large within-group variation of Results B.

The analysis of variance provides us with a more formal comparison of the variation between the average results per condition and the average variation within the different conditions. In this analysis, as we see next, a ratio (called the **F ratio**, or **F test**) is formed. In Chapter 13, we stated that one way to think about the t test is that if the null hypothesis were true, the most likely value of t would be 0. The F ratio, on the other hand, usually has values close to 1.0 when the variation between conditions is not different from the variation within the different conditions (i.e., when the H_0 is true); we explain later why this is so. The larger the F ratio, the greater is the dispersion of group means relative to the dispersion of scores within groups. In other words, as with t, most researchers generally prefer larger F values because they are associated with smaller p levels.

How Is Variability Apportioned in a One-Way ANOVA?

The calculation of F tests is one purpose of the analysis of variance. A more general purpose is to divide up the variation of all the observations into a number of separate sources of variance. In this illustration of comparing the four samples in a one-way ANOVA, the total variation among the 12 scores is broken into two sources: (a) systematic variation between groups or conditions (the *signal* variation) and (b) error variation within groups or conditions (the *noise* variation).

It will be useful here to look again at the basic idea of variance, as defined in Chapter 10 by the following formula:

$$S^2 = \frac{\Sigma(X - M)^2}{N - 1},$$

where S^2 is the unbiased estimate of the population value of σ^2, and $N = $ total number of units. As noted in Chapter 10, the quantity S^2 is also called the **mean square** (abbreviated as *MS*), because when $\Sigma(X - M)^2$ (which gives the sum of the squares) is divided by $N - 1$ (the *df*), the result is the squared deviation per *df*, representing a kind of average.

In the analysis of variance, we are especially interested in the numerators of these various S^2 values (e.g., for between conditions and for within conditions). This interest has to do with the additive property of the numerators, or the **sum of squares** (abbreviated as *SS*) of the deviations about the mean. These *SS* values add up to the total sum of squares in the following way:

Total $SS = $ Between-conditions $SS + $ Within-conditions SS.

In one-way between-subjects designs, analysis of variance requires calculation of the between-conditions SS and the within-conditions SS. If you are using a calculator to try the examples in this chapter, compute the total SS as a check on your arithmetic. Let us look at the formulas for each of these three sums of squares.

First, the total SS is defined as the sum of squares of all the measurements' deviations from the grand mean. What goes into the total SS is given by the following formula:

Total $SS = \Sigma(X - M_G)^2,$

where X is each observation and M_G is the grand mean (i.e., the mean of all N scores).

Second, the between-conditions SS is defined as the sum of squares of the deviations of the condition means from the grand mean, as given by the following formula:

Between $SS = \Sigma[\,n_k(M_k - M_G)^2\,],$

where n_k is the number of observations in the kth condition (and k is *any* particular condition), M_k is the mean of the kth condition, and M_G is again the grand mean.

Third, the within-conditions SS is defined as the sum of squares of the deviations of the measurements from their condition means, as given by the following formula:

Within $SS = \Sigma(X - M_k)^2,$

where X is each observation and M_k is again the mean of the condition to which X belongs.

We will now use these formulas to compute an overall ANOVA on the scores of Results A in Table 14.1. Table 14.2 provides the basic data for this analysis, with the addition of two new symbols: M_k for the group or the condition mean and M_G for the grand mean. First, we compute the total sum of squares by

Total $SS = \Sigma(X - M_G)^2,$

	Group 1 Zero	Group 2 Milk	Group 3 Vitamins	Group 4 Hot lunch
	8	10	13	17
	10	12	15	19
	12	14	17	21
M_k	10	12	15	19

Table 14.2   Data for ANOVA Based on Results A in Table 14.1

$$M_G = \frac{10 + 12 + 15 + 19}{4} = 14$$

which instructs us to subtract the grand mean from each individual score and then add up the squared deviations:

$$\text{Total } SS = (8 - 14)^2 + (10 - 14)^2 + (12 - 14)^2$$
$$+ (10 - 14)^2 + (12 - 14)^2 + (14 - 14)^2$$
$$+ (13 - 14)^2 + (15 - 14)^2 + (17 - 14)^2$$
$$+ (17 - 14)^2 + (19 - 14)^2 + (21 - 14)^2$$
$$= 170$$

Next, we compute the between-conditions sum of squares by

$$\text{Between } SS = \Sigma[\,n_k(M_k - M_G)^2\,],$$

which instructs us to subtract the grand mean from each condition mean and then add up the weighted squared deviations:

$$\text{Between } SS = 3(10 - 14)^2$$
$$+ 3(12 - 14)^2$$
$$+ 3(15 - 14)^2$$
$$+ 3(19 - 14)^2$$
$$= 138$$

And finally, we compute the within-conditions sum of squares by

$$\text{Within } SS = \Sigma(X - M_k)^2,$$

which instructs us to subtract the appropriate condition mean from each individual score and then add up the squared deviations:

$$\text{Within } SS = (8 - 10)^2 + (10 - 10)^2 + (12 - 10)^2$$
$$+ (10 - 12)^2 + (12 - 12)^2 + (14 - 12)^2$$
$$+ (13 - 15)^2 + (15 - 15)^2 + (17 - 15)^2$$
$$+ (17 - 19)^2 + (19 - 19)^2 + (21 - 19)^2$$
$$= 32$$

As a check on our arithmetic, we add the sum of squares between conditions to the sum of squares within conditions to make sure their total equals the total sum of squares, that is,

$$\text{Total } SS = \text{ Between } SS + \text{ Within } SS$$

$$170 \quad = \quad 138 \quad + \quad 32$$

 How Are ANOVA Summary Tables Set Up and Interpreted?

The results of a one-way ANOVA, as traditionally displayed in the form of a summary table, are shown in Table 14.3. The rows label the specific sources of variation, which in this case are the variation between conditions and the variation within conditions. Listed in the SS column are sum-of-squares values for each source of variation. The degrees of freedom (df) are listed in the next column (see also Box 14.2). As there were four independent conditions (symbolized as $k = 4$), three of the means were free to vary once the grand mean (M_G, or mean of the means) was determined. We define the degrees of freedom between conditions as

$$df_{\text{between}} = k - 1,$$

which in this case is $df_{\text{between}} = 4 - 1 = 3$.

We obtain the degrees of freedom within conditions from the df within each condition (defined as $n - 1$) and then adding them. The reason we have $n - 1$ degrees of freedom within each condition is that all scores but one are free to vary within each condition once the mean of that condition is determined, and so we eliminate 1 df within each condition. Thus, the degrees of freedom within conditions are found by

$$df_{\text{within}} = N - k,$$

where N is the total number of measurements or sampling units and k is the number of conditions, giving us $df_{\text{within}} = 12 - 4 = 8$.

The total degrees of freedom (not shown in Table 14.3) are defined as the total number of measurements minus 1, that is,

$$df_{\text{total}} = N - 1,$$

which gives us $df_{\text{total}} = 12 - 1 = 11$. After we have computed df_{between} and df_{within}, we can check our calculations by adding these df to see whether they agree with the df_{total}. In the present case, we have

$$df_{\text{total}} = df_{\text{between}} + df_{\text{within}}$$

$$11 \quad = \quad 3 \quad + \quad 8$$

The MS column shows the mean squares, which we find by dividing the sums of squares by the corresponding df. We divide 138 by 3 to get $MS_{\text{between}} = 46$, and we divide 32 by 8 to get $MS_{\text{within}} = 4$. These MS values can be seen as the amounts of the total variation (measured in SS) attributable to each df. The larger the MS for the between-conditions source of variance (the signal) relative to the within-conditions source of variance (the noise), the less likely becomes the null

Table 14.3   Summary ANOVA for Results in Table 14.2

Source	SS	df	MS	F	p
Between conditions	138	3	46	11.50	.003
Within conditions	32	8	4		

BOX 14.2 When to Report Effect Sizes

Previously, we described *F* tests with 1 *df* in the numerator as **focused statistical tests** (because they address specific statistical questions) and effect sizes indexed in association with focused tests as *one-degree-of-freedom effects*. We described *F* tests with numerator *df* > 1 as **omnibus statistical procedures** (because they address diffuse, or unfocused, questions) and effect sizes indexed in association with omnibus tests as *multiple-degree-of-freedom effects*. As one-degree-of-freedom effects are more interpretable than multiple-degree-of-freedom effects, effect sizes should almost always be reported for focused statistical tests.

hypothesis of no difference between the conditions. If the null hypothesis were true, the *SS* variation per *df* should be roughly the same for the *df* between groups and the *df* within groups. The *F* value in the next column provides this information. We obtained this *F* by dividing the mean square between conditions by the mean square within conditions; the result is a signal-to-noise ratio of $F = 46/4 = 11.5$.

To review, *F* is called the *F* ratio to reflect the fact that it is a ratio of two mean squares (i.e., two variances, as noted in Box 14.1). The denominator mean square (i.e., the mean square for error) serves as a kind of base rate for noise level, or typical variation. The numerator (the signal) is a reflection of both the size of the effect and the size of the study. In other words, a numerator *MS* may be large relative to a denominator *MS* because (a) the obtained effect is large, (b) the *n* per condition is large, or (c) both are large. Thus, large *F* values should not automatically be seen as indicating the presence of large effects. No effect size is noted, because a general rule of thumb is to report effect size indices only for one-degree-of-freedom effect sizes (Box 14.2). Therefore, we report the effect size associated with *F* when the numerator *df* = 1, as in a comparison of two conditions or as in a contrast *F* test on more than two groups (illustrated later in this chapter).

The final value in Table 14.3 is the probability that an *F* of this size or larger, with this number of degrees of freedom (3 in the numerator and 8 in the denominator), might occur if the null hypothesis of no difference among the means were true. In Chapter 13, we noted that the distribution of *t* values is different for every value of the degrees of freedom. The situation for *F* is similar but more complicated, because *two* relevant *df* values must be taken into account for every *F* ratio. One is the degrees of freedom between conditions and the other is the degrees of freedom within conditions. For every combination of df_{between} and df_{within}, there is a different curve. As with *t*, smaller values of *F* are likely when the null hypothesis of no difference between conditions is true, whereas larger values of *F* are less likely and are therefore used as evidence to suggest that the null hypothesis is probably false.

Another important difference between *t* and *F* curves was alluded to earlier: The expected value of *t* is 0 when the null hypothesis is true, but the expected value of *F* is generally a little more than 1 when the null hypothesis is true in most cases that behavioral researchers are likely to encounter. The symmetrical bell shape of *t* curves means that they are centered at 0, with negative values running to negative infinity and positive values running to positive infinity. However, *F* curves are positively skewed, with values beginning at the null of 0 and ranging upward to positive infinity. Thus, *F* is intrinsically one-tailed as a test of significance. When the null hypothesis of 0 is true, the expected value of *F* is $df/(df - 2)$, where these are *df* for within conditions. The last column in Table 14.4 lists expected values of *F* when the null hypothesis is true, and notice that the values decrease until they are a little more than 1.0.

Table 14.4 enables us to locate the *p* value of a given *F*. A more comprehensive table can be found in Appendix B (see pp. 329–333). In Table 14.4, notice that the values of *F* required to reach the .05 and .01 levels decrease as the df_{within} value increases for any given df_{between} value. Similarly,

Table 14.4 F Values Required for Significance at the .05 (Upper Entry) and .01 Levels

Degrees of freedom within conditions (denominator)	Degrees of freedom between conditions (numerator)						Expected value of F when H_0 is true
	1	2	3	4	6	∞	
1	161	200	216	225	234	254	—
	4052	4999	5403	5625	5859	6366	
2	18.5	19.0	19.2	19.3	19.3	19.5	—
	98.5	99.0	99.2	99.3	99.3	99.5	
3	10.1	9.55	9.28	9.12	8.94	8.53	3.00
	34.1	30.8	29.5	28.7	27.9	26.1	
4	7.71	6.94	6.59	6.39	6.16	5.63	2.00
	21.2	18.0	16.7	16.0	15.2	13.5	
5	6.61	5.79	5.41	5.19	4.95	4.36	1.67
	16.3	13.3	12.1	11.4	10.7	9.02	
6	5.99	5.14	4.76	4.53	4.28	3.67	1.50
	13.7	10.9	9.78	9.15	8.47	6.88	
8	5.32	4.46	4.07	3.84	3.58	2.93	1.33
	11.3	8.65	7.59	7.01	6.37	4.86	
10	4.96	4.10	3.71	3.48	3.22	2.54	1.25
	10.0	7.56	6.55	5.99	5.39	3.91	
15	4.54	3.68	3.29	3.06	2.79	2.07	1.15
	8.68	6.36	5.42	4.89	4.32	2.87	
20	4.35	3.49	3.10	2.87	2.60	1.84	1.11
	8.10	5.85	4.94	4.43	3.87	2.42	
25	4.24	3.38	2.99	2.76	2.49	1.71	1.09
	7.77	5.57	4.68	4.18	3.63	2.17	
30	4.17	3.32	2.92	2.69	2.42	1.62	1.07
	7.56	5.39	4.51	4.02	3.47	2.01	
40	4.08	3.23	2.84	2.61	2.34	1.51	1.05
	7.31	5.18	4.31	3.83	3.29	1.80	
∞	3.84	2.99	2.60	2.37	2.09	1.00	1.00
	6.64	4.60	3.78	3.32	2.80	1.00	

Note: For a more complete table, see Appendix B, Table B.3.

the critical values of F decrease as the $df_{between}$ value increases for any given df_{within}, except for the special cases of $df_{within} = 1$ or 2. For $df_{within} = 1$, a substantial increase in the F value is required to reach the .05 and .01 levels as the $df_{between}$ value increases from 1 to infinity. For $df_{within} = 2$, only a very small increase in the F values is required to reach the .05 and .01 levels as the $df_{between}$ values increase from 1 to infinity. In practice, however, there are very few studies with large $df_{between}$ and only 1 or 2 df_{within}.

BOX 14.3 Using *t* to Boost Power

The *F* tests we have looked at so far are all omnibus tests, and we cannot take the square root of an omnibus *F* and get *t*. But, as noted earlier, taking the square root of a focused *F* (i.e., *F* with numerator $df = 1$) gives us *t*. An interesting characteristic of *F* distributions is that the *p* values, although naturally one-tailed, translate into two-tailed *p* values in *t* curves. Suppose you have a focused *F* and find

$p = .06$ in the predicted direction. If you plan to report *t*, you may have the option of reporting $p = .03$ one-tailed (because you predicted the direction) or $p = .06$ two-tailed (if you choose a more conservative *p*), but you do not have this option with *F*. There is, of course, not much difference between $p = .06$ and $p = .03$, except that they fall on either side of the coveted $p = .05$.

To look up our *F* of 11.50 in Table 14.4, we put a finger on the intersection of $df_{between} = 3$ and $df_{within} = 8$. The two values are 4.07 (the *F* value required for significance at $p = .05$) and 7.59 (the *F* value required for significance at $p = .01$). Because our obtained *F* is larger than 7.59, we know that the corresponding *p* must be less than .01. As indicated by Table B.3 on pp. 329–333, the *p* is approximately .003. Performing similar calculations on Results B in Table 14.1, we find *F* to be 1.28 (again with 3 and 8 degrees of freedom). Looking up this value in Table B.3, we find it to be too small to be significant at even the .20 level. The *p* is approximately .35.

What do these approximate *p* values tell us? The *p* value of .003 for Results A implies that, with numerator $df = 3$ and denominator $df = 8$, we would obtain an *F* of 11.50 or larger only 3 in 1,000 times if we repeatedly conducted this study under the same conditions and if there really were no overall differences between the four groups (i.e., if the null hypothesis were true). The *p* value of .35 for Results B implies that, with numerator $df = 3$ and denominator $df = 8$, we would obtain an *F* of 1.28 once every 3 times if we conducted the study under these conditions over and over, and if the null hypothesis were true. In reporting the *p* value, there is no need to state that it is one-tailed, because this fact is implicit in *F* (see also Box 14.3).

 ## How Can I Test for Simple Effects After an Omnibus F?

For the basic data that were previously shown in Table 14.2, knowing that the four groups differ significantly does not tell us whether milk helps in and of itself and whether vitamins help in and of themselves. To address these questions, we need to compare (a) the results in Group 2 with the results in Group 1 (the zero control) and (b) the results in Group 3 with the zero control. These comparisons are called **tests of simple effects**, and an easy way to do them is by *t* tests. Using the formula for comparing independent means given in Chapter 13, we continue to define S^2 as the pooled value (as described in Chapter 13), but we now find this value simply from our ANOVA because it is the MS_{within} denominator of our *F* ratio.

To illustrate the test of simple effects using the results in Table 14.2, we substitute the values of Groups 1 and 3 in the general formula for the independent *t* test:

$$t = \frac{M_3 - M_1}{\sqrt{\left(\dfrac{1}{n_3} + \dfrac{1}{n_1}\right)S^2}} = \frac{15 - 10}{\sqrt{\left(\dfrac{1}{3} + \dfrac{1}{3}\right)4}} = 3.06,$$

where M_3 is the mean of Group 3; M_1 is the mean of Group 1; n_3 and n_1 are the sample sizes of these groups; and S^2 is the value of the within-conditions *MS* that was previously shown in Table 14.3. However, in testing this *t* for statistical significance, we base our *df* not on $n_3 + n_1 - 2$ (as we did previously), but on *df* equal to the within-conditions *SS* (i.e., 8 *df*), because we are using a pooled estimate of S^2. Referring to Table B.2 (see pp. 327–328), we find the significance of $t = 3.06$ to be less than $p = .01$ but more than $p = .005$ one-tailed (succinctly stated as $.005 < p_{\text{one-tailed}} < .01$). More precisely, the one-tailed p is .008, and therefore the two-tailed p is .016.

Had we planned from the beginning to compute a specific t test, we could do so whether our overall F is statistically significant or not. We do not have to engage in a kind of "Simon says" game in which we seek "permission" from the p value associated with an omnibus test before we examine the effect of interest. However, if we are going to explore for large differences that we did not specifically predict, our t test results will be much more interpretable if our overall F is significant. The reason is that if we use a lot of t tests to go on a fishing expedition for significant differences, some of them will turn out to be significant by chance. One procedure that researchers sometimes use to try to avoid an excess of findings of significant t values when there are lots of possible t tests, or the t tests were unplanned, is to work with a more conservative level of significance, such as .01 instead of .05, or an even more conservative .005 or .001 (all listed in Table B.2).

However, we recommend not placing all your emphasis on the significance level. Instead, we recommend also paying attention to the effect size and its corresponding confidence interval. To calculate the effect size correlation from our t, we use the same formula as before, but we define the degrees of freedom from the groups being compared, that is,

$$r_{\text{effect size}} = \sqrt{\frac{t^2}{t^2 + df}} = \sqrt{\frac{(3.06)^2}{(3.06)^2 + 4}} = .84,$$

where df is based on the fact that there were 3 subjects in Group 3 and 3 subjects in Group 1, and therefore $df = n_3 + n_1 - 2 = 4$. The confidence interval of this effect size is computed as described in Chapter 13.

How Is Variability Apportioned in a Two-Way ANOVA?

R. A. Fisher (Box 14.1) noticed that it is sometimes possible to rearrange a one-way design to form a two-way design of much greater power to reject certain null hypotheses. We turn now to an analysis of the simplest two-way design, one in which there are two levels of each factor (i.e., a 2 × 2 factorial). An example is essential, and we study again the hypothetical effects of nutrition on academic performance. However, we will slightly change the question we asked earlier about the differences among our four nutritional conditions. Instead we ask the following questions:

1. What is the effect on academic performance of the intake of daily milk?
2. What is the effect on academic performance of the intake of daily vitamins?
3. What is the effect on academic performance of both milk and vitamins (i.e., the hot lunch includes both milk and vitamins)?
4. Is the effect of vitamins different when milk is also given from when milk is not given?
5. Is the effect of milk different when vitamins are also given from when vitamins are not given?

We can answer all these questions by using a two-way design of the kind shown in Table 14.5. Notice that this table uses the same scores as those previously shown in Table 14.2, which should give you further insight into the two-way factorial by comparing its summary ANOVA with the one-way ANOVA computed previously. Table 14.6 shows the group means of the sets of scores in Table 14.5. Table 14.6 also illustrates how this 2 × 2 design allows us to answer more questions than the omnibus ANOVA on the 1 × 4 design. For example, we can learn whether the effect of one of our factors is much the same for each of the two or more conditions of the other factor. As noted before, another name for the difference between group means is **simple effects**. In this example, a comparison of the differences between the simple effects tells us that there is a two-unit effect

Table 14.5 Raw Scores of a Two-Way Design

Vitamin treatment	Milk treatment		Row means
	Present	Absent	
Present	17, 19, 21	13, 15, 17	17
Absent	10, 12, 14	8, 10, 12	11
Column means	15.5	12.5	14

(12 − 10 = 2) of milk when no vitamins are given, and that there is a four-unit effect (19 − 15 = 4) of milk when vitamins are given. Similarly, there is a five-unit effect (15 − 10 = 5) of vitamins when no milk is given and a seven-unit effect (19 − 12 = 7) of vitamins when milk is given.

Another characteristic of factorial designs is that the study participants serve double duty, increasing the power $(1 - \beta)$ to reject certain null hypotheses regarding overall effects if the null hypotheses are false. That is, more of the participants available for the study are able to contribute to the major comparisons (milk vs. no milk; vitamins vs. no vitamins). In this case, half of all the participants of the experiment are in the milk conditions instead of the quarter of all participants that would be in the milk condition in a one-way design. Thus, half the participants can be compared to the remaining half, who received no milk, so that all the participants of the experiment shed light on the question of the effect of drinking milk. The overall effect (**main effect**) of milk is assessed by a comparison of the milk and no-milk column means (15.5 and 12.5, respectively). At the same time that all of the participants provide information on the milk comparison, they also provide information on the effect of vitamins. The main effect of vitamins is assessed by a comparison of the vitamin and no-vitamin marginal values in the rows (means of 17 and 11, respectively).

As described next, factorial designs also give us information about **interaction effects** (i.e., assuming they are really of interest to us). They represent the "leftover" combination of the independent variables after the removal of the main effects, and because they are leftover effects, they are called **residuals**. In the 2 × 2 example that we have been discussing, the interaction is designated as "rows × columns" (stated as "rows by columns") or "vitamins × milk" (stated as "vitamins by milk") to describe this combination. Once you understand these ideas, you will have a better sense of when you have actually hypothesized an interaction (in the statistical sense of ANOVA) and when all you are really interested in is the pattern of the group means, which we turn to later in this chapter.

Table 14.6 Means and Effects of Results in Table 14.5

Vitamin treatment	Milk treatment		Row means	Row effects
	Present	Absent		
Present	19	15	17	+3.0
Absent	12	10	11	−3.0
Column means	15.5	12.5	14 (grand mean)	
Column effects	+1.5	−1.5		

How Do I Interpret Main and Interaction Effects?

To help explain further what main and interaction effects can tell us in a factorial ANOVA, it is useful to begin by examining how the analysis of variance divides up the variance of all the observations into a number of separate sources of variance. We think of the group means (as well as the individual scores) as comprising a number of separate statistical components. In a two-way ANOVA (such as the 2 × 2 design in Tables 14.5 and 14.6), the group means (and individual measurements) can be broken into (a) the grand mean, (b) the row effects, (c) the column effects, (d) the interaction effects, and (e) error. We will start by examining how the first four components (the grand mean, the row effect, the column effect, and the interaction effect) are conceptualized in terms of an **additive model** (i.e., a model in which the components sum to the group means).

As noted previously, the *grand mean* (M_G) is the mean of all N scores, and so $M_G = 14$ in this example. As shown in Table 14.6, the **row effect** for each row is the mean of that row (M_r) minus the grand mean:

$$\text{Row effect} = M_r - M_G.$$

Thus, the row effects are computed as $17 - 14 = +3.0$ for vitamins present and $11 - 14 = -3.0$ for vitamins absent. The **column effect** of each column is the mean of that column (M_c) minus the grand mean:

$$\text{Column effect} = M_c - M_G,$$

which gives us $15.5 - 14 = +1.5$ for milk present and $12.5 - 14 = -1.5$ for milk absent. Each set of effects sums to zero when totaled over all conditions, a result that is characteristic of all row, column, and interaction effects.

Not visible in Table 14.6 are the interaction effects (the residuals, or leftover effects). These effects are what remain after the grand mean, row effect, and column effect are subtracted from the group mean. In other words,

$$\text{Interaction effect} = \text{Group mean} - \text{Grand mean} - \text{Row effect} - \text{Column effect},$$

so for these data, the interaction effects for the vitamins-plus-milk group (VM), the vitamins-only group (V), the milk-only group (M), and the zero control (O) are computed as shown in Table 14.7. What can we learn about the results of our experiment by studying this table? The grand mean tells us the general level of our measurements and is usually not of great intrinsic interest. The +3 and −3 row effects indicate that the groups receiving vitamins (VM and V) did better than those not receiving vitamins (M and O). The +1.5 and −1.5 column effects indicate that the groups receiving milk (VM and M) did better than those not receiving milk (V and O). The column of +0.5 and −0.5 interaction effects indicate that the group receiving *both* vitamins and milk (VM) and the group

Table 14.7 Interaction Effects Revealed When Group Means Are Decomposed

	Group mean	−	Grand mean	−	Row effect	−	Column effect	=	Interaction
VM	19	−	14	−	3.0	−	1.5	=	0.5
V	15	−	14	−	3.0	−	(−1.5)	=	(−0.5)
M	12	−	14	−	(−3.0)	−	1.5	=	(−0.5)
O	10	−	14	−	(−3.0)	−	(−1.5)	=	0.5
Sum	56	−	56	−	0.0	−	0.0	=	0.0

BOX 14.4 The Additive Model

We said that the idea of ANOVA is based on an additive model; that is, components sum to the row, column, and interaction effects with one another. The statistical advantage is that it makes *F* tests possible.

The conceptual advantage of the additive structure is that it provides a baseline that allows you to compare group means. You can see this more clearly when you total all four conditions of the two-way table.

	Group mean	=	Grand mean	+	Row effect	+	Column effect	+	Interaction effect
VM	19	=	14	+	3.0	+	1.5	+	0.5
V	15	=	14	+	3.0	+	(−1.5)	+	(−0.5)
M	12	=	14	+	(−3.0)	+	1.5	+	(−0.5)
O	10	=	14	+	(−3.0)	+	(−1.5)	+	0.5
Sum	56	=	56	+	0.0	+	0.0	+	0.0

receiving *neither* vitamins nor milk (O) did better than the groups receiving *either* vitamins (V) *or* milk (M). Though it is slightly better from the viewpoint of the interaction effect alone to receive neither treatment, this statistical advantage in the interaction effect (0.5) is more than offset by the statistical disadvantage in the row effect (−3.0) and the column effect (−1.5) of receiving neither treatment. (See also Box 14.4.)

How Do I Compute a Two-Way ANOVA and Set Up a Summary Table?

Earlier, when we analyzed the results of the present study as a one-way ANOVA, we computed the total sum of squares as

$$\text{Total } SS = \Sigma(X - M_G)^2 = 170,$$

where X is each observation or measurement, and M_G is the mean of all the N scores. We computed the within-conditions SS as

$$\text{Within } SS = \Sigma(X - M_k)^2 = 32,$$

where M_k is the mean of the group or condition to which each observation or measurement (X) belongs. For our two-way ANOVA, we use the same (above) formulas, but we need to compute the sums of the squares of the rows, the columns, and the interaction.

The sum of squares of the rows is defined as

$$\text{Row } SS = \Sigma[nc(M_r - M_G)^2],$$

where n is the number of observations in each condition; c is the number of columns contributing to the computation of M_r (the mean of the rth row); and M_G is again the grand mean. The sum of squares of the columns is defined as

$$\text{Column } SS = \Sigma[nr(M_c - M_G)^2],$$

where n is the number of observations in each condition; r is the number of rows contributing to the computation of M_c (the mean of the cth column); and M_G is the grand mean. And finally, the interaction sum of squares is defined as

$$\text{Interaction } SS = \text{Total } SS - (\text{Row } SS + \text{Column } SS + \text{Within } SS).$$

Table 14.8   Two-Way ANOVA on Results in Table 14.5

Source	SS	df	MS	F	p	$r_{effect\ size}$
Vitamins (rows)	108	1	108	27.0	8.3^{-4}	.88
Milk (columns)	27	1	27	6.75	.03	.68
Interaction	3	1	3	.75	.41	.29
Within error	32	8	4			

At the same time that we compute the formulas above, we can take apart the individual scores to help us understand better the various terms of the analysis of variance. The ANOVA summary is presented in Table 14.8, and Table 14.9 shows at an individual level where the *SS* values came from. The only new values in Table 14.8 are those for *error*, which for each subject is computed as the person's raw score minus the group mean. The term *error*, as used in this context, means that the size of the deviations of raw scores from their group mean reflects how "poorly" we have predicted scores from a knowledge of group or condition membership. In other words, the score reflects a large error if it falls far from the mean of its group and a small error if it falls close to the mean of its group. We can now write **error** as

$$Error = Score - Group\ mean.$$

Thus, for the VM subject in Table 14.5 who scored 17, Table 14.9 shows that we subtract 19 (the mean of this group) to get the error score of −2. Rearranging the relationship above, we have

$$Score = Group\ mean + Error,$$

and because

$$Group\ mean = Grand\ mean + Row\ effect + Column\ effect + Interaction\ effect,$$

it follows that

$$Score = Grand\ mean + Row\ effect + Column\ effect + Interaction\ effect + Error,$$

as is also indicated by the column headings in Table 14.9.

Table 14.9   Effects for Computing ANOVA on Results in Table 14.5

Group	Score	=	Grand mean	+	Row effect	+	Column effect	+	Interaction effect	+	Error
VM	17	=	14	+	3.0	+	1.5	+	0.5	+	(−2)
VM	19	=	14	+	3.0	+	1.5	+	0.5	+	0
VM	21	=	14	+	3.0	+	1.5	+	0.5	+	2
V	13	=	14	+	3.0	+	(−1.5)	+	(−0.5)	+	(−2)
V	15	=	14	+	3.0	+	(−1.5)	+	(−0.5)	+	0
V	17	=	14	+	3.0	+	(−1.5)	+	(−0.5)	+	2
M	10	=	14	+	(−3.0)	+	1.5	+	(−0.5)	+	(−2)
M	12	=	14	+	(−3.0)	+	1.5	+	(−0.5)	+	0
M	14	=	14	+	(−3.0)	+	1.5	+	(−0.5)	+	2
O	8	=	14	+	(−3.0)	+	(−1.5)	+	0.5	+	(−2)
O	10	=	14	+	(−3.0)	+	(−1.5)	+	0.5	+	0
O	12	=	14	+	(−3.0)	+	(−1.5)	+	0.5	+	2
ΣX	168	=	168	+	0	+	0	+	0	+	0
ΣX^2	2,522	=	2,352	+	108	+	27	+	3	+	32

Below each column in Table 14.9 are shown the sums of the listed values (ΣX) and the sums of squares of the listed values (ΣX^2), and we can now see where the SS values for Vitamins (rows), Milk (columns), Interaction, and Within error in Table 14.8 came from. Summing all of the SS values in Table 14.8 gives $108 + 27 + 3 + 32 = 170$, the total SS, previously defined as the sum of the squared deviations between every single score and the grand mean, that is, $(17 - 14)^2 + (19 - 14)^2 + \ldots + (12 - 14)^2 = 170$. In Table 14.9, subtracting the sum of the squared grand means (shown as 2,352) from the sum of the squared scores (shown as 2,522) gives us the same value (i.e., total $SS = 2{,}522 - 2{,}352 = 170$). Looking again at Table 14.3 reminds us that, in the one-way ANOVA, the total SS is allocated to two sources of variance: a between-conditions source and a within-conditions source. In the move from a one-way to a two-way ANOVA, the within-conditions source of variance (i.e., the source attributable to error) remains unchanged (i.e., "Within error" or "Within conditions" $SS = 32$ in Tables 14.3, 14.8, and 14.9). However, the between-conditions source of variance in the one-way ANOVA (shown in Table 14.3 as 138) is, in the two-way table (Table 14.8), now broken down into three components: a row effect SS, a column effect SS, and an interaction effect SS.

Let us also compute these values using our formulas and the raw scores in Table 14.5. First, we obtain the row effect sum of squares from

$$\text{Row } SS = \Sigma[nc(M_r - M_G)^2]$$
$$= [(3)(2)(17 - 14)^2] + [(3)(2)(11 - 14)^2]$$
$$= 108,$$

where Table 14.5 shows $n = 3$ scores in each group, $c = 2$ columns, row means (M_r) of 17 and 11, and a grand mean (M_G) of 14. The resulting value is, of course, the same value shown in Table 14.8 and in the bottom row of Table 14.9.

Next, we obtain the column effect sum of squares from

$$\text{Column } SS = \Sigma[nr(M_c - M_G)^2]$$
$$= [(3)(2)(15.5 - 14)^2] + [(3)(2)(12.5 - 14)^2]$$
$$= 27,$$

where the only new values from Table 14.5 are $r = 2$ rows and the column means (M_c) of 15.5 and 12.5. Again, the resulting value is the same as that in Table 14.8 and in the bottom row of Table 14.9.

Finally, we obtain the sum of squares of the interaction from

$$\text{Interaction } SS = \text{Total } SS - (\text{Row } SS + \text{Column } SS + \text{Within } SS),$$

which gives us

$$\text{Interaction } SS = 170 - (108 + 27 + 32) = 3,$$

and, as anticipated, it is the value shown in Table 14.8 and in the bottom row of Table 14.9.

The logic of computing the degrees of freedom of the two-way ANOVA is the same as that in the one-way analysis, but we must apportion the between-conditions df to the row main effect, the column main effect, and the interaction. The definition of the degrees of freedom for rows in Table 14.8 is

$$df_{\text{rows}} = r - 1,$$

where r is the number of rows (thus, $df_{\text{rows}} = 2 - 1 = 1$). The definition of the degrees of freedom for columns is

$$df_{\text{columns}} = c - 1,$$

where c is the number of columns (thus, $df_{columns} = 2 - 1 = 1$). The definition of the degrees of freedom for the interaction is

$$df_{interaction} = (r - 1)(c - 1),$$

which gives us $df_{interaction} = (2 - 1)(2 - 1) = 1$.

The degrees of freedom for the "Within error" are the same as those in Table 14.3, defined as

$$df_{within} = N - k,$$

where N is the total number of observations or measurements, and k is the number of groups or conditions (thus, $df_{within} = 12 - 4 = 8$). In other words, this is the number of units in each group or condition minus 1 totaled over all groups, or $df_{within} = (3 - 1) + (3 - 1) + (3 - 1) + (3 - 1) = 8$. As a check on the degrees of freedom, we compute the df of the total SS as $df_{total} = N - 1$ and find this result ($df_{total} = 12 - 1 = 11$) to be identical to the sum of the df in Table 14.8 (i.e., $1 + 1 + 1 + 8 = 11$).

As before, we obtain the mean square (MS) values in Table 14.8 by dividing the sums of squares by the corresponding df. That is, we divide 108 by 1 to get 108, and we divide 32 by 8 to get 4 (the amount of the total variation, measured in SS, attributable to each df). We compute the F ratios by dividing the mean squares for rows, columns, and interaction (the signals) by the mean square within conditions (the noise). Thus, we divide 108 by 4 to get 27.0, and we divide 27 by 4 to get 6.75, and we divide 3 by 4 to get 0.75.

Because F ratios with 1 df in the numerator are focused tests, we can indicate one-degree-of-freedom effect sizes. Since our F is a comparison of two groups, and in two-group comparisons we know that $\sqrt{F} = t$, we obtain the effect size of each F by the formula given at the beginning of this chapter:

$$r_{effect\ size} = \sqrt{\frac{F}{F + df_{within}}}.$$

We interpret these results as we would any effect size correlation, including using the confidence interval.

Table 14.8 shows the values of p. The F of 6.75 for the effect of milk could have occurred by chance about 3 times in 100, and the F of 27.0 for the effect of vitamins could have occurred by chance far less often ($p = 8.3^{-4}$, or 8.3 times in 10,000, or 83 times in 100,000), if the null were true. By contrast, the F for the interaction was so small ($F < 1$) that it could easily have occurred by chance. However, if the interaction were of interest, we would analyze it as before (as a comparison between the residuals of the diagonal cells). The effect sizes tell us that both milk and vitamins have a beneficial effect, and that more of the effect is attributable to vitamins than to milk. We can also calculate t tests of simple effects by using the procedure described previously.

What Are Contrasts, and How Do I Compute Them on More Than Two Groups?

Not too long ago, more than 500 active psychological researchers were asked about the proper way to think about interaction effects in analysis of variance. About a third of them answered incorrectly, mistaking the pattern of the group means for the interaction residuals (Zuckerman, Hodgins, Zuckerman, & Rosenthal, 1993). However, you know that group means are made up of the grand mean, the row effect, the column effect, and the interaction (Box 14.4). The interaction effects are what are left over after the removal of those other effects from the group means. The confusion may come from the common usage of *interaction* to imply a "combination of things," which is true of statistical interactions. But a statistical interaction in analysis of variance also has a specialized meaning, as you learned in the preceding discussion. If you are not interested in the residuals but are more interested in a predicted pattern of the group means in designs with more than two conditions,

Table 14.10	Summary ANOVA (Omnibus F) for Results A and B in Table 14.1				
Results A:					
Source	SS	df	MS	F	p
Between conditions	138	3	46	11.50	.003
Within conditions	32	8	4		
Results B:					
Source	SS	df	MS	F	p
Between conditions	138	3	46	1.28	.35
Within conditions	288	8	36		

the most powerful and precise way to assess such a prediction is by means of a **contrast**, meaning a statistical procedure for asking focused questions of data.

To illustrate, we refer to the hypothetical data (A and B) that we presented earlier in this chapter (Table 14.1). The overall analysis of variance of each set (A and B) is summarized in Table 14.10. You now know that the reason the omnibus F is so much larger for Results A than for Results B is that the within-conditions variability is so much smaller in Results A than in B. However, saying there was "no difference" between the four groups in Results B would make no sense intuitively, because in Table 14.1 we clearly see a gradual increment in the scores from Group 1 to Group 4.

Suppose we had hypothesized a linear pattern of regularly increasing means from Group 1 to Group 4. Because we would get the same omnibus F no matter how the groups were arranged, the omnibus F would be a poor choice to test our hypothesis. A better choice would be to compute a contrast t or F that is specifically addressed to the predicted linear trend. To do so, we state our prediction in simple integers, called **lambda weights** (λ), also called **contrast weights**. The only stipulation is that the lambdas (i.e., the contrast weights) must sum to zero (i.e., $\Sigma\lambda = 0$). Because we hypothesized an increasing linear trend in the four groups, we might choose λs of $-3, -1, +1, +3$ to represent our prediction. Next, we compare these lambda weights with the obtained scores by using the following formula:

$$t_{\text{contrast}} = \frac{\Sigma M\lambda}{\sqrt{MS_{\text{within}}\left(\Sigma \dfrac{\lambda^2}{n}\right)}},$$

where M in the numerator refers to a specific condition mean; MS_{within} in the denominator refers to the within-conditions mean square in Table 14.10; n is the number of observations in a given condition; and λ refers to the contrast weight required by our prediction for that condition.

Using this formula with Results A, we find

$$t_{\text{contrast}} = \frac{(10)(-3) + (12)(-1) + (15)(+1) + (19)(+3)}{\sqrt{4\left[\dfrac{(-3)^2}{3} + \dfrac{(-1)^2}{3} + \dfrac{(+1)^2}{3} + \dfrac{(+3)^2}{3}\right]}}$$

$$= \frac{30}{\sqrt{(4)(6.667)}} = 5.809,$$

which, with 8 df (the degrees of freedom for MS_{within}, or $N - k$), has an associated $p = .0002$ one-tailed (or in scientific notation, $p = 2.0^{-4}$ one-tailed). For Results B, applying this same formula yields

$$t_{contrast} = \frac{(10)(-3) + (12)(-1) + (15)(+1) + (19)(+3)}{\sqrt{36\left[\dfrac{(-3)^2}{3} + \dfrac{(-1)^2}{3} + \dfrac{(+1)^2}{3} + \dfrac{(+3)^2}{3}\right]}}$$

$$= \frac{30}{\sqrt{(36)(6.667)}} = 1.936,$$

which, with 8 df, has an associated $p = .044$ one-tailed. The reason that we prefer these results to those in Table 14.10 is that the $t_{contrast}$ addresses the hypothesized linear trend, whereas the F tests in Table 14.10 are not focused on the predicted trend.

You will recall that squaring t always gives F. Thus, because squaring these two contrast t values produces contrast F values, we find that $F_{contrast} = (5.809)^2 = 33.74$ for Results A and that $F_{contrast} = (1.936)^2 = 3.75$ for Results B. To obtain the p levels of these F values, we consult Table B.3 with numerator $= 1$ and denominator $= 8$ degrees of freedom. Suppose we want to report a summary ANOVA table that shows the contrast F carved out of the between-conditions sum of squares. There are several ways to obtain the information we need. One option is to compute the contrast mean square ($MS_{contrast}$) from

$$MS_{contrast} = \frac{nL^2}{\Sigma\lambda^2},$$

where

$$L = M_1\lambda_1 + M_2\lambda_2 + M_3\lambda_3 + M_4\lambda_4.$$

To illustrate with Results B, we solve for L as follows:

$$L = (10)(-3) + (12)(-1) + (15)(+1) + (19)(+3) = 30$$

and then substitute in the previous equation to find

$$MS_{contrast} = \frac{nL^2}{\Sigma\lambda^2} = \frac{3 \times (30)^2}{(-3)^2 + (-1)^2 + (+1)^2 + (+3)^2} = \frac{2,700}{20} = 135.$$

We know that $MS = SS/df$, and because $df = 1$ for all contrasts, $MS_{contrast} = SS_{contrast}$.

Table 14.11 shows the linear contrast sum of squares that we carved out of the between-conditions sum of squares. The contrast F is $MS_{contrast}/MS_{within} = 135/36 = 3.75$, the same result as squaring the contrast t. New to this table is the noncontrast sum of squares (3), which is simply the remainder after subtraction of the contrast sum of squares (135) from the between-conditions sum of squares (138). The $F_{noncontrast}$ of .04 came from dividing the mean square noncontrast (1.5) by the mean square within (36).

Table 14.11   Linear Contrast Carved Out of ANOVA on Results B in Table 14.10

Source	SS	df	MS	F	p
Between conditions	138	3	46	1.28	.35
Contrast	135	1	135	3.75	.089
Noncontrast	3	2	1.5	.04	
Within conditions	288	8	36		

What Do $r_{\text{effect size}}$, r_{alerting}, and r_{contrast} Tell Me?

In Chapter 13, we stated that when comparing two groups by an independent-sample t, we can use Cohen's d or the point-biserial r between the subjects' group membership (dummy-coded 0 or 1) and their scores on the dependent measure. When contrasts are computed on three or more groups or conditions, neither Cohen's d nor the point-biserial r is relevant, and $r_{\text{effect size}}$ is now defined as the correlation between each subject's score (Y) on the dependent variable and the contrast weight (λ) assigned to the condition to which the subject belongs. This index is also denoted as $r_{Y\lambda}$, and it can be computed from the results in Table 14.11 by

$$r_{\text{effect size}} = r_{Y\lambda} = \sqrt{\frac{F_{\text{contrast}}}{F_{\text{contrast}} + F_{\text{noncontrast}}\left(df_{\text{noncontrast}}\right) + df_{\text{within}}}},$$

with terms defined in that table (R. Rosenthal et al., 2000). Substituting in this equation, we find

$$r_{\text{effect size}} = \sqrt{\frac{3.75}{3.75 + .04(2) + 8}} = \sqrt{\frac{3.75}{11.83}} = .563.$$

Another informative r-type effect size when contrasts are computed on three or more groups is the **alerting r** (or r_{alerting}), which is the correlation between the condition means (M) and their respective contrast (λ) weights, also denoted as $r_{M\lambda}$. It takes its name from the idea that it alerts us to trends of possible interest and, when squared, reveals the proportion of the sum of squares between conditions that can be accounted for by the contrast weights. It is easy to compute the alerting r if you have a calculator that gives you correlations when you punch in the raw scores and tap the correlation key. Table 14.12, which shows the alerting r calculated in the tabular format of Chapter 11, is a reminder that this r is simply a product-moment correlation. That is,

$$r_{M\lambda} = \frac{\Sigma z_1 z_2}{N} = \frac{3.956}{4} = .989.$$

Squaring the alerting r gives us $(.989)^2 = .978$, which indicates the proportion of the between-conditions sum of squares that is accounted for by our linear contrast (see also Box 14.5).

Table 14.12 Product-Moment r Between Group Means and Linear Contrast Weights for Results B in Table 14.1

Groups	Group means		λ weights		Product of z_1 and z_2 scores
	Mean	z_1 score	Lambda	z_2 score	
1 (Zero)	10	−1.1795	−3	−1.3416	1.582
2 (Milk)	12	−0.5898	−1	−0.4472	.264
3 (Vitamins)	15	+0.2949	+1	+0.4472	.132
4 (Hot lunch)	19	+1.4744	+3	+1.3416	1.978
Sum (Σ)	56	0	0	0	3.956
Mean (M)	14	0	0	0	.989
SD (σ)	3.3912	1.0	2.2361	1.0	

BOX 14.5 Computing Contrasts From Other Researchers' Omnibus *F* Tests

Suppose you read a research article about an experiment with more than two groups, and all that is reported is group means and an overall *F* with numerator *df* > 1 (an omnibus *F*, as described in Box 14.2). A linear relationship was predicted but never precisely tested. Given the information in that article, you can compute a contrast *F* in four easy steps and decide for yourself whether the researcher's results were consistent with a linear prediction. Assume that (as in Results B in Table 14.1 and Table 14.10) the reported group means are 10, 12, 15, 19 and the omnibus *F* is 1.28. First, you need to create a set of contrast (λ) weights to represent

the predicted linear trend, and let's say you choose weights of $-3, -1, +1, +3$. Second, you will correlate these weights with their respective group means and find an alerting *r* of .989. Third, you will multiply the omnibus *F* by its numerator *df* to find the maximum possible value of any contrast *F* carved out of the $SS_{between}$, which in this case is $F(3,8) = 1.28 \times 3 = 3.84$. The final step is to multiply the squared alerting *r* of $(.989)^2$ times the maximum-possible-contrast *F* of 3.84 to produce the linear contrast *F*. The answer is $F_{contrast} = (.989)^2 \times 3.84 = 3.75$, the same result as was shown in Table 14.11.

When the alerting *r* approaches 1.0, we can use a familiar formula to estimate $r_{effect\ size}$ from *F*:

$$r = \sqrt{\frac{F}{F + df_{within}}},$$

which we refer to more generally as the **contrast *r*** (or $r_{contrast}$) rather than (as in our discussion of two-group comparisons) the effect size *r*. The contrast *r* is understood as a *partial* correlation, in this case, the correlation between subjects' (*Y*) scores on the dependent measure and the contrast weights (λ values) associated with their groups after the elimination of all between-group sources of variability other than the contrast in question (R. Rosenthal et al., 2000). This *r*-type index can also be denoted as $r_{Y\lambda \cdot NC}$, where NC means that all the *noncontrast variation* has been removed (or partialed out). Because in two-group designs there is no noncontrast variation to be eliminated, $r_{contrast} = r_{effect\ size}$ in all two-group comparisons. In the case of Results B, where $r_{alerting} = .989$, and $r^2_{alerting} = .978$, we find

$$r_{contrast} = r_{Y\lambda \cdot NC} = \sqrt{\frac{F_{contrast}}{F_{contrast} + df_{within}}} = \sqrt{\frac{3.75}{3.75 + 8}} = .565.$$

Not surprisingly, given that $r^2_{alerting}$ was close to 1.0 (i.e., we found $r_{M\lambda}$ was .989, and squared it gave us $r^2_{alerting} = .978$), the contrast correlation is nearly identical to the value of $r_{effect\ size}$ that we found to be .563. Usually, $r_{contrast}$ is larger than $r_{effect\ size}$, and the difference is sometimes quite substantial. The value of $r_{alerting}$ tends to be larger than $r_{effect\ size}$ and $r_{contrast}$, but it need not be so. Reporting the entire family of *r*-type effect size indices when working with more than two groups captures the different meanings of the contrast in a way that cannot be exactly communicated by any single effect size measurement (see also Rosnow, Rosenthal, & Rubin, 2000).

How Are Contrasts on Multiple Repeated Measures Computed?

So far in our discussion of statistical tests, whether those tests involved comparing two means (*t* tests) or more than two groups (*F* tests), each of the participants, or other units, contributed only a single score, measurement, or observation. It often happens that we *must* measure participants more

Table 14.13	Cognitive Performance Measured on Four Occasions				
	Occasion of measurement				
Student	First	Second	Third	Fourth	Mean
1	1	3	7	5	4.0
2	0	6	2	4	3.0
3	2	4	6	8	5.0
Mean	1.00	4.33	5.00	5.67	4.0

than once to address the question of interest, described as *intrinsically repeated-measures research* (R. Rosenthal et al., 2000). Suppose we want to learn the degree to which students' performance on a cognitive task improves over time (i.e., over repeated occasions of measurement). There is no alternative to measuring the participants repeatedly (twice, or three times, or more, depending on the particular research question). We might predict, for example, that on a particular cognitive task, the students will improve by an equal amount each time they perform the task over four measurement occasions, say, 1 month apart. Table 14.13 shows the results of a hypothetical study of three students, and Table 14.14 shows the summary ANOVA.

As in any two-way ANOVA, Table 14.14 displays a row effect (between subjects in this example), a column effect (occasions in this example), and an interaction effect (an occasions × subjects interaction in this example). The mean square (*MS*) for subjects (4.00) tells us how far apart the three subjects' means are on average. The mean square for occasions (12.89) tells us how far apart the four occasions' means are on average. The occasions × subjects interaction mean square (3.56) tells us how different the subjects' effects are on different occasions or, equivalently, how different the occasions' effects are for different subjects; we think of these results as the heterogeneity of the patterns or profiles of four scores among the three subjects. Had all three subjects shown identical patterns over the four occasions of measurement, the interaction *MS* would have been zero. Figure 14.1 shows that the three patterns (or profiles) are not identical but do show similarities. Had they been identical, all three profiles would have been exactly parallel to one another over the four occasions of measurement. To illustrate, Figure 14.2 shows how the three profiles might have looked had there been no interaction at all.

Though the three profiles of Figure 14.1 are certainly different from one another, what they do have in common is that all three students' second, third, and fourth performance scores are higher than their first scores. This finding is consistent with our prediction that performance would improve with each successive measurement, but it is not quite the same as our prediction. We predicted that students would improve by an equal amount on each occasion of measurement. Using what we have learned about contrasts, we can create a contrast score for each student. This contrast score, or *L* score, tells us the degree to which the student behaved in accordance with our

Table 14.14	Analysis of Variance of Data of Table 14.13				
Source	SS	df	MS	$F_{(3,6)}$	p
Between subjects	8.00	2	4.00	—	
Within subjects	60.00	9			
Occasions	38.67	3	12.89	3.62	.08
Occasions × subjects	21.33	6	3.56		

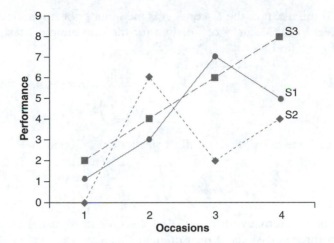

Figure 14.1   Profiles of three students' performance measured on four occasions.

prediction. The *L* score is simply the sum of the products of the contrast (λ) weights, multiplied by the student's actual performance, or

$$L = \Sigma Y\lambda = Y_1\lambda_1 + Y_2\lambda_2 + \ldots + Y_k\lambda_k.$$

We form the contrast (λ) weights for the occasions of measurement by writing down the value we predict and then subtracting the mean of the four predictions from each individual prediction to meet the requirement that, for any contrast, the sum of the λ weights must equal zero. Suppose our prediction was that, over four occasions, students' scores would go from 1 to 3 to 5 to 7. The mean of these four predicted values is 4, which we subtract from each of our four predicted values, obtaining λ weights of −3, −1, +1, +3. Then, for Student 1 (S1) the *L* score is

$$L = \Sigma Y\lambda = 1(-3) + 3(-1) + 7(+1) + 5(+3) = 16.$$

The analogous *L* scores for Students 2 and 3 are 8 and 20, respectively.

We can now compute a one-sample *t* test on these three *L* scores by using the following formula:

$$t_{(df)} = \frac{M_L}{\sqrt{\left(\dfrac{1}{N}\right)S_L^2}},$$

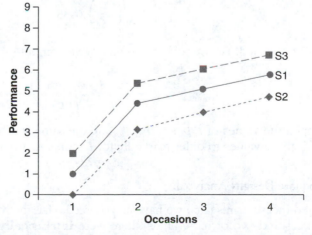

Figure 14.2   Profiles of three students' performance showing zero interaction.

where M_L is the mean of the L scores, N is the number of students, S_L^2 is the variance of the L scores, and df refers to the degrees of freedom for the one-sample t test, usually $N - 1$. For the data of Table 14.13, we find

$$t_{(2)} = \frac{14.67}{\sqrt{\left(\frac{1}{3}\right)37.33}} = 4.16$$

and $p = .027$ one-tailed. For our effect size index, we compute

$$r_{contrast} = \sqrt{\frac{t^2}{t^2 + df}} = \sqrt{\frac{(4.16)^2}{(4.16)^2 + 2}} = .95.$$

There is an alternative to the use of L scores in repeated-measures analyses as long as there are at least three occasions of measurement. We can use r values, the correlations of the repeated measures with their associated λ weights. For Student 1, given the following data:

Occasion	1	2	3	4
Score (Y)	1	3	7	5
λ	-3	-1	$+1$	$+3$

we find that the product-moment correlation of Student 1's scores (1, 3, 7, 5) and the associated λ weights ($-3, -1, +1, +3$) over the 4 occasions is $r = .80$. Analogous correlations for Students 2 and 3 are .40 and 1.00, respectively. We now compute a one-sample t test on these three r values as follows:

$$t_{(df)} = \frac{\bar{r}}{\sqrt{\left(\frac{1}{N}\right)S_r^2}},$$

where $\bar{r}$ is the mean of the r values, N is the number of students, S_r^2 is the variance of the r values, and df refers to the degrees of freedom for the one-sample t test, usually $N - 1$. For the data of Table 14.13, we find

$$t_{(2)} = \frac{.73}{\sqrt{\left(\frac{1}{3}\right).0933}} = 4.14$$

and $p = .027$ one-tailed. For our effect size index, we compute

$$r_{contrast} = \sqrt{\frac{t^2}{t^2 + df}} = \sqrt{\frac{(4.14)^2}{(4.14)^2 + 2}} = .95.$$

In this example, the values of t, p, and $r_{contrast}$ are the same for the L scores and the r values, but it is possible for these values to differ markedly for L scores versus r values.

How Are Latin Square Designs Analyzed?

In the repeated-measures research we have considered so far, the research question *required* that each student be measured two or more times (there were **intrinsically repeated measures**). In another use of repeated measures, it is *not required* in principle that a repeated-measures design be used.

| Table 14.15 | Four Conditions Administered to Each of Four Patients |

	Four conditions			
	1	2	3	4
Patients	None	Placebo	Old	New
Patient 1				
Patient 2				
Patient 3				
Patient 4				

Such a design is used to increase the efficiency, precision, and statistical power of the study by administering several treatments to each of the participants or other sampling units. We call this arrangement **nonintrinsically repeated measures** research (R. Rosenthal et al., 2000).

Suppose we are interested in a rare disorder and want to compare the measured effects of (a) a new medical treatment, (b) an old or standard medical treatment, (c) a placebo control, and (d) a no-treatment (zero) control condition. But we have available only four patients with the rare disorder. Although we could randomly assign one patient to each of those four conditions, we could learn little by using that approach. We would never know whether observed differences in outcomes were due to differences in the four conditions or instead to individual differences among the four patients. In other words, treatment conditions would be confounded with patients' individual differences.

Perhaps we could administer all four conditions to all four patients with the rare disorder, as outlined in Table 14.15. All four patients would begin by having no treatment (say, for 1 month), then have a month of placebo, then a month of the standard treatment, and finally a month of the new treatment. This kind of repeated-measures design would give us 16 observations, with 4 per treatment, instead of just 1 per treatment, but our results would still be confounded. However, this time the order of presentation (first vs. second vs. third vs. fourth) would be completely confounded with the treatment condition. We would never be able to disentangle the effects of being fourth-administered, for example, from the effects of the new medical treatment.

To separate order effects from condition effects, we can counterbalance the design by the use of the Latin square described in Chapter 7. Table 14.16 shows the Latin square rearrangement of the four conditions in Table 14.15. All four conditions (A, B, C, and D) are administered to each of the four patients, but the sequence is different for each patient. The sequences are arranged so that each condition occurs only once in each row (which we call the *Sequence* factor) and once in each column (which we call the *Order* factor). This arrangement allows us to uncover general differences among the four conditions, the four orders of presentation, and the four sequences or subjects (the patients). Sequences and subjects are confounded, but as we are rarely interested in either sequence or subject effects, this confounding poses no problem of any immediate concern.

| Table 14.16 | Latin Square Design for the Conditions of Table 14.15 |

	Order of administration			
	1	2	3	4
Sequence 1	A	B	C	D
Sequence 2	B	C	D	A
Sequence 3	C	D	A	B
Sequence 4	D	A	B	C

Table 14.17   Data Obtained for the Latin Square of Table 14.16

	Order of administration				
	1	2	3	4	Σ
Sequence 1	2	7	10	7	26
Sequence 2	4	8	10	5	27
Sequence 3	6	9	5	8	28
Sequence 4	9	4	8	10	31
Σ	21	28	33	30	112

Condition sums (each based on 4 scores)

A	B	C	D
16	27	34	35

Table 14.17 displays the hypothetical results of a study of the type we have been discussing, and Table 14.18 summarizes the analysis of variance. We will not describe the technical details of this analysis here, but they are available in our advanced text (Rosenthal & Rosnow, 2008). Here it is enough to note that there is a substantial F for both the order effect and the condition effect, but both are omnibus F tests. You know that omnibus tests are diffuse, and these tests tell us little of what we really want to know specifically about the condition effect or the order effect. The most efficient way to investigate treatment effects is to use the L scores method described in the preceding section. For each patient, we compute the appropriate L score. For example, if our prediction had been that a placebo would be a lot better than no treatment at all, and that the old treatment would be somewhat better than a placebo, and that the new treatment would be better than the old treatment, we might predict relative outcome scores of 2, 5, 6, and 7, respectively, for no treatment, placebo, old treatment, and new treatment. The mean of these predicted scores is 5, which we now subtract from each predicted score to give us contrast (λ) weights that sum to zero.

In this example, our contrast weights are -3, 0, $+1$, $+2$, respectively. Subject 1 (who is listed as Sequence 1 in Table 14.17) has an L score of 18, computed as

$$L = \Sigma Y\lambda = 2(-3) + 7(0) + 10(+1) + 7(+2) = 18.$$

Subjects 2, 3, and 4 have L scores of 13, 9, and 16, respectively. The t test examining our prediction yields

$$t_{(3)} = \frac{M_L}{\sqrt{\left(\dfrac{1}{N}\right)S_L^2}} = \frac{14}{\sqrt{\left(\dfrac{1}{4}\right)15.33}} = 7.15,$$

Table 14.18   Analysis of Variance of the Data of Table 14.17

Source	SS	df	MS	$F_{(3,6)}$	p
Sequences	3.50	3	1.17	—	
Orders	19.50	3	6.50	4.11	.066
(Sequences × orders)	(67.00)	(9)	(7.44)		
Conditions	57.50	3	19.17	12.13	5.9^{-3}
Residual (S × O)	9.50	6	1.58		

and $p = 2.8^{-3}$ one-tailed. For our effect size index, we compute

$$r_{\text{contrast}} = \sqrt{\frac{t^2}{t^2 + df}} = \sqrt{\frac{(7.15)^2}{(7.15)^2 + 3}} = .97,$$

a huge (and highly significant) effect size.

We could, of course, compute L scores for somewhat different predictions or hypotheses. For example, if our more simplified prediction had been that the two treatment conditions (old and new) would do better than the two control conditions (no treatment and placebo), we might have used contrast weights of $+1, +1, -1, -1$, respectively, for those four conditions. Had we examined that prediction, we would have found L scores of 8, 9, 2, 7 for Patients 1, 2, 3, 4, respectively, giving us $t_{(3)} = 4.18$, $p = .012$, and $r_{\text{contrast}} = .92$. Had we wanted to investigate order effects, we could have done so in analogous fashion. For example, had we hypothesized that patients would tend to improve over time, we might have predicted a linear trend indicated by contrast weights of $-3, -1, +1, +3$. Had we used these weights to investigate order effects, we would have found $t_{(3)} = 2.29$, $p = .053$, and $r_{\text{contrast}} = .80$. (We leave it to readers to verify that these values are correct!)

Summary of Ideas

1. The *F test* used in a between-conditions *analysis of variance (ANOVA)* is a ratio of the spread of mean scores around the grand mean (the signal) to the spread of scores within each condition (the noise) (also Box 14.1).

2. For the special case of the comparison of two groups, $F = t^2$, and in that particular case, we can calculate the effect size correlation for F as

$$r_{\text{effect size}} = \sqrt{\frac{F}{F + df_{\text{within}}}}.$$

   However, later in this chapter, we called this formula the *contrast r* when applied to focused tests on more than two groups, and in two-group comparisons $r_{\text{contrast}} = r_{\text{effect size}}$.

3. *F* tests with numerator $df = 1$ and all *t* tests are characterized as *focused statistical tests*, and effect sizes indexed in association with them are called *one-degree-of-freedom effects*. All *F* tests with numerator $df > 1$ are called *omnibus statistical tests*, and the effect sizes indexed in association with them are called *multiple-degree-of-freedom effects* (Box 14.2).

4. When computing *t* tests on *simple effects* after the omnibus *F*, we define S^2 in the *t* formula as the *MS* within (the pooled error term) in the ANOVA summary table.

5. When computing effect size *r* values on simple effects after computing the omnibus *F*, we define *df* in the $r_{\text{effect size}}$ formula by the size of the groups being compared ($df = n_1 + n_2 - 2$).

6. In *factorial designs*, because two or more levels of each factor (or independent variable) are administered in combination with two or more levels of every other factor, these designs use the units more efficiently and address more questions than do ordinary one-way ANOVA designs. However, they may not address the focused question of interest to the researcher.

7. The *error* of individual scores (the deviation of each score from the mean of the group) represents the extent to which the score can be predicted from a knowledge of group membership.

8. The summary table for the factorial ANOVA differs from the summary table for the one-way ANOVA in reflecting the subdivision of the between-conditions *SS* into *main* and *interaction SS*.

9. The additive model is based on the idea that each group mean is the sum of the grand mean, the *row effect*, the *column effect*, and the *interaction effect*. The model thus provides a baseline that allows us to compare these effects with one another (Box 14.4).

10. *Interaction effects* in two-way ANOVA are the effects that are left over (*residuals*) after the row and column effects are removed from the group means. Removing the grand mean will reveal the pure residuals.

11. *Contrast t and F tests* are focused procedures that compare (*contrast*) an obtained pattern of means with a predicted pattern that is expressed in the form of lambda (λ) weights that sum to zero ($\Sigma\lambda = 0$).

12. The r_{alerting} effect size index is the correlation between the group means and their respective λ weights, and thus is also symbolized as $r_{M\lambda}$. The r_{contrast} is the (partial) correlation between the scores on the dependent variable and their respective λ weights with noncontrast sources of variation removed, and thus is also symbolized as $r_{Y\lambda \cdot NC}$.

13. Squaring the alerting r reveals the proportion of the between-conditions sum of squares that is accounted for by the particular contrast (λ) weights. If this value approaches 1.0, we can use the formula in (2) above to estimate $r_{\text{effect size}}$ from F. The alerting r is also useful in computing contrasts from reported group means and an omnibus F (Box 14.5).

14. In *intrinsically repeated-measures research*, we *must* measure the participants more than once to address

the question of interest. We can use either the L score or the r value method to compute contrasts, but it is possible for contrast r values obtained from these two methods to differ markedly.

15. In *nonintrinsically repeated-measures research*, it is *not essential* that we use a repeated-measures design, but it increases efficiency, precision, and statistical power to do so. An example is the Latin square design described at the end of this chapter.

Key Terms

additive model   p. 269
alerting r (r_{alerting} or $r_{M\lambda}$)   p. 276
analysis of variance (ANOVA)   p. 258
column effect   p. 269
contrast   p. 274
contrast (λ) weights   p. 274
contrast r (r_{contrast} or $r_{Y\lambda \cdot NC}$)   p. 277
effect size r ($r_{\text{effect size}}$ or $r_{Y\lambda}$)   p. 258
error   p. 271

focused statistical tests   p. 264
F ratio   p. 260
F test   p. 260
interaction effects   p. 268
intrinsically repeated measures   p. 280
lambda (λ) weights   p. 274
main effect   p. 268
mean square (S^2, or MS)   p. 261
multiple-degree-of-freedom effects   p. 259

nonintrinsically repeated measures   p. 281
omnibus statistical procedures   p. 264
one-degree-of-freedom effects   p. 259
residuals   p. 268
row effect   p. 269
simple effects   p. 267
sum of squares (SS)   p. 261
tests of simple effects   p. 266

Multiple-Choice Questions for Review

1. When comparing only two groups, $F =$ _____. (a) t; (b) $2t$; (c) t^2; (d) $t/2$.

2. A "one-way ANOVA" has only one _____. (a) degree of freedom; (b) between-group SS; (c) variance; (d) treatment condition.

3. S^2 is also called _____. (a) sum of squares; (b) σ^2; (c) F ratio; (d) mean square.

4. Total $SS =$ _____ $SS +$ _____ SS. (a) Experimental; Control; (b) Dependent; Independent; (c) Between; Within; (d) all of the above

5. In a two-way factorial, the between $SS =$ _____. (a) Main effects SS; (b) Main effects $SS +$ Interaction SS; (c) Main effects $SS +$ Interaction $SS +$ Error SS; (d) none of the above.

6. A student at the University of Tennessee conducts an experiment with three groups. Each group contains four subjects. How many between-conditions degrees of freedom will there be? (a) 2; (b) 3; (c) 4; (d) 11

7. In the study above, what are the total degrees of freedom? (a) 2; (b) 3; (c) 4; (d) 11

8. A student at Southern Illinois University conducts a study with two groups and five subjects in each group. She calculates that $F = 5$. According to Table 14.4, what is the appropriate p value? (a) $p > .05$; (b) $p < .05$; (c) $p < .01$; (d) cannot be determined

9. A student at the University of Arizona conducts an experiment with four groups. He calculates an F test to examine the overall differences between the groups. He then computes t tests to compare each group to each of the others. These t tests are said to be tests of (a) within-subjects effects; (b) main effects; (c) repeated-measures effects; (d) simple effects.

10. Both F with numerator $df = 1$ and any t test are (a) focused tests; (b) unfocused tests; (c) omnibus tests; (d) diffuse tests.

Discussion Questions for Review

1. From a population of 50 male professional runners, an Ohio State researcher randomly assigns 10 to each of five groups. Each group receives a different brand

of running shoe. The brands are coded A, B, C, D, E. Each member of a group receives a new pair of the top-of-the-line shoe made by a shoe company and then rates the shoe for comfort. Below are the mean comfort ratings (on a scale from 1 to 20) given to the different brands:

Brand	Rating
A	19
B	13
C	17
D	9
E	10

Suppose the researcher performs an analysis of variance, and the within-shoe-brands mean square is 94, whereas the mean square for between-shoe-brands is 188. What is the value of the omnibus F testing the significance of the overall difference among the shoe brands? What are the associated degrees of freedom?

2. A University of Pittsburgh researcher has the following two sets of data, each of which contains three independent groups. The 12 subjects in each set were randomly assigned to the groups; 4 subjects were assigned to each group. The numbers are scores on some dependent measure.

Set A:

	Group 1	Group 2	Group 3
	2	5	11
	3	5	10
	2	4	9
	1	6	10
Mean	2	5	10

Set B:

	Group 1	Group 2	Group 3
	9	11	23
	-6	-10	10

(*continued*)

	4	0	-2
	1	19	9
Mean	2	5	10

Which set of data is likely to yield a larger F ratio in an analysis of variance? How can you be sure?

3. A University of Colorado student obtains the following set of means in a study that measures the benefits of vacations in rural versus urban areas for participants who live in rural or urban areas. Higher numbers indicate greater benefits. Figure out the row effects, the column effects, and the interaction residuals, and then decide how they should be interpreted.

	Urban participants	Rural participants
Urban vacations	5	3
Rural vacations	11	1

4. A University of Maine student obtains the data shown in Table 14.2 and computes the ANOVA shown in Table 14.3. His primary interest, however, is in whether the scores of the hot lunch group on average are significantly better than the average scores of the remaining three groups. How would you advise him to address his question?

5. A McGill University student who computed a contrast F is advised by her instructor to look at the alerting r before estimating the effect size r from $\sqrt{(F)/(F + df)}$. Why?

6. A University of Maryland–Baltimore County student who used a repeated-measures design in his research is advised by his instructor to compute a contrast using L scores. What are they, and how can the student form a set of lambda weights?

Answers to Review Questions

Multiple-Choice Questions

1. c	**3.** d	**5.** b	**7.** d	**9.** d
2. b	**4.** c	**6.** a	**8.** a	**10.** a

Discussion Questions

1. An appropriate table of variance for this study is

Source	SS	df	MS	F	p
Between brands	752	4	188	2.0	.11
Within brands	4,230	45	94		

The researcher finds F from MS between divided by MS within and then finds df from $k - 1$ for numerator df and $N - k$ for denominator df. The researcher does not report $r_{\text{effect size}}$ because this is an omnibus F test (i.e., numerator $df > 1$).

2. Set A would yield a larger F because its within-condition variability is much smaller than that of Set B. Since the means of Sets A and B are equal, the MS between for Sets A and B are equal. Therefore, the results with the smaller MS within will yield the larger F.

3. The following table shows the means, row effects, and column effects (as in Table 14.6):

Type of vacation	Type of participants Urban (UP)	Rural (RP)	Row means	Row effects
Urban (UV)	5	3	4	−1
Rural (RV)	11	1	6	+1
Column means	8	2	5	
Column effects	+3	−3		

The interaction effects for each of the four conditions are computed from:

	Group mean	−	Grand mean	−	Row effect	−	Column effect	=	Interaction effect
UV, UP	5	−	5	−	(−1)	−	3	=	(−2)
UV, RP	3	−	5	−	(−1)	−	(−3)	=	2
RV, UP	11	−	5	−	1	−	3	=	2
RV, RP	1	−	5	−	1	−	(−3)	=	(−2)
Sum	20	−	20	−	0.0	−	0.0	=	0.0

If we disregard matters of statistical significance, these results show that the type of participants made the largest difference, the type of vacation made the smallest difference, and the interaction made an intermediate amount of difference. The urban participants benefited more than the rural participants, the rural

vacations were associated with greater benefits than were the urban vacations, and the interaction showed greater benefits for those vacationing in the setting in which they did *not* reside.

4. A t test following the F would address the question appropriately. The two means to be compared would be the hot lunch mean and the mean of the means of the remaining three groups, that is, $(10 + 12 + 15)/3 = 12.33$. The two required sample sizes, n_1 and n_2, would be the n for the hot lunch (i.e., 3) and the n for the children in the remaining three groups (i.e., $3 + 3 + 3 = 9$). As in the case of most t tests computed after the ANOVA, the S^2 used in computing t is the S^2 obtained from the ANOVA, the MS within. Thus

$$t = \frac{19 - 12.33}{\sqrt{\left(\frac{1}{3} + \frac{1}{9}\right)4}} = 5.00,$$

with $df = 8, p = .0005$. Whenever we compute t, or F with 1 df in the numerator, we want to know the effect size. So we compute the effect size correlation from

$$r_{\text{effect size}} = \sqrt{\frac{t^2}{t^2 + df}} = \sqrt{\frac{(5.0)^2}{(5.0)^2 + 8}} = .87,$$

which is a jumbo-sized effect. An alternative way to address this question is by means of t_{contrast}, which in this case would involve contrast (λ) weights of $+3, -1, -1, -1$, reflecting our prediction that the mean of the hot lunch would be higher than the other three means, which in turn would not differ from each other. As we would expect, the value of t_{contrast} is identical to our sample t value of 5.00, that is,

$$t_{\text{contrast}} = \frac{\Sigma M \lambda}{\sqrt{MS_{\text{within}}\left(\Sigma \frac{\lambda^2}{n}\right)}}$$

$$= \frac{19(+3) + 10(-1) + 12(-1) + 15(-1)}{\sqrt{4\left[\frac{(+3)^2}{3} + \frac{(-1)^2}{3} + \frac{(-1)^2}{3} + \frac{(-1)^2}{3}\right]}}$$

$$= \frac{20}{\sqrt{16}} = 5.00.$$

5. In the context of contrast analysis, the formula she wanted to use to estimate the effect size r from her contrast F is referred to more generally as the contrast r rather than the effect size r. However, it can be used to estimate the effect size r if the squared alerting r

approaches 1, as it would imply that there is very little noncontrast variation to be concerned about.

6. L scores are the contrast scores for each participant in a repeated-measures contrast, defined as the sum of the products of the contrast (λ) weights multiplied by the participant's performance scores (the Y scores). A convenient way to form a set of λ weights is to write down your prediction in integers and then to subtract the mean from each integer. For example, if the student had predicted that the scores would go from 3 to 9 and then back to 3, he would subtract the mean of 5 from each predicted value, finding λ weights of $-2, +4, -2$. Though not required, the student could simplify the computations a little by dividing the contrast weights by 2 to yield the simpler weights of $-1, +2, -1$.

CHAPTER 15

The Analysis of Frequency Tables

Preview Questions

- What is the purpose of chi-square (χ^2)?

- How do I compute 1-*df* chi-squares?

- How do I obtain the *p* value, effect size, and confidence interval?

- What is the relationship between 1-*df* χ^2 and phi?

- How do I deal with tables larger than 2 × 2?

- How is standardizing the margins done, and what can it tell me?

- What is a binomial effect-size display used for?

What Is the Purpose of Chi-Square (χ^2)?

The statistic we discuss in this final chapter is the **chi-square**, symbolized as χ^2, pronounced "ki (rhymes with *eye*) square." Invented in 1900 by Karl Pearson (who also invented the product-moment *r*), it is a statistic that, like *t* and *F*, tells us (with the aid of a table, computer program, or scientific calculator) how unlikely it is that the relationship investigated has occurred by chance (see also Box 15.1). Also like *t* and *F*, chi-square does not tell us immediately about the strength of the relationship between the variables. Just as in the case of *t* and *F*, any given value of χ^2 is associated with a stronger degree of relationship when it is based on a smaller number of units or observations. In other words, a relationship must be quite strong to result in a large χ^2 (or *t* or *F*) with only a small number of sampling units.

We compute χ^2 for tables of independent frequencies (also called *counts*), and therefore χ^2 can be thought of as a comparison of independent counts. This assumption of the *independence of the observed frequencies (or counts)* is fundamental when you are computing chi-square. Chi-square does its job of testing the relationship between two variables by focusing on the discrepancy between the obtained or **observed frequency (f_o)** and the theoretically **expected frequency (f_e)**. In other words, χ^2 differs from the other significance tests we have examined in that it can be used for dependent variables that are not scored or scaled. In all the earlier examples of *t* and *F*, participants' responses were recorded as scores in such a way that some could be regarded as so many units larger or smaller than other scores. Because χ^2 is a comparison of counts, it allows us to deal with categories of response that are not usually scaled, ordered, or scored.

Like *F*, the chi-square can be a focused or an omnibus test. Chi-squares with 1 *df* are focused tests, and chi-squares with *df* > 1 are omnibus tests. Earlier, we illustrated the calculation of the phi coefficient from a 2 × 2 table of counts, and in this chapter we will show how phi can also be computed directly from a 1-*df* chi-square. Focused statistical tests are generally more readily interpretable than omnibus tests, but we will suggest strategies for interpreting χ^2 tables of counts when

BOX 15.1 Fisher as Detective

In the 19th century, Gregor Mendel, the legendary Austrian botanist, performed experiments that became the basis of the modern science of genetics. Working with garden peas, he showed that their characteristics could be predicted from the characteristics of their "parents." In a famous piece of scientific detective work, R. A. Fisher (the inventor of the *F* test and the null hypothesis) later used the chi-square to ask whether Mendel's data may have been manipulated so that they would seem to be more in line with his theory. Fisher used the chi-square as a "goodness-of-fit" test of Mendel's reported findings compared with the statistically expected values. Fisher found Mendel's data *too perfect* to be plausible! Fisher speculated that Mendel had been deceived by a research assistant, someone who knew what Mendel wanted to find and who manipulated the data *too* well.

the *df* > 1. One strategy that we illustrate later, called *standardizing the margins*, generates row totals that are equal to each other and also column totals that are equal to each other, making it far easier to interpret cell counts. The chapter concludes by illustrating another kind of standardization process, in which a 2 × 2 display, called a *binomial effect-size display* (or BESD), is used to exhibit the "success rate" of the experimental treatment in a hypothetical population, where the row and column totals of the BESD are all preset at 100 each.

How Do I Compute 1-*df* Chi-Squares?

Imagine we wanted to study the food preferences of students who belong to two eating clubs, the Junk Food Junkies (JFJ) and the Green Earthies (GE). We give each of the students a menu with a choice of one of two meals: a juicy grilled hamburger with onions, pickles, relish, and barbecue sauce on a sesame seed bun (called a Big Jack) or a grilled soyburger with lettuce and tomato on whole wheat bread. Our expectation (or hypothesis) is that the Junk Food Junkies are more likely to select the Big Jack, whereas the Green Earthies are more likely to select the grilled soyburger, but it is possible that some of each group might do the opposite simply out of curiosity. Table 15.1 provides the imaginary results, which we need to compute chi-square from a 2 × 2 table of independent counts. The results in Section A are the observed frequencies (counts), where the entries correspond to a food choice (the row variable) and the club to which a student belongs (the column variable). As this table shows, 24 out of 36 members of the Junk Food Junkies chose a Big Jack, and the remaining 12 chose a soyburger, and of the members of the Green Earthies, 13 out of 43 chose a Big Jack, and the remaining 30 chose a soyburger.

The following general formula summarizes the steps we will take in applying a chi-square to these data:

$$\chi^2 = \sum \frac{(f_o - f_e)^2}{f_e},$$

where f_o is the observed frequency in each cell, and f_e is the expected frequency in that cell. This formula instructs us to sum (Σ) the squared differences between the observed frequencies (f_o) and the expected frequencies (f_e) after first dividing each squared difference by the expected frequency. If the null hypothesis of no relationship between the rows and columns is true, we expect the f_o and f_e values to be similar in magnitude. In other words, observed frequencies that are substantially larger and smaller than the expected frequencies are needed to cast doubt on the null hypothesis, because the value of chi-square will be small when the $f_o - f_e$ difference is small.

Table 15.1   Basic Data for 2 × 2 Chi-Square

A. Observed frequencies (f_o)

Food choice	JFJ	GE	Row sums
Big Jack	24	13	37
Soyburger	12	30	42
Column sums	36	43	79

B. Expected frequencies (f_e)

Food choice	JFJ	GE	Row sums
Big Jack	16.861	20.139	37.000
Soyburger	19.139	22.861	42.000
Column sums	36.000	43.000	79.000

C. $(f_o - f_e)^2 / f_e$ values

Food choice	JFJ	GE	Row sums
Big Jack	3.023	2.531	5.554
Soyburger	2.663	2.229	4.892
Column sums	5.686	4.760	10.446

To use this formula, we must first determine for each of the observed frequencies the number of "expected" entries, that is, the number that would be expected if the null hypothesis of no relationship between the row and column variables were true. To calculate this expected frequency (f_e) for each cell, we multiply the column total by the row total where that row and that column intersect in that cell. We then divide this quantity by the grand total of entries. That is,

$$f_e = \frac{(\text{Column total})(\text{Row total})}{\text{Grand total}}.$$

For example, the upper-left cell in Section A of Table 15.1 is at the intersection of the JFJ column and the Big Jack row. Multiplying the appropriate totals together and dividing by the grand total gives us $f_e = (36 \times 37)/79 = 16.861$.

Section B shows all the expected frequencies computed in this way. These f_e values, row by row, are

$$(36 \times 37)/79 = 16.861$$

$$(43 \times 37)/79 = 20.139$$

$$(36 \times 42)/79 = 19.139$$

$$(43 \times 42)/79 = 22.861$$

As a check on our arithmetic, notice that the row totals, the column totals, and the grand total of all the values in Section B are equal to the corresponding totals of the values in Section A. Substituting in the general formula for chi-square, we add up the $(f_o - f_e)^2/f_e$ values (i.e., for each cell, the square of the difference between the observed and expected frequency divided by the expected frequency):

$$\chi^2 = \sum \frac{(f_o - f_e)^2}{f_e} = \frac{(24 - 16.861)^2}{16.861} + \frac{(13 - 20.139)^2}{20.139} + \frac{(12 - 19.139)^2}{19.139} + \frac{(30 - 22.861)^2}{22.861}$$

$$= 3.023 + 2.531 + 2.663 + 2.229 = 10.446.$$

Table 15.2	2 × 2 Contingency Table	
A	B	(A + B)
C	D	(C + D)
(A + C) (B + D)	(N = A + B + C + D)	

The $(f_o - f_e)^2/f_e$ values for each cell also appear in Section C of Table 15.1, which serves as a reminder that the total of all those values is the chi-square.

Though the formula we have been using to compute χ^2 will work in any situation, there is an easier way to compute the 1-*df* chi-square directly from the observed frequencies (f_o) in a 2 × 2 table:

$$\chi^2_{(1)} = \frac{N(BC - AD)^2}{(A + B)(C + D)(A + C)(B + D)},$$

where the letters are defined in Table 15.2. For the observed frequencies in Part A of Table 15.1, we find

$$\chi^2_{(1)} = \frac{79[(13 \times 12) - (24 \times 30)]^2}{(37)(42)(36)(43)} = \frac{79(318,096)}{2,405,592} = 10.446.$$

 How Do I Obtain the *p* Value, Effect Size, and Confidence Interval?

As was the case for *t* and *F*, there is a different chi-square curve for every value of the degrees of freedom. The degrees of freedom (*df*) of chi-square are defined as

$$df = (\text{rows} - 1)(\text{columns} - 1),$$

that is, the number of rows minus 1 multiplied by the number of columns minus 1. The larger the value of χ^2, the less likely are the observed frequencies to differ from the expected frequencies by chance. Table 15.3 provides a sample listing of χ^2 values with 1 to 5 degrees of freedom for *p* = .10, .05, and .01. A more comprehensive listing is in Table B.4 (p. 334). Notice that the value of χ^2 must be larger than the degrees of freedom to cast doubt on the null hypothesis.

In this example, the 1-*df* chi-square of 10.446 is larger than the largest value shown for *df* = 1 (6.64 for *p* = .01). The rounded *p* is approximately .001, which means that a chi-square value this large or larger would occur 1 time in 1,000 repeated samplings if the null hypothesis were true. In other words, there is about 1 chance in 1,000 that a chi-square this large would

Table 15.3	Chi-Square Values for Significance at .10, .05, and .01		
df	*p* = .10	*p* = .05	*p* = .01
1	2.71	3.84	6.64
2	4.61	5.99	9.21
3	6.25	7.82	11.34
4	7.78	9.49	13.28
5	9.24	11.07	15.09

BOX 15.2 Chi-Square and the Null Hypothesis

Reminiscent of F, all chi-square curves also begin at zero and range upward to infinity. You will recall that the expected value of t is zero when the null hypothesis is true, and the expected value of F is $df/(df-2)$, where df are for the denominator mean square (Table 14.4 in Chapter 14). For chi-square distributions, the expected value (when the null hypothesis is true) is equivalent to the df defining the particular chi-square distribution, that is, $df = (\text{rows} - 1)(\text{columns} - 1)$. Thus, for chi-squares based on 2×2, 2×3, and 2×4 tables, the average value of the χ^2 if the null hypothesis were true would be 1, 2, and 3, respectively. The maximum possible value of χ^2 is equivalent to the total N.

occur if there really were no relationship between group membership and food choice in Table 15.1 (see also Box 15.2).

We now estimate the effect size. As these are frequency data in a 2×2 table, it should be obvious that we will estimate the effect size by the **phi coefficient (ϕ)**. To compute phi directly from a 1-df chi-square table, we again use the general formula that was introduced in Chapter 11 as

$$\phi = \frac{BC - AD}{\sqrt{(A + B)(C + D)(A + C)(B + D)}},$$

with the letters defined in Table 15.2. Substituting the data in Section A (observed frequencies) of Table 15.1, we find

$$\phi = \frac{(13 \times 12) - (24 \times 30)}{\sqrt{(37)(42)(36)(43)}} = \frac{-564}{1,551} = .36.$$

The convention (from meta-analysis) is to report an effect size r as positive ($+$) when the finding is in the hypothesized direction and to report it as negative ($-$) when the finding is in the opposite direction. In this case, the finding is consistent with our hypothesis, and we report $r_{\text{effect size}} = .36$ (the positive sign is implicit).

And finally, we compute a 95% confidence interval (CI) around the observed effect using the procedure described in Chapter 12 (although we are not limited to a 95% confidence interval and can choose any level of confidence we feel comfortable with). To review, we first consult Table B.6 (p. 336) to convert our $r_{\text{effect size}} = .36$ into Fisher $z_r = .377$. Step 2 substitutes the value of $N = 79$ in the expression

$$\left(\frac{1}{\sqrt{N - 3}} \right) 1.96 = \left(\frac{1}{\sqrt{79 - 3}} \right) 1.96 = .2248,$$

where (as described in Chapter 12) 1.96 is the standard score for z for $p = .05$ two-tailed, and the other value defines the standard error of a Fisher z_r. In Step 3, we subtract .2248 from .377 (the value in Step 1) and also add .2248 to .377 to find the lower and upper limits of the Fisher z_r values. The lower limit is $.377 - .2248 = .1522$ (rounded to .15), and the upper limit is $.377 + .2248 = .6018$ (rounded to .60). In the final step, we convert these scores back into the metric of the effect size r (using Table B.7 on p. 337) and conclude, with 95% confidence, that the $r_{\text{effect size}}$ is between .15 and .54. Had the total sample size been larger, or had we chosen to work with 90% confidence, the interval would have been narrower.

What Is the Relationship Between 1-*df* χ^2 and Phi?

If the sample size (N) is not too small ($N > 20$), and if the smallest expected frequency is not too small (e.g., less than 3 or so), we can assess the statistical significance of phi coefficients by chi-square tests, because

$$\chi^2 = \phi^2 \times N.$$

This equation also serves as another example of the conceptual relationship described as

$$\text{Significance test} = \text{Size of effect} \times \text{Size of study,}$$

which reminds us that χ^2 (like t and F) is the product of an effect size and the study size. Hence, the larger the effect or the more sampling units in the chi-square table (i.e., the larger the total N), the greater will be the value of χ^2. This relationship underscores the importance of doing a power analysis (as described in Chapter 12). It also implies that, as in the case of the t and F, a relationship must be very strong (the effect size must be sizable) to result in a large chi-square with only a small total N. Substituting in the equation above, we find

$$\chi^2 = (.3636^2)(79) = 10.44,$$

which, not surprisingly, is the same value of chi-square that we obtained before (within rounding error).

More often, researchers compute χ^2 first and then estimate the effect size for focused chi-squares (i.e., chi-squares with $df = 1$). To obtain the value of the effect size correlation (phi) from the 1-*df* chi-square, rearranging the formula above gives us

$$\phi = \sqrt{\frac{\chi^2}{N}}$$

which is our operational definition of $r_{\text{effect size}}$ for any chi-square with $df = 1$. In our continuing example, substituting in this formula gives us

$$\phi = \sqrt{\frac{\chi^2}{N}} = \sqrt{\frac{10.446}{79}} = .36,$$

which, also not surprisingly, is the same value of phi that we calculated directly from the table of counts.

How Do I Deal With Tables Larger Than 2 × 2?

When there are many cells in a table of counts, chi-square may be more difficult to interpret than in a 2 × 2 table. Table 15.4 illustrates this situation in a 2 × 4 table that we created by the addition of two new groups to Table 15.1. One new group (designated as PC) consists of 35 members of the Psychology Club, and the other new group consists of 11 members of the Mathematics Club (MC). The hypothesis is that psychology and mathematics students will be more like Junk Food Junkies than Green Earthies in choosing grilled beef over grilled soy.

Turning to Table 15.5, we find that Section A shows the expected frequencies (f_e) computed from the observed frequencies in Table 15.4. For example, Table 15.4 showed that 21 out of the 35 students who belong to the Psychology Club chose grilled beef. To obtain the expected frequency shown as 18.480 in Table 15.5, we multiplied the appropriate row total (shown as 66 in Table 15.4) by the appropriate column total (35) and divided the product by the total number of counts (125) to find $(66 \times 35)/125 = 18.480$. Notice that the row and column sums in Section A of Table 15.5 are identical to the corresponding values in Table 15.4 (confirming the accuracy of our calculations).

Table 15.4	Obtained Frequencies (f_o) for 2 × 4 Chi-Square				
Food choice	PC	MC	JFJ	GE	Row sums
Big Jack	21	8	24	13	66
Soyburger	14	3	12	30	59
Column sums	35	11	36	43	125

The calculation of the chi-square for this 2 × 4 contingency table (and therefore $df = 3$) uses the same formula given earlier:

$$\chi^2 = \sum \frac{(f_o - f_e)^2}{f_e}.$$

The cell entries shown in Section B of Table 15.5 are the $(f_o - f_e)^2/f_e$ values that go into this formula. In other words, the resulting chi-square value is the grand total of these cell entries in Section B, or 14.046. The exact p value of this chi-square (with 3 df) is .0028 (or in scientific notation, $p = 2.8^{-3}$).

The larger the value of an obtained chi-square, the less likely are the observed frequencies to differ from the expected frequencies by chance, and this chi-square is interestingly large. However, all it tells us is that *somewhere* in the data the observed frequencies depart noticeably from the expected values. In a way, it reminds us of the case of analysis of variance with $df > 1$ in the numerator of F. That is, a significant omnibus F tells us there is some difference, but it does not tell us where the difference is. In Chapter 14, we illustrated the use of t tests of simple effects, along with one-degree-of-freedom effect sizes, to help us identify and interpret specific differences. A number of alternative options are available to help us interpret chi-square tables with $df > 1$ (Rosenthal & Rosnow, 2008, Ch. 19).

Among these alternatives, one option is to inspect closely the $(f_o - f_e)^2/f_e$ results, as these results show which of the cells contributed most to the overall large chi-square. A large cell entry in such a table indicates that the cell in question is "surprising" given the magnitude of the row and column totals associated with that cell. That is, the cell is "unexpected" in terms of chance or likelihood—not necessarily in terms of our research hypothesis, however. In Table 15.5, the largest values in Section B suggest that Green Earthies reacted in a less likely way than would be expected by chance on the basis of the choices of the other three groups.

Table 15.5	Expected Frequencies (f_e) and $(f_o - f_e)^2/f_e$ Values				
A. Expected frequencies (f_e)					
Food choice	PC	MC	JFJ	GE	Row sums
Big Jack	18.480	5.808	19.008	22.704	66.000
Soyburger	16.520	5.192	16.992	20.296	59.000
Column sums	35.000	11.000	36.000	43.000	125.000
B. ($f_o - f_e)^2/f_e$ values					
Food choice	PC	MC	JFJ	GE	Row sums
Big Jack	0.344	0.827	1.311	4.148	6.630
Soyburger	0.384	0.925	1.467	4.640	7.416
Column sums	0.728	1.752	2.778	8.788	14.046 (grand total)

A second option might be to subdivide the large table into more interpretable smaller tables. In this procedure, called **partitioning of tables**, we compute additional chi-squares based on portions of the overall table. Both the number and the size of the subtables are guided by statistical rules, and the calculations also call for certain statistical adjustments. You will find a discussion and detailed illustration in our advanced text (Rosenthal & Rosnow, 2008, pp. 609–614).

In a third option, which we turn to next, the idea is to take the size of the row and column totals (called the *margins*) into account by generating row margins that are equal to each other and also generating column margins that are equal to each other, a process called *standardizing the margins* (Mosteller, 1968).

 ## How Is Standardizing the Margins Done, and What Can It Tell Me?

In **standardizing the margins**, the term *standardizing* does not mean that z scores are used; instead it means that uniform (or "standardized") row margins and uniform column margins are produced by a process of successive repetitions (called *iterations*). The reason for standardizing the row and column margins is that one of the problems of trying to understand the pattern of results in tables of counts larger than 2×2 is that we are likely to be fooled by the absolute magnitude of the frequencies displayed (the f_0 data). To illustrate, suppose we were to ask of the counts in Table 15.4 which group of students is most overrepresented in the Big Jack category. We note that Psychology Club members (PC) and Junk Food Junkies (JFJ) have the greatest frequency of occurrence in that category. Thus, we might conclude that one of these groups is most overrepresented in the Big Jack category.

Our conclusion would be wrong, however. The reason is that we inspected only the interior of the table and not, at the same time, the sums in the row and column margins. A look at these margins suggests that the PC and JFJ groups *should* have larger obtained frequencies in the Big Jack category than the Mathematics Club members (MC) because the PC and JFJ groups have more members than the MC group. In addition, there are slightly more students in general in the Big Jack category than in the soyburger category. Taking all these margins into account simultaneously would show us that it is actually the MC students who are most overrepresented in the Big Jack category. The practical problem, however, is that "taking the margins into account" in large tables becomes a difficult matter without the use of systematic aids to eye and mind. The process of standardizing the margins allows us to adjust (or "correct") for the unequal column and row margins and thus provides us with a systematic procedure for taking the unequal margins into account.

Table 15.6 shows the steps taken to adjust for the unequal column and row margins in Table 15.4. Section A of Table 15.6 gives the results of the first step in this process, which consisted of dividing each obtained frequency (in Table 15.4) by its column sum. For instance, to obtain the "corrected" values for 21 and 14 in Table 15.4, we divided each by 35; to obtain the "corrected" values for 8 and 3 in Table 15.4, we divided each by 11; and so on. These calculations produced the results in Section A of Table 15.6. Notice that although the column margins have been equalized, the row margins remain very unequal. Thus, the next step is to adjust the row margins, and we do this by dividing each of the new values in Section A by its row margin. To obtain the "corrected" values for .600, .727, .667, and .302, we divided each by 2.296. To obtain the "corrected" values for .400, .273, .333, and .698, we divide each by 1.704. The results appear in Section B of Table 15.6.

Section B has equalized the row margins, at least within rounding error, but the column margins are no longer equal. By now, we know what to do about that: Simply divide each entry of Section B by its new column margin. That process will equalize the column margins but *might* make our new row margins unequal. We repeat this procedure until further iterations (repetitions) no longer affect the margins. For these data, the final results obtained by successive iterations are shown in Section C of Table 15.6, which shows margins equalized within rounding error and allows us to interpret the table entries without worrying about the confusing effects of variations in margins. It clearly shows that, in the Big Jack category, the Mathematics Club (MC) is overrepresented most, whereas in the soyburger category, the Green Earthies (GE) are the ones most overrepresented.

Table 15.6	Steps in Standardizing the Margins

A. Results "corrected" for unequal column margins in Table 15.4

Food choice	PC	MC	JFJ	GE	Row sums
Big Jack	0.600	0.727	0.667	0.302	2.296
Soyburger	0.400	0.273	0.333	0.698	1.704
Column sums	1.000	1.000	1.000	1.000	4.000

B. Results "corrected" for unequal row margins in A (above)

Food choice	PC	MC	JFJ	GE	Row sums
Big Jack	0.261	0.317	0.291	0.132	1.001
Soyburger	0.235	0.160	0.195	0.410	1.000
Column sums	0.496	0.477	0.486	0.542	2.001

C. Final "corrected" results

Food choice	PC	MC	JFJ	GE	Row sums
Big Jack	0.517	0.657	0.589	0.238	2.001
Soyburger	0.483	0.343	0.411	0.762	1.999
Column sums	1.000	1.000	1.000	1.000	4.000

D. Results in C (above) shown as deviations from an expected value of .500

Food choice	PC	MC	JFJ	GE	Row sums
Big Jack	+0.017	+0.157	+0.089	−0.262	+0.001
Soyburger	−0.017	−0.157	−0.089	+0.262	−0.001
Column sums	0.000	0.000	0.000	0.000	0.000

There is one additional step we can take to throw the results into bolder relief: We can show the cell entries as deviations from the values we would expect if there were no differences whatever among the groups in their representation in the Big Jack and soyburger categories. If there were no such differences, and given the margins of Section C, all the values in the table would be .500. In forming our final table, we subtract this expected value of .500 from each entry in Section C. The final results are shown in Section D of Table 15.6, and the interpretation is fairly direct. Besides the big difference between the Green Earthies, who are overrepresented very heavily in the soyburger category, and all the other groups, which are more modestly overrepresented in the Big Jack category, there are other differences that help us to interpret our earlier results. For example, even though some of the sample sizes are too small to be very stable, we can also raise some tentative questions about differences among the three groups overrepresented in the Big Jack category. The Mathematics Club is substantially more overrepresented in the Big Jack category than the Psychology Club, which is virtually not overrepresented at all. The Junk Food Junkies fall almost exactly midway between the PC and MC groups in their degree of overrepresentation in the Big Jack category.

What Is a Binomial Effect-Size Display Used For?

The object of standardizing the margins was to generate row totals that were equal to each other and also column totals that were equal to each other, and we turn now to another approach that is predicated on the assumption of uniform marginal values. Called a **binomial effect-size display** (or **BESD**), it is called a *display* because it converts "success rates" in experimental and control groups into a 2 × 2 table, and it is called a *binomial* display (which means "two-term") because both the row and column variables are displayed as dichotomous. Unlike the results of standardizing the margins, the row and column marginal totals of a BESD are all preset at 100 each.

To illustrate how the BESD works, we draw upon the final results of a highly publicized double-blind, placebo-controlled, clinical trial designed in part to determine whether low-dose aspirin decreases cardiovascular mortality. The participants were more than 22,000 male physicians, who were randomly assigned to receive low dose aspirin (325 mg) every other day or a placebo. The outcome (dependent) variable that we will focus on was whether they experienced a heart attack (referred to as *myocardial infarction*, or MI) over the course of this clinical trial. At a special meeting held in December 1987, it was decided to end the study earlier than had been scheduled because it had become so profound that low-dose aspirin prevents heart attacks (and death from heart attacks) that it would be unethical to continue giving half of the study participants a placebo (Steering Committee of the Physicians' Health Study Research Group, 1988, 1989). The way that aspirin works to reduce mortality from heart attacks is to promote circulation even when fatty deposits have collected along the walls of the coronary arteries. That is, aspirin does not reduce the chances of clotting but, by thinning the blood, eases transportation of blood as the arteries get narrower. The raw counts in the final report are shown in Part A of Table 15.7. The 1-*df* chi-square computed on these results is 26.9 ($p = 2.1^{-7}$), and therefore

$$\phi = \sqrt{\frac{\chi^2}{N}} = \sqrt{\frac{26.9}{22,071}} = .035.$$

The binomial effect-size display recasts *r* as a 2 × 2 contingency table, in which all the row and column totals are preset at 100. Part B of Table 15.7 illustrates the BESD based on an *r* of .035. The 48.25% in cell A was computed from 100(.500 − *r*/2), and the 51.75% in cell B was computed from 100(.500 + *r*/2). In other words, the *r* of .035 is equivalent to the aspirin regimen's improvement of the success rate from 48.25% to 51.75%. The difference between these rates corresponds to the value of *r* times 100. These percentages should not, of course, be mistaken for raw percentages in the actual data in Part A; rather, they should be interpreted as the "standardized" percentages, given that all the margins sum to 100. Another way of saying this is that the effect size *r* of .035 amounts to a difference between the rates of 48.25% and 51.75%, if one half the population

---

Table 15.7	Effect on Heart Attack of 325 mg of Aspirin Every Other Day		

A. Raw counts

Condition	Heart attack	No heart attack	Total
Aspirin	139	10,898	11,037
Placebo	239	10,795	11,034
Total	378	21,693	22,071

B. Binomial effect-size display of $r_{effectsize} = .035$

Condition	Heart attack	No heart attack	Total
Aspirin	48.25	51.75	100
Placebo	51.75	48.25	100
Total	100	100	200

Source: The raw counts in Part A are based on results reported in 1989 by the Steering Committee of the Physicians' Health Study, "Final Report on the Aspirin Component of the Ongoing Physicians' Health Study," *New England Journal of Medicine, 318*, pp. 262–264.

| Table 15.8 | Values of r and χ^2 Associated with Various Binomial Effect-Size Displays | | | |

| BESD cells | | | | |
A	B	C	D	$r_{\text{effect size}}$
0	100	100	0	1.00
5	95	95	5	.90
10	90	90	10	.80
15	85	85	15	.70
20	80	80	20	.60
25	75	75	25	.50
30	70	70	30	.40
35	65	65	35	.30
40	60	60	40	.20
45	55	55	45	.10
50	50	50	50	.00

received low-dose aspirin and one half did not, and if one half the population suffered a heart attack and one half did not.

Table 15.8 provides a general summary of the relation between the BESD and various values of $r_{\text{effect size}}$ (Rosenthal et al., 2000). Continuing with the clinical trials example, let us assume that (as in Table 12.5 on p. 231) A and B refer to the presence and absence of some specified adverse event, respectively, in the treated group, and C and D refer to the presence and absence of such an event, respectively, in the control group. The values listed in the column labeled $r_{\text{effect size}}$ are equivalent to dividing the difference between the listed high and low BESD-outcome rates by 100.

In this example, the effect size r was the phi coefficient, but the BESD can also be used with the point-biserial r computed from an independent-sample t, with the partial r computed from a paired t, and with the contrast r, alerting r, and effect size r associated with contrasts on three or more groups. However, the interpretation is more subtle than in a two-group design (for further discussion, see Rosenthal et al., 2000).

A Journey Begun

The *beginning* in the title of this book is intended to have a double meaning. It not only describes the level of the text but also conveys the idea of a journey. For some students, the journey embarked on at the start of this course is now complete. For others, the journey has just begun. In either case, it should be recognized that, particularly in some of their statistical aspects, the design of experiments and the comparison of research conditions constitute a very specialized and highly developed field. The purpose of Chapters 10–15 was to further your understanding of the logic and meaning of the statistical procedures and concepts associated with the application of the scientific method, an understanding that may have been initiated in a basic statistics course. Professional researchers regard a thorough knowledge of the characteristics of both the data obtained and the statistics used as essential to sound scientific practice. Whether the conclusion of this chapter represents the start or the end of your journey in behavioral or social (or some other area of) research, you should now have a deeper understanding of the applicability and limits of the scientific method. Many of the procedures you have learned about in these final chapters can be used to address questions you have about the scientific results reported in newspapers and magazines (or that you hear about in chat groups on the Internet) and to address many everyday questions that can be framed in ways that will allow you to reach beyond other people's conclusions and, using empirical reasoning, decide for yourself what is true.

Summary of Ideas

1. *Chi-square* (χ^2) is used to test the degree of agreement between the data actually obtained (the *observed frequency*) and the data expected (the *expected frequency*) under a particular hypothesis (e.g., the null hypothesis), on the assumption of independent observed frequencies.

2. The larger the value of chi-square, the less likely are the observed frequencies to differ from the expected frequencies only by chance.

3. The expected value of chi-square when the null hypothesis is true is equal to the degrees of freedom defining the particular chi-square distribution, where $df = (\text{rows} - 1)(\text{columns} - 1)$.

4. The effect size r for 2×2 chi-squares (i.e., *focused chi-squares*) is phi (ϕ), which is computed directly from the 1-*df* chi-square by

$$r_{\text{effect size}} = \phi = \sqrt{\frac{\chi^2}{N}}.$$

5. If the sample size is not too small, and if the smallest expected frequency is not too small, we test the significance of the effect size r by $\chi^2 = (\phi^2)(N)$, which also

reflects the conceptual relationship that Significance test = Size of effect $\times$ Size of study.

6. As in the case of t and F, a relationship must be quite strong to result in a large chi-square with only a small number of sampling units.

7. One option in interpreting larger tables of counts is to inspect the $(f_o - f_e)^2/f_e$ results, because they show which of the cells in the table of counts contributed most to the overall chi-square.

8. A second option is to *partition* the larger table of counts into smaller (e.g., 2×2) chi-square tables (discussed elsewhere).

9. A third option is to *standardize the margins* (totals) by making all row margins equal and, at the same time, making all column margins equal.

10. The *binomial effect-size display* (BESD) recasts the effect size r in a 2×2 contingency table, where the row and column totals are all fixed at 100, and r is interpreted as the difference in rates of success (or improvement) if half the population received the treatment and half did not, and if half the population improved and half did not.

Key Terms

binomial effect-size display
  (BESD)   p. 296
chi-square (χ^2)   p. 288

expected frequency (f_e)   p. 288
observed frequency (f_o)   p. 288
partitioning of tables   p. 295

phi coefficient (ϕ)   p. 292
standardizing
  the margins   p. 295

Multiple-Choice Questions for Review

1. Chi-square differs from significance tests such as t and F in that it is specifically designed for use when (a) there are multiple dependent variables; (b) there are multiple independent variables; (c) the dependent variables are not necessarily ordered, scored, or scaled beyond two levels; (d) none of the above.

2. Chi-squares are calculated from the differences between _____ and _____ frequencies. (a) expected, obtained; (b) theoretical, operational; (c) between, within; (d) none of the above

3. In the following 2×2 table, what is the expected frequency in the upper-left cell, where the column variable refers to those in Group A and Group B who volunteered to participate in research but did not versus did eventually show up? (a) 1; (b) 4; (c) 19; (d) 25

	No-shows	Shows
Group A	4	1
Group B	1	19

4. A student at Kutztown University examines a 2×2 table of counts and calculates the chi-square to be 6. According to Table 15.3, what is the appropriate p value? (a) <.10; (b) <.05; (c) <.01; (d) cannot be determined from this information

5. The same student examines a 4×2 table of counts and calculates the chi-square to be 6. According to Table 15.3, what is the appropriate p value? (a) >.10; (b) <.10; (c) <.05; (d) cannot be determined from this information

6. The effect size measure typically associated with 1-*df* chi-square is (a) ϕ; (b) f_e; (c) f_o; (d) d.

7. $\chi^2 =$ _____ × _____. (a) ϕ^2, N; (b) row total, column total; (c) rows -1, columns -1; (d) none of the above

8. Chi-square data tables are also called tables of (a) means; (b) ANOVAs; (c) counts; (d) unequaled margins.

9. A study is conducted that yields a 3 × 4 chi-square table. The overall chi-square is found to be significant. To interpret the results more fully, the researcher decides to examine a table of $(f_o - f_e)^2/f_e$ scores. In this table, the cells with _____ numbers indicate "unexpected" results. (a) small; (b) positive; (c) no; (d) large

10. A study is conducted that yields a 3 × 4 chi-square table. To interpret the results more fully, the researcher uses successive iterations to generate row totals that equal each other and also column totals that equal each other. This procedure is called (a) partitioning; (b) examining a table of $(f_o - f_e)^2/f_e$ scores; (c) standardizing the margins; (d) binary analysis.

Discussion Questions for Review

1. A clinical psychologist at the University of Alabama examines the relation of three types of psychopathology to socioeconomic status (SES) in 100 patients. Her table of counts is:

SES	Schizophrenic	Neurotic	Depressed
High	5	5	20
Medium	5	15	20
Low	10	10	10

How should she test the hypothesis that this table of counts is significantly different from what would be expected by chance if there were no relation between these variables? How many degrees of freedom will an overall chi-square have? In what way will the p value she obtains address only incompletely her wish to examine the relationship between type of psychopathology and SES?

2. A Brigham Young University student obtained the following data, where the numbers are frequencies (counts). How should she plan to standardize the margins?

Annual carrot consumption (lb.)	Visual acuity		
	High	Average	Low
11–20	9	3	1
1–10	5	8	2
0	1	8	7

3. A researcher at Rochester Institute of Technology asks 10 engineering students each from the freshman, sophomore, junior, and senior classes whether they plan to attend graduate school. The results are:

	Frosh	Sophs	Juniors	Seniors
Want advanced degree	7	6	3	1
Want out of school	3	4	7	9

How many degrees of freedom would the chi-square for this table have? How should the researcher calculate the expected frequencies? What is the nature of the relation between year in college and wanting an advanced degree?

4. Three students at the College of New Jersey each conduct the same study with the following results:

	χ^2 (1-*df*)	N	p
Student 1	2.00	20.00	.16
Student 2	3.00	30.00	.08
Student 3	4.00	40.00	.05

Student 3 claims a significant relationship between the two levels of her independent variable (0, 1) and the two levels of her dependent variable (0, 1). Students 1 and 2 chide her, saying that they have not found a significant effect and that her results are therefore undependable and unreplicable. How should Student 3 reply?

5. In Chapter 12, Table 12.6 (on page 232) showed the hypothetical results of six 2 × 2 clinical trials. The table shows comparisons of effect size indicators, but it does not show chi-square results or their associated p levels. Eyeballing Studies 1, 2, and 3 in that table, which would you predict probably has the largest chi-square value and which has the smallest chi-square value? Now do the same for Studies 4, 5, and 6. Next, comparing Studies 1 and 4, which would you predict has the larger chi-square value? Now do the same for Studies 2 and 5, and then for Studies 3 and 6.

6. A page-one story in *The New York Times*, headlined "Safe Therapy Is Found for Blood-Clot Risk," describes a clinical trial involving 508 patients who were at high risk of blood clots, half of whom had been given low-dose warfarin (Coumadin) and the other half, a placebo (Grady, 2003). The story continues, "Of the 253 on placebos, 37 developed blood clots, as compared with only 14 of 255 on the drug" (p. A22). The drug was considered so beneficial that "the study itself was halted ahead of schedule by its sponsor, the National Heart, Lung and Blood Institute, because a safety board found such a benefit to treatment that it would have been unethical to keep giving placebos to people in the control group" (p. A1). Given this information, re-create the table of counts, calculate chi-square, then the effect size r (phi) from chi-square, and recast your obtained r as a BESD. And finally, as a

refresher on what you learned in Chapter 12, compute the risk difference (RD) and use it to estimate (a) the number of patients that need to be treated (NNT) in order to prevent a single blood clot case and (b) the number of such patients that would benefit from the treatment in a group of 10,000. From your findings, would you agree with the sponsor's decision to halt the study ahead of schedule?

Answers to Review Questions

Multiple-Choice Questions

1. c	**3.** a	**5.** a	**7.** a	**9.** d
2. a	**4.** b	**6.** a	**8.** c	**10.** c

Discussion Questions

1. She would compute a χ^2 for which the df would be (rows − 1)(columns − 1) = (3 − 1)(3 − 1) = 4. Because her χ^2 is based on $df > 1$ (i.e., $df = 4$), its p value will tell her nothing about the nature of the relationship between type of psychopathology and SES. She should therefore consider inspecting the $(f_o - f_e)^2/f_e$ results, partitioning her table, and/or standardizing the margins.

2. Following the procedures of Table 15.6, she would arrive at this approximate solution:

Annual carrot consumption (lb.)	Visual acuity			
	High	Average	Low	Sum
11–20	.64	.20	.14	.98
1–10	.31	.45	.23	.99
0	.05	.34	.62	1.01
Sum	1.00	.99	.99	2.98

She can display these results as deviations from an expected value of .33 (i.e., the total of 3.00 divided by 9 cells = 3/9 = .33), yielding the following:

Annual carrot consumption (lb.)	Visual acuity			
	High	Average	Low	Sum
11–20	.31	−.13	−.19	−.01
1–10	−.02	.12	−.10	.00
0	−.28	.01	.29	.02
Sum	+.01	.00	.00	.01

These results show that high-visual-acuity individuals are relatively overrepresented among high carrot consumers, whereas low-visual-acuity individuals are relatively overrepresented among low carrot

consumers. As a corollary, we see that high-visual-acuity individuals are underrepresented among low carrot consumers, whereas low-visual-acuity individuals are relatively underrepresented among high carrot consumers. Unless this was a randomized experiment, the student should be cautious about inferring causality. Though it is possible that eating more carrots leads to better visual acuity, it may also be that better visual acuity leads to finding more carrots in the darker regions of the refrigerator.

3. The df for this χ^2 are obtained from (rows − 1)(columns − 1) = (2 − 1)(4 − 1) = 3. The expected frequencies are obtained from

$$f_e = \frac{(\text{Row total})(\text{Column total})}{\text{Grand total}},$$

which, for these data, results in:

	Frosh	Sophs	Juniors	Seniors
Want degree	4.25	4.25	4.25	4.25
Want out	5.75	5.75	5.75	5.75

With each advancing year, a greater proportion of students want out, a result shown clearly in the final results, in deviation form, of standardizing the margins:

	Frosh	Sophs	Juniors	Seniors
Want degree	.26	.20	−.10	−.36
Want out	−.26	−.20	.10	.36

Once again, we must be careful in our interpretation of the results, because we cannot distinguish differences in year at college from cohort differences (discussed in Chapter 8).

4. Student 3 should ask that all three students compute the effect size correlation that is associated with their results, using the following formula:

$$r_{\text{effect size}} = \phi = \sqrt{\frac{\chi^2}{N}}.$$

When the three students compute their r values, they all find the same magnitude of effect ($r_{\text{effect size}}$ = .316). Student 3 shows thereby that the three studies agree with one another remarkably well.

5. The chi-square values (and their associated p levels) for the six studies in Table 12.6 are as follows:

Study 1: Chi-square = 16.36, $p <$ .0001

Study 2: Chi-square = 540.0, $p <$ .0001

Study 3: Chi-square = 1,620.0, $p <$ .0001

Study 4: Chi-square = 0.2, $p =$ .89

Study 5: Chi-square = 6.67, $p <$ .01

Study 6: Chi-square = 20.0, $p <$ .0001.

6. The table of counts re-created from the basic ingredients in the newspaper story is as follows:

Condition	Blood clot	No blood clot	Total
Low-dose warfarin	14	241	255
Placebo	37	216	253
Total	51	457	508

Chi-square ($df =$ 1) is 11.7, and using Table B.4 we find $p <$ .001 (the more exact p is .0006), and the effect size r computed from 1-df chi-square is

$$r_{\text{effect size}} = \sqrt{\frac{\chi^2}{N}} = \sqrt{\frac{11.73}{508}} = .15.$$

To recast the effect size r of .15 into a BESD, we use 100[.50 ± (r/2)], which gives us the following binomial effect-size display:

Condition	Blood clot	No blood clot	Total
Low-dose warfarin	42.5	57.5	100
Placebo	57.5	42.5	100
Total	100	100	200

The difference between 57.5 and 42.5 tells us the "success rate" of low-dose warfarin would be 15% if half the population of patients received low-dose warfarin and half did not, and if half that population experienced a blood clot and half did not. In other words, the effect size r of .15 is equivalent to increasing the success rate from 42.5% to 57.5% in such a standardized population. Computing the risk difference (RD), and using this result to estimate the number needed to treat (NNT) to avoid a single case of the adverse event (blood clot) and the number of patients that would benefit from the treatment in a group of 10,000 yields:

$$\text{RD} = \left(\frac{A}{A + B}\right) - \left(\frac{C}{C + D}\right)$$

$$= \left(\frac{14}{255}\right) - \left(\frac{37}{253}\right) = -0.0913$$

$$\text{NNT} = 1/\text{RD} = 1/0.0913 = 11 \,(\text{rounded})$$

$$\text{RD}(10,000) = 0.0913(10,000) = 913$$

The collective results of all these effect size indicators are consistent in confirming the wisdom of the sponsor's decision to halt the study ahead of schedule, in order not to deprive the control group of the benefits of the treatment.

APPENDIX A

Reporting Your Research Results

 ### Research Reports in APA Style

For scientists in all fields, the research process is not complete until the results have been reported in a peer-reviewed journal. Undergraduate students in behavioral science courses with research requirements are also required to report their results, but the primary audience is usually the instructor. It is rare for undergraduate students to submit their research results to a scientific journal, as the rejection rates of many peer-reviewed scientific journals are daunting (70%, 80%, and higher). Because even most professional researchers have experienced rejection, they do not lightly encourage undergraduate students to strike out on their own without the skilled guidance of an experienced hand. If, however, you are that rare individual encouraged by your instructor to submit a paper to a journal, then your instructor will also advise you about the precise style required for journal submissions. In research methods courses in psychology and some related disciplines in which students are expected to present their empirical results to the instructor in the form of a written report, it is usually expected to be in the *APA style*, that is, the style recommended in the sixth edition of the *Publication Manual of the American Psychological Association* (2010; hereafter called the APA Manual).

The purpose of this appendix is to provide an example of what a student's research report in APA style might look like, though with a few departures from the strict APA style required of *copy manuscripts* that are submitted for publication. Copy manuscripts are in a provisional form, but written reports submitted for class assignments are *final manuscripts* in a finished form. With that distinction in mind, the title page of Mary Jones's final manuscript (at the end of this appendix) has a layout similar to that of an APA-style copy manuscript, but the content of each part of Mary's title page is specifically addressed to the instructor. Another departure from the strict APA style is that Mary's report ends with an appendix section that reports her raw scores. Not all instructors require such an appendix section, but many do. Mary uses the appendix not only to report the raw scores but also to provide additional details about the statistical data analyses that she performed.

Incidentally, the APA style is not the only formatting style that students are likely to encounter in college. In English, language, and literature classes, instructors often have students write "research papers" in the style recommended by the Modern Language Association (called the *MLA style*). The term *research* is used differently in those courses than in research methods courses. In an English class, "research" is a way of saying "I looked things up," but in research methods courses, you are saying that you did an empirical investigation.

In the remainder of this appendix, we will shepherd you through the major sections of the research report of an individual study, using Mary Jones's research report as a frame of reference. Some colleges have Web sites that provide psychology students with guidance on writing papers in the APA style. The APA has a 280-page "Official Pocket Style Guide" titled *Concise Rules of APA Style*, and it also has a blog at http://blog.apa.style.org (or http://twitter.com/APA_style). The modified APA style on which Mary Jones's report was based (along with other suggestions mentioned in this discussion) was adapted from Rosnow and Rosnow's (2012) *Writing Papers in Psychology*.

Getting Started

As we frequently refer to Mary Jones's research report, we suggest you start by looking at Mary's sample report, which begins on page 306. The report illustrates a number of APA style points and (as noted above) some suggested modifications for student papers, but not everything in the sample report will be needed in every student paper. For example, you may not need footnotes, or you may be using more than one table or one or more figures, or your instructor may not require an appendix section. Thus, it is important at the outset to know what the instructor expects of you.

For example, do you know exactly when the final report is due? Is there a specified length for the final report? Are you required to turn in intermediate drafts or outlines, and when are they due? Are sample reports available to provide a further idea of what is expected? You can speak with other students to get their impressions, but that approach may stress you out even more. The best person to consult is the instructor, teaching assistant, or grader to make sure that you are on the right track. Incidentally, the raw scores in the sample report are real-world data (provided by Dr. Bruce Rind). We have included this research in previous editions of this book and each time have edited the report to keep it fresh and timely (as we did again this time).

If your instructor requires that you adhere strictly to the APA style for fonts and lettering, the APA Manual recommends a serif font (such as 12-point Times New Roman) for all parts of the manuscript except the lettering of figures. (*Serif fonts* have a tiny stroke at the beginning and end of each letter.) For the lettering of figures, the APA Manual recommends a sans serif font (*sans* means "without"). Use double spacing between all text lines, and leave margins of at least 1 inch at the top, bottom, and both sides of every page. Use a maximum line length of 6 ½ inches, and don't use hyphenation to break a word at the end of the line. Leave all the right margins uneven (called a *ragged* margin), as in Mary's report. You can use the default setting of the tab key, or you can set the tab key at ½ inch or 5–7 spaces to indent the first line of every paragraph.

We turn next to a description of each part of the basic structure of the report of a single study, but remember that not all research reports will require all these parts:

Title page (numbered page 1)

Abstract (numbered page 2)

Introduction (starts on page 3, with the full title repeated)

Method (no page break)

Results (no page break)

Discussion (no page break)

References (starts on a separate page)

Footnotes (starts on a separate page)

Tables (each table starts on a separate page)

Figures (each figure starts on a separate page)

Appendix (starts on a separate page)

A final piece of advice before we start: Try to begin early, so that you don't feel rushed as the deadline approaches and so you will have time to revise and polish your work well before the due dates. Here are some suggestions about tasks to put on your calendar:

- Finish gathering references
- Draft a research proposal
- Due date of polished proposal
- Completion of ethics review
- Begin collecting the data

- Begin the data analysis
- Write a first draft
- Polish the draft in APA style
- Proofread the final manuscript
- Due date of final manuscript

 Title Page

Glancing at the title page of Mary Jones's report, notice that there is a *page header* consisting of two words in caps (taken from the full title) in the top left corner on the same line as the page number in the right corner. This abbreviated title is repeated on the top of every page (and is also called a *running head*) so the instructor can easily identify pages that may become separated from the rest. Using the abbreviated title as the page header in students' final manuscripts is a remnant of the peer review convention of masking the names of authors of *copy manuscripts* submitted for publication. (Because Mary's *final manuscript* satisfies a course requirement and is not a "copy manuscript" submitted to a journal for a blind review, the instructor may prefer having the student's name as the page header, as shown in the sample proposal in Chapter 2.)

The full title of the report summarizes the main idea of the research and is centered near the top of the title page. (Notice that the full title appears again on page 3 of the report.) Below the full title is the student's name (called the *byline*), and below that is the name of the educational institution.

The next section of the title page is the Author Note, which is divided into two parts. In the first part, Mary Jones takes responsibility for the originality of the research reported and identifies the course. She then acknowledges the assistance provided by others. The second part of the Author Note is Mary's contact information.

On the bottom of the page, centered and set off from the author note, the student indicates the date that this final manuscript is submitted to the instructor.

 Abstract

The *abstract* (the word is capitalized, centered, and in boldface) appears on page 2 of the report. Its purpose is to give the reader (the instructor) a distillation in one paragraph (not indented) of the important points in the body of the research report, so write it after you have written the rest of the report. The APA Manual lists four essentials of good abstracts. First, they are accurate reporting the purpose and content of the research. Second, they report but do not evaluate that information (the evaluation is saved for the results section). Third, they contain no jargon. Fourth, they are concise in describing the objective of the research, the participants, the method used, the basic findings, and the conclusions.

Here are five questions to guide you as you draft your abstract after you have written your report:

- What was the objective of the research?
- Who were the participants?
- What empirical method did you use?
- What were the findings?
- What did you conclude?

 Introduction

The introduction (the first section after the abstract page) has no section heading but leads by repeating the full title of the report (centered, but not in bold). This section emphasizes linking the problem investigated and related ideas to past research and/or empirically grounded theories, and it

(*text continues on p. 320*)

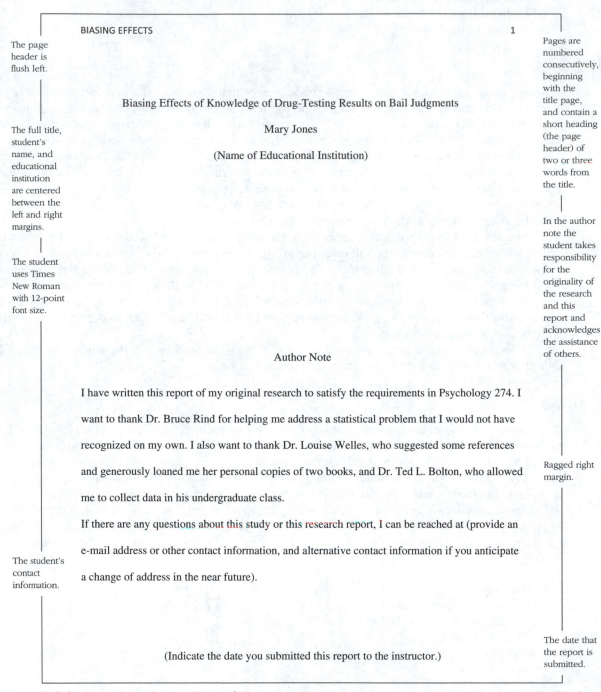

BIASING EFFECTS   1

The page header is flush left.

Pages are numbered consecutively, beginning with the title page, and contain a short heading (the page header) of two or three words from the title.

Biasing Effects of Knowledge of Drug-Testing Results on Bail Judgments

Mary Jones

(Name of Educational Institution)

The full title, student's name, and educational institution are centered between the left and right margins.

In the author note the student takes responsibility for the originality of the research and this report and acknowledges the assistance of others.

The student uses Times New Roman with 12-point font size.

Author Note

I have written this report of my original research to satisfy the requirements in Psychology 274. I want to thank Dr. Bruce Rind for helping me address a statistical problem that I would not have recognized on my own. I also want to thank Dr. Louise Welles, who suggested some references and generously loaned me her personal copies of two books, and Dr. Ted L. Bolton, who allowed me to collect data in his undergraduate class.

If there are any questions about this study or this research report, I can be reached at (provide an e-mail address or other contact information, and alternative contact information if you anticipate a change of address in the near future).

Ragged right margin.

The student's contact information.

(Indicate the date you submitted this report to the instructor.)

The date that the report is submitted.

Exhibit A.1   Mary Jones's Research Report

(*continued*)

BIASING EFFECTS   2

The page
header is on
every page.

The abstract
begins on
page 2.

Abstract

The research reported here was inspired by a debate over the mandatory drug testing of suspects on arrest. The issue contested was whether having knowledge of this testing would have biasing effects on bail judgments in legal proceedings. My hypothesis, which was grounded in an aspect of correspondent inference theory, was that harsher bail judgments are more likely when judges have been informed that the defendant tested positive for drug usage. This research was intended to simulate such a situation by using college students as the "judges." The students were assigned (at random) to one of two scenarios, both of which described a defendant who had been arrested as a suspected burglar. In the experimental condition, the scenario stated that the defendant's blood test while in custody revealed that he had recently used drugs. In the control condition, the scenario made no mention of the drug test information. The students in both conditions were told to imagine that they were the bail judge and to set a dollar amount from $0 to $50,000. The data were analyzed by an independent-sample t and afterward, because of observed heterogeneity of variance, by an alternative approach known as Satterthwaite's method. All these results were in the predicted direction, and the effect size correlation was approximately .35. In the discussion section, I point out some limitations of this study and propose ideas for future research.

Ragged right
margin on
every page.

The abstract
tells why the
research was
done, what
was hypothe-
sized, what the
results were,
and what else
appears in the
discussion.

The abstract
is written
after the rest
of the report
is completed.

Exhibit A.1   *(continued)*

Biasing Effects of Knowledge of Drug-Testing Results on Bail Judgments

The main task of the bail judge is to set bail at a level that will make it likely the defendant will appear for trial. In making this decision, the judge will perhaps consider factors suggestive of the defendant's traits, with the idea that some traits should predict whether the defendant will skip bail or show up for the trial. In this regard, attribution theory is specifically concerned with factors that influence how observers infer the traits of particular actors (Jones & Davis, 1965; Kelley, 1972) and how this trait information is used to make decisions or judgments regarding actors (Baron & Byrne, 1987). For example, Jones and Davis's classic work on correspondent inference theory provided a conceptual framework for the description of how observers go about inferring traits of actors. According to Jones and Davis, observers tend to focus on certain types of behavior on the assumption that certain actions are indicative of some traits. Three questions that observers may ask themselves, according to Jones and Davis, are (a) Was the behavior freely chosen? (b) Did the behavior produce uncommon effects? and (c) Was the behavior low in social desirability?[1]

Consider, for example, a situation in which the bail judge was informed of the positive drug testing result of the accused person prior to the judge's making a bail ruling. Would knowing that the accused person had tested positive be likely to bias the bail ruling, possibly even in instances in which there was no connection between the person's drug usage and the crime for which the person would be tried? Lawyers may disagree, however, about the likely consequences of drug-testing results on bail judgments. Some might contend that bail judges would not be swayed by this information, whereas others might argue that drug testing could pose a threat to individual rights because knowledge of positive results is likely to bias judges' decisions on how much bail to impose. I think of my research as primarily exploratory given the nature of the sample and the

The text begins on page 3 and opens with a repetition of the full title.

Each paragraph is indented.

Ragged right margins on every page.

Superscript for the footnote.

The introduction sets the stage and flows into the hypotheses and/or exploratory questions.

Exhibit A.1   *(continued)*

BIASING EFFECTS   4

simulation used, but I did have an expectation of the direction of the results

My expectation was based on the assumption that drug usage is generally perceived as

a freely chosen behavior that produces uncommon effects and is low in social desirability by our

societal standards. Thus, it could be argued that this behavior is likely to be heavily weighted in

predicting the actor's future behavior or, in the real world situation in which I was interested, in

whether a defendant is likely to appear for trial. Given this line of reasoning, my hypothesis was

that providing "judges" with information about positive results from a drug test is likely to result

in harsher bail judgments than when such information is not made available.

Method

Participants

The research participants consisted of 31 male and female students in an undergraduate

course. I received permission from the instructor to conduct this study during a regular meeting

of the class, as the instructor explained to the class that it would give those who wished to take

part in my study an opportunity to have a firsthand experience of what it is like to participate in

psychological research. The participation was, however, voluntary and there was no penalty for

not participating. It turned out that all the students participated, and 15 were randomly assigned

to the experimental condition and 16 to the control condition (as described below).

Materials

The materials were one-page questionnaires, which began by asking for the student's age,

sex, year in college, grade point average, and major. This was followed by the instruction: "Now

please read the following paragraph carefully, and then answer the question that follows it."

In the experimental condition, the paragraph that followed for the participant to read next

stated:

The student's hypothesis concludes the introduction and leads into the method section, which follows without a page break.

First-level headings are centered and in boldface.

Second-level headings are flush left and in boldface.

Exhibit A.1   *(continued)*

A man was arrested as a suspected burglar. He fit the description of a man seen running from

the burglarized house. While in custody the man submitted to a blood test, and it was

determined that he had very recently used drugs.

In the control condition, the following paragraph was substituted for the paragraph the students

in the experimental condition read:

A man was arrested as a suspected burglar. He fit the description of a man seen running from

the burglarized house. He spent enough time in custody so that he received two meals and

made three phone calls.

In both conditions, the paragraphs were immediately followed by this question:

If you were the bail judge, what bail would you set? Choose a dollar amount from $0 to

$50,000:

_____ amount of bail

Design and Procedure

The class was told that this was a study to explore the question of the amount of bail they

thought was appropriate in a hypothetical court case. The two versions of the questionnaire were

mixed together and distributed at the same time. The students were told there was no penalty for

not participating in this study, in which case all that they need do was to keep the questionnaire

until I asked for it at the end of the study. If they were willing to participate, they were instructed

to complete the information at the top of the page, read the scenario that followed, and then write

down their bail judgment. When it was apparent that students had completed the questionnaires,

they were instructed to fold them in half so only the blank side showed and to pass them forward.

The purpose of this procedure was to shield the results from the other students. I also thought it

would be a way of protecting the identity of those who chose not to complete the questionnaire,

Margin notes:

Double-spacing is used throughout the text of the report.

Second-level heading.

Exhibit A.1   (*continued*)

but (as noted above) it turned out that all of the students had chosen to participate.

Results

The results section of the text follows without a page break.

First-level heading is centered and in boldface.

The descriptive results are summarized in Table 1, which shows the mean (*M*) judgment in each condition, the square root (*S*) of the unbiased estimator of the population value of σ^2, the corresponding variance (S^2), the standard deviation (σ) of each set of scores, and the sample size (*n*) in each condition. Using an independent-sample *t* test (described in the appendix section later in this report) to compare the two means, the result was $t(29) = 2.08$, $p = .046$ two-tailed, $r_{\text{effect size}} = .36$, and 95% CI[.01,.63].

The results section describes the findings, beginning with those that are most relevant to the hypotheses.

One of the assumptions underlying *t* tests used to compare two groups is that the *t* value will be more accurate as the variances (the S^2 values) of the populations from which the sampling units were drawn are more nearly equal in variance (Rosenthal & Rosnow, 2008). One traditional way to test this assumption is by using Hartley's F_{max}, in which the larger of the two S^2 values is divided by the smaller S^2 value and the quotient is referred to a special statistics table that takes into account the number of groups being compared and the degrees of freedom (*df*). Dividing the larger of the two S^2 values in Table 1 by the smaller S^2 yielded $F(14,15) = 9.0$, $p = 6.3^{-5}$, which is an indication of the violation of the homogeneity of variance required by the *t* test (Rosenthal & Rosnow, 2008).

Enough information is reported for others to make sense of the data and reach their own conclusions.

As described in more detail in the appendix of this report, one way of dealing with this problem was to use Satterthwaite's approximate method. By this method, the *t* is calculated using a modified formula and the *df* are adjusted. Taking this approach, I obtained $t(16) = 2.03$, $p = .06$ two-tailed, $r_{\text{effect size}} = .34$, and 95% CI[-.02,.62]. The reason that the confidence interval crosses slightly into the negative side is that the procedure I used to compute the 95% CI (as described in Rosnow & Rosenthal, 2009, p. 10) had .05 as the two-tailed *p*, and the obtained *p* of .06 (or more

Exhibit A.1   (*continued*)

precisely, .059) did not quite make the .05 level. A more detailed discussion of this approach can be found in the appendix at the end of this report, including all my calculations and the raw data on which the calculations (and Table 1) are based.

The discussion follows without a page break. It begins by reiterating the original expectation and describing the results that are most relevant to that expectation.

Discussion

First-level heading.

Although I still view this simulation study as primarily exploratory, I did begin with the expectation that knowledge of positive results from the (fictitious) defendant's drug test would result in harsher bail judgments than when that information was unavailable to participants who played the role of a "bail judge." Both my original analysis and a subsequent analysis proposed by the instructor were consistent with the hypothesis above. On the surface, this finding implies that the goal of being just and unbiased, which is one objective of our criminal justice system, is potentially compromised when drug testing and the reporting of its results are legally mandated. However, inasmuch as I was unable to use real judges and had to use college students, the results may not be applicable to the "real world" behavior of actual bail judges. Interestingly, a similar concern as to the generalizability of the simulated behavior in an experimental laboratory to real world behavior was also recently raised by Leavitt and List (2007) in another context.

Future research might be designed to address that potential problem of external invalidity and possibly other plausible threats to external and internal validity as well (Strohmetz, 2008). Future research might also be considered to assess the participants' inferences of corresponding traits from socially undesirable behavior. It is interesting that although the participants seemingly judged the suspect more harshly when the drug information was included, there was actually no logical connection emphasized between the drug usage and the burglary. Perhaps the participants were drawing on a stereotype to assume that the association was likely, because the media often report property crimes that are motivated by the need to get money to purchase drugs. Followup

Conclude with the limitations and the implications for future research.

Exhibit A.1 (*continued*)

BIASING EFFECTS   8

research could use crime scenarios that are not stereotypically associated with drugs to determine

whether biasing effects occur and are general in nature. Finally, I have not attempted to focus on

the legal issue of whether the mandatory testing of someone "innocent until proved guilty" could

possibly be unconstitutional on the grounds that it is a violation of a person's civil rights. Clearly

there are interesting and important questions still waiting to be addressed, but perhaps that might

be said of all research.

The discussion ties everything together.

Exhibit A.1   (*continued*)

BIASING EFFECTS   9

References

Baron, R. A., & Byrne, D. (1987). *Social psychology: Understanding human interaction*. Boston, MA: Allyn & Bacon.

Jones, E. E., & Davis, K. E. (1965). From acts to dispositions: The attribution process in person perception. In L. Berkowitz (Ed.), *Advances in experimental social psychology* (Vol. 2, pp. 219-266). New York, NY: Academic Press. doi:10.1016/S0065-2601(08)60107-0

Kelley, H. H. (1972). Attribution in social interaction. In E. E. Jones, D. E. Kanouse, R. E. Nisbett, S. Valins, & B. Weiner (Eds.), *Attribution: Perceiving the causes of behavior* (pp. 1-26). Morristown, NJ: General Learning Press.

Leavitt, S. D., & List, J. A. (2007). What do laboratory experiments measuring social preferences reveal about the real world? *Journal of Economic Perspectives, 21,* 153-174. doi:10.1257/jep.21.2.153

Rosenthal, R., & Rosnow, R. L. (2008). *Essentials of behavioral research: Methods and data analysis* (3rd ed.). New York: McGraw-Hill.

Rosnow, R. L., & Rosenthal, R. (2009). Effect sizes: Why, when, and how to use them. *Zeitschrift fur Psychologie/Journal of Psychology, 217,* 6-14. doi:10.1027/0044-3409.217.1.6

Strohmetz, D. B. (2008). Research artifacts and the social psychology of psychological experiments. *Social and Personality Psychology Compass* 2(2008): 10.111/j.1751-9004.2007.00072.x

VandenBos, G. R. (Ed.). (2007). *APA dictionary of psychology*. Washington, DC: American Psychological Association.

Hanging indents are used for all references.

The references begin on a new page.

The doi is the Digital Object Identifier.

Every article and book cited in the report is listed in the references, and every reference is cited in the report.

Exhibit A.1   (*continued*)

BIASING EFFECTS   10

Footnotes

[1]In my research proposal, I mentioned only that I had consulted my notes from a social

psychology course that I took last semester. Dr. Rind advised me to meet with the instructor to

make sure I was representing her lecture accurately and, if she agreed, to then acknowledge her

assistance in an author note. I did, in fact, meet with the instructor, Dr. Louise Welles, who also

generously loaned me her personal copies of Baron and Byrne (1987) and Jones et al. (1972, in

which the chapter by Kelley was published), as neither book was available in the college library

and there was no guarantee that I would be able to obtain them through an interlibrary loan in a

reasonable amount of time.

Superscript
for the
footnote
number.

The footnotes
begin on a
new page.

Exhibit A.1   (*continued*)

Table number and title (which is in italics) are flush left.

The table begins a new page.

Table 1

Mean, Variability, and Sample Size in Each Condition

Results	Experimental group	Control group
M	$16,146.67	$6,990.63
S	16,645.07	5,549.60
S^2	277,058,355.31	30,798,060.16
σ	16,080.67	5,373.38
n	15	16

The numerical values are arranged in an orderly display of columns and rows.

The note is flush left with no paragraph indentation.

Note. Median values were 10,000 and 5,000 in the experimental and control groups, respectively. The individual bail judgments on which the values in this table were based are in the appendix at the end of this report.

Exhibit A.1　(*continued*)

BIASING EFFECTS   12

Appendix

The following table shows the raw scores (i.e., the individual bail judgments) of the 31

students who were randomly assigned to the experimental and control conditions:

Experimental	Control
50,000	20,000
50,000	15,000
30,000	10,000
30,000	10,000
20,000	10,000
12,500	10,000
10,000	10,000
10,000	5,000
10,000	5,000
10,000	5,000
5,000	5,000
2,000	4,000
2,000	1,500
500	500
200	500
	350

Shown below are the basic equations I began with and my calculations for each of the

equations, starting with the independent-sample *t* test on the raw scores above:

$$t = \frac{M_1 - M_2}{\sqrt{\left(\frac{1}{n_1} + \frac{1}{n_2}\right) S^2_{pooled}}} = \frac{16{,}146.67 - 6{,}990.63}{\sqrt{\left(\frac{1}{15} + \frac{1}{16}\right) 149{,}682{,}340.575}} = 2.08,$$

and the effect size correlation computed from *t*:

Exhibit A.1   (*continued*)

$$r_{\text{effect size}} = \sqrt{\frac{t^2}{t^2 + df}} = \sqrt{\frac{(2.08)^2}{(2.08)^2 + 29}} = .36.$$

I met with Dr. Rind after I collected the data and showed him the descriptive statistics in

Table 1. He said that if I were interested in learning about the "robustness of the t test," he could

suggest an additional analysis but I would need to read a few pages in an advanced textbook. As

I was interested, he also told me to calculate F_{max} by dividing the larger of my two variances (S^2

= 277,058,355.31 experimental) by the smaller variance (S^2 = 30,798,060.16 control group) and

then to follow the instructions in Rosenthal and Rosnow (2008, p. 431) and calculate the t test by

Satterthwaite's method (pp. 401-403). The results of all the analyses and what I learned about the

robustness of the t test are described in this appendix.

Mary uses citation and quote to buttress the discussion in the appendix.

Turning first to the *APA Dictionary of Psychology*, I learned that the term *robustness* was

defined as "the ability of a hypothesis-testing or estimation procedure to produce valid results in

spite of violations of the assumptions upon which the methodology is based" (VandenBos, 2007,

p. 803). Dividing the larger of the two variances by the smaller variance gave $F(14,15) = 8.996$,

$p = 6.3^{-5}$, indicating violation of the homogeneity of variance required by the t test. As explained

in Rosenthal and Rosnow (2008):

Block quotation is indented.

For the t test situation in which two groups are being compared, the t obtained will be more

accurate if the variances of the populations from which the data were drawn are more nearly

equal. Only if the population variances are very different *and* if the two sample sizes are very

different is the violation of this assumption [of homogeneity of variance] likely to lead to

serious consequences. (p. 401)

Ragged right margin.

I next tried "Satterthwaite's approximate method," which Rosenthal and Rosnow (2008)

described as "a serviceable way to make an independent t more accurate" (p. 401). This method

uses a modified computational formula for t and an estimate of the adjusted degrees of freedom

Exhibit A.1   (*continued*)

BIASING EFFECTS   14

for use with the modified t. Using the following formulas given in Rosenthal and Rosnow (2008,

p. 402) yielded:

$$t_{\text{Satterthwaite}} = \frac{M_1 - M_2}{\sqrt{\dfrac{S_1^2}{n_1} + \dfrac{S_2^2}{n_2}}} = \frac{16{,}146.67 - 6{,}990.63}{\sqrt{\dfrac{277{,}058{,}355.305}{15} + \dfrac{30{,}798{,}060.16}{16}}} = 2.03$$

Equations can be written by hand if that is easier than formatting them using the word processor.

and

$$df_{\text{Satterthwaite}} = \frac{\left(\dfrac{S_1^2}{n_1} + \dfrac{S_2^2}{n_2}\right)^2}{\left[\dfrac{\left(\dfrac{S_1^2}{n_1}\right)^2}{n_1 - 1}\right] + \left[\dfrac{\left(\dfrac{S_2^2}{n_2}\right)^2}{n_2 - 1}\right]} = \frac{\left(\dfrac{277{,}058{,}355.305}{15} + \dfrac{30{,}798{,}060.16}{16}\right)^2}{\left[\dfrac{\left(\dfrac{277{,}058{,}355.305}{15}\right)^2}{15 - 1}\right] + \left[\dfrac{\left(\dfrac{30{,}798{,}060.16}{16}\right)^2}{16 - 1}\right]} = 16.90.$$

Following instructions in Rosenthal and Rosnow (2008, p. 402), I "truncated" the 16.90

df to the next lower integer, 16. The t of 2.03 was slightly smaller than the unadjusted t of 2.08

that I obtained originally; the p value of the adjusted t used Satterthwaite's degrees of freedom

($df = 16$) and was $p = .059$ two-tailed. For the effect size r, I used the t value of 1.96 associated

with the adjusted p noted above and, following instructions, used the original degrees of freedom

(29), which gave me:

$$r_{\text{effect size}} = \sqrt{\frac{t^2}{t^2 + df}} = \sqrt{\frac{(1.96)^2}{(1.96)^2 + 29}} = .34.$$

This effect size value was only slightly smaller than the one I calculated originally as .36. These

statistical analyses taught me that t was relatively robust even in the face of the violation of the

homogeneity of variance assumption.

Exhibit A.1   (*continued*)

is expected to flow into your hypothesis or research question and (in the next section) the method used. In other words, a good "evidence-based" introduction tells the reader about the point of the research and provides a persuasive framework for what follows. The idea is to lead the reader to the thought, "Yes, of course, that is what this researcher *had* to do to answer the question or test the hypothesis."

Here are some questions to help you plan the introduction:

- What was the purpose of your research, and why did it seem important to choose this particular problem?
- What were your hypotheses and/or expectations, and what were your reasoning and grounds for those hypotheses or expectations?
- Are there terms that you need to define for the reader who may be unfamiliar with this area?
- If you had more than one hypothesis, how are your hypotheses interconnected (so they don't seem fragmented)?
- When you turn to the method section afterward, will it be clear from your introduction that the empirical procedures you used were a natural consequence of the questions you wanted to answer?

 Method

In the method section, you describe the research participants, the materials or instruments used, and the research design and procedure. It is customary to subdivide this section, possibly in the way that the sample report is subdivided into "Participants," "Materials," and "Design and Procedure." However, no ironclad rule states that you must use these particular subdivisions and headings if you have a clearer, more logical, and more fluid way of describing what you did. Notice also that each section heading ("Method") is centered and in bold, whereas the subsection headings ("Participants," etc.) are flush left, in bold, and separated from the paragraph that follows. The center heading is called a *first-level heading*, and the subsection heading is a *second-level heading*. If you need a *third-level heading*, it should be indented and in boldface, only the first letter of the first word should be in uppercase, and the heading should end with a period followed by the text.

In the first subsection, Mary tells us about the students who "participated" in her research. The question of whether to call these people "participants" or "subjects" (a commonly used term in many research fields) is a matter of some sensitivity in psychology. Calling them "subjects," it has been said, makes them seem like mindless robots rather than sentient and active beings with their own needs, expectations, anxieties, and sensitivities to task-orienting cues (called *demand characteristics* in Chapter 7). The APA Manual advises that researchers write about the people in their study "in a way that acknowledges their participation but is also consistent with the traditions of the field" (American Psychological Association, 2010, p. 73). We would only add that they must be described clearly, accurately, and in sufficient detail to prevent any misunderstanding about the sample of people who participated in the research, as this information pertains directly to the degree of generalizability (the *external validity*).

Another sensitive problem is avoiding sexist language in describing the people who participate. It would be a mistake, for example, to use the word *man* as a general term for both sexes, as the word creates a mental picture that is simply inaccurate (Dumond, 1990). On the other hand, if the people who participated were only men, it would be misleading *not* to describe them by sex (and by other relevant characteristics, such as age and level of education). When this issue first gained prominence some years ago, many writers used contrived words such as *s/he* and *he/she* to avoid sexist language when referring to both men and women. You can avoid awkward terms like these by using plural pronouns (*they, them, their*) when you are referring to both genders. The basic rule, however, is not to mislead readers by creating the wrong mental picture when describing the people who participated in your research.

The next subdivision of Mary's method section describes the questionnaire she developed for use in her research. If you used well-known tests or standardized measures of some kind, this is the section of your report where you provide information about the known reliability and validity of the instruments and cite your sources. If you are referring to reliability, you will need to specify which type of reliability you mean: the test-retest reliability, the alternate-form reliability, or the internal-consistency reliability (each explained in Chapter 6). Similarly, if you refer to the term *validity,* you will need to specify which type of validity you mean (also in Chapter 6). The final subdivision of Mary's method section is where she describes in detail the design of her research and the procedure she used for implementing it.

 Results

You describe your findings in the results section, beginning with the results that are most relevant to your hypotheses. You might, as Mary does, present the summary results in a table. We will have more to say about tables and the appendix section of the student's report later in this discussion, but notice that Mary mentions there is a Table 1 and also calls attention to the appendix section. In the following paragraphs, Mary mentions another data analysis, thus going from the general findings to the statistical procedures she used to evaluate her hypothesis. It was not necessary for her to repeat in her narrative text every detail in the table, but she tells enough to explain why she did the secondary analysis using the procedure called Satterthwaite's approximate method.

It is important to report enough information for others to make sense of the data and reach their own conclusions. The APA Manual suggests reporting at least (a) the number of units, or participants, in the samples and subsamples; (b) the sample and subsample means or, in chi-square designs, frequencies; and (c) the standard deviation or pooled within-cell variances. For statistical tests such as t, F, and chi-square, the APA Manual calls for the reporting of (d) the exact value of the test statistic; (e) the degrees of freedom; (f) the statistical probability (p level); and (g) the effect size indices associated with single degree-of-freedom statistical tests (what we described as "focused statistical tests" in Chapter 14; see also the glossary). Also recommended in the APA Manual are (h) reporting the confidence intervals for estimations of population means and effect sizes and (i) basing those confidence intervals on a prespecified level (such as 95% CI or 99% CI), which is then consistently used in the report.

The APA Manual notes, "Historically, researchers in psychology have relied heavily on null hypothesis significance testing (NHST) as a starting point for many…[data] analytic approaches" (p. 33). The manual goes on to state that "APA stresses that NHST is but a starting point and that additional reporting elements such as effect sizes, confidence intervals, and extensive description are needed to convey the most complete meaning of the results" (p. 33). Not all instructors consider NHST a starting point, but most would probably agree with the rest of the statement above. All of the recommended information is reported in Mary's paper.

A trick to help you pull the results together before you start writing is to set down a list of your statistical findings. Divide the list into coherent sets of results, and then decide the sequence according to their order of importance or relevance to your hypotheses, questions, and objectives. Experienced authors try to anticipate the concerns that readers may have, particularly inquiries about ambiguous results that call for clarification or further analysis. Here are some questions to help you organize this section:

- What did you find, and what is the order of importance of your findings?
- Can you describe what you found in a careful, detailed way?
- Have you left out anything important?
- Are there details that belong in the appendix rather than in the results section?
- Is there enough information for a reader to draw his or her own conclusions?

Discussion

In the discussion section, you integrate and interpret your findings in a way that will pull everything together. If you had a sudden insight or an unexpected idea, the discussion section is also the place to write about it. Without being overly repetitive, Mary begins by reminding us of the background that she developed in the introduction. She recapitulates her original hypothesis, underscoring the logical continuity of her presentation. She writes "defensively" in that she plays her own devil's advocate by pointing out the limitations of her study. She raises some potential implications and future directions of her research and thus further indicates to the instructor that she has thought deeply about her research.

As you begin to write a first draft of this section, here are some questions to consider:

- What was the major purpose of your study, and were there any secondary objectives?
- How do your results relate to that purpose and those objectives?
- Were there any unexpected findings of interest, and how do you plan to show their relevance to this project and to possible follow-up research?
- How valid and generalizable are your findings, and what are their limitations?
- What can you say about the wider implications of the results?

References

The title page and abstract are each on separate pages, and the first page of the introduction (page 3 of Mary's paper) begins on a separate page, but the method section, results, and discussion section follow one another without any page breaks. The reference section also begins on a separate page. The basic rule is that every article, chapter, and book that you cited anywhere in your report must be listed in the references section, and every reference you list must be cited somewhere in your report. If at the last minute you need to recheck the author, title, or publisher of a book that you cited, you can go to the Library of Congress Web site (http://catalog.loc.gov). If you need to recheck a published article (e.g., for page numbers of quoted material), you can use your college library's electronic full-text databases.

Here is a condensed list of the APA Manual's rules about how to reference books and articles:

- List authors' names in the exact order in which they appear on the title page of the publication and by last name, then first initial and middle initial.
- Authors' names are separated by commas; use an ampersand (&) before the last author.
- Give the year the work was copyrighted (the year and month for magazine articles and the year, month, and day for newspaper articles).
- For titles of books, chapters in books, and journal articles, generally capitalize only the first word of the title and of the subtitle (if any) as well as any proper names.
- Italicize the title of a book or a journal and the volume number of a journal article.
- Give the city and state for a book's publisher in the United States, using postal abbreviations for the state. For a foreign city, give the country name.
- If what you are referencing has a digital objective identifier (doi), list it at the end of the reference as "doi:xxxxx" without a period.
- If there is no doi and you retrieved the information electronically, the APA style is to list the "http" (for "hypertext transfer protocol") address (called the URL, for Universal Resource Locator) for the journal or other source of information.

Footnotes

The purpose of footnotes is to add essential details or enlarge on something in a way that cannot be easily fitted into the narrative text of the research report without disrupting the flow of the presentation. Use footnotes only if you believe that they are absolutely essential, however. Mary uses a footnote to go into detail that would be of interest only in a paper written for this course assignment; it is not the kind of footnote that would be in an article published in an APA journal. Notice that the "footnotes" section (Mary has one footnote) starts on a new page, and the heading is centered but not in boldface. The number of the footnote is in superscript, and the footnote is indented. Going back to the end of the first paragraph of Mary's introduction (page 3 of her report), you will see another superscript referencing this footnote.

Tables and Figures

By the term *tables*, the APA Manual means displays that "usually show numerical values or textual information … arranged in an orderly display of columns and rows" (p. 125). If you decided to include more than one table, each would begin on a new page. The table number and the title of the table are flush left, and only the title is in italics. To include a note expanding on some point or explaining something, type the word *Note* (italicized and followed by a period) before the note. Everything is flush left, and there is no paragraph indentation. As illustrated in the sample report, each column of Mary's Table 1 has a heading that defines the items below, and all of the row and column information is clear, concise, and informative.

The difference between tables and figures, as these terms are explained in the APA Manual, is that "any type of illustration other than a table is referred to as a *figure*" (p. 125). If you are wrestling with whether to use a table as opposed to a bar graph or line graph, keep in mind that exact values can be given in a table (or in a stem-and-leaf chart), but readers can make only an educated guess about the exact values in a bar graph or line graph. For poster presentations, where people do not usually want to stand around in a cramped area with relatively poor lighting and study detailed information, simple bar graphs and line graphs are an effective way of presenting an overall picture of your results. However, because even the most interested viewers are unlikely to want to take extensive notes, have a handout with information they can take with them (e.g., Rosnow & Rosnow, 2012, pp. 152–153).

Appendix

The final section in Mary Jones's report, the appendix, also starts on a new page. As the material included in the appendix of a student's research report can vary greatly, the formatting style should be determined by the information reported. It is usually preferable to have a separate appendix for each general type of information or material. For example, Mary might have used one appendix for the questionnaires and another appendix for the scores and calculations. Had she done so, she would have labeled one Appendix A and the other Appendix B, and she would also have titled them to describe the contents of each.

The appendix in Mary's report takes the instructor through the logic of her data analysis and shows that Mary's analysis was done properly and that she has a clear understanding of the procedures used. If there is a mistake, the instructor can trace the inaccuracy and not penalize the student for making what might seem a misstep in interpretation or understanding when it was a less serious mistake, such as an overlooked typographical error.

Writing and Revising

Now that you know what is expected, it is time to begin writing a first draft. A good way to begin is to compose a *self-motivator statement* that you can refer to as a way of focusing your thoughts. In a short paragraph, remind yourself what your report will be about. This statement may also be useful to you when you write the abstract after you have written the rest of the report. At that point, it will be a reminder of what you viewed as the emphasis of your research. We can imagine the following as the self-motivator statement that Mary might have composed before she began the first draft of her research report:

> I'm going to describe why I conducted this research and what I learned about the biasing effect of knowledge of drug-testing results on bail judgments. I will open my report by explaining the problem and what I hypothesized. After describing the participants, questionnaires, and research procedure, I will give the main results and then the follow-up analysis that was suggested by the instructor. In the discussion, I will sum up my conclusions, mention the limitations of this simulation study and the sampling units studied, and possibly suggest future directions.

If you are someone who has trouble getting started, one useful trick is to begin not at the beginning but with the section you feel will be easiest to write. Once the ideas begin to flow, you can tackle the introductory section. This approach will also bolster flagging spirits, because you can reread the sections that you have already written when you begin to feel a loss of energy or determination. Try not to fall into the trap of napping, tweeting, or escaping into the blogosphere. If you recognize those counterproductive moves for what they are, you should be able to avoid them.

Here are three helpful hints to make the writing go more smoothly:

- Find a quiet, well-lighted place in which to write, and do your writing in 2-hour stretches.
- Print out a copy of your first draft so you can get an idea of what it will look like to the instructor.
- Pace your work so that you can complete the first draft and let it rest for at least 24 hours before you revise and polish what will be your final draft.

To help you catch misspellings, you can use a spell checker. Be sure that the spell checker has not missed any misspelled technical terms, however. It may not catch typos such as a capital *I* when you meant to type *in*. Using the grammar checker should catch that kind of mistake, but the grammar checker can drive some writers to distraction by querying almost every phrase and line they write. Grammar checkers are also notorious for catching "mistakes" that are not mistakes at all.

Put the final manuscript aside for a day or two, and then look at it again to make sure that no gremlins in the computer program introduced any weird changes. Make sure the print is dark enough to be easily read; you don't want to frustrate the grader by submitting a paper with typescript so light or blurry that it taxes the eyes. Make sure all the pages are in order, that there are no omissions or misspellings, that the numbers are correct, and that all references cited in the body of the paper are listed in the reference section. You should feel the satisfaction of a job well done.

APPENDIX B

Statistical Tables

Appendix B

Table B.1 z Values and Their Associated One-Tailed p Values

					Second digit of z					
z	.00	.01	.02	.03	.04	.05	.06	.07	.08	.09
.0	.5000	.4960	.4920	.4880	.4840	.4801	.4761	.4721	.4681	.4641
.1	.4602	.4562	.4522	.4483	.4443	.4404	.4364	.4325	.4286	.4247
.2	.4207	.4168	.4129	.4090	.4052	.4013	.3974	.3936	.3897	.3859
.3	.3821	.3783	.3745	.3707	.3669	.3632	.3594	.3557	.3520	.3483
.4	.3446	.3409	.3372	.3336	.3300	.3264	.3228	.3192	.3156	.3121
.5	.3085	.3050	.3015	.2981	.2946	.2912	.2877	.2843	.2810	.2776
.6	.2743	.2709	.2676	.2643	.2611	.2578	.2546	.2514	.2483	.2451
.7	.2420	.2389	.2358	.2327	.2296	.2266	.2236	.2206	.2177	.2148
.8	.2119	.2090	.2061	.2033	.2005	.1977	.1949	.1922	.1894	.1867
.9	.1841	.1814	.1788	.1762	.1736	.1711	.1685	.1660	.1635	.1611
1.0	.1587	.1562	.1539	.1515	.1492	.1469	.1446	.1423	.1401	.1379
1.1	.1357	.1335	.1314	.1292	.1271	.1251	.1230	.1210	.1190	.1170
1.2	.1151	.1131	.1112	.1093	.1075	.1056	.1038	.1020	.1003	.0985
1.3	.0968	.0951	.0934	.0918	.0901	.0885	.0869	.0853	.0838	.0823
1.4	.0808	.0793	.0778	.0764	.0749	.0735	.0721	.0708	.0694	.0681
1.5	.0668	.0655	.0643	.0630	.0618	.0606	.0594	.0582	.0571	.0559
1.6	.0548	.0537	.0526	.0516	.0505	.0495	.0485	.0475	.0465	.0455
1.7	.0446	.0436	.0427	.0418	.0409	.0401	.0392	.0384	.0375	.0367
1.8	.0359	.0351	.0344	.0336	.0329	.0322	.0314	.0307	.0301	.0294
1.9	.0287	.0281	.0274	.0268	.0262	.0256	.0250	.0244	.0239	.0233
2.0	.0228	.0222	.0217	.0212	.0207	.0202	.0197	.0192	.0188	.0183
2.1	.0179	.0174	.0170	.0166	.0162	.0158	.0154	.0150	.0146	.0143
2.2	.0139	.0136	.0132	.0129	.0125	.0122	.0119	.0116	.0113	.0110
2.3	.0107	.0104	.0102	.0099	.0096	.0094	.0091	.0089	.0087	.0084
2.4	.0082	.0080	.0078	.0075	.0073	.0071	.0069	.0068	.0066	.0064
2.5	.0062	.0060	.0059	.0057	.0055	.0054	.0052	.0051	.0049	.0048
2.6	.0047	.0045	.0044	.0043	.0041	.0040	.0039	.0038	.0037	.0036
2.7	.0035	.0034	.0033	.0032	.0031	.0030	.0029	.0028	.0027	.0026
2.8	.0026	.0025	.0024	.0023	.0023	.0022	.0021	.0021	.0020	.0019
2.9	.0019	.0018	.0018	.0017	.0016	.0016	.0015	.0015	.0014	.0014
3.0	.0013	.0013	.0013	.0012	.0012	.0011	.0011	.0011	.0010	.0010
3.1	.0010	.0009	.0009	.0009	.0008	.0008	.0008	.0008	.0007	.0007
3.2	.0007									
3.3	.0005									
3.4	.0003									
3.5	.00023									
3.6	.00016									
3.7	.00011									
3.8	.00007									
3.9	.00005									
4.0	.00003									

Source: S. Siegel, *Nonparametric Statistics*, 1st edition, McGraw-Hill. Copyright © 1956 The McGraw-Hill Companies. Reprinted with permission.

Table B.2   *t* Values and Their Associated One-Tailed and Two-Tailed *p* Values

p df	.50 .25	.20 .10	.10 .05	.05 .025	.02 .01	.01 .005	.005 .0025	.002 .001	
	.50	.20	.10	.05	.02	.01	.005	.002	two-tailed
	.25	.10	.05	.025	.01	.005	.0025	.001	one-tailed
1	1.000	3.078	6.314	12.706	31.821	63.657	127.321	318.309	
2	.816	1.886	2.920	4.303	6.965	9.925	14.089	22.327	
3	.765	1.638	2.353	3.182	4.541	5.841	7.453	10.214	
4	.741	1.533	2.132	2.776	3.747	4.604	5.598	7.173	
5	.727	1.476	2.015	2.571	3.365	4.032	4.773	5.893	
6	.718	1.440	1.943	2.447	3.143	3.707	4.317	5.208	
7	.711	1.415	1.895	2.365	2.998	3.499	4.029	4.785	
8	.706	1.397	1.860	2.306	2.896	3.355	3.833	4.501	
9	.703	1.383	1.833	2.262	2.821	3.250	3.690	4.297	
10	.700	1.372	1.812	2.228	2.764	3.169	3.581	4.144	
11	.697	1.363	1.796	2.201	2.718	3.106	3.497	4.025	
12	.695	1.356	1.782	2.179	2.681	3.055	3.428	3.930	
13	.694	1.350	1.771	2.160	2.650	3.012	3.372	3.852	
14	.692	1.345	1.761	2.145	2.624	2.977	3.326	3.787	
15	.691	1.341	1.753	2.131	2.602	2.947	3.286	3.733	
16	.690	1.337	1.746	2.120	2.583	2.921	3.252	3.686	
17	.689	1.333	1.740	2.110	2.567	2.898	3.223	3.646	
18	.688	1.330	1.734	2.101	2.552	2.878	3.197	3.610	
19	.688	1.328	1.729	2.093	2.539	2.861	3.174	3.579	
20	.687	1.325	1.725	2.086	2.528	2.845	3.153	3.552	
21	.686	1.323	1.721	2.080	2.518	2.831	3.135	3.527	
22	.686	1.321	1.717	2.074	2.508	2.819	3.119	3.505	
23	.685	1.319	1.714	2.069	2.500	2.807	3.104	3.485	
24	.685	1.318	1.711	2.064	2.492	2.797	3.090	3.467	
25	.684	1.316	1.708	2.060	2.485	2.787	3.078	3.450	
26	.684	1.315	1.706	2.056	2.479	2.779	3.067	3.435	
27	.684	1.314	1.703	2.052	2.473	2.771	3.057	3.421	
28	.683	1.313	1.701	2.048	2.467	2.763	3.047	3.408	
29	.683	1.311	1.699	2.045	2.462	2.756	3.038	3.396	
30	.683	1.310	1.697	2.042	2.457	2.750	3.030	3.385	
35	.682	1.306	1.690	2.030	2.438	2.724	2.996	3.340	
40	.681	1.303	1.684	2.021	2.423	2.704	2.971	3.307	
45	.680	1.301	1.679	2.014	2.412	2.690	2.952	3.281	
50	.679	1.299	1.676	2.009	2.403	2.678	2.937	3.261	
55	.679	1.297	1.673	2.004	2.396	2.668	2.925	3.245	
60	.679	1.296	1.671	2.000	2.390	2.660	2.915	3.232	
70	.678	1.294	1.667	1.994	2.381	2.648	2.899	3.211	
80	.678	1.292	1.664	1.990	2.374	2.639	2.887	3.195	
90	.677	1.291	1.662	1.987	2.368	2.632	2.878	3.183	
100	.677	1.290	1.660	1.984	2.364	2.626	2.871	3.174	
200	.676	1.286	1.652	1.972	2.345	2.601	2.838	3.131	
500	.675	1.283	1.648	1.965	2.334	2.586	2.820	3.107	
1,000	.675	1.282	1.646	1.962	2.330	2.581	2.813	3.098	
2,000	.675	1.282	1.645	1.961	2.328	2.578	2.810	3.094	
10,000	.675	1.282	1.645	1.960	2.327	2.576	2.808	3.091	
∞	.674	1.282	1.645	1.960	2.326	2.576	2.807	3.090	

Appendix B

(*continued*)

Table B.2		*t* Values and Their Associated One-Tailed and Two-Tailed *p* Values					
p	.001	.0005	.0002	.0001	.00005	.00002	two-tailed
df	.0005	.00025	.0001	.00005	.000025	.00001	one-tailed
1	636.619	1,273.239	3,183.099	6,366.198	12,732.395	31,830.989	
2	31.598	44.705	70.700	99.992	141.416	223.603	
3	12.924	16.326	22.204	28.000	35.298	47.928	
4	8.610	10.306	13.034	15.544	18.522	23.332	
5	6.869	7.976	9.678	11.178	12.893	15.547	
6	5.959	6.788	8.025	9.082	10.261	12.032	
7	5.408	6.082	7.063	7.885	8.782	10.103	
8	5.041	5.618	6.442	7.120	7.851	8.907	
9	4.781	5.291	6.010	6.594	7.215	8.102	
10	4.587	5.049	5.694	6.211	6.757	7.527	
11	4.437	4.863	5.453	5.921	6.412	7.098	
12	4.318	4.716	5.263	5.694	6.143	6.756	
13	4.221	4.597	5.111	5.513	5.928	6.501	
14	4.140	4.499	4.985	5.363	5.753	6.287	
15	4.073	4.417	4.880	5.239	5.607	6.109	
16	4.015	4.346	4.791	5.134	5.484	5.960	
17	3.965	4.286	4.714	5.044	5.379	5.832	
18	3.922	4.233	4.648	4.966	5.288	5.722	
19	3.883	4.187	4.590	4.897	5.209	5.627	
20	3.850	4.146	4.539	4.837	5.139	5.543	
21	3.819	4.110	4.493	4.784	5.077	5.469	
22	3.792	4.077	4.452	4.736	5.022	5.402	
23	3.768	4.048	4.415	4.693	4.972	5.343	
24	3.745	4.021	4.382	4.654	4.927	5.290	
25	3.725	3.997	4.352	4.619	4.887	5.241	
26	3.707	3.974	4.324	4.587	4.850	5.197	
27	3.690	3.954	4.299	4.558	4.816	5.157	
28	3.674	3.935	4.275	4.530	4.784	5.120	
29	3.659	3.918	4.254	4.506	4.756	5.086	
30	3.646	3.902	4.234	4.482	4.729	5.054	
35	3.591	3.836	4.153	4.389	4.622	4.927	
40	3.551	3.788	4.094	4.321	4.544	4.835	
45	3.520	3.752	4.049	4.269	4.485	4.766	
50	3.496	3.723	4.014	4.228	4.438	4.711	
55	3.476	3.700	3.986	4.196	4.401	4.667	
60	3.460	3.681	3.926	4.169	4.370	4.631	
70	3.435	3.651	3.962	4.127	4.323	4.576	
80	3.416	3.629	3.899	4.096	4.288	4.535	
90	3.402	3.612	3.878	4.072	4.261	4.503	
100	3.390	3.598	3.862	4.053	4.240	4.478	
200	3.340	3.539	3.789	3.970	4.146	4.369	
500	3.310	3.504	3.747	3.922	4.091	4.306	
1,000	3.300	3.492	3.733	3.906	4.073	4.285	
2,000	3.295	3.486	3.726	3.898	4.064	4.275	
10,000	3.292	3.482	3.720	3.892	4.058	4.267	
∞	3.291	3.481	3.719	3.891	4.056	4.265	

Source: From "Extended Tables of the Percentage Points of Student's *t*-Distribution," by E. T. Federighi, 1959. *Journal of the American Statistical Association, 54,* pp. 683–688. Reprinted by permission of the American Statistical Association.

Table B.3   *F* Values and Their Associated *p* Values

df_2 \ df_1	p	1	2	3	4	5	6	8	12	24	∞
1	.001	405284	500000	540379	562500	576405	585937	598144	610667	623497	636619
	.005	16211	20000	21615	22500	23056	23437	23925	24426	24940	25465
	.01	4052	4999	5403	5625	5764	5859	5981	6106	6234	6366
	.025	647.79	799.50	864.16	899.58	921.85	937.11	956.66	976.71	997.25	1018.30
	.05	161.45	199.50	215.71	224.58	230.16	233.99	238.88	243.91	249.05	254.32
	.10	39.86	49.50	53.59	55.83	57.24	58.20	59.44	60.70	62.00	63.33
	.20	9.47	12.00	13.06	13.73	14.01	14.26	14.59	14.90	15.24	15.58
2	.001	998.5	999.0	999.2	999.2	999.3	999.3	999.4	999.4	999.5	999.5
	.005	198.50	199.00	199.17	199.25	199.30	199.33	199.37	199.42	199.46	199.51
	.01	98.49	99.00	99.17	99.25	99.30	99.33	99.36	99.42	99.46	99.50
	.025	38.51	39.00	39.17	39.25	39.30	39.33	39.37	39.42	39.46	39.50
	.05	18.51	19.00	19.16	19.25	19.30	19.33	19.37	19.41	19.45	19.50
	.10	8.53	9.00	9.16	9.24	9.29	9.33	9.37	9.41	9.45	9.49
	.20	3.56	4.00	4.16	4.24	4.28	4.32	4.36	4.40	4.44	4.48
3	.001	167.5	148.5	141.1	137.1	134.6	132.8	130.6	128.3	125.9	123.5
	.005	55.55	49.80	47.47	46.20	45.39	44.84	44.13	43.39	42.62	41.83
	.01	34.12	30.81	29.46	28.71	28.24	27.91	27.49	27.05	26.60	26.12
	.025	17.44	16.04	15.44	15.10	14.89	14.74	14.54	14.34	14.12	13.90
	.05	10.13	9.55	9.28	9.12	9.01	8.94	8.84	8.74	8.64	8.53
	.10	5.54	5.46	5.39	5.34	5.31	5.28	5.25	5.22	5.18	5.13
	.20	2.68	2.89	2.94	2.96	2.97	2.97	2.98	2.98	2.98	2.98
4	.001	74.14	61.25	56.18	53.44	51.71	50.53	49.00	47.41	45.77	44.05
	.005	31.33	26.28	24.26	23.16	22.46	21.98	21.35	20.71	20.03	19.33
	.01	21.20	18.00	16.69	15.98	15.52	15.21	14.80	14.37	13.93	13.46
	.025	12.22	10.65	9.98	9.60	9.36	9.20	8.98	8.75	8.51	8.26
	.05	7.71	6.94	6.59	6.39	6.26	6.16	6.04	5.91	5.77	5.63
	.10	4.54	4.32	4.19	4.11	4.05	4.01	3.95	3.90	3.83	3.76
	.20	2.35	2.47	2.48	2.48	2.48	2.47	2.47	2.46	2.44	2.43
5	.001	47.04	36.61	33.20	31.09	29.75	28.84	27.64	26.42	25.14	23.78
	.005	22.79	18.31	16.53	15.56	14.94	14.51	13.96	13.38	12.78	12.14
	.01	16.26	13.27	12.06	11.39	10.97	10.67	10.29	9.89	9.47	9.02
	.025	10.01	8.43	7.76	7.39	7.15	6.98	6.76	6.52	6.28	6.02
	.05	6.61	5.79	5.41	5.19	5.05	4.95	4.82	4.68	4.53	4.36
	.10	4.06	3.78	3.62	3.52	3.45	3.40	3.34	3.27	3.19	3.10
	.20	2.18	2.26	2.25	2.24	2.23	2.22	2.20	2.18	2.16	2.13
6	.001	35.51	27.00	23.70	21.90	20.81	20.03	19.03	17.99	16.89	15.75
	.005	18.64	14.54	12.92	12.03	11.46	11.07	10.57	10.03	9.47	8.88
	.01	13.74	10.92	9.78	9.15	8.75	8.47	8.10	7.72	7.31	6.88
	.025	8.81	7.26	6.60	6.23	5.99	5.82	5.60	5.37	5.12	4.85
	.05	5.99	5.14	4.76	4.53	4.39	4.28	4.15	4.00	3.84	3.67
	.10	3.78	3.46	3.29	3.18	3.11	3.05	2.98	2.90	2.82	2.72
	.20	2.07	2.13	2.11	2.09	2.08	2.06	2.04	2.02	1.99	1.95
7	.001	29.22	21.69	18.77	17.19	16.21	15.52	14.63	13.71	12.73	11.69
	.005	16.24	12.40	10.88	10.05	9.52	9.16	8.68	8.18	7.65	7.08
	.01	12.25	9.55	8.45	7.85	7.46	7.19	6.84	6.47	6.07	5.65
	.025	8.07	6.54	5.89	5.52	5.29	5.12	4.90	4.67	4.42	4.14
	.05	5.59	4.74	4.35	4.12	3.97	3.87	3.73	3.57	3.41	3.23
	.10	3.59	3.26	3.07	2.96	2.88	2.83	2.75	2.67	2.58	2.47
	.20	2.00	2.04	2.02	1.99	1.97	1.96	1.93	1.91	1.87	1.83

(continued)

Table B.3 *F* Values and Their Associated *p* Values

df_2 \ df_1	p	1	2	3	4	5	6	8	12	24	∞
8	.001	25.42	18.49	15.83	14.39	13.49	12.86	12.04	11.19	10.30	9.34
	.005	14.69	11.04	9.60	8.81	8.30	7.95	7.50	7.01	6.50	5.95
	.01	11.26	8.65	7.59	7.01	6.63	6.37	6.03	5.67	5.28	4.86
	.025	7.57	6.06	5.42	5.05	4.82	4.65	4.43	4.20	3.95	3.67
	.05	5.32	4.46	4.07	3.84	3.69	3.58	3.44	3.28	3.12	2.93
	.10	3.46	3.11	2.92	2.81	2.73	2.67	2.59	2.50	2.40	2.29
	.20	1.95	1.98	1.95	1.92	1.90	1.88	1.86	1.83	1.79	1.74
9	.001	22.86	16.39	13.90	12.56	11.71	11.13	10.37	9.57	8.72	7.81
	.005	13.61	10.11	8.72	7.96	7.47	7.13	6.69	6.23	5.73	5.19
	.01	10.56	8.02	6.99	6.42	6.06	5.80	5.47	5.11	4.73	4.31
	.025	7.21	5.71	5.08	4.72	4.48	4.32	4.10	3.87	3.61	3.33
	.05	5.12	4.26	3.86	3.63	3.48	3.37	3.23	3.07	2.90	2.71
	.10	3.36	3.01	2.81	2.69	2.61	2.55	2.47	2.38	2.28	2.16
	.20	1.91	1.94	1.90	1.87	1.85	1.83	1.80	1.76	1.73	1.67
10	.001	21.04	14.91	12.55	11.28	10.48	9.92	9.20	8.45	7.64	6.76
	.005	12.83	9.43	8.08	7.34	6.87	6.54	6.12	5.66	5.17	4.64
	.01	10.04	7.56	6.55	5.99	5.64	5.39	5.06	4.71	4.33	3.91
	.025	6.94	5.46	4.83	4.47	4.24	4.07	3.85	3.62	3.37	3.08
	.05	4.96	4.10	3.71	3.48	3.33	3.22	3.07	2.91	2.74	2.54
	.10	3.28	2.92	2.73	2.61	2.52	2.46	2.38	2.28	2.18	2.06
	.20	1.88	1.90	1.86	1.83	1.80	1.78	1.75	1.72	1.67	1.62
11	.001	19.69	13.81	11.56	10.35	9.58	9.05	8.35	7.63	6.85	6.00
	.005	12.23	8.91	7.60	6.88	6.42	6.10	5.68	5.24	4.76	4.23
	.01	9.65	7.20	6.22	5.67	5.32	5.07	4.74	4.40	4.02	3.60
	.025	6.72	5.26	4.63	4.28	4.04	3.88	3.66	3.43	3.17	2.88
	.05	4.84	3.98	3.59	3.36	3.20	3.09	2.95	2.79	2.61	2.40
	.10	3.23	2.86	2.66	2.54	2.45	2.39	2.30	2.21	2.10	1.97
	.20	1.86	1.87	1.83	1.80	1.77	1.75	1.72	1.68	1.63	1.57
12	.001	18.64	12.97	10.80	9.63	8.89	8.38	7.71	7.00	6.25	5.42
	.005	11.75	8.51	7.23	6.52	6.07	5.76	5.35	4.91	4.43	3.90
	.01	9.33	6.93	5.95	5.41	5.06	4.82	4.50	4.16	3.78	3.36
	.025	6.55	5.10	4.47	4.12	3.89	3.73	3.51	3.28	3.02	2.72
	.05	4.75	3.88	3.49	3.26	3.11	3.00	2.85	2.69	2.50	2.30
	.10	3.18	2.81	2.61	2.48	2.39	2.33	2.24	2.15	2.04	1.90
	.20	1.84	1.85	1.80	1.77	1.74	1.72	1.69	1.65	1.60	1.54
13	.001	17.81	12.31	10.21	9.07	8.35	7.86	7.21	6.52	5.78	4.97
	.005	11.37	8.19	6.93	6.23	5.79	5.48	5.08	4.64	4.17	3.65
	.01	9.07	6.70	5.74	5.20	4.86	4.62	4.30	3.96	3.59	3.16
	.025	6.41	4.97	4.35	4.00	3.77	3.60	3.39	3.15	2.89	2.60
	.05	4.67	3.80	3.41	3.18	3.02	2.92	2.77	2.60	2.42	2.21
	.10	3.14	2.76	2.56	2.43	2.35	2.28	2.20	2.10	1.98	1.85
	.20	1.82	1.83	1.78	1.75	1.72	1.69	1.66	1.62	1.57	1.51
14	.001	17.14	11.78	9.73	8.62	7.92	7.43	6.80	6.13	5.41	4.60
	.005	11.06	7.92	6.68	6.00	5.56	5.26	4.86	4.43	3.96	3.44
	.01	8.86	6.51	5.56	5.03	4.69	4.46	4.14	3.80	3.43	3.00
	.025	6.30	4.86	4.24	3.89	3.66	3.50	3.29	3.05	2.79	2.49
	.05	4.60	3.74	3.34	3.11	2.96	2.85	2.70	2.53	2.35	2.13
	.10	3.10	2.73	2.52	2.39	2.31	2.24	2.15	2.05	1.94	1.80
	.20	1.81	1.81	1.76	1.73	1.70	1.67	1.64	1.60	1.55	1.48

(continued)

Table B.3											

Table B.3 *F* Values and Their Associated *p* Values

df_2	df_1 p	1	2	3	4	5	6	8	12	24	∞
15	.001	16.59	11.34	9.34	8.25	7.57	7.09	6.47	5.81	5.10	4.31
	.005	10.80	7.70	6.48	5.80	5.37	5.07	4.67	4.25	3.79	3.26
	.01	8.68	6.36	5.42	4.89	4.56	4.32	4.00	3.67	3.29	2.87
	.025	6.20	4.77	4.15	3.80	3.58	3.41	3.20	2.96	2.70	2.40
	.05	4.54	3.68	3.29	3.06	2.90	2.79	2.64	2.48	2.29	2.07
	.10	3.07	2.70	2.49	2.36	2.27	2.21	2.12	2.02	1.90	1.76
	.20	1.80	1.79	1.75	1.71	1.68	1.66	1.62	1.58	1.53	1.46
16	.001	16.12	10.97	9.00	7.94	7.27	6.81	6.19	5.55	4.85	4.06
	.005	10.58	7.51	6.30	5.64	5.21	4.91	4.52	4.10	3.64	3.11
	.01	8.53	6.23	5.29	4.77	4.44	4.20	3.89	3.55	3.18	2.75
	.025	6.12	4.69	4.08	3.73	3.50	3.34	3.12	2.89	2.63	2.32
	.05	4.49	3.63	3.24	3.01	2.85	2.74	2.59	2.42	2.24	2.01
	.10	3.05	2.67	2.46	2.33	2.24	2.18	2.09	1.99	1.87	1.72
	.20	1.79	1.78	1.74	1.70	1.67	1.64	1.61	1.56	1.51	1.43
17	.001	15.72	10.66	8.73	7.68	7.02	6.56	5.96	5.32	4.63	3.85
	.005	10.38	7.35	6.16	5.50	5.07	4.78	4.39	3.97	3.51	2.98
	.01	8.40	6.11	5.18	4.67	4.34	4.10	3.79	3.45	3.08	2.65
	.025	6.04	4.62	4.01	3.66	3.44	3.28	3.06	2.82	2.56	2.25
	.05	4.45	3.59	3.20	2.96	2.81	2.70	2.55	2.38	2.19	1.96
	.10	3.03	2.64	2.44	2.31	2.22	2.15	2.06	1.96	1.84	1.69
	.20	1.78	1.77	1.72	1.68	1.65	1.63	1.59	1.55	1.49	1.42
18	.001	15.38	10.39	8.49	7.46	6.81	6.35	5.76	5.13	4.45	3.67
	.005	10.22	7.21	6.03	5.37	4.96	4.66	4.28	3.86	3.40	2.87
	.01	8.28	6.01	5.09	4.58	4.25	4.01	3.71	3.37	3.00	2.57
	.025	5.98	4.56	3.95	3.61	3.38	3.22	3.01	2.77	2.50	2.19
	.05	4.41	3.55	3.16	2.93	2.77	2.66	2.51	2.34	2.15	1.92
	.10	3.01	2.62	2.42	2.29	2.20	2.13	2.04	1.93	1.81	1.66
	.20	1.77	1.76	1.71	1.67	1.64	1.62	1.58	1.53	1.48	1.40
19	.001	15.08	10.16	8.28	7.26	6.61	6.18	5.59	4.97	4.29	3.52
	.005	10.07	7.09	5.92	5.27	4.85	4.56	4.18	3.76	3.31	2.78
	.01	8.18	5.93	5.01	4.50	4.17	3.94	3.63	3.30	2.92	2.49
	.025	5.92	4.51	3.90	3.56	3.33	3.17	2.96	2.72	2.45	2.13
	.05	4.38	3.52	3.13	2.90	2.74	2.63	2.48	2.31	2.11	1.88
	.10	2.99	2.61	2.40	2.27	2.18	2.11	2.02	1.91	1.79	1.63
	.20	1.76	1.75	1.70	1.66	1.63	1.61	1.57	1.52	1.46	1.39
20	.001	14.82	9.95	8.10	7.10	6.46	6.02	5.44	4.82	4.15	3.38
	.005	9.94	6.99	5.82	5.17	4.76	4.47	4.09	3.68	3.22	2.69
	.01	8.10	5.85	4.94	4.43	4.10	3.87	3.56	3.23	2.86	2.42
	.025	5.87	4.46	3.86	3.51	3.29	3.13	2.91	2.68	2.41	2.09
	.05	4.35	3.49	3.10	2.87	2.71	2.60	2.45	2.28	2.08	1.84
	.10	2.97	2.59	2.38	2.25	2.16	2.09	2.00	1.89	1.77	1.61
	.20	1.76	1.75	1.70	1.65	1.62	1.60	1.56	1.51	1.45	1.37
21	.001	14.59	9.77	7.94	6.95	6.32	5.88	5.31	4.70	4.03	3.26
	.005	9.83	6.89	5.73	5.09	4.68	4.39	4.01	3.60	3.15	2.61
	.01	8.02	5.78	4.87	4.37	4.04	3.81	3.51	3.17	2.80	2.36
	.025	5.83	4.42	3.82	3.48	3.25	3.09	2.87	2.64	2.37	2.04
	.05	4.32	3.47	3.07	2.84	2.68	2.57	2.42	2.25	2.05	1.81
	.10	2.96	2.57	2.36	2.23	2.14	2.08	1.98	1.88	1.75	1.59
	.20	1.75	1.74	1.69	1.65	1.61	1.59	1.55	1.50	1.44	1.36

(continued)

Appendix B

Table B.3 *F* Values and Their Associated *p* Values

df_2	p \ df_1	1	2	3	4	5	6	8	12	24	∞
22	.001	14.38	9.61	7.80	6.81	6.19	5.76	5.19	4.58	3.92	3.15
	.005	9.73	6.81	5.65	5.02	4.61	4.32	3.94	3.54	3.08	2.55
	.01	7.94	5.72	4.82	4.31	3.99	3.76	3.45	3.12	2.75	2.31
	.025	5.79	4.38	3.78	3.44	3.22	3.05	2.84	2.60	2.33	2.00
	.05	4.30	3.44	3.05	2.82	2.66	2.55	2.40	2.23	2.03	1.78
	.10	2.95	2.56	2.35	2.22	2.13	2.06	1.97	1.86	1.73	1.57
	.20	1.75	1.73	1.68	1.64	1.61	1.58	1.54	1.49	1.43	1.35
23	.001	14.19	9.47	7.67	6.69	6.08	5.65	5.09	4.48	3.82	3.05
	.005	9.63	6.73	5.58	4.95	4.54	4.26	3.88	3.47	3.02	2.48
	.01	7.88	5.66	4.76	4.26	3.94	3.71	3.41	3.07	2.70	2.26
	.025	5.75	4.35	3.75	3.41	3.18	3.02	2.81	2.57	2.30	1.97
	.05	4.28	3.42	3.03	2.80	2.64	2.53	2.38	2.20	2.00	1.76
	.10	2.94	2.55	2.34	2.21	2.11	2.05	1.95	1.84	1.72	1.55
	.20	1.74	1.73	1.68	1.63	1.60	1.57	1.53	1.49	1.42	1.34
24	.001	14.03	9.34	7.55	6.59	5.98	5.55	4.99	4.39	3.74	2.97
	.005	9.55	6.66	5.52	4.89	4.49	4.20	3.83	3.42	2.97	2.43
	.01	7.82	5.61	4.72	4.22	3.90	3.67	3.36	3.03	2.66	2.21
	.025	5.72	4.32	3.72	3.38	3.15	2.99	2.78	2.54	2.27	1.94
	.05	4.26	3.40	3.01	2.78	2.62	2.51	2.36	2.18	1.98	1.73
	.10	2.93	2.54	2.33	2.19	2.10	2.04	1.94	1.83	1.70	1.53
	.20	1.74	1.72	1.67	1.63	1.59	1.57	1.53	1.48	1.42	1.33
25	.001	13.88	9.22	7.45	6.49	5.88	5.46	4.91	4.31	3.66	2.89
	.005	9.48	6.60	5.46	4.84	4.43	4.15	3.78	3.37	2.92	2.38
	.01	7.77	5.57	4.68	4.18	3.86	3.63	3.32	2.99	2.62	2.17
	.025	5.69	4.29	3.69	3.35	3.13	2.97	2.75	2.51	2.24	1.91
	.05	4.24	3.38	2.99	2.76	2.60	2.49	2.34	2.16	1.96	1.71
	.10	2.92	2.53	2.32	2.18	2.09	2.02	1.93	1.82	1.69	1.52
	.20	1.73	1.72	1.66	1.62	1.59	1.56	1.52	1.47	1.41	1.32
26	.001	13.74	9.12	7.36	6.41	5.80	5.38	4.83	4.24	3.59	2.82
	.005	9.41	6.54	5.41	4.79	4.38	4.10	3.73	3.33	2.87	2.33
	.01	7.72	5.53	4.64	4.14	3.82	3.59	3.29	2.96	2.58	2.13
	.025	5.66	4.27	3.67	3.33	3.10	2.94	2.73	2.49	2.22	1.88
	.05	4.22	3.37	2.98	2.74	2.59	2.47	2.32	2.15	1.95	1.69
	.10	2.91	2.52	2.31	2.17	2.08	2.01	1.92	1.81	1.68	1.50
	.20	1.73	1.71	1.66	1.62	1.58	1.56	1.52	1.47	1.40	1.31
27	.001	13.61	9.02	7.27	6.33	5.73	5.31	4.76	4.17	3.52	2.75
	.005	9.34	6.49	5.36	4.74	4.34	4.06	3.69	3.28	2.83	2.29
	.01	7.68	5.49	4.60	4.11	3.78	3.56	3.26	2.93	2.55	2.10
	.025	5.63	4.24	3.65	3.31	3.08	2.92	2.71	2.47	2.19	1.85
	.05	4.21	3.35	2.96	2.73	2.57	2.46	2.30	2.13	1.93	1.67
	.10	2.90	2.51	2.30	2.17	2.07	2.00	1.91	1.80	1.67	1.49
	.20	1.73	1.71	1.66	1.61	1.58	1.55	1.51	1.46	1.40	1.30
28	.001	13.50	8.93	7.19	6.25	5.66	5.24	4.69	4.11	3.46	2.70
	.005	9.28	6.44	5.32	4.70	4.30	4.02	3.65	3.25	2.79	2.25
	.01	7.64	5.45	4.57	4.07	3.75	3.53	3.23	2.90	2.52	2.06
	.025	5.61	4.22	3.63	3.29	3.06	2.90	2.69	2.45	2.17	1.83
	.05	4.20	3.34	2.95	2.71	2.56	2.44	2.29	2.12	1.91	1.65
	.10	2.89	2.50	2.29	2.16	2.06	2.00	1.90	1.79	1.66	1.48
	.20	1.72	1.71	1.65	1.61	1.57	1.55	1.51	1.46	1.39	1.30

(continued)

| Table B.3 | | F Values and Their Associated p Values | | | | | | | | | |

df_2 \ df_1	p	1	2	3	4	5	6	8	12	24	∞
29	.001	13.39	8.85	7.12	6.19	5.59	5.18	4.64	4.05	3.41	2.64
	.005	9.23	6.40	5.28	4.66	4.26	3.98	3.61	3.21	2.76	2.21
	.01	7.60	5.42	4.54	4.04	3.73	3.50	3.20	2.87	2.49	2.03
	.025	5.59	4.20	3.61	3.27	3.04	2.88	2.67	2.43	2.15	1.81
	.05	4.18	3.33	2.93	2.70	2.54	2.43	2.28	2.10	1.90	1.64
	.10	2.89	2.50	2.28	2.15	2.06	1.99	1.89	1.78	1.65	1.47
	.20	1.72	1.70	1.65	1.60	1.57	1.54	1.50	1.45	1.39	1.29
30	.001	13.29	8.77	7.05	6.12	5.53	5.12	4.58	4.00	3.36	2.59
	.005	9.18	6.35	5.24	4.62	4.23	3.95	3.58	3.18	2.73	2.18
	.01	7.56	5.39	4.51	4.02	3.70	3.47	3.17	2.84	2.47	2.01
	.025	5.57	4.18	3.59	3.25	3.03	2.87	2.65	2.41	2.14	1.79
	.05	4.17	3.32	2.92	2.69	2.53	2.42	2.27	2.09	1.89	1.62
	.10	2.88	2.49	2.28	2.14	2.05	1.98	1.88	1.77	1.64	1.46
	.20	1.72	1.70	1.64	1.60	1.57	1.54	1.50	1.45	1.38	1.28
40	.001	12.61	8.25	6.60	5.70	5.13	4.73	4.21	3.64	3.01	2.23
	.005	8.83	6.07	4.98	4.37	3.99	3.71	3.35	2.95	2.50	1.93
	.01	7.31	5.18	4.31	3.83	3.51	3.29	2.99	2.66	2.29	1.80
	.025	5.42	4.05	3.46	3.13	2.90	2.74	2.53	2.29	2.01	1.64
	.05	4.08	3.23	2.84	2.61	2.45	2.34	2.18	2.00	1.79	1.51
	.10	2.84	2.44	2.23	2.09	2.00	1.93	1.83	1.71	1.57	1.38
	.20	1.70	1.68	1.62	1.57	1.54	1.51	1.47	1.41	1.34	1.24
60	.001	11.97	7.76	6.17	5.31	4.76	4.37	3.87	3.31	2.69	1.90
	.005	8.49	5.80	4.73	4.14	3.76	3.49	3.13	2.74	2.29	1.69
	.01	7.08	4.98	4.13	3.65	3.34	3.12	2.82	2.50	2.12	1.60
	.025	5.29	3.93	3.34	3.01	2.79	2.63	2.41	2.17	1.88	1.48
	.05	4.00	3.15	2.76	2.52	2.37	2.25	2.10	1.92	1.70	1.39
	.10	2.79	2.39	2.18	2.04	1.95	1.87	1.77	1.66	1.51	1.29
	.20	1.68	1.65	1.59	1.55	1.51	1.48	1.44	1.38	1.31	1.18
120	.001	11.38	7.31	5.79	4.95	4.42	4.04	3.55	3.02	2.40	1.56
	.005	8.18	5.54	4.50	3.92	3.55	3.28	2.93	2.54	2.09	1.43
	.01	6.85	4.79	3.95	3.48	3.17	2.96	2.66	2.34	1.95	1.38
	.025	5.15	3.80	3.23	2.89	2.67	2.52	2.30	2.05	1.76	1.31
	.05	3.92	3.07	2.68	2.45	2.29	2.17	2.02	1.83	1.61	1.25
	.10	2.75	2.35	2.13	1.99	1.90	1.82	1.72	1.60	1.45	1.19
	.20	1.66	1.63	1.57	1.52	1.48	1.45	1.41	1.35	1.27	1.12
∞	.001	10.83	6.91	5.42	4.62	4.10	3.74	3.27	2.74	2.13	1.00
	.005	7.88	5.30	4.28	3.72	3.35	3.09	2.74	2.36	1.90	1.00
	.01	6.64	4.60	3.78	3.32	3.02	2.80	2.51	2.18	1.79	1.00
	.025	5.02	3.69	3.12	2.79	2.57	2.41	2.19	1.94	1.64	1.00
	.05	3.84	2.99	2.60	2.37	2.21	2.09	1.94	1.75	1.52	1.00
	.10	2.71	2.30	2.08	1.94	1.85	1.77	1.67	1.55	1.38	1.00
	.20	1.64	1.61	1.55	1.50	1.46	1.43	1.38	1.32	1.23	1.00

Source: Table V of R. A. Fisher and F. Yates, Statistical Tables for Biological (6th ed.), 1974, Longman "Tables of Percentage Points of the Inverted Beta (β) Distribution," Biometrika, Vol. 33 (April 1943), pp. 73–88. Used with permission.

Appendix B

Table B.4 Chi-square Values and Their Associated *p* Values

							Probability							
df	.99	.98	.95	.90	.80	.70	.50	.30	.20	.10	.05	.02	.01	.001
1	.000157	.000628	.00393	.0158	.0642	.148	.455	1.074	1.642	2.706	3.841	5.412	6.635	10.827
2	.0201	.0404	.103	.211	.446	.713	1.386	2.408	3.219	4.605	5.991	7.824	9.210	13.815
3	.115	.185	.352	.584	1.005	1.424	2.366	3.665	4.642	6.251	7.815	9.837	11.345	16.268
4	.297	.429	.711	1.064	1.649	2.195	3.357	4.878	5.989	7.779	9.488	11.668	13.277	18.465
5	.554	.752	1.145	1.610	2.343	3.000	4.351	6.064	7.289	9.236	11.070	13.388	15.086	20.517
6	.872	1.134	1.635	2.204	3.070	3.828	5.348	7.231	8.558	10.645	12.592	15.033	16.812	22.457
7	1.239	1.564	2.167	2.833	3.822	4.671	6.346	8.383	9.803	12.017	14.067	16.622	18.475	24.322
8	1.646	2.032	2.733	3.490	4.594	5.527	7.344	9.524	11.030	13.362	15.507	18.168	20.090	26.125
9	2.088	2.532	3.325	4.168	5.380	6.393	8.343	10.656	12.242	14.684	16.919	19.679	21.666	27.877
10	2.558	3.059	3.940	4.865	6.179	7.267	9.342	11.781	13.442	15.987	18.307	21.161	23.209	29.588
11	3.053	3.609	4.575	5.578	6.989	8.148	10.341	12.899	14.631	17.275	19.675	22.618	24.725	31.264
12	3.571	4.178	5.226	6.304	7.807	9.034	11.340	14.011	15.812	18.549	21.026	24.054	26.217	32.909
13	4.107	4.765	5.892	7.042	8.634	9.926	12.340	15.119	16.985	19.812	22.362	25.472	27.688	34.528
14	4.660	5.368	6.571	7.790	9.467	10.821	13.339	16.222	18.151	21.064	23.685	26.873	29.141	36.123
15	5.229	5.985	7.261	8.547	10.307	11.721	14.339	17.322	19.311	22.307	24.996	28.529	30.578	37.697
16	5.812	6.614	7.962	9.312	11.152	12.624	15.338	18.418	20.465	23.542	26.296	29.633	32.000	39.252
17	6.408	7.255	8.672	10.085	12.002	13.531	16.338	19.511	21.615	24.769	27.587	30.995	33.409	40.790
18	7.015	7.906	9.390	10.865	12.857	14.440	17.338	20.601	22.760	25.989	28.869	32.346	34.805	42.312
19	7.633	8.567	10.117	11.651	13.716	15.352	18.338	21.689	23.900	27.204	30.144	33.687	36.191	43.820
20	8.260	9.237	10.851	12.443	14.578	16.266	19.337	22.775	25.038	28.412	31.410	35.020	37.566	45.315
21	8.897	9.915	11.591	13.240	15.445	17.182	20.337	23.858	26.171	29.615	32.671	36.343	38.932	46.797
22	9.542	10.600	12.338	13.041	16.314	18.101	21.337	24.939	27.301	30.813	33.924	37.659	40.289	48.268
23	10.196	11.293	13.091	14.848	17.187	19.021	22.337	26.018	28.429	32.007	35.172	38.968	41.638	49.728
24	10.856	11.992	13.848	15.659	18.062	19.943	23.337	27.096	29.553	33.196	36.415	40.270	42.980	51.179
25	11.524	12.697	14.611	16.473	18.940	20.867	24.337	28.172	30.675	34.382	37.652	41.566	44.314	52.620
26	12.198	13.409	15.379	17.292	19.820	21.792	25.336	29.246	31.795	35.563	38.885	42.856	45.642	54.052
27	12.879	14.125	16.151	18.114	20.703	22.719	26.336	30.319	32.912	36.741	40.113	44.140	46.963	55.476
28	13.565	14.847	16.928	18.939	21.588	23.647	27.336	31.391	34.027	37.916	41.337	45.419	48.278	56.893
29	14.256	15.574	17.708	19.768	22.475	24.577	28.336	32.461	35.139	39.087	42.557	46.693	49.588	58.302
30	14.953	16.306	18.493	20.599	23.364	25.508	29.336	33.530	36.250	40.256	43.773	47.962	50.892	59.703

Source: Reproduced from Table III of R. A. Fisher, *Statistical Methods for Research Workers* (14th ed.), 1973, copyright by Oxford University Press, England. Used by permission of Oxford University Press (originally published by Oliver and Boyd, Ltd.).

| Table B.5 | r Values and Their Associated p Values |

Probability level					
(N − 2)	.10	.05	.02	.01	.001
1	.988	.997	.9995	.9999	1.000
2	.900	.950	.980	.990	.999
3	.805	.878	.934	.959	.991
4	.729	.811	.882	.917	.974
5	.669	.754	.833	.874	.951
6	.622	.707	.789	.834	.925
7	.582	.666	.750	.798	.898
8	.549	.632	.716	.765	.872
9	.522	.602	.685	.735	.847
10	.497	.576	.658	.708	.823
11	.476	.553	.634	.684	.801
12	.458	.532	.612	.661	.780
13	.441	.514	.592	.641	.760
14	.426	.497	.574	.623	.742
15	.412	.482	.558	.606	.725
16	.400	.468	.542	.590	.708
17	.389	.456	.528	.575	.693
18	.378	.444	.516	.561	.679
19	.369	.433	.503	.549	.665
20	.360	.423	.492	.537	.652
22	.344	.404	.472	.515	.629
24	.330	.388	.453	.496	.607
25	.323	.381	.445	.487	.597
30	.296	.349	.409	.449	.554
35	.275	.325	.381	.418	.519
40	.257	.304	.358	.393	.490
45	.243	.288	.338	.372	.465
50	.231	.273	.322	.354	.443
55	.220	.261	.307	.338	.424
60	.211	.250	.295	.325	.408
65	.203	.240	.284	.312	.393
70	.195	.232	.274	.302	.380
75	.189	.224	.264	.292	.368
80	.183	.217	.256	.283	.357
85	.178	.211	.249	.275	.347
90	.173	.205	.242	.267	.338
95	.168	.200	.236	.260	.329
100	.164	.195	.230	.254	.321
125	.147	.174	.206	.228	.288
150	.134	.159	.189	.208	.264
175	.124	.148	.174	.194	.248
200	.116	.138	.164	.181	.235
300	.095	.113	.134	.148	.188
500	.074	.088	.104	.115	.148
1,000	.052	.062	.073	.081	.104
2,000	.037	.044	.052	.058	.074

Note: All p values are two-tailed in this table.

Source: From *Some Extensions of Student's t and Pearson's r Central Distributions*, by A. L. Sockloff and J. N. Edney, May 1972, Unpublished Technical Report 72-5, Temple University Measurement and Research Center. Reprinted with the permission of Alan Sockloff.

Table B.6   Transformations of r to Fisher z_r

r	.00	.01	.02	.03	.04	.05	.06	.07	.08	.09
				Second	digit of r					
.0	.000	.010	.020	.030	.040	.050	.060	.070	.080	.090
.1	.100	.110	.121	.131	.141	.151	.161	.172	.182	.192
.2	.203	.213	.224	.234	.245	.255	.266	.277	.288	.299
.3	.310	.321	.332	.343	.354	.365	.377	.388	.400	.412
.4	.424	.436	.448	.460	.472	.485	.497	.510	.523	.536
.5	.549	.563	.576	.590	.604	.618	.633	.648	.662	.678
.6	.693	.709	.725	.741	.758	.775	.793	.811	.829	.848
.7	.867	.887	.908	.929	.950	.973	.996	1.020	1.045	1.071
.8	1.099	1.127	1.157	1.188	1.221	1.256	1.293	1.333	1.376	1.422

r	.000	.001	.002	.003	.004	.005	.006	.007	.008	.009
				Third	digit of r					
.90	1.472	1.478	1.483	1.488	1.494	1.499	1.505	1.510	1.516	1.522
.91	1.528	1.533	1.539	1.545	1.551	1.557	1.564	1.570	1.576	1.583
.92	1.589	1.596	1.602	1.609	1.616	1.623	1.630	1.637	1.644	1.651
.93	1.658	1.666	1.673	1.681	1.689	1.697	1.705	1.713	1.721	1.730
.94	1.738	1.747	1.756	1.764	1.774	1.783	1.792	1.802	1.812	1.822
.95	1.832	1.842	1.853	1.863	1.874	1.886	1.897	1.909	1.921	1.933
.96	1.946	1.959	1.972	1.986	2.000	2.014	2.029	2.044	2.060	2.076
.97	2.092	2.109	2.127	2.146	2.165	2.185	2.205	2.227	2.249	2.273
.98	2.298	2.323	2.351	2.380	2.410	2.443	2.477	2.515	2.555	2.599
.99	2.646	2.700	2.759	2.826	2.903	2.994	3.106	3.250	3.453	3.800

Source: Statistical Methods, G.W. Snedecor, W.G. Cochran. John Wiley & Sons, Inc., 1989. Used with permission.

Table B.7	Transformations of Fisher z_r to r								
z_r	.00	.01	.02	.03	.04	.05	.06	.07	.08	.09
.0	.000	.010	.020	.030	.040	.050	.060	.070	.080	.090
.1	.100	.110	.119	.129	.139	.149	.159	.168	.178	.187
.2	.197	.207	.216	.226	.236	.245	.254	.264	.273	.282
.3	.291	.300	.310	.319	.327	.336	.345	.354	.363	.371
.4	.380	.389	.397	.405	.414	.422	.430	.438	.446	.454
.5	.462	.470	.478	.485	.493	.500	.508	.515	.523	.530
.6	.537	.544	.551	.558	.565	.572	.578	.585	.592	.598
.7	.604	.611	.617	.623	.629	.635	.641	.647	.653	.658
.8	.664	.670	.675	.680	.686	.691	.696	.701	.706	.711
.9	.716	.721	.726	.731	.735	.740	.744	.749	.753	.757
1.0	.762	.766	.770	.774	.778	.782	.786	.790	.793	.797
1.1	.800	.804	.808	.811	.814	.818	.821	.824	.828	.831
1.2	.834	.837	.840	.843	.846	.848	.851	.854	.856	.859
1.3	.862	.864	.867	.869	.872	.874	.876	.879	.881	.883
1.4	.885	.888	.890	.892	.894	.896	.898	.900	.902	.903
1.5	.905	.907	.909	.910	.912	.914	.915	.917	.919	.920
1.6	.922	.923	.925	.926	.928	.929	.930	.932	.933	.934
1.7	.935	.937	.938	.939	.940	.941	.942	.944	.945	.946
1.8	.947	.948	.949	.950	.951	.952	.953	.954	.954	.955
1.9	.956	.957	.958	.959	.960	.960	.961	.962	.963	.963
2.0	.964	.965	.965	.966	.967	.967	.968	.969	.969	.970
2.1	.970	.971	.972	.972	.973	.973	.974	.974	.975	.975
2.2	.976	.976	.977	.977	.978	.978	.978	.979	.979	.980
2.3	.980	.980	.981	.981	.982	.982	.982	.983	.983	.983
2.4	.984	.984	.984	.985	.985	.985	.986	.986	.986	.986
2.5	.987	.987	.987	.987	.988	.988	.988	.988	.989	.989
2.6	.989	.989	.989	.990	.990	.990	.990	.990	.991	.991
2.7	.991	.991	.991	.992	.992	.992	.992	.992	.992	.992
2.8	.993	.993	.993	.993	.993	.993	.993	.994	.994	.994
2.9	.994	.994	.994	.994	.994	.995	.995	.995	.995	.995

Source: Statistical Methods, G.W. Snedecor, W.G. Cochran. John Wiley & Sons, Inc., 1989. Used with permission.

Appendix B

APPENDIX C

Introduction to Meta-Analysis

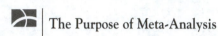

The Purpose of Meta-Analysis

The term **meta-analysis** was coined in 1976 by Gene V Glass (no middle name, only the letter *V*) to mean the "statistical analysis of a large collection of analysis results from individual studies for the purpose of integrating the findings" (p. 3). The expression "analysis results" refers not to the prose conclusions drawn by investigators in their research reports, but to the degree of relationship between any variable *X* and any variable *Y* of interest. The *degree of relationship* is indicated by (a) an appropriate effect size measure and (b) the accuracy or reliability of the estimated effect size (e.g., a confidence interval placed around the effect size estimate). In this appendix, we will give you a sense of the reasoning and a sample of several procedures used to compare and combine effect sizes and to estimate overall *p* values when they are of interest. We primarily emphasize *r*-type indices in this discussion because they can be useful in situations to which other effect size indices are not naturally suited, but it is also common to see standardized difference indices in meta-analyses of two-group designs (such as Cohen's *d*, described in Chapter 13).

Although the term *meta-analysis* is of relatively recent vintage, the analysis of analyses (the literal meaning of *meta-analysis*) is actually older than the *t* test, which (as noted in Chapter 13) dates back to William Sealy Gosset ("Student," his pen name) in 1908. In a forerunner of meta-analysis (and also the prophetic use of a correlation coefficient as an effect size indicator, more than a half-century before the term *effect size* was coined by Jacob Cohen), Karl Pearson (1904) published a brief report in the *British Medical Journal*, in which he integrated the findings of individual studies for the purpose of assessing the degree to which inoculation against smallpox saved lives. A few decades later, there were other visionary examples of the statistical analysis of analyses in other research areas (e.g., Lush, 1931) as well as the beginning of the development of specialized statistical procedures for the integration of analysis results (e.g., Cochran, 1937; Yates & Cochran, 1938).

If you are interested in learning more about meta-analysis, Morton Hunt's book *How Science Takes Stock* (1997) is a most engaging introduction. You will also find up-to-date information and guidance on a range of issues in research synthesis and meta-analysis in Cooper, Hedges, and Valentine's (2009) comprehensive handbook. In this appendix, we draw on two overviews of meta-analysis published by Rosenthal and DiMatteo (2001, 2002) and also on a further discussion in our advanced text (Rosenthal & Rosnow, 2008, Ch. 21). For a recent discussion of reporting standards and ethical issues in meta-analyses, see the chapter by Cooper and Dent (2011) in Panter and Sterba's (2011) handbook on ethical issues in quantitative methods.

Some Pro and Con Arguments

Among the advantages of doing meta-analyses is an emphasis on the cumulative results of different studies that build on one another in a continuing cycle of discovery and justification (a topic discussed in Chapters 1 and 2). Another benefit is that *moderator variables* (defined in Chapter 2 as "conditions that may strengthen or weaken the relationships" between variables) may be more easily spotted and evaluated in the context of a quantitative research summary. The reason is that a meta-analysis requires more than merely perusing abstracts and discussion sections. It is essential to look closely at the numbers and, very often, to compute relevant effect sizes oneself and to explore plausible moderators (e.g., using back-to-back stem-and-leaf charts, illustrated in Chapter 10).

Critics of meta-analysis have argued there is an *irretrievability problem*; that is, retrieved results might not be representative of the results that were unpublished because they failed to reach statistical significance. Mindful of this concern, researchers have developed and refined procedures for retrieving hard-to-find studies (M. C. Rosenthal, 1994, 2006). If statistical significance is a primary concern, there is also a procedure (described later in this appendix) that involves estimating the number of statistically nonsignificant studies that it would take to nudge a statistically significant overall p level for the retrieved studies to $p > .05$.

Another criticism is that integrating the results of independent studies is likely to muddle the overall conclusions because the integrated studies are not uniform. Glass (1978) called this criticism the "apples and oranges issue." As he put it, apples and oranges are actually *good* things to mix when we are trying to generalize to fruit. Furthermore, if we as researchers are willing to generalize over participants *within* studies (as most experimenters routinely do), why should we not be willing to generalize *across* studies? If participants behave very differently within studies, there are basic designs that allow us to focus on participant characteristics to help us figure out why. Just as it is informative to make statements about fruit, it is informative to make general statements about apples, about oranges, and about the differences between them. There is nothing inherent in meta-analytic procedures to prevent us from doing so.

 Comparing Two Effect Sizes

Suppose we think of two studies as conceptually similar. For example, a student might have tried to replicate a published finding, or another experimenter might have begun a program of research by computing Killeen's p_{rep} statistic (discussed at the end of Chapter 12) on some relevant published findings and then deciding to try to replicate the effect with the highest p_{rep} value. Assuming the original study (Study 1) and the replication study (Study 2) are *conceptually* similar, now we might also be interested in comparing the effect size in Study 1 with the effect size in Study 2 to see whether the two effects constitute a homogeneous set *statistically*.

First, assuming the replication produced an effect size correlation in the same direction as the original experiment, we will give both effect size values the same sign. Had the results of the replication been in the opposite direction, we would have given them different signs. Next, we find for each $r_{\text{effect size}}$ the Fisher z_r, which (as you learned in Chapter 12) is the log transformation of r indicated in Table B.6 (p. 336). Third, we substitute in the following formula to get the standard normal deviate (z) corresponding to the difference between the Fisher z_r scores:

$$z \text{ of difference} = \frac{z_{r1} - z_{r2}}{\sqrt{\dfrac{1}{N_1 - 3} + \dfrac{1}{N_2 - 3}}},$$

where z_{r1} and z_{r2} are the log transformations of effect size correlations in the original experiment (Study 1) and the replication (Study 2), respectively, and N_1 and N_2 are the total sample sizes in Study 1 and Study 2, respectively. The final step is to look up the result in Table B.1 (p. 326), which gives us the associated one-tailed p of the z of difference. Let us try some examples.

Example 1. Suppose you were the student who did the follow-up study, and you computed the effect size on the originally reported independent-sample t to be $r_{\text{effect size}} = .50$ based on only $N_1 = 10$ participants. In your study, you used a total of 100 participants (N_2) and found $r_{\text{effect size}} = .31$, but your finding was in the opposite direction of the one previously reported. You code your effect as negative to reflect the fact that it is in the opposite direction, and then you consult Table B.6 (p. 336) to find the Fisher z_r corresponding to each $r_{\text{effect size}}$. For $r_1 = .50$, you find $z_{r1} = .549$ in Table B.6 at the intersection of the .5 row and the .00 column. For $r_2 = -.31$, you find $z_{r2} = .321$ at the .3 row and the .01 column intersection, and you code the result as $-.321$ because it was in the opposite direction from the earlier result.

Next, from the previous formula, you compute

$$z \text{ of difference} = \frac{(.549) - (-.321)}{\sqrt{\dfrac{1}{7} + \dfrac{1}{97}}} = \frac{.870}{.391} = 2.22$$

as the z of the difference between the two effect sizes. Looking up the p value associated with $z = 2.22$ in Table B.1 (p. 326), you find $p = .0132$ one-tailed, which you can round to .01 one-tailed or .03 two-tailed (i.e., $.0132 \times 2 = .03$ rounded). Although both r_1 and r_2 effects are sizable, you would consult with your instructor before combining the two results meta-analytically without careful thought and comment. In describing the results of both studies considered together, you would report the differences between them and give a provisional explanation for the differences (possibly proposing a moderator variable that could be explored in a third study).

Example 2. Alternatively, suppose your result is in the same direction as the original one and of a similar magnitude, and you have used the same number of participants. This time, let's suppose the original $r_1 = .45$ ($N = 120$) and your $r_2 = .40$ ($N = 120$). Following the procedure as in Example 1, you find in Table B.6 the z_r values corresponding to the effect size r values to be .485 and .424, respectively. From the preceding formula you compute

$$z \text{ of difference} = \frac{.485 - .424}{\sqrt{\dfrac{1}{117} + \dfrac{1}{117}}} = \frac{.061}{.131} = .47$$

as your obtained z of the difference. In Table B.1 you find the p value associated with $z = .47$ to be .3192 one-tailed. Here, then, is an example of two studies that do not disagree significantly in their estimates of the size of the relationship between X and Y and are quite similar in magnitude. In other words, they can be routinely combined by means of a simple meta-analytic technique, as shown next.

Combining Two Effect Sizes

Given two effect size r values that can be combined on conceptual and statistical grounds, we find the typical (or average) effect size by using the following formula:

$$\bar{z}_r = \frac{z_{r1} + z_{r2}}{2},$$

where z_{r1} and z_{r2} are as defined previously (log transformations of the effect sizes in the original experiment and the replication, respectively). We afterward transform the resulting Fisher z_r into the metric of an effect size correlation. In this formula the denominator is the number of z_r scores in the numerator. The resulting value is an average Fisher z_r (symbolized here as $\bar{z}_r$, where the bar over the z_r signifies that it is a mean value). Example 3 gives an illustration of this procedure of combining two effect sizes.

Example 3. In Example 2, r_1 was .45 and r_2 was .40 (both coded as positive to show that both results were in the predicted direction). You found the Fisher z_r scores corresponding to the effect size r values to be $z_{r1} = .485$ and $z_{r2} = .424$. From the formula above you compute

$$\bar{z}_r = \frac{.485 + .424}{2} = .45$$

as the average Fisher z_r. Finally, looking in Table B.7 (p. 337), you find that a Fisher z_r of .45 is associated with an r of .422, which is the $r_{\text{effect size}}$ estimate of the two studies combined. By using the average of r_1 and r_2, you weighted the two effect sizes equally. Often, meta-analysts want, in addition, to weight the means by their sample sizes, in which case the following formula can be used:

$$\bar{z}_r \ (weighted\ mean) = \frac{[(n_1 - 3)z_{r1}] + [(n_2 - 3)z_{r2}]}{n_1 + n_2 - 6}.$$

 ## Obtaining an Overall Significance Level

Although meta-analysts are generally more interested in effect sizes and confidence intervals than in p values, remember that a nonsignificant result is not equivalent to finding "zero effect." We mentioned earlier in this book that it is prudent (and protection against Type I and Type II error) to routinely accompany effect size estimates (when possible) with interval estimates. In Chapter 12, we described how to create a confidence interval around $r_{\text{effect size}}$, and in Chapter 13, we showed how to do the same thing for Cohen's d on two independent groups. In Chapter 12, we described the null-counternull interval, which is a kind of confidence interval except that it involves the null hypothesis and the obtained p value (Rosenthal & Rubin, 1994). The counternull statistic is another good way of protecting yourself against falling into the error trap of failing to reject the null hypothesis when it is false.

Suppose, however, that you are interested in reporting the overall statistical significance of a set of comparable studies. It is an easy matter to combine the p values and get an overall estimate of the probability that the p values might have been obtained if the null hypothesis of no relationship between X and Y were true. You first need to obtain an accurate p value for each study (accurate, say, to two digits, not counting zeros before the first nonzero value, such as $p = .43$ or .024 or .0012). That is, if t (with 30 df) = 3.03, we record p as .0025, not as $p < .05$. Extended tables of the t distribution may be helpful (such as Table B.2 on pp. 327–328), but more helpful still is a computer program or a good calculator that gives accurate p values at the touch of a few keys. For each p value, you would find z (not the Fisher z_r, but the standard normal deviate z in Table B.1 of Appendix B). Both p values should also be one-tailed. You would give the corresponding z values the same sign if both studies showed effects in the same direction, but different signs if the results were in the opposite direction.

In our continuing example of working with two studies, the formula used to combine the two z values is as follows:

$$Combined\ z = \frac{z_1 + z_2}{\sqrt{2}}.$$

That is, the sum of the two z values when divided by the square root of the number of z values combined yields a new z. This new z corresponds to the p value of the two studies combined if the null hypothesis of no relationship between X and Y were true.

Example 4. As an illustration, suppose we assume that Studies 1 and 2 are a combinable set with results in the same direction, but neither is statistically significant. One p value is .121, and the other is .084. Their z values are 1.17 and 1.38, respectively. From the preceding formula we have

$$Combined\ z = \frac{1.17 + 1.38}{\sqrt{2}} = \frac{2.55}{1.41} = 1.81$$

as our combined z. The p associated with this combined z is .035 one-tailed (or .07 two-tailed).

Detective-Like Probing of Reported Data

For our illustrations of meta-analytic comparisons and combinations of effect size r and p values, we have concentrated on the case of only two independent results. Meta-analysts typically work with many more results to be coded, compared, and combined, however. The procedures used are similar in spirit to the procedures described above, but various adjustments are often made on the effect size estimates. You will find descriptions in the handbooks and texts cited earlier. Even if there is limited information to work with, it is frequently possible to re-create a summary table for all the original findings and to compute our own contrasts and effect sizes from the reconstituted summary. There are examples in this text, such as computing a contrast from a reported omnibus F test (Chapter 14) and then computing your own r-type effect size indices (Chapter 14), or computing effect sizes from news reports of biomedical trials (Chapter 12).

When all we have are the total N and an accurate p value, we can often estimate an equivalent effect size d or r (R. Rosenthal & Rubin, 2003). We mentioned this in Chapter 12 (Box 12.5). Suppose we have a nonparametric test that gives us the exact p value, but there is no generally accepted effect size index for the test. If we are interested in reporting the effect size as a point-biserial r, and the reported p value is .008 one-tailed, we would find the value of t corresponding to the exact p and df and then substitute in the following familiar formula (Chapter 13):

$$r_{equivalent} = \sqrt{\frac{t^2}{t^2 + df}},$$

where the result is indicated as $r_{equivalent}$ because it is analogous to $r_{effect\ size}$ between the treatment indicator (e.g., with the treatment dummy-coded 1 and the control coded 0) and the continuous outcome measure with $N/2$ units in each group. In this example, where $p = .008$ and $N = 9$, the t value for 7 degrees of freedom is 3.16, and substituting in the formula above gives us $r_{equivalent} = .77$.

The File Drawer Problem

Previously, we mentioned the problem that statistically nonsignificant results frequently go unpublished (Bakan, 1967; Sterling, 1959). If there were a substantial number of such studies in researchers' file drawers, the meta-analyst's evaluation of the overall significance level might be unduly optimistic. We conclude by illustrating one solution to the **file drawer problem**, which is to estimate the number of studies averaging null results that would be required to push the significance level for *all* studies (retrieved and unretrieved combined) to the less coveted side of $p = .05$ (R. Rosenthal, 1979, 1983, 1991). If the overall significance level computed on the basis of retrieved studies can be brought down to $p > .05$ by the addition of just a few more null results, the original estimate of p is clearly *not robust* (i.e., not resistant to the file drawer threat).

Table C.1 illustrates the results of such calculations. It shows *tolerance values* in which the rows represent the number of retrieved (i.e., meta-analyzed) studies and the columns represent three different levels of the average statistical significance of the retrieved studies. The intersection of any row and column shows the sum of old and new studies required to bring the p for all studies (retrieved *and* unretrieved) down to the level of being barely "nonsignificant" at $p > .05$.

Suppose we have meta-analyzed 8 studies and found the average (not the combined, but the mean) p value to be .05. The 64 in Table C.1 tells us that it will take an additional 56 unretrieved studies averaging null results to bring the original average $p = .05$ based on 8 studies ($64 - 8 = 56$) down to $p > .05$. As a general rule, it has been suggested that we regard as robust any combined

Table C.1	Tolerances for Future Null Results		
	Original average significance level		
Retrieved studies	.05	.01	.001
1	1	2	4
2	4	8	15
3	9	18	32
4	16	32	57
5	25	50	89
6	36	72	128
7	49	98	173
8	64	128	226
9	81	162	286
10	100	200	353
15	225	450	795
20	400	800	1,412
25	625	1,250	2,206
30	900	1,800	3,177
40	1,600	3,200	5,648
50	2,500	5,000	8,824

Note: Entries in this table are the total number of old and new studies required to bring an original average p of .05, .01, or .001 down to an overall $p > .05$ (i.e., just barely to "nonsignificance").

results for which the tolerance level reaches $5(k) + 10$, where k is the number of studies retrieved (R. Rosenthal, 1991). In our example of 8 studies retrieved, this means that we will be satisfied that the original estimate of $p \leq .05$ is robust if we think that there are fewer than an additional $5(8) + 10 = 50$ studies with null results squirreled away in file drawers. Because this table shows a tolerance for an additional 56 studies, we conclude that the original estimate is robust.

Appendix C

Glossary of Terms

A-B design   Simplest single-case design, in which the dependent variable is measured throughout the pretreatment or baseline period (the A phase) and the treatment period (the B phase). (8)

A-B-A design   Single-case design in which there are repeated measures before the treatment (the A phase), during the treatment (the B phase), and then with the treatment withdrawn (the final A phase). (8)

A-B-A-B design   Single-case design in which there are two types of occasions (B to A and A to B) for demonstrating the effects of the treatment variable. (8)

A-B-A-B-A design   Single-case design in which there are repeated measures before, during, and after treatment (the B phase). (8)

A-B-BC-B design   Single-case design in which there are repeated measures before the introduction of the treatments (the A phase), then during Treatment B, during the combination of Treatments B and C, and, finally, during Treatment B alone; the purpose of the design is to tease out the effect of B both in combination with C and apart from C. (8)

A-B-C design   General term for single-case design in which B and C are two different treatments. (8)

abscissa   The horizontal axis (the *x* axis) of a distribution. (10)

absolute risk reduction   See *risk difference*.

abstract   Brief, comprehensive summary of the content of a report or paper. (Appendix A)

accidental plagiarism   Unintentionally misrepresenting someone else's work as one's own. (3)

account for conflicting results   One of several hypothesis-generating heuristics. (2)

acquiescent response set   The tendency of an individual to go along with any request or attitudinal statement. (5)

active deception   Sometimes described as *deception by commission*, it involves actively manipulating the truth by presenting the research participants with false information or using some other ruse to directly trick them (e.g., having them unsuspectingly interact with confederates who pretend to be other participants). (3)

additive model   Statistical model in which the components sum to the group means in ANOVA. (14)

ad hoc hypothesis   A conjecture or speculation developed on the spot to explain a result. (1)

aesthetic aspect of science   The beauty or elegance of scientific theories, experiments, or other facets of science. (1)

after-only design   Any research design in which the participants are measured after the treatment but not before; also called a *posttest-only design*.

alerting r (r_{alerting})   The correlation between the group means (M) and contrast (λ) weights; also symbolized as $r_{M\lambda}$. (14)

alpha (α)   Probability of a Type I error. (12)

alpha coefficient   See *Cronbach's alpha*.

alternate-form reliability   The correlation between two forms of a test with different items that are measuring the same attribute. (6)

alternative hypothesis (H_1)   The investigator's working hypothesis (also called the *experimental hypothesis*), which in null hypothesis significance testing (NHST) is in opposition to the null hypothesis (H_0). (12)

analogies and metaphors   Linguistic forms that are used in reasoning to explain or describe one thing in terms of another. (2)

analysis of variance (ANOVA)   Subdivision of the total variance of a set of scores into its components. (14)

ANOVA   See *analysis of variance*.

APA   American Psychological Association. (1)

APA style   The style recommended in the *Publication Manual of the American Psychological Association*. (Appendix A)

a priori method   C. S. Peirce's term for reliance on pure reason and logic as a basis of explanation. (1)

APS   Association for Psychological Science. (2)

archival material   Documents, pictorial records, or other information stored in accessible repositories. (4)

area probability sampling   Sampling in which the subclasses are geographic areas. (9)

arithmetic mean (M)   The simple average of a set of values (more commonly called the *mean*). (10)

ARR   See *risk difference*.

artifact Systematic error or a confounded aspect of the scientist's observations that, if ignored, or left uncontrolled, can jeopardize the validity of the scientist's conclusions regarding the question or hypothesis of interest. (7)

asymmetrical distribution A distribution of scores in which there is not an exact correspondence in arrangement on the opposite sides of the middle line. (10)

attrition See *bias due to attrition*.

autonomy Independence, which in the context of research ethics refers to a prospective participant's right as well as ability to choose whether to participate in the study, or to continue in the study. (3)

back-to-back stem-and-leaf chart A display of two distributions of data values, where each of the values is split between the leading digit (called the "stem") and the first trailing digit (called the "leaf"), and the finished display resembles two back-to-back histograms, except that all original values are displayed. (10)

back-translation See *translation and back-translation*.

bar graphs Graphic distributions where the height or length of the bars typically indicates some quantity such as the total number or percentage of scores. (10)

before-after design A research design in which the participants are measured before and after treatment; also called a *pre-post design*.

behavior What someone does or how someone acts.

behavioral baseline The comparison base, generally defined in single-case research as the continuous, and continuing, performance of a single unit. (8)

behavioral diary Data collection technique in which the research participant keeps a record of events at the time they occur. (5)

behavioral research The empirical investigation of how and why people act, perceive, reason, think, and feel as they do. (1)

behavioral science A general term that encompasses a number of disciplines in which empirical research is performed to study the nature, antecedents, and consequences of people's actions and reactions in a range of contexts. (1)

Belmont Report A landmark report by a national commission in the 1970s delegated the responsibility to protect the rights and welfare of human participants in biomedical and behavioral research. (3)

beneficence The aspirational ideal to "do good," for example, by maximizing the societal and scientific benefits of research, one of several ethical principles discussed in this book. (3)

BESD See *binomial effect-size display*.

beta (β) Probability of a Type II error. (12)

between-subjects design Statistical design in which the sampling units are exposed to one condition each (also described as a *nested design* because the sampling units are said to be "nested" within their own condition). (7)

bias Net systematic error. (9)

bias due to attrition A threat to internal validity owing to the possibility that differential loss of sampling units results in substantially dissimilar groups (e.g., treatment and control group). (7)

bias due to history A threat to internal validity owing to the possibility that an event other than, but concurrent with, the treatment might be responsible for the observed effect. (7)

bias due to maturation A threat to internal validity owing to the possibility that certain naturally occurring changes over time in the research participants (as opposed to the treatment variable) might be responsible for the observed effect. (7)

bias due to testing A threat to internal validity owing to the possibility that merely being measured, tested, or observed initially (or repeatedly) might affect participants' reactions or performance on the dependent variable. (7)

biased selection The consequence of selecting a sample that is not representative of the population of interest. (7)

Big Five factors (OCEAN) The collective name for five broad domains of individual personality: (a) openness to experience, (b) conscientiousness, (c) extraversion, (d) agreeableness, and (e) neuroticism. (5)

bimodal A distribution showing two modes. (10)

binomial effect-size display (BESD) A 2×2 representation of the "success rate" of the experimental treatment in a hypothetical population, where the row and column totals are all preset at 100 each (used with effect size correlations). (15)

bipolar rating scales Scales in which the cue words at each end are extreme opposites. (5)

blind experimenters Experimenters who are unaware of which participants have been assigned to particular conditions (e.g., treatment vs. control condition). (7)

byline The author's name as it appears on the title page. (Appendix A)

CATI Computer-assisted telephone interviewing. (5)

causal inference Reasoning that X causes Y. (7)

causation The relation of cause to effect. (7)

ceiling effect A testing or measurement condition in which there is little opportunity for upward movement (or improvement), as when test items are too easy and participants' scores were very high to begin with. (5)

central tendency Location of the bulk of a distribution; measured by means, medians, modes, and trimmed means. (10)

central tendency bias A type of response set in which the respondent is reluctant to give extreme ratings and instead rates in the direction of the mean of the total group. (5)

certificate of confidentiality A formal agreement between the investigator and the government agency sponsoring the research that requires the investigator to keep the data confidential. (3)

chi-square (χ^2) A statistical procedure that assesses the degree of agreement between the frequency data obtained and the expected frequencies under a particular hypothesis (e.g., the null hypothesis). (15)

closed items See *fixed-choice items*.

clusters See *strata*.

coefficient of determination (r^2) Proportion of variance shared by two variables. (13)

cognitive heuristics Information-processing rules of thumb. (1)

Cohen's *d* A descriptive index of effect size calibrated in standard deviation units. (13)

coherence The high degree to which the components of a theory or hypothesis "stick together" logically. (2)

cohort A sociological term for a collection of individuals who were born in the same period, implying a "generation" that has experienced certain similar life events at the same period. (8)

column effect Column mean minus grand mean. (14)

composite reliability The aggregate reliability of two or more items or judges' ratings. (6)

concealed measurement The use of hidden observations or measurements, such as an out-of-sight recording device that eavesdrops on conversations. (4)

conceptual definitions See *theoretical definitions*.

concurrent validity The extent to which test results are correlated with a specified criterion in the present. (6)

confidence interval The estimated lower and upper bounds of the population value of a statistic, where confidence is defined as $1 - \alpha$. (9, 10, 12)

confidentiality Protection of research participants' or survey respondents' disclosures against unwarranted access. (3)

confirmatory data analysis Analysis of data for the purpose of testing hypotheses. (10)

confounded hypotheses (in panel designs) The inability to separate the effect attributed to one hypothesis from the effect attributed to another hypothesis in cross-lagged panel designs. (8)

construct Abstract expression, term, or concept that is formulated ("constructed") to serve as a causal or descriptive explanation. (2)

construct validity A type of test or research validity that addresses the question of what is really being assessed by a particular test, or manipulated or investigated in an experiment, for example, the validity of an abstract expression, term, or concept that is presumed to explain or give meaning to the relationship between X and Y in experimental research. (6)

content analysis A method of decomposing written messages and pictorial documents. (4)

content validity A type of test validity that addresses the degree to which the test adequately samples the relevant material. (6)

context of discovery Includes the initial hunches, questions, or insights and the resulting conjectural statements or suppositions that give direction to researchers' observations. (2)

context of justification Includes the empirical evaluation of conjectural statements or suppositions and the evidence-based defense of conclusions and generalizations. (2)

contingency table A table of frequencies (counts) coded by row and column variables. (11)

continuous variable It is possible to imagine another value falling between any two adjacent scores. (11)

contrast A statistical procedure (or significance test) for asking a focused question of data, including any *t* test, any *F* test with numerator $df = 1$, and any 1-*df* chi-square test. (14)

contrast *r* ($r_{contrast}$) The pure correlation between individual scores or data values on the dependent variable (Y) and their corresponding lambda (λ) weights after removal of any other patterns in the data; also symbolized as $r_{Y\lambda \cdot NC}$, where "NC" denotes the removal of noncontrast variation. (14)

contrast weights See *lambda weights*.

contrived observation Unobtrusive observation of the effect of some variable intentionally introduced into a situation. (4)

control group A condition with which the effects of the experimental or test condition are compared. (7)

convergent validity Validity supported by a substantial correlation of conceptually similar measures. (6)

corrected range See *extended range*.

correlated replicators Nonindependent replicators. (6)

correlated-sample *t* See *paired t*.

correlation coefficient An index of the degree of association between two variables, typically Pearson *r* or related product-moment correlation. (11)

correlation (or *r*-type) family A category of effect size indices, including phi, the point-biserial *r*, the alerting *r*, the contrast *r*, and the effect size *r*. (12)

correlational research Another common name for relational research, that is, investigations in which two or more variables or conditions are measured and related to one another. (1)

correspondence with reality The extent to which an idea or a hypothesis is presumed to agree with "accepted truths" (which in science usually means established facts). (2)

counterbalancing A within-subjects design in which the sequence of conditions (or treatments) is rotated; for example, in a Latin square design with two treatments, some of the sampling units (e.g., research subjects) receive Treatment A before Treatment B, and the others receive B before A. (7)

counternull statistic A measure of the non-null magnitude of the effect size that is supported by the same amount of evidence as the null value of the effect size. (12)

counts Frequencies. (11, 15)

covariation The principle that, in order to demonstrate causality, there must be evidence indicating that what is labeled as the "cause" is, in fact, correlated with what is presumed to be the "effect." (7)

criterion validity The extent to which a measure correlates with one or more criterion variables. (6)

critical incident technique Open-ended method that instructs the respondent to describe an observable action (a) the purpose of which is fairly clear to the respondent and (b) the consequences of which are sufficiently definite to leave little doubt about its effects. (5)

Cronbach's alpha A measure of internal consistency reliability. (6)

crossed design Another name for the basic within-subjects design, because the sampling units are said to be "crossed" by conditions, that is, observed under two or more conditions rather than "nested" within a condition. (7)

cross-lagged correlations Correlations of degrees of association between two sets of variables, of which one is treated as a lagged (time-delayed) value. (8)

cross-lagged panel design A relational research design using cross-lagged correlations, cross-sectional correlations repeated over time, and test-retest correlations. (8)

cross-sectional design Research that compares sampling units on one or more variables at one point in time. (8)

crude range Highest score minus lowest score. (10)

cue words Guiding labels that define particular points or categories of response. (5)

debriefing The process of disclosing to participants more about the full nature of the research in which they participated and, if an active or passive deception was used, why it was believed to be necessary. (3)

deception by commission See *active deception*.

deception by omission See *passive deception*.

degrees of freedom (*df*) The number of observations minus the number of restrictions limiting the observations' freedom to vary. (13)

demand characteristics The mixture of task-orienting cues that govern the participant's perceptions of (a) his or her role as a research subject and (b) the experimenter's hypothesis or scientific objective. (7)

dependent variable A variable the changes in which are viewed as dependent on changes in one or more other variables. (2)

descriptive measure Statistics that are used to directly measure population values (such as σ, σ^2, and Cohen's *d*). (10)

descriptive research An empirical investigation in which the objective is to map out (describe) a situation or set of events. (1)

df See *degrees of freedom*.

dichotomous variable A variable that is divided into two classes or two discrete parts. (11)

difference family A category of effect size indices, including Cohen's *d* and the risk difference. (12)

digital object identifier (DOI) An identification number used for intellectual property in the digital environment. (Appendix A)

discovery H. Reichenbach's general term for the origin, creation, or invention of ideas for investigation. (2)

discrete variable A variable taking on two or more distinct values. (11)

discriminant validity Validity supported by a lack of correlation between conceptually unrelated measures. (6)

dispersion Spread or variability. (10)

doi See *digital object identifier*.

double-blind procedures Procedures (typically used in randomized clinical trials) in which neither the experimenter nor the research participants are aware of which participants were randomly assigned to a particular condition (e.g., treatment vs. placebo control). (7)

double deception A deception embedded in what the research participant thinks is the official debriefing; double deception is unethical because it leaves participants with a lie. (3)

dummy coding Assigning arbitrary numerical values (often 0 and 1) to the two levels of a dichotomous variable. (11)

effective power The associated or actual resulting power (i.e., $1 - \beta$) of the statistical test used. (12)

effective sample size The net equivalent sample size that the researcher ends up with. (9)

effect size The magnitude of a specified effect, as indicated by a correlation (*r*-type) indicator, a difference-type indicator (such as Cohen's *d* or the risk difference), or a ratio-type indicator (such as the odds ratio or the relative risk). (12, 13, 14, 15)

effect size *r* ($r_{\text{effect size}}$) The magnitude of the relationship between two variables, such as *X* and *Y*, or the correlation between a set of obtained scores on *Y* and their respective contrast (lambda) weights ($r_{Y\lambda}$). (12, 13, 14, 15)

efficient causality The idea that a propelling or instigating event or condition or force sets some other event in motion or alters another condition to some degree. (7)

empirical Controlled observation and measurement. (1)

empirical reasoning A combination of systematic (organized) observation (e.g., measurement) and logical reasoning that is open to scrutiny. (1)

equivalence, coefficient of The correlation between alternate measures of the same construct. (6)

error Fluctuation in measurements; also deviation of a score from the mean of the group or condition. (14)

error of estimate Closeness of estimate to actual value. (9)

errors of measurement Random errors in classical test theory. (6)

ethical principles Accepted or professed rules of action to help researchers decide what aspects of a study might pose an ethical problem and, in general terms, how to avoid it. (3)

ethics The moral values by which behavior is judged. (3)

evaluation apprehension M. J. Rosenberg's term for the experience of feeling discomfort about the possibility of being negatively evaluated or not positively evaluated. (5)

evaluation, potency, and activity The three primary dimensions of subjective meaning measured by the semantic differential method. (5)

expectancy control design A factorial design in which an expectancy variable can be analyzed separately from, as well as in interaction with, a treatment variable of interest. (7)

expected frequency (f_e) Counts expected under specified row and column conditions if certain hypotheses (e.g., the null hypothesis) are true. (15)

Glossary

expedited review An evaluation, without undue delay, of proposed research of minimal risk by an institutional review board (IRB). (3)

experimental group A group or condition in which research participants undergo a manipulation or some other experimental intervention. (7)

experimental hypothesis The experimenter's working hypothesis; also an alternative to the null hypothesis (H_0) in null hypothesis significance testing. (2)

experimental research A study designed to explain "what leads to what," or in which the objective implies a causal explanation. (1)

experimenter expectancy bias Another name for the experimenter expectancy effect. (2)

experimenter expectancy effect A type of bias (or artifact) that results when the working hypothesis or experimental expectation held by the experimenter leads unintentionally to behavior toward the participants that, in turn, increases the likelihood that the hypothesis or expectation will be confirmed. (7)

exploratory data analysis The use of simple arithmetic and visual techniques (such as the stem-and-leaf chart) to change our point of view by looking below the surface of any body of data and, as J. W. Tukey (1977) put it, "to make it more easily and effectively handleable by minds" (p. v). (10)

exploratory research An empirical investigation guided more by general questions than by specific hypotheses. (2)

extended range (corrected range) Crude range plus one unit. (10)

external validity The degree of generalizability to particular populations, settings, treatment variables, and measurement variables. (6)

extraneous effect The result of an unaccounted-for variable. (7)

$F_{contrast}$ The F test used to address a focused prediction involving more than two groups or conditions. (14)

$F_{noncontrast}$ The result of dividing the mean square noncontrast by the mean square within. (14)

face-to-face interview An interview in which the interviewer and the respondent directly interact with one another face to face. (5)

face validity The extent to which a test (or some other instrument) seems on its surface to be measuring something it purports to measure. (6)

factor A general name for a variable, the independent variable. (7)

factorial design A research design with more than one factor and two or more levels of each factor. (7)

fair-mindedness Impartiality. (3)

falsifiability (refutability) Karl Popper's proposition that a conjecture or theoretical assertion is scientific only if it can be stated in such a way that it can, if incorrect, be refuted by some empirical means. (2)

field experiments Experimental research that is done in a naturalistic setting. (4)

file drawer problem The concern that a substantial number of studies with nonsignificant results are tucked away in file drawers. (Appendix C)

final causality An emphasis on the end goal, objective, or purpose of an action. (7)

finite Term applied when all the units or events can, at least in theory, be completely counted. (10)

Fisher z_r The log transformation of r, as shown in Table B.6. (12, Appendix B, Appendix C)

fixed-choice items Questions or measures with fixed response options (also called *structured*, *precoded*, or *closed*). (5)

floor effect Condition in which the opportunity for change downward is limited by the lower boundary of a measure. (5)

focused chi-square χ^2 with 1 *df*. (15)

focused statistical tests Statistical procedures that ask focused questions of data, including any t test, 1-*df* χ^2, or F test with numerator $df = 1$. (14)

forced-choice scales Measures that use an item format requiring the respondent to select a single item (or a specified number of items) from a presented set of choices, even when the respondent finds no choice or more than one of the choices acceptable. (5)

formal causality An emphasis on the implicit form or development that gives meaning to an action. (7)

frames Sampling lists in survey research. (9)

F ratio Ratio of mean squares that are distributed as F when the null hypothesis is true, where F is a test of significance used to judge the tenability of the null hypothesis of no relationship between two or more variables (or of no difference between two or more variabilities). (14)

frequency distribution A chart that summarizes the number of times each score or measurement occurs in a set of data. (10)

F test See *F ratio*.

full-text database Information databank that contains the entire work, not just an abstract.

good subject M. T. Orne's term for a research participant who is overly sensitive to and compliant with demand characteristics. (7)

grand mean (M_G) The mean of all observations. (14)

graphic scales Rating scales in the form of a straight line with cue words attached. (5)

halo effect A biased response set in which a judge overextends a positive central trait to a person's other characteristics and thus forms an overall favorable impression of that person. (5)

harmonic mean sample size (n_h) The reciprocal of the arithmetic mean of sample sizes that have been transformed to their reciprocals. (13)

heterogeneous Dissimilarity among the elements of a set. (9)

heuristic Something general that stimulates interest, thought, and possibly empirical investigation. (2)

history See *bias due to history*. (7)

homogeneity of variance Equality of the population variances of the groups to be compared. (13)

homogeneous Similarity among the elements of a set. (9)

hypothesis A conjectural statement or supposition. (2)

hypothesis-generating heuristics Strategies or circumstances that lead to testable hypotheses. (2)

Implicit Attitude Test (IAT) An indirect attitudinal assessment method that focuses on the respondent's automatic associations to specific target concepts and the time it takes to make those associations. (5)

improve on older ideas One of several hypothesis-generating heuristics. (2)

independent-sample *t* test A two-sample test of statistical significance that is used to judge the tenability of the null hypothesis of no relation between two variables. (13)

independent variable A variable on which the dependent variable depends; in experiments, a variable that the experimenter manipulates to determine the degree to which there are effects on another variable. (2)

inferential measure A statistic or measure (such as S and S^2) that is used to estimate population values based on a sample of values. (10)

infinite Boundless, or without limits. (10)

informed consent The procedure in which prospective research participants, who have been told what they will be getting into by volunteering, formally agree to participate in the research. (3)

institutional review board (IRB) A group set up to make risk-benefit analyses of proposed studies and, on the basis of such analyses, approve or reject research proposals (and also monitor the research). (3)

instrumentation bias A plausible threat to internal validity that occurs when changes in the measuring instrument (e.g., deterioration of the instrument) bias the results. (7)

intensive case study In-depth examination of a particular incident, individual, or phenomenon. (2)

interaction effects (residuals) In factorial designs, condition means minus grand mean, row effects, and column effects. (14)

interaction of independent variables The mutually moderating effects of two or more independent variables. (2)

interactions See *interaction of independent variables*.

intercoder reliability The extent to which the raters or judges who are coding data are in agreement. (4)

interitem correlation (r_{ii}) The relationship of the responses to one item with the responses to another item. (6)

internal-consistency reliability Reliability based on the intercorrelation among components of a test, such as subtests or all the individual test items (also termed *reliability of components*). (6)

internal validity Traditional term for whether an experimental treatment did in fact make a difference in a specific

experimental instance, or whether instead a rival condition might account for the observed covariation between X and Y. (6, 7)

interquartile range The difference between the 75th and 25th percentiles. (10)

interrupted time-series design A design in which there is a string of data points (observations or measures) before and after an inserted condition or intervention. (8)

interval estimates The extent to which point estimates are likely to be in error. (9)

intervention An experimental treatment or condition, or episodic event, or some other form of experimental event or action.

interview schedule A script that contains the questions the interviewer will ask. (5)

intrinsically repeated measures Measurements that *must* be repeated to address the question of interest. (14)

introspection The individual's reflection on his or her sensations and perceptions. (5)

IRB See *institutional review board*.

item analysis A procedure used for selecting items (e.g., for a Likert attitude scale). (5)

item-to-item reliability (r_{ii}) The relationship of responses to one item with those to another item, an estimate of the reliability of any single item on average. (6)

iterations Repetitions, as in standardizing the margins of a large table of counts. (15)

judges Coders, raters, decoders, or others who assist in describing and categorizing ongoing events or existing records of events. (4)

judge-to-judge reliability (r_{jj}) The relationship of one judge's responses to those of another judge, an estimate of the reliability of any single judge on average. (6)

judgment study The use of observers (judges or raters) to scale, sort, or rate specified variables (e.g., aspects of observable behavior). (4)

justice The aspirational ideal of impartiality (e.g., the fair distribution of benefits and burdens), one of the ethical principles discussed in this book. (3)

justification H. Reichenbach's term for the defense or confirmation of hypotheses, theories, or other proposed explanations. (2)

K-R 20 A traditional measure of internal-consistency reliability that is used with items that are scored dichotomously (G. F. Kuder & M. W. Richardson's 20th-numbered formula). (6)

lambda (λ) weights Values that sum to zero ($\Sigma \lambda = 0$) and are used to state a prediction. (14)

Latin square design A within-subjects design with counterbalanced conditions. (7)

lazy writing Written work that is saturated with quoted material that, with a little more effort, could be paraphrased (and, of course, referenced). (3)

leading questions Questions that can constrain responses and produce biased answers. (5)

leftover effects See *residual effects*.

Glossary

leniency bias   A type of rating error in which the judge's or observer's ratings are consistently more positive than they should be. (5)

Lie (L) Scale   A set of items in the MMPI that were designed to identify respondents who are deliberately trying to appear "better" than they believe they are. (5)

Likert scales   Attitude scales constructed by the method of summated ratings, developed by R. Likert. (5)

linearity   Relationship between two variables that resembles a straight line. (11)

line graphs   Visual displays of changes in the frequency or proportion of scores over time. (10)

literature search   Retrieval of background information. (2)

logical error in rating   A type of response set in which the judge gives similar ratings for variables or traits that are only intuitively related. (5)

longitudinal study   Research in which the same subjects are studied over a period of time. (8)

main effect   The effect of an independent variable apart from its interaction with other independent variables. (14)

margin of error   Interval within which an anticipated value is expected to occur. (9)

Marlowe-Crowne Social Desirability Scale (MCSD scale)   D. Marlowe and D. Crowne's standardized test that measures social desirability responding and need for social approval. (6)

matched-pair *t*   See *paired t*.

matching   The pairing of sampling units on certain relevant variables. (7)

material causality   An emphasis on the material composition of something that leads to an action. (7)

maturation   A shorthand term for a plausible threat to internal validity that occurs when results not using randomization are contaminated by the participants' having, for instance, grown older, wiser, stronger, or more experienced between the pretest and the posttest. See also *bias due to maturation*. (7)

MCSD   See *Marlowe-Crowne social desirability scale*.

Mdn   See *median*.

mean (*M*)   The arithmetic average of a set of scores. (10)

mean square (*MS*)   Variance (S^2 or σ^2). (10, 14)

mean square for error   Variance (S^2) used as the denominator of F ratios. (14)

median (*Mdn*)   The midmost score of a distribution. (10)

meta-analysis   The "analysis of analyses," or the use of quantitative and graphic methods to summarize the results from individual studies for the purpose of integrating the findings and identifying moderator variables. (Appendix C)

metaphor   A word or phrase applied to a concept or phenomenon it does not literally denote. (2)

method of agreement   J. S. Mill's "If *X*, then *Y*" proposition, which implies that if we find two or more instances in which *Y* occurs, and if only *X* is present on each occasion, then *X* is suspected to be a sufficient condition of *Y*. (7)

method of authority   C. S. Peirce's term for the belief that something is true because someone in a position of power or authority says it is. (1)

method of difference   J. S. Mill's "If not-*X*, then not-*Y*" proposition, which implies that if a presumed effect (*Y*) does not occur when the presumed cause (*X*) is absent, then *X* is suspected to be a necessary condition of *Y*. (7)

method of equal-appearing intervals   A traditional attitude-scaling technique in which values are obtained for items on the assumption that the underlying intervals are equidistant; also called a *Thurstone scale*. (5)

method of self-report   The procedure of having the research participants describe their own behavior or state of mind (e.g., used in interviews, questionnaires, and behavioral diaries). (5)

method of tenacity   C. S. Peirce's term for clinging stubbornly to an idea merely because it has been around for a while. (1)

methodological pluralism   In science, the use of multiple methods of controlled observation to study different facets of complex phenomena from more than one methodological vantage point. (1)

methodological triangulation   Zeroing in on phenomena of interest from more than one vantage point or methodological perspective. (4)

Milgram experiments   A set of experiments performed by Stanley Milgram in which he investigated the willingness of participants to give "electric shocks" to another subject, actually a confederate who pretended to receive the electric shocks. (3)

Mill's methods   Logical propositions popularized by the 19th-century English philosopher J. S. Mill, exemplified by the method of agreement and the method of difference. (7)

minimal risk   Studies in which the likelihood and extent of harm to the participants are believed to be no greater than those typically experienced in everyday life; such studies are generally eligible for an expedited review by an institutional review board. (3)

Minnesota Multiphasic Personality Inventory (MMPI)   A structured personality test containing hundreds of statements that reflect general health, sexual attitudes, religious attitudes, emotional state, and so on. (5)

mixed factorial design   A statistical design with two or more factors, with at least one between and one within subjects. (7)

MMPI   See *Minnesota Multiphasic Personality Inventory*.

modal representativeness index   An indicator of the modal value and the proportion of *N* scores falling on the mode. (10)

mode   The score occurring with the greatest frequency. (10)

moderator variables   Conditions that alter the relationship between independent and dependent variables. (2, Appendix C)

MS   See *mean square*.

***MS*contrast**   The contrast mean square, which is also equivalent to the contrast sum of squares. (14)

multiple-degree-of-freedom effects Effect sizes indexed in association with omnibus statistical procedures. (14)

mutually exclusive Describing this condition: If A is true, then not-A is false. (12)

N The total number of scores in a study; the number of scores in one condition or subgroup is denoted as *n*.

naturalistic observation Research that looks at behavior in its usual natural environment. (4)

necessary condition A requisite or essential condition. (7)

need for social approval The desire to be positively evaluated, or approved of. (6)

negatively skewed distribution An asymmetrical distribution in which the pointed end is toward the left (i.e., toward the negative tail). (10)

nested design Another name for the basic between-subjects design, because the units (e.g., participants) are "nested" within their own groups or conditions. (7)

network analysis See *social network analysis*.

NHST See *null hypothesis significance testing*.

NNT See *number needed to treat*.

***N*-of-1 experimental research** Single-case or single-unit experimental designs. (8)

noise Random error, or the variability within the samples. (6, 13, 14)

nonequivalent-groups designs Nonrandomized research in which the responses of a treatment group and a control group are compared on measures collected at the beginning and end of the study. (8)

nonintrinsically repeated measures Repeated-measures research in which it is not actually essential to use repeated measures, but their use increases the efficiency, precision, and power of the study. (14)

nonlinearity Relationship between two variables that does not resemble a straight line. (11)

nonmaleficence The aspirational ideal to "do no harm," one of several ethical principles discussed in this book. (3)

nonreactive observation Methods of observation or measurement that do not affect what is being observed or measured. (4)

nonresponse bias Systematic error that can be traced to nonresponse or nonparticipation. (9)

nonskewed distribution A symmetrical distribution. (10)

normal distribution Bell-shaped curve that is completely described by its mean and standard deviation. (10)

norm-referenced Indicating that a standardized test has norms (i.e., typical values), so that a person's score can be compared with the scores of a reference group. (5)

norms Tables of values representing the typical performance of a given group. (9)

no-shows People who volunteer for research but fail to keep their scheduled research appointments. (7)

null-counternull interval Range extending from the null value to the counternull value of an observed effect size. (13)

null hypothesis (H_0) The hypothesis to be nullified; usually states that there is no relationship between two or more variables. (12)

null hypothesis significance testing (NHST) The use of statistics and probabilities to evaluate the null hypothesis. (12)

number needed to treat (NNT) The number of patients needed to be treated by a drug in order for one patient to benefit. (12)

numerical scales Rating scales in which the respondent works with a sequence of defined numbers. (5)

observational studies Longitudinal investigations that simply observe the participants, without introducing an intervention or experimental manipulation. (4)

observed frequency (f_0) Counts obtained in specific rows and columns. (15)

observed scores Raw scores. (6)

observer bias The systematic overestimation or underestimation of observable events. (4)

Occam's razor The principle that explanations should be as parsimonious as possible (William of Occam, or Ockham). (2)

odds ratio (OR) Relative indication of the odds for a binary variable (e.g., adverse event present vs. absent) in two groups of participants (e.g., treated subjects and control subjects). (12)

omnibus chi-square χ^2 with $df > 1$. (15)

omnibus statistical procedures Statistical procedures that ask unfocused (diffuse) questions of data, such as F with numerator $df > 1$, or χ^2 with $df > 1$. (14)

one-degree-of-freedom effects Effect sizes indexed in association with focused statistical procedures. (14)

one-group pre-post design (O-X-O) A single-group design in which reactions of the group are observed (O) both before and after an event or intervention (X). (7)

one-sample *t* test See *paired t*.

one-shot case study (X-O) A single-group design in which reactions of the group are observed (O) only after an event or intervention (X). (7)

one-tailed *p* value The *p* value associated with a result supporting the prediction of that research result's specific direction, such as $M_A > M_B$, or the sign of r is positive. (12)

one-way design A statistical design in which two or more groups comprise a single dimension. (7)

open-ended items Questions or statements that offer respondents an opportunity to express their feelings, motives, opinions, or reactions spontaneously. (5)

operational definition The meaning of a variable in terms of the operations (empirical conditions) used to measure it or the experimental method involved in its determination. (2)

opportunity samples The selection of participants largely on the basis of their availability and convenience (as opposed to probability sampling). (9)

ordinate The vertical axis (the *y*-axis) of a distribution. (10)

outliers Scores lying far outside the normal range. (10)

O-X-O See *one-group pre-post design*.

Glossary

p_{rep}   P. R. Killeen's proposed statistic for estimating the replicability of an obtained effect. (12)

paired t (also called *correlated-sample t, matched-pair t,* or *one-sample t***)**   The t test computed on nonindependent samples. (13)

paradoxical incident   An occurrence characterized by seemingly self-contradictory aspects. (2)

parsimony   The quality of economy in a statement or proposition, so that it is not overly wordy or unduly complex; see also *Occam's razor.* (2)

partial concealment   Observation in which the researcher conceals only who or what is being specifically observed. (4)

participant observation   Studying a group or a community from within and recording behavior as it occurs. (4)

partitioning of tables   Statistical procedure for subdividing larger chi-square tables into smaller tables (e.g., into 2×2 tables). (15)

passive deception   Deceiving research subjects by omission, such as withholding certain details of the study, or not informing them of the meaning of their responses when they are given a projective test. (3)

payoff potential   A subjective assessment of the likelihood that a prediction or an experimental hypothesis will be corroborated because it is consistent with the literature. (2)

Pearson r   K. Pearson's standard (product-moment) index of the linear relationship between two variables. (11)

peer-reviewed journals   Journals in which articles submitted for publication are reviewed by experts in the field. (1)

percentile   A point in a distribution of scores below and above which a specified percentage of scores falls. (10)

perceptibility   The use of images in the form of analogies and metaphors to explain things. (1)

phi coefficient (ϕ)   Pearson r where both variables are dichotomous. (11, 15)

physical traces   Material evidence of behavior. (4)

pilot testing   The evaluation of some aspect of the research before the study is implemented.

placebo   A substance without any pharmacological benefit given as a pseudomedicine to a control group. (7)

placebo control group   A control group that receives a placebo. (7)

placebo effects   The "healing" effects of inert substances or nonspecific treatments. (7)

plagiarism   Representing someone else's work as one's own. (3)

plausible rival hypotheses   Propositions, or sets of propositions, that provide a reasonable alternative to the working hypothesis. (4, 6)

point-biserial correlation (r_{pb})   Pearson r where one of the variables is continuous and the other is dichotomous. (11)

point estimates   Estimates of particular (usually average) characteristics of the population (e.g., the number of times an event occurs). (9)

population   The universe of elements from which sample elements are drawn, or the universe of elements to which we want to generalize. (9)

positively skewed distribution   An asymmetrical distribution in which the pointed end is toward the right (i.e., the positive tail). (10)

posttest-only design   See *after-only design.*

power ($1 - \beta$)   In significance testing, the probability of not making a Type II error. (12)

power analysis   Estimation of the statistical power of a significance test, or of the sample size needed to detect an effect given a specified level of power. (12)

power of a test   The probability, when using a particular test statistic (e.g., t, F, χ^2), of not making a Type II error. (12)

precoded items   See *fixed-choice items.*

predictive validity   The extent to which a test can predict future outcomes. (6)

preexperimental designs   Designs in which the total absence of a suitable control makes the results especially vulnerable to causal misinterpretations. (7)

pre-post design   See *before-after design.*

preratings   The ratings made before an experimental treatment. (2)

pretest   The measurement made before an experimental manipulation or intervention. (5)

probability   The mathematical chance of an event's occurring. (9)

probability sampling   The random selection of sampling units so that the laws of mathematical probability apply. (9)

product-moment correlation   Standard index of linear relationship, or Pearson r. (11)

projective test   A psychological measure that operates on the principle that the respondent's spontaneous responses are a projection of some unconscious aspect of his or her life experience and emotions onto ambiguous stimuli (e.g., the Rorschach test and the Thematic Apperception Test). (5)

propensity score   A composite variable that summarizes differences between "treated" and "untreated" sampling units on a number of different variables. (8)

proportion of variation explained   See *coefficient of determination.*

proposal   See *research proposal.*

prospective data   Information collected by following the participant's behavior or reaction forward in time. (8)

pseudoscience   Bogus claims masquerading as scientific facts. (1)

PsycARTICLES   The American Psychological Association's full-text database of articles. (2)

PsycINFO   The American Psychological Association's main informational database. (2)

push polls   An insidious form of negative political campaigning disguised as opinion polling but designed to push opinions in a particular direction. (9)

p **value** Probability value or level obtained in a test of significance. (12)

qualitative research Studies in which the raw data exist in a nonnumerical form. (4)

quantitative research Studies in which the raw data exist in a numerical form. (4)

quasi-control subjects M. T. Orne's term for research participants who are invited to reflect on the context in which an experiment is conducted and to speculate on the ways in which the context (e.g., demand characteristics) might influence their own and other subjects' behaviors. (7)

quasi-experimental A traditional term used to describe study designs that resemble randomized experimental designs (i.e., having treatments, outcome measures, and experimental units) but that lack random assignment, which would create the comparisons from which treatment-caused changes could be inferred, as in randomized experimental designs. (7)

quota sampling In this once-traditional (but long viewed as highly problematic) procedure, the questioner is assigned a quota of people to be interviewed and then attempts to build up a sample that is supposed to be representative of the population. (9)

r^2 See *coefficient of determination.*

$r_{alerting}$ See *alerting r.*

$r_{contrast}$ See *contrast r.*

$r_{counternull}$ See *counternull statistic.*

$r_{effect\ size}$ See *effect size r.*

random assignment, rule of The plan according to which random allocation is implemented. (1, 7)

random digit dialing Sampling households for telephone interviews by, for example, selecting the first three digits of telephone numbers and using a computer program to select the last four digits at random. (9)

random error The effects of uncontrolled variables that cannot be specifically identified; such effects are, theoretically speaking, self-canceling in that the average of the errors will equal zero in the long run. (6)

random sampling Selecting a sample by chance procedures and with known probabilities of selection. (1, 9)

random selection Another name for random sampling. (1)

randomization Random allocation of sampling units to groups or conditions. (7)

randomized experiments Experimental designs that use randomization. (7)

randomized trials Another name for randomized experiments in biomedical and other clinical contexts. (1, 7)

range Distance between the highest and lowest score. (10)

rater biases See *rating errors.*

rating errors Systematic errors in responses on rating scales (also called *response biases* or *rater biases*). (5)

rating scales The common name for a variety of measuring instruments on which the observer or judge gives a numerical value (either explicitly or implicitly) to certain judgments or assessments. (5)

ratio family A category of effect size indices (including the odds ratio and relative risk). (12)

raw scores Observed (obtained) scores. (6)

RD See *risk difference.*

reactive observation An observation or measurement that affects what is being observed or measured. (4)

refutability A synonym for *falsifiability.* (2)

relational research An empirical investigation in which the objective is to identify relationships among variables. (1)

relative risk (RR) A ratio of the incidence rate of a specified adverse event among participants administered a treatment to the incidence rate of such an event in the participants that were not given the treatment. (12)

relative risk reduction (RRR) The reduction in relative risk (RR) expressed as a percentage. (12)

reliability The extent to which observations or measures are consistent or stable. (6)

reliability of components See *internal-consistency reliability.* (6)

repeated-measures design Statistical design in which the sampling units generate two or more measurements. (7)

replicate To repeat or duplicate. (1)

replication Research designed to assess the repeatability of a result. (2, 6)

representative Typical, such as when a segment is representative (or typical) of the larger pool. (9)

r-**equivalent** An estimation of the effect size equivalent to a sample point-biserial *r.* (12)

research proposal Detailed account of what a researcher proposes to study and how the researcher plans to go about it. (2)

residuals Leftover effects when appropriate components are subtracted from scores or means. (14)

response biases See *rating errors.*

retest reliability See *test-retest reliability.*

retrospective data Information collected by going back in time. (8)

rhetoric The language of a given field, which in science encompasses the proper use of technical terms. (1)

rhetoric of justification The language and line of reasoning used by scientists to substantiate an evidence-based conclusion. (1)

risk-benefit analysis An evaluation of the potential risks of harm and the projected (societal and scientific) benefits of proposed studies. (3)

risk difference (RD) The difference between the risk of a specified adverse event in (a) the treated group and (b) the control group (also called *absolute risk reduction,* ARR). (12)

rival interpretations Competing explanations, hypotheses, or predictions of a specific result. (4)

root mean square Square root of the mean square. (10)

Rorschach test   A projective test that consists of a set of inkblots on pieces of cardboard. (5)

row effect   Row mean minus grand mean. (14)

RR   See *relative risk.*

RRR   See *relative risk reduction.*

r-type indices   See *effect size.*

sample   A subset of the population. (9)

sampling frames   Lists of sampling units, also called *sampling lists.* (9)

sampling plan   A design, scheme of action, or procedure that specifies how the participants are to be selected in a survey study. (9)

sampling units   The elements that make up the sample. (9)

sampling with replacement   A type of random sampling in which the selected units are placed in the selection pool again and may be reselected in subsequent draws. (9)

sampling without replacement   A type of random sampling in which a previously selected unit cannot be chosen again and must be disregarded in any later draw. (9)

Satterthwaite's method   A procedure used to make *t* tests more accurate when suitable transformations are unavailable or ineffective. (13, Appendix A)

scatter diagram   See *scatter plot.*

scatter plot (scatter diagram)   A visual representation of the correlation between two variables, resembling a cloud of scattered dots. (11)

scientific method   General expression for the methodology of science, or a systematic research approach or outlook emphasizing the use of empirical reasoning. (1)

secondary observation   Information that is twice removed from the source. (4)

segmented graphic scale   A rating scale in the form of a line that is broken into segments. (5)

selection   A shorthand term for a plausible threat to the internal validity of research not using randomization, when the kinds of research participants selected for one treatment group are different from those selected for another group. See also *biased selection.* (7)

self-fulfilling prophecy   R. Merton's term for a prediction that is fulfilled because those aware of the prediction then act accordingly. (1)

self-report measures   Respondents' or participants' description or report of their own behavior or state of mind. (5)

semantic differential method   Traditional rating procedure in which the subjective meaning of stimuli or target concepts is judged in terms of several dimensions, usually evaluation, potency, and activity. (5)

seminal theories   Conceptualizations that shape or stimulate further work. (2)

serendipity   Making a chance discovery. (2)

signal   Information. (13, 14)

signal-to-noise ratio   A ratio of information to lack of information, for example, the ratio of the variability between samples (the signal) to the variability within the samples (the noise). (13, 14)

significance level   The probability of a Type I error. (12)

Significance test = Size of effect × Size of study   The basic conceptual form of all significance tests. (13, 15)

simple effects   Differences between group or condition means. (14)

simple observation   Unobtrusive observation of events without any attempt to affect them. (4)

simple random sampling   The most basic probability-sampling plan, in which the respondents are initially selected individually on the basis of a randomized procedure. (9)

single-case experimental research   Studies using repeated-measures designs in which $N = 1$ participant or 1 group (also called *small-N experimental research* or *N-of-1 experimental research*). (8)

size of the study   The number of sampling units or some index of that number. (13)

small-N experimental research   Studies using repeated-measures designs in which the treatment effect is evaluated within the same subject (or participant) or a small number of subjects. (8)

social network analysis (SNA)   The use of visual and quantitative techniques to map networks of interpersonal communication or social interactions. (4)

social psychology of the experiment   The study of the ways in which participant-related and experimenter-related artifacts operate. (7)

socially desirable responding   The tendency to respond in ways that seem to elicit a favorable evaluation. (5, 6)

Spearman-Brown prophecy formula   A traditional equation (originally published independently by C. Spearman and W. Brown) that measures overall internal-consistency reliability of a test from knowledge of the reliability of its components. (6)

Spearman rho (r_s)   Correlation computed on scores in ranked form. (11)

spread   Dispersion or variability. (10)

stability   The extent to which a set of measurements does not vary. (9)

standard deviation   An index of the variability of a set of data around the mean value in a distribution. (10)

standard normal curve   Normal curve with mean $= 0$ and $\sigma = 1$. (10)

standard score (z score)   Score converted to a standard deviation unit. (10)

standardized measures   Measurements, such as psychological tests (e.g., of ability, personality, judgment, and attitude), requiring that certain rules be followed in the development, administration, and scoring of the measuring instrument. (5)

standardizing the margins   A successive-iteration procedure for setting all the row totals equal to each other and all the column totals equal to each other in large tables of counts. (15)

statistical-conclusion validity The relative accuracy of drawing statistical conclusions. (6)

statistical power See *power*.

stem-and-leaf chart The display of a distribution of data values (resembling a histogram, except that all of the original data values are preserved), where each data value is split between the leading digit (called the "stem") and the first trailing digit (called the "leaf"). (10)

strata (clusters) Subpopulations (or layers) in survey sampling. (9)

stratified random sampling Probability sampling plan in which a separate sample is randomly selected within each homogeneous stratum (or layer) of the population. (9)

structured items See *fixed-choice items*.

Student's *t* The pen name used by the inventor of the *t* test, W. S. Gosset, was "Student." (13)

subclassification on propensity scores Using *propensity scores* to form matched subgroups of "treated" and "untreated" participants or units. (8)

sufficient condition A condition that is adequate to bring about some effect or result. (7)

sum of squares (*SS*) The sum of the squared deviations from the mean in a set of scores. (14)

summated ratings method A method of attitude scaling, developed by R. Likert, that uses item analysis to select the best items for a Likert scale. (5)

symmetrical distribution A distribution of scores in which there is a close correspondence in arrangement on the opposite sides of the middle line. (10)

synchronous correlations In cross-lagged panel designs, correlations of the degree of relationship of variables at a specific point in time. (8)

syndrome A set of symptoms. (2)

systematic error The effect of uncontrolled variables that often can be specifically identified; such effects are, theoretically speaking, not self-canceling (in contrast to the self-canceling nature of *random errors*). (6)

systematic observation Observation that is guided or influenced by preexisting questions or hypotheses, and that also follows a particular plan or involves a system that can be evaluated on the basis of accepted scientific standards. (4)

$t_{contrast}$ The symbol used in this book to denote a *t* test that is used to address a focused question or hypothesis in a comparison of more than two groups or conditions. (14)

tally sheets Recording materials for counting frequencies.

target population The group or population to which sampled findings are intended to be generalized. (1)

TAT See *Thematic Apperception Test*.

t distribution Family of curves, each resembling the standard normal distribution, for every possible value of the degrees of freedom (*df*) of the *t* test. (13)

teleological causality The cause when the action is goal-directed. (7)

telephone interview Survey interview conducted by telephone. (5)

temporal precedence The principle that the presumed "cause" must be shown to have occurred before the presumed "effect." (7)

testing See *bias due to testing*.

test-retest correlations Correlations that represent the stability of a variable over time. (8)

test-retest reliability The degree of consistency of a test or measurement, or the characteristic it is designed to measure, from one administration to another (also simply called *retest reliability*). (6)

tests of simple effects Significance tests of the difference between two groups or two condition means in a multigroup design. (14)

Thematic Apperception Test (TAT) A classic projective test consisting of pictures of people in different life contexts. (5)

theoretical (conceptual) definition The meaning of a variable in abstract or conceptual terms. (2)

theoretical ecumenism Framing the conjectural explanation for a complex phenomenon from more than one theoretical perspective. (1)

theory A set of proposed explanatory statements or propositions connected by logical arguments and by explicit and implicit assumptions. (2)

third-variable problem A condition in which a variable correlated with *X* and *Y* is suspected to be the cause of both. (4, 8)

three Rs principle (of humane animal experimentation) The widely accepted proposition (in experimental research in which animals are used to test various treatments) that scientists should (a) *reduce* the number of animals used in the research, (b) *refine* their animal experiments so that the animals suffer less, and (c) *replace* animals with other procedures whenever possible. (3)

Thurstone scales See *method of equal-appearing intervals*.

time-series designs Studies in which the effects of an intervention are inferred from a comparison of the outcome measures obtained at different time intervals before and after an intervention. (8)

transformation Conversion of data to another mathematical form. (10)

translation and back-translation Procedure used when the language of those questioned is not the native language of the investigators. The questionnaire items and instructions are translated from the source to the target language and then independently translated back into the source language. The original version is compared with the twice-translated version to ensure that nothing of importance was lost in the translations. (4)

treatments The procedures or conditions of an experiment. (7)

trials Term for randomized controlled experiments designed to test the efficacy of pharmaceuticals or other clinical interventions. (7)

trimmed mean The mean of a distribution from which a specified highest and lowest percentage of scores has been dropped. (10)

trust   The establishment of a relationship of integrity with the research participants. (3)

t **test**   A test of significance used to judge the tenability of the null hypothesis of no relationship between two variables. (13)

two-by-two factorial design   ANOVA design with two rows and two columns. (7)

two-tailed *p* value   The *p* value associated with a result supporting the prediction of a nonspecific direction for that result. (12)

two-way design (two-way factorial)   ANOVA design in which each entry in the table is associated with a row variable and a column variable. (14)

two-way factorial   See *two-way design*.

Type I error   The error of rejecting the null hypothesis when it is true. (12)

Type II error   The error of failing to reject the null hypothesis when it is false. (12)

unbiased   A term describing the condition in which the average of the sample values coincides with the corresponding "true" population value. (9)

unbiased estimator of the population value of σ^2   A statistic usually written as S^2. (10, 13)

unbiased sampling plan   Survey design in which the range of the sample values coincides with the corresponding "true" population values. (9)

unipolar rating scales   Scales in which one end represents a great deal of a quality and the other end represents a complete absence of that quality. (5)

unobtrusive observation   Measurements or observations used to study behavior when the subjects are unaware of being measured or observed. (4)

unstructured measures   See *open-ended items*.

validity   The degree to which what was observed or measured is the same as what was purported to be observed or measured. (6)

variability   See *spread*.

variable   An event or a condition the researcher observes or measures or plans to investigate that is likely to vary. (2)

variables   Attributes of sampling units, events, or conditions that can take on two or more values, or observed or measured events or conditions that vary or are likely to vary. (2)

variance (mean square)   The mean of the squared deviations of scores from their means in a population, or its unbiased estimate. (10)

varied replication   Repeating (replicating) a previous study but with some new twist. (2)

visualization   Seeing things in the "mind's eye"; also called *perceptibility* in this book. (1)

volunteer bias   Systematic error resulting when volunteers for research participation respond differently from the way individuals in the general population would respond. (9)

WAIS   See *Wechsler Adult Intelligence Scale*.

wait-list control group   A control group in which the participants wait to be given the experimental treatment until after it has been administered to the experimental group. (8)

Wechsler Adult Intelligence Scale (WAIS)   The most widely used of the individual intelligence tests; divided into verbal and performance scores. (6)

wild scores   Extreme scores that result from computational or recording mistakes. (10)

within-subjects design   Statistical design in which each sampling unit (e.g., each research participant) receives two or more conditions. (7)

working hypothesis   An empirically testable supposition, the experimental hypothesis. (2)

***x* axis (abscissa)**   The horizontal axis of a distribution. (10)

X-O   See *one-shot case study*.

***y* axis (ordinate)**   The vertical axis of a distribution. (10)

yea-sayers   Respondents who are overly agreeable; for example, they may answer questions consistently in the affirmative. See also *acquiescent response set*. (5)

$\bar{z}_r$ The average Fisher z_r. (Appendix B, Appendix C)

zero control group   A group that receives no treatment of any kind. (7)

***z* score**   See *standard score*.

References

Abelson, R. P. (1985). A variance explanation paradox: When a little is a lot. *Psychological Bulletin, 97,* 129–133.

Adair, J. G. (1973). *The human subject: The social psychology of the psychological experiment.* Boston, MA: Little, Brown.

Adair, R. K. (1990). *The physics of baseball.* New York, NY: Harper & Row.

Aditya, R. N. (1996). *The not-so-good subject: Extent and correlates of pseudovolunteering in research.* Unpublished M.A. thesis, Temple University Department of Psychology, Philadelphia.

Aiken, L. R., Jr. (1963). Personality correlates of attitude toward mathematics. *Journal of Educational Research, 56,* 576–580.

Ainsworth, M. D. S., Blehar, M. C., Waters, E., & Wall, S. (1978). *Patterns of attachment.* Hillsdale, NJ: Erlbaum.

Allaman, J. D., Joyce, C. S., & Crandall, V. C. (1972). The antecedents of social desirability response tendencies of children and young adults. *Child Development, 43,* 1135–1160.

Allport, G. W. (1935). Attitudes. In C. Murchison (Ed.), *Handbook of social psychology* (pp. 798–884). Worcester, MA: Clark University Press.

Allport. G. W. (1954). *The nature of prejudice.* Reading, MA: Addison-Wesley.

Allport, G. W., & Postman, L. (1947). *The psychology of rumor.* New York, NY: Holt, Rinehart & Winston.

Altman, D. A., Machin, D., Bryant, T. N., & Gardner, M. J. (Eds.). (2000). *Statistics with confidence* (2nd ed.). London, England: British Medical Journal Books.

American Association for the Advancement of Science. (1988). *Project on scientific fraud and misconduct.* Washington, DC: Author.

American Psychological Association. (2002). Ethical principles of psychologists and code of conduct. *American Psychologist, 57,* 1060–1073.

American Psychological Association. (2010). *Publication manual of the American Psychological Association* (6th ed.). Washington, DC: Author.

Anastasi, A., & Urbina, S. (1997). *Psychological testing* (7th ed.). Upper Saddle River, NJ: Prentice Hall.

Anderson, C. A., & Bushman, B. J. (1997). External validity of "trivial" experiments: The case of laboratory aggression. *Review of General Psychology, 1,* 19–41.

Anderson, D. C., Crowell, C. R., Hantula, D. A., & Siroky, L. M. (1988). Task clarification and individual performance posting for improving cleaning in a student-managed university bar. *Journal of Organizational Behavior Management, 9,* 73–90.

Arceneaux, K. (2010). The benefits of experimental methods for the study of campaign effects. *Political Communication, 27,* 199–215.

Aronson, E., & Carlsmith, J. M. (1968). Experimentation in social psychology. In G. Lindzey & E. Aronson (Eds.), *The handbook of social psychology* (2nd ed., Vol. 2, pp. 1–79). Reading, MA: Addison-Wesley.

Asch, S. E. (1952). Effects of group pressure upon the modification and distortion of judgments. In G. E. Swanson, T. M. Newcomb, & E. L. Hartley (Eds.), *Readings in social psychology* (Rev. ed., pp. 393–401). New York, NY: Holt, Rinehart & Winston.

Atkinson, L. (1986). The comparative validities of the Rorschach and MMPI: A meta-analysis. *Canadian Psychology, 27,* 238–247.

Atwell, J. E. (1981). Human rights in human subjects research. In A. J. Kimmel (Ed.), *Ethics of human subject research* (pp. 81–90). San Francisco, CA: Jossey-Bass.

Axinn, S. (1966). Fallacy of the single risk. *Philosophy of Science, 33,* 154–162.

Babad, E. (1993). Pygmalion—25 years after interpersonal expectations in the classroom. In P. D. Blanck (Ed.), *Interpersonal expectations: Theory, research, and applications* (pp. 125–153). New York, NY: Cambridge University Press.

Bailey, P., & Bremer, F. (1921). Experimental diabetes insipidus. *Archives of Internal Medicine, 28,* 773–803.

Bakan, D. (1967). *On method: Toward a reconstruction of psychological investigation.* San Francisco, CA: Jossey-Bass.

Baldwin, W. (2000). Information no one else knows: The value of self-report. In A. A. Stone, J. S. Turkkan, C. A. Bachrach, J. B. Jobe, H. S. Kurtzman, & V. S. Cain (Eds.), *The science of self-report: Implications for research and practice* (pp. 1–7). Mahwah, NJ: Erlbaum.

Bales, R. F. (1950a). A set of categories for analysis of small group interaction. *American Sociological Review, 15,* 257–263.

Bales, R. F. (1950b). *Interaction process analysis: A method for the study of small groups.* Cambridge, MA: Addison-Wesley.

Bales, R. F. (1955). How people interact in conferences. *Scientific American, 192,* 18(March), 31–35.

Bales, R. F., & Cohen, S. P. (1979). *Symlog: A system for the multiple level observation of groups.* New York, NY: Free Press.

Baltimore, D. (1997, January 27). Philosophical differences. *New Yorker,* p. 8.

Barker, P. (1996). *Psychotherapeutic metaphors: A guide to theory and practice.* New York, NY: Brunner/Mazel.

Barrass, R. (1978). *Scientists must write.* London, England: Chapman & Hall.

Bartoshuk, L. (2002). Self-reports and across-group comparisons: A way out of the box. *APS Observer, 15*(3), 7, 26–28.

Bauer, M. I., & Johnson-Laird, P. N. (1993). How diagrams can improve reasoning. *Psychological Science, 4,* 372–378.

Baumrind, D. (1964). Some thoughts on ethics of research: After reading Milgram's "Behavioral Study of Obedience." *American Psychologist, 19,* 421–423.

Beck, A. T., Rush, A. J., Shaw, B. F., & Emery, D. (1979). *Cognitive therapy of depression.* New York, NY: Guilford Press.

Beck, A. T., Steer, R. A., & Garbin, G. M. (1988). Psychometric properties of the Beck Depression Inventory. *Journal of Clinical Psychology, 40,* 77–100.

Beck, S. J., Beck, A., Levitt, E., & Molish, H. (1961). *Rorschach's test: Vol. 1. Basic processes.* New York, NY: Grune & Stratton.

Beecher, H. K. (1970). *Research and the individual.* Boston, MA: Little, Brown.

Benjamin, L. T., Jr., & Simpson, J. A. (2009). The power of the situation: The impact of Milgram's obedience studies on personality and social psychology. *American Psychologist, 64,* 12–19.

Bergum, B. O., & Lehr, D. J. (1963). Effects of authoritarianism on vigilance performance. *Journal of Applied Psychology, 47,* 75–77.

Bernard, H. B., & Killworth, P. D. (1970). Informant accuracy in social network data, Part 2. *Human Communication Research, 4,* 3–18.

Bernard, H. B., & Killworth, P. D. (1980). Informant accuracy in social network data: 4. A comparison of clique-level structure in behavioral and cognitive network data. *Social Networks, 2,* 191–218.

Bernstein, D. A. (1969). Modification of smoking behavior: An evaluative review. *Psychological Bulletin, 71,* 418–440.

Bersoff, D. M., & Bersoff, D. N. (2000). Ethical issues in the collection of self-report data. In A. A. Stone, J. S. Turkkan, C. A. Bachrach, J. B. Jobe, H. S. Kurtzman, & V. S. Cain (Eds.), *The science of self-report: Implications for research and practice* (pp. 9–24). Mahwah, NJ: Erlbaum.

Billow, R. M. (1977). Metaphor: A review of the psychological literature. *Psychological Bulletin, 84,* 81–92.

Biocca, F., & Levy, M. R. (Eds.). (1995). *Communication in the age of virtual reality.* Hillsdale, NJ: Erlbaum.

Blanck, P. D. (Ed.). (1993). *Interpersonal expectations: Theory, research, and applications.* New York: Cambridge University Press.

Blanck, P. D., Bellack, A. S., Rosnow, R. L., Rotheram-Borus, M. J., & Schooler, N. R. (1992). Scientific rewards and conflicts of ethical choices in human subjects research. *American Psychologist, 47,* 959–965.

Blanck, P., Schartz, H. A., Ritchie, H., & Rosenthal, R. (2006). Science and ethics in conducting, analyzing, and reporting disability policy research. In D. A. Hantula (Ed.), *Advances in social and organizational psychology* (pp. 141–159). London, England: Psychology Press/Taylor & Francis.

Blass, T. (2004). *The man who shocked the world: The life and legacy of Stanley Milgram.* New York, NY: Basic Books.

Blass, T. (2009). From New Haven to Santa Clara: A historical perspective on the Milgram obedience experiments. *American Psychologist, 64,* 37–45.

Blastland, M., & Dilnot, A. (2009). *The numbers game.* New York, NY: Gotham Books.

Blumberg, M., & Pringle, C. D. (1983). How control groups can cause loss of control in action research: The case of Rushton coal mine. *Journal of Applied Behavioral Science, 19,* 409–425.

Bok, S. (1978). *Lying: Moral choice in public and private life.* New York, NY: Pantheon.

Bonanno, G. A., Galea, S., Bucciarelli, A., & Vhahov, D. (2006). Psychological resilience after disaster: New York City in the aftermath of the September 11th terrorist attack. *Psychological Science, 17,* 181–186.

Boorstein, D. J. (1985). *The discoverers.* New York, NY: Vintage.

Bordia, P., & Rosnow, R. L. (1998). Rumor rest stops on the information highway: Transmission patterns in a computer-mediated rumor chain. *Human Communication Research, 25,* 163–179.

Borgatti, S. P., Mehra, A., Brass, D. J., & Labianca, G. (2009). Network analysis in the social sciences. *Science, 323,* 892–895.

Boring, E. G. (1957). *A history of experimental psychology.* New York, NY: Appleton-Century-Crofts.

Bradburn, N. M. (1982). Question-wording effects in surveys. In R. Hogarth (Ed.), *New directions for methodology of social and behavioral science: Question framing and response contingency* (No. 11, pp. 65–76). San Francisco, CA: Jossey-Bass.

Braun, H. I., & Wainer, H. (1989). Making essay test scores fairer with statistics. In J. M. Tanur, F. Mosteller, W. H. Kruskal, E. L. Lehmann, R. F. Link, R. S. Pieters, & G. S. Rising (Eds.), *Statistics: A guide to the unknown* (3rd ed., pp. 178–187). Pacific Grove, CA: Wadsworth & Brooks/Cole.

Brehmer, B., & Dörner, D. (1993). Experiments with computer-simulated microworlds: Escaping both the narrow straits of the laboratory and the deep blue sea of the field study. *Computers in Human Behavior, 9,* 171–184.

Brody, J. E. (2002, October 22). Separating gold from junk in medical studies. *The New York Times,* p. F7.

Brody, J. E. (2009, August 26). Symptom list helps to gauge head injuries. *The New York Times,* p. D7.

Broome, J. (1984). Selecting people randomly. *Ethics, 95,* 38–55.

Brown, R. (1965). *Social psychology.* New York, NY: Free Press.

Brown, W. (1910). Some experimental results in the correlation of mental abilities. *British Journal of Psychology, 3,* 296–322.

Brownlee, K. A. (1955). Statistics of the 1954 Polio vaccine trials. [Electronic version]. *Journal of the American Statistical Association, 272,* 1005–1013.

Bureau of Labor Statistics. (2010–2011). *Occupational outlook handbook.* Retrieved from http://www.bls.gov/oco/ocos162.htm

Burger, J. M. (2009). Replicating Milgram: Would people still obey today? *American Psychologist, 64,* 1–11.

Burnham, J. R. (1966). *Experimenter bias and lesion labeling.* Unpublished manuscript, Purdue University, West Lafayette, IN.

Buunk, B. P., & Gibbons, F. X. (Eds.). (1997). *Health, coping, and well-being: Perspectives from social comparison theory.* Mahwah, NJ: Erlbaum.

Campbell, D. T. (1957). Factors relevant to the validity of experiments in social settings. *Psychological Bulletin, 54,* 297–312.

Campbell, D. T., & Boruch, R. F. (1975). Making the case for randomized assignment to treatments by considering the alternatives: Six ways in which quasi-experimental evaluations in compensatory education tend to underestimate effects. In C. A. Bennett & A. Lumsdaine (Eds.), *Evaluation and experiments: Some critical issues in assessing social programs* (pp. 195–296). New York, NY: Academic Press.

Campbell, D. T., & Fiske, D. W. (1959). Convergent and discriminant validation by the multitrait-multimethod matrix. *Psychological Bulletin, 56,* 81–105.

Campbell, D. T., & Kenny, D. A. (1999). *A primer on regression artifacts.* New York, NY: Guilford Press.

Campbell, D. T., & Stanley, J. C. (1963). *Experimental and quasi-experimental designs for research.* Chicago, IL: Rand McNally.

Carr, K., & England, R. (Eds.). (1995). *Simulated and virtual realities: Elements of perception.* London, England: Taylor & Francis.

Ceci, S. J. (1990). *On intelligence ... more or less: A bio-ecological treatise on intellectual development.* Englewood Cliffs, NJ: Prentice Hall.

Ceci, S. J. (1996). *On intelligence: A bioecologial treatise on intellectual development* (Expanded ed.). Cambridge, MA: Harvard University Press.

Ceci, S. J., & Bruck, M. (1993). Suggestibility of the child witness: A historical review and synthesis. *Psychological Bulletin, 113,* 403–439.

Ceci, S. J., & Bruck, M. (1995). *Jeopardy in the courtroom: A scientific study of children's testimony.* Washington, DC: American Psychological Association.

Ceci, S. J., Peters, D., & Plotkin, J. (1985). Human subjects review, personal values, and the regulation of social science research. *American Psychologist, 40,* 994–1002.

Chalmers, I., & Altman, D. G. (1995). *Systematic reviews.* London, England: BJM Publishing Group.

Chambers, J. M., Cleveland, W. S., Kleiner, B., & Tukey, P. A. (1983). *Graphical methods for data analysis.* Pacific Grove, CA: Wadsworth.

Chandrasekhar, S. (1987). *Truth and beauty: Aesthetics and motivations in science.* Chicago, IL: University of Chicago Press.

Chein, I. (1948). Behavior theory and the behavior of attitudes: Some critical comments. *Psychological Review, 55,* 175–188.

Cho, A. (2006). Math clears up an inner-ear mystery: Spiral shape pumps up the bass. *Science, 311,* 1087.

Clark, R. W. (1971). *Einstein: The life and times.* New York, NY: World.

Cochran, W. G. (1937). Problems arising in the analysis of a series of similar experiments. *Journal of the Royal Statistical Society 4* (Supplement), 102–118.

Cochran, W. G. (1963). *Sampling techniques* (2nd ed.). New York, NY: Wiley.

Cochran, W. G. (1968). The effectiveness of adjustment by subclassification in removing bias in observational studies. *Biometrics, 24,* 295–313.

Cochran, W. G. (1977). *Sampling techniques* (3rd ed.). New York, NY: Wiley.

Cohen, J. (1969). *Statistical power analysis for the behavioral sciences.* New York, NY: Academic Press.

Cohen, J. (1988). *Statistical power analysis for the behavioral sciences* (2nd ed.). Hillsdale, NJ: Erlbaum.

Cohen, J. (1990). Things I have learned (so far). *American Psychologist, 45,* 1304–1312.

Cohen, J. (1994). The earth is round ($p < .05$). *American Psychologist, 49,* 997–1003.

Committee on Science, Engineering, and Public Policy. (2009). *On being a scientist: A guide to responsible conduct in research* (3rd ed.). Washington, DC: National Academies Press.

Conant, J. B. (1957). Introduction. In J. B. Conant & L. K. Nash (Eds.), *Harvard case studies in experimental science* (Vol. 1, pp. vii–xvi). Cambridge, MA: Harvard University Press.

Conrath, D. W. (1973). Communications environment and its relationship to organizational structure. *Management Science, 20,* 586–603.

Conrath, D. W., Higgins, C. A., & McClean, R. J. (1983). A comparison of the reliability of questionnaire versus diary data. *Social Networks, 5,* 315–322.

Converse, J. M., & Presser, S. (1986). *Survey questions: Handcrafting the standardized questionnaire.* Beverly Hills, CA: Sage.

Cook, T. D., & Campbell, D. T. (1976). The design and conduct of quasi-experiments and true experiments in field settings. In M. D. Dunnette (Ed.), *Handbook of industrial and organizational psychology* (pp. 223–326). Chicago, IL: Rand McNally.

Cook, T. D., & Campbell, D. T. (1979). *Quasi-experimentation: Design and analysis issues for field settings.* Chicago, IL: Rand McNally.

Cooper, H. (2010). *Research synthesis and meta-analysis: A step-by-step approach* (4th ed.). Thousand Oaks, CA: Sage.

Cooper, H., & Dent, A. (2011). Ethical issues in the conduct and reporting of meta-analysis. In A. T. Panter & S. K. Sterba (Eds.), *Handbook of ethics in quantitative methodology* (pp. 417–443). New York, NY: Routledge.

Cooper, H., & Hedges, L. V. (Eds.). (1994). *The handbook of research synthesis.* New York, NY: Russell Sage Foundation.

Cooper, H., Hedges, L. V., & Valentine, J. C. (Eds.). (2009). *The handbook of research synthesis and meta-analysis* (2nd ed.). New York, NY: Russell Sage Foundation.

Crabb, P. B., & Bielawski, D. (1994). The social representation of maternal culture and gender in children's books. *Sex Roles, 30,* 69–79.

Crabb, P. B., & Marciano, D. L. (2011). Representations of material culture and gender in award-winning children's books: A twenty-year follow-up. *Journal of Research in Childhood Education, 25,* 390–398.

Crancer, J., Dille, J., Delay, J., Wallace, J., & Haybin, M. (1969). Comparison of the effects of marijuana and alcohol on simulated driving performance. *Science, 164,* 851–854.

Cronbach, L. J. (1951). Coefficient alpha and the internal structure of tests. *Psychometrika, 16,* 297–334.

Cronbach, L. J., & Meehl, P. E. (1955). Construct validity in psychological tests. *Psychological Bulletin, 52,* 281–302.

Cronbach, L. J. & Quirk, T. J. (1971). Test validity. In L. C. Deighton (Ed.), *Encyclopedia of education* (Vol. 9, pp. 165–175). New York, NY: Macmillan & Free Press.

Crowne, D. P. (1979). *The experimental study of personality.* Hillsdale, NJ: Erlbaum.

Crowne, D. P. (1991). From response style to motive. *Current Contents: Social and Behavioral Sciences, 23*(30), 10.

Crowne, D. P., & Marlowe, D. (1964). *The approval motive: Studies in evaluative dependence.* New York, NY: Wiley.

Cryer, J. D. (1986). *Time series analysis.* Boston, MA: PWS-Kent.

Csikszentmihalyi, M., & Larson, R. (1984). *Being adolescent: Conflict and growth in the teenage years.* New York, NY: Basic Books.

Cumming, G. (2010). Replication, prep, and confidence intervals: Comment prompted by Iverson, Wagenmakers, and Lee (2010); Lecoutre, Lecoutre, and Poitevineau (2010); and Maraun and Gabriel (2010). *Psychological Methods, 15,* 192–198.

Darley, J. M., & Latané, B. (1968). Bystander intervention in emergencies. *Journal of Personality and Social Psychology, 8,* 377–383.

Davis, J. D., Gallagher, R. L., & Ladove, R. (1967). Food intake controlled by blood factors. *Science, 156,* 1247–1248.

Day, D. D., & Quackenbush, O. F. (1942). Attitudes toward defensive, cooperative, and aggressive wars. *Journal of Social Psychology, 16,* 11–20.

Deighton, L. C. (Ed.). (1971). *The encyclopedia of education* (Vols. 1–10). New York, NY: Macmillan & Free Press.

Delgado, J. M. R. (1963). Cerebral heterostimulation in a monkey colony. *Science, 141,* 161–163.

DePaulo, B. M., & Kashy, D. A. (1998). Everyday lies in close and casual relationships. *Journal of Personality and Social Psychology, 74,* 63–79.

DePaulo, B. M., Kashy, D. A., Kirkendol, S. E., Wyer, M. M., & Epstein, J. A. (1996). Lying in everyday life. *Journal of Personality and Social Psychology, 70,* 979–995.

De Vos, G. A., & Boyer, L. B. (1989). *Symbolic analysis cross-culturally: The Rorschach test.* Berkeley: University of California Press.

de Wolff, M. S., & Van Ijzendoorn, M. H. (1997). Sensitivity and attachment: A meta-analysis on parental antecedents of infant attachment. *Child Development, 68,* 571–591.

Diener, E. (2000). Subjective well-being. *American Psychologist, 55,* 34–43.

DiFonzo, N. (2008). *The watercooler effect: A psychologist explores the extraordinary power of rumors.* New York: NY: Avery.

DiFonzo, N., & Bordia, P. (2006). Rumor in organizational contexts. In D. A. Hantula (Ed.), *Advances in social and organizational psychology* (pp. 249–274). London, England: Psychology Press/Taylor & Francis.

DiFonzo, N., & Bordia, P. (2007). *Rumor psychology: Social and organizational approaches.* Washington, DC: American Psychological Association.

DiFonzo, N., Bordia, P., & Rosnow, R. L. (1994). Reining in rumors. *Organizational Dynamics, 23,* 47–62.

DiFonzo, N., Hantula, D. A., & Bordia, P. (1998). Microworlds for experimental research: Having your (control and collection) cake and realism too. *Behavior Research Methods, Instruments, and Computers, 30,* 278–286.

Diggle, P. J., Liang, K. Y., & Zeger, S. L. (1996). *Analysis of longitudinal data* (reprinted with corrections). Oxford, England: Oxford University Press.

Dorn, L. D., Susman, E. J., & Fletcher, J. C. (1995). Informed consent in children and adolescents: Age, maturation and psychological state. *Journal of Adolescent Health, 16,* 185–190.

Downs, C. W., Smeyak, G. P., & Martin, E. (1980). *Professional interviewing.* New York, NY: Harper & Row.

Dumond, V. (1990). *The elements of nonsexist language.* New York, NY: Prentice Hall.

Dunning, D., Heath, C., & Suls, J. M. (2004). Flawed self-assessment: Implications for health, education, and the workplace. *Psychological Science in the Public Interest, 5*(3), 69–106.

Ebbinghaus, H. (1885). *Über das Gedächtnis: Untersuchungen zur experimentellen Psychologie* [*On memory: A contribution to experimental psychology*]. Leipzig, Germany: Duncker & Humblot.

Emerson, J. D., & Hoaglin, D. C. (1983). Stem-and-leaf displays. In D. C. Hoaglin, F. Mosteller, & J. W. Tukey (Eds.), *Understanding robust and exploratory data analysis* (pp. 7–32). New York, NY: Wiley.

Entwisle, D. R. (1961). Interactive effects of pretesting. *Educational and Psychological Measurement, 21,* 607–620.

Ericsson, K. A., & Simon, H. A. (Eds.). (1993). *Protocol analysis: Verbal reports as data* (Rev. ed.). Cambridge, MA: MIT Press.

Esposito, J. L., Agard, E., & Rosnow, R. L. (1984). Can confidentiality of data pay off? *Personality and Individual Differences, 5,* 477–480.

Evans, M. A., & Saint-Aubin, J. (2005). What children are looking at during shared storybook reading. *Psychological Science, 16,* 913–920.

Everitt, B. (2006). *Medical statistics from A to Z: A guide for clinicians and medical students* (2nd ed.). Cambridge, England: Cambridge University Press.

Exline, J. J. (2002). Stumbling blocks on the religious road: Fractured relationships, nagging vices, and the inner struggle to believe. *Psychological Inquiry, 13,* 182–189.

Exner, J. E. (1993). *The Rorschach: A comprehensive system* (3rd ed., Vol. 1). New York, NY: Wiley.

Fairbanks, L. A. (1993). What is a good mother? Adaptive variation in maternal behavior of primates. *Current Directions in Psychological Science, 2,* 179–183.

Federighi, E. T. (1959). Extended tables of the percentage points of Student's *t* distribution. *Journal of the American Statistical Association, 54,* 683–688.

Ferster, C. B., & Skinner, B. F. (1957). *Schedules of reinforcement.* New York, NY: Appleton-Century-Crofts.

Festinger, L. (1954). A theory of social comparison processes. *Human Relations, 7,* 117–140.

Festinger, L. (1957). *A theory of cognitive dissonance.* Evanston, IL: Row Peterson.

Festinger, L. (1962). *A theory of cognitive dissonance.* Stanford, CA: Stanford University Press.

Festinger, L., Schachter, S., & Riecken, H. (1956). *When prophecy fails.* Minneapolis: University of Minnesota Press.

Feyerabend, P. (1988). *Against method* (Rev. ed.). London, England: Verso.

Feynman, R. P. (1988). *"What do I care what other people think?" Further adventures of a curious character*. New York, NY: Bantam Books.

Fienberg, S. E., & Tanur, J. M. (1989). Combining cognitive and statistical approaches to survey design. *Science, 243*, 1017–1022.

Fine, G. A., & Deegan, J. G. (1996). Three principles of Serendip: Insight, chance, and discovery in qualitative research. *Qualitative Studies in Education, 9*, 434–447.

Fine, G. A., & Turner, P. A. (2001). *Whispers on the color line: Rumor and race in America*. Berkeley: University of California Press.

Finkner, A. L. (1950). Methods of sampling for estimating commercial peach production in North Carolina. *North Carolina Agricultural Experiment Station Technical Bulletin, 91* (whole).

Fisher, R. A. (1960). *The design of experiments* (7th ed.). Edinburgh, Scotland: Oliver & Boyd.

Fisher, R. A. (1971). *The design of experiments* (8th ed.). New York, NY: Hafner.

Fisher, R. A. (1973a). *Statistical methods and scientific inference* (3rd ed.). New York, NY: Hafner.

Fisher, R. A. (1973b). *Statistical methods for research workers* (14th ed.). London, England: Oliver and Boyd.

Fisher, R. A., & Yates, F. (1974). *Statistical tables for biological, agricultural, and medical research* (6th ed.). London, England: Longman.

Fisher, R. J. (1993). Social desirability bias and the validity of indirect questioning. *Journal of Consumer Research, 20*, 303–315.

Fiske, D. W. (2000). Artifact in assessment. In A. E. Kazdin (Ed.), *Encyclopedia of psychology* (Vol. 1, pp. 245–248). New York, NY: Oxford University Press & American Psychological Association.

Flanagan, J. C. (1954). The critical incident technique. *Psychological Bulletin, 51*, 327–358.

Forrest, D. W. (1974). *Francis Galton: The life and work of a Victorian genius*. New York, NY: Taplinger.

Fossey, D. (1981). Imperiled giants of the forest. *National Geographic, 159*, 501–604.

Fossey, D. (1983). *Gorillas in the mist*. Boston, MA: Houghton Mifflin.

Foster, E. K., & Rosnow, R. L. (2006). Gossip and network relationships. In D. C. Kirkpatrick, S. Duck, & M. K. Foley (Eds.), *Relating difficulty: The process of constructing and managing difficult interaction* (pp. 161–180). Mahwah, NJ: Erlbaum.

Fowler, F. J., Jr. (1993). *Survey research methods* (2nd ed.). Newbury Park, CA: Sage.

Francis, Jr., T., Korns, R. F., Voight, R. B., Boisen, M., Hemphill, F., Napier, J., & Tolchinsky, E. (1955). An evaluation of the 1954 poliomyelitis vaccine trials—summary report. *American Journal of Public Health, 45*(5), 1–63.

Freedman, D., Pisani, R., Purves, R., & Adhikari, A. (1991). *Statistics* (2nd ed.). New York, NY: Norton.

Frey, J. H. (1986). An experiment with a confidentiality reminder in a telephone survey. *Public Opinion Quarterly, 50*, 26–269.

Friedman, A. F., Lewak, R., Nichols, D. S., & Webb, J. T. (2001). *Psychological assessment with the MMPI-2*. Mahwah, NJ: Erlbaum.

Friedman, H. (Ed.). (1998). *Encyclopedia of mental health* (Vols. 1–3). San Diego, CA: Academic Press.

Fuerbringer, J. (1997, March 30). Why both bulls and bears can act so bird-brained: Quirky behavior is becoming a realm of economics. *The New York Times,* Section 3, pp. 1, 6.

Funke, J. (1991). Dealing with dynamic systems: Research strategy, diagnostic approach and experimental results. *German Journal of Psychology, 16*, 24–43.

Gallup, G. (1976, May 21). *Lessons learned in 40 years of polling*. Paper presented before National Council on Public Polls.

Galton, F. (1869). *Hereditary genius*. London, England: Macmillan.

Garb, H. N., Wood, J. M., Lilienfeld, S. O., & Nezworski, M. T. (2002). Effective use of projective techniques in clinical practice: Let the data help with selection and interpretation. *Professional Psychology: Research and Practice, 33*, 454–463.

Garb, H. N., Wood, J. M., Lilienfeld, S. O., & Nezworski, M. T. (2005). Roots of the Rorschach controversy. *Clinical Psychology Review, 25*, 97–118.

Gardner, H. (1983). *Frames of mind: The theory of multiple intelligences*. New York, NY: Basic Books.

Gardner, H. (1986). *The mind's new science: A history of the cognitive revolution*. New York, NY: Basic Books.

Gardner, H. (Ed.). (1993). *Multiple intelligences: The theory in practice*. New York, NY: Basic Books.

Gardner, H., Kornhaber, M. L., & Wake, W. K. (1996). *Intelligence: Multiple perspective*. Ft. Worth, TX: Harcourt Brace.

Gardner, M. (1957). *Fads and fallacies in the name of science*. New York, NY: Dover.

Garfield, E. (1989a). Art and science: 1. The art-science connection. *Current Contents, 21*(8), 3–10.

Garfield, E. (1989b). Art and science: 2. Science for art's sake. *Current Contents, 21*(9), 3–8.

Gazzaniga, M. S., & LeDoux, J. E. (1978). *The integrated mind*. New York, NY: Plenum Press.

Geller, D. M. (1982). Alternatives to deception: Why, what, and how? In J. E. Sieber (Ed.), *The ethics of social research: Surveys and experiments* (pp. 39–55). New York, NY: Springer-Verlag.

Gentner, D., Holyoak, K. J., & Kokinov, B. N. (Eds.). (2001). *The analogical mind: Perspectives from cognitive science*. Cambridge, MA: MIT Press.

Gentner, D., & Markman, A. B. (1997). Structure mapping in analogy and similarity. *American Psychologist, 52*, 45–56.

Gerber, A. S., & Green, D. P. (2000). The effects of canvassing, telephone calls, and direct mail on voter turnout: A field experiment. *American Political Science Review, 94*, 653–663.

Gibson, E. J., & Walk, R. D. (1960, April). The visual cliff. *Scientific American, 202*(4), 64–71.

Gigerenzer, G. (1991). From tools to theories: A heuristic of discovery in cognitive psychology. *Psychological Review, 98*, 254–267.

Gigerenzer, G., Gaissmaier, W., Kurz-Milcke, E., Schwartz, L. M., & Woloshin, S. (2008). Helping doctors and patients make sense of health statistics. *Psychological Science in the Public Interest, 8*, 53–96.

Gigerenzer, G., Swijtink, Z., Porter, T., Daston, L., Beatty, J., & Krüger, L. (1989). *The empire of chance: How probability* changed science and everyday life. New York, NY: Cambridge University Press.

Gilovich, T. (1991). *How we know what isn't so: The fallibility of human reason in everyday life.* New York, NY: Free Press.

Glass, G. V (1976). Primary, secondary, and meta-analysis of research. *Educational Researcher, 5,* 3–8.

Glass, G. V (1978). In defense of generalization. *Behavioral and Brain Sciences, 3,* 394–395.

Glass, G. V, McGaw, B., & Smith, M. L. (1981). *Meta-analysis in social research.* Beverly Hills, CA: Sage.

Goldberg, L. R. (1993). The structure of phenotypic personality traits. *American Psychologist, 48,* 26–34.

Goldman, B. A., & Mitchell, D. F. (1995). *Directory of unpublished experimental mental measures* (Vol. 6). Washington, DC: American Psychological Association.

Goldman, B. A., & Mitchell, D. F. (2003). *Directory of unpublished experimental mental measures* (Vol. 8). Washington, DC: American Psychological Association.

Goldman, B. A., Mitchell, D. F., & Egelson, P. (Eds.). (1997). *Directory of unpublished experimental mental measures* (Vol. 7). Washington, DC: American Psychological Association.

Goldman, B. A., Osborne, W. L., & Mitchell, D. F. (1996). *Directory of unpublished experimental mental measures* (Vols. 4–5). Washington, DC: American Psychological Association.

Goldman, B. A., Saunders, J. L., & Busch, J. C. (1996). *Directory of unpublished experimental mental measures* (Vols. 1–3). Washington, DC: American Psychological Association.

Gombrich, E. H. (1963). *Meditations on a hobby horse.* London, England: Phaidon.

Gottman, J. M. (1979). Detecting cyclicity in social interaction. *Psychological Bulletin, 86,* 338–348.

Gottman, J. M. (1981). *Time-series analysis: A comprehensive introduction for social scientists.* Cambridge, England: Cambridge University Press.

Gould, M. S., & Shaffer, D. (1986). The impact of suicide in television movies: Evidence of imitation. *New England Journal of Medicine, 315,* 690–694.

Greenwald, A. G., & Banaji, M. R. (1995). Implicit social cognition: Attitudes, self-esteem, and stereotypes. *Psychological Review, 102,* 4–27.

Greenwald, A. G., McGhee, D. E., & Schwartz, J. L. K. (1998). Measuring individual differences in implicit cognition: The implicit association test. *Journal of Personality and Social Psychology, 74,* 1464–1480.

Gross, A. G. (1990). *The rhetoric of science.* Cambridge, MA: Harvard University Press.

Groves, R. M., & Mathiowetz, N. A. (1984). Computer assisted telephone interviewing: Effects on interviewers and respondents. *Public Opinion Quarterly, 48,* 356–369.

Guilford, J. P. (1954). *Psychometric methods* (2nd ed.). New York, NY: McGraw-Hill.

Gulliksen, H. (1950). *Theory of mental tests.* New York, NY: Wiley.

Hall, J. A. (1984). *Instructor's manual to accompany Rosenthal/Rosnow: Essentials of behavioral research.* New York, NY: McGraw-Hill.

Hall, R. V., Lund, D., & Jackson, D. (1968). Effects of teacher attention on study behavior. *Journal of Applied Behavior Analysis, 1,* 1–12.

Hantula, D. A. (Ed.). (2006). *Advances in social and organizational psychology.* London, England: Psychology Press/Taylor & Francis.

Hantula, D. A., Stillman, F. A., & Waranch, H. R. (1992). Can a mass-media campaign modify tobacco smoking in a large organization? Evaluation of the Great American Smokeout in an urban hospital. *Journal of Organizational Behavior Management, 13,* 33–47.

Harmon, A. (2010, Sept. 18). New drugs stir debate on rules of clinical trials. *The New York Times,* pp. 1, 20–21.

Harris, B. (1988). Key words: A history of debriefing in social psychology. In J. Morawski (Ed.), *The rise of experimentation in American psychology* (pp. 188–212). New Haven, CT: Yale University Press.

Härtel, C. E. J. (1993). Rating format research revisited: Format effectiveness and acceptability depend on rater characteristics. *Journal of Applied Psychology, 78,* 212–217.

Hartmann, G. W. (1936). A field experiment on the comparative effectiveness of "emotional" and "rational" political leaflets in determining election results. *Journal of Abnormal and Social Psychology, 31,* 99–114.

Hedges, L. V., & Olkin, I. (1985). *Statistical methods for meta-analysis.* New York, NY: Academic Press.

Heise, G. A., & Miller, G. A. (1951). Problem solving by small groups using various communication nets. *Journal of Abnormal and Social Psychology, 46,* 327–331.

Hellweg, S. A. (1987). Organizational grapevines. In B. Dervin & M. J. Voigt (Eds.), *Progress in communication sciences* (Vol. 8, pp. 213–230). Norwood, NJ: Ablex.

Hersen, M., & Barlow, D. H. (1976). *Single-case experimental designs: Strategies for studying behavior change.* Oxford, England: Pergamon Press.

Higbee, K. L., & Wells, M. G. (1972). Some research trends in social psychology during the 1960s. *American Psychologist, 27,* 963–966.

Higgins, J. J. (2004). *Introduction to modern nonparametric statistics.* Belmont, CA: Wadsworth.

Hiller, J. B., Rosenthal, R., Bornstein, R. F., Berry, D. T. R., & Brunell-Neuleib, S. (1999). A comparative meta-analysis of Rorschach and MMPI validity. *Psychological Assessment, 11,* 278–296.

Hineline, P. H. (2005). The aesthetics of behavioral arrangements. *Behavior Analyst, 28,* 15–28.

Hineline, P. N., & Lattal, K. A. (2000). Single-case experimental design. In A. E. Kazdin (Ed.), *Encyclopedia of psychology* (Vol. 7, pp. 287–289). New York, NY: Oxford University Press & American Psychological Association.

Hirsh-Pasek, K., & Golinkoff, R. M. (1993). Skeletal supports for grammatical learning: What infants bring to the language learning task. In C. Rovee-Collier & L. P. Lipsitt (Eds.), *Advances in infancy research* (Vol. 8, pp. 299–315). Norwood, NJ: Ablex.

Hirsh-Pasek, K., & Golinkoff, R. M. (1996). *The origins of grammar: Evidence from early language comprehension.* Cambridge, MA: MIT Press.

Hodges, B. H., & Geyer, A. L. (2006). A nonconformist account of the Asch experiments: Values, pragmatics, and moral dilemmas. *Personality and Social Psychology Review, 10,* 2–19.

Hogan, R., Hogan, J., & Roberts, B. W. (1996). Personality measurement and employment decisions. *American Psychologist, 51,* 469–477.

Holyoak, K. J., & Thagard, P. (1997). The analogical mind. *American Psychologist, 52,* 35–44.

Hoover, K., & Donovan, T. (1995). *The elements of social scientific thinking* (6th ed.). New York, NY: St. Martin's Press.

Hoyt, W. T. (2000). Rater bias in psychological research: When is it a problem and what can we do about it? *Psychological Methods, 5,* 64–86.

Hult, C. A. (1996). *Researching and writing in the social sciences.* Boston, MA: Allyn & Bacon.

Hume, D. (1978). *A treatise of human nature.* Oxford, England: Oxford University Press. (Original work published 1739–1740).

Hunt, M. (1997). *How science takes stock: The story of meta-analysis.* New York, NY: Russell Sage Foundation.

Hunter, J. E., & Schmidt, F. L. (2004). *Methods of meta-analysis* (2nd ed.). Thousand Oaks, CA: Sage.

Huprich, S. K. (Ed.). (2006). *Rorschach assessment of the personality disorders.* Mahwah, NJ: Erlbaum.

Imber, S. D., Glanz, L. M., Elkin, I., Sotsky, S. M., Boyer, J. L., & Leber, W. R. (1986). Ethical issues in psychotherapy research: Problems in a collaborative clinical trials study. *American Psychologist, 41,* 137–146.

Iversen, I. H., & Lattal, K. A. (1991). *Techniques in the behavioral and neural sciences: Vol. 6. Experimental analysis of behavior.* Amsterdam, Netherlands: Elsevier.

Iversen, L. L. (2000). *The science of marijuana.* Oxford, England: Oxford University Press.

Iverson, G. J., Wagenmakers, E.-J., & Lee, M. D. (2010). A model-averaging approach to replication: The case of prep. *Psychological Methods, 15,* 172–181.

Jacobs, J. (1961). *The death and life of great American cities.* New York, NY: Random House.

Jaeger, M. E., & Rosnow, R. L. (1988). Contextualism and its implications for psychological inquiry. *British Journal of Psychology, 79,* 63–75.

Jammer, M. (1966). *The conceptual development of quantum mechanics.* New York, NY: McGraw-Hill.

Janis, I. L., & Mann, L. (1965). Effectiveness of emotional role-playing in modifying smoking habits and attitudes. *Journal of Experimental Research in Personality, 1,* 181–186.

Johnson, G. (2002, September 24). Here they are, science's 10 most beautiful experiments. *The New York Times,* Section F, p. 3.

Johnson-Laird, P. N. (1983). *Mental models: Towards a cognitive science of language, inference, and consciousness.* Cambridge, MA: Harvard University Press.

Johnson-Laird, P. N., & Byrne, R. M. J. (1991). *Deduction.* Hove, England: Erlbaum.

Johnston, J. M., & Pennypacker, H. S. (Eds.). (1993a). *Readings for strategies and tactics of behavioral research* (2nd ed.). Hillsdale, NJ: Erlbaum.

Johnston, J. M., & Pennypacker, H. S. (1993b). *Strategies and tactics of behavioral research* (2nd ed.). Hillsdale, NJ: Erlbaum.

Jones, E. E., & Gerard, H. B. (1967). *Foundations of social psychology.* New York, NY: Wiley.

Jones, J. H. (1993). *Bad blood: The Tuskegee syphilis experiment* (Rev. ed.). New York, NY: Free Press.

Judd, C. M., & Kenny, D. A. (1981). *Estimating the effects of social interventions.* Cambridge, England: Cambridge University Press.

Jung, J. (1969). Current practices and problems in the use of college students for psychological research. *Canadian Psychologist, 10,* 280–290.

Kagay, M. R. (1996, December 15). Experts say refinements are needed in the polls. *The New York Times,* p. 34.

Kahane, H. (1989). *Logic and philosophy: A modern introduction* (6th ed.). Belmont, CA: Wadsworth.

Kahneman, D., Slovic, P., & Tversky, A. (Eds.). (1982). *Judgment under uncertainty: Heuristics and biases.* New York, NY: Cambridge University Press.

Kahneman, D., & Tversky, A. (1973). On the psychology of prediction. *Psychological Review, 80,* 237–251.

Kanner, L. (1943). Autistic disturbances of affective contact. *Nervous Child, 2,* 217–250.

Kaplan, A. (1964). *The conduct of inquiry: Methodology for behavioral science.* Scranton, PA: Chandler.

Kaptchuk, T. J., Kelley, J. M., Conboy, L. A., Davis, R. B., Kerr, C. E., Jacobson, E. E., Kirsch, I., Schyner, R. N., Nam, B. H., Nguyen, L. T., Park, M., Rivers, A. L., McManus, C., Kokkotou, E., Drossman, D. A., Goldman, P., & Lembo, A. J. (2008). Components of placebo effect: Randomised controlled trial in patients with irritable bowel syndrome. *British Medical Journal, 336*(7651), 999–1003.

Katz, D. (1972). *Experimentation with human beings.* New York, NY: Russell Sage Foundation.

Katz, D., & Cantril, H. (1937). Public opinion polls. *Sociometry, 1,* 155–179.

Kazdin, A. E. (1976). Statistical techniques for single-case experimental designs. In M. Hersen & D. H. Barlow (Eds.), *Single case experimental designs: Strategies for studying behavior change* (pp. 265–316). Oxford, England: Pergamon Press.

Kazdin, A. E. (1992). *Research design in clinical psychology* (2nd ed.). Boston, MA: Allyn & Bacon.

Kazdin, A. E. (Ed.). (2000). *Encyclopedia of psychology* (Vols. 1–8). New York, NY: Oxford University Press & American Psychological Association.

Kelley, H. H., & Thibaut, J. W. (1969). Group problem solving. In G. Lindzey & E. Aronson (Eds.), *The handbook of social psychology* (2nd ed., Vol. 4, pp. 1–101). Reading, MA: Addison-Wesley.

Kelley, S. R. (2004). *Rumors in Iraq: A guide to winning hearts and minds.* Master's thesis. Monterey, CA: Naval Postgraduate School.

Kelman, H. C. (1968). *A time to speak: On human values and social research.* San Francisco, CA: Jossey-Bass.

Kendon, A. (1967). Some functions of gaze direction in social interaction. *Acta Psychologica, 26,* 1–47.

Kenny, D. A. (1979). *Correlation and causality.* New York, NY: Wiley.

Kenny, D. A., & Campbell, D. T. (1984). Methodological considerations in the analysis of temporal data. In K. Gergen & M. Gergen (Eds.), *Historical social psychology* (pp. 125–138). Mahwah, NJ: Erlbaum.

Kenny, D. A., & Campbell, D. T. (1989). On the measurement of stability in over-time data. *Journal of Personality, 57,* 445–481.

Kerner, O., et al. (1968). *Report of the National Advisory Commission on Civil Disorders.* New York, NY: Bantam.

Kidder, L. H., Kidder, R. L., & Snyderman, P. (1976). *A cross-lagged correlational analysis of the causal relationship between police employment and crime rates.* Paper presented at the meeting of the American Psychological Association, Washington, DC.

Kilborn, P. T. (1994, January 23). Alarming trend among workers: Surveys find clusters of TB cases. *The New York Times,* pp. A1, A16.

Killeen, P. R. (2005). An alternative to null-hypothesis significance tests. *Psychological Science, 16,* 345–353.

Killeen, P. R. (2010). prep replicates: Comment prompted by Iverson, Wagenmakers, and Lee (2010); Lecoutre, Lecoutre, and Poitevineau (2010); and Maraun and Gabriel (2010). *Psychological Methods, 15,* 199–202.

Kimmel, A. J. (Ed.). (1981). *Ethics of human subjects research.* San Francisco, CA: Jossey-Bass.

Kimmel, A. J. (1988). *Ethics and values in applied social research.* Beverly Hills, CA: Sage.

Kimmel, A. J. (1991). Predictable biases in the ethical decision making of American psychologists. *American Psychologist, 46,* 786–788.

Kimmel, A. J. (1996). *Ethical issues in behavioral research: A survey.* Oxford, England: Blackwell.

Kimmel, A. J. (2004). *Rumors and rumor control: A manager's guide to understanding and combating rumors.* Mahwah, NJ: Erlbaum.

Kimmel, A. J. (2006). From artifacts to ethics: The delicate balance between methodological and moral concerns in behavioral research. In D. A. Hantula (Ed.), *Advances in social and organizational psychology* (pp. 113–140). London, England: Psychology Press/Taylor & Francis.

Kimmel, A. J. (2007). *Ethical issues in behavioral research: Basic and applied perspectives* (2nd ed.). Oxford, England: Blackwell.

Kimmel, A. J., & Audrain-Pontevia, A.-F. (2010). Analysis of commercial rumors from the perspective of marketing managers: Rumor prevalence, effects, and control tactics. *Journal of Marketing Communications, 16,* 239–253.

Kirk, R. E. (1995). *Experimental design: Procedures for the behavioral sciences* (3rd ed.). Pacific Grove, CA: Brooks/Cole.

Kirk, R. E. (2000). Randomized experiments. In A. E. Kazdin (Ed.), *Encyclopedia of psychology* (Vol. 6, pp. 502–505). New York, NY: Oxford University Press & American Psychological Association.

Kish, L. (1965). *Survey sampling.* New York, NY: Wiley.

Kleinmuntz, B. (1982). *Personality and psychological assessment.* New York, NY: St. Martin's Press.

Knapp, R. H. (1944). A psychology of rumor. *Public Opinion Quarterly, 8,* 22–27.

Koch, S. (1959). General introduction to the series. In S. Koch (Ed.), *Psychology: A study of a science* (Vol. 1, pp. 1–18). New York, NY: McGraw-Hill.

Kolata, G. B. (1986). What does it mean to be random? *Science, 231,* 1068–1070.

Kolodner, J. L. (1997). Educational implications of analogy: A view from case-based reasoning. *American Psychologist, 52,* 57–66.

Komaki, J., & Barnett, F. T. (1977). A behavioral approach to coaching football: Improving the play execution of the offensive backfield on a youth football team. *Journal of Applied Behavior Analysis, 10,* 657–664.

Kossinets, G., Kleinberg, J., & Watts, D. (2008, August 24–27). The structure of information pathways in a social communication network. *Proceedings of the 14th ACM SIGKDD International Conference on Knowledge Discovery and Data Mining.* Las Vegas, NV (Report No. arXiv:0806.3201).

Kossinets, G., & Watts, D. J. (2006). Empirical analysis of an evolving social network. *Science, 311,* 88–90.

Kosslyn, S. M. (1994). *Elements of graph design.* New York, NY: W. H. Freeman.

Kragh, H. (2002, August). Paul Dirac: Seeking beauty. *Physics World,* pp. 27–31.

Kratochwill, T. R., & Levin, J. R. (Eds.). (1992). *Single-case research design and analysis: New directions for psychology and education.* Hillsdale, NJ: Erlbaum.

Kuder, G. F., & Richardson, M. W. (1937). The theory of estimation of test reliability. *Psychometrika, 2,* 151–160.

Kuhn, T. S. (1962). *The structure of scientific revolutions.* Chicago, IL: University of Chicago Press.

Kuhn, T. S. (1977). *The essential tension.* Chicago, IL: University of Chicago Press.

Labaw, P. (1980). *Advanced questionnaire design.* Cambridge, MA: ABT Books.

LaGreca, A. M. (Ed.). (1990). *Through the eyes of the child: Obtaining self-reports from children and adolescents.* Boston, MA: Allyn & Bacon.

Lakoff, G., & Johnson, M. (1980). *Metaphors we live by.* Chicago, IL: University of Chicago Press.

Lana, R. E. (1959). Pretest-treatment interaction effects in attitudinal studies. *Psychological Bulletin, 56,* 293–300.

Lana, R. E. (1969). Pretest sensitization. In R. Rosenthal & R. L. Rosnow (Eds.), *Artifact in behavioral research* (pp. 119–141). New York, NY: Academic Press.

Lana, R. E. (1991). *Assumptions of social psychology: A reexamination.* Hillsdale, NJ: Erlbaum.

Lana, R. E., & Rosnow, R. L. (1972). *Introduction to contemporary psychology.* New York, NY: Holt, Rinehart & Winston.

Lando, H. A. (1976). On being sane in insane places: A supplemental report. *Professional Psychology, 7,* 47–52

Lane, F. W. (1960). *Kingdom of the octopus.* New York, NY: Sheridan House.

Latané, B., & Darley, J. M. (1968). Group inhibition of bystander intervention in emergencies. *Journal of Personality and Social Psychology, 10,* 215–221.

Latané, B., & Darley, J. M. (1970). *The unresponsive bystander: Why doesn't he help?* New York, NY: Appleton-Century-Crofts.

Laupacis, A., Sackett, D. L., & Roberts, R. S. (1988). An assessment of clinically useful measures of the consequences of treatments. *New England Journal of Medicine, 318,* 1728–1733.

Lavelle, J. M., Hovell, M. F., West, M. P., & Wahlgren, D. R. (1992). Promoting law enforcement for child protection: A community analysis. *Journal of Applied Behavior Analysis, 25,* 885–892.

Lavrakas, P. J. (1987). *Telephone survey methods: Sampling, selection, and supervision.* Beverly Hills, CA: Sage.

Leary, D. E. (Ed.). (1990). *Metaphors in the history of psychology.* Cambridge, England: Cambridge University Press.

Lecoutre, B., Lecoutre, M.-P., & Poitevineau, J. (2010). Killeen's probability of replication and predictive probabilities: How to compute, use, and interpret them. *Psychological Methods, 15,* 159–171.

Lee, R. M. (1993). *Doing research on sensitive topics.* London, England: Sage.

Levav, J., & Fitzsimons, G. J. (2006). When questions change behavior: The role of ease of representation. *Psychological Science, 17,* 207–213.

Levin, J. R. (2011). Ethical issues in professional research, writing, and publishing. In A. T. Panter & S. K. Sterba (Eds.), *Handbook of ethics in quantitative methodology* (pp. 463–492). New York, NY: Routledge.

Levitt, S. D., & List, J. A. (2007). What do laboratory experiments measuring social preferences reveal about the real world? *Journal of Economic Perspectives, 21,* 153–174.

Lewin, T. (1994, January 7). Prize in an unusual lottery: A scarce experimental drug. *The New York Times,* pp. A1, A17.

Lewis-Beck, M., Bryman, A., & Liao, T. F. (2003). *Encyclopedia of research methods for the social sciences.* Thousand Oaks, CA: Sage.

Li, H., Rosenthal, R., & Rubin, D. B. (1996). Reliability of measurement in psychology: From Spearman-Brown to maximal reliability. *Psychological Methods, 1,* 98–107.

Li, H., & Wainer, H. (1998). Toward a coherent view of reliability in test theory. *Journal of Educational and Behavioral Statistics, 23,* 478–484.

Lieberman, M. D., & Eisenberger, N. I. (2009). Pains and pleasures of social life. *Science, 323,* 890–892.

Light, R. J., & Pillemer, D. B. (1984). *Summing up: The science of reviewing research.* Cambridge, MA: Harvard University Press.

Likert, R. A. (1932). A technique for the measurement of attitudes. *Archives of Psychology, 140,* 1–55.

Lindquist, E. F. (1953). *Design and analysis of experiments in psychology and education.* Boston, MA: Houghton Mifflin.

Linsky, A. S. (1975). Stimulating responses to mailed questionnaires: A review. *Public Opinion Quarterly, 39,* 83–101.

Lipsey, M. W., & Wilson, D. B. (2001). *Practical meta-analysis.* Thousand Oaks, CA: Sage.

Liss, M. B. (1994). Child abuse: Is there a mandate for researchers to report? *Ethics and Behavior, 4,* 133–146.

Loftus, E. F. (1975). Leading questions and the eyewitness report. *Cognitive Psychology, 7,* 560–572.

Loomis, J. M., Blascovich, J., & Beall, A. C. (1999). Immersive virtual environments as a basic research tool in psychology. *Behavioral Research Methods, Instruments and Computers, 31,* 557–564.

Lush, J. L. (1931). Predicting gains in feeder cattle and pigs. *Journal of Agricultural Research, 42,* 853–881.

Mahler, I. (1953). Attitude toward socialized medicine. *Journal of Social Psychology, 38,* 273–282.

Main, M., & Solomon, J. (1990). Procedures for identifying infants as disorganized/disoriented during the Ainsworth Strange Situation. In M. T. Greenberg, D. Cichetti, & E. M. Cummings (Eds.), *Attachment in the preschool years* (pp. 121–160). Chicago, IL: University of Chicago Press.

Mann, L. (1967). The effects of emotional role playing on smoking attitudes and behavior. *Journal of Experimental Social Psychology, 3,* 334–348.

Mann, L., & Janis, I. L. (1968). A follow-up study on the long-term effects of emotional role playing. *Journal of Personality and Social Psychology, 8,* 339–342.

Mann, T. (1994). Informed consent for psychological research: Do subjects comprehend consent forms and understand their legal rights? *Psychological Science, 5,* 140–143.

Marascuilo, L. A., & McSweeney, M. (1977). *Nonparametric and distribution-free methods for the social sciences.* Belmont, CA: Brooks/Cole.

Maraun, M., & Gabriel, S. (2010). Killeen's (2005) prep coefficient: Logical and mathematical problems. *Psychological Methods, 15,* 182–191.

Mark, M. M., Eyssell, K. M., & Campbell, B. (1999). The ethics of data collection and analysis. In J. L. Fitzpatrick & M. Morris (Eds.), *Ethical issues in program evaluation* (pp. 47–56). San Francisco, CA: Jossey-Bass.

Marks, G., & Miller, N. (1987). Ten years of research on the false-consensus effect: An empirical and theoretical review. *Psychological Bulletin, 102,* 72–90.

Martin, D. (2001, March 25). Charles Johnson, 76, proponent of flat earth. *The New York Times,* p. 44.

Maurer, T. J., Palmer, J. K., & Ashe, D. K. (1993). Diaries, checklists, evaluations, and contrast effects in measurement of behavior. *Journal of Applied Psychology, 78,* 226–231.

Maxwell, S. E., & Delaney, H. D. (2000). *Designing experiments and analyzing data: A model comparison perspective.* Mahwah, NJ: Erlbaum.

McClelland, D. C., Atkinson, J. W., Clark, R. A., & Lowell, E. L. (1953). *The achievement motive.* New York, NY: Appleton-Century-Crofts.

McCrae, R. R., & Costa, P. T., Jr. (1997). Personality trait structure as a human universal. *American Psychologist, 52,* 509–516.

McGuire, W. J. (1964). Inducing resistance to persuasion: Some contemporary approaches. In L. Berkowitz (Ed.), *Advances in experimental social psychology* (Vol. 1, pp. 191–229). New York, NY: Academic Press.

McGuire, W. J. (1973). The yin and yang of progress in social psychology: Seven koan. *Journal of Personality and Social Psychology, 26,* 446–456.

McGuire, W. J. (1997). Creative hypothesis generating in psychology: Some useful heuristics. *Annual Review of Psychology, 48,* 1–30.

McGuire, W. J. (2006). Twenty questions for perspective epistemologists. In D. A. Hantula (Ed.), *Advances in social and organizational psychology* (pp. 329–358). London, England: Psychology Press/Taylor & Francis.

McNemar, Q. (1946). Opinion-attitude methodology. *Psychological Bulletin, 43,* 289–374.

Medawar, P. B. (1969). *Induction and intuition in scientific thought* (Jayne Lectures for 1968). Philadelphia, PA: American Philosophical Society.

Meier, P. (1988). The biggest public health experiment ever: The 1954 field trial of the Salk poliomyelitis vaccine. In J. M.

Tanur, F. Mosteller, W. H. Kruskal, E. L. Lehmann, R. F. Link, R. S. Pieters, & G. R. Rising (Eds.), *Statistics: A guide to the unknown* (3rd ed., pp. 3–14). Pacific Grove, CA: Wadsworth.

Melton, G. B., Levine, R. J., Koocher, G. P., Rosenthal, R., & Thompson, W. C. (1988). Community consultation in socially sensitive research: Lessons from clinical trials of treatments for AIDS. *American Psychologist, 43,* 573–581.

Merton, R. K. (1948). The self-fulfilling prophecy. *Antioch Review, 8,* 193–210.

Merton, R. K. (1968). *Social theory and social structure.* New York, NY: Free Press.

Michener, W., Rozin, P., Freeman, E., & Gale, L. (1999). The role of low progesterone and tension as triggers of perimenstrual chocolate and sweets craving: Some negative experimental evidence. *Physiology and Behavior, 67,* 417–420.

Milgram, S. (1963). Behavioral study of obedience. *Journal of Abnormal and Social Psychology, 67,* 371–378.

Milgram, S. (1967, May). The small world problem. *Psychology Today, 1*(1), 60–67.

Milgram, S. (1974). *Obedience to authority: An experimental view.* New York, NY: Harper & Row.

Milgram, S. (1977). *The individual in a social world: Essays and experiments.* Reading, MA: Addison-Wesley.

Mill, J. S. (1965). *A system of logic* (8th ed.). London, England: Longmans Green.

Miller, A. I. (1986). *Imagery in scientific thought: Creating 20th century physics.* Cambridge, MA: MIT Press.

Miller, A. I. (1996). *Insights of genius: Imagery and creativity in science and art.* New York, NY: Springer-Verlag.

Miller, G. A., & Newman, E. B. (1958). Tests of a statistical explanation of the rank-frequency relation for words in written English. *American Journal of Psychology, 71,* 209–258.

Miller, J. D. (2007). Finding clinical meaning in cancer data. *Journal of the National Cancer Institute, 99*(24), 1832–1835.

Miller, P. V., & Cannell, C. F. (1982). A study of experimental techniques for telephone interviewing. *Public Opinion Quarterly, 46,* 250–269.

Millham, J., & Jacobson, L. I. (1978). The need for approval. In H. London & J. E. Exner (Eds.), *Dimensions of personality* (pp. 365–390). New York, NY: Wiley.

Mitchell, J. (1985). *Eccentric lives and peculiar notions.* New York, NY: Harcourt Brace Jovanovich.

Mook, D. G. (1983). In defense of external invalidity. *American Psychologist, 38,* 379–387.

Moreno, J. L. (1934). *Who shall survive?* Washington, DC: Nervous and Mental Disease Publishing.

Mosteller, F. (1968). Association and estimation in contingency tables. *Journal of the American Statistical Association, 63,* 1–28.

Mueller, C. G. (1979). Some origins of psychology as a science. *Annual Review of Psychology, 30,* 9–29.

Murphy, K. R., Jako, R. A., & Anhalt, R. L. (1993). Nature and consequences of halo effect: A critical analysis. *Journal of Applied Psychology, 78,* 218–225.

Myers, D. G. (2000). The funds, friends, and faith of happy people. *American Psychologist, 55,* 56–67.

National Commission for the Protection of Human Subjects of Biomedical and Behavioral Research. (1979). *The Belmont report: Ethical principles and guidelines for the protection of human subjects of research.* Washington, DC: Government Printing Office.

National Commission on Research. (1980). Accountability: Restoring the quality of the partnership. *Science, 207,* 1177–1182.

National Heart Institute. (1966). *The Framingham heart study: Habits and coronary heart disease.* Public Health Service Publication No. 1515. Bethesda, MD: National Heart Institute.

Neuringer, A. (1992). Choosing to vary and repeat. *Psychological Science, 3,* 246–250.

Neuringer, A. (1996). Can people behave "randomly"? The role of feedback. *Journal of Experimental Psychology: General, 115,* 62–75.

Neuringer, A., & Voss, C. (1993). Approximating chaotic behavior. *Psychological Science, 4,* 113–119.

Nisbet, R. (1976). *Sociology as an art form.* London, England: Oxford University Press.

Nisbett, R. E., & Wilson, T. D. (1977). Telling more than we can know: Verbal reports on mental processes. *Psychological Review, 84,* 231–259.

Norwick, R., Choi, Y. S., & Ben-Shachar, T. (2002). In defense of self-reports. *APS Observer, 15*(3), 7, 24.

Nouri, H., Blau, G., & Shahid, A. (1995). The effect of socially desirable responding (SDR) on the relation between budgetary participation and self-reported job performance. *Advances in Management Accounting, 4,* 163–177.

Nunnally, J. C., & Bernstein, I. H. (1994). *Psychometric theory* (3rd ed.). New York, NY: McGraw-Hill.

Offer, D., Kaiz, M., Howard, K. I., & Bennett, E. S. (2000). The altering of reported experiences. *Journal of the American Academy of Child and Adolescent Psychiatry, 39,* 735–743.

Omodei, M. M., & Wearing, A. J. (1995). The Fire Chief microworld generating program: An illustration of computer-simulated microworlds as an experimental paradigm for studying complex decision-making behavior. *Behavior Research Methods, Instruments, and Computers, 27,* 303–316.

Ones, D. S., Viswesvaran, C., & Reiss, A. D. (1996). Role of social desirability in personality testing for personnel selection: The red herring. *Journal of Applied Psychology, 81,* 660–679.

Oppenheimer, R. (1956). Analogy in science. *American Psychologist, 11,* 127–135.

Orne, M. T. (1959). The nature of hypnosis: Artifact and essence. *Journal of Abnormal and Social Psychology, 58,* 277–299.

Orne, M. T. (1962). On the social psychology of the psychological experiment: With particular reference to demand characteristics and their implications. *American Psychologist, 17,* 776–783.

Orne, M. T. (1969). Demand characteristics and the concept of quasi-controls. In R. Rosenthal & R. L. Rosnow (Eds.), *Artifact in behavioral research* (pp. 143–179). New York, NY: Academic Press.

Orne, M. T. (1970). Hypnosis, motivation, and the ecological validity of the psychological experiment. In W. J. Arnold & M. M. Page (Eds.), *Nebraska symposium on motivation* (pp. 187–265). Lincoln: University of Nebraska Press.

Osgood, C. E., & Luria, Z. (1954). A blind analysis of a case of multiple personality using the semantic differential. *Journal of Abnormal and Social Psychology, 49,* 579–591.

Osgood, C. E., Suci, G. L., & Tannenbaum, P. H. (1957). *The measurement of meaning.* Urbana: University of Illinois Press.

Otten, M. W., & Van de Castle, R. L. (1963). A comparison of set "A" of the Holtzman inkblots with the Rorschach by means of the semantic differential. *Journal of Projective Techniques and Personality Assessment, 27,* 452–460.

Ozer, D. J. (1985). Correlation and the coefficient of determination. *Psychological Bulletin, 97,* 307–315.

Panter, A. T., & Sterba, J. K. (Eds.). (2011). *Handbook of ethics in quantitative methodology.* New York, NY: Routledge.

Pargament, K. I. (2002). The bitter and the sweet: An evaluation of the costs and benefits of religiousness. *Psychological Inquiry, 13,* 168–181.

Parker, K. C. H., Hanson, R. K., & Hunsley, J. (1988). MMPI, Rorschach, and WAIS: A meta-analytic comparison of reliability, stability, and validity. *Psychological Bulletin, 103,* 367–373.

Paul, E. F., Miller, F. D., & Paul, J. (Eds.). (2000). *Why animal experimentation matters: The use of animals in medical research.* New Brunswick, NJ: Transaction.

Paulhus, D. L. (1991). Measurement and control of response bias. In J. P. Robinson, P. R. Shaver, & L. S. Wrightsman (Eds.), *Measures of personality and social psychological attitudes* (pp. 17–59). San Diego, CA: Academic Press.

Paulos, J. A. (1990). *Innumeracy: Mathematical illiteracy and its consequences.* New York, NY: Vintage Books.

Paulos, J. A. (1991, April 24). Math moron myths. *The New York Times OP-ED,* p. 25.

Paulos, J. A. (2003). *A mathematician plays the stock market.* New York, NY: Basic Books.

Pearl, J. (2000). *Causality: Models, reasoning, and inference.* Cambridge, England: Cambridge University Press.

Pearson, K. (1904). Report on certain enteric fever inoculation statistics. *British Medical Journal, 2,* 1243–1246.

Peirce, C. S. (1966). *Charles S. Peirce: Selected writings (Values in a universe of chance).* (P. P. Weiner, Ed.). New York, NY: Dover.

Pelz, D. C., & Andrew, F. M. (1964). Detecting causal priorities in panel study data. *American Sociological Review, 29,* 836–848.

Pera, M., & Shea, W. R. (Eds.). (1991). *Persuading science: The art of scientific rhetoric.* Canton, MA: Science History.

Perloff, R. (2006). An Rx for advancing and enriching psychology. In D. A. Hantula (Ed.), *Advances in social and organizational psychology* (pp. 315–327). London, England: Psychology Press/Taylor & Francis.

Pessin, J. (1933). The comparative effects of social and mechanical stimulation on memorizing. *American Journal of Psychology, 45,* 263–270.

Phillips, D. P., & Carstensen, M. S. (1986). Clustering of teenage suicides after television news stories about suicide. *New England Journal of Medicine, 315,* 685–689.

Phillips, D. P., & Glynn, L. M. (2000). Field study. In A. E. Kazdin (Ed.), *Encyclopedia of psychology* (Vol. 3, p. 370). New York, NY: Oxford University Press & American Psychological Association.

Phillips, D. P., Lesyna, K., & Paight, D. J. (1992). Suicide and the media. In R. W. Maris, A. L. Berman, J. T. Maltsberger, & R. I. Yufit (Eds.), *Assessment and prediction of suicide* (pp. 499–519). New York, NY: Guilford Press.

Phillips, D. P., & Paight, B. A. (1987). The impact of televised movies about suicide: A replicative study. *New England Journal of Medicine, 317,* 809–811.

Pierce, C. A., & Aguinis, H. (1997). Using virtual reality technology in organizational behavior research. *Journal of Organizational Behavior, 18,* 407–410.

PLoS Medicine Editors (2009, Sept.). Ghostwriting: The dirty little secret of medical publishing that just got bigger. *PloS Medicine, 6* (9), e10000156. Retrieved September 19, 2009 from http://www.plosmedicine.org/static/ghostwriting.action

Poarch, R., & Monk-Turner, E. (2001). Gender roles in children's literature: A review of non-award-winning "easy-to-read" books. *Journal of Childhood Education, 16,* 70–76.

Popper, K. R. (1934). *Logik der Forschung.* Vienna, Austria: Springer-Verlag

Popper, K. R. (1961). *The logic of scientific inquiry.* New York, NY: Basic Books.

Popper, K. R. (1963). *Conjectures and refutations: The growth of scientific knowledge* (Rev. ed.). London, England: Routledge.

Popper, K. R. (1972). *Objective knowledge: An evolutionary approach.* Oxford, England: Oxford University Press.

Postman, L., Bruner, J. S., & McGinnies, E. (1948). Personal values as selective factors in perception. *Journal of Abnormal and Social Psychology, 43,* 142–154.

Powell, F. A. (1962). Open- and closed-mindedness and the ability to differentiate source and message. *Journal of Abnormal and Social Psychology, 65,* 61–64.

Principe, G. F., Kanaya, T., Ceci, S. J., & Singh, M. (2006). Believing is seeing: How rumors can engender false memories in preschoolers. *Psychological Science, 17,* 243–248.

Rand Corporation. (1955). *A million random digits with 100,000 normal deviates.* New York, NY: Free Press.

Randhawa, B. S., & Coffman, W. E. (Eds.). (1978). *Visual learning, thinking, and communication.* New York, NY: Academic Press.

Raudenbush, S. W. (1984). Magnitude of teacher expectancy effects on pupil IQ as a function of the credibility of expectancy induction: A synthesis of findings from 18 experiments. *Journal of Educational Psychology, 76,* 85–97.

Reed, S. K. (1988). *Cognition: Theory and applications* (2nd ed.). Pacific Grove, CA: Brooks/Cole.

Regis, E. (1987). *Who got Einstein's office? Eccentricities and genius at the Institute for Advanced Study.* Reading, MA: Addison-Wesley.

Reichenbach, H. (1938). *Experience and prediction.* Chicago: University of Illinois Press.

Rind, B., & Bordia, P. (1996). Effect on restaurant tipping of male and female servers drawing a happy, smiling face on the backs of customers' checks. *Journal of Applied Social Psychology, 26,* 218–225.

Roberts, C. W. (Ed.). (1997). *Text analysis for the social sciences: Methods for drawing statistical inferences from texts and transcripts.* Mahwah, NJ: Erlbaum.

Robin, H. (1993). *The scientific image: From cave to computer*. New York, NY: W. H. Freeman.

Robinson, J. P., Shaver, P. R., & Wrightsman, L. S. (Eds.). (1991). *Measures of personality and social psychological attitudes*. San Diego, CA: Academic Press.

Rogosa, D. (1980). A critique of cross-lagged correlation. *Psychological Bulletin, 88*, 245–258.

Rokeach, M. (1960). *The open and closed mind*. New York, NY: Basic Books.

Rosenbaum, P. R., & Rubin, D. B. (1983). The central role of the propensity score in observational studies for causal effects. *Biometrika, 70*, 41–55.

Rosenberg, M. J. (1969). The conditions and consequences of evaluation apprehension. In R. Rosenthal & R. L. Rosnow (Eds.), *Artifact in behavioral research* (pp. 279–349). New York, NY: Academic Press.

Rosenhan, D. L. (1973). On being sane in insane places. *Science, 179*, 250–258.

Rosenthal, A. M. (1964). *Thirty-eight witnesses*. New York, NY: McGraw-Hill.

Rosenthal, A. M. (1999). *Thirty-eight witnesses: The Kitty Genovese case*. Berkeley: University of California Press.

Rosenthal, M. C. (1994). The fugitive literature. In H. Cooper & L. V. Hedges (Eds.), *The handbook of research synthesis* (pp. 85–94). New York, NY: Russell Sage Foundation.

Rosenthal, M. C. (2006). Retrieving literature for meta-analysis: Can we really find it all? In D. A. Hantula (Ed.), *Advances in social and organizational psychology* (pp. 75–92). London, England: Psychology Press/Taylor & Francis.

Rosenthal, R. (1966). *Experimenter effects in behavioral research*. New York, NY: Appleton-Century-Crofts.

Rosenthal, R. (1973). Estimating effective reliability in studies that employ judges' ratings. *Journal of Clinical Psychology, 29*, 342–345.

Rosenthal, R. (1976). *Experimenter effects in behavioral research* (Enlarged ed.). New York, NY: Irvington.

Rosenthal, R. (1979). The "file drawer problem" and tolerance for null results. *Psychological Bulletin, 86*, 638–641.

Rosenthal, R. (1982). Conducting judgment studies. In K. R. Scherer & P. Ekman (Eds.), *Handbook of methods in nonverbal behavior research* (pp. 287–361). New York, NY: Cambridge University Press.

Rosenthal, R. (1983). Meta-analysis: Toward a more cumulative social science. In L. Bickman (Ed.), *Applied social psychology annual* (Vol. 4, pp. 65–93). Beverly Hills, CA: Sage.

Rosenthal, R. (1985). From unconscious experimenter bias to teacher expectancy effects. In J. B. Dusek (Ed.), *Teacher expectancies* (pp. 37–65). Hillsdale, NJ: Erlbaum.

Rosenthal, R. (1987). *Judgment studies: Design, analysis, and meta-analysis*. Cambridge, England: Cambridge University Press.

Rosenthal, R. (1990a). Evaluation of procedures and results. In K. W. Wachter & M. L. Straf (Eds.), *The future of meta-analysis* (pp. 123–133). New York, NY: Russell Sage Foundation.

Rosenthal, R. (1990b). How are we doing in soft psychology? *American Psychologist, 45*, 775–777.

Rosenthal, R. (1990c). Replication in behavioral research. *Journal of Social Behavior and Personality, 5*, 1–30.

Rosenthal, R. (1991). *Meta-analytic procedures for social research* (Rev. ed.). Newbury Park, CA: Sage.

Rosenthal, R. (1993). Interpersonal expectations: Some antecedents and some consequences. In P. D. Blanck (Ed.), *Interpersonal expectations: Theory, research, and applications* (pp. 3–24). Cambridge, England: Cambridge University Press.

Rosenthal, R. (1994a). Parametric measures of effect size. In H. Cooper & L. V. Hedges (Eds.), *The handbook of research synthesis* (pp. 231–244). New York, NY: Russell Sage Foundation.

Rosenthal, R. (1994b). Science and ethics in conducting, analyzing, and reporting psychological research. *Psychological Science, 5*, 127–134.

Rosenthal, R. (1995a). Progress in clinical psychology: Is there any? *Clinical Psychology: Science and Practice, 2*, 133–150.

Rosenthal, R. (1995b). Writing meta-analytic reviews. *Psychological Bulletin, 118*, 183–192.

Rosenthal, R., & DiMatteo, M. R. (2001). Meta-analysis: Recent developments in quantitative methods for literature reviews. *Annual Review of Psychology, 52*, 59–82.

Rosenthal, R., & DiMatteo, M. R. (2002). Meta-analysis. In H. Pashler & J. Wixted (Eds.), *Stevens' handbook of experimental psychology: Vol. 4. Methodology in experimental psychology* (pp. 391–428). New York, NY: Wiley.

Rosenthal, R., & Fode, K. L. (1963). The effect of experimenter bias on the performance of the albino rat. *Behavioral Science, 8*, 183–189.

Rosenthal, R., Hall, J. A., DiMatteo, M. R., Rogers, P. L., & Archer, D. (1979). *Sensitivity to nonverbal communication: The PONS test*. Baltimore, MD: Johns Hopkins University Press.

Rosenthal, R., & Jacobson, L. (1968). *Pygmalion in the classroom: Teacher expectation and pupils' intellectual development*. New York, MD: Holt, Rinehart & Winston.

Rosenthal, R., & Lawson, R. (1964). A longitudinal study of experimenter bias on the operant learning of laboratory rats. *Journal of Psychiatric Research, 2*, 61–72.

Rosenthal, R., & Rosnow, R. L. (Eds.). (1969). *Artifact in behavioral research*. New York, NY: Academic Press.

Rosenthal, R., & Rosnow, R. L. (1975a). *Primer of methods for the behavioral sciences*. New York, NY: Wiley.

Rosenthal, R., & Rosnow, R. L. (1975b). *The volunteer subject*. New York, NY: Wiley.

Rosenthal, R., & Rosnow, R. L. (1984). Applying Hamlet's question to the ethical conduct of research: A conceptual addendum. *American Psychologist, 39*, 561–563.

Rosenthal, R., & Rosnow, R. L. (1985). *Contrast analysis: Focused comparisons in the analysis of variance*. Cambridge, England: Cambridge University Press.

Rosenthal, R., & Rosnow, R. L. (1991). *Essentials of behavioral research: Methods and data analysis* (2nd ed.). New York, NY: McGraw-Hill.

Rosenthal, R., & Rosnow, R. L. (2008). *Essentials of behavioral research: Methods and data analysis* (3rd ed.). Boston, MA: McGraw-Hill.

Rosenthal, R., & Rosnow, R. L. (2009). *Artifacts in behavioral research*. New York, NY: Oxford University Press.

Rosenthal, R., Rosnow, R. L., & Rubin, D. B. (2000). *Contrasts and effect sizes in behavioral research: A correlational approach.* Cambridge, England: Cambridge University Press.

Rosenthal, R., & Rubin, D. B. (1978). Interpersonal expectancy effects: The first 345 studies. *Behavioral and Brain Sciences, 3,* 377–386.

Rosenthal, R., & Rubin, D. B. (1979a). Comparing significance levels of independent studies. *Psychological Bulletin, 86,* 1165–1168.

Rosenthal, R., & Rubin, D. B. (1979b). A note on percent variance explained as a measure of the importance of effects. *Journal of Applied Social Psychology, 9,* 395–396.

Rosenthal, R., & Rubin, D. B. (1982a). Comparing effect sizes of independent studies. *Psychological Bulletin, 92,* 500–504.

Rosenthal, R., & Rubin, D. B. (1982b). A simple general purpose display of magnitude of experimental effect. *Journal of Educational Psychology, 74,* 166–169.

Rosenthal, R., & Rubin, D. B. (1989). Effect size estimation for one-sample multiple-choice type data: Design, analysis, and meta-analysis. *Psychological Bulletin, 106,* 332–337.

Rosenthal, R., & Rubin, D. B. (1994). The counternull value of an effect size: A new statistic. *Psychological Science, 5,* 329–334.

Rosenthal, R., & Rubin, D. B. (2003). $r_{equivalent}$: A simple effect size indicator. *Psychological Methods, 8,* 492–496.

Rosenzweig, S. (1933). The experimental situation as a psychological problem. *Psychological Review, 40,* 337–354.

Rosnow, R. L. (1968). A "spread of effect" in attitude formation. In A. G. Greenwald, T. C. Brock, & T. M. Ostrom (Eds.), *Psychological foundations of attitudes* (pp. 89–107). New York, NY: Academic Press.

Rosnow, R. L. (1972, March). Poultry and prejudice. *Psychology Today,* pp. 53–56.

Rosnow, R. L. (1978). The prophetic vision of Giambattista Vico: Implications for the state of social psychological theory. *Journal of Personality and Social Psychology, 36,* 1322–1331.

Rosnow, R. L. (1980a). Psychology of rumor reconsidered. *Psychological Bulletin, 87,* 578–591.

Rosnow, R. L. (1980b). Rumor as communication: A contextualist approach. *Journal of Communication, 38*(1), 12–28.

Rosnow, R. L. (1981). *Paradigms in transition: The methodology of social inquiry.* New York, NY: Oxford University Press.

Rosnow, R. L. (1986). Shotter, Vico and fallibilistic indeterminacy. *British Journal of Social Psychology, 25,* 215–216.

Rosnow, R. L. (1990). Teaching research ethics through role-play and discussion. *Teaching of Psychology, 17,* 179–181.

Rosnow, R. L. (1991). Inside rumor: A personal journey. *American Psychologist, 46,* 484–496.

Rosnow, R. L. (1993). The volunteer problem revisited. In P. D. Blanck (Ed.), *Interpersonal expectations: Theory, research, applications* (pp. 418–436). New York, NY: Cambridge University Press.

Rosnow, R. L. (1997). Hedgehogs, foxes, and the evolving social contract in psychological science: Ethical challenges and methodological opportunities. *Psychological Methods, 2,* 345–356.

Rosnow, R. L. (2000a). Longitudinal research. In A. E. Kazdin (Ed.), *Encyclopedia of psychology* (Vol. 5, pp. 76–77).

Washington, DC: American Psychological Association and Oxford University Press.

Rosnow, R. L. (2000b). Semantic differential. In A. E. Kazdin (Ed.), *Encyclopedia of psychology* (Vol. 7, pp. 224–225). Washington, DC: American Psychological Association and Oxford University Press.

Rosnow, R. L. (2001). Rumor and gossip in interpersonal interaction and beyond: A social exchange perspective. In R. M. Kowalski (Ed.), *Behaving badly: Aversive behaviors in interpersonal relationships* (pp. 203–232). Washington, DC: American Psychological Association.

Rosnow, R. L. (2002). Experimenter and subject artifacts. In N. J. Smelser & P. B. Baltes (Eds.), *International encyclopedia of the social and behavioral sciences* (pp. 5120–5124). Amsterdam, Netherlands: Pergamon Press.

Rosnow, R. L., Esposito, J. L., & Gibney, L. (1987). Factors influencing rumor spreading: Replication and extension. *Language and Communication, 7,* 1–14.

Rosnow, R. L., & Fine, G. A. (1974, August). Inside rumors. *Human Behavior,* pp. 64–68.

Rosnow, R. L., & Fine, G. A. (1976). *Rumor and gossip: The social psychology of hearsay.* New York, NY: Elsevier.

Rosnow, R. L., & Georgoudi, M. (Eds.). (1986). *Contextualism and understanding in behavioral science.* New York, NY: Praeger.

Rosnow, R. L., Goodstadt, B. E., Suls, J. M., & Gitter, A. G. (1973). More on the social psychology of the experiment: When compliance turns to self-defense. *Journal of Personality and Social Psychology, 27,* 337–343.

Rosnow, R. L., Holper, H. M., & Gitter, A. G. (1973). More on the reactive effects of pretesting in attitude research: Demand characteristics or subject commitment? *Educational and Psychological Measurement, 33,* 7–17.

Rosnow, R. L., & Kimmel, A. J. (2000). Rumors. In A. E. Kazdin (Ed.), *Encyclopedia of psychology* (Vol. 7, pp. 122–123). Washington, DC: American Psychological Association and Oxford University Press.

Rosnow, R. L., & Rosenthal, R. (1970). Volunteer effects in behavioral research. In K. H. Craik, B. Kleinmuntz, R. L. Rosnow, R. Rosenthal, J. A. Cheyne, & R. H. Walters, *New directions in psychology* (No. 4, pp. 211–277). New York, NY: Holt, Rinehart & Winston.

Rosnow, R. L., & Rosenthal, R. (1976). The volunteer subject revisited. *Australian Journal of Psychology, 28,* 97–108.

Rosnow, R. L., & Rosenthal, R. (1988). Focused tests of significance and effect size estimation in counseling psychology. *Journal of Counseling Psychology, 35,* 203–208.

Rosnow, R. L., & Rosenthal, R. (1989a). Definition and interpretation of interaction effects. *Psychological Bulletin, 105,* 143–146.

Rosnow, R. L., & Rosenthal, R. (1989b). Statistical procedures and the justification of knowledge in psychological science. *American Psychologist, 44,* 1276–1284.

Rosnow, R. L., & Rosenthal, R. (1991). If you are looking at the cell means, you're not looking at *only* the interaction (unless all main effects are zero). *Psychological Bulletin, 110,* 574–576.

Rosnow, R. L., & Rosenthal, R. (1995). "Some things you learn aren't so": Cohen's paradox, Asch's paradigm, and the interpretation of interaction. *Psychological Science, 6, 3–9.*

Rosnow, R. L., & Rosenthal, R. (1996). Computing contrasts, effect sizes, and counternulls on other people's published data: General procedures for research consumers. *Psychological Methods, 1,* 331–340.

Rosnow, R. L., & Rosenthal, R. (1997). *People studying people: Artifacts and ethics in behavioral research.* New York, NY: W. H. Freeman.

Rosnow, R. L., & Rosenthal, R. (2002). Contrasts and correlations in theory assessment. *Journal of Pediatric Psychology, 27,* 59–66.

Rosnow, R. L., & Rosenthal, R. (2003). Effect sizes for experimenting psychologists. *Canadian Journal of Experimental Psychology, 57,* 221–237.

Rosnow, R. L., & Rosenthal, R. (2007). Assessing the effect size of outcome research. In A. M. Nezu & C. M. Nezu (Eds.), *Evidence-based outcome research: A practical guide to conducting randomized controlled trials for psychosocial interventions* (pp. 379–401). New York, NY: Oxford University Press.

Rosnow, R. L., & Rosenthal, R. (2009). Effect sizes: Why, when, and how to use them. *Zeitschrift für Psychologie/Journal of Psychology, 217,* 6–14.

Rosnow, R. L., & Rosenthal, R. (2011). Ethical principles in data analysis: An overview. In A. T. Panter & J. K. Sterba (Eds.), *Handbook of ethics in quantitative methodology* (pp. 37–58). New York, NY: Routledge.

Rosnow, R. L., & Rosenthal, R. (2012). Quantitative methods and ethics. In T. Little (Ed.), *The Oxford handbook of quantitative methods.* New York, NY: Oxford University Press.

Rosnow, R. L., Rosenthal, R., & Rubin, D. B. (2000). Contrasts and correlations in effect size estimation. *Psychological Science, 11,* 446–453.

Rosnow, R. L., & Rosnow, M. (2012). *Writing papers in psychology* (9th ed.). Belmont, CA: Wadsworth/Cengage Learning.

Rosnow, R. L., Rotheram-Borus, M. J., Ceci, S. J., Blanck, P. D., & Koocher, G. P. (1993). The institutional review board as a mirror of scientific and ethical standards. *American Psychologist, 48,* 821–826.

Rosnow, R. L., Skleder, A. A., Jaeger, M. E., & Rind, B. (1994). Intelligence and the epistemics of interpersonal acumen: Testing some implications of Gardner's theory. *Intelligence, 19,* 93–116.

Rosnow, R. L., Strohmetz, D., & Aditya, R. (2000). Artifact in research. In A. E. Kazdin (Ed.), *Encyclopedia of psychology* (Vol. 1, pp. 242–245). New York, NY: Oxford University Press & American Psychological Association.

Rosnow, R. L., & Suls, J. M. (1970). Reactive effects of pretesting in attitude research. *Journal of Personality and Social Psychology, 15,* 338–343.

Ross, L., Greene, D., & House, P. (1977). The "false-consensus effect": An egocentric bias in social perception and attribution processes. *Journal of Experimental Social Psychology, 13,* 279–301.

Rossi, P. H., Wright, J. D., & Anderson, A. B. (1983). Sample surveys: History, current practice, and future prospects. In P. H. Rossi, J. D. Wright, & A. B. Anderson (Eds.), *Handbook of survey research* (pp. 1–20). New York, NY: Academic Press.

Rothenberg, R. (1990, October 5). Surveys proliferate, but answers dwindle. *The New York Times,* pp. A1, D4.

Rozelle, R. M., & Campbell, D. T. (1969). More plausible rival hypotheses in the cross-lagged panel correlation technique. *Psychological Bulletin, 71,* 74–80.

Rozin, P., Fischler, C., Imada, S., Sarubin, A., & Wrzesniewski, A. (1999). Attitudes to food and the role of food in life in the U.S.A., Japan, Flemish Belgium and France: Possible implications for the diet-health debate. *Appetite, 33,* 163–180.

Rubin, D. B. (1973). The use of matched sampling and regression adjustment to control bias in observational studies. *Biometrics, 29,* 184–203.

Rubin, D. B. (1974). Estimating causal effects of treatments in randomized and nonrandomized studies. *Journal of Educational Psychology, 66,* 688–701.

Rubin, D. B. (2006). Estimating treatment effects from nonrandomized studies using subclassification on propensity scores. In D. A. Hantula (Ed.), *Advances in social and organizational psychology* (pp. 41–59). London, England: Psychology Press/Taylor & Francis.

Rubin, D. B., & Thomas, N. (1996). Matching using estimated propensity scores: Relating theory to practice. *Biometrics, 52,* 249–264.

Russell, M. S., & Burch, R. L. (1959). *The principles of humane experimental technique.* London, England: Methuen.

Ryder, N. B. (1965). The cohort as a concept in the study of social change. *American Sociological Review, 30,* 843–861.

Saks, M. J., & Blanck, P. D. (1992). Justice improved: The unrecognized benefits of aggregation and sampling in the trial of mass torts. *Stanford Law Review, 44,* 815–851.

Sales, B. D., & Folkman, S. (Eds.). (2000). *Ethics in research with human participants.* Washington, DC: American Psychological Association.

Salsburg, D. (2001). *The lady tasting tea: How statistics revolutionized science in the twentieth century.* New York, NY: W. H. Freeman.

Saris, W. E. (1991). *Computer-assisted interviewing.* Thousand Oak, CA: Sage.

Sartre, J.-P. (1956). *Being and nothingness: A phenomenological essay on ontology.* New York, NY: Washington Square Press.

Saxe, L. (1991). Lying: Thoughts of an applied social psychologist. *American Psychologist, 46,* 409–415.

Schachter, S. (1968). Obesity and eating. *Science, 161,* 751–756.

Schacter, D. L. (1999). The seven sins of memory: Insights from psychology and cognitive neuroscience. *American Psychologist, 54,* 182–203.

Schaeffer, N. C. (2000). Asking questions about threatening topics: A selective overview. In A. A. Stone, J. S. Turkkan, C. A. Bachrach, J. B. Jobe, H. S. Kurtzman, & V. S. Cain (Eds.), *The science of self-report: Implications for research and practice* (pp. 105–121). Mahwah, NJ: Erlbaum.

Schultz, D. P. (1969). The human subject in psychological research. *Psychological Bulletin, 72,* 214–228.

Schuman, H., & Presser, S. (1996). *Questions and answers in attitude surveys: Experiments on question form, wording, and content.* Thousand Oaks, CA: Sage.

Scott, W. A. (1968). Attitude measurement. In G. Lindzey & E. Aronson (Eds.), *The handbook of social psychology* (2nd ed., Vol. 2, pp. 204–272). Reading, MA: Addison-Wesley.

Scott-Jones, D., & Rosnow, R. L. (1998). Ethics and mental health research. In H. Friedman (Ed.), *Encyclopedia of mental health* (Vol. 2, pp. 149–160). Palo Alto, CA: Academic Press.

Sears, D. O. (1986). College sophomores in the laboratory: Influences of a narrow database on social psychology's view of human nature. *Journal of Personality and Social Psychology, 51,* 515–530.

Serlin, R. C. (2010). Regarding prep: Comment prompted by Iverson, Wagenmakers, and Lee (2010); Lecoutre, Lecoutre, and Poitevineau (2010); and Maraun and Gabriel (2010). *Psychological Methods, 15,* 203–208.

Shadish, W. R. (2010). Campbell and Rubin: A primer and comparison of their approaches to causal inference in field settings. *Psychological Methods, 15,* 3–17.

Shadish, W. R., Cook, T. D., & Campbell, D. T. (2002). *Experimental and quasi-experimental designs for generalized causal inference.* Boston, MA: Houghton Mifflin.

Shapiro, J., Anderson, J., & Anderson, A. (1997). Diversity in parental storybook reading. *Early Child Development and Care, 127–128,* 47–59.

Sharkey, K. J., & Ritzler, B. A. (1985). Comparing diagnostic validity of the TAT and a new picture projection test. *Journal of Personality Assessment, 49,* 406–412.

Shaw, M. E., & Wright, J. M. (1967). *Scales for the measurement of attitudes.* New York, NY: McGraw-Hill.

Sherman, S. J., Presson, C., & Chassin, L. (1984). Mechanisms underlying the false consensus effect: The special role of threats to the self. *Personality and Social Psychology Bulletin, 10,* 127–138.

Shermer, M. (1997). *Why people believe weird things: Pseudoscience, superstition, and other confusions of our time.* New York, NY: W. H. Freeman.

Sidman, M. (1960). *Tactics of scientific research: Evaluating experimental data in psychology.* New York, NY: Basic Books.

Sieber, J. E. (1982a). Deception in social research: 1. Kinds of deception and the wrongs they may involve. *IRB: A Review of Human Subjects Research, 3,* 1–2, 12.

Sieber, J. E. (Ed.). (1982b). *The ethics of social research* (Vols. 1–2). New York, NY: Springer-Verlag.

Sieber, J. E (1983). Deception in social research: 2. Factors influencing the magnitude of potential for harm or wrong. *IRB: A Review of Human Subjects Research, 4,* 1–3, 12.

Sieber, J. E. (1992). *Planning ethically responsible research.* Newbury Park, CA: Sage.

Sieber, J. E. (1994). Scientists' responses to ethical issues in science. In W. Shadish & S. Fuller (Eds.), *The social psychology of science* (pp. 286–299). New York, NY: Guilford Press.

Sieber, J. E., & Saks, M. J. (1989). A census of subject pool characteristics and policies. *American Psychologist, 44,* 1053–1061.

Siegel, S. (1956). *Nonparametric statistics.* New York, NY: McGraw-Hill.

Siegel, S., & Castellan, Jr., N. J. (1988). *Nonparametric statistics for the behavioral sciences* (2nd ed.). New York, NY: McGraw-Hill

Sigall, H., Aronson, E., & Van Hoose, T. (1970). The cooperative subject: Myth or reality? *Journal of Experimental Social Psychology, 6,* 1–10.

Silverman, I. (1977). *The human subject in the psychological experiment.* New York, NY: Pergamon Press.

Simonton, D. K. (2000). Archival research. In A. E. Kazdin (Ed.), *Encyclopedia of psychology* (Vol. 1, pp. 234–235). New York, NY: Oxford University Press & American Psychological Association.

Singer, E., Hippler, H.-J., & Schwarz, N. (1992). Confidentiality assurances in surveys: Reassurance or threat? *International Journal of Public Opinion, 4,* 256–268.

Singer, E., Von Thurn, D. R., & Miller, E. R. (1995). Confidentiality assurances and response: A quantitative review of the experimental literature. *Public Opinion Quarterly, 59,* 66–77.

Skinner, B. F. (1938). *The behavior of organisms: An experimental analysis.* New York, NY: Appleton-Century-Crofts.

Skinner, B. F. (1948a). Superstition in the pigeon. *Journal of Experimental Psychology, 38,* 168–172.

Skinner, B. F. (1948b). *Walden II.* New York, NY: Macmillan.

Skoller, C. E. (2008). *Twisted confessions: The true story behind the Kitty Genovese and Barbara Kralik murder trials.* Austin, TX: Bridgeway Books.

Slife, B., & Rubinstein, J. (Eds.). (1992). *Taking sides: Clashing views on controversial psychological issues* (7th ed.). Guilford, CT: Dushkin.

Slovic, P. (1987). Perception of risk. *Science, 236,* 280–285.

Smart, R. G. (1966). Subject selection bias in psychological research. *Canadian Psychologist, 7a,* 115–121.

Smelser, N. J, & Baltes, P. B. (Eds.). (2002). *International encyclopedia of the social and behavioral sciences* (Vols. 1–26). Amsterdam, Netherlands: Pergamon Press.

Smith, C. (1980). *Selecting a source of local television news in the Salt Lake City SMSA: A multivariate analysis of cognitive and affective factors for 384 randomly-selected news viewers.* Unpublished doctoral dissertation, Temple University School of Communication, Philadelphia, PA.

Smith, C. P. (Ed.). (1992). *Motivation and personality: Handbook of thematic content analysis.* Cambridge, England: Cambridge University Press.

Smith, M. B. (1969). *Social psychology and human values.* Chicago, IL: Aldine.

Smith, M. B. (2000). Moral foundations in research with human participants. In B. D. Sales & S. Folkman (Eds.), *Ethics in research with human participants* (pp. 3–10). Washington, DC: American Psychological Association.

Smith, N. C., Kimmel, A. J., & Klein, J. G. (2009). Social contract theory and the ethics of deception in consumer research. *Journal of Consumer Psychology, 19,* 486–496.

Smith, T. W. (1997, April 20). Punt, pass and ponder the questions. *The New York Times,* p. 11.

Snedecor, G. W., & Cochran, W. G. (1989). *Statistical methods* (8th ed.). Ames: Iowa State University Press.

Sockloff, A. L., & Edney, J. N. (1972). *Some extensions of Student's t and Pearson's r central distributions.* Technical Report 72–5. Temple University Measurement and Research Center, Philadelphia, PA.

Solomon, R. L. (1949). An extension of control group design. *Psychological Bulletin, 46,* 137–150.

Solomon, R. L., & Howes, D. (1951). Word frequency, personal values, and visual duration thresholds. *Psychological Review, 58,* 256–270.

Solomon, R. L., & Lessac, M. S. (1968). A control group design for experimental studies developmental processes. *Psychological Bulletin, 70,* 145–150.

Sonneck, G., Etzersdorfer, E., & Nagel-Kuess, S. (1994). Imitative suicide on the Viennese subway. *Social Science and Medicine, 38,* 453–457.

Spearman, C. (1910). Correlation calculated from faulty data. *British Journal of Psychology, 3,* 271–295.

Sperry, R. W. (1968). Hemisphere deconnection and unity in conscious awareness. *American Psychologist, 23,* 723–733.

Spielmans, G. I. & Parry, P. I. (2010). From evidence-based medicine to marketing-based medicine: Evidence from internal industry documents. *Journal of Bioethical Inquiry, 7*(1), 13–29.

Stanley, J. C. (1971). Test reliability. In L. C. Deighton (Ed.), *The encyclopedia of education* (Vol. 9, pp. 143–153). New York, NY: Macmillan & Free Press.

Steering Committee of the Physicians' Health Study Research Group. (1988). Preliminary report: Findings from the aspirin component of the ongoing Physicians' Health Study. *New England Journal of Medicine, 318,* 262–264.

Steering Committee of the Physicians' Health Study Research Group. (1989). Final report on the aspirin component of the ongoing Physicians' Health Study. *New England Journal of Medicine, 321,* 129–135.

Steinberg, J. (2005, January 20). Study cites human failings in election day poll system. *The New York Times,* A14.

Sterling, T. D. (1959). Publication decisions and their possible effects on inferences drawn from tests of significance—or vice versa. *Journal of the American Statistical Association, 54,* 30–34.

Sternberg, R. J. (1985). *Beyond IQ: A triarchic theory of human intelligence.* Cambridge, England: Cambridge University Press.

Sternberg, R. J. (1990). *Metaphors of mind: Conceptions of the nature of intelligence.* Cambridge, England: Cambridge University Press.

Sternberg, R. J. (1997). The concept of intelligence and its role in lifelong learning and success. *American Psychologist, 52,* 1030–1037.

Sternberg, R. J. (2000). Research dissemination. In A. E. Kazdin (Ed.), *Encyclopedia of psychology* (Vol. 7, pp. 76–80). New York, NY: Oxford University Press & American Psychological Association.

Sternberg, R. J., & Detterman, D. K. (Eds.). (1986). *What is intelligence? Contemporary viewpoints on its nature and definition.* Norwood, NJ: Ablex.

Steuer, J. (1992). Defining virtual reality: Dimensions determining telepresence. *Journal of Communication, 42,* 73–93.

Stigler, S. M. (1986). *The history of statistics: The measurement of uncertainty before 1900.* Cambridge, MA: Belknap/Harvard.

Stone, A. A., Turkkan, J. S., Bachrach, C. A., Jobe, J. B., Kurtzman, H. S., & Cain, V. S. (Eds.). (2000). *The science of self-report: Implications for research and practice.* Mahwah, NJ: Erlbaum.

Stone, P. (1997). Thematic text analysis: New agendas for analyzing text content. In C. W. Roberts (Ed.), *Text analysis for the social sciences: Methods for drawing statistical inferences from texts and transcripts.* Mahwah, NJ: Erlbaum.

Stone, P. (2000). Content analysis. In A. E. Kazdin (Ed.), *Encyclopedia of psychology.* New York, NY: American Psychological Association & Oxford University Press.

Street, E., & Carroll, M. B. (1989). Preliminary evaluation of a new food product. In J. M. Tanur, F. M. Mosteller, W. H. Kruskal, E. L. Lehmann, R. F. Link, R. S. Pieters, & G. R. Rising (Eds.), *Statistics: A guide to the unknown* (3rd ed., pp. 161–169). Pacific Grove, CA: Wadsworth & Brooks/Cole.

Strickland, B. R. (1977). Approval motivation. In T. Blass (Ed.), *Personality variables in social behavior* (pp. 315–356). Hillsdale, NJ: Erlbaum.

Strohmetz, D. B. (2006). Rebuilding the ship at sea: Coping with artifacts in behavioral research. In D. A. Hantula (Ed.), *Advances in social and organizational psychology* (pp. 93–112). London, England: Psychology Press/Taylor & Francis.

Strohmetz, D. B., & Rosnow, R. L. (1994). A mediational model of artifacts. In J. Brzeziński (Ed.), *Probability in theory-building: Experimental and non-experimental approaches to scientific research in psychology* (pp. 177–196). Amsterdam, Netherlands: Rudopi.

Stryker, J. (1997, April 13). Tuskegee's long arm still touches a nerve. *The New York Times,* p. E4.

Student. (1908). The probable error of a mean. *Biometrika, 6,* 1–25.

Suls, J. M., Martin, R., & Wheeler, L. (2000). Three kinds of opinion comparison: The triadic model. *Personality and Social Psychology Review, 4,* 219–237.

Suls, J. M., & Miller, R. L. (Eds.). (1977). *Social comparison processes: Theoretical and empirical perspectives.* Washington, DC: Hemisphere.

Suls, J. M., & Rosnow, R. L. (1988). Concerns about artifacts in psychological experiments. In J. Morawski (Ed.), *The rise of experimentation in American psychology* (pp. 163–187). New York, NY: Oxford University Press.

Susman, E. J., Dorn, L. D., & Fletcher, J. C. (1992). Participation in biomedical research: The consent process as viewed by children, adolescents, young adults, and physicians. *Journal of Pediatrics, 121,* 547–552.

Symonds, P. M. (1925). Notes on rating. *Journal of Applied Psychology, 9,* 188–195.

Takooshian, H. (2009, March 11). The 1964 Kitty Genovese tragedy: Still a valuable parable. *PsycCRITIQUES, 54,* 1554-0138. Release 10, Article 2.

Tanur, J. M. (Ed.). (1994). *Questions about questions: Inquiries into the cognitive bases of surveys.* New York, NY: Russell Sage Foundation.

Thomas, C. B., Jr., Hall, J. A., Miller, F. D., Dewhirst, J. R., Fine, G. A., Taylor, M., & Rosnow, R. L. (1979). Evaluation apprehension, social desirability, and the interpretation of test correlations. *Social Behavior and Personality, 7,* 193–197.

Thorndike, E. L. (1920). A constant error in psychological ratings. *Journal of Applied Psychology, 4,* 25–29.

Thurstone, L. L. (1929). Theory of attitude measurement. *Psychological Bulletin, 36,* 222–241.

Thurstone, L. L. (1929–1934). *The measurement of social attitudes.* Chicago, IL: University of Chicago Press.

Tolman, E. C. (1959). Principles of purposive behavior. In S. Koch (Ed.), *Psychology: A study of a science* (Vol. 2, pp. 92–157). New York, NY: McGraw-Hill.

Tourangeau, R. (2000). Remembering what happened: Memory errors and survey reports. In A. A. Stone, J. S. Turkkan, C. A. Bachrach, J. B. Jobe, H. S. Kurtzman, & V. S. Cain (Eds.), *The science of self-report: Implications for research and practice* (pp. 29–47). Mahwah, NJ: Erlbaum.

Travers, J., & Milgram, S. (1969). An experimental study of the small world problem. *Sociometry, 32,* 425–443.

Tryfos, P. (1996). *Sampling methods for applied research: Text and cases.* New York, NY: Wiley.

Tufte, E. R. (1983). *The visual display of quantitative information.* Cheshire, CT: Graphics Press.

Tufte, E. R. (1990). *Envisioning information.* Cheshire, CT: Graphics Press.

Tukey, J. W. (1977). *Exploratory data analysis.* Reading, MA: Addison-Wesley.

Turk, D. C., & Melzack, R. (Eds.). (1992). *Handbook of pain assessment.* New York, NY: Guilford Press.

Turkkan, J. S., & Brady, J. V. (2000). Placebo effect in research design. In A. E. Kazdin (Ed.), *Encyclopedia of psychology* (Vol. 6, pp. 210–212). New York, NY: Oxford University Press & American Psychological Association.

Tversky, A., & Kahneman, D. (1974). Judgment under uncertainty: Heuristics and biases. *Science, 185,* 1124–1131.

U.S. Department of Health and Human Services. (1983). Protection of human subjects. *Code of Federal Regulations, 45,* Section 46.115.

VandenBos, G. R. (Ed.). (2007). *APA dictionary of psychology.* Washington, DC: American Psychological Association.

Vinacke, W. E. (1954). Deceiving experimental subjects. *American Psychologist, 9,* 155.

Wachter, K. W., & Straf, M. L. (Eds.). (1990). *The future of meta-analysis.* New York, NY: Russell Sage Foundation.

Wainer, H. (1972). Draft of Appendix for R. E. Lana & R. L. Rosnow's *Introduction to contemporary psychology.* New York, NY: Holt, Rinehart & Winston.

Wainer, H. (1984). How to display data badly. *American Statistician, 38,* 137–147.

Wainer, H. (1997). *Visual revelations: Graphical tales of fate and deception from Napoleon Bonaparte to Ross Perot.* Mahwah, NJ: Erlbaum.

Wainer, H. (2009). *Picturing the uncertain world.* Princeton, NJ: Princeton University Press.

Wainer, H., & Thissen, D. (1993). Combining multiple-choice and constructed-response test scores: Toward a Marxist theory of test construction. *Applied Measurement in Education, 6*(2), 103–118.

Walker, R. (2006, January 8). Cold call. *The New York Times Magazine,* Section 6, p. 24.

Wallis, W. A., & Roberts, H. V. (1956). *Statistics: A new approach.* New York, NY: Free Press.

Watson, E. K., Firman, D. W., Heywood, A., Hauquitz, A. C., & Ring, I. (1995). Conducting regional health surveys using a computer-assisted telephone interviewing method. *Australian Journal of Public Health, 19,* 508–511.

Watson, J. D. (1969). *The double helix.* New York, NY: Mentor.

Watson, J. D. (1993). Succeeding in science: Some rules of thumb. *Science, 261,* 1812–1813.

Watts, D. J. (2003). *Six degrees: The science of a connected age.* New York, NY: W. W. Norton.

Weaver, C. (1972). *Human listening.* Indianapolis, IN: Bobbs-Merrill.

Webb, E. J., Campbell, D. T., Schwartz, R. F., & Sechrest, L. (1966). *Unobtrusive measures: Nonreactive research in the social sciences.* Chicago, IL: Rand McNally.

Webb, E. J., Campbell, D. T., Schwartz, R. F., Sechrest, L., & Grove, J. B. (1981). *Nonreactive measures in the social sciences* (2nd ed.). Boston, MA: Houghton Mifflin.

Webber, R. A. (1970). Perception of interactions between superiors and subordinates. *Human Relations, 23,* 235–248.

Wechler, J. (Ed.). (1978). *On aesthetics in science.* Cambridge, MA: MIT Press.

Weick, K. E. (1968). Systematic observational methods. In G. Lindzey & E. Aronson (Eds.), *The handbook of social psychology* (2nd ed., Vol. 2, pp. 357–451). Reading, MA: Addison-Wesley.

Weinberger, D. A. (1990). The construct validity of the repressive coping style. In J. L. Singer (Ed.)., *Repression and dissociation: Implications for personality theory, psychopathology, and health* (pp. 337–386). Chicago, IL: University of Chicago Press.

Weiner, B. (1991). Metaphors in motivation and attribution. *American Psychologist, 46,* 921–930.

Weiner, I. B. (2003). *Principles of Rorschach interpretation.* Mahwah, NJ: Erlbaum.

Weisberg, R. W. (1994). Genius and madness? A quasi-experimental test of the hypothesis that manic-depression increases creativity. *Psychological Science, 5,* 361–367.

Werner, H. C., & Kaplan, B. (1963). *Symbol formation: An organismic-developmental approach to language and the expression of thought.* New York, NY: Wiley.

Westen, D., & Rosenthal, R. (2003). Quantifying construct validity: Two simple measures. *Journal of Personality and Social Psychology, 84,* 608–618.

Wheeler, L., Martin, R., & Suls, J. (1997). The proxy model of social comparison for self-assessment of ability. *Personality and Social Psychology Review, 1,* 54–61.

White, D. M. (1950). The "gate keeper": A case study in the selection of news. *Journalism Quarterly, 27,* 383–390.

White, L., Tursky, B., & Schwartz, G. (Eds.). (1985). *Placebo: Clinical phenomena and new insights.* New York, NY: Guilford Press.

White, T. L., Leichtman, M. D., & Ceci, S. J. (1997). The good, the bad, and the ugly: Accuracy, inaccuracy, and elaboration in preschoolers' reports about a past event. *Applied Cognitive Psychology, 11,* S37–S54.

Wickesberg, A. K. (1968). Communication networks in a business organization structure. *Journal of the Academy of Management, 11,* 253–262.

Wiggins, J. S. (Ed.). (1996). *The five-factor model of personality.* New York, NY: Guilford Press.

Wilcox, R. R. (2005). New methods for comparing groups: Strategies for increasing the probability of detecting true differences. *New Directions in Psychological Science, 14,* 272–275.

Wilkinson, L., & Engelman, L. (1996). Descriptive statistics. In L. Wilkinson (Ed.), *SYSTAT 9: Statistics I* (pp. 205–225). Chicago, IL: SPSS.

Wilkinson, L., and the Task Force on Statistical Inference. (1999). Statistical methods in psychology journals. *American Psychologist, 54,* 594–604.

Willis, G., Brittingham, A, Lee, L., Tourangeau, R., & Ching, P. (1999). *Response errors in children's surveys of immunization.* Vital and Health Statistics, Series 6, No. 8, Hyattsville, MD: National Center for Health Statistics.

Wolman, B. B. (Ed.). (1977). *International encyclopedia of psychiatry, psychology, psychoanalysis, and neurology* (Vols. 1–12). New York, NY: Van Nostrand Reinhold.

Wood, J. (1989). Theory and research concerning social comparisons of personal attributes. *Psychological Bulletin, 106,* 231–248.

Woodrum, E. (1984). "Mainstreaming" content analysis in social science: Methodological advantages, obstacles, and solutions. *Social Science Research, 13,* 1–19.

Yaden, D. B., Smolkin, L. B., & MacGillivray, L. (1993). A psychogenetic perspective on children's understanding about letter associations during alphabet book reading. *Journal of Reading Behaviour, 25,* 43–68.

Yates, F., & Cochran, W. G. (1938). The analysis of groups of experiments. *Journal of Agricultural Science, 28,* 556–580.

Yonge, C. D. (Ed.). (1854). *The deipnosophists or the banquet of the learned of Athenaeus* (Vol. 1). London, England: Henry G. Bohn.

Zajonc, R. F. (1965). Social facilitation. *Science, 149,* 269–274.

Zechmeister, E. G., & Nyberg, S. E. (1982). *Human memory: An introduction to research and theory.* Monterey, CA: Brooks/Cole.

Zipf, G. K. (1935). *The psycho-biology of language.* Boston, MA: Houghton Mifflin.

Zipf, G. K. (1949). *Human behavior and the principle of least effort.* Reading, MA: Addison-Wesley.

Zuckerman, M., Hodgins, H. S., Zuckerman, A., & Rosenthal, R. (1993). Contemporary issues in the analysis of data: A survey of 551 psychologists. *Psychological Science, 4,* 49–53.

Name Index

A

Abelson, R. P., 247, 357
Adair, J. G., 45, 357
Adair, R. K., 74, 137, 357
Adhikari, A., 109, 172, 357, 361
Aditya, R. N., 142, 191, 357, 370
Agard, E., 83, 360
Aguinis, H., 75, 367
Aiken, L. R. Jr., 89, 357
Ainsworth, M. D. S., 114, 357
Allaman, J. D., 122, 357
Allport, G. W., 25, 89, 357
Altman, D. A., 231, 357
Altman, D. G., 359
American Association for Public Opinion Research, 173
American Psychiatric Association, 29, 37, 65
American Psychological Association, 41, 43, 54, 59, 191, 303–324, 350, 357
Anastasi, A., 118, 119, 120, 357
Anderson, A. B., 72, 100, 172, 370, 371
Anderson, D. C., 158, 357
Anderson, J., 72, 371
Andrew, F. M., 160, 367
Anhalt, R. L., 91, 366
Arceneaux, K., 78, 357
Archer, D., 69, 368
Aristotle, 6, 137, 146
Aronson, E., 15, 55, 357, 371
Asch, S. E., 8, 9, 17, 51, 52, 61, 62, 121, 357
Ashe, D. K., 102, 365
Athenaeus of Naucratis, 6
Atkinson, J. W., 87, 365
Atkinson, L., 113, 357
Atwell, J. E., 43, 357
Audrain-Pontevia, A.-F., 15, 26
Axinn, S., 223, 357

B

Babad, E., 14, 357
Bachrach, C. A., 83, 101, 372
Bailey, P., 32, 357
Bakan, D., 342, 357

Baldwin, W., 82, 357
Bales, R. F., 69–71, 79, 357
Baltes, P. B., 29, 371
Baltimore, D., 3, 358
Banaji, M. R., 88, 102, 362
Barker, P., 11, 358
Barlow, D. H., 157, 362
Barnett, F. T., 156, 364
Barrass, R., 16, 358
Bartoshuk, L., 84, 358
Bauer, M. I., 11, 358
Baumrind, D., 52, 358
Beall, A. C., 75, 365
Beatty, J., 130, 239, 361
Beck, A. T., 30, 87, 358
Beck, S. J., 87, 358
Beecher, H. K., 43, 358
Bellack, A. S., 49, 51, 55, 180, 358
Benjamin, L. T. Jr., 51, 358
Bennett, E. S., 84, 366
Ben-Shachar, T., 84, 366
Bergum, B. O., 24, 358
Bernard, H. B., 101, 358
Bernstein, D. A., 89, 358
Bernstein, I. H., 111, 366
Berry, D. T. R., 113, 362
Bersoff, D. M., 84, 358
Bersoff, D. N., 84
Bielawski, D., 71, 72, 359
Billow, R. M., 11, 358
Biocca, F., 75, 358
Blanck, P. D., 48, 49, 50, 51, 55, 165, 180, 358, 370
Blascovich, J., 75, 365
Blass, T., 51, 358
Blastland, M., 2, 358
Blau, G., 93, 366
Blehar, M. C., 114, 357
Blumberg, M., 48, 358
Boisen, M., 129, 132, 361
Bok, S., 42, 49, 358
Bonanno, G. A., 165, 358
Boorstein, D. J., 3, 358
Bordia, P., 15, 26, 44, 75, 99, 358, 360, 367
Borgatti, S. P., 66, 358
Boring, E. G., 7, 358

Bornstein, R. F., 113, 362
Boruch, R. F., 359
Boyer, J. L., 44, 363
Boyer, L. B., 87, 360
Bradburn, N. M., 98, 100, 358
Brady, J. V., 133, 373
Brass, D. J., 66, 358
Braun, H. I., 113, 358
Brehmer, B., 75, 358
Bremer, F., 32, 357
Brittingham, A., 84, 374
Brody, J. E., 2, 82, 358
Broome, J., 168, 358
Brownlee, K. A., 129, 139, 358
Brown, R., 15, 358
Brown, W., 112, 354, 358
Bruck, M., 8, 359
Brunell-Neuleib, S., 113, 362
Bruner, J. S., 75, 76, 367
Bryant, T. N., 31, 357
Bryman, A., 29, 365
Bucciarelli, A., 165, 358
Burch, R. L., 57, 370
Bureau of Labor Statistics, 44, 358
Burger, J. M., 54–55, 358
Burnham, J. R., 144, 358
Busch, J. C., 362
Bushman, B. J., 357
Buunk, B. P., 31, 358
Byrne, R. M. J., 11, 363

C

Cain, V. S., 83, 101, 372
Campbell, B., 365
Campbell, D. T., 63, 75, 77, 78, 116, 117, 120, 122, 123, 139–141, 146, 153, 160, 359, 363, 364, 370, 371, 373
Cannell, C. F., 101, 366
Cantril, H., 171, 363
Carlsmith, J. M., 55, 357
Carr, K., 75, 359
Carroll, M. B., 372
Carstensen, M. S., 154, 367
Castellan, N. J. Jr., 226, 371
Cattell, J. M., 7
Ceci, S. J., 8–9, 15, 17, 48, 114, 359, 367, 370, 373

Subject Index

CHAPTER 13 (pp. 247–248)
Cohen's d converted to point-biserial r when $n_1 \neq n_2$: $r = \dfrac{d}{\sqrt{d^2 + 4\left(\dfrac{\overline{n}}{n_h}\right)}}$

which, when $n_1 = n_2$, simplifies to: $r = \dfrac{d}{\sqrt{d^2 + 4}}$

CHAPTER 13 (p. 249)
95% confidence interval (CI) for Cohen's d on independent-sample means:

$$95\%\,\text{CI} = d \pm t_{(.05)}(S_{\text{Cohen's d}})$$

and $S_{\text{Cohen's d}} = \sqrt{\left[\dfrac{n_1 + n_2}{n_1 n_2} + \dfrac{d^2}{2(df)}\right]\dfrac{n_1 + n_2}{df}}$

CHAPTER 13 (pp. 251–252)
Paired (correlated) t and population variance estimate:

$$t = \dfrac{M_D}{\sqrt{\left(\dfrac{1}{N}\right)S_D^2}}, \text{and}\ \ S_D^2 = \dfrac{\Sigma(D - M_D)^2}{N - 1}$$

CHAPTER 13 (pp. 252–253)
Cohen's d for paired observations computed on original data or obtained from paired t:

$$d = \dfrac{M_D}{\sigma_D}, \text{ and } \sigma_D = \sqrt{\dfrac{\Sigma\left(D - M_D\right)^2}{N}}$$

$$d = \dfrac{t}{\sqrt{N - 1}} = \dfrac{t}{\sqrt{df}}$$

CHAPTER 14 (pp. 261–263)
Sums of squares (SS) and degrees of freedom (df) in ANOVA:

$$\text{Total } SS = \Sigma(X - M_G)^2 \qquad df_{\text{total}} = N - 1$$
$$\text{Between } SS = \Sigma[n_k(M_k - M_G)^2] \qquad df_{\text{between}} = k - 1$$
$$\text{Within } SS = \Sigma(X - M_k)^2 \qquad df_{\text{within}} = N - k$$

CHAPTER 14 (pp. 263–266)
Mean squares (MS) and F ratio in one-way ANOVA:

$$MS_{\text{between}} = \dfrac{\text{Between } SS}{df_{\text{between}}} \qquad MS_{\text{within}} = \dfrac{\text{Within } SS}{df_{\text{within}}} \qquad F = \dfrac{MS_{\text{between}}}{MS_{\text{within}}}$$

CHAPTER 14 (pp. 270–273)
Row, column, within, and interaction SS and df in two-way ANOVA:

$$\text{Row } SS = \Sigma[nc\,(M_r - M_G)^2] \qquad df_{\text{rows}} = \text{rows} - 1$$
$$\text{Column } SS = \Sigma[nr\,(M_c - M_G)^2] \qquad df_{\text{columns}} = \text{columns} - 1$$
$$\text{Within } SS = \Sigma(X - M_k)^2 \qquad df_{\text{within}} = N - k$$
$$\text{Interaction } SS = \text{Total } SS - (\text{Row } SS + \text{Column } SS + \text{Within } SS) \qquad df_{\text{interaction}} = (\text{rows} - 1)(\text{columns} - 1)$$